Family Dollar Stores, Inc., a *Fortune 500* company, is the second integrated case. Most students are familiar with—and have likely shopped in—a local Family Dollar Store. This example provides students with a focus for analyzing a real company by using actual financial statements that beginning students can understand.

Family Dollar Stores, Inc. and Subsidiaries
Consolidated Income Statement
For the Year Ended August 30, 2003 (in thousands)

Net sales	$4,750,171
Costs and expenses:	
Cost of sales	3,145,788
Selling, general and administrative	1,214,658
	4,360,446
Income before income taxes	389,725
Income taxes	142,250
Net income	$ 247,475

Terrell and Terrell's unique presentation of two integrated examples:

✓ Makes learning easier for students through immediate application

✓ Peaks student interest in later chapters as they follow the stories behind these two cases

✓ Takes student through the entire accounting cycle, from planning to financial statements, from internal to external analysis

✓ Gives students the ability to identify with the cases and personalize the learning

SURVEY OF
ACCOUNTING
Making Sense of Business

SURVEY OF

ACCOUNTING
Making Sense of Business

Katherene P. Terrell
University of Central Oklahoma

Robert L. Terrell
University of Central Oklahoma

PEARSON

Prentice
Hall

Upper Saddle River, New Jersey 07458

Library of Congress Cataloging-in-Publication Data

Terrell, Katherene P.
    Survey of accounting : making sense of business / Katherene P. Terrell, Robert L. Terrell.
      p. cm.
    Includes bibliographical references and index.
    ISBN 0-13-091184-4 (hc : alk. paper)
    1. Accounting. 2. Managerial accounting. I. Terrell, Robert L., 1947- II. Title.

    HF5635.T38 2004
    657—dc22

                        2004053394

Senior Acquisitions Editor: Bill Larkin
Editor-in-Chief: Jeff Shelstad
Assistant Editor: Sam Goffinet
Editorial Assistant: Jane Avery
Media Project Manager: Caroline Kasterine
Marketing Manager: Beth Toland
Marketing Assistant: Melissa Owens
Managing Editor (Production): Cynthia Regan
Production Editor: Carol Samet
Permissions Supervisor: Charles Morris
Manufacturing Buyer: Michelle Klein
Design Manager: Maria Lange
Designer: Steven Frim
Interior Design: Karen Quigley
Cover Design: Steven Frim
Cover Illustration/Photo: Tom Stillo/Index Stock Imagery
Illustrator (Interior): Matrix Art Services
Manager, Print Production: Christy Mahon
Full-Service Project Management: nSight, Inc.
Composition: Laserwords
Printer/Binder: Courier-Westford
Typeface: 10.5/12 Times Roman

Credits and acknowledgments borrowed from other sources and reproduced, with permission, in this textbook appear on appropriate page within text.

Pearson Education LTD.
Pearson Education Singapore, Pte. Ltd
Pearson Education, Canada, Ltd
Pearson Education–Japan
Pearson Education, Upper Saddle River, NJ

Pearson Education Australia PTY, Limited
Pearson Education North Asia Ltd
Pearson Educación de Mexico, S.A. de C.V.
Pearson Education Malaysia, Pte. Lt.

10 9 8 7 6 5 4 3 2 1
ISBN 0-13-091184-4

To our family
Rob and Melissa, Jon and Heidi,
Katherene, John, Theresa, Robert,

and

Our students

Dedicated to
John W. Peoples, Jr.
An example of bravery in the face of adversity
and the triumph of the human spirit.

BRIEF CONTENTS

CONTENTS

CHAPTER 3 Organizing a Business: Equity and Debt Financing 60

We live in a time of dynamic change in the accounting profession and accounting education. Members of the profession face daily challenges in discovering fraud and maintaining ethical values. The U.S. Congress has charged the Securities and Exchange Commission (SEC) and the Financial Accounting Standards Board (FASB) with developing and maintaining principle-based accounting rules, placing substance over form. As information becomes more available to the general public via the Internet, it becomes increasingly important for people to become educated so they can understand what accounting information provides and what it does not. For many reasons, colleges and universities require most students to take at least one accounting course. This poses a dilemma for accounting educators who want to teach it all but find they have only one semester in which to do so.

Pedagogical Philosophy

Faced with the challenge of shortening a two-semester pedagogy into one, we analyzed the typical accounting principles curriculum to determine the segments of accounting knowledge that are most elemental for a non-accounting major. This text is appropriate for all majors as an introduction to accounting. Our assumption here is that anything good for non-accounting majors is good for accounting majors, too. By integrating financial and managerial topics and creating a new accounting learning cycle, we condensed the material into 13 chapters.

Our accounting learning cycle is grounded in the conceptual framework of accounting, and it steps through accounting concepts in a logical, natural order that learners can absorb

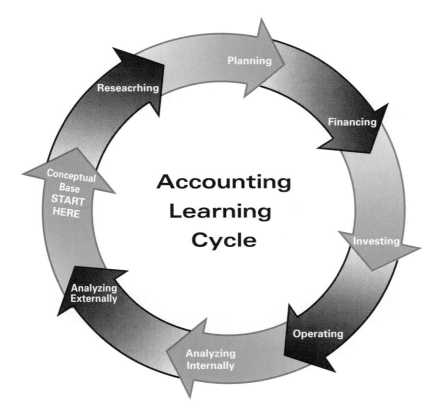

and integrate with the real world of business. Rather than approach accounting education from a balance sheet or income statement perspective, we took a just-in-time approach to teaching how accounting provides information that managers need to operate a business. Instead of a contrived topic order, this learning cycle corresponds to a natural business flow. The accounting learning cycle illustration shows the business cycle of a start-up company.

❖ **Conceptual Base**—Chapter 1 introduces the conceptual base by describing the business environment and the role of accounting in business. Chapter 2 establishes the four major financial statements through the conceptual framework of accounting.

❖ **Researching**—Chapter 3 illustrates researching the business parameters, initiating strategic planning, and designing internal controls, and begins the discussion of the methods available to secure financing. The appendix describes how to compute the selling price of bonds and prepare amortization tables.

❖ **Planning**—Chapter 4 establishes the basis of the planning stage by introducing basic cost-volume-profit analysis, strategic planning, and initial planning budgets.

❖ **Financing**—Chapters 3 and 4 discuss financing methods and illustrate how initial financing occurs in a business.

❖ **Investing**—Chapter 5 delineates the initial investments and starting operations that launch the business.

❖ **Operating**—Chapters 5 and 6 describe the operations of the business through the first month and illustrate the accounting cycle and financial statement presentation.

❖ **Analyzing Internally**—Chapter 7 begins the internal analysis of the business with preparation of the cash flow statement and other forms of cash analysis. Chapter 8 continues with analytical review procedures. Chapter 9 explores relevant decision making for a growing business. Chapter 10 details the budgeting process and includes an appendix on variance analysis. Chapter 11 completes the internal analysis process with capital budgeting and an appendix on present value techniques.

❖ **Analyzing Externally**—Chapters 12 and 13 complete the learning cycle with external analysis of companies. Chapter 12 focuses on issues that differ among companies, such as inventory and depreciation methods. Chapter 13 looks at more complex issues for public companies.

❖ **Continuous Cycle**—The cycle does not end because a real business repeats it again and again.

This pedagogy makes teaching students easy. Because information is presented just in time, it holds their attention and peaks their curiosity about the next step. By using a fictitious company, Elevation Sports, Inc. for a continuous problem throughout the majority of the book, we integrate the story and the information from chapter to chapter. In addition, we integrate Family Dollar Stores, Inc., a *Fortune 500* company, throughout most of the book. Students can understand this national company using its simple financial statements from the first to the last chapters of the book. Students find these two companies interesting, and the order of the learning steps has a natural progression instead of a contrived order.

The authors believe this text presents accounting as a true information system that enables managers to collect, store, retrieve, and analyze the information necessary for them to effectively operate a business, all in a way that students can understand and utilize.

Pedagogical Highlights of Chapters

Chapter 1—The Business Environment

"I very much like the flow from concept to internal operations – to external reporting."
John L. Norman, Jr., Keller School of Management

Chapter 1 lays a foundation for understanding business in a global economy. Assuming that this may be the only business course taken by non-business majors, the chapter defines key business terms about the four factors of production, types of businesses, types of business organization, social responsibility, business reputation, and the types of business relationships. The chapter concludes with the role of accounting in business and the responsibilities of accountants.

Chapter 2—Basic Concepts of Accounting and Financial Reporting

Chapter 2 explains the conceptual framework of accounting, which is the basis for decisions in transaction analysis. Using this conceptual framework, we introduce the four financial statements with the intent of tying the framework to accounting information in the students' minds. We teach our students accounting this way, stressing that transaction analysis depends upon the concepts in the framework. Chapter 2 helps students learn to recognize the four basic financial statements and associate the appropriate accounting elements with each. Critical-thinking skills are enhanced by problems associated with the qualitative characteristics of accounting information.

"The Family Dollar Stores, Inc. information is extremely helpful in amplifying and explaining chapter information."
Terrence Willyard, Baker College

Chapter 3—Organizing a Business: Equity and Debt Financing

Chapter 3 introduces the stages of developing a new business. It includes corporate organizational structure, raising capital through equity and debt, researching an industry, preparing a strategic plan, designing internal controls, and understanding the cost of debt financing. The chapter teaches students to think before they act by using a systematic model. Students meet the characters of Elevation Sports and study four young people's dreams for owning their own business. The chapter appendix takes students who are ready to use a financial calculator through the computations to determine bond pricing, cost of borrowing, and amortization tables.

Chapter 4—Planning for and Predicting Performance

Chapter 4 helps students learn to prepare initial operating and capital budgets so they can determine the feasibility of a business plan. Careful guidance through basic cost behavior concepts enables students to learn to predict costs of future products and business expenses necessary to open and run a business. This is a natural place to focus on break-even analysis to assess the risk of business failure. Sensitivity analysis allows students to plan at various levels of production or under different condition assumptions. The potential owners of Elevation Sports use all these tools to determine if they can make their dream a reality.

"The use of Elevation Sports, Inc. weaves a familiar element into the chapter."   Terrence Willyard, Baker College

Chapter 5—Recording Accounting Data

Chapter 5 opens with a conceptual illustration of the accounting cycle. After a discussion about the meaning and purpose of debits and credits, it portrays the first month of operation of Elevation Sports, beginning with the investment by the owners, purchase of equipment, and other opening transactions. As it is needed, the narrative provides information about these transactions; purchase discounts and freight terms are two examples. The chapter illustrates one month's transaction analysis for the first stages of the accounting cycle through the trial balance. Instructors who wish to bypass the bookkeeping can do so and still introduce the accounting cycle and the other concepts presented in the chapter.

"I consider the assignment material to be one of the strongest aspects of this text. I have worked with many texts that had problem sections with either too few problems or material unrepresentative of what was covered in the chapter. The problems follow the material covered in the chapters. There are enough problems that an instructor will have a variety of choices when choosing what to assign."
Robert D. Patterson, Penn State – Erie

Chapter 6—Completing the Accounting Cycle and Preparing the Financial Statements

Continuing the cycle begun in Chapter 5, Chapter 6 begins with a trial balance for the end of Elevation Sports' first year. We provide just-in-time learning so students see the adjusting process and the preparation of the balance sheet, income statement, and statement of stockholders' equity. The chapter concludes with the remaining steps of the cycle, finishing with the closing of the temporary accounts and a post-closing trial balance. Additional topics that help complete the cycle include bank reconciliation, bad debt analysis, application of the matching principle, statement of cost of goods manufactured, and computation of basic earnings per share. Instructors who wish to ignore the bookkeeping can still use the chapter to teach the cycle and the other topics covered.

Chapter 7—Using Analytical Data Review for Internal Financial Decisions and Planning for Cash

Chapter 7 describes the internal users of analytical data review techniques and the types of decisions they make. Students learn to perform analytical review techniques, including trend analysis and common size statements, and how to interpret each of them. Continuing with the Elevation Sports and Family Dollar illustrations, the chapter demonstrates how to prepare the statement of cash flows and includes an analysis of the information provided by the statement. The chapter concludes with a discussion of cash ratios and the importance of cash management.

"I loved your discussion of the cash flow statement, and I would recommend this text based solely on your coverage of this one area. End of chapter problems were right on target." Robert Dunn, Auburn University

Chapter 8—Analyzing Financial Statements for Profitability, Liquidity, and Solvency

Chapter 8 continues the discussion of analytical procedures. Using both Elevation Sports and Family Dollar, students learn to compute and understand the meaning of liquidity, solvency, and profitability ratios. Students discover how to locate industry averages for comparison purposes and how to evaluate a real company using the techniques learned in Chapters 7 and 8. The chapter concludes with a discussion of the basic limitations inherent in the use of financial statement ratios.

"The analysis of Elevation Sports and Family Dollar Stores at the end of the chapter should enhance the students' understanding that ratios are best analyzed in groups and in trend analysis." Robert D. Patterson, Penn State – Erie

Chapter 9—Using Relevant Information for Internal Operations

Chapter 9 continues the analysis process for internal operations by introducing students to relevant decision-making concepts. Continuing the Elevation Sports story and other illustrations, students learn to determine fixed and variable components of cost elements using the high-low method and the results of regression analysis. We only ask students to interpret regression results, not to calculate them. The chapter delves into the characteristics of relevant costs and revenues and explains the concept of sunk costs. The chapter concludes by having students evaluate relevant costs and solve various business problems using these concepts.

"It is helpful that the decisions are presented in a step-by-step approach that emphasizes that although what's relevant depends on the decision situation, the basic procedure is the same. I also think it's important that doing nothing is included as an option." Robert D. Patterson, Penn State – Erie

Chapter 10—Internal Planning and Measurement Tools

Chapter 10 explores the operating budgeting process. Students learn the types and benefits of budgeting. The Elevation Sports team work through the entire process of developing a detailed operating budget from the sales budget through to the budgeted financial statements. The chapter concludes with an optional appendix that illustrates the concepts of variance analysis for a standard cost system.

"The extended step-by-step discussion of variances utilizing Elevation Sports, Inc. was the best explanation of variances that I've seen." Terrence Willyard, Baker College

Chapter 11—Internal Allocation of Scarce Resources

Chapter 11 is the final chapter covering the internal analysis process. Chapter 11 continues the Elevation Sports scenario to introduce the capital budgeting process using the payback, net present value, profitability index, and a special case of the internal rate of return. The text explains how and why businesses must budget for their fixed asset acquisitions. The chapter also contains an appendix that covers a concise presentation of the basics of present value techniques.

"The presentation is excellent. The introduction concisely described the nature of capital projects. There is an excellent discussion of the important elements of these projects and the methods used to evaluate them. The appendix provides a concise discussion of the time value of money—present and future. However, what sets this text apart from others is the presentation of cost of capital and blended cost of capital. In similar texts this topic is either ignored or presented as very complex. The discussion here is concise and appropriate to the level of the text."
Theodore Tully, DeVry University – Freemont

Chapter 12—External Reporting Issues

Chapter 12 begins the external analysis cycle. The chapter describes the importance of external financial information to users and explains different valuation methods used for external financial reporting. This chapter teaches students how to calculate the various depreciation methods and how to determine inventory valuation. The students are asked to compare and contrast the effects of these various accounting methods on the financial statements using Elevation Sports, Family Dollar, and other real companies. The chapter concludes with descriptions of disclosure requirements for external reporting with examples from real companies.

"I have not seen a presentation like this one with the major topics that impact the differences in external reporting brought together in one chapter. Makes a lot of sense, and Bravo for your presentation. This is the area of greatest difficulty for my students." Robert Dunn, Auburn University

Chapter 13 – External Reporting for Public Companies

Chapter 13 opens with detailed coverage of ethics in business reporting and the implications of the Sarbanes-Oxley Act of 2002. Students examine the information found in the typical annual report and the required information in the Form 10-K. The chapter explains how to obtain an annual report and how to interpret items found on the balance sheets of large or complex companies using real companies' disclosures. The chapter details the reporting of recurring and nonrecurring items on the income statement, and explains net of tax disclosures for discontinued operations, extraordinary items, and accounting changes. The chapter concludes with a discussion of the importance of skepticism when using financial information. The end-of-chapter materials contain both a long and short version of an annual report project. These projects have been classroom tested for a decade and are always a highlight of the semester for our students.

"Chapters 12 and 13 on external reporting issues were also very well written and timely. These chapters introduce a number of issues that should be of interest to both accounting and non-accounting majors."
Robert D. Patterson, Penn State – Erie

Unique Features of the Text

❖ **Conceptual** The text is grounded in the conceptual framework and rooted in practical application, analysis, and synthesis. The use of the conceptual framework to introduce the financial statements is intended to help the students internalize the framework and better understand its importance.

❖ **Analytical** The text details the whys, not just the hows. The authors carefully provide both internal and external analysis techniques.

❖ **Stand alone debits and credits** With the inclusion of a conceptual introduction to the accounting cycle, professors can choose to skip the accounting procedures and focus on the analysis. If the professor chooses to use the companion text by Parrish and Sheets, he or she can also concentrate on accounting procedures.

❖ **Focus on ethics and Sarbanes-Oxley Act** The text provides students with a critical perspective about recent events. The exercises in each chapter contain an ethics problem for students to ponder.

❖ **Elevation Sports, Inc.** The case study of Elevation Sports is utilized throughout Chapters 3 to 12 to provide the student with a view of how business issues are actually addressed in the real world. Its best features are that it:
  ✦ is easy to understand
  ✦ is about a company that is feasible for the average student who might dream of one day owning a business
  ✦ ties the chapters together so students do not learn isolated facts that are easily forgotten
  ✦ becomes a familiar part of the text that peaks interest in later chapters
  ✦ sets a context that does not have to be relearned as subjects change
  ✦ treats financial and managerial accounting issues with the same level of importance and illustrates how integrated the issues are for a business trying to make decisions
  ✦ takes students through the entire accounting cycle, from planning to financial statements, from internal to external analysis
  ✦ completes financial statement analysis and analytical review
  ✦ takes students through the complete budgeting process

❖ **Relevant** Contains relevant decision-making and capital budgeting problems for students to grasp easily.

❖ **Real-world companies** Each chapter contains references to real-world companies and examples. Margin notes contain many references to company Web sites to stimulate student interest.

❖ **Family Dollar Stores, Inc.** Features "the little company who could" and its experience of phenomenal growth in physical size and earnings while maintaining minimal debt. This *Fortune* 500 company appears in Chapter 2 to 13 and is easy for students of varying levels to understand.

❖ **Pedagogy progression** The text progresses from simple companies to complex subjects in Chapters 12 and 13 for students ready to grasp more advanced topics.

❖ **Challenging variety of student activities** The text contains a variety of questions and problems including:

 computer analysis,

 Internet challenges,

real-world companies to analyze in real time, and critical-thinking exercises.

* **"What Do You Think?"** Questions contained in the body of each chapter ask critical-thinking questions perfect for classroom discussion or written responses.
* **Two annual report projects** Contains one short project for lower-level students and a much longer project for higher-level students. These projects can be started early in the semester for a term project or used as a comprehensive review for the end of the semester. Both projects have been used in the authors' classrooms for a decade and are very effective in synthesizing the material.
* **Written on multiple levels** The text is easy enough for freshmen or sophomores, yet challenging enough to add depth and meaning for graduate students. The variety of student activities allows professors to select the level of detail, procedures, and analysis that is best suited to their students.

Instructor Resources

 Instructor's Resource CD contains PowerPoint Slides, Test Item File, Instructor's Manual, and the Solutions Manual.

* **PowerPoint Slides** A ready-made chapter presentation appropriate for lectures.
* **Test Item File** Written by Dr. Natalie Strouse, Notre Dame College of Ohio. More than 1,000 psychometrically-sound questions are available to test student learning.
* **TestGen Software** Computerized testing software utilizing the questions in the Test Item File for ease of use.
* **Instructor's Manual** Written by Dr. Bambi Hora, University of Central Oklahoma. Includes classroom-tested learning and instruction techniques, pre-tests, quizzes, student activities, and solutions to the "What Do You Think?" questions contained in the chapters.
* **Solutions Manual** Written by the textbook authors, Drs. Robert and Katherene Terrell, University of Central Oklahoma. Solutions to end-of-chapter Review of Concepts and Application Exercises suitable for classroom presentation.

Instructor's Resource Center

 Available at *www.prenhall.com/terrell*. This one-stop resource center hosts all of the instructor supplements.

Student Resources

 Companion Web Site Contains quizzes, exercises, PowerPoint slides at *www.prenhall.com/terrell*.

 Ask the Tutor On-line help from an accounting instructor at *www.prenhall.com/askthetutor*.

 On Location! Videos Enhance student learning in the classroom and peak students' interest.

Student Study Guide and Working Papers Written by Dr. Barbara Parrish, University of Central Oklahoma. Helpful guide to student learning containing chapter summaries, demonstration problems, and quizzes to reinforce student learning.

Acknowledgments

The authors wish to thank the following reviewers for their insightful comments and encouragement in producing this text.

Tim Alzheimer, *Montana State University-Bozeman*
Florence Atiase, *University of Texas at Austin*
Thomas Badley, *Baker College*
Rosalind Cranor, *Virginia Polytechnic Institute and State University*
Michael L. Davis, *Pepperdine University*
Robert Dunn, *Auburn University*
Leslie B. Fletcher, *Georgia Southern University*
Kimberly Frank, *University of Nevada-Las Vegas*
William T. Geary, *College of William and Mary*
John L. Norman, Jr., *Keller Graduate School of Management*
Robert D. Patterson, *Pennsylvania State University-Erie*
Janet F. Phillips, *Southern Connecticut State University*
Theodore Tully, *DeVry University-Fremont*
Terrence Willyard, *Baker College*

Special thanks to our supplement authors and reviewers:

Natalie Strouse, *Notre Dame College of Ohio*
Bambi Hora, *University of Central Oklahoma*
Barbara Parrish, *University of Central Oklahoma*
Dan Haskin, *University of Central Oklahoma*

Thanks to Kumen Jones and Michael Werner for their contributions to this project.

Thanks for the support, encouragement, and faith of Bill Larkin, Jane Avery, Elisa Adams, Debbie Hoffman, and Tempe Goodhue. Each of you was invaluable to us in completing this project.

Special thanks to Dr. James Enderby Bidlack, Karen Price, Orjola Jolldashi, and Dr. Michael Haselkorn for your contributions to the manuscript's correctness.

Katherene P. Terrell and Robert L. Terrell
University of Central Oklahoma

ACCOUNTING

Making Sense of Business

CHAPTER 1

LEARNING OBJECTIVES

After completing this chapter you should be able to:

1 Define business activity and the profit motive.

2 Distinguish among the three major types of business activities and hybrid-type businesses.

3 Distinguish among the three basic forms of business organizations and describe the advantages and disadvantages of each.

4 Identify the stakeholders of a business and describe social responsibility.

5 Identify the attributes and evaluate the importance of business reputation and ethical behavior.

6 Compare and contrast the relationships between a business and its employees, other businesses, consumers, and government.

7 Discuss the effect of e-commerce on business practices.

8 Define accounting and distinguish among the different roles of accountants.

The Business Environment

Gone are the days when a business could achieve success by opening a location and waiting for customers to walk in and buy its products or services. A business today can sell to local, national, and international customers simultaneously not only by using its normal selling space, but also through communications such as telephone, catalogs, e-mail, and the Internet. Business professionals who compete in the global marketplace find it very complex due to the variety of sales avenues, cultures, and legal systems among countries. They must be able to make decisions that enable their companies to survive fierce global competition while maintaining ethical business practices.

To make sound business decisions, managers need relevant, reliable information. The accounting function in a firm provides information necessary to operate a successful business. To comprehend accounting, we must first understand the basic elements of the 21st century's business environment. The contemporary business environment includes firms engaged in different types of business activities, several forms of business ownership, and a complex web of relationships every company maintains with its employees, customers, suppliers, competitors, society, and governments. For an increasing number of firms, business today also includes the global and electronic marketplaces. The business owner or manager continuously juggles these components to plan and execute a successful business strategy.

One of the most successful business strategies an owner establishes is, "Good ethics is good business." Ethics is a system of standards of conduct and moral judgment. Ethical values vary from one society to another, and in a global economy it is

View the Nike® Accounting Environment video on the Web site *www.prenhall.com/terrell.*

● **ethics**
A system of standards of conduct and moral judgment.

difficult to judge a company's ethics by one particular set of values. As you will see later in this chapter, those companies that maintain the highest ethical standards enjoy the best reputations. In the last half of the 20th century, even as management scientists taught that ethical business behavior was important to longevity and success, the public saw some of the largest frauds and business failures occur. Throughout the history of business enterprise, fraud and greed have always tempted some business people to take shortcuts to success. They seldom succeed.

We will examine each of the components of the business environment to understand the business context for which accounting provides useful information. We will define accounting and briefly look at the accounting profession and its role in the business environment. Let's begin with the types of business activity.

Business Activity

● **business**
The process of producing and distributing goods and services to those who desire them.

● **profit**
The excess of revenues over expenses.

● **not-for-profit firms**
Generally benevolent organizations formed to serve the needs of society instead of earning profits to distribute to owners.

● **factors of production**
The four major items needed to support economic activity: natural resources, human resources, physical capital, and entrepreneurship.

● **natural resources**
Include air currents, water, land, and things that come from the earth such as timber, minerals, oil, and natural gas.

● **human resources**
Mental and physical efforts of all workers who produce the goods and services for a society.

● **physical capital**
Buildings, equipment, tools, and infrastructure required to produce goods and services.

● **entrepreneurship**
Creativity, willingness to accept risk, and management skills necessary to combine natural resources, human resources, and physical capital into business activity.

● **business plan**
Details of a firm's business goals and its action plan to achieve those goals.

Business is the process of producing and distributing goods and services to those who desire them. Production and distribution occur when entrepreneurs employ physical capital to combine labor and natural resources into products and services. A primary motivation for entrepreneurs to engage in business activity is **profit**, the excess of revenues over expenses. Profits represent the reward for those who take risks in business investments. Some organizations do not exist to earn profits for owners. **Not-for-profit firms** are, generally, benevolent organizations formed to serve the needs of society instead of earning profits to distribute to owners. If "profits" occur, the organization uses them to advance its goals. For-profit firms pay income taxes on profits but not-for-profit firms are exempt from certain portions of income taxes.

The **factors of production** are the four major items needed to support economic activity: natural resources, human resources, physical capital, and entrepreneurship. **Natural resources** include air currents, water, land, and things that come from the earth such as timber, minerals, oil, and natural gas. **Human resources** consist of the mental and physical efforts of all workers who produce the goods and services for a society. **Physical capital** consists of buildings, equipment, tools, and infrastructure required to produce goods and services. **Entrepreneurship** is the creativity, willingness to accept risk, and management skills necessary to combine natural resources, human resources, and physical capital into business activity. The success of an economy depends on the availability and use of the four factors of production within its economic system.

Just as an economy must utilize the four factors of production to function, so must an individual business determine the amount of each of the factors necessary to carry out its business purpose. Business owners (or prospective owners) prepare a **business plan** that details a firm's business goals and its action plan to achieve those goals. The U.S. Small Business Administration recommends that a business plan contain the following information:

1 statement of purpose;
2 description of the business including the type of business activity;
3 marketing plan including information on competition;
4 operations plan including information on personnel and insurance coverage; and
5 financial plan, which is the longest section of the plan and includes many types of accounting information.[1]

---

1. U.S. Small Business Administration, "The Business Plan, Road Map to Success," *www.SBAONLINE.SBA.gov/ starting/indexbusplans.html.*

Part of the analysis required to prepare the financial portion of any business plan describes the sources and costs of each of the factors of production and how each will be incorporated into operations. The Small Business Administration requires a business plan from prospective entrepreneurs. Creating the business plan makes entrepreneurs research and plan how to operate the business before they make the investment, lessening the risk of failure.

What Do You Think?

1-1   Think of a type of business you would enjoy owning and managing. Describe the specific human resources, natural resources, and physical capital you would need to successfully begin and operate this business.

Businesses require different levels of each factor of production because of the type of business activity conducted. We will examine those types of business activity and try to draw conclusions about the relationship between business activity and the need for factors of production.

Types of Business Activity

How the factors of production are combined to form a successful business depends on the type of business being formed. We can classify a company by its type of business activity. The three broad classifications of business activity are manufacturing, merchandising, and service. Although a single company can be involved in all three business activities, usually one constitutes the company's major focus.

Manufacturing Companies

Manufacturing is the business activity that converts raw materials into a tangible, physical product. A manufacturing company purchases raw materials from a supplier, and with physical capital and workers, transforms them into saleable products. Raw materials consist of either unprocessed natural resources or completely finished products manufactured by others. For example, Dell Computer Corporation purchases processors from Intel and disc drives from Seagate to use in construction of its computers. These processors and disc drives, while raw materials to Dell, are manufactured finished products for Intel and Seagate.

● **manufacturing**
The business activity that converts raw materials into a tangible, physical product.

A manufacturing company normally requires a large physical capital investment and a sufficient number of trained workers. The right combination of quality raw materials, manufacturing equipment, and well-trained workers will facilitate effective, efficient production. Efficiency and effectiveness contribute to higher profits.

Merchandising Companies

Merchandising is the business activity of selling finished goods produced by other companies. Like a manufacturer, a merchandising company sells tangible, physical products, called merchandise, as its major business activity. Instead of manufacturing the product it sells, a merchandising company buys it from suppliers in a finished form.

There are two kinds of merchandisers:

● **merchandising**
The business activity of selling finished goods produced by other companies.

1   **Wholesale merchandiser**—A wholesaler buys its product from a manufacturer (or from another wholesaler) and then sells that product to another business that eventually sells it to the **final consumer**, the final user of a product. Examples of wholesale merchandisers are C & S Wholesale Grocers, Inc., a national grocery wholesaler, and W. W. Grainger, Inc., a major wholesale merchandiser of tools. C & S Wholesale Grocers sells to retail grocery stores such as Piggly Wiggly, A & P, and Safeway. Grainger sells tools

● **final consumer**
The final user of a product.

Visit the C&S and Grainger Web sites to learn more about wholesale distribution systems at **www.cswg.com** and **www.grainger.com.**

directly to businesses for use in operations or for resale to retail customers. As a consumer, you may not recognize the names of these wholesalers because you most often buy from a retailer. Wholesalers provide a valuable service to retailers by making the retailer's purchasing convenient and cost effective.

2   Retail merchandiser—A retailer buys its product from a wholesaler or manufacturer and sells the product to the final consumer. Major national retailers are Barnes & Noble, Wal-Mart, and Gap Inc. Other retail chains focus on specific regions of the country, such as Family Dollar Stores. Still other successful retailers have one location, such as gift shops and specialty stores.

A typical merchandising company requires a large investment in inventory, a lesser investment in physical capital, and a smaller workforce than a manufacturer. A typical manufacturing company makes a significant investment in property, plant, and equipment; a smaller investment in raw materials; and requires a large workforce. A manufacturer's investment in physical capital is long term (5 to 30 years), whereas a merchandiser's investment in inventory turns over very quickly (usually 10 to 120 days).

Service Companies

● **service**
A business activity that provides specific work or a job function as its major operation.

Service is the business activity that provides specific work or a job function as its major operation. A service company does not sell tangible products, but performs a service for businesses or consumers as its major business activity. Doctors, lawyers, dentists, and accountants provide professional work instead of tangible products. Computer service centers, plumbers, auto mechanics, janitorial companies, and copier repair technicians provide services to both businesses and consumers.

Service providers usually have significantly lower physical capital requirements than manufacturers or merchandisers. Although they usually require fewer employees than a manufacturing operation, the employees may be highly educated professionals and technicians.

Hybrid Companies

● **hybrid company**
A company that participates significantly in more than one type of business activity.

A company that participates significantly in more than one type of activity is known as a **hybrid company**. For example, a new car dealership sells automobiles and trucks and is, therefore, classified as a merchandiser. In addition, a new-car dealer normally generates significant sales by providing repair services. Therefore, an automobile dealership is a hybrid of merchandising and service activities.

In the future we can expect the distinctions among manufacturing, merchandising, and service companies to become even more blurred. As the struggle for survival in the global marketplace becomes increasingly intense, many companies find it beneficial to diversify. By involving themselves in a wide variety of business activities, these businesses offer a broad mixture of products and services to protect a company's overall well-being when a downturn occurs in a particular market segment.

The latest business census from the U.S. Census Bureau provides the information contained in Exhibit 1-1 about the number and characteristics of U.S. business firms. The Census Bureau lists firms by major business activities according to the North American Industrial Classification System (NAICS). Because the NAICS considers only the major activity of a firm, we cannot determine how many companies engage in hybrid business activities.

Notice that manufacturing posts the largest number of workers, but not the largest amount of receipts. Wholesale trade accounts for 25 percent of receipts, but has less than 10 percent of the number of firms and only six percent of the workers. Compare the retail and health care industries. Both have approximately the same number of workers, but retail has almost twice the number of firms as health care, and almost three times the amount of receipts.

The owners of a new business select the type of activity for their firm. Equally important is the selection of the form of business organization because each business form operates in different legal and structural environments.

Exhibit 1-1
U.S. Business Firms Statistics

U.S. Business Firms			
	NUMBER OF FIRMS	**NUMBER OF EMPLOYEES**	**RECEIPTS (IN MILLIONS)**
All Industries	6,417,035	101,372,992	$17,808,277
Mining	25,000	509,006	$173,989
Utilities	15,513	702,703	$411,713
Construction	656,434	5,664,840	$858,581
Manufacturing	363,753	16,888,016	$3,842,061
Wholesale Trade	453,470	5,796,557	$4,059,658
Retail Trade	1,118,447	13,991,103	$2,460,886
Transportation, Warehousing	178,025	2,920,777	$318,245
Information	114,475	3,066,167	$623,214
Financial, Insurance	395,203	5,835,214	$2,197,771
Realty, Rentals, Leasing	288,273	1,702,420	$240,918
Professional, Scientific, Technological Services	621,129	5,361,210	$595,251
Management of Companies, Enterprises	47,319	2,617,527	$92,473
Support, Waste Management, Remediation	276,393	7,347,366	$295,936
Education	40,936	321,073	$20,239
Health Care, Social Assistance	645,853	13,561,579	$885,054
Arts, Entertainment, Recreation	99,099	1,587,660	$104,715
Accommodation, Food Services	545,068	9,451,226	$350,399
Other Services	519,715	3,256,178	$265,898
Auxiliaries, Subsidiaries, Managing Offices	12,930	792,370	$11,276

Source: 1997 Business Census, U.S. Census Bureau

What Do You Think?

1-2   Examine the information in Exhibit 1-1. Prepare a table that reclassifies the groups into manufacturing, merchandising, and service firms. Explain the reasoning for your choices.

1-3   After reclassifying the data in Exhibit 1-1 into merchandising, manufacturing, and service firms, which of the three has the largest number of:

(a) firms?
(b) employees?
(c) estimated receipts?
(d) employees per firm?
(e) estimated receipts per employee?

1-4   Visit the Web sites of the following companies to determine if each is a manufacturing, merchandising, service, or hybrid company. In your analysis, identify the primary business activity or activities for each company.

(a) Daimler Chrysler (*www.daimlerchrysler.com*)
(b) Johnson & Johnson (*www.johnsonandjohnson.com*)
(c) Procter & Gamble (*www.pg.com*)
(d) Nordstrom (*www.nordstom.com*)
(e) Snap-On Incorporated (*www.snapon.com*)
(f) Dollar Thrifty Auto Group, Inc. (*www.DollarThrifty.com*)

Forms of Business Organization in the United States

The three basic forms of business organization in the United States are sole proprietorships, partnerships, and corporations.

Sole Proprietorships

● **sole proprietorship**
A business that is owned by a single individual and is not legally separate from the owner.

A common American dream is to own a business. Often this dream becomes reality with a sole proprietorship, the simplest business form. A **sole proprietorship**, or proprietorship, is a business that is owned by a single individual and is not legally separate from the owner. A common misconception about this form of business is that it is always small. Although most sole proprietorships are small, the classification suggests nothing about the size of the business, only that it has a single owner.

A sole proprietorship is easy and inexpensive to organize. No special legal requirements are associated with starting a sole proprietorship. The only legal barrier to establishing a proprietorship is to obtain any necessary licenses and permits, which usually cost several hundred dollars or less. A single owner has total ownership of after-tax profits and total control over running the business. A sole proprietor has the independence to determine the quantity and quality of business effort. From a legal standpoint, a sole proprietorship is simply an extension of its owner and pays no separate income tax. The earnings of the company are considered the earnings of the owner and become a part of his or her personal taxable income. Sole proprietors can end their business as easily as they can start them. If the owner decides to cease operations, he or she must notify the appropriate licensing agent of the state and local governments and satisfy all business debts.

It may seem that owning a sole proprietorship provides the owner with a lot of control and few problems. Working alone without additional financial support, however, presents the owner with numerous challenges concerning liability, resources, talent, and time commitment. Because a sole proprietorship is legally an extension of its owner, all business obligations become the owner's legal obligations. Because the owner's liability is unlimited, if the company fails to pay its debts, the creditors can sue the owner for the owner's personal property, including his or her house, car, boat, or other holdings. The amount of capital available to a sole proprietorship is limited to the amount of personal assets the owner can contribute to the business or the amount the owner can borrow on a personal loan. A sole proprietor operates with personal talents and expertise and, consequently, many proprietorships fail because the owner lacks skills or expertise in areas critical to the survival of the company. In addition, running a business is hard work, and a sole proprietor works very long hours—probably longer hours than if he or she were employed elsewhere. Unless the company is sold to another entity or is passed on to the owner's heirs, the life of the business cannot legally exceed the life of the owner.

Nearly 71 percent of U.S. companies are sole proprietorships. Because most of them are small businesses, only about 6 percent of all business revenues earned in the United States come from this form of business.

Partnerships

● **partnership**
A business with two or more owners who all share in the risks and profits of the entity.

A **partnership** is a business with two or more owners who all share in the risks and profits of the entity. Many people incorrectly assume that all partnerships are small businesses. In fact, some partnerships are quite large. Most large public accounting firms, such as KPMG LLP or Deloitte & Touche LLP, are partnerships, and some of them have as many as 1,500 partners and 20,000 employees.

People form a partnership to overcome some of the challenges of a sole proprietorship while they retain some advantages of a proprietorship. From a legal standpoint, partners can form a partnership almost as easily as a proprietorship. Although not legally required, partners should commit the ownership and profit-sharing structure of the partnership to a formal partnership agreement, signed by each partner, to clarify their consensus about these issues. Wise partners will also include clauses about adding or dismissing partners and partnership dissolution. In delineating the profit-sharing arrangement, the partners usually consider the amount of capital each partner invests in the partnership, how much time each partner regularly commits, and any special expertise a partner may contribute. Partners may select any profit-sharing arrangement on which all can agree. A well-written partnership agreement helps to resolve future conflicts and problems.

Partners often form partnerships because each has skills in a critical area of business that complement the others' skills. Combining those areas of expertise into a partnership enhances the business's chances of success. Having more than one person involved in the ownership of the business usually increases access to capital. In fact, many partnerships form to combine one partner's special expertise with another's capital.

A partnership is not legally separate from its owners, replicating many of the challenges of a proprietorship. A partnership does not pay separate income taxes from its owners. Rather, the partnership files a tax return that allocates the business profits, according to the profit-sharing agreement, among the partners. Each partner includes his or her share of the profits on the partner's personal tax return.

When a partner dies or withdraws from the partnership, the legal life of that partnership ends. The heirs inherit the value of the partnership interest but not the right to be partners in the firm. For all practical purposes, however, the business generally does not need to cease operations. The partnership must settle with the heirs, and the partnership agreement may allow the remaining partner or partners either to continue with one less partner or to admit another partner to the firm.

Although the partnership form helps overcome some disadvantages of a proprietorship, it also creates new ones. The troublesome unlimited liability is common to both proprietorships and partnerships. In fact, in most instances, each partner is personally liable for the total obligations of the partnership. This means that if any partner makes a decision that obligates the partnership, all the other partners become liable, even if they knew nothing about the decision. This adds an additional risk to being a partner.

Another serious risk in a partnership is what may happen when conflicts arise among the partners. Suppose one partner wants the company to begin selling a new product and another partner disagrees. If the two partners have equal power, gridlock results. The bases for conflicts among partners range from personal habits to overall business philosophy. Most conflicts are minor, but severe conflicts may require dissolution of the partnership if the partners cannot resolve them. Ending a partnership severs personal and professional ties and can be a devastating emotional experience. If individuals forming a partnership are wise, they will include specific provisions for dissolution in the original partnership agreement when all the partners have positive attitudes toward one another. You might think of this as the business version of a prenuptial agreement: The parties forming the business agree on how the business marriage will end. Although the partnership form solves some problems of being a sole proprietor, many people believe the potential risks outweigh them. Only about one percent of all U.S. businesses are partnerships, and they account for just about four percent of all business revenues.

Modern business practice managed to overcome the worst of the partnership's disadvantages by creating two new partnership forms. A **limited partnership** consists of at least one general partner and one or more limited partners. The general partners have unlimited liability and operate the partnership. The limited partners enjoy limited liability, but they are precluded from having a decision-making role in the organization. Financiers, such as Merrill Lynch, frequently use limited partnerships for investment ventures.

A **limited liability partnership (LLP)** limits the liability of a general partner to his or her own negligence or misconduct, or the behavior of persons he or she controls. Many professional partnerships of accountants and lawyers use the LLP business form, such as Grant Thornton LLP and Ernst & Young LLP.

● **limited partnership**
A partnership that consists of at least one general partner and one or more limited partners.

● **limited liability partnership (LLP)**
A partnership that limits the liability of a general partner to his or her own negligence or misconduct, or the behavior of persons he or she controls.

Separate Entity Assumption

● **separate entity assumption**
The assumption that economic activity can be identified with a particular economic entity and that the results of the activities will be separately recorded.

From a record-keeping and accounting perspective, proprietorships, partnerships, and corporations are considered to be completely separate from their owners. This view reflects the **separate entity assumption** that economic activity can be identified with a particular economic entity and that the results of the activities will be separately recorded. This is true whether the entity is an individual, proprietorship, corporation, or even a division of a business. However, from a legal standpoint, the corporation is the only form of business considered to be a separate legal entity from its owners.

Corporations

● **corporation**
A separate legal entity with the rights and obligations of a person.

In 1819 Chief Justice John Marshall issued a ruling that made the **corporation** a separate legal entity with the rights and obligations of a person, including the right to enter into contracts and the right to buy, own, and sell property. The law requires a corporation to discharge its obligations lawfully, and creditors can sue for recovery if it does not. A corporation can be taken to court if it breaks the law, and it is obligated to pay taxes like any other person. In addition to the legal obligations of corporations, the moral obligation of corporations to be socially responsible has been a topic of widespread discussion in recent years.

● **stock**
Certificates of ownership in a corporation.

● **stockholder**
A person or entity who owns shares of stock in a corporation and usually has the right to vote on how to operate the business and to receive profit distributions. Also called a shareholder.

Individuals, partnerships, or other corporations can organize a corporation. Investors buy certificates of ownership in a corporation called **stock**. The **stockholder**, or shareholder, is a person or entity who owns shares of stock in a corporation and usually has the right to vote on how to operate the business and to receive profit distributions.

The corporate business form solves the major problem of ownership in a proprietorship or a partnership—unlimited liability. Because a corporation is a separate legal entity from its stockholders, the owners are not personally liable for the corporation's obligations. With limited liability, stockholders limit their losses to the amount of their investment in the corporation and not everything else they own.

By dividing the ownership of the firm into relatively low-cost shares of stock, a corporation can attract a great number of investors, raise capital, and have life independent of the owners. Some U.S. corporations have more than one million stockholders. Many small corporations, and a few large ones, have only one stockholder. Because ownership shares in a corporation usually cost less than $100, individual investors buy and sell shares much more easily than they could trade an ownership interest in a proprietorship or partnership. Freely traded stock requires no approval or permission from other shareholders for trading, unlike the approval required to accept a partner into a business. Being separate from its owners, a corporation continues to exist even when ownership changes completely. Transferring shares of stock has no effect on the life of a corporation.

● **board of directors**
A group of people who have ultimate responsibility for managing the corporation.

The stockholders exercise their voting privileges to elect a **board of directors**, who have ultimate responsibility for managing the corporation. In almost all proprietorships and in most partnerships, the owners manage the business according to their wishes. In large corporations, few stockholders participate in the daily operations of the business. The board of directors hires professional managers to operate the company on behalf of the owners. Professional managers frequently have greater expertise in business than proprietors, but sometimes operate the company in their own interests, rather than the owners' interest.

● **dividend**
A distribution of part of the firm's after-tax profit to the shareholders.

● **limited liability company (LLC)**
A corporation in which stockholders enjoy the limited liability status of a corporation but are taxed as partners in a partnership.

Creating a legal entity causes several disadvantages that both cost money and create complications for the business. Unlike a proprietorship or partnership, a corporation must pay a federal income tax, and in many states it also pays state and local income taxes. The board of directors can distribute part of the firm's after-tax profit to the shareholders as a **dividend**. Stockholders report dividends received as personal income and pay personal income taxes on them. We refer to this process as double taxation, and it has been the subject of fierce debate for many years in the United States. Recent regulations created a new type of corporation termed a **limited liability company (LLC)**. In an LLC, stockholders enjoy the limited liability status of a corporation but are taxed as partners in a partnership, thus avoiding double taxation.

Government subjects corporations to significantly more control than either sole proprietorships or partnerships. In addition to federal and state income tax returns, many corporations file numerous reports with other federal and state regulatory bodies. Filing these reports costs time and money.

Although corporations represent a small percentage of the total number of U.S. businesses, corporations transact approximately nine times as much business as all proprietorships and partnerships combined. Corporations also control the majority of business resources in the United States.

What Do You Think?

1-5   If you were to start a business, what form of business organization would you select? State the reasons for your choice.

The business environment consists of all forms of business entities that interact with other businesses and a number of individuals and groups. Business behavior plays an important part in shaping the tone of the business environment.

Business Stakeholders

A **stakeholder** is any person or entity affected by the way a company conducts its business. A company's reputation develops from the way its stakeholders view its performance. Stakeholders of a business entity include:

- **Customers**—Customers want quality products and services at reasonable prices. Customers have a right to receive products and services that are truthfully marketed and pose no health or safety risks.
- **Employees**—Employees want fair wages, safe working conditions, job security, opportunities to advance, and reasonable benefits.
- **Stockholders**—Stockholders have invested savings and taken a risk on a company. In return, they expect the company to be a good steward of the investment by making a reasonable profit and protecting its assets. Stockholders also want returns in the form of dividends and growth in the market price of the stock. Both dividends and price growth increase stockholders' wealth.
- **Competitors**—Competitors expect fair competition. U.S. trade laws require that a company not engage in predatory pricing, price fixing, price discrimination, or monopolistic practices. **Predatory pricing** is marking prices so low that competitors are forced to drop out of the market because they cannot remain profitable. A large company can sometimes operate more cheaply than its competitors. When the large company intentionally lowers its sales price below its competitors' cost to drive the competitors out of the market, it becomes a predator. **Price fixing** occurs when a group of competitors agree to set a uniform market price to increase their profits. Price fixing blocks the normal competitive market forces that tend to hold consumer prices to reasonable amounts. Price discrimination also interrupts normal competitive market forces. **Price discrimination** occurs when a business charges different prices to different customers to lessen competition.

   A monopoly occurs when only one producer exists for a particular product or service. **Monopolistic practices** take advantage of consumers by raising prices unfairly because a business is the main supplier of a particular good or service.
- **Government**—Governments (federal, state, local, and foreign) have a stake in a company because they collect taxes from the profits of the business activity it generates. Government regulations also help protect the public from fraudulent business practices, pollution, and unsafe conditions.

● **stakeholder**
Any person or entity affected by the way a company conducts its business.

● **predatory pricing**
Marking prices so low that competitors are forced to drop out of the market because they cannot remain profitable.

● **price fixing**
A group of competitors agree to set a uniform market price to increase their profits.

● **price discrimination**
Charging different prices to different customers to lessen competition.

● **monopolistic practices**
Taking advantage of consumers by raising prices unfairly because a business is the main supplier of a particular good or service.

● **Community**—The community (local, state, national, and global) has a vested interest in business. The community depends on a business for employment and taxes, and the business plays a major role in shaping the communities in which it operates. To be a good business citizen, a firm must first do no harm; then it must exhibit social responsibility. **Social responsibility** encompasses the attitudes and actions that exhibit sensitivity to social and environmental concerns. Social responsibility entails working as an essential contributor to the community's well-being. A firm exhibits social responsibility by encouraging its employees to participate in community programs, making monetary contributions to charitable organizations, and sponsoring various civic and charitable events.

● **social responsibility**
Attitudes and actions that exhibit sensitivity to social and environmental concerns.

The business environment reflects how ethical and socially responsible members of the business community behave toward their stakeholders. As social scientists began to study the characteristics of successful businesses in the 20th century, they discovered that long-term successful firms enjoyed good reputations that included the ethical treatment of others.

Business Reputation and Ethical Behavior

In seeking success, the business community takes note of the attributes of successful companies. A business builds a successful reputation with such attributes as:

● **corporate culture**
An organization's values and beliefs.

1   An enduring corporate culture—**Corporate culture** reflects an organization's values and beliefs. It drives reputation. An enduring culture provides a framework for growth and change that remains true to core values and ethics. Robert Waterman, in *What America Does Right: Learning from Companies That Put People First,* indicates that "corporate cultures that tend to put their three constituencies—shareholders, customers, and employees—on the same plane, as opposed to putting shareholders first, are perversely the ones that do best for shareholders."[2]

2   Product and service quality—A company's reputation will be no better than what it gives to its customers.

3   Innovation—To remain competitive and viable in a global marketplace, a company must innovate and stay at the cutting edge of customer needs and technology.

4   Financial strength—Financially strong companies have resources to attract talented people, innovate, and pay attention to product and service quality.

5   Attraction and retention of talented people—A company cannot produce quality goods and services without hiring and keeping talented and dedicated employees. Good reputations, in turn, motivate employees.

6   Social responsibility—Ethical involvement with all levels of community enhances business relationships with employees, customers, stockholders, and competitors.

Donald Lessard, deputy dean of the Sloan School of Business at the Massachusetts Institute of Technology, lists reputation as the number one risk a business must manage. He asserts that management often focuses on protecting financial and physical assets instead of its more vulnerable reputation, business model, human capital, intellectual property, and business relationships. For example, a damaged reputation often reduces the market value of stock. When children in Belgium became sick from a Coke product in 1999, Coca-Cola suffered $103 million in costs and the market value of its stock fell $34 billion in the third quarter of 1999.[3]

Managers earn a good reputation for a company in the business world when they conduct business in an ethical manner. A good reputation helps a company to maintain or increase its market share with customers, encourages potential investors to buy company stocks and bonds, and helps attract good employees.

---

2. Robert Waterman, *What America Does Right: Learning from Companies That Put People First* (New York: Norton, 1994).
3. Thomas A. Stewart. "Managing Risk in the 21st Century," *Fortune* 141 (February 7, 2000):202ff.

Fortune attempts to measure the business reputation of large U.S. businesses each year when it publishes a list of the most admired and least admired companies. It bases the list on an annual survey of more than 10,000 directors, executives, and security analysts. The respondents rank companies on eight key attributes of innovativeness, quality of management, employee talent, financial stability, wise use of corporate assets, social responsibility, quality of products and services, and long-term investment value. All attributes were equally weighted in the rankings. Exhibit 1-2

For more information about the ranking of U.S. businesses, go to *Fortune*'s Web site at **www.fortune.com.**

Exhibit 1-2
Fortune's Most and Least Admired Companies, for 1999 Through 2002

		Fortune's Most Admired Companies		
RANK	**1999**[1]	**2000**[2]	**2001**[3]	**2002**[4]
1	General Electric	General Electric	General Electric	General Electric
2	Coca-Cola	Microsoft	Cisco Systems	Southwest Airlines
3	Microsoft	Dell Computer	Wal-Mart Stores	Wal-Mart Stores
4	Dell Computer	Cisco Systems	Southwest Airlines	Microsoft
5	Berkshire Hathaway	Wal-Mart Stores	Microsoft	Berkshire Hathaway
6	Wal-Mart Stores	Southwest Airlines	Home Depot	Home Depot
7	Southwest Airlines	Berkshire Hathaway	Berkshire Hathaway	Johnson & Johnson
8	Intel	Intel	Charles Schwab	FedEx
9	Merck	Home Depot	Intel	Citigroup
10	Disney	Lucent Technologies	Dell Computer	Intel

				Fortune's Least Admired Companies					
RANK	**1999**[1]	**RANK**	**2000**[2]	**RANK**	**2001**[3]	**RANK**	**2002**[4]
460	Foundation Health	495	Humana	526	TWA	520	Merisel
461	Fruit of the Loom	496	Revlon	527	Trump Resorts	521	Kmart
462	Viad	497	TWA	528	Kmart	522	UAL
463	Olsten	498	CKE Restaurants	529	Bridgestone	523	Microage
464	U.S. Industries	499	CHS Electronics	530	America West	524	Winn-Dixie Stores
465	Stone Container	500	Rite Aid	531	LTV	525	Comdisco
466	Oxford Health Plans	501	Trump Resorts	532	US Airways Group	526	Consolidated Freightways
467	MedPartners	502	Fruit of the Loom	533	Federal-Mogul	527	Federated-Mogul
468	Shoney's	503	Amerco	534	Warnaco Group	528	LTV
476	Flagstar	469	Trump Resorts Casinos	535	CKE Restaurants	529	Warnarco Group

1. Eryn Brown and Len A. Costa, "America's Most Admired Companies," *Fortune* 139 (March 1, 1999):68+.
2. Geoffrey Colvin and Ahmad Diba, "America's Most Admired Companies," *Fortune* 141 (February 21, 2000):108+.
3. Ahmad Diba and Lisa Munoz, "America's Most Admired Companies," *Fortune* 143 (February 19, 2001):64+.
4. Jessica Sung and Christopher Tkaczyk, "Who's on Top and Who Flopped," *Fortune* 145 (March 4, 2002):75+.

summarizes the top 10 most admired and least admired U.S. companies according to *Fortune*'s survey for 1999 through 2002. By studying these organizations, we might learn how they achieve success.

What Do You Think?

1-6   What do you believe are the three most important attributes that give a company a good reputation? Do not limit yourself the companies listed in Exhibit 1-2.

1-7   Name three companies in your community you most admire. Discuss the qualities each business possesses that you consider important in your determination.

1-8   Would you trade with a company that has a bad reputation? If so, under what circumstances?

Now that we have examined some facets of business reputation, let's discover more about the important relationships a business maintains with its employees, customers, other businesses, and governments.

Business Relationships

To operate in the 21st century business environment, a business must maintain ethical and appropriate relationships with its employees, its customers, other businesses, and governments. If management can successfully create ethical relationships with these groups, owners and shareholders will prosper.

Employees

An organization is no better than its weakest link. Each employee, from the shipping clerk to the president, affects how the organization functions and serves its customers. If a company expects to have the best personnel it can afford, it must find ways to attract, and keep, high-functioning people to carry out the company's mission and help the stockholders prosper. The corporate culture sets the tone for personal behavior in an organization. A wholesome culture that operates in an atmosphere of mutual trust creates relationships beneficial to both employee and employer. How does the company's management know how to treat employees? Beyond general rules of fairness, ethics, and equity, it is hard to know because each group of employees is different.

We can gain insights into building good employee relationships from studying the way successful companies treat employees. Each January since 1997, *Fortune* has published the "100 Best Companies to Work For" in the United States. Although the study is about U.S.-based businesses, many of the businesses operate internationally. The study focuses on the characteristics that U.S. workers find most attractive in employers. More than 36,000 employees completed surveys in 2000 to determine the best employers. Although this survey does not examine every U.S. company, 36,000 employees give us a reasonable sample of valued employment factors. According to the surveys, employees place a good working environment—corporate culture—at the top of the list. Even more important than salary levels, employees value flexible work schedules, onsite child-care services, tuition reimbursement plans, a variety of group insurance plans, home-purchasing assistance, and personal financial counseling. Exhibit 1-3 presents the top 20 companies of 2000 through 2003.

The top 100 companies represent 20 different fields, including many in the fields of technology and finance. But the list includes retailers, manufacturing, airlines, and pharmaceutical companies. *Fortune*'s writers discovered that these companies possess the following characteristics: a diverse workforce that competes for these positions;

For more information on these companies and the complete list of the top 100 companies, visit *Fortune's* Web site at **www.fortune.com.**

Exhibit 1-3
Top 20 of *Fortune*'s 100 Best Companies to Work For, 2000–2003

	Top 20 Companies to Work For			
RANK	**2000**[1]	**2001**[2]	**2002**[3]	**2003**[4]
1	Container Store	Container Store	Edward Jones	Edward Jones
2	Southwest Airlines	SAS Institute	Container Store	Container Store
3	Cisco Systems	Cisco Systems	SAS Institute	Alston & Bird Institute
4	TDIndustries	Southwest Airlines	TDIndustries	Xilinx
5	Synovus Financial	Charles Schwab	Synovus Financial	Adobe Systems
6	SAS Institute	TDIndustries	Xilinx	American Cast Iron Pipe
7	Edward Jones	Fenwick & West	Plante & Moran	TDIndustries
8	Charles Schwab	Synovus Financial	Qualcomm	J.M. Smucker
9	Goldman Sachs	Edward Jones	Alston & Bird	Synovus Financial
10	MBNA	Plante & Moran	Baptist Health Care	Wegmans Food Markets
11	CDW	CDW	Frank Russell	Plante & Moran
12	Scitor	Born Information Services	Hypertherm	Pella
13	Frank Russell	Frank Russell	CDW	CDW
14	Qualcomm	Xilinx	Fenwick & West	JM Family Enterprises
15	Great Plains	Goldman Sachs	Cisco Systems	Baptist Health Care
16	Finova Group	WRQ	Graniterock	Vision Service Plan
17	Plante & Moran	Graniterock	Beck Group	Republic Bancorp
18	AFLAC	Continental Airlines	East Alabama Medical Center	Qualcomm
19	Graniterock	Vision Service Plan	Goldman Sachs	SAS Institute
20	Pfizer	American Century Investment	JM Family Enterprises	Microsoft

1. Robert Levering and Milton Moslowitz, "The 100 Best Companies to Work For," *Fortune* 141 (January 10, 2000):82–110.
2. Robert Levering and Milton Moslowitz, "The 100 Best Companies to Work For," *Fortune* 143 (January 8, 2001):148–168.
3. Robert Levering and Milton Moslowitz, "The 100 Best Companies to Work For," *Fortune* 145 (February 4, 2002):72–90.
4. Robert Levering and Milton Moslowitz, "The 100 Best Companies to Work For," *Fortune* 147 (January 20, 2003):127–152.

low turnover of personnel; employee benefits that include stock ownership, flexible working hours, educational opportunities, and onsite day care; longevity of the organization and top leadership; and higher than average profitability.

What Do You Think?

1-9 List the qualities you desire in an employer in order of importance. Explain why each quality is important to you.

1-10 What are the five most important benefits you seek from a prospective employer?

After looking at the characteristics of highly valued employers, their management teams seem to recognize that employees have complicated lives. By helping employees better their lives, management finds that employees with well-balanced lives perform better and help the company become more profitable. After establishing a good relationship with employees, management must pay careful attention to its relationship with customers. Customers come in two basic forms: other businesses and consumers. The relationships with business customers and consumers differ for most companies. Let's look closely at each.

Business to Business

In any business-to-business (B2B) transaction, one firm is the seller and the other takes the customer role, such as C & S Wholesale Grocers and A & P. In some instances, Bidlack Co. may sell to and buy from Sheets, Inc., making this relationship more complex. The management of Bidlack Co. must be both a good vendor to and a good customer of Sheets, Inc., and Sheets, Inc. faces the same challenge.

To maintain good business relationships, management prefers to trade with other companies that it can trust in an atmosphere of mutual respect. Although management wants to spend the least amount for its input materials, many managers realize that small cost savings can be eliminated by the cost of dealing with unprincipled or ruthless companies. The adage, "If it seems too good to be true, it probably is," still applies. Many a businessperson has learned to heed that warning after buying a low-cost alternative only to learn it was not the required quality of material.

Trading with other businesses offers a firm expanding opportunities. The cheapest and most effective form of advertising is networking and word-of-mouth. Business executives and managers build a large relationship network with others who work for vendors, customers, and even competitors. This network can be a valuable source of new vendors and customers.

Business customers frequently buy in large quantities. Selling 10,000 units of product to one business customer normally takes less time than selling 100 units to many consumers. Even though businesses are often given lower prices than are consumers, a large volume of sales to business customers can increase the company profits faster than the same amount of sales to individual consumers because making large sales usually costs less per unit.

Take for example Sandy Smith, who makes a $7,000 sale to Roger Corporation with one day's work including a short drive and buying a nice lunch for Roger's purchasing agent. The total cost for Sandy's work is $400 including her five percent commission. Tony Holden makes $20,000 in sales to 20 individuals in a week. His cost of making these sales is $1,300 including his five percent commission.

What Do You Think?

1-11   What are Sandy's and Tony's potential sales for the month if each can average the performance given in the example?

1-12   Ignoring all other costs except those given in the example, how much do Sandy and Tony contribute to business profits in a four-week (20 working-day) period?

1-13   Per dollar of sales, which of the two contributes more to business profits? Why?

As you may have discovered in answering the discussion questions, the large sales become more profitable in dollars and percentage of sales. Look at an analysis of Sandy's and Tony's sales:

	Sandy	Tony
Monthly sales	$140,000	$80,000
Costs:		
5% Commission	7,000	4,000
Other	1,000	1,200
Sales less costs	$132,000	$74,800
Percent cost/sales	5.71%	6.50%

Not only do the business sales add up quickly, but the selling cost per dollar of sales is less, making the B2B sales more profitable per sales dollar.

Why are Sandy's other costs less than Tony's? Part of this may be because she spends less time with the business customer per dollar of sales. The purchasing agent she met with at Roger Corporation did not have a lot of time to spend with Sandy. The business buyer may also be more knowledgeable about the product. They met; came to an agreement on price, delivery, and other important issues; and closed the $7,000 deal.

Tony had to deal with 20 individuals to close his sales. He had to go through the same process 20 times and each time closed a $1,000 deal. The time spent per deal is less, but there is less reward for the time.

Some companies make only B2B sales, others sell only to consumers, or business to customer (B2C), and others do both, as we illustrated in our example. Do companies market differently to consumers than to businesses?

Business to Consumers

Companies that focus on business-to-consumer (B2C) sales include various levels of service. Self-service operations, such as grocers and discount stores, provide little personal service and focus energies on keeping products on the shelves. At the opposite end of the spectrum, custom-designed clothing and jewelry stores are service-intensive merchandisers that utilize a many-to-one employee ratio with each customer.

Traditional B2C firms operate with many venues. Some firms have single fixed locations, others offer multiple locations, some have mobile locations, and others serve customers in their choice of location. Catalog sales have offered customers choices in the privacy of their homes for more than a century. Each venue has its unique costs, benefits, and sacrifices to both the company and the customer.

Sandy's sales:	
$7,000 x 20 days	
Tony's sales:	
$20,000 x 4 weeks	
Sandy's commission:	
5% x $140,000	
Tony's commission:	
5% x $80,000	
Sandy's other costs:	
Daily cost	$ 400
	x 20 days
	$8,000
Commission	−7,000
Other costs	$1,000
Tony's other costs:	
Weekly cost	$1,300
	x 4 weeks
	$5,200
Commission	−4,000
Other costs	$1,200

What Do You Think?

1-14 For each of the following marketing strategies, think of a real business you have patronized that uses this strategy. Describe what you believe are the customer benefits and disadvantages for each:

  (a) **single store**
  (b) **multiple store locations**
  (c) **mobile or traveling operation**
  (d) **catalog sales**

1-15 What do you believe might be the unique costs or sacrifices for the seller for each type of marketing listed in question 1-14?

Management must decide what is the proper mix of company costs and customer benefits to maintain its profitability and stability. In determining this mix, management attempts to create a profitable relationship with its customers. Relationship marketing seeks to create optimum customer satisfaction to maximize sales because satisfied, valued customers become repeat customers. Management must find cost-effective ways to satisfy the greatest number of customers who purchase the largest amount of products and services. How does management determine who these customers are and what they want? Market research plays a critical role in providing such information.

A firm's accounting and information systems can provide a wealth of market data such as the time, day, and month customers make purchases; the number of items purchased per transaction; the zip code of the purchaser; and so on. These data give management information about peak selling times to help schedule the right amount of help. Market research specialists have numerous ways of adding more information to company databases about customers' family income, ages of family members, hobbies, customer tastes and preferences, and desirable services and products the company does not currently offer. All such information adds to the likelihood that management can tailor products and services to match the desires of their customers. Remember that customer data are normally specific to a small region or even a single location.

Knowledge about customer needs and wants are not enough to maximize sales and profits, however. Management must have an action plan to transform that knowledge into sales. If a company builds its reputation on low prices, customers must find the lowest prices in that store. When a firm guarantees special service, its management must provide service-minded employees. Relationship management techniques can build strong customer loyalty, which gives that company a strategic advantage over the competition.

What Do You Think?

1-16   Can you name two businesses for which you have such loyalty that you will pay more for an item to buy it there? Why?

1-17   Have you ever stopped doing business with a company with which you had a loyal relationship? Describe the incident(s) that led to your decision to break the relationship. What could the company do to get you back as a loyal customer?

Government agencies (local, state, and federal) comprise another group of potential customers. Businesses have unique relationships with government entities.

Business to Governments

Governments are among the largest consumers of products and services businesses offer. Business entities, in turn, provide a tax base for local, state, and federal governments. Governments levy sales and service taxes that consumers pay on business transactions, tax business profits, tax employers on salaries paid to workers, and levy tariffs (taxes on imports and exports). Government regulation of business practices increases expenses for reporting and compliance.

Society as a whole benefits from the regulations that monitor unethical or illegal business practices, safety in the workplace, pollution, product safety, and so forth. Consumers, however, pay for these costs in higher product prices and higher taxes. Both companies and governments must raise income, prices, and taxes to pay for these costs. A business cannot continue to operate unless it makes a profit.

A business must maintain a good relationship with the governments with which it interacts. Most businesses accomplish this by being good corporate citizens operating within laws and obeying regulations. When a business disrupts its relationship with employees, vendors, or customers, it loses sales and sacrifices profits. When a business enters into an adversarial relationship with a government agency, the agency can impose restrictions and penalties on business activities. Such penalties can lead to the company's demise.

Therefore, the relationship between businesses and governments remains complicated. Governments must help keep business and the economy strong and healthy while at the same time controlling business abuses. A company must operate profitably while tiptoeing through a minefield of government regulations. It can be quite a challenge.

Business relationships with customers and governments evolve over time. New technologies in the late 20th century dramatically changed the traditional relationship between companies and customers.

E-Commerce

In the 1990s the introduction of the World Wide Web brought the information technology of the Internet into homes and businesses. Soon thereafter businesses and customers realized that business could be conducted over the Internet in much the same way as catalog and television shopping channels operated during the 20th century. Business transactions that are conducted electronically through the Internet and other electronic media are called **e-commerce**. The use of the information technology can reduce both the time required and the cost of business transactions in a number of ways.

First, communication time declines from days to minutes. E-mail delivers business letters and orders within a few minutes and eliminates the cost of stationery and postage. Purchase delivery time is reduced just by the time saved in preparing and mailing the order form. Prior to the Internet, many used the telephone, which was also fast. But long-distance telephone calls are expensive and require preparing and mailing printed order confirmations. Telephone communication also requires a person to receive the call. E-mail can be sent 24 hours a day and received at the convenience of the recipient.

Second, Internet catalogs save color printing costs and mailing fees. Even at third-class postage rates, the cost of printing and mailing catalogs is enormous. Online catalogs have the same visual effect of glossy printing. In addition, some companies have created Web technology that can project three-dimensional images.

Third, the Internet allows sellers to process payments instantly through credit cards and bank debits. This both accelerates cash collection and reduces the risk of nonpayment for the seller. Customers' risk increases because payment is rendered before receipt of the goods. The buyers also assume the risk of dealing with a seller they may not know or trust. Some organizations provide consumers protection by certifying the safety of a Web site.

● **e-commerce**
Business transactions that are conducted electronically through the Internet and other electronic media.

Visit the Web site of Lands' End at **www.Landsend.com** to see its unique virtual catalog.

What Do You Think?

1-18 Have you ever purchased anything:

(a) **from a catalog?**
(b) **on the Internet?**
(c) **over the telephone?**

Describe your purchases and your satisfaction with the process.

1-19 If Wal-Mart began to sell its entire product line through its Web site, do you think you would buy online? What types of items would you buy and why?

All this new technology sounds great for both buyer and seller. Products should be cheaper and profits higher for the businesses. Does e-commerce really produce cost savings or increase sales? Companies with physical locations must determine if Internet sales are additional sales or simply current customers who use the Web site for convenience. Virtual companies, which operate only on the Internet, struggle to remain profitable. Currently, only one percent of the international economy occurs on the Internet, leaving tremendous opportunity for growth.[4] Not all companies that use the Internet do so just to make new sales. At the beginning of 1999, General Electric's chief executive officer (CEO), Jack Welch, launched a technology initiative to improve the delivery of GE products to the consumer. In the process, GE streamlined its sales distribution system, reduced the cost of paper work and warehousing, and improved its quality control mechanisms for its customers. By reducing the time taken to get help for its customers and improving the flow of useful information to them, GE also improved its sales through customer satisfaction.[5]

---

4. Steven M. Glover, Stephen W. Liddle and Douglas F. Prawitt, *E-business: Principles & Strategies for Accountants* (Upper Saddle River, NJ: Prentice Hall, 2001).

5. Geoffrey Colvin and Ahmad Diba, "America's Most Admired Companies," *Fortune* 141 (February 21, 2000):108ff.

E-commerce has changed the traditional business and customer relationships and will continue to do so into the future. Considering what happened in one decade, can you imagine what the next decade may bring? So where does accounting fit into this maze of business and business relationships? As we indicated, accounting provides information necessary to operate a successful business.

Accounting in the Business Environment

● **accounting**
A system for analyzing and recording business transactions, transforming the resulting data into information useful for decision making, and reporting to the proper stakeholders.

● **internal decision makers**
People within the organization who make decisions *for* the company and have almost unlimited access to accounting information.

● **external decision makers**
People outside the company who make decisions *about* the company from limited information furnished by the entity's management.

● **financial accounting**
Provides historical financial information to internal and external decision makers.

● **management accounting**
Provides detailed financial information and nonfinancial information to internal decision makers.

● **accountant**
An information specialist who provides a variety of accounting and consultation services to businesses and individuals.

The purpose of accounting is to provide useful information to decision makers. **Accounting** is a system for analyzing and recording business transactions, transforming the resulting data into information useful for decision making, and reporting to the proper stakeholders. Stakeholders of accounting information are both internal decision makers and external decision makers. **Internal decision makers** are people within the organization who make decisions *for* the company and have almost unlimited access to accounting information. They include the members of the board of directors, management, and other employees of the organization. **External decision makers** are people outside the company who make decisions *about* the company from limited information furnished by the entity's management. External decision makers include stockholders, creditors, regulatory or government agents, and potential investors.

The two main types of accounting are financial accounting and management accounting. **Financial accounting** provides historical financial information to internal and external decision makers. Financial information given to external decision makers is generally summarized in a report format. **Management accounting** provides detailed financial information and nonfinancial information to internal decision makers. Internal decision makers can normally request management accounting information, in any format they wish, to use the data for their distinct purpose.

An **accountant** is an information specialist who provides a variety of accounting and consultation services to businesses and individuals. Accountants play a critical role in providing information to internal and external parties. Because accounting information is used to make decisions, the quality of the decisions depends on the quality of the accounting information. Accounting is considered a profession and accountants are professionals. Let's look at what professionalism in accounting means to the business community.

Development of the Accounting Profession

● **Securities and Exchange Commission (SEC)**
The government agency empowered by Congress to regulate securities sales and establish accounting rules, standards, procedures, and the form of published financial reporting.

When the U.S. stock market crashed in 1929, the U.S. Congress realized that investors and lenders needed reliable accounting information to make prudent decisions about companies. Prior to 1929, potential investors or stockholders were given little information about the company's resources, debts, and profitability. Instead of making sound investments in worthwhile companies, investors risked their fortunes on rumor and speculation.

After the events in 1929 and the resulting Great Depression, Congress enacted two important laws that changed dramatically financial reporting laws and the accounting profession—the Securities Act of 1933 and the Securities Exchange Act of 1934. The 1934 act created the **Securities and Exchange Commission**

(SEC), a government agency empowered by Congress to regulate securities sales and establish accounting rules, standards, procedures, and the form of published financial reporting. The SEC regulates the public trading of corporate securities but has delegated the authority for establishing accounting principles to the accounting profession through the **Financial Accounting Standards Board (FASB)**, the organization principally responsible for establishing accounting guidelines and rules in the United States. The SEC believes the members of the accounting profession possess the expertise, experience, and research ability to best define accounting standards.

During the last two-thirds of the 20th century the accounting profession, through the American Institute of Certified Public Accountants (AICPA) and the FASB, has developed a set of standards for financial reporting. The result is known as **generally accepted accounting principles (GAAP)**, which are guidelines for presentation of financial accounting information designed to serve external decision makers' need for consistent and comparable information. Only SEC-regulated companies are legally required to follow GAAP. Because the SEC regulates only publicly traded companies, nonregulated firms technically do not have to conform to GAAP. We will examine GAAP more closely in Chapter 2.

Accounting is dynamic and changes with the natural evolution of business and technology. The SEC monitors the accounting rules and reporting decisions made by the FASB and sometimes encourages the FASB to study new or developing topics. Today, the FASB continues to focus on the issues that affect financial reporting and the needs of financial report users.

With the blessing of most developed countries, the **International Accounting Standards Board (IASB)**, an independent organization responsible for establishing international accounting standards and rules of statement presentation, acts as the international counterpart of FASB. Accounting standards vary among countries, but international standards may prevail throughout the world within a decade or two. U.S. GAAP dominates current IASB standards, so U.S. accountants would not find a change to international standards a dramatic departure from current U.S. GAAP.

Visit the SEC Web site at *www.sec.gov.*

● **Financial Accounting Standards Board (FASB)**
The organization principally responsible for establishing accounting guidelines and rules in the United States.

Learn more about the FASB at *www.FASB.org.*

● **generally accepted accounting principles (GAAP)**
Guidelines for presentation of financial accounting information designed to serve external decision makers' need for consistent and comparable information.

● **International Accounting Standards Board (IASB)**
An independent organization responsible for establishing international accounting standards and rules of statement presentation.

Visit the IASB's Web site at *www.iasb.org.*

Ethical Standards for Accountants

The SEC oversees the accounting profession's activities. In light of recent financial reporting scandals, Congress passed the Sarbanes-Oxley Act of 2002, which created stricter penalties for both management and auditors for reporting errors and fraudulent financial statements. The act also created a new Public Companies Accounting Oversight Board (PCOAB) to oversee both the accounting profession and the SEC.

The Sarbanes-Oxley Act of 2002 created no new accounting principles. It did, however, request that GAAP remain principle-based to avoid the tendency to follow the letter of the rules instead of the substance of the rules. The irony is that GAAP *are* principle-based. It is the interpretations of the principles by FASB and SEC, rather, which have become so rule-based.

One of the reasons that the SEC has allowed the accounting profession to establish accounting principles is that it is a profession. A profession is characterized by a code of ethics, a code of professional conduct, educational requirements, continuing professional

NOTE
See Chapter 13 for more details about the Sarbanes-Oxley Act of 2002.

● **certified public accountant (CPA)**

An individual who meets educational and professional criteria to be licensed by a state board of accountancy.

education, and licensing by a government unit. A **certified public accountant (CPA)** is an individual who meets educational and professional criteria to be licensed by a state board of accountancy.

Strict ethical standards have been a cornerstone for CPAs and, consequently, accountants are considered to be conservative. How do we explain, then, the debacles of 2001 and 2002? The failures included SEC investigations of numerous public companies, shredding of important documents that led to the complete collapse of a century-old top five international accounting firm, and top managers of *Fortune* 500 companies being escorted away in handcuffs. In the past, individual CPAs have been convicted of fraud, companies have declared bankruptcy, and CEOs have been arrested for fraud. The 1980s saw headlines for savings and loan failures. The collapse, however, of companies such as Enron, WorldCom, Adelphia, and others was not expected because the runaway bull stock market hid a lot of the problems. It was also the first time that accountants were accused of knowingly participating in the fraud and deceit for personal profit on such a large scale.

If accounting is a profession and its code of ethics is a criterion for a profession, how is it that some individuals in the accounting profession failed so miserably in upholding the profession's code of professional conduct? Of course, the profession comprises more than 300,000 CPAs, yet only a few individuals were responsible for all the problems that arose. A few CPAs lost sight of their ethics and compromised the welfare of all the members. Unfortunately, those few had the capacity to wreak havoc on hundreds of thousands of investors.

The accounting profession, and auditors in particular, spent much effort during the 1990s investigating their clients and clients' managers because auditors must rely on the overall integrity of management. That some managers were less concerned with the truth or the overall fairness of the financial statements than they were their own agendas has become painfully obvious. Some auditors were only interested in protecting themselves. Accountants' primary motivation for entering the profession should be the welfare of the public they agree to protect, not personal financial rewards. Accountants must police their profession and rid it of unscrupulous members.

Now let's turn our attention to the role of accountants in business.

Roles of Accountants

For more information on accountants' roles in business, visit these Web sites:
www.AICPA.org.
www.IMA.org.
www.IIA.org.

Accountants interact with every business, whether the accountant works internally for a private business, externally as a consultant, or for a regulatory agency. Accountants perform a variety of services for the general public, private employers, governments, and educational institutions. Accountants enter the profession after meeting the minimum education requirements of a bachelor's degree and passing at least one of numerous certifying examinations.

Accountants' roles in business fall into four major categories of assurance services, taxation, consulting services, and management accounting. Within these four broad categories are myriad activities.

Assurance Services

● **assurance services**

Independent professional services that improve the quality of information, or its context, for decision makers.

● **independence**

A requirement that an accountant have no personal or financial interest (direct or indirect) in the client being examined.

The AICPA Special Committee on Assurance Services defines **assurance services** as "independent professional services that improve the quality of information, or its context, for decision makers." [6] Rule 101 of the AICPA Code of Professional Conduct requires that assurance providers be independent in *fact* and *appearance* while rendering professional assurance services. **Independence** is a requirement that an accountant have no personal or financial interest (direct or indirect) in the client being examined.

---

6. American Institute of Certified Public Accountants, "Definitions," *www.aicpa.org/members/glossary/a.html/*.

The requirement that accountants be independent allows the public to trust the examiner. The majority of assurance services CPAs perform are attestation services. **Attestation** involves the evaluation of one party's assertion to a third party. For example, management asserts that the company has complied with all environmental protection laws. After examining a sufficient amount of evidence and comparing that to the government regulations, a CPA could attest to the government that the company has complied (or not complied) with these laws. The examination process is called auditing.

Auditing is a process of gathering objective evidence, evaluating the evidence against specific criteria, and reporting the results to the users of the information. The SEC requires that publicly held companies provide audited accounting information to stockholders, the SEC, and other stakeholders. The most important attestation function of CPAs is a financial statement audit. A **financial statement audit** is an examination by an independent CPA of enough of a company's records to determine whether the financial statements were prepared in accordance with GAAP and demonstrate a fair representation of the company's financial condition. Financial statement users rely on an audit report for assurance that they can believe what they read in the financial statements. During an audit, the auditor examines financial statements the client's management prepared, along with its internal policies, procedures, and supporting documentation, to determine whether the financial statements present a fair picture of the client's financial condition in accordance with GAAP.

To give auditors confidence in the client's information, they assess the internal control structure. The **internal control structure** is a process designed to provide assurance that an entity can report reliable financial information, comply with laws and regulations, operate efficiently and effectively, and safeguard its assets. Organizations that utilize an effective internal control structure reduce the chances of fraud, employee theft, and manipulation of financial information. Auditors rely on statistical theory and sampling methods to test some of the records and determine the probability that the records as a whole verify the fairness of the financial statement numbers.

After conducting the audit, the auditor must issue a report that states his or her opinion about the fairness of the company's financial statements. Sometimes a client hires an accountant to help prepare the financial information, instead of auditing it. In this case, the CPA's report indicates that he or she cannot express an opinion because no audit was performed. Wise users of financial statements always read the auditor's report to determine whether the statements were audited and what opinion, if any, the accountant expressed.

Taxation

Considering that individuals and businesses pay up to 50 percent or more of income in obvious and hidden taxes from birth through death, planning to legally and ethically reduce taxes makes sound economic sense. CPAs help to reduce overall taxation first by knowing the tax laws and using that knowledge to plan how to structure ownership, business deals, and property transfers, and second by determining the most advantageous timing of such transactions to minimize taxes. After planning, the CPA attempts to prepare tax returns that legally minimize tax assessments.

CPAs save clients tax dollars and represent their clients in matters before the Internal Revenue Service (IRS) and many state and local taxing agencies. Practice before government agencies and in tax court requires special expertise gained through postgraduate education and experience.

Consulting Services

Accountants offer consulting services (sometimes called management advisory services) ranging from short conferences that might last 15 minutes to large research projects that might last several months or years. **Consulting services** encompass a range

● **attestation**
Involves the evaluation of one party's assertion to a third party.

● **auditing**
A process of gathering objective evidence, evaluating the evidence against specific criteria, and reporting the results to the users of the information.

● **financial statement audit**
An examination by an independent CPA of enough of a company's records to determine whether the financial statements were prepared in accordance with GAAP and demonstrate a fair representation of the company's financial condition.

● **internal control structure**
A process designed to provide assurance that an entity can report reliable financial information, comply with laws and regulations, operate efficiently and effectively, and safeguard its assets.

● **consulting services**
Activities in which an accountant provides data, decision information, and other advice that helps the client manage the business.

of activities in which the CPA provides data, decision information, and other advice that helps the client manage the business. Frequently the client, especially a small business, considers the CPA its primary source of information and help.

Accountants study a wide variety of business subjects and must have a clear understanding of how successful businesses operate. They possess the competency to consult with clients on business investments, real estate investments, lease or buy decisions, starting a business, selling or closing businesses or business segments, adding new product lines, make-or-buy decisions, retirement plans, health and life insurance plans, and a host of other issues. As the accounting profession develops, this list of competencies grows.

Management Accounting

● **chief financial officer (CFO)**
A person who directs the firm's financial affairs.

A business organization must record its transactions, pay bills, deposit receipts, prepare various tax returns, make important decisions, and report to stockholders. The **chief financial officer (CFO)**, who directs the firm's financial affairs, forms an accounting department to employ accountants to oversee these many tasks. Accountants ordinarily hire accounting clerks to perform routine duties such as paying bills, depositing income, and recording normal transactions. Accountants prepare tax returns, prepare external accounting reports, solve problems, design information systems, and prepare analyses for internal decision making.

In addition to their expertise in financial accounting, management accountants assemble a wide range of detailed information to aid managers in making well-informed decisions. They help in the planning process by preparing operating and capital budgets. They formulate decision models and provide information for making important decisions concerning projects and major investments. Management accountants analyze costs to increase profitability. A business cannot afford to do without these functions if it wishes to become or remain profitable.

● **cost accounting**
A narrow application of management accounting dealing specifically with procedures designed to determine how much a particular item (usually a unit of manufactured product) costs.

Cost accounting is a narrow application of management accounting dealing specifically with procedures designed to determine how much a particular item (usually a unit of manufactured product) costs. Cost accountants design and maintain cost accounting software that determines product costs, help analyze data that comes from the financial accounting and cost accounting software, and work with other employees to determine where cost savings are possible. Even savings of a fraction of a penny per unit may be important when thousands or millions of units are produced. To find every possible cost savings, accountants examine the minute details of various operations and their costs.

Responsibilities of Accountants

Accountants with professional certifications have responsibilities to meet rigorous standards for expertise in their field and to abide by a written code of ethics demanding the highest standards of professional behavior. In addition, virtually every accounting certification requires accountants to update their knowledge periodically through continuing education. CPAs licensed by the state have legal responsibilities to clients and third parties who rely on financial information associated with the CPA. CPAs can be sued for malpractice much like doctors or dentists. Courts can award monetary settlements to plaintiffs who prove that their reliance on financial information associated with a CPA, which was intentionally or negligently misleading, caused them financial injury. A state board of accountancy can take away a CPA's license for such acts or for failure to meet certain continuing education requirements, ethical violations, or numerous other reasons.

Professional Organizations and Certifications

More than 50 professional accounting organizations exist worldwide. Each state and U.S. territory has a Board of Accountancy that governs the licensing of CPAs. Although all accounting certifications provide evidence of the accountant's knowledge, abilities, and professional conduct, the CPA designation is the only accounting certification that is actually licensed by a government entity. The need for state licensing is due to the CPA's function as an independent auditor of financial information for use by third parties. Additionally, 50 state societies of CPAs exist that promote professionalism, offer continuing professional education, and function as a liaison with the AICPA between the profession and government agencies.

For links to accounting organizations' Web sites, visit the Web site *www.prenhall.com/terrell.*

As you now understand after reading this chapter, business is complex with many facets. Information and communication are vital to the business world to operate effectively and reduce the risk of failure. In Chapter 2 we look closely at the theories and practices used in financial accounting recording and reporting, and we introduce the basic accounting reports.

CHAPTER SUMMARY

Business is the process of producing and distributing goods and services. A primary business motive is profit, the reward for making investments in an enterprise. Free economies utilize four factors of production: natural resources, human resources, physical capital, and entrepreneurship. The success of an economy or a business depends on the proper mix of the factors of production for the type of business activity.

The three major classifications of business activity are manufacturing, merchandising, and service. A manufacturing business converts raw materials into a saleable physical product. A merchandising business sells tangible, physical products, either as a wholesaler that sells to other businesses who in turn resell or as a retailer that sells to final consumers. A service business performs a service as its major business activity. A business that participates in more than one type of activity is a hybrid.

In the United States, businesses organize in one of several ways. A sole proprietorship is a business owned by a single individual that is not legally separate from the owner. A partnership is a business with two or more owners who share all the risks and profits of the entity. A limited partnership has at least one general partner and one or more limited partners who enjoy limited liability. An LLP is a partnership in which the liability of each general partner is limited to actions and behavior that he or she controls. Under the separate entity assumption, all economic activity can be identified with a particular economic entity. A corporation is the only business form that is a separate legal entity. The corporation is a legal person that possesses many of the rights and obligations of a person. Each business form has several advantages and disadvantages.

Corporation owners are called stockholders or shareholders. Corporations pay tax on net income and the stockholders pay tax on dividends from the corporation creating double taxation. An LLC provides the shareholders with limited liability, but taxes them as partners in a partnership to eliminate double taxation.

Each business has an effect on its community. The way a business operates affects its stakeholders. A business must be a good citizen and carefully guard its good reputation to generate sustained profits. Reputation evolves from the company's corporate culture, product quality, innovation, financial strength, talented employees, and social responsibility. Social responsibility represents management's attitudes and actions that exhibit sensitivity to social and environmental concerns.

In building reputation, a business builds relationships with four key groups: employees, other businesses, consumers, and governments. A business builds a good relationship with these groups when it behaves ethically, legally, and exhibits social responsibility. A business attracts and retains good employees when it helps improve the overall quality of their lives. When conducting ethical business dealings with other firms and building sound relationship networks, a business finds many opportunities. A firm that utilizes relationship marketing with customers builds a loyal customer base. Government agencies are large consumers of business products and services that also tax business transactions and profits. Governments are responsible for keeping the economy and the business environment healthy while protecting society and the environment from abuses. This creates a complex relationship between government and business.

E-commerce has changed the way many businesses relate to business customers and consumers. Regardless of selling method, a business keeps its customers happy by fulfilling their demands at fair prices in a convenient fashion.

After the stock market crash in 1929, Congress passed the Securities Act of 1933 and the Securities Exchange Act of 1934 to form the SEC. During the 20th century, the accounting profession defined its basic theories and principles and implemented sophisticated standards for financial reporting.

Accountants provide assurance, tax, and consulting services to their clients. The distinguishing function of CPAs is auditing financial statements for third-party use. Management accountants provide a wide variety of decision-making information to an organization including cost accounting.

Professional accountants owe more responsibility to employers than the average employee because of professional codes of conduct. Accountants have professional liability to the public and third parties for opinions expressed on financial statements. Accountants have formed numerous professional organizations that promote the development of the accounting profession.

Visit the Web site *www.prenhall.com/terrell* for additional study help with the Online Study Guide.

REVIEW OF CONCEPTS

A   Distinguish between *business* and *a business.*

B   Contrast profit in for-profit and not-for-profit organizations.

C   Explain the interactions of the four factors of production in a business.

D   Describe the purpose and components of a business plan.

E   Distinguish among the three classifications of business activity and a hybrid company.

F   Identify the three basic forms of business organization and discuss the advantages and disadvantages of each.

G   Discuss how an LLP differs from a partnership and how an LLC differs from a corporation.

H   Distinguish between a *stakeholder* and a *stockholder.*

I   How does a business exhibit social responsibility?

J   Describe a least six characteristics of business reputation and discuss why a good reputation is important to a business.

K   Discuss the importance of a business relationship with employees.

L   Describe the types of relationships one business might have with another and how it uses those relationships to market its company's goods and services.

M Define *e-commerce* and discuss the changes it has made in business in the past decade.

N Distinguish between *internal users* and *external users* of accounting information and the responsibility of CPAs to each.

O Define the legal authority of the SEC in U.S. accounting standards and describe how it has chosen to participate in determining U.S. GAAP.

P Distinguish between an *accountant* and a *CPA*.

Q What are generally accepted accounting principles?

R Distinguish among *assurance*, *attestation*, and *auditing*.

S Describe what independence means to an auditor.

T Describe the characteristics of a profession.

APPLICATION EXERCISES

1-20 Define the following terms and give examples of each.

1. entrepreneurship
2. human resources
3. business
4. ethics
5. factors of production
6. natural resources
7. physical capital
8. profit motive

LO 1
Terminology

1-21

a. If you assume that not-for-profit organizations earn a profit, is earning a profit as important for a not-for-profit organization as it is for a for-profit organization? Why or why not?

b. Do you think that a not-for-profit organization needs management accounting information? Why or why not?

LO 1
Profit Motive

1-22 Pick two companies with which you are familiar. Compare and contrast the two in terms of the factors of production that they employ; for example, an airline will require a large investment in physical capital (airplanes), whereas an oil company will require a large investment in natural resources. Be sure to comment on all four factors of production. Information about the companies you choose may be readily available on each company's Web site.

LO 2
Business Activity

1-23 Phil Jackson owns and operates a jewelry store. During the past month, he sold a necklace to a customer for $2,500. Phil paid $1,800 for the necklace.

a. What type of business does Phil own (manufacturer, wholesaler, retailer, etc.)? Explain how you determined your response.

b. Determine Phil's profit on the sale of the necklace.

c. Identify four costs besides the cost of the necklace that Phil might incur in the operation of his jewelry store.

LO 1, 2
Business Activity and Profit

1-24 The Digital Center of America (DCA) manufactures and sells high-definition televisions. During October the center produced and sold 1,000 televisions. The sale of

LO 1, 2
Business Activity and Profit

the televisions generated $1,000,000 in sales. DCA spent $300,000 for the parts to build the televisions and paid $200,000 for the labor to assemble the televisions. DCA also paid $100,000 for all other costs (overhead) necessary to construct the televisions and spent $50,000 on other operating expenses.

Based on this information:
a. What type of business does the DCA operate (i.e., manufacturing, merchandising, or service)?
b. What is the amount of profit for October?

LO 1, 2
Business Activity and Profit

1-25   Utilizing Exhibit 1-1, prepare a computer spreadsheet to calculate:
a. the average number of employees per firm for each industry listed.
b. the average estimated receipts per firm for each industry listed.
c. the average receipts per employee for each industry listed.
d. What does your analysis tell you about the intensity of labor in each industry segment?

LO 2
Business Activity

1-26   The chapter discussed five types of business in the United States: manufacturer, wholesale merchandiser, retail merchandiser, service, and hybrid.
a. Explain in your own words the major characteristics of each type of business.
b. Name two businesses that might best function using each type of business model. Do not use any examples given in the chapter, and explain how you determined your answer.

LO 2
Business Activity

1-27   Professor Agnes Moore is starting up a publishing company to publish and distribute accounting textbooks throughout the United States. She feels this will be a successful venture because the textbooks will be based on a revolutionary new format of accounting education. Moore has extended an invitation to all her students to invest in her new business. She is offering shares of stock for a mere $10 each.
a. What form of business is Professor Moore proposing?
b. Briefly explain four advantages of operating the business in this form.

LO 4
Stakeholders

1-28   Consider that you are a stockholder in a business that provides the public with electricity generated from nuclear power.
a. What is the difference between a stakeholder and a stockholder?
b. Are all stockholders stakeholders?
c. Are all stakeholders stockholders?
d. Who are the stakeholders of this business and what is their stake in the organization?

LO 4
Social Responsibility

1-29   Imagine that you own a midsize business in your hometown. Describe specifically how you would demonstrate social responsibility to your local community.

LO 4
Social Responsibility

1-30   Go to the Web site at *www.prenhall.com/terrell* and select two companies from among the links listed.
Go to the respective Web sites and answer the following questions:
a. What does each company do to demonstrate its commitment to social responsibility?
b. What would you describe as the most distinguishing characteristic of each business?

LO 4
Social Responsibility

1-31   Locate a recent article about the social responsibility a company exhibited. Summarize the article describing how the company exhibited social responsibility and the value it gave the community.

1-32 Locate a recent news article about the failure of a company to act in a manner that is socially responsible.

    a. Describe the criticism leveled at the company and decide if the criticism is deserved.

    b. Discuss how the company could have avoided the problem.

LO 4
Social Responsibility

1-33 If you were to establish your own business, describe the type of corporate culture you would develop. Give a brief statement of the values and beliefs you would embrace in your organization.

LO 5
Corporate Culture

1-34 Go to the Web site for one of the following organizations:

Dollar General Stores
Johnson & Johnson
Wal-Mart
Winnebago

Write the corporation's mission, values, and beliefs statements. How do these statements affect your perception about this company?

LO 5
Corporate Culture

1-35 Go to the Web site for *Fortune* and locate the listing of the *Fortune* 500.

    a. What is the *Fortune* 500?

    b. What criteria are used to determine how companies rank in the listing?

    c. Explain why a company's ranking on this list would or would not make you more likely to invest in, buy from, or work for the company?

LO 5
Business Reputation

1-36 Describe the relationship the following companies try to build with their customers. Use any personal knowledge you have of these companies and visit their Web sites to learn more about how they value customers.

    a. Gap Inc.

    b. Nordstrom

    c. Sears

LO 6
Business Relationships

1-37 Determine at least five criteria that are important to you in selecting a company to join after graduation.

    a. Choose a company you would like to work for and locate the company's Web site.

    b. See how much information you can find about the company to determine whether it meets each criterion you require for accepting a position with this company.

    c. Based on your analysis, would you wish to work for this company?

LO 6
Business Relationships

1-38 From Exhibit 1-3, choose any two companies from *Fortune*'s top 20 employers in 2003 you find interesting.

    a. Go to their Web site to find information about their employment practices.

    b. Write a brief report outlining information you find about the companies that might explain why employees admire these companies.

LO 6
Business Relationships

1-39 Locate several articles on the topic of e-commerce. Write a two-page paper describing how e-commerce is changing the way business is conducted.

LO 7
e-Commerce

1-40 Write a paper that describes the way e-commerce affected your buying habits. For example, have you ever made a purchase over the Internet? If not, why not? What would convince you to do so?

LO 6
e-Commerce

LO 8
Internal vs. External Decision Makers

1-41   For each of the following, decide if the person is an internal or external decision maker for the Tiny Tot Toy Company. Label each item with **I** for internal or **E** for external:
   a. a bank loan officer at Tiny Tot's bank
   b. Tiny Tot's manufacturing supervisor
   c. Tiny Tot's CFO
   d. credit manager of the plastics firm that supplies Tiny Tot with materials
   e. the CPA who audits Tiny Tot
   f. Tiny Tot's credit manager
   g. a traveling salesperson for Tiny Tot
   h. an IRS auditor

LO 8
Development of GAAP

1-42   The SEC allows the accounting profession to establish GAAP through the FASB. Do you believe that the SEC should set the rules? Why or why not?

LO 8
Professions

1-43
   a. List the characteristics of a profession.
   b. Using two professions as examples, describe how society as a whole benefits from these groups being subject to professional standards.

LO 8
Independence

1-44
   a. Define the independence required of an auditor.
   b. Do you believe that such independence is important to the public? Why or why not?

LO 8
Cost Accounting

1-45   Assume that Kenfield Corporation sells two billion bolts each year. A cost accountant believes that once a new manufacturing technique is in place, the company will save one penny for each bolt produced.
   a. How much could the company save in one year by using the new technique?
   b. Suppose that new equipment to implement the change will cost $10 million and last for four years. Does that change your analysis of the cost savings in part a? Should management implement the change?
   c. What if the equipment cost $100 million? Should management implement the change?

LO 4
Ethics

1-46   Fred Smoot, CPA, is contacted by a member of the board of directors of Salmon Company to bid on the current year's audit of Salmon. The director explains that the audit is to be used primarily by the board of directors and is not for the use of any outsiders.

Required:

Discuss Smoot's professional obligation as an auditor and a CPA in light of this request by a board member.

FOR ADDITIONAL READING

Baum, Geoff. "Introducing the New Value Creation Index." April 3, 2000. *www.forbes.com/asap/2000/0403/140_print.html*

Dennis, Anita. "No One Stands Still in Public Accounting," *Journal of Accountancy*, 189, 6, 66–74.

Glover, Steven M., Stephen W. Liddle, and Douglas F. Prawitt. *E-business: Principles & Strategies for Accountants*. Upper Saddle River, NJ: Prentice Hall, 2001.

"Guide to Corporate Scandals: Companies under the Microscope, A." January 18, 2003. *www.msnbc.com/news/wld/business/brill/CorporateScandal_DW.asp*

Keys, E. Theodore Jr., Ed. *How to Save Millions*. Altamonte Springs, FL: Institute of Internal Auditors, 1988.

Leaf, Clifton. "Send Them to Jail." *Fortune* 145 (March 18, 2002):60–76.

Magill, Harry T., Gary J. Previts, and Thomas R. Robinson. *The CPA Profession: Opportunities, Responsibilities, and Services*. Upper Saddle River, NJ: Prentice Hall, 1998.

McLean, Bethany. "Why Enron Went Bust." *Fortune* 144 (December 24, 2001):58–68.

Previts, Gary J., and Barbara D. Merino. *A History of Accountancy in the United States*. Columbus, Ohio: The Ohio State University Press, 1998.

CHAPTER 2

LEARNING OBJECTIVES

After completing this chapter you should be able to:

1 Describe the objectives of accounting and useful accounting information.

2 Define the qualitative characteristics of accounting information and determine the effect of each on information.

3 Define the elements of accounting and construct the accounting equation.

4 Recognize a balance sheet, income statement, statement of equity, and statement of cash flows and determine which accounting elements comprise each statement.

5 Identify the underlying assumptions of accounting and describe how they affect financial reporting.

6 Define the underlying principles of accounting and determine the appropriate application of each.

7 Identify the underlying constraints of accounting and describe how they affect accounting decisions and reporting.

Basic Concepts of Accounting and Financial Reporting

The Conceptual Framework of Accounting

One of the first tasks of the FASB during the last quarter of the 20th century was to develop the accounting profession's foundation, called the conceptual framework of accounting. Accounting's conceptual framework sets forth its objectives, supported by consistent beliefs and values, based on certain principles and assumptions. It might be compared to a building with a roof, supported by columns, and a foundation that supports the whole structure as shown in Exhibit 2-1. The objective of accounting is to provide useful information to decision makers. This objective cannot stand alone, and like the roof of the building, it must be supported by a cohesive structure of accounting concepts and elements. We will navigate through the conceptual framework in this chapter as a way to introduce you to the basic concepts of accounting.

The conceptual framework has four structural components:

1 objectives;
2 qualitative characteristics of accounting information;
3 accounting elements; and
4 principles, assumptions, and constraints.

We will examine these one component at a time. Let's begin our look at the framework by focusing on the objectives of financial accounting information.

Accounting Objectives

A company generates accounting data with every business transaction. **Accounting data** are raw results of economic transactions and events. When data are in an unorganized form, they are of little use to decision makers; **information** is data that are put into some useful form for decision making. **Accounting information** is the product of accountants' organization, classification, and summarization of economic transactions and events so that it is useful to economic decision makers.

● **accounting data**
The raw results of economic transactions and events.

● **information**
Data that are put into some useful form for decision making.

● **accounting information**
The product of accountants' organization, classification, and summarization of economic transactions and events so that it is useful to economic decision makers.

People make business decisions every day. Both internal and external users of accounting information depend on financial information to make many of those decisions. The FASB, in its *Statement of Financial Accounting Concepts No. 1, Objectives of Financial Reporting by Business Enterprises,* lists three aims of accounting information. Financial accounting information should be useful to:

1 stockholders, potential investors, creditors, and other users for making investment, credit, and other important business decisions provided they have a reasonable understanding of economic activity and will diligently study the information;

2 stockholders, potential investors, creditors, and other users in assessing the certainty, timing, and amounts of future cash available to pay such things as debts and operating costs; and

3 financial statement users' understanding about the entity's resources, claims to those resources, and the changes that take place in each over a time period.[1]

Exhibit 2-1 shows these objectives as the roof structure.

Exhibit 2-1
Conceptual Framework of Accounting

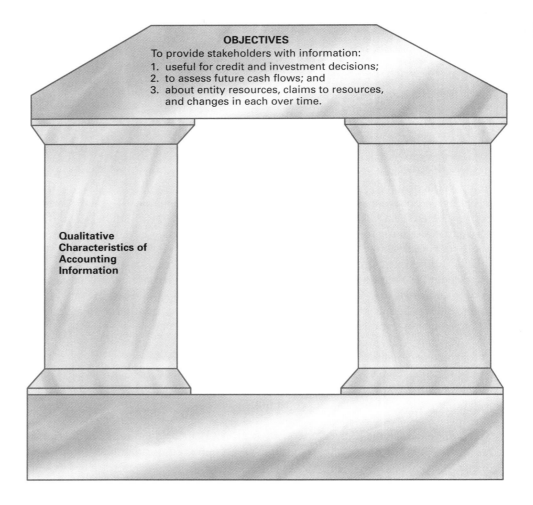

OBJECTIVES
To provide stakeholders with information:
1. useful for credit and investment decisions;
2. to assess future cash flows; and
3. about entity resources, claims to resources, and changes in each over time.

Qualitative
Characteristics of
Accounting
Information

---

1. Financial Accounting Standards Board, *Statement of Financial Accounting Concepts No. 1, Objectives of Financial Reporting by Business Enterprises* (Norwalk, CT: Financial Accounting Standards Board, November 1978).

Qualitative Characteristics of Accounting Information

As the architects of the conceptual framework, the FASB defined certain qualities that accounting information should possess to ensure the integrity of financial reporting in its *Statement of Financial Accounting Concepts No. 2, The Qualitative Characteristics of Accounting Information*. The qualitative characteristics of accounting information are relevance, reliability, comparability, and consistency.[2] As Exhibit 2-1 shows, just as the columns of a building support its roof, the qualitative characteristics of accounting work to support financial accounting objectives to provide useful information for decision makers. For most information to contain one characteristic is not difficult, but accountants require accounting information to meet multiple qualitative tests. Let's explore each of the qualitative characteristics of accounting information to determine how to measure information by these criteria.

The primary qualities that make accounting information useful are relevance and reliability. If either of these qualities is missing, the information will not be useful.

Relevance and Reliability

Relevance is a characteristic of useful accounting information that requires the information to pertain to and make a difference in a particular decision situation. Relevant information possesses *at least* two characteristics:

1 **Timeliness**—Having information before it is too late to influence decisions. If a decision maker receives important information too late, perhaps after the decision has been made, the information has no value. To keep information relevant, accountants sometimes sacrifice perfect accuracy for timeliness.

2 **Predictive value *or* feedback value**—Relevant information must be timely, and it must possess *at least one* of the following two characteristics:

○ **Predictive value**—A quality of information that assists users to increase the probability of correctly forecasting the results of past or present events. Before economic decision makers commit resources to one alternative instead of another, they must satisfy themselves that a reasonable expectation of accomplishing their goals exists. Accounting information with predictive value helps to reduce the uncertainty of that expectation. For example, if an investor can track the performance of a stock over time, the past results may help the investor predict future performance.

○ **Feedback value**—The quality of information that allows users to substantiate or amend prior expectations. Good decision makers should evaluate the results of their decision after the fact to determine whether they made a wise choice. Accounting information that provides input for those evaluations has feedback value.

Reliability is a characteristic of useful accounting information that requires the information to be reasonably unbiased and accurate. For example, to a prospective home buyer, information about the recent repairs and maintenance on the home would be relevant because the information would be helpful in deciding whether or not to purchase the home. If the source of the information were a disinterested third party rather than the current owner, the prospective buyer would probably consider the information more reliable. To be considered reliable, accounting information must possess **three** qualities:

● **Verifiability**—The ability of information to be substantiated by unbiased measures. Accounting information is considered verifiable if several qualified individuals, working independently of one another, would arrive at similar

● **relevance**
A characteristic of useful accounting information that requires the information to pertain to and make a difference in a particular decision situation.

● **timeliness**
Having information before it is too late to influence decisions.

● **predictive value**
The quality of information that assists users to increase the probability of correctly forecasting the results of past or present events.

● **feedback value**
The quality of information that allows users to substantiate or amend prior expectations.

● **reliability**
A characteristic of useful accounting information that requires the information to be reasonably unbiased and accurate.

● **verifiability**
The ability of information to be substantiated by unbiased measures.

---

2. Financial Accounting Standards Board, *Statement of Financial Accounting Concepts No. 2, Qualitative Characteristics of Accounting Information* (Norwalk, CT: Financial Accounting Standards Board, May 1980).

conclusions using the same data. For example, if we asked two people to determine the amount of Michelle Miller's wages this year, they should both come to the same conclusion: A simple review of payroll records should provide verifiable information for the amount. If however, payroll records were unavailable or did not include all the wages paid to Miller, the wages for the year would not be verifiable.

● **representational faithfulness**
Validity or agreement between a measure or description and the event that it represents.

● **Representational faithfulness**—Validity or agreement between a measure or description and the event that it represents. A small variation between reality and the amount accounting information reports does not compromise representational faithfulness. For example, if a company's accounting information reports sales of $5,000 and the accounting records reflect sales of $4,999, the accounting information is representationally faithful; however, if the accounting records reflect sales of only $3,590, the accounting information lacks representational faithfulness.

● **neutrality**
Absence of bias to influence reported information.

● **Neutrality**—The absence of bias to influence reported information. Accounting information should neither depict a situation as better or worse than it really is, nor should it be slanted to further some ulterior motive. Making decisions is difficult enough without having to rely on slanted information.

What Do You Think?

2-1 Assume that you will soon graduate from college and two firms have offered you attractive positions. One firm is a *Fortune* 500 company and the other is a local company. If you could ask only five questions of one person at each company, what would they be, and what is the title of the person you would select to answer the questions?

2-2 What part did relevance and reliability play in your choice of questions and the person you selected?

Comparability and Consistency

According to the FASB, the two secondary qualitative characteristics that make accounting information useful are comparability and consistency.

● **comparability**
The quality of information that allows users to identify similarities in and differences between two sets of accounting information.

● **Comparability**—The quality of information that allows users to identify similarities in and differences between two sets of accounting information. Economic decision makers evaluate alternatives. Accounting information for one alternative must be commensurate with accounting information for the other. For example, assume you intend to make an investment in one of two companies. If you review accounting information from each company, and the companies used very different accounting methods, you would find making a meaningful comparison difficult.

● **consistency**
Conformity from period to period with accounting policies and procedures.

● **Consistency**—Conformity from period to period with accounting policies and procedures. Evaluating the financial progress of an investment would be difficult if the company used different accounting methods each year. Consistency in the application of accounting techniques over time increases the usefulness of the information provided.

Students often confuse comparability and consistency. Comparability is a quality that is needed to meaningfully assess accounting information of two or more *different entities* or *decision alternatives*. Consistency is a quality that is needed to meaningfully assess accounting information from the *same entity* or *decision alternative* over time. To achieve comparability, accounting rules require that companies provide accounting information that conforms to a relatively uniform structure. To comply with GAAP, all companies use the same basic classification and valuation structure and issue the same set of financial reports. A company may choose from alternative accounting techniques and formats, so the information from one company will not be exactly the same as another, but it will be similar enough to be comparable.

Comparability and consistency often have similar effects on the decision-making process. Their presence increases the decision maker's confidence in his or her decision. The absence of these qualities decreases confidence or confounds the decision maker's ability to make an informed decision. We can expand the column representing the qualitative characteristics of accounting information in our conceptual framework model in Exhibit 2-2 to include all its components of relevance, reliability, comparability, and consistency.

Now you know that accounting information should be relevant, reliable, comparable, and consistent. In accounting there are four reports, called financial statements, that should embody these qualitative characteristics. To understand them we need to turn our attention to the basic accounting building blocks of the financial statements, called accounting elements. These elements form the right support column of the accounting framework in Exhibit 2-2. We will examine each element to see how the elements form the various financial statements.

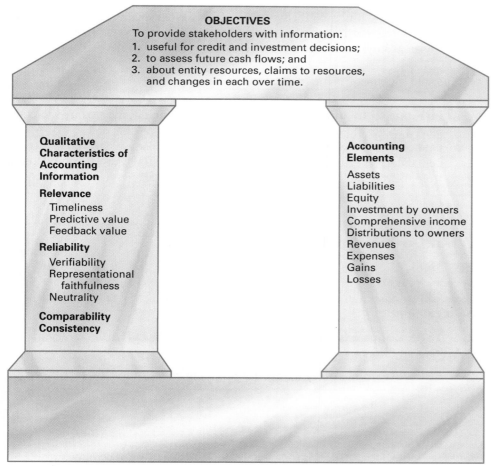

Exhibit 2-2
Conceptual Framework of Accounting

Accounting Elements

Accountants use an accounting system to transform accounting data into useful accounting information. Transactions create accounting data. Accountants group these elements to prepare four interrelated financial statements that summarize the present status and the past performance of a business enterprise. The first financial statement is the balance sheet.

The Balance Sheet

The **balance sheet** provides information about the present condition of a business at a specific point in time. It consists of three accounting elements: assets, liabilities, and equity. The FASB defines these elements in its *Statement of Financial Accounting Concepts No. 6, Elements of Financial Statements*.[3] Let's examine simple definitions of each of these elements:

- **Assets** are things an entity owns or controls that have future value. Examples include cash, merchandise held for resale, equipment, land, and buildings.
- **Liabilities** are the obligations of an entity to transfer assets to, or perform services for, a third party. Most liabilities require payment of cash to a creditor to satisfy an obligation. A liability may be an obligation to transfer assets other than cash, or to provide goods or services to a customer who paid for those goods or services in advance. Liabilities arise from past transactions, not events that might occur in the future. An entity must, however, settle or pay liabilities some time in the future.
- **Equity** is the difference between the entity's assets and its liabilities and represents the portion of the assets that the owner(s) own free and clear. Consequently, equity can also be called *net assets*.

Equity in a company comes from two sources:

- **investments by owners**, which represent the amount invested by the company's owner(s) to get it started or to finance its expansion; and
- **earned equity**, which is the total amount a company has earned since its beginning, less any amounts distributed to its owner(s). Earned equity comes from the profitable operation of a company over time.

● balance sheet
The financial statement that provides information about the present condition of a business at a specific point in time. A balance sheet consists of three accounting elements: assets, liabilities, and equity.

● assets
Things an entity owns or controls that have future value.

● liabilities
The obligations of an entity to transfer assets to, or perform services for, a third party.

● equity
The difference between the entity's assets and its liabilities.

● investments by owners
The amount invested by the company's owner(s) to get it started or to finance its expansion.

● earned equity
The total amount a company has earned since its beginning, less any amounts distributed to its owner(s).

What Do You Think?

2-3   Think about the things of value you own. Prepare a list of your personal assets. Your list should include two columns with the descriptions of the assets in the left column and the cost of the assets in the right column.

2-4   Think about any debts you owe. Prepare a list of your personal liabilities similar to the list you prepared in 2-3.

2-5   Calculate your equity using the answers to 2-3 and 2-4.

---

3. Financial Accounting Standards Board, *Statement of Financial Accounting Concepts No. 6, Elements of Financial Statements* (Norwalk, CT: Financial Accounting Standards Board, December 1985), paragraphs 25–82.

The Accounting Equation

A constant relationship exists among the assets, liabilities, and equity on the balance sheet. Recall that the assets of an entity are things that the entity owns or controls, and equity is the difference between its assets and its liabilities. Both creditors and owners have claims on those assets. Therefore, the company's assets will be equal to the claims that are made on those assets—creditors' claims (liabilities), or the owners' claims (equity). This relationship can be stated as an equation called the **accounting equation**:

$$\text{ASSETS} = \text{LIABILITIES} + \text{EQUITY}$$

● **accounting equation**
Assets equal liabilities plus equity.

Accounting uses this equation to measure the financial reality of business. Because the equation has all the properties of a mathematical equation, we can rearrange it as:

$$\text{ASSETS} - \text{LIABILITIES} = \text{EQUITY}$$

This reordering of the equation shows equity for what it is: the owners' residual interest in the company. (See Exhibit 2-3.)

A balance sheet is an expanded accounting equation, and the term *balance sheet* comes from the fact that both sides of the equation must be kept in balance. Exhibit 2-4 (see p. 38) shows a condensed balance sheet for Family Dollar Stores, Inc. with its important components:

Visit the Family Dollar Stores Web site at *www.familydollar.com*.

A the name of the entity for which the statement provides the financial condition;
B the title "balance sheet";
C the date of the balance sheet;
D the list of assets, liabilities, and equity; and
E an indication that the total of the assets equals the total of liabilities and owner's equity.

Note that the date of the balance sheet refers to one specific date. It is like a financial snapshot of a company. Like any snapshot, it only shows what existed on the day it

Exhibit 2-3
Accounting Equation

> If you buy an automobile by paying $5,000 in cash and borrowing $8,000 from the bank, both you and the bank have a claim against the car.
>
> | Assets | = | Liabilities | + | Equity |
> |--------|---|-------------|---|--------|
> | Car | = | Bank Loan | + | Equity |
> | $13,000 | = | $8,000 | + | $5,000 |
>
> By rearranging the equation to
>
> | Assets | – | Liabilities | = | Equity |
> |--------|---|-------------|---|--------|
> | $13,000 | – | $8,000 | = | $5,000 |
>
> you can see that in this situation, you have a car worth $13,000, the bank has an $8,000 claim against the car, and you have a $5,000 equity in the automobile.

Exhibit 2-4
Balance Sheet of Family Dollar
Stores, Inc. and Subsidiaries

Family Dollar Stores, Inc. and Subsidiaries
Consolidated Balance Sheet
August 30, 2003 (in thousands)

Assets

Cash and cash equivalents	$ 206,731
Merchandise inventories	854,370
Other current assets	95,391
Property and equipment (net)	812,123
Other assets	17,080
	$1,985,695

Liabilities and Shareholders' Equity

Liabilities

Accounts payable	$ 401,799
Other liabilities	193,532
Deferred income taxes	79,395
	$ 674,726
Shareholders' equity	1,310,969
	$1,985,695

Notice that these two amounts are equal.
Assets = Liabilities + Equity

Accompanying notes are an integral part of the consolidated financial statements.

was taken. By the next day, business transactions will change the assets, liabilities, and owner's equity, although they will remain in balance.

Notice that the information provides few details. For example, it does not show a description of the equipment or the bank name for the company's cash. The information is aggregated or summarized for external users, and such details are not required for them.

What Do You Think?

2-6 Using Exhibit 2-4 as a guide, prepare your personal balance sheet from the information you provided in 2-3, 2-4, and 2-5.

2-7 Use the accounting equation to determine the missing amounts in the following information.

	Assets	Liabilities	Equity
A	$ 50,000	$ 35,000	?
B	$120,000	?	$ 25,000
C	?	$230,000	$ 95,000
D	$278,000	?	$(35,000)

Visit the Web site
www.prenhall.com/terrell to
examine financial statements for
proprietorships and partnerships.

Balance Sheet Presentation

In Chapter 1 we discussed the three major forms of business organizations: proprietorships, partnerships, and corporations. Each form requires a slightly different presentation of the balance sheet to depict the differences in ownership structure. Because most

Jason's Furniture Gallery
Balance Sheet
December 31, 2004

Exhibit 2-5
Balance Sheet for a
Corporation

Assets		Liabilities		
Cash	$ 29,000	Accounts payable	$100,000	
Investments	75,000	Mortgage payable	200,000	
Inventory	200,000	**Total Liabilities**		$300,000
Land	80,000			
Building	300,000	**Stockholders' Equity**		
Equipment	60,000	Common stock	$200,000	
		Retained earnings	244,000	
		Total Stockholders' Equity		444,000
		Total Liabilities		
Total Assets	$744,000	**and Stockholders' Equity**		$744,000

business is conducted in the corporate form in the United States, we will present only the corporate financial statements.

Examine the balance sheet in Exhibit 2-5 for Jason's Furniture Gallery, Inc. It is fairly easy to figure out that Jason's Furniture Gallery has cash, investments, merchandise, land, building, and equipment. It owes some suppliers on account, listed as accounts payable, and a mortgage on the building. The title of the equity section is "Stockholders' Equity," and it lists no individuals' names but includes "Common Stock" and "Retained Earnings."

What Do You Think?

2-8 If you were a banker, would it be useful for you to know the assets, liabilities, and stockholders' equity of a company applying to you for a $500,000 loan? Why or why not?

We have examined the balance sheet, the first of the four financial statements. Next, let's focus on the income statement and the four accounting elements it includes.

The Income Statement

The **income statement** is a financial report that provides information about an entity's financial performance during a specific time period. The purpose of the income statement is to measure the results of performance for some specific time period. Remember that the balance sheet depicts financial condition at a specific *point* in time, but the income statement depicts results of business activity for a *period* of time. The elements of the income statement are:

- **Revenues** are increases in net assets (equity) that occur as a result of an entity's selling or producing products and performing services for its customers. Revenues are the reward of doing business. Revenues from manufacturing or selling products are called sales. Revenues from rendering services are designated service revenue.

● **income statement**
A financial report that provides information about an entity's financial performance during a specific time period.

● **revenues**
Increases in net assets (equity) that occur as a result of an entity's selling or producing products and performing services for its customers.

● **expenses**
Sacrifices of the future value of assets used to generate revenues from customers.

● **cost of goods sold**
The cost of merchandise transferred to a customer in the entity's primary business activity.

● **gains**
Increases in net assets (equity) that result from incidental or other peripheral events that affect the entity, except for normal revenues and investments by owners.

● **losses**
Decreases in net assets (equity) that result from incidental or other peripheral events that affect the entity, except for normal expenses and distributions to owners.

● **net income**
The difference between the rewards (revenues and gains) and the sacrifices (expenses and losses) for a given period of activity.

● **net loss**
Occurs when the expenses and losses for the period are greater than the revenues and gains for the period.

● **Expenses** are sacrifices of the future value of assets used to generate revenues from customers. A company's merchandise is an asset because it has a future sales value. When a customer purchases one of the company's products, the company transfers the item to the customer, and it has no more future value to the company. The cost of merchandise transferred to a customer in the entity's primary business activity is an expense called **cost of goods sold**. Other operating expenses include selling expenses and administrative expenses.

● **Gains** are increases in net assets (equity) that result from incidental or other peripheral events that affect the entity, except for normal revenues and investments by owners.

● **Losses** are decreases in net assets (equity) that result from incidental or other peripheral events that affect the entity, except for normal expenses and distributions to owners.

The most common gains and losses occur when an enterprise sells the assets it uses in its trade or business or that it holds for investments. Equipment, land, buildings, and other assets have a limited usefulness to a business and will be sold or scrapped when they are no longer needed. Likewise, the company's management may buy and sell securities and other investments when they have excess cash. Sales of these kinds of assets give rise to gains and losses. Why do we not consider them revenues and expenses? Because the company's primary function is to sell its goods and services, not its assets.

Income Statement Equation

The difference between the rewards (revenues and gains) and the sacrifices (expenses and losses) for a given period of activity is the net reward of doing business called **net income**. Accountants also call net income *earnings, net earnings,* or *net profit*. When the expenses and losses for the period are greater than the revenues and gains for the period, the result is a **net loss**. The following equation, called the net income equation, represents the relationship among revenues, expenses, gains, losses, and either net income or net loss:

$$\text{Revenues} - \text{Expenses} + \text{Gains} - \text{Losses} = \text{Net Income (or Net Loss)}$$

What Do You Think?

2-9 Consider your personal transactions for the past month. Identify those that resulted in revenues and those that resulted in expenses.

2-10 Use the income statement equation to determine whether you had a gain or a loss for the month.

Income Statement Presentation

Just as the balance sheet is an expanded accounting equation, the income statement is an expanded net income equation. Examine Exhibit 2-6, which contains the income statement for Family Dollar Stores, Inc. for the year ended August 30, 2003. Notice how it follows the income statement equation to present revenues minus expenses to

Exhibit 2-6
Income Statement for Family
Dollar Stores, Inc. and
Subsidiaries

Family Dollar Stores, Inc. and Subsidiaries **Consolidated Income Statement** **For the Year Ended August 30, 2003 (in thousands)**	
Net sales	$4,750,171
Costs and expenses:	
Cost of sales	3,145,788
Selling, general and administrative	1,214,658
	4,360,446
Income before income taxes	389,725
Income taxes	142,250
Net income	$ 247,475

Accompanying notes are an integral part of the consolidated financial statements.

arrive at net income while giving pertinent information about the name of the organization and the period reported. Let's take a closer look at the income statement organization and its components.

Income Statement Organization

Exhibit 2-7 contains the income statement for Jason's Furniture Gallery for the year
ended December 31, 2004. We added a few intermediate steps to the income statement equation, as discussed below, to provide information that most income statement readers want.

Exhibit 2-7
Income Statement for a
Corporation

Jason's Furniture Gallery, Inc. **Income Statement** **For the Year Ended December 31, 2004**		
Sales Revenues		$455,000
Cost of Goods Sold		245,000
Gross Profit		$210,000
Operating Expenses		
Selling expenses	$105,000	
Administrative expenses	60,000	
Total Operating Expenses		165,000
Operating Income		$ 45,000
Other Revenues and Expenses		
Gain on the sale of equipment	$ 25,000	
Loss on investments sold	(8,000)	17,000
Income before Taxes		$ 62,000
Income Taxes		21,000
Net Income		$ 41,000

- **Revenues** include the primary business activities of the organization. Jason sells furniture, so his revenue comes from merchandise sales. A doctor's primary business activity stems from services performed, so her revenue would be service fees.
- **Cost of goods sold** appears only on merchandising or hybrid companies' income statements. Service companies have no goods to sell.

● **gross profit**
Sales minus cost of goods sold.

- **Gross profit** is the sales minus cost of goods sold. If Jason buys a sofa for $300 and sells it for $500, he makes a $200 gross profit. Notice that gross profit ignores all other costs of operating the business. The following formula can be used to calculate a gross profit percentage:

$$\frac{\text{Gross}}{\text{Profit }\%} = \frac{\text{Sales} - \text{Cost of Goods Sold}}{\text{Sales}} = \frac{\$500 - \$300}{\$500} = 40\%$$

The gross profit amount and the gross profit percentage are important information for merchandisers. Most merchandisers know what gross profit percentage they must achieve to have a successful month or year.

- **Operating expenses** consist of the selling and administrative costs of running the business, such as sales and administrative salaries, accounting fees, advertising, and insurance.
- **Operating income** describes the income (before income taxes) from the primary business activity.
- **Other revenue and expenses** include revenues and expenses associated with incidental or peripheral business operations. For most firms, examples would encompass gains and losses from the sale of business assets and investments and interest revenue or expense.
- **Income taxes** are corporate income taxes.
- **Net income** is the final amount that remains after all expenses, including income taxes for a corporation, are deducted from all revenues. Remember that sole proprietors and partners pay income taxes on business net income with their personal tax returns, so the expense does not appear on the business income statement.

Having looked at the balance sheet and income statement, now let's turn our attention to the third financial statement, the statement of stockholders' equity.

Statement of Stockholders' Equity

Equity has three main components:

1 investments by owners;
2 comprehensive income; and
3 distributions to owners.

To continue our discussion, we need to define two new accounting elements:

● **comprehensive income**
The change in equity arising from any non-owner source.

- **Comprehensive income** is the change in equity arising from any non-owner sources. It includes net income, which comprises revenues, expenses, gains and losses, and other comprehensive income. Frequently it is equal to net income on the income statement. (For companies that invest in certain types of securities, operate globally, and offer pension plans to their employees, accounting complexities create other items of comprehensive income not reported on the income statement. For the purposes of this book, we will not address these accounting technicalities referred to as *other comprehensive income*.)

● **distributions to owners**
Transfers of cash or other company assets to owners that result in a reduction of equity.

- **Distributions to owners** are transfers of cash or other company assets to owners that result in a reduction of equity. In a corporation, distributions to owners are dividends.

Regardless of organizational form, investments by owners and positive comprehensive income *increase* equity; distributions to owners and negative comprehensive income *decrease* equity.

Exhibit 2-8
Statement of Shareholders' Equity for Family Dollar Stores, Inc. and Subsidiaries

Family Dollar Stores, Inc. and Subsidiaries
Consolidated Statement of Stockholders' Equity
For the Year Ended August 30, 2003 (in thousands)

	COMMON STOCK	CAPITAL IN EXCESS OF PAR	RETAINED EARNINGS	TREASURY STOCK	TOTAL EQUITY
Balance, August 31, 2002	$18,583	$63,294	$1,118,015	$ 44,944	$1,154,948
Net Income for the year			247,475		247,475
Issuance of stock under ESOP	108	24,098			24,206
Purchase of treasury shares				65,851	(65,851)
Issuance of stock under an outside directors plan		65		(16)	81
Less Dividends on common stock			(49,890)		(49,890)
Balance, August 30, 2003	$18,691	$87,457	$1,315,600	$110,779	$1,310,969

Accompanying notes are an integral part of the consolidated financial statements.

Statement of Stockholders' Equity Presentation

The **statement of stockholders' equity** is the financial statement that reports the change in the entity's equity during a period of time. It shows how the equity changed from the beginning of the reporting period to the end of the period. All changes in equity come from changes in its three components—contributions by owners, comprehensive income, and distributions to owners. Examine closely Exhibits 2-8 and 2-9.

Exhibit 2-8 illustrates a condensed statement of stockholders' equity from Family Dollar Stores that bridges the income statement and balance sheets shown in Exhibits 2-4 and 2-6 and Exhibit 2-9 does the same for Jason's Furniture Gallery. It defines the nature of the changes in the components of equity from the beginning of the year to the end of the year. In both statements, changes arise from net income, issuance of stock, and declaration of dividends. Note that all the statements for each entity follow and detail the 10 accounting elements.

● **statement of stockholders' equity**
The financial statement that reports the change in the entity's equity during a period of time.

Jason's Furniture Gallery, Inc.
Statement of Stockholders' Equity
For the Year Ended December 31, 2004

Exhibit 2-9
Statement of Stockholders' Equity

	COMMON STOCK	RETAINED EARNINGS	TOTAL STOCKHOLDERS' EQUITY
Balance, January 1, 2004	$150,000	$233,000	$383,000
Stock issued	50,000		50,000
Net income		41,000	41,000
Dividend distributions		(30,000)	(30,000)
Balance, December 31, 2004	$200,000	$244,000	$444,000

We have now looked at all 10 accounting elements that complete the second column of the conceptual framework of accounting. We also introduced 3 of the 4 financial statements that use those 10 elements. The last financial statement, the statement of cash flows, focuses only on one asset: cash.

Statement of Cash Flows

Because we have used all 10 elements of accounting, why do we need another statement that focuses entirely on cash? We examined resources, claims, and equity on the balance sheet; performance on the income statement; and owner's transactions in the statement of changes in owners' equity. Each tells an important part of a company's financial picture. But the reality is, a business runs on cash. Even though a business may be profitable, if it runs out of cash it will be unable to continue to operate. Only cash pays the bills and keeps the company in business. The secret to becoming a street-smart user of accounting information is to balance the complexity of business with the simple rule of keeping your eye on cash flow.

● **statement of cash flow**
A financial statement that details cash provided and used by the three major functions of a firm—to operate, to invest resources, and to finance the operations and investments.

You can monitor cash flow by learning to read and understand a cash flow statement. The **statement of cash flows** details cash provided and used by the three major functions of a firm—to operate, to invest resources, and to finance the operations and investments. The statement reveals the sources and uses of cash from the primary operations, called *operating activities*. It details the investments purchased and sold in the section designated *investing activities*. And finally it describes the sources of financing from investments by owners and borrowed cash, repayments of debt, and distributions to owners in the *financing activities*. The statement as a whole delineates the sources and uses of cash in the organization during the same period as the income statement. When we know how a company uses its cash, we learn about its priorities. Exhibit 2-10 illustrates the statement of cash flows for Jason's Furniture Gallery.

Exhibit 2-10
Statement of Cash Flows

Jason's Furniture Gallery, Inc. Statement of Cash Flows For the Year Ended December 31, 2004		
Operating Activities:		
Cash received from customers		$455,000
Cash paid for:		
Merchandise	$ 160,000	
Operating expenses	150,000	
Income taxes	21,000	331,000
Cash provided by operating activities		$124,000
Investing Activities:		
Purchase of equipment	$ (35,000)	
Purchase of building	(300,000)	
Cash used by investing activities		(335,000)
Financing Activities:		
Sale of common stock	$ 50,000	
Proceeds of mortgage on building	200,000	
Dividends paid	(30,000)	
Cash provided by financing activities		220,000
Net change in cash		$ 9,000
Cash balance, January 1, 2004		20,000
Cash balance, December 31, 2004		$ 29,000

Financial Statement Articulation

The four financial statements are intertwined, and the linkage between them is known as **articulation**. Net income shown on the income statement is the same net income that appears on the statement of equity. Net income usually accounts for most of the change in equity during a period. The statement of equity shows the beginning and ending equity of the entity, both of which are indicated on comparative balance sheets. Thus, the statement of equity becomes a bridge between the income statement and the balance sheet. The balance sheet and cash flow statement articulate through the cash account. Likewise, both the beginning and ending cash balance mirror one another on the cash flow statement and balance sheet. If you think that this might not be important, imagine how you as a reader would react if you saw net income on the income statement in the amount of $41,000, but the statement of equity indicated it was $46,000. Then you looked at the balance sheet and located the current cash balance of $29,000, but the cash flow statement indicated that it was $32,000. You would probably realize that the statements contradicted one another. You would probably not have any confidence that these statements were accurate; neither would you know which of them to believe. Exhibit 2-11 illustrates articulation among the financial statements of Jason's Furniture Gallery.

Finally, we turn to the foundation of our accounting structure. The foundation consists of the basic assumptions, principles, and constraints of accounting theory. (See Exhibit 2-12 on p. 47.) We will begin our discussion of this foundation with the four assumptions accountants use as a basis for economic measurement and reporting.

● **articulation**
The linkage between the financial statements.

Assumptions

Accountants assume the following when providing information for financial accounting.

- **Separate entity assumption**—Economic transactions and activities of a business can be accounted for separately and apart from the personal activities of the owners. From an accounting standpoint, the business is viewed as a separate entity whether it is a proprietorship, partnership, or corporation.
- **Going-concern assumption**—In the absence of any information to the contrary, a business entity will continue to remain in existence for an indefinite period of time. If this assumption could not be made, a business would have no assets because nothing it possessed would have future value.
- **Monetary unit assumption**—Economic activities are measured and expressed in terms of the appropriate legal currency for a business. For example, dollars are the legal currency of the United States. U.S. GAAP assumes that the purchasing power of the dollar remains relatively stable over time and therefore ignores the effects of inflation or deflation for accounting purposes.
- **Periodicity assumption**—We measure economic activity over an arbitrary time period, such as a year or a month, for the purpose of providing useful information. The SEC and the IRS began requiring annual reporting periods in the 20th century for reporting and taxing purposes. Since then, publicly held companies report to the SEC quarterly and annually, and of course, tax returns must be filed annually. Without this assumption, however, financial analysts and investors would not receive meaningful information necessary to determine an entity's profitability trend over a number of years.

● **going-concern assumption**
In the absence of any information to the contrary, a business entity will continue to remain in existence for an indefinite period of time.

● **monetary unit assumption**
Economic activities are measured and expressed in terms of the appropriate legal currency for a business.

● **periodicity assumption**
Measurement of economic activity over an arbitrary time period, such as a year or month, for the purpose of providing useful information.

Exhibit 2-11
Financial
Statement
Articulation

Jason's Furniture Gallery, Inc.
Income Statement
For the Year Ended December 31, 2004

Sales Revenues		$455,000
Cost of Goods Sold		245,000
Gross Profit		$210,000
Operating Expenses		
Selling expenses	$105,000	
Administrative expenses	60,000	
Total Operating Expenses		165,000
Operating Income		$ 45,000
Other Revenues and Expenses		
Gain on the sale of equipment	$ 25,000	
Loss on investments sold	(8,000)	
		17,000
Income before Taxes		$ 62,000
Income Taxes		21,000
Net Income		$ 41,000

Jason's Furniture Gallery, Inc.
Statement of Stockholders' Equity
For the Year Ended December 31, 2004

	COMMON STOCK	RETAINED EARNINGS	TOTAL STOCKHOLDERS' EQUITY
Balance, January 1, 2004	$150,000	$233,000	$383,000
Stock issued	50,000		50,000
Net income		41,000	41,000
Dividend distributions		(30,000)	(30,000)
Balance, December 31, 2004	$200,000	$244,000	$444,000

Net income is the same on both the income statement and the statement of equity.

Jason's Furniture Gallery, Inc.
Balance Sheet
December 31, 2004

Assets		**Liabilities**		
Cash	$ 29,000	Accounts payable	$100,000	
Investments	75,000	Mortgage payable	200,000	
Inventory	200,000	**Total Liabilities**		$300,000
Land	80,000			
Building	300,000	**Stockholders' Equity**		
Equipment	60,000	Common stock	$200,000	
		Retained earnings	244,000	
		Total Stockholders' Equity		444,000
Total Assets	$744,000	**Total Liabilities and Stockholders' Equity**		$744,000

The equity balance on the statement of equity agrees with the balance sheet.

Jason's Furniture Gallery, Inc.
Statement of Cash Flows
For the Year Ended December 31, 2004

Operating Activities:		
Cash received from customers		$455,000
Cash paid for:		
Merchandise	$160,000	
Operating expenses	150,000	
Income taxes	21,000	331,000
Cash provided by operating activities		$124,000
Investing Activities:		
Purchase of equipment	$(35,000)	
Purchase of building	(300,000)	
Cash used by investing activities		(335,000)
Financing Activities:		
Sale of common stock	$ 50,000	
Proceeds of mortgage on building	200,000	
Dividends paid	(30,000)	
Cash provided by financing activities		220,000
Net change in cash		$ 9,000
Cash balance, January 1, 2004		20,000
Cash balance, December 31, 2004		$ 29,000

The cash balance on the balance sheet agrees with the ending cash amount on the cash flow statement.

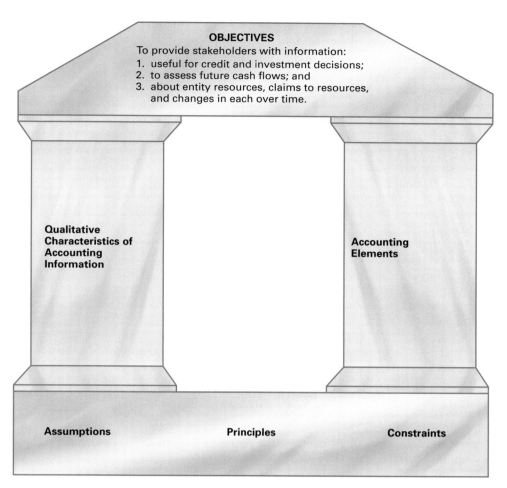

Exhibit 2-12
Conceptual Framework of Accounting

Over time, accountants have embraced the assumptions above as a necessity for meaningful financial reporting. Next we examine the basic principles that accountants follow as they record the transactions of a business enterprise. The accounting principles help us to understand how accountants identify, measure, and report the various accounting elements.[4]

Principles

Accountants observe the following principles when providing information for financial accounting.

● The **historical cost principle** requires that balance sheet items be reported at the total cost at acquisition instead of a current value. Historical cost represents the most verifiable and objective value at which to report the assets and liabilities of a business enterprise. Historical cost is often more determinable and better defined than reporting at a current value.

● **Revenue recognition** occurs when the revenue is earned and an enforceable claim exists to receive the asset traded for the revenue. To satisfy the requirement of being earned, a company must have substantially completed the terms of the sale or service. Most often substantial completion occurs at delivery of the goods or services.

● **historical cost principle**
Requires that balance sheet items be reported at the total cost at acquisition instead of a current value.

● **revenue recognition principle**
Revenue recognition occurs when the revenue is earned and an enforceable claim exists to receive the asset traded for the revenue.

---

4. Financial Accounting Standards Board, *Statement of Financial Accounting Concepts No. 5, Recognition and Measurement of Financial Statement of Business Enterprises* (Norwalk, CT: Financial Accounting Standards Board, December 1984), paragraphs 63–85.

● **account receivable**
A customer's legal promise to pay cash in the future.

● **matching principle**
Requirement that a company match revenue with the expense of producing that revenue.

● **depreciation**
The allocation of the cost of long-lived assets to the periods benefited by its use.

● **full disclosure principle**
Requirement that information necessary for an informed user of the financial statements of a business enterprise to make an economic decision must be made available to the statement users.

To satisfy the second requirement of an enforceable claim, there must be a transfer of cash or a customer's legal promise to pay cash in the future, called an **account receivable**. Both criteria must be met to recognize revenue.

● The **matching principle** requires that a company match revenue with the expense of producing that revenue. In that way, the income statement will reflect the revenue earned during the time period and the expenses required to earn that revenue. This helps to paint a realistic picture of the company's performance during the period.

When no direct cause and effect between the revenues and expenses exists, a firm either recognizes the expense when incurred or allocates it to future periods of benefit. For example, when a company pays a two-year premium for insurance coverage, it creates a prepaid insurance asset, a benefit to future periods. Furthermore, we can clearly estimate which of those future periods benefit from the policy—the next 24 months. As time passes during the two years, we systematically transfer the cost of the prepaid insurance asset to expense.

If a purchased item has no discernible future benefit, or the periods benefited cannot be reasonably estimated, we immediately recognize the cost of the item as an expense. For example, Honda's television advertising, intended to increase sales of the Civic, provides Honda with immediate benefits and some lasting benefits of name recognition and such. Television ads purchased and presented to the public in one period probably benefit future periods, but we cannot reasonably estimate how many periods or how much benefit occurs in each of those periods. Thus, we usually recognize the cost of television advertising as an expense in the periods when the ads are presented to consumers.

When a firm acquires assets that will benefit the company for more than one accounting period, the cost is recorded as an asset (unexpired cost) on the balance sheet. As time passes, the cost is transferred to expense on the income statement. The allocation of the cost of long-lived assets to the periods benefited by its use is **depreciation**. Depreciation is applied to a variety of long-lived assets such as machinery, buildings, and equipment.

● The **full disclosure principle** requires that information necessary for an informed user of the financial statements of a business enterprise to make an economic decision must be made available to the statement users. The information included should be important enough to make a difference to the user and should be adequate to aid the users in decision making.

Constraints

The final items in the foundation of the theoretical structure of accounting are four constraints that sometimes cause a departure from the use of the basic principles and assumptions.

● **materiality**
Something that will influence the judgment of a reasonable person.

● **cost-benefit relationship**
The benefit of knowing information should exceed the cost of providing information.

● **Materiality** relates to something that will influence the judgment of a reasonable person. When the amount of a particular item is not large enough to make a difference to the decision maker, it is not material. Often this judgment is relative. If the General Motors balance sheet has a $20,000 error in the amount listed for cash, the reader may not even notice it because the GM balance sheet is presented in millions of dollars. Such an error, however, would make a significant difference on the balance sheet of a small used car dealer with owner's equity of $30,000. Deciding whether or not an item is material requires an accountant's professional judgment.

● The **cost-benefit relationship** requires that the benefit of knowing information should exceed the cost of providing information. For example, information that costs $5 to obtain and saves a company only $2 is not worth providing. Sometimes the benefit is difficult to determine. If a government agency requires a company to provide certain information about air pollution, the only benefit to the company is the avoidance of fines or penalties. The true benefit may be to society as a whole when the government agency uses the information to control or reduce pollution.

- For an accountant, **conservatism** means choosing alternatives that are least likely to overstate assets and income or understate liabilities when uncertainty or doubt exists. Paramount in this definition is the phrase *when uncertainty or doubt exists.* When an accountant must adopt a conservative accounting treatment because no clearly correct decision can be made, a conservative position is least likely to mislead financial statement users to believe a company is worth more or is more profitable than it really is.

- **Industry practices** develop because certain industries may require departure from GAAP because of the peculiar nature of the industry or a particular transaction, to ensure fair presentation of the financial information within that industry. A company that explores for oil and gas conducts business very differently from a company that makes wooden chairs. The AICPA publishes guides for these special industries to help companies select the most appropriate accounting methods for the particular industry.

● **conservatism**
Choosing alternatives that are least likely to overstate assets and income or understate liabilities when uncertainty or doubt exists.

● **industry practices**
Certain industries may require departure from GAAP because of the peculiar nature of the industry or a particular transaction, to ensure fair presentation of the financial information within that industry.

Exhibit 2-13 shows the complete conceptual framework of accounting including the objectives of financial reporting; the qualitative characteristics of accounting information; the accounting elements; and the assumptions, principles, and constraints of accounting. This conceptual framework is the foundation of U.S. GAAP. By understanding these concepts, you will have a perspective for what you learn in future chapters. We will begin to apply these concepts as we start a business in Chapter 3.

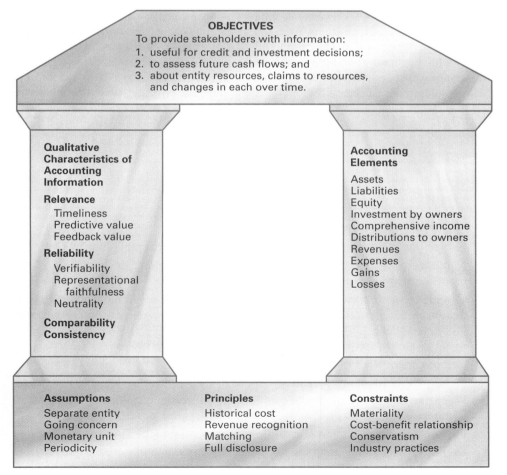

Exhibit 2-13
Conceptual Framework of Accounting

OBJECTIVES
To provide stakeholders with information:
1. useful for credit and investment decisions;
2. to assess future cash flows; and
3. about entity resources, claims to resources, and changes in each over time.

Qualitative Characteristics of Accounting Information

Relevance
Timeliness
Predictive value
Feedback value

Reliability
Verifiability
Representational faithfulness
Neutrality

Comparability Consistency

Accounting Elements

Assets
Liabilities
Equity
Investment by owners
Comprehensive income
Distributions to owners
Revenues
Expenses
Gains
Losses

Assumptions	Principles	Constraints
Separate entity	Historical cost	Materiality
Going concern	Revenue recognition	Cost-benefit relationship
Monetary unit	Matching	Conservatism
Periodicity	Full disclosure	Industry practices

CHAPTER SUMMARY

The overarching purpose of financial reporting is expressed in the accounting objectives of the conceptual framework of accounting. The purpose of accounting is to provide useful information necessary to enable decision makers to reach appropriate conclusions in business decisions, to assess the potential for future cash flows, and to understand an entity's resources and the claims against those resources and the changes in them over time.

The qualitative characteristics of accounting information include the primary characteristics of relevance (timeliness, feedback value, and predictive value) and reliability (verifiability, representational faithfulness, and neutrality) and the secondary characteristics of consistency and comparability. The qualitative characteristics of accounting information serve to ensure the usefulness of the information.

The 10 elements of accounting information attempt to measure the present status and the past performance of a business enterprise. Assets, liabilities, and equity comprise the balance sheet, which reports the present condition of the business entity. The balance sheet organization represents the accounting equation (Assets = Liabilities + Equity). The income statement provides information about a company's performance and profitability and comprises revenues, expenses, gains, and losses. The statement of stockholders' equity provides a summary of the change in equity between the beginning amount and the ending amount. The statement of stockholders' equity provides the link between the income statement and the balance sheet called articulation.

The statement of cash flows presents the changes in cash during the period, classified into three major functions of a business: operating, investing, and financing. By analyzing how a company uses its cash, we better understand its priorities.

Assumptions, principles, and constraints form the foundation of the accounting framework. The assumptions (separate entity, going concern, monetary unit, and periodicity) form the bases for economic measurement and reporting. The principles (historical cost, revenue recognition, matching, and full disclosure) help us understand how accountants identify, measure, and report the various accounting elements. The constraints (materiality, cost-benefit relationship, conservatism, and industry practice) represent items that may cause a departure from the use of the basic principles and assumptions.

Visit the Web site *www.prenhall.com/terrell* for additional study help with the Online Study Guide.

REVIEW OF CONCEPTS

A Identify the objectives of financial reporting.

B Explain the difference between accounting data and accounting information.

C Name the primary qualitative characteristics of accounting information and discuss the importance of each to financial statement users.

D Compare and contrast the specific characteristics necessary for accounting information to be relevant with the characteristics necessary for accounting information to be reliable.

E Identify the secondary qualities of useful accounting information and discuss how they are interrelated.

F Identify the accounting elements presented in each of the four financial statements.

G Write the basic accounting equation. Rewrite the accounting equation using all 10 accounting elements.

H Explain why the statement of cash flows is important to the information user.

I Define the accounting assumptions and determine which of the principles or constraints rely on each assumption.

J Define the accounting principles and provide an example not used in the text of how each principle would satisfy a real-world uncertainty.

K List and define the underlying constraints of accounting information and provide a real-world example for each.

APPLICATION EXERCISES

2-11 List the three objectives of accounting and describe which financial statements satisfy each objective.

LO 1
Objectives of Accounting

2-12 Aunt Mary died recently and left you your choice of one of her two businesses. Whichever one you reject, your cousin Pat will inherit. You know little about these businesses. Her will directs that you must select the business after asking no more than 10 questions. Write your 10 questions.

LO 1
Information

2-13 Fred Zink is the chief accountant of Hunter Company. He is trying to decide whether to extend credit to Freed Company, a new customer. Hunter does most of its business on credit, but is very strict in granting credit terms. Frank Freed, owner and president of Freed Company, sent the following items for Zink to look at as he performs his evaluation:

LO 2
Qualitative Characteristics of Accounting Information

1. all company bank statements for the past 7 years (84 bank statements);
2. a detailed analysis showing the amount of sales the company expects to have in the coming year and its estimated profit;
3. another, less detailed analysis outlining projected company growth over the next 20 years;
4. a biographical sketch of each of the company's officers and a description of the function each performs in the company;
5. letters of reference from 10 close friends and relatives of the company's officers;
6. a report of the company's credit history that company employees prepared on Freed Company letterhead; and
7. a letter signed by all company officers expressing their willingness to personally guarantee the credit Hunter extends to Freed. (You may assume this is a legally binding document.)

Required:

Analyze each item Freed sent in light of the primary qualitative characteristics of relevance (including timeliness, predictive value, and feedback value) and reliability (including verifiability, representational faithfulness, and neutrality). Explain how each item either possesses or does not possess these characteristics.

2-14 You are in the market for a used motorcycle. You notice a promising advertisement in the local newspaper and make an appointment to meet with the seller, whose name is Roaddog. During your meeting you obtain the following information:

LO 2
Chapter Concepts

1. The cycle is a 1998 Harley Sportster model.
2. Roaddog said he has used the motorcycle only for commuting to and from work.
3. You notice the motorcycle has out-of-state license tags.
4. The odometer reading is 65,319 miles.
5. Roaddog reports that he has had the oil changed every 3,000 miles since he bought the motorcycle new.
6. Roaddog says this is the greatest motorcycle he has ever owned.
7. The saddle bag contains a maintenance record prepared by a licensed mechanic.

Required:

a. Evaluate each of the preceding items in terms of its relevance (specifically, predictive value and timeliness) to your decision about whether to buy Roaddog's motorcycle.
b. Evaluate each of the preceding items in terms of its reliability (verifiability, representational faithfulness, and neutrality) for deciding whether to buy Roaddog's motorcycle.

LO 2
Qualitative Characteristics of Accounting Information

2-15 The chapter states that to be useful, accounting information must possess the primary qualitative characteristics of relevance (timeliness and predictive value or feedback value) and reliability (verifiability, representational faithfulness, and neutrality). These characteristics are also applicable to other types of information. Suppose that prior to taking your midterm exam in this course, your instructor gives you two options:

Option 1: One week before the midterm exam you will be given a rough idea of what is going to be on the exam.
Option 2: On the day following the exam, you will be given a copy of the actual midterm exam with an answer key.

Assume further that you have two goals:

Goal 1: To prepare for the midterm exam.
Goal 2: To evaluate your performance on the midterm exam.

Required:

Within the context of each goal, evaluate both options using the primary qualitative characteristics. Be sure to explain how the primary characteristics are present or absent and how such presence or absence affects you as a rational decision maker.

LO 2
Qualitative Characteristics of Accounting Information

2-16 Suppose you are about to buy a new car. The car you want is a Ford Mustang. You have $25,000 in the bank to spend on a new car. You obtain the following items of information:
1. On your first visit to Quality Ford, a salesperson casually tells you that the price of a new Mustang is $22,500.
2. A friend tells you he heard that someone was selling a three-year-old Mustang for $16,000.
3. Another friend just bought a new Chevy pickup truck for $22,000.
4. The sticker price of a Mustang with the options you want is $24,800.
5. A Ford dealer in the area is advertising a new Mustang with the options you want for $21,200.
6. A friend tells you she heard that someone bought a new Mustang a couple months ago for around $20,000.

Assume that you are about to visit a Ford dealership and your goal is to buy a new Mustang for the best price. You intend to use the preceding information to evaluate whether or not the price you get is a good deal.

Required:

a. Evaluate each of the preceding items in terms of its relevance (feedback value, predictive value, and timeliness). Explain how the presence or absence of the characteristics affects your ability to use the information to determine if this is a good deal.
b. Evaluate each of the preceding items in terms of its reliability (verifiability, representational faithfulness, and neutrality). Explain how the presence or absence of these characteristics affects your ability to use the information to determine if you are getting a good deal.

LO 2
Qualitative Characteristics of Accounting Information

2-17 Exactly three weeks from today you must take the midterm exam for this class. You feel you are in trouble because you cannot seem to grasp exactly how you should prepare for the exam. As you are walking across campus, you see the following notice pinned to a bulletin board:

TAKING ACCOUNTING 201? I CAN HELP!!!
I GUARANTEE AN "A" OR "B"
WILL TUTOR FOR $15 PER HOUR

Qualifications:

- **Got an "A" in the course myself.**
- **Have outlines of all chapters of the text.**
- **Have more than 120 satisfied customers from previous semesters.**
- **Know the professor personally.**
- **Know the authors of the text personally.**
- **Working on a graduate degree in history.**

Call Bill Austin at 555–5555

Required:

a. Evaluate each of Bill's claimed qualifications in relation to the primary characteristic of relevance (including timeliness and predictive value or feedback value).
b. Evaluate each of Bill's claimed qualifications in relation to the primary characteristic of reliability (including verifiability, representational faithfulness, and neutrality).
c. Prepare three additional questions of Bill that would give you better information to make your decision and explain why each would help relevance, reliability, or both.

2-18   You are conducting research for a term paper in a field of interest. Your instructor demands that all research be conducted through the Internet. Assuming you only select relevant information, write an analysis of how you will judge the information you find on the basis of:

a. reliability
b. relevance
c. comparability
d. consistency

Please be specific.

LO 2
Qualitative Characteristics of Accounting Information

2-19

a. Write out the basic accounting equation.
b. Define each element of the equation in your own words and give at least two examples of each from your own life.

LO 3
Accounting Equation

2-20   Presented below is a list of three accounting elements, followed by partial definitions of those items in random order.

            a. Assets   b. Liabilities   c. Equity

1. _____ debts of the company
2. _____ probable future economic benefits
3. _____ "things" of value a company has
4. _____ the residual interest in the assets of an entity that remains after deducting its liabilities
5. _____ probable future sacrifices of economic benefits
6. _____ what the company owes
7. _____ what the company has less what it owes
8. _____ the owner's interest in the company

LO 3
Accounting Elements

Required:

For each partial definition, identify the element (a, b, or c) to which it refers.

LO 3
Accounting Equation

2-21   Write the basic equation to define net income or net loss. In your own words define each of the elements used in this equation and give examples of each from your own life.

LO 3
Accounting Elements

2-22   Write the basic accounting equation for the statement of stockholders' equity for a corporation. In your own words, define each element used in your equation.

LO 3
Accounting Elements

2-23   Fill in the missing amounts in the following table.

Assets	=	Liabilities	+	Equity
10,000	=	15,000	+	?
25,000	=	?	+	5,000
?	=	75,000	+	20,000
95,000	=	25,000	+	?

LO 4
Balance Sheet

2-24   The following balance sheet of Sally Clark and Associates was compiled at the end of its first year of operations:

Sally Clark and Associates
Balance Sheet
December 31, 2004

Assets		Liabilities and Equity	
Cash	$40,000	Note payable—Central Bank	$10,000
Land	20,000	Common stock	15,000
		Retained earnings	35,000
Total Assets	$60,000	Total Liabilities and Equity	$60,000

Required:

a. Describe what this balance sheet tells you about the financial position of the company.
b. What type of business organization is Sally Clark and Associates?
c. From the information provided, can you determine how much profit the company made in the first year? If not, where can you find this information?

LO 4
Balance Sheet

2-25   On January 2, 2004, Kyle Dover started an appliance repair business. Assume that the business organized on January 2, 2004, was a corporation Kyle and his brother Lyle started, which they have named K&L Enterprises, Inc. Kyle invested $2,000 and received 200 shares of common stock. Lyle invested $3,000 and received 300 shares of common stock.

Required:

Prepare a balance sheet as of January 2, 2004, for the company to reflect the stockholders' investments.

LO 4
Balance Sheet and Statement of Stockholders' Equity

2-26   On July 1, 2005, Sandy and Dennis Spears started a business. Assume that the business organized on July 1, 2005, was a corporation Sandy and his other brother Dennis started, which they have named S&D Enterprises, Inc. Sandy invested $40,000 cash and a piece of land valued at $10,000 for which he received 5,000 shares of common stock. Dennis invested $30,000 for which he received 3,000 shares of common stock.

Required:

a. Prepare a balance sheet as of July 1, 2005, for the company to reflect the stockholders' investment.
b. Prepare a statement of stockholders' equity.
c. Describe the advantages of forming a corporation rather than a partnership.

2-27   Presented below is a list of items relating to the concepts discussed in this chapter, followed by definitions and examples of those items in random order.

a. Assets   c. Equity   e. Expenses

b. Liabilities   d. Revenues

1. ____ debts of the company
2. ____ sales
3. ____ probable future economic benefits
4. ____ inflows of assets from delivering or producing goods, rendering services, or other activities
5. ____ "things" of value a company has
6. ____ the residual interest in the assets of an entity that remains after deducting its liabilities
7. ____ probable future sacrifices of economic benefits
8. ____ outflows or other using up of assets from delivering or producing goods, rendering services, or carrying out other activities
9. ____ costs that have no future value
10. ____ what the company owes
11. ____ what the company has less what it owes
12. ____ the owner's interest in the company

Required:

Match the letter next to each item to the appropriate numbered term.

2-28   Compare and contrast each of the following pairs of terms:
a. revenue and expense
b. net income and net loss
c. net profit and gross profit

2-29   Fill in the missing pieces of information for each income statement.

	a.	b.	c.	d.
Sales	$50,000	$80,000	$75,000	?
Cost of goods sold	34,000	?	?	$40,000
Gross profit	?	50,000	?	60,000
Operating expenses	?	?	10,000	20,000
Net income	7,000	20,000	15,000	?

2-30   Karen Allen and Company, Inc. had $75,985 in sales revenue during 2003. In addition to the regular sales revenue, Allen sold a small building it owned and made a gain of $4,800. Cost of goods sold for the year totaled $31,812. Other administrative and selling expenses for the year were as follows:

Rent	$10,500
Utilities	2,195
Advertising	4,265
Wages	12,619

Required:

Prepare a 2003 income statement for Karen Allen and Company, Inc.

LO 4
Income Statement

2-31 Geri Kenfield and Company had $245,000 in sales revenue during 2004. In addition, Kenfield sold a plot of land it owned at a loss of $7,600. Cost of goods sold for the year totaled $102,000. Other administrative and selling expenses for the year were:

Rent	$24,000
Wages	13,500
Advertising	2,200
Utilities	2,900

Required:

Prepare a 2004 income statement for Geri Kenfield and Company.

LO 4
**Income Statement
and Statement of
Stockholder's Equity**

2-32 The following information is from the accounting records of Graham's Pet Store, Inc. for 2004:

Sales	$830,000
Cost of goods sold	440,000
Wages	280,000
Utilities	34,000
Rent	28,000
Advertising	22,000

Required:

a. Prepare a 2004 income statement for Graham's Pet Store.
b. Prepare the statement of stockholder's equity for Graham's Pet Store for 2004 assuming that Graham is the sole stockholder who paid $20,000 for his stock in 2003; the January 1, 2004, retained earnings balance is $21,000; and the corporation paid a dividend of $12,000 during 2004.

LO 4
**Income Statement
and Stockholders'
Equity**

2-33 The Aaron McLeroy Company, Inc. reported the following information in its records for 2004:

Sales	$250,000
Cost of goods sold	120,000
Salaries	70,000
Utilities	4,000
Rent	3,000
Advertising	1,000
Dividends paid	5,000

Required:

a. Prepare the income statement for the Aaron McLeroy Company for 2004.
b. Explain how the resulting income statement will affect the stockholder's equity for the year.

LO 4
Statements of Equity

2-34 Fill in the missing information for each statement of equity.

	a.	b.	c.	d.
Beginning balance	$10,000	$12,000	$15,000	?
Owner investment	15,000	?	12,000	$11,000
Net income or (loss)	?	11,000	(9,000)	10,000
Distributions	12,000	10,000	?	14,000
Ending balance	25,000	35,000	18,000	13,000

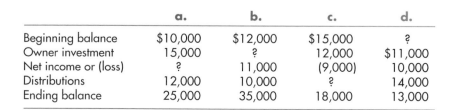

2-35 Fill in the missing information for each statement of shareholders' equity.

LO 4
Analysis of
Shareholders' Equity

	a.	b.	c.	d.
Beginning balance	$200,000	$100,000	$300,000	?
Stock issued	100,000	?	200,000	$100,000
Net income	?	250,000	100,000	(90,000)
Dividend distributions	0	150,000	?	0
Ending balance	400,000	225,000	400,000	700,000

2-36 Examine Exhibit 2-10. Describe how the management of Jason's Furniture Gallery used its cash in 2004 and from what sources the cash came.

LO 4
Statement of Cash
Flows

2-37 Describe in your own words why and how the statement of cash flows gives insight into the priorities of a business' management.

LO 4
Statement of Cash
Flows

2-38 Presented below are terms relating to the concepts discussed in this chapter, followed by statements about those items in random order.

LO 5, 6, 7
Principles,
Assumptions,
Constraints

a. going concern   c. monetary unit   e. historical cost   g. matching

b. separate entity   d. periodicity   f. revenue recognition   h. full disclosure

1. _____ the assumption that measures economic activity over arbitrary time periods
2. _____ the assumption that economic transactions can be accounted for apart from personal activities of owners
3. _____ the assumption that a business entity will continue for an indefinite period of time
4. _____ the assumption that economic activities are measured in terms of appropriate legal currency
5. _____ the principle that states when an enforceable claim exists revenue may be recognized
6. _____ the principle that states it is the most objective value to report assets and liabilities
7. _____ the principle that requires that information necessary for an informed user to make an economic decision must be provided
8. _____ the principle that requires a proper association of revenues and expenses in a given period

Required:

Match the letter next to each item on the list with the appropriate definition. Each letter will be used only once.

2-39 Presented below are terms relating to the concepts discussed in this chapter, followed by definitions of those items in random order.

LO 5, 6, 7
Principles,
Assumptions,
Constraints

a. materiality   c. industry practice   e. monetary unit

b. cost-benefit relationship   d. conservatism

1. _____ the concept that takes into account the benefits to be received in relation to costs incurred
2. _____ the size of an item is not large enough to make a difference in a decision
3. _____ the prudent reaction to uncertainty to ensure that risk is adequately considered
4. _____ the particular nature of a business may dictate the accounting practices of a business
5. _____ the economic activities are measured in the appropriate currency

Required:

Match the letter next to each item on the list with the appropriate definition. Each letter will be used only once.

LO 6
Revenue Recognition

2-40 In each of the following situations decide when revenue should be recognized.
a. A customer buys a case of soda at the local convenience store and pays cash.
b. A customer buys a dress at the local department store and uses a credit card for payment.
c. A customer buys a suit at the local department store and charges the purchase on his store account.
d. A CPA prepares a tax return for a client on February 10, the client picks it up on February 12, and the client pays the CPA on April 10.

LO 5, 6, 7
Principles,
Assumptions,
Constraints

2-41 A client who manufactures gold jewelry comes to you for advice. He tells you of a new device that he can place in his drains to capture gold shavings that are being washed down the drains. The device will cost $5,000 installed. What points might you advise your client to consider before making the decision?

LO 4
Articulation

2-42 Examine Exhibits 2-4, 2-6, and 2-8 for the Family Dollar Stores, Inc. Indicate how the balance sheet, income statement, and statement of stockholders' equity articulate. Be specific.

LO 4
Financial Statements

2-43 Go the Web site *www.prenhall.com/terrell* and link to a company assigned by your instructor.
a. From the balance sheet, determine:
1. total assets
2. total liabilities
3. total stockholders' equity
(Be sure that your accounting equation balances.)
b. From the income statement, determine:
1. net sales
2. gross profit
3. net income
c. From the statement of stockholders' equity, determine:
1. the amount of dividends declared
2. the amount of new stock sold or issued
d. From the cash flow statement, determine:
1. total cash provided (used) by operations activities
2. total cash provided (used) by investing activities
3. total cash provided (used) by financing activities
e. What is your initial impression of this company from looking at these financial statements?

Ethics Case

2-44 Amy Boggs, CPA, was engaged in a discussion with the CEO of a new client. Amy was trying to explain to the CEO the importance of the conceptual framework of accounting. The CEO could not understand why accounting had to have a framework because he knew there seemed to be accounting rules for every accounting situation that he encountered.

Required:

Explain the need for a conceptual framework of accounting and discuss how it helps accountants provide more useful information.

FOR ADDITIONAL READING

Lundholm, Russell J. "Reporting on the Past: A New Approach to Improving Accounting Today." *Accounting Horizons* 13 (December 1999):315–322.

Ottenheimer, Jack L. "Cutting Financial Reports Down to Size." *Journal of Accountancy* 187 (March 1999):45–48.

Penn, Robert. "A Glimpse of the Future." *Journal of Accountancy* 188 (July 1999):35–40.

CHAPTER 3

LEARNING OBJECTIVES

After completing this chapter you should be able to:

1 Identify the steps to organizing a business.

2 Describe a corporate organization structure and define the equity structure of a corporation.

3 Compare and contrast the characteristics of common stock and preferred stock.

4 Research an industry for its particular characteristics and identify its major competitors.

5 Prepare a strategic plan for a business.

6 Outline internal controls for operations.

7 Define borrowing terms and compute the cost of borrowing.

8 Compute and distinguish between nominal and effective interest rates.

9 Compute the selling price of bonds with a calculator.

Organizing a Business: Equity and Debt Financing

Decision time! How long has it been since someone asked you what you were going to do when you . . . grow up . . . graduate from college . . . get married? Probably not long ago. That is why friends, parents, and grandparents exist—to cajole us into making decisions we sometimes would rather avoid. Many people dream of flexing entrepreneurial muscles and owning their own business. In the remaining chapters of this book, we will observe the experience of four people who work together to make their dream of owning a snowboard manufacturing company come true.

Visit the *www.prenhall.com/terrell* Web site to view the Lands' End video, Part I.

First, some background on our four adventurers: Rob, Megan, Jon, and Angie. They met on the slopes of a ski resort during spring break of their junior year at State University. They immediately became friends, sharing an avid interest in snowboarding. One year later, after graduating, the four interviewed with numerous firms for career positions. Rob accepted a position with an advertising firm and learned how to create effective advertising copy and place ads with various media. Angie went to a dot-com company where she used her computer programming skills. Jon found a challenging position with a mechanical engineering firm and gained invaluable experience with CAD/CAM programs for production assembly lines. Megan joined a large international CPA firm as a staff accountant, passed her CPA exam, and quickly rose to the rank of senior auditor.

Three years after graduation, the quartet met for their annual New Year's week on the slopes. With a quarter of a century of life behind them, they pondered

Exhibit 3-1
Checklist to Consider Before
Beginning Operations

> **International Accounting Associates LLP**
> **Client Checklist Before Beginning Operations**
>
> 1. Find competent people to be responsible for the four functions of the firm.
> 2. Decide upon the organizational form for the business.
> 3. Research the industry and the product.
> 4. Prepare a strategic plan.
> 5. Design internal controls for operations and information.
> 6. Secure financing.
> 7. Prepare initial capital and operating budgets.

their futures. Among the consensus was appreciation of their rich experience in their chosen field, a need to pursue their own dreams, and a longing to have more free time to pursue their passion in life—snowboarding. Rob began doodling snowboard ads on a pad of paper. Jon started reengineering the drawing. Megan began mapping out costs and sales projections, and Angie mentally began creating a Web site. By Sunday, when it was time to return to the real world, they had created the germ of a plausible idea—starting their own snowboard company. Being realistic, they decided to consider the idea for two months, and meet during the first week of March to see if there was any way their dream could become reality.

Megan used her connections with the accounting firm to get a checklist of important considerations before venturing into a new business, shown in Exhibit 3-1. Megan sent the checklist to the others and asked them to gather information for their March meeting. They each agreed to use this checklist as a model. Megan answered many of her friends' questions during those intervening months.

We will walk through their process of gathering the right information to determine whether or not they can start their business in Chapters 3 and 4. We will cover steps one through six in Chapter 3 and complete step seven in Chapter 4.

The Four Functions of the Firm

In Chapter 2 you learned that three primary functions of a firm were operating, investing, and financing. The fourth vitally important function of a company is making decisions. How can a company make decisions? Only its management can. A sole proprietorship has a very simple management structure—the proprietor makes all final decisions unless he or she delegates that power to an employee. Partnerships usually rely on partners' votes when all partners do not agree. A corporate structure usually contains a hierarchy of people who have decision-making authority.

As they analyzed their situation, they decided the operating functions could be shared by Rob, Jon, and Angie. Rob would lead the marketing effort, Jon run the manufacturing plant, and Angie control the information system. Megan, being the CPA, would oversee investing and financing. All four would participate in the decision-making process.

Selecting the Organizational Form

One issue quickly settled was to operate as a corporation. Four cannot form a sole proprietorship, so the only choice was between partnership and corporation. Each member realized the potential for product liability with recreational equipment. As you recall from Chapter 1, the corporate form limits the investor's liability and protects the owners' other personal assets, so they chose to incorporate. Megan volunteered to see how insurance could provide additional protection. Megan sent everyone information on corporate structure so they could become familiar with it.

Forming a Corporation

Forming a corporation requires **incorporators** to submit a formal application to create a corporation and file it with the appropriate state agency. The application, called the **articles of incorporation**, generally includes:

1 basic information about the corporation and its purpose;
2 the names of the incorporators; and
3 details concerning the types and amounts of corporate stock authorized for sale. **Corporate stock** is evidence of a share of ownership in the corporation.

If the state agency approves the application, it issues a **corporate charter**, which is a certificate that creates a legal corporate entity and entitles the corporation to begin operations. The incorporators sell stock to investors to raise capital. Once they buy stock, the investors become stockholders who formulate the **corporate bylaws**, which serve as basic rules for management to follow in conducting the corporation's business. Stockholders also elect a board of directors. The directors meet to elect a chairperson and appoint a president and such other officers as they deem necessary to manage the company.

Corporate Organizational Structure

In the preceding section, we referred to several groups of people within the corporate structure. Because these groups are critical to the successful operation of a corporation, we will discuss each of them in detail.

- **Stockholders**—The stockholders own the corporation. Stockholders provide cash or other assets to the corporation in exchange for ownership shares in the company. In most corporations, the stockholders do not participate in the daily management of the company unless they have been elected to the board of directors or have been appointed as officers or managers.
    When stockholders invest in the corporation they receive a **stock certificate**, a legal document providing evidence of ownership and containing the provisions of the stock ownership agreement (see Exhibit 3-2). The stockholders meet no less than annually to elect members to the board of directors and conduct other important corporate business.
- **Board of directors**—The board of directors has ultimate responsibility for managing the corporation. In practice, however, most boards restrict themselves to formulating very broad corporate policy, planning, and appointing officers to conduct the corporation's daily operations. The board serves as a link between the stockholders and the officers of the company. If the officers are not managing the corporation in the best interests of the stockholders, the board of directors, acting on behalf of the stockholders, can replace the officers. The board of directors elects a chairperson.

● **incorporators**
Persons who submit a formal application to create a corporation and file it with the appropriate state agency.

● **articles of incorporation**
An application for incorporation that generally includes: (1) basic information about the corporation and its purpose; (2) the names of the incorporators; and (3) details concerning the types and amounts of corporate stock authorized for sale.

● **corporate stock**
Evidence of a share of ownership in a corporation.

● **corporate charter**
A certificate that creates a legal corporate entity and entitles the corporation to begin operations.

● **corporate bylaws**
Basic rules for management to follow in conducting the corporation's business.

● **stock certificate**
A legal document providing evidence of ownership and containing the provisions of the stock ownership agreement.

Exhibit 3-2
Corporate Stock Certificate

Corporations issue stock certificates to their owners as evidence of the investment made by stockholders. This historical stock certificate represents 100 shares of stock.

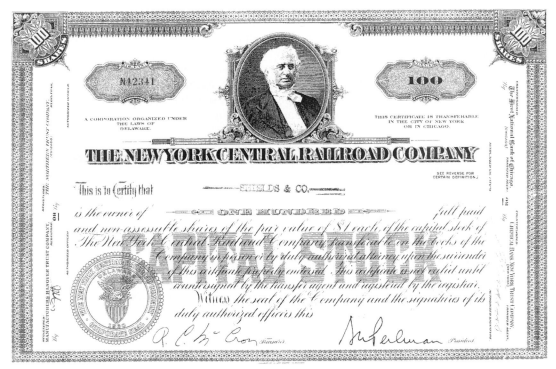

● **chief operating officer (COO)**
The corporate officer who directs the daily operations of the corporation.

● **treasurer**
The corporate officer who is responsible for managing the company's cash.

● **corporate secretary**
The corporate officer who maintains the minutes of the board of directors' and stockholders' meetings and may also represent the company in legal proceedings.

● **Corporate officers**—A corporation's CEO, normally chairperson of the board of directors and sometimes concurrently the corporate president, is responsible for all activities of the company. The **chief operating officer (COO)** may be the president or a vice president who directs the daily operations of the corporation. In addition to the president, most corporations have one or more vice presidents who are responsible for specific functions of the company, such as marketing, finance, and production. Many corporations name a CFO, who directs the corporation's financial affairs. Other corporate officer positions include the controller, who is the chief accountant; the **treasurer**, who is responsible for managing the company's cash; and the **corporate secretary**, who maintains the minutes of meetings of the board of directors and stockholders and may represent the company in legal proceedings. Exhibit 3-3 illustrates typical relationships among the various groups in the corporate structure.

Very small corporations with only a few stockholders operate more like sole proprietorships and partnerships. The CEO may be the chairperson of the board of directors,

Exhibit 3-3
Corporate Structure

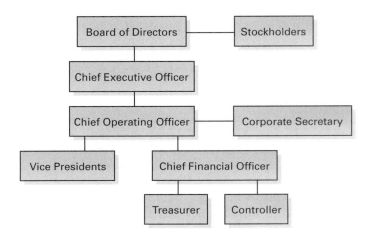

president, and sole stockholder, and may empty the trashcans at the end of the day. A business of any size may assume the corporate form, provided it meets the legal requirements of the state in which it operates. Although we may focus on larger, publicly held corporations in some chapter materials, the concepts apply to corporations of any size.

Corporate Capital Structure

As part of the formal application to create a corporation, the incorporators must include details of their plans to sell shares of stock. They request the authority to sell, or issue, a certain number of shares of stock. **Authorized shares** are the maximum number of shares the charter allows the corporation to issue. The corporate officers may request authorization of additional shares during the life of the corporation. Shares of stock sold to stockholders are **issued shares**. **Outstanding shares** are shares of stock currently held by stockholders. In many instances, issued shares and outstanding shares will be the same number. Occasionally, however, a corporation reacquires shares of stock it has previously issued to reduce the number of shares outstanding to give to employees as rewards or bonuses, for pensions, or for various other legal and financial reasons. **Treasury stock**, shares of stock reacquired by the corporation and held in the treasury, will cause the numbers of issued shares and outstanding shares to differ. For example, assume a corporation issued 100,000 shares of its stock and later reacquired 2,000 of those shares for its pension plan. The company still has 100,000 shares issued, but now has only 98,000 outstanding shares. The cash paid to reacquire the treasury stock is deducted from both cash and total stockholders' equity to keep the accounting equation in balance.

The two basic classes of stock are common stock and preferred stock.

Common Stock

Common stock is the voting stock of the corporation. Common stockholders are the residual owners of the corporation. They own the residue, or what is left after all other claims to assets are settled. Each share of common stock represents an equal share in the ownership of the corporation; therefore, the stockholders' equity portion of a corporate balance sheet will show information about common stock.

Common stock may or may not have a par value. **Par value** is an arbitrary dollar amount placed on the stock by the incorporators at the time they make application for the corporate charter. To protect investors and creditors, states used to require a par value to set the minimum legal limits of liability for stockholders.[1] Par value does not describe the selling price, or the market value, of the stock. All 50 states have now removed the par value requirement. So why do we discuss par value if it is no longer required? Because most large U.S. corporations were formed before the requirement was eliminated, and they issued **par value stock**, or stock that carries a par value. Also, many incorporators elect to issue par value stock in newly formed corporations.

Most corporations set the par value of their stock considerably below its market value because most states do not allow stock to be sold for less than its par value. (See Exhibit 3-4 for a comparison of par and market values for some major corporations' stocks.) Par values of $1 per share or even lower are not unusual. Tiffany & Co., for example, has a par value on its stock of $0.01 per share. Stock authorized without a par value is **no-par stock**. Choosing to issue no-par stock instead of stock with a par value has no effect on the market value of the shares.

Preferred Stock

Preferred stock offers certain preferential treatment to its owners over common stockholders for dividends and in the event of liquidation. Although preferred stockholders do not have voting rights, they receive other types of benefits, which

- **authorized shares**
The maximum number of shares the charter allows the corporation to issue.

- **issued shares**
Shares of stock sold to stockholders.

- **outstanding shares**
The number of shares of stock currently held by stockholders.

- **treasury stock**
Shares of stock reacquired by the corporation and held in the treasury.

- **common stock**
The voting stock of a corporation.

- **par value**
An arbitrary dollar amount placed on the stock by the incorporators at the time of incorporation.

- **par value stock**
Stock that carries a par value.

- **no-par stock**
Stock authorized without a par value.

- **preferred stock**
Stock that offers certain preferential treatment to its owners over common stockholders for dividends and in the event of liquidation.

1. If you recall, corporations protect stockholders' personal assets from the liabilities of the corporation through limited liability. The stockholder's minimum liability risked with the purchase of stock is the stock's par value. Therefore, if a stock had a par value of $10 and the corporation sold it to a stockholder for $8, the stockholder has a potential liability to creditors of $2 if the corporation defaults on a debt and closes the business.

Exhibit 3-4
Comparison of Par Values
and Market Values

COMPANY	PAR VALUE	MARKET VALUE DECEMBER 1, 2003
Saks, Inc.	$0.10	$15.71
IBM	0.20	91.01
J. C. Penny	0.50	25.77
Tiffany & Co.	0.01	45.20
Dow Chemical	2.50	38.50
Snap-On Inc.	1.00	30.54
Avery Dennison	1.00	55.30
Southwest Airlines	1.00	18.44
Dell Computer	0.01	34.89

are outlined in the stock agreement. Two benefits of ownership normally found in preferred stock agreements are:

1. Owners of preferred stock must receive a dividend before any dividend is paid to owners of common stock.
2. If a corporation is liquidated, preferred stockholders receive a distribution of assets before any assets can be distributed to common stockholders. **Liquidation** is the process of going out of business: The corporation is shut down, all assets are sold, and all liabilities are settled.

● **liquidation**
The process of going out of business when all assets are sold and all liabilities are settled.

Preferred stock usually carries a par value. Although par value has little meaning for common stock, the par value of preferred stock is important because dividends are usually stated as a percentage of par value. For example, if a corporation issued 8% preferred stock with a par value of $100 per share, the annual dividend would be $8 per share ($100 × 8% = $8). Most corporations must offer a reasonable dividend to encourage investors to buy their preferred stock. The preferred stock's market value fluctuates more with the dividend rate than any other measure.

● **additional paid-in capital**
The amount paid to a corporation for stock in excess of its par value.

Additional paid-in capital represents the amount paid to a corporation for common or preferred stock in excess of its par value. If an investor pays $25 for a $10 par value stock, $15 is attributed to additional paid-in capital.

Predictably, Megan did a good job in teaching everyone about corporations. Each of our group members has much to think about in organizing this new corporation. As they contemplate organizational and capital structure, they also need to move to the next step on the list, researching the industry.

Researching the Industry

● **industry**
A group of companies that form a sector of the economy.

Most companies operate within an **industry**, a group of companies that form a sector of the economy. We can find a lot of information about an industry, but we must determine the best industry data to examine. Snowboarding is too small to be a whole industry; it is a subset of the recreation industry.

How does one research an industry? Fortunately today we can have information available in minutes that 20 years ago might have taken weeks or months to obtain. We do, however, have to determine who provides reliable information about an industry. The best sources include trade organizations, industry guides, business periodicals, and information from members of the industry.

● **trade organizations**
Organizations that collect information about an industry, act as a spokesperson for the industry, interface with government agencies, and promote the products and services marketed by the industry.

● **Trade organizations**—Some industries have **trade organizations** such as the AICPA and the Cotton Council. Trade organizations collect information about an industry, act as a spokesperson for the industry, interface with government agencies, and promote the products and services marketed by the industry.

How do you find such organizations? The easiest way is to ask someone in the industry if such an organization exists. Another involves searching the Internet. Search engines, such as Yahoo! or Google, help locate trade organizations. A business reference librarian can also assist you in such a search.

Trade organizations collect a variety of data about sales, operating profits, special problems, government regulations, and product research. Trade groups share some of this information only with members and publish or sell other information.

- **Market research firms**—American Sports Data Inc. and Sports Business Research Network both specialize in research in sports data and the sporting goods industry. Research firms normally require fee-based membership in their organization to access the information.

- **Industry guides**—A number of organizations produce useful periodicals: Mergent FIS, Inc. issues *Mergent Industry Review*; Standard & Poor publishes *Standard & Poor's Industry Surveys*; and the Gale Group issues *Manufacturing & Distribution USA, Industry Analyses, Statistics, and Leading Companies*. Once you have defined the industry you seek, you can find good information in these publications, which can be found in the reference section of a library. Each industry has a NAICS six-digit number, and information is often listed by industry number.

- **Business periodicals**—Publications such as *Fortune, Business Week, The Wall Street Journal*, and *Forbes* offer reasonably unbiased news articles about international business. These publications provide a great deal of industry- and company-specific information for large industries such as automakers, technology, petrochemicals, accounting and financial services, retail, and insurance.

Use the *Business Periodical Index* in a library or go online to find a number of articles to meet your information needs. Search engines on the Internet can also help you locate articles in these publications about certain industries. The Web sites for *Fortune, Business Week, The Wall Street Journal*, and *Forbes* can also help you. Both *Fortune* and *Forbes* have search engines for articles on the Internet and allow you to print them without charge.

Rob agreed to research snowboarding to see what he could find concerning the industry outlook, the number of competitors, the identity of trade associations, and avenues for marketing their new product.

Megan reminded everyone that the next item on the checklist was to develop a strategic plan. Angie volunteered to provide more information about strategic planning.

What Do You Think?

3-1   Name three trade organizations other than the AICPA and the Cotton Council that regularly advertise an industry in the media and discuss how their activities might influence you.

3-2   In addition to the ways mentioned in the text, how might a trade organization benefit its members?

3-3   Using the Internet, locate a trade organization for snowboard manufacturers.

Developing a Strategic Plan

Standard & Poor's Industry Surveys contains a segment on "How to Analyze a Leisure Products Company." The first qualitative factor it suggests you examine is whether or not the company has a clearly defined strategic plan.

● **strategic plan**
The plan that describes the organizational approach the senior management of a company will employ to fulfill the corporate mission and vision and achieve the stated goals by allocating financial resources and directing human resources.

● **corporate mission**
A statement that describes the organization's purpose.

● **corporate vision**
A statement that articulates the organization's values and intentions.

● **internal environment**
An organization's culture and resources.

● **core competency**
An activity at the center of the organization's purpose that it performs very well.

● **external environment**
The industry environment and the macroenvironment in which a company operates.

● **industry environment**
A company's relationships and relative power position with its customers, suppliers, competitors, special interest groups, and the extent of substitute products and services.

● **macroenvironment**
The current and future state of, and likely changes in, the economic climate, the political climate, demographics, technology, and societal trends and attitudes.

Angie soon discovered that strategic planning has been a top priority for large businesses in the past two decades. She asked her mentor, "Should a small business prepare a strategic plan?" His answer was, "Absolutely!" So Angie did her homework and sent the following information to her future partners.

A **strategic plan** describes the organizational approach the senior management of a company will employ to fulfill the corporate mission and vision and achieve the stated goals by allocating financial resources and directing human resources. Strategic planning is the process used to develop a strategic plan, and it consists of seven steps:

1   Develop a clearly articulated mission and vision. The **corporate mission** describes the organization's purpose, and the **corporate vision** articulates the organization's values and intentions.

2   Set measurable goals and objectives. Goals describe what the organization wishes to achieve, and objectives explain how the organization plans to achieve its goals.

3   Scan the internal environment to assess strengths and weaknesses and the external environment to assess opportunities and threats. The **internal environment** consists of the organization's culture and resources. The beliefs, values, and expectations of the organization's personnel influence its ability to carry out the mission. This value system becomes the organizational culture. A new organization can influence the culture that develops by defining its value system and operating true to those values. The organization's resources include its core competencies, financial resources, human resources, management information system, marketing abilities, manufacturing or operating capabilities, and its research and development. A **core competency** is an activity at the center of the organization's purpose that it performs very well. When the organization excels in a core competency compared to other members of its industry, its core competency may become so distinctive that it gives the company an advantage over its competitors. Distinctive core competencies contribute to a company becoming an industry leader. Strategic planners look for the strengths and weaknesses in an organization. Weaknesses must be addressed and strengths maintained for an organization to remain strong and grow.

The **external environment** consists of the industry environment and the macroenvironment in which a company operates. The **industry environment** consists of a company's relationships and relative power position with its customers, suppliers, competitors, special interest groups, and the extent of substitute products and services. The **macroenvironment** includes the current and future state of, and likely changes in, the economic climate, the political climate, demographics, technology, and societal trends and attitudes. Planners continually scan the external environment to look for threats and opportunities. Every threat has an opportunity for enterprising visionaries. Every opportunity carries with it certain threats to the status quo.

4   Formulate alternative strategies. Formulate strategies that can accomplish goals capitalizing on strengths and opportunities to overcome weaknesses and threats. Brainstorming can be very productive.

5   Develop the plan. Select the best alternative(s) and develop actions that can best accomplish the stated goals.

6   Implement the plan. Develop working plans and put them into motion.

7   Evaluate the results of the implementation and return to step 1. Constantly monitor the success of the plan and return to step 1. Make use of the lessons learned in the prior plan to formulate new plans. Most companies set strategic plans every one to three years.[2]

---

2. Stephen P. Robbins and Mary Coulter, *Management* (Upper Saddle River, NJ: Prentice Hall, 1999):238–241.

As Angie learned, strategic planning is a continuous process throughout the corporation's life. Angie asked that each person think about the mission, vision, and goals of this venture as they began formulating a strategic plan. Another critical management function is to plan and create internal controls for the firm's operations and private information. Let's look at why internal controls deserve such attention.

Designing Internal Controls for Operations and Information

As defined in Chapter 2, the internal control structure helps to protect the business against preventable losses and to promote efficient operations by creating checks and balances within the accounting and operating processes. You participate in internal control systems each time you purchase something in a retail store. Some stores offer you a reward when a cashier fails to give you a register receipt because the employee is then required to ring up the sale and can't steal your cash. Displaying the amount at a drive-through order restaurant allows you to verify the accuracy and amount of the order to keep the cashier from charging you the wrong amount and pocketing the difference. Electronic inventory tags help to prevent shoplifting. These are physical examples of internal controls designed to protect a business from theft or embezzlement.

Internal controls develop as a business grows. Right now our budding entrepreneurs need some help with establishing internal controls early in their project, so we will look at the most important internal control concerns for a new business. Megan checked with experts on internal controls and learned that the three areas of major importance in internal controls are protecting physical assets, protecting proprietary information, and creating an environment that respects internal controls.

Protecting Physical Assets

To protect physical assets, management can insure against theft, fire, and natural disasters. They can secure physical assets with appropriate locks, alarms, guards, and other physical barriers. Inventory can be secured with electronic tags that activate when removed from the premises. An important consideration is to hire employees with integrity who are well qualified for the specific position. In addition, management can segregate duties so that each employee has controlled access to assets. Employees with access to assets should have no opportunity to alter record keeping for that asset. Finally, if a company pays appropriate wages, employees are less likely to feel justified in stealing company assets, including time, supplies, raw materials, inventory, information, or cash. None of these methods require a lot of money or extensive time requirements. For internal controls to work, however, they require consistent application.

Protecting Proprietary Information

Assets are not limited to inventory, buildings, and machinery. They include engineering designs, strategic plans, financial information, and management information. How do we protect information? Some controls are easy to implement. For example, install virus protection software and keep it updated. Use password protection for computer programs, data files, and other information files. Segregate duties so that persons who enter data (from computer terminals or cash registers) have no ability to interrupt or change computer programs and vice versa. Possibly the best protection for proprietary information is to hire appropriate people for each position, train them well, and pay them fairly. Finally, secure daily back-up copies of all important information, data files, and program files to protect them against theft and physical destruction. Consider also using offsite locations such as data storage services.

Creating the Right Environment

No matter what internal controls management installs, none will work without the proper atmosphere. Senior management sets the tone for internal controls in an organization. If senior managers circumvent controls, their example filters down to lower level employees, who will also circumvent controls.

Internal controls afford protection, but cannot guarantee protection without the cooperation of the participants. If managers scoff at controls or frequently bypass them, the controls eventually become ineffective. Even more important, management must clearly communicate the internal control policies and procedures to each employee. Finally, management should prosecute any person who breaks internal control policies and procedures and causes the business to experience losses through theft or embezzlement. Our entrepreneurs discuss how they can meet each of these internal control challenges. They also pledged to maintain an attitude consistent with a strong internal control structure to help to protect their investments.

Next we will discuss how to secure resources to finance the company formation. Megan agreed to chart these alligator-infested waters for the group and sent the following report.

Securing Financing

● **equity financing**
Acquiring funds for business operations by selling ownership interests in the company.

● **debt financing**
Borrowing funds for business operations.

● **short-term financing**
Borrowing that must be repaid within five years.

● **long-term financing**
Borrowing with a repayment period that extends past five years.

All companies have one thing in common: Each must obtain capital money to support operations. In the long run, a company must employ internal financing by providing funds for the operation of a company with the profits from its operations. When just starting out or during a time of expansion, almost all companies find it necessary to seek funds from outside the company. To obtain these funds, companies can sell ownership shares or borrow funds. **Equity financing** acquires funds for business operations by selling ownership interests in the company. Most businesses begin their operations using cash the owners invested. Borrowing funds for business operations is **debt financing**.

Small businesses have two primary sources of debt financing—owners and banks or other financial institutions. Owners can make loans to the business that must be repaid, in addition to purchasing an equity interest in the business. Business firms normally seek bank financing after the owners' resources have been depleted. The need for external funding does not indicate a weakness. On the contrary, companies often need additional funding because the company is growing even faster than expected.

A company needs short-term financing to run its day-to-day operations and long-term financing to achieve its long-range goals. From a financial market perspective, **short-term financing** is any borrowing that must be repaid within five years. **Long-term financing** has a repayment period that extends past five years. Good cash management relies on the coordination of short-term activities with short-term financing and long-term activities with long-term financing to effectively manage the cash inflows and outflows. Several sources provide these two types of financing to businesses.

Borrowing from Financial Institutions

The commercial banking industry includes many types of financial institutions that serve a broad range of customers, such as savings and loan associations (S&Ls), mutual savings banks (MSBs), credit unions (CUs), and commercial banks. Commercial banks primarily lend to business firms and earn profits by renting money to customers. The bank rents money from its depositors and then in turn rents it out to borrowers. Logic dictates that the rent the bank pays to depositors must be less than the rent it receives from borrowers if it is to be profitable. A bank can only remain in business when it earns a profit. **Interest** is the cost of borrowing, or renting, another's money. It is revenue to the lender and expense to the borrower.

Borrowing with Notes Payable

If a company needs to borrow short-term funds, a bank may lend it money and require it to sign a **note payable**. This is a written agreement or debt instrument between a lender and a borrower that creates a liability for the borrower to repay both principal and interest. The bank's lending policies and the judgment of the lending officer determine the amount of money lent and the **term**, the length of time between borrowing and repaying a loan. Borrowing cash by signing a note payable adds to the assets of the company, but at the same time it creates a liability. Thus assets and liabilities both increase and keep the accounting equation in balance.

ASSETS = LIABILITIES + OWNERS' EQUITY
Increase $10,000 = Increase $10,000 + $0 No Change

A note payable generally requires the signing of a **promissory note**, a legal promise to repay a loan. In addition, the lender may require collateral to secure the loan. **Collateral** is something of value that must be forfeited to the lender if the borrower fails to make payments as agreed. Failure to repay a loan as agreed or to abide by other requirements of the lending agreement is called **default**. For example, if you borrow money from a local bank to buy a new car, the car usually serves as collateral. If you fail to make the payments, the bank can repossess the car and sell it to get its money back. By offering collateral, companies may be able to borrow more funds for a greater length of time. This type of larger, longer term collateralized note payable includes an additional document called a mortgage. The **mortgage** is a document that states the agreement between a lender and a borrower who has secured the loan with collateral.

The Cost of Borrowing

The difference between what one borrows and what one repays is the cost of borrowing or interest. Any borrower attempts to minimize interest cost. We can determine the cost of borrowing by using the terms of the note payable.

For example:

Kenfield, Inc. borrowed $5,000 on March 2, 2002, by signing an 8 percent, three-year note. The lender requires annual interest payments to be made on the anniversary of the note.

The important note information is:

1 Date of the note: March 2, 2002
2 Amount received from the loan: $5,000
3 Interest rate: 8 percent
4 Loan length: 3 years, due on March 2, 2005
5 Interest payments due annually on March 2

The rate of interest is always stated as an annual percentage. Therefore, 8 percent refers to the amount of interest the lender requires for a full year, regardless of the terms of the loan. Interest is calculated on the amount of funds actually borrowed, the **principal**. The formula to determine the annual interest amount is:

Principal × Rate = Annual Interest

● **interest**
The cost of borrowing money that represents rent paid to use another's money. It is revenue to the lender and expense to the borrower.

● **note payable**
A written agreement or debt instrument between a lender and a borrower that creates a liability for the borrower to repay both principal and interest.

● **term**
The length of time between borrowing and repaying a loan.

● **promissory note**
A legal promise to repay a loan.

● **collateral**
Something of value that must be forfeited to the lender if the borrower fails to make payments as agreed.

● **default**
Failure to repay a loan as agreed or to abide by other requirements of the lending agreement.

● **mortgage**
A document that states the agreement between a lender and a borrower who has secured the loan with collateral.

On January 31, 2004, Dillards, Inc. owed $59.75 million in mortgage notes. Land, buildings, and building improvements with a book value of $39.60 million were pledged as collateral for the mortgages.

● **principal**
In the case of notes and mortgages, the amount of funds actually borrowed.

In our example of the Kenfield, Inc. note, the amount of interest due each year is calculated as:

$$\text{Principal} \times \text{Rate} = \text{Annual Interest}$$
$$\$5,000 \times .08 = \$400$$

The note terms require the following payments:

Date	Interest Payments	Principal Payments	Total Payments
March 2, 2003	$ 400		$ 400
March 2, 2004	400		400
March 2, 2005	400	$5,000	5,400
Totals	$1,200	$5,000	$6,200

Remember that the difference between what is borrowed and what is paid back represents the cost of borrowing:

Amount repaid	$6,200
Amount received from the loan	5,000
Cost of borrowing or interest	$1,200 for three years

The length of notes payable varies. If Kenfield, Inc. needed to borrow the funds from the bank for a shorter time, the note might have been described as a $5,000, 8 percent, three-month note. This terminology suggests that the $5,000 must be repaid three months from the day the funds were borrowed. On that day, Kenfield, Inc. would pay the lender the principal ($5,000) and the interest due. Recall that interest rates are stated in annual terms, so 8 percent indicates the amount of interest that would be due if the funds were held for one year. If the funds were held for three months, only a portion of the year's interest would be due.

We can refine our formula to account for the length of time the funds are held:

$$\text{Principal} \times \text{Rate} \times \text{Time} = \text{Interest}$$
$$P \times R \times T = I$$

If the funds are borrowed for 3 months, time is represented by 3/12, indicating 3 months of the 12 months in a year. The calculation to determine the interest owed by Kenfield, Inc. is:

$$P \times R \times T = I$$
$$\$5,000 \times .08 \times 3/12 = \$100$$

If, however, the note read $5,000, 8 percent, 90-day note, the calculation of interest would be:

$$P \times R \times T = I$$
$$\$5,000 \times .08 \times 90/365 = \$98.63$$

How do we calculate the due date of a 90-day loan made on March 2? Determine how many days the note will be outstanding, not counting the first day, for each month until you reach 90 days.

March (31 days minus 2 days)	29
April	30
May	31
Total days	90

Therefore, the due date is May 31. Did you guess June 2? Remember that not all three-month intervals contain the same number of days.

The cost of borrowing describes the total dollars of interest paid on a loan. We also compare the interest rate stated in the loan terms with the true interest rate paid by the borrower. Let's see how to measure the true rate and what makes it differ from the stated rate.

Effective Interest Rate

Lenders write loan terms to conform to the specific needs of the lender or the borrower. Therefore, not all terms are the same for each customer or for all loans made to one customer. Look at the following loan information:

Kenfield, Inc. deposited $9,000 as the loan proceeds of a $10,000 discounted note due one year from today.

The lender deducted the 10 percent interest on the loan in advance. A loan arrangement in which a bank deducts the full interest in advance from the loan proceeds is a **discounted note**. The bank charged Kenfield $1,000 for interest, which is 10 percent of the $10,000 loan. Kenfield, however, only had the use of $9,000, not $10,000, for the year. Return to our analysis model for the cost of borrowing:

● **discounted note**
A loan arrangement in which a bank deducts the full interest in advance from the loan proceeds.

Amount repaid	$10,000
Amount received from the loan	9,000
Cost of borrowing (interest)	$ 1,000

Using the interest formula, we can solve for the true interest rate of the discounted note:

$$P \times R = I$$
$$R = \frac{I}{P} = \frac{\$1,000}{\$9,000} = 11.11\%$$

As you can see, the calculated rate is not the 10 percent the bank quoted, but 11.11 percent. The **effective interest rate** is the actual interest rate the lender earns and the borrower pays. The act of discounting the note, deducting the interest from the proceeds, effectively increases the true interest paid on the amount the borrower uses. Is the bank lying about the interest? No, because each lender must indicate clearly the true cost of borrowing, the annual percentage rate (APR), on the face of the note. The bank will disclose the effective interest rate of 11.11 percent. The business community understands the implications of a discounted note and the fact that it increases the effective interest rate of the loan.

● **effective interest rate**
The actual interest rate the lender earns and the borrower pays.

What Do You Think?

3–4 A bank has offered to help you open a business by loaning you $10,000. You currently have no other funds available for this business, so the bank includes a restriction in the loan that you must keep at least $3,000 in your checking account at all times.

(a) How much of the loan can you utilize?
(b) On how much of the loan will you pay interest?
(c) How might this restriction affect the effective interest rate of your loan?

3–5 A credit card company offers to grant you $1,000 of credit at an APR of 21% in a special offer for first-time credit card holders. It also requires that you deposit $500 in a savings account paying 5%, from which you may not make withdrawals as long as the credit card has a balance. Comment on the effective interest rate on the credit card assuming that your balance is the full $1,000.

Borrowing Through the Financial Markets

Large corporations, such as those among the *Fortune* 500, need to borrow larger sums than most banks can accommodate. These corporations have the ability to borrow large sums for short terms of five years or less from the investing public by the use of

● **commercial paper**
A corporate promissory note that investors buy from the corporation.

● **bond**
A type of long-term note payable, usually a $1,000 interest-bearing debt instrument.

● **bond indenture**
A legal document that details the agreement between the company issuing the bonds and the buyers of the bonds, including the timing and amount of the interest payments and repayment of the bond principal.

● **par value for a bond**
The principal of the loan, which is the amount that must be repaid at maturity.

● **nominal interest rate**
The interest rate that the issuing corporation agreed to pay in the bond indenture, stated as a percentage of the par value of the bond.

● **effective interest rate of a bond**
The actual interest rate that the bondholder will earn over the life of the bond, also called the **yield rate** or **market interest rate**.

● **selling price of a bond**
The amount for which a bond actually sells. Also called the **market price**.

● **discount**
Occurs when a bond sells for less than par value.

commercial paper. **Commercial paper** is a corporate promissory note that investors buy from the corporation, which in turn agrees to repay the notes plus interest at the end of the specified term.

When a large corporation needs to borrow money for long periods of time, the debt markets have yet another source of financing available. A **bond** is a type of long-term note payable, usually a $1,000 interest-bearing debt instrument. The main differences between a bond and a note payable to a bank are the length of time the debt will be outstanding and the amount of money borrowed. Unlike five-year notes, bonds payable can have a term of 40 years or more. Corporations sell bonds to borrow money from many different parties, so the total amount borrowed can exceed what one bank could lend. Large U.S. corporations use bonds as a major source of external financing and typically have millions or billions in long-term debt on their balance sheets. For example, Johnson & Johnson had long-term bonds outstanding of $2.24 billion as of December 31, 2003. The SEC regulates bond issuances and requires each bond issue to provide detailed information to investors in its **bond indenture**. This legal document details the agreement between the company issuing the bonds and the buyers of the bonds, including the timing and amount of the interest payments and repayment of the bond principal.

Bonds are issued in a set denomination, generally $1,000 for each bond. The denomination sets the **par value** or the principal of the loan, which is the amount that must be repaid at maturity. The **nominal interest rate** is the interest rate that the issuing corporation agreed to pay in the bond indenture, stated as a percentage of the par value of the bond. For example, an 8 percent, $1,000 bond pays $80 per year interest to the buyer.

$$P \times R = I$$
$$\$1,000 \times .08 = \$80$$

Unlike the nominal rate, which is determined by the issuing company, the effective rate is determined by the investors in the financial markets. The **effective interest rate of a bond** denotes the actual interest rate that the bondholder will earn over the life of bond, also called the **yield rate** or **market interest rate**. Because bonds exceed more than one year of life, the effective rate of interest must be computed using present-value techniques, which you will study in Chapter 10. (Financial calculators can also help you find the selling price of bonds or the effective interest rate. See the appendix to this chapter for instructions.) Financial market investors determine what rate they require for a company's bond based on the credit risk of the company and other current market rates available. The investors compare their required rate with the nominal rate the company offers and make an offer to purchase based on present-value calculations.

The **selling price of a bond** is the amount for which a bond actually sells; it is also called the **market price**. If the market-required interest rate and the nominal interest rate are the same, a bond sells at par or 100, meaning at 100 percent of its face or par value. When bond buyers require a higher rate of interest than the nominal rate, the bond will sell at a **discount**, or less than par value. For instance, a selling price of 95 means the bond is selling at 95 percent of its par value. If you think about it, you will realize why. If you are trying to sell a bond that pays a rate lower than the market-required rate, you will be forced to lower the price. Only then will you attract the buyers you need.

If Yoko Industries issues one thousand $1,000, 10 percent, 20-year bonds when the market demands a 10.6 percent rate of return on investment, the bonds will only sell for 95, or 95 percent of par value. Apply the cost-of-borrowing model to the Yoko Industries bonds:

Amount repaid:	
Maturity value ($1,000 × 1,000)	$1,000,000
Interest paid	
($1,000,000 × 10% × 20 years)	2,000,000
	$3,000,000
Bond proceeds:	
(1,000 bonds × $1,000 × .95)	950,000
Total cost of borrowing for 20 years	$2,050,000

As you can see, the total cost of borrowing for 20 years, $2,050,000, exceeds the cash payments for interest, $2,000,000. Therefore the yield rate of interest is higher than the 10 percent nominal rate.

When a bond's nominal rate of interest is more than the market-required interest rate, a bond may sell for more than its par value, or at a **premium**. If Yoko Industries issues one thousand $1,000, 12 percent, 20-year bonds at a time when the market only requires an 11.3 percent rate of return on investment, the bonds will sell for 104 or 104 percent of par value. Look again at the cost-of-borrowing model:

● **premium**
Occurs when a bond sells for more than par value.

Amount repaid:	
Maturity value ($1,000 × 1,000)	$1,000,000
Interest paid	
($1,000,000 × 12% × 20 years)	2,400,000
	$3,400,000
Bond proceeds	
(1,000 bonds × $1,000 × 1.04)	1,040,000
Total cost of borrowing for 10 years	$2,360,000

The total cost of borrowing for 20 years, $2,360,000, is less than the cash interest paid, $2,400,000, indicating that the bonds yield less than the 12 percent cash interest paid.

What Do You Think?

3–6 If Easley Corporation sells one thousand, 10-year, 9%, $1,000 bonds at 98, what are the proceeds of the bond issue?

3–7
(a) Calculate the total cost of borrowing over the life of the bonds in 3–6.
(b) What is the annual cash payment for interest?
(c) Is the effective interest rate more or less than 9%?
(d) How can you determine this?

3–8 How would your answers to 3–6 and 3–7 change if the bonds sold at 103?

3–9 If you wish to earn 10% on a bond investment, does it matter whether you buy a bond at a discount price or a bond at a premium price if the yield is 10%? Explain your answer.

One last item to remember about stocks and bonds: The company receives money only when the corporation originally issues the securities in the primary securities market. The **primary securities market** involves sales of newly issued stocks and bonds between the issuing corporation and investors where the corporation receives the proceeds of sales. The organized stock exchanges, such as the New York Stock Exchange (NYSE), the American Stock Exchange (AMEX), and National Association of Securities Dealers Automatic Quotations (NASDAQ) comprise the **secondary securities market**. All the trading that occurs on the secondary securities market takes place among buying and selling investors, and the corporation receives nothing from these trades.

Our group certainly needs to consider both equity and debt financing for their venture. Megan asked each member of the group to figure out how much equity capital each could contribute and to be prepared with answers when they next meet. She also requested that each inquire about sources for debt financing for their equipment needs. Each of the group members agreed to gather the information needed to complete step

● **primary securities market**
Sales of newly issued stocks and bonds between the issuing corporation and investors where the corporation receives the proceeds of sales.

● **secondary securities market**
Trading that occurs on organized stock exchanges among buying and selling investors, and the corporation receives nothing from these trades.

seven for their meeting in March. (We will go through the details of those steps in Chapter 4.) Meanwhile, we will fast forward to their March meeting and look at how our four dealt with making decisions about organizational structure and form, researching the industry and product, preparing the strategic plan, and searching for financing opportunities.

The Summit

Our four adventurers met in Vail, Colorado, during the first week of March. Jon had located an abandoned warehouse on the perimeter of the town that included a small showroom at the ski base village. The city of Vail offered special rental rates for this property of $20,000 per year for both locations, with the first six months rent free for a business that would operate year-round. They decide to check out the location, make their reports, and make some important decisions.

Rob's Report on the Industry

Industry Information. To his surprise, Rob discovered a lot of information on the sports equipment industry in three publications:

1 *Standard & Poor's Industry Surveys*—Standard & Poor's believes that snowboarding will be an enduring part of leisure activity, especially among youths, partly because snowboarding is now an Olympic sport. Consumer purchases for snowboards were $164 million in 1998, $184 million in 1999, and $246 million in 2000. From 1994 to 1999, the number of people participating in snowboarding rose 58 percent; during the same time, Alpine skiing declined 30 percent. Approximately 3,635,000 young people, age 7 to 17, participated frequently in snowboarding. Standard & Poor's predicts that the population of those between age 5 and 19 will fall from 21.6 percent of the population in 2000 to 20.7 percent by 2015. The age demographics directly influence the sales of certain sport products.

The report stressed that new product introductions were key to successful growth in the sporting goods industry. Most new products boast improvements that make the product bigger or better.[3] Unfortunately, this report was the last that Standard & Poor's made on the leisure products industry. It does, however, include reports for many other industries.

2 *Manufacturing USA: Industry Analyses, Statistics, and Leading Companies*—This publication gives statistics of all kinds from production by state, to leading companies, to types of materials used in production by NAICS number (339920 for sporting and athletic goods manufacturing). The number of establishments grew 35 percent from 1992 to 2003 while sales increased 76 percent to $13,316,000,000.[4]

3 *Mergent Industry Review*—This semiannual publication gives comparative statistics and financial ratios for companies in an industry. One interesting recreation company was Vail Resorts, Inc. which was eighth in the industry in revenues and net income. The company showed a 21.7 percent growth in revenue and 16.78 percent growth in operating income from 1997 to 2002.[5]

Trade associations. Rob discovered three trade associations related to snowboard manufacturing: U. S. Ski and Snowboard Association (USSA), which is the national governing

---

3. Tom Graves, CFA, "Leisure Products," *Standard & Poor's Industry Surveys* (New York, NY: October 19, 2000):1–32.
4. Arsen J. Darnay, ed., "Sporting and Athletic Goods Manufacturing," *Manufacturing and Distribution USA: Industry Analyses, Statistics, and Leading companies* (Detroit, MI: Gale Research, 2003):2338–2342.
5. Mergent FIS, "Recreation," *Mergent Industry Review* (New York, NY: July 2002–January 2003):433–435.

body for Olympic snowboarding competition and athletic programs; Sporting Goods Manufacturers Association (SGMA), which promotes the growth of the industry and encourages participation in sports activities; and the National Sporting Goods Association (NSGA), the world's largest association for retailers and manufacturers of sporting goods with 25,000 members. The USSA Web site provides a wide array of links to other Web pages and a variety of information about the sport of snowboarding.

Other industry information. Subaru is a committed sponsor for snow sports. In past years Subaru has sponsored the Ski Dazzle Ski and Snowboard Show in Los Angeles and Chicago. Many resorts and manufacturers exhibited their products at this meeting with a lot of entertainment and demonstrations. A recent *Fortune* article about marketing skis and snowboards focuses on K2, a company that produces different types of bindings and boots for snowboarders. The company netted $27.5 million in 1997 with sales of $661 million.[6] A May 2000 *Forbes* article highlights Steen Strand, the head of Freebord Manufacturing, which makes a skateboard that mimics a snowboard. It offers good insights on the rigors of starting a new business.[7]

Visit the USSA, SGMA, and NSGA Web sites to learn about their activities.
www.usaa.org
www.sgma.com
www.nsga.org

Megan's Report on Insurance

Megan discovered that product liability insurance will cost $5,000 for the year plus $1 for each snowboard manufactured. This insurance will protect against losses from product liability.

Jon's Report on Manufacturing Equipment

Jon located a bank that had repossessed manufacturing equipment that can fulfill the company's needs for the first few years because it can make several sizes of snowboards and skis. Although new equipment would cost about $250,000, the bank will sell this equipment for $75,000. The best part of the deal is that a Vail bank will finance the equipment over four years with a down payment of $15,000. Each year the company must pay 10 percent interest and make another principal payment of $15,000.

Angie's Report on Software and Technology

Angie found appropriate computer hardware for $3,000 and needed software for accounting, manufacturing, and online work that cost $1,500. She will also write a few small programs to customize the purchased software. Because of the small costs involved and the short lives of computers and software, Angie's bank will finance the purchase for only one year.

Equity Investment and Financing

Equity investments—After careful consideration, our intrepid four decided they could each contribute between $18,000 and $30,000 for their stock in the company.

Financing—All four discovered that it would be difficult to borrow money for start-up costs. From what Megan learned, it would be wise to use direct financing for equipment and software and save their equity investments for operating costs. Another financing resource would be to negotiate terms with raw material suppliers to preserve operating cash.

---

6. Ed Brown, "Marking Tracks in the Sports-Equipment Business," *Fortune* 137 (February 2, 1998):36ff.
7. Kelly Barron, "Wheeler-dealer," *Forbes* (May 1, 2000) *http://www.forbes.com/forbes/00/0501/6510136a.htm.*

The Decisions

After three days of intensive discussion on mission, vision, and goals, the group decided to go for it. Each will give notice to their employers and begin on June 1. Jon also located two, two-bedroom condominiums on the square in Vail that the city would lease to the group free until October 1 in conjunction with the free rent on the warehouse. That will give them time to locate permanent housing in the area before the busy season. With life decisions behind them, business decisions followed.

Corporate Structure

The new venture, Elevation Sports, Inc., will incorporate by authorizing 100,000 shares of $10 par value common stock. Each of the four originators will contribute $25,000 for 1,000 shares of common stock and will serve on the board of directors. The group elected Megan as CEO and president, Rob as vice president of Marketing, Angie as vice president of Information Technology, and Jon as vice president of Manufacturing.

Strategic Planning

Mission, Vision, and Goals. The group spent two days of their meeting working on the strategic plan. After much thought, they developed the mission, vision, goals, and objectives contained in Exhibit 3-5.

Environmental Scan. *Strengths and weaknesses of the internal environment.* With a start-up company, there is not much to analyze. The strengths include four officers/owners and their talent, education, and enthusiasm. Their financial resources are modest and mostly equity. They will acquire good production equipment and the latest information

Exhibit 3-5
Mission, Vision, Goals, and Objectives

ELEVATION SPORTS, INC.

Mission
Elevation Sports, Inc. builds safe, quality products for sports enthusiasts.

Vision
Elevation Sports, Inc. will produce technologically innovative, safe, environmentally friendly sports equipment that gives our customers value and quality.

Goals and Objectives
Goal 1: Be operational by August 15.
    Objective 1: Begin manufacturing by July 15.
    Objective 2: Attend the next ski industrial show with at least 100 boards for sale.
    Objective 3: Open the Vail shop by Thanksgiving with at least four weeks' inventory.
Goal 2: Have the Web site operational by July 1.
    Objective 1: Register the Web site and get an address.
    Objective 2: Prepare to receive sales online.
    Objective 3: Arrange for lowest price shipping with a dependable carrier.
Goal 3: Be profitable in first year and each year thereafter.
    Objective 1: Prepare operating and capital budgets.
    Objective 2: Get as much free publicity as possible.
    Objective 3: Keep sales prices as high as possible and costs low.
Goal 4: Keep debt low.
    Objective 1: Borrow as little as possible.
    Objective 2: Repay debt as quickly as possible.
Goal 5: Grow at a healthy and safe rate.
    Objective 1: Expand the breadth and depth of the product line over time.
    Objective 2: Open additional outlets as opportunities arise.

technology. Among the four, they possess expertise in accounting/finance, engineering, marketing, and information technology. Weaknesses include a lack of specific experience in owning and running a company, limited capital resources, and the inherent issues in a seasonal business.

Opportunities and threats in the external environment. Information that Rob gathered showed that snowboarding increased about 58 percent in the last half of the 1990s and the number of manufacturers rose about 29 percent in the last decade. Opportunity requires innovation and frequently rolling out new and improved products. The largest markets for sports equipment are the North American Free Trade Association (NAFTA) countries, Western Europe, Japan, and China. The sports industry grew about 2.8 percent annually through 2003. Almost two-thirds of sales occur in sports shops and discount stores. The inclusion of snowboarding in the Olympics has increased the popularity of the sport.

Threats include the slowly declining population between the ages of 5 and 19 predicted until 2015. Also, the 29 percent increase in the number of manufacturers may pose a threat because the industry may become too saturated with manufacturers and create too much supply in the marketplace for all to make a reasonable profit. The group has one more general opportunity that they may explore in the future. Snowboards are closely aligned with skateboards and the new mountain boards, which are skateboards designed to go into off-road terrains. Mountain boards, in particular, may become the summer version of snowboards and give the company a natural way to expand its product line.

> Remember the steps of a strategic plan:
>
> 1. Develop mission and vision.
> 2. Set goals and objectives.
> 3. Scan internal and external environments.
> 4. Formulate alternative strategies.
> 5. Develop the plan.
> 6. Implement the plan.
> 7. Evaluate the results.

Formulate alternative strategies. Rob, Megan, Jon, and Angie considered the following strategies.

Manufacturing:

1 Manufacture one snowboard and gradually add different boards to the product line.
2 Manufacture one snowboard that can be customized for buyers and make only snowboards.
3 Manufacture a line of snowboards from the beginning and expand the product line into related products (skateboards and mountain boards) as quickly as possible.
4 Manufacture one snowboard, grow the product line steadily, and expand into related products as opportunities arise.

Marketing:

1 Market only through the sales office in Vail and over the Internet directly to consumers.
2 Market primarily over the Internet to wholesale accounts and in Vail to customers.
3 Market to consumers in Vail and over the Internet and solicit wholesale customers at trade shows and with manufacturers' representatives.
4 Promote the boards by offering special pricing to ski rental shops.

Develop the plan. After reviewing their goals and possible strategies, and after lengthy discussions, the group settled on the following plan:

1 Engineer one innovative board that can be customized. Continuously plan for new products, including mountain boards, and introduce them as they generate customer interest.
2 Use the Internet to market to consumers and make a second Web site available for wholesale orders. Attend trade shows to generate wholesale sales and sales to ski shops that rent boards. Give special wholesale prices to Colorado ski rental shops to promote the new brand.

We will see how they begin to implement and evaluate their basic plan in the coming chapters.

Our intrepid adventurers left Vail with high levels of anticipation and anxiety. On June 1, they will each bring $25,000 of hard-earned savings to begin their dream and sign papers to commit to loans and leases. They realize that any dream can end in failure, but they would rather try and fail, than not try at all. At this point in their lives, they have few responsibilities beyond themselves, and probably have less to lose than at any future point in their lives. In Chapter 4 the four entrepreneurs deal with the realities of building both their product and budgets. Join them in learning the basics of putting the numbers together to set their strategic plans in motion.

USING A FINANCIAL CALCULATOR TO COMPUTE BOND INFORMATION

Computing the Selling Price of Bonds

Financial calculators make it possible to compute the effective interest rate, or yield, and the selling price of a bond. Different models of calculators operate somewhat differently, but most are similar. To find the selling price of a bond, you must enter the following information according to the instructions for your model:

n = the number of interest payment periods

i = effective interest rate per period

FV = maturity value

pmt = cash interest paid each period (some calculators require you to enter the interest payments as a negative number)

cpt **PV** = selling price of the bonds

Example:

If Jupiter Corporation wanted to sell $1,000,000 of 20-year bonds with a nominal rate of 11 percent when the market expects to receive 10.5 percent interest, what would the bonds' selling price be?

If Jupiter pays interest once per year, we can calculate the selling price by entering the following:

20 **n** = the number of interest payment periods

10.5 **i** = effective interest rate per period

$1,000,000 **FV** = maturity value

$110,000 **pmt** = cash interest paid each period ($1,000,000 × .11)

Enter these four items and then select:

cpt **PV** = selling price of the bonds

The calculator will give you the answer 1041154.50, which equals a selling price of $1,041,154.50.

If the bonds pay interest twice a year, the calculation will be different. If the bonds pay interest twice a year, it pays interest 40 times instead of 20, at half of the rate, and pays half the amount of $55,000. Recalculate the selling price:

40	**n**	=	the number of interest payment periods (2 x 20)
5.25	**i**	=	effective interest rate per period (10.5/2)
$1,000,000	**FV**	=	maturity value
$55,000	**pmt**	=	cash interest paid each period ($110,000/2)

Enter these four items and then select:

cpt	**PV**	=	selling price of the bonds

The calculator will give you the answer 1041468.70, which equals a selling price of $1,041,468.70.

Computing Other Bond Information

As long as you have any four of the five input items for bonds, you can compute the missing item with the calculator. Assume that:

Torrie Corporation sells 2,000, 10 percent, 5-year, $1,000 bonds on January 1, 2004, for $1,926,080. The bonds pay interest annually on December 31.

What is the effective interest rate?

5	**n**	=	the number of interest payment periods
$1,926,080	**PV**	=	selling price of the bonds
$2,000,000	**FV**	=	maturity value
$200,000	**pmt**	=	cash interest paid each period

Enter these four items and then select:

cpt	**i**	=	effective interest rate per period

The calculator will give you the answer 11.000029. This equates to an 11 percent effective interest rate.

If the bonds paid interest twice a year, our calculation would change and the effective interest would also change:

40	**n**	=	the number of interest payment periods (2 x 20)
10	**n**	=	the number of interest payment periods (5 x 2)
$1,926,080	**PV**	=	selling price of the bonds
$2,000,000	**FV**	=	maturity value
$100,000	**pmt**	=	cash interest paid each period ($200,000/2)

Enter these four items and then select:

cpt	**i**	=	effective interest rate per period

The calculator will give you the answer 5.4901074. When we multiply by 2, for twice a year, this equates to 10.98 percent effective interest rate.

Exhibit 3-6
Amortization Table

YEAR	A CASH PAID MATURITY × 10%	B INTEREST EXPENSE D × 11%	C DISCOUNT AMORTIZATION B – A	D BOOK VALUE
				$1,926,080 ←Bond Selling Price
2004	$ 200,000	$ 211,869	$11,869	1,937,949
2005	200,000	213,174	13,174	1,951,123
2006	200,000	214,624	14,624	1,965,747
2007	200,000	216,232	16,232	1,982,979
2008	200,000	218,021*	18,021	2,000,000 ←Maturity Value
Totals	$1,000,000	$1,073,920	$73,920	
	↕	↕	↕	
	Total Interest Paid	Total Cost of Borrowing	Discount on Selling Price	

*rounded

Exhibit 3-7
Comparison of Cost-of-Borrowing Model to Amortization Table

Amount repaid:
    Maturity value ($1,000 × 2,000) $2,000,000 = Ending Carrying Value
    Interest paid ($200,000 × 5 years)   1,000,000 = Total Column A
    Total repaid $3,000,000
Bond proceeds: 1,926,080 = Beginning Book Value
Total cost of borrowing for 20 years $1,073,920 = Total Column B

Amortization Table

Lenders frequently provide an amortization table that details the payments of principal and interest on loans. Exhibit 3-6 contains an amortization table for the Torrie Corporation bonds that pay annual interest.

Exhibit 3-6 contains all of the information pertinent to the bond. Column A contains the annual interest payment of $200,000. Column B contains the amount of the effective interest expense for each year. It can be computed by multiplying the book value in column D times the effective interest rate. Column C is the difference between the annual nominal interest and the effective interest, called the *discount amortization*. The amount of column C is added each year to the book value of the bonds in column D. The book value begins with the selling price of the bonds and equals the maturity value at the due date of the bonds. Compare the amortization table with the cost-of-borrowing model shown in Exhibit 3-7.

You should notice that the information contained in the amortization table is consistent with the cost-of-borrowing model.

CHAPTER SUMMARY

Organizing a business requires numerous planning steps to create the possibility of a successful venture. The first step is to appoint effective people to perform the four functions of the firm: operating, investing, financing, and making decisions.

The second step is for the entrepreneur(s) to decide on the form of business organization. Formation of a corporation requires following appropriate state laws to sell stock to owners (stockholders). The organizational structure of a corporation consists of the stockholders, the board of directors, and the corporate officers.

The corporate capital structure consists of the authorized, issued, and outstanding shares of stock. Common stock is the voting stock of the corporation and it may or may not have a par value. Another type of stock is preferred stock, which has certain preferences over the common stock for dividends and in liquidation. Additional paid-in capital is the amount received from the sale of stock above the par value of the stock. Treasury stock is any of the corporation's own stock that has been reacquired.

The third step in organizing a business requires researching the industry in which a business operates. The industry poses threats to and holds opportunities for business success. Trade organizations, industry guides, and business periodicals provide helpful resources for such research.

The fourth step is to develop a strategic plan. Strategic planning is a seven-step process to achieve organizational goals by allocating financial resources and directing human resources. Steps include developing the corporate mission, setting goals and objectives, scanning the internal environment for strengths and weakness and the external environment for opportunities and threats, formulating alternative strategies, selecting the best alternatives to form the plan, implementing the plan, evaluating the results of the implementation, and returning to the beginning to start the process over again.

Fifth, the design and implementation of internal controls in a new business will help to protect the business against preventable losses and promote efficient operations. Internal controls should be developed to protect physical assets and proprietary information. Internal controls are effective only when a proper control environment is established and promoted by top management.

Sixth, the business leaders must obtain financing from internal or external sources. Internal financing is provided from the earnings of the business. External financing comes from two primary sources, equity investors (stockholders) or debt financing. Banks and financial institutions provide debt financing through short-term and long-term borrowing. Businesses borrow short-term loans with promissory notes, whereas long-term financing frequently requires collateral with a mortgage on that collateral.

The cost of borrowing, the difference between what one borrows and what one repays, is called *interest*. Lenders structure loans to conform to the needs of borrowers. These varying structures may cause the note to be discounted and the effective interest rate to differ from the rate actually quoted. Large corporations use commercial paper to borrow funds for short periods or bonds to borrow for longer periods. Bonds are notes payable that the corporation sells to, or borrows from, investors in the financial markets. Bonds frequently have a maturity or par value of $1,000. The corporation pays nominal interest on the bond each year and, when the bond matures, pays the investor $1,000. When investors require different interest rates than the bonds pay, they offer a premium or discount on the par value of the bond to create the effective interest rate (yield) that they wish to earn.

 Visit the Web site *www.prenhall.com/terrell* for additional study help with the Online Study Guide.

REVIEW OF CONCEPTS

A   Describe the four functions of a firm and how they are related to the financial statements.

B   Describe the steps in forming a corporation.

C Identify and describe the groups associated with a corporation.

D Describe the duties of the board of directors.

E Identify the various corporate officers and describe their duties.

F Explain the differences among authorized, issued, and outstanding shares of stock.

G Define treasury stock and explain the ways a corporation might use it.

H Describe how to research an industry.

I Discuss the steps in developing a strategic plan and how strategic planning benefits a corporation.

J Describe the importance of internal controls for an Internet sales environment.

K Discuss the importance of management's attitudes toward internal controls.

L Distinguish between internal and external financing.

M Identify the two external sources of capital and discuss whether a corporation should use one or both.

N Define *note payable*, *promissory note*, *collateral*, *default*, and *mortgage*.

O Describe how to compute the cost of borrowing.

P Discuss the meaning of *effective interest rate*.

Q Define *commercial paper* and describe how it is used.

R Explain why bonds are sometimes necessary to meet the borrowing needs of businesses.

S Explain the terms *par value* and *stated rate* as they pertain to bonds.

T Explain how the nominal rate and the market rate of bonds differ.

U Explain what causes a bond to sell either at a premium or at a discount.

V Explain how the primary and secondary bond markets differ.

APPLICATION EXERCISES

3-10 Determine for each of the following whether it pertains to the operating, investing, financing, or decision-making function of a firm.

  a. purchasing equipment to produce snowboards
  b. obtaining a loan from a bank to purchase equipment
  c. selling stock to raise capital
  d. paying monthly operating expenses
  e. hiring an engineer to design the company's products
  f. selling bonds to provide cash to build a manufacturing facility
  g. paying for the construction of a manufacturing facility
  h. hiring a management team

LO 1
Functions of a Firm

3-11 List the steps of organizing a business presented in the chapter. What benefits would each step give the entrepreneur in achieving business success?

LO 1
Organizing a Business

3-12 Krim Corporation began operations in 1972 by issuing 20,000 shares of its no-par common stock for $5 per share. The following details provide information about the company's stock in the years since that time:

  1. In 1992 the company issued an additional 50,000 shares of common stock for $15 per share.
  2. Krim Corporation stock is traded on the NYSE. During an average year, about 25,000 shares of its common stock are sold by one set of investors to another.

LO 2
Terminology of the Corporate Business Form

3. On December 31, 2000, Krim Corporation common stock was quoted on the NYSE at $38 per share.
4. On December 31, 2002, Krim Corporation common stock was quoted on the NYSE at $55 per share.

Required:

a. Which of the stock transactions described above involved the primary stock market and which ones involved the secondary stock market?
b. How much money has Krim Corporation received in total from the sales of its common stock since it was incorporated in 1972?
c. When Krim Corporation prepares its balance sheet as of December 31, 2002, what dollar amount will it show in the owners' equity section for common stock?
d. How many shares of stock are outstanding at December 31, 2002?
e. What, if anything, can you infer about Krim Corporation's performance during 2001 from the price of its common stock on December 31, 2000, and December 31, 2002?

LO 2
Common Stock
Issuances

3-13   Shiner Corporation began operations in 1988 by issuing 35,000 shares of its common stock for $10 per share. The following details provide information about the company's stock in the years since that time:
1. In 1992 the company issued an additional 80,000 shares of common stock for $15 per share.
2. Shiner Corporation stock is traded on the AMEX. During an average year, about 40,000 shares of its common stock are sold by one group of investors to another.
3. On December 31, 2000, Shiner Corporation common stock was quoted on the AMEX at $79 per share.
4. On December 31, 2001, Shiner Corporation common stock was quoted on the AMEX at $45 per share.

Required:

a. Which of the stock transactions described above involved the primary stock market and which ones involved the secondary stock market?
b. How much money has Shiner Corporation received in total from the sales of its common stock since it was incorporated in 1988?
c. When Shiner Corporation prepares its balance sheet as of December 31, 2001, what dollar amount will it show in the owners' equity section for common stock?
d. What, if anything, can you infer about Shiner Corporation's performance during 2001 from the price of its common stock on December 31, 2000, and December 31, 2001?

LO 2
Common Stock
Issuances

3-14   La Forge Corporation began operations in January 1992 by issuing 90,000 shares of its no-par common stock for $25 per share and 10,000 shares of its $100 par value 6% preferred stock. The following details provide information about the company's stock in the years since that time:
1. In January 1993 the company issued an additional 50,000 shares of common stock for $35 per share and 5,000 shares of preferred stock for $150 per share.
2. La Forge Corporation stock is traded on the NYSE. During an average year, about 100,000 shares of its common stock and 6,000 shares of preferred stock are sold by one group of investors to another.
3. On December 31, 2002, La Forge Corporation common stock was quoted on the NYSE at $55 per share. The preferred stock was quoted at $135 per share.
4. On December 31, 2003, La Forge Corporation common stock was quoted on the NYSE at $65 per share. The preferred stock was quoted at $150 per share.

Required:

a. Which of the stock transactions described above involved the primary stock market and which ones involved the secondary stock market?

b. How much money has La Forge Corporation received in total from the sales of its stock since it was incorporated in 1992?

c. When La Forge Corporation prepares its balance sheet as of December 31, 2003, what dollar amount will it show in the owners' equity section for common stock and for preferred stock?

d. What is the market value of LaForge's stock on December 31, 2002, and December 31, 2003?

e. How much has LaForge Corporation earned in profits since incorporation?

f. How much has LaForge Corporation paid in dividends to common shareholders and preferred shareholders since incorporation?

3-15   Bennett Corporation began operations in 1979 by issuing 40,000 shares of its no-par common stock for $5 per share. The following details provide information about the company's stock in the years since that time:

1. In 1992 the company issued an additional 70,000 shares of common stock for $15 per share.

2. Bennett Corporation stock is traded on the NYSE. During an average year, about 50,000 shares of its common stock are sold by one set of investors to another.

3. On January 1, 1995, Bennett Corporation repurchased 10,000 shares of common stock at $20 per share.

4. On December 31, 2002, Bennett Corporation common stock was quoted on the NYSE at $56 per share.

5. On December 31, 2004, Bennett Corporation common stock was quoted on the NYSE at $35 per share.

Required:

a. Which of the stock transactions described above involved the primary stock market and which ones involved the secondary stock market?

b. How much money has Bennett Corporation received in total from the sales of its common stock since it was incorporated in 1979?

c. When Bennett Corporation prepares its balance sheet as of December 31, 2004, what dollar amount will it show in the owners' equity section for common stock?

d. How many shares of outstanding common stock does Bennett Corporation have at December 31, 2004?

3-16   Gaylord Corporation began operations on July 10, 2003, by issuing 10,000 shares of $5 par value common stock and 2,000 shares of $100 par value preferred stock. The common stock sold for $10 per share and the preferred stock sold for $130 per share.

Required:

a. Prepare a balance sheet for Gaylord Corporation at July 10, 2003, immediately after the common stock and preferred stock were issued.

b. Assume that both preferred and common stock are no-par stock. Prepare a balance sheet for Gaylord Corporation at July 10, 2003, immediately after the common stock and preferred stock were issued.

3-17   Sheets Corporation began operations on May 5, 2002, by issuing 150,000 shares of $2 par value common stock and 25,000 shares of $100 par value preferred stock. The common stock sold for $10 per share and the preferred stock sold for $150 per share.

Required:

a. Prepare a balance sheet for Sheets Corporation at May 5, 2002, immediately after the common stock and preferred stock were issued.

b. Prepare a statement of stockholders' equity immediately after the stock issuances.

LO 2
Common Stock Issuances with Treasury Stock

LO 2
Balance Sheet Effects of Common and Preferred Stock Issuances

LO 2
Effects of Common and Preferred Stock Issuances on Financial Statements

LO2
Balance Sheet Effects of Common and Preferred Stock Issuances

3-18   Mayes Corporation began operations on April 15, 2004, by issuing 200,000 shares of no-par common stock and 20,000 shares of $50 par value preferred stock. The common stock sold for $25 per share and the preferred stock sold for $125 per share.

Required:

Prepare a balance sheet for Mayes Corporation at April 15, 2004, immediately after the common stock and preferred stock were issued.

LO 2
Effect of Common Stock Issuances

3-19   The balance sheet of Reagan Inc. contains the following information in its equity section:

Stockholders' Equity:

Common Stock, $5 par value, 1,000,000 shares authorized, 800,000 shares issued and outstanding	$ 4,000,000
Additional paid-in capital	4,800,000
Retained earnings	2,000,000
Total Stockholders' Equity	$10,800,000

Required:

a. How many shares of stock could Reagan issue if the board of directors wished to do so?
b. At what average price did Reagan sell its stock?
c. If the board of directors declared a $1.25 per share dividend, how much cash would be required to issue the dividend?
d. If Reagan has distributed $3,500,000 to shareholders since its formation, how much profit has the corporation earned since its formation?

LO 2
Corporate Form of Organization

3-20   The following is an excerpt from the equity section of the balance sheet of the Joan Revell Corporation:

Stockholders' Equity:

Common stock, $10 par value, 1,000,000 shares authorized, 800,000 shares issued and 750,000 shares outstanding	$ 8,000,000
Additional paid-in capital	8,000,000
Retained earnings	9,500,000
	$25,500,000
Less: Treasury stock (at cost)	4,100,000
Total Stockholders' Equity	$21,400,000

Required:

a. How many shares are in the treasury? How can you determine this?
b. How many shares of stock could Revell sell if the board of directors desired to do so?
c. At what average price did Revell sell its stock?
d. If the board of directors declared a $2 per share dividend, how much cash would be required to issue the dividend?
e. If Revell has distributed $5,500,000 to shareholders since its formation, how much profit has the corporation earned since its formation?
f. What was the average cost per share of the treasury stock?
g. If the board of directors wished to raise $5,000,000, how much would it have to sell stock for if all available shares were sold?

3-21 The following is an excerpt from the equity section of the balance sheet of Jorge Ruiz Corporation:

LO 2
Corporate Form of Organization

Stockholders' Equity:

Common stock, $10 par value, 1,000,000 shares authorized and issued, 950,000 shares outstanding	$10,000,000
Additional paid-in capital	8,000,000
Retained earnings	9,500,000
	$27,500,000
Less: Treasury stock (at cost)	2,500,000
Total Stockholders' Equity	$25,000,000

Required:

a. How many shares are in the treasury?
b. How many shares of stock could Ruiz sell if the board of directors desired to do so?
c. At what average price did Ruiz sell its stock?
d. If the board of directors declared a $1.50 per share dividend, how much cash would be required to issue the dividend?
e. If Ruiz has earned $9,500,000 since its formation, how much profit has the corporation distributed to stockholders in the form of dividends since its formation?
f. What was the average cost per share of the treasury stock?
g. If the current market price of the stock is $60 per share, how much cash could the board of directors raise if it sold all available shares?

3-22 Assume you have $20,000 to invest, and you are trying to decide between investing in the preferred stock of Arbo Company and the common stock of Arbo Company.

LO 2
Corporate Form of Organization

Required:

a. List and briefly explain at least two reasons why you would invest in the preferred stock rather than the common stock of Arbo Company.
b. List and briefly explain at least two reasons why you would invest in the common stock rather than the preferred stock of Arbo Company.

3-23 Discuss the characteristics of investors who invest in:
a. common stock
b. preferred stock
Include in your discussion willingness to take risk, desire for current income, and desire for capital appreciation in addition to other factors.

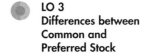
LO 3
Differences between Common and Preferred Stock

3-24
a. Find a list of trade associations for the boating industry.
b. Identify and write out the mission statement for one organization.
c. Discuss the contributions this organization makes to the boating industry.

LO4
Researching the Industry

3-25 Using sources listed in the chapter, search for the following information on the information technology industry:
1. projected growth for the next five years
2. highest users of information technology
3. number of competitors in the market

LO 4
Researching the Industry

Required:

a. List the information you found in your search.
b. Discuss what insights this information gives you about the information technology industry and how this information would help you to formulate a strategy to enter the information technology business.
c. Discuss how the information would help you if you were already in the information technology business.

LO 4
Researching the Industry

3-26 Using the *Mergent Industry Review*, find a list of the competitors in the recreation industry. Select the top five firms according to:
1. sales
2. net profits
3. five-year growth in revenues

Required:
a. List the top five firms for each category of information.
b. Determine whether or not the same names appear in each list and whether or not they are in the same order.
c. Select which firm you believe is the leading firm in the industry and explain why you selected that company. Be sure to defend your criteria for selecting that company.

LO 5
Strategic Planning

3-27
a. List and describe the steps necessary to complete a strategic plan.
b. Which step in the planning process do you believe is most important? Discuss the reasons for your choice.

LO 5
Strategic Planning

3-28 Locate the mission statement of your college or university.
a. In your opinion, does your school strive to meet its mission?
b. Identify ways in which you believe that it does and ways that it does not.
c. In what ways does your answer to question b influence your opinion of the school?

LO 7
Effect of Interest on the Bank and the Borrower

3-29 Susan Ryan decided to buy a new computer system to use in her business. The system will cost $10,000, and Susan plans to borrow 75% of the purchase price from her bank.

Required:
a. If the bank charges Susan 12% interest, how much interest will the bank earn during the first year of the loan?
b. If Susan makes a $2,000 principal payment at the end of year 1 and the bank continues to charge 12% interest, how much interest will the bank earn for the second year of the loan?
c. If Susan makes a $4,000 principal payment at the end of year 1, how much interest will she save in year 2?

LO 7
Effect of Interest on the Balance Sheet and the Borrower

3-30 Fred and Ethel formed F&E Enterprises, Inc., on January 2, 2004. Fred invested $20,000 and received 2,000 shares of common stock. Ethel invested $10,000 and received 1,000 shares of common stock. The common stock has a par value of $5 per share. The following balance sheet was prepared immediately after the corporation was formed:

F&E ENTERPRISES, INC.
Balance Sheet
January 2, 2004

Assets:		
Cash		$30,000
Total Assets		$30,000
Liabilities:		$ 0
Liabilities and Stockholders' Equity:		
Common stock	$15,000	
Additional paid-in capital	15,000	
Total Stockholders' Equity		30,000
Total Liabilities and Stockholders' Equity		$30,000

On January 3, 2004, F&E Enterprises borrowed $20,000 from the Second National Bank by signing a one-year, 8% note. The principal and interest on the note must be paid to the bank on January 2, 2005.

Required:

a. Prepare a new balance sheet for F&E at January 3, 2004, to reflect the $20,000 note payable.
b. Calculate the amount of interest F&E must pay on January 2, 2005.
c. Think about the three questions all economic decision makers are trying to answer (Will I be paid? When? How much?). Assuming Second National Bank has satisfied itself with regard to the first question, how would the bank answer the second and third questions regarding the loan to F&E?

3-31   Assume the same facts as set forth in question 3-30, except that the note is for three months rather than one year, so it must be repaid on April 2, 2004.

LO 7
Effect of Interest on the Balance Sheet and the Borrower

Required:

a. Prepare a new balance sheet for F&E at January 3, 2004, to reflect the $20,000 note payable.
b. Calculate the amount of interest F&E must pay on April 2, 2004.
c. If the note were for 90 days instead of 3 months, what would be the due date? How much interest would be due the bank on the due date?
d. Think about the three questions all economic decision makers are trying to answer (Will I be paid? When? How much?). Assuming second National Bank has satisfied itself with regard to the first question, how would the bank answer the second and third questions regarding the loan to F&E?

3-32   Fred and Ethel formed F&E Enterprises, Inc., on January 2, 2004. Fred invested $20,000 and received 2,000 shares of common stock. Ethel invested $10,000 and received 1,000 shares of common stock. The common stock has a par value of $5 per share. The following balance sheet was prepared immediately after the corporation was formed:

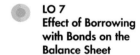

LO 7
Effect of Borrowing with Bonds on the Balance Sheet

F&E ENTERPRISES, INC.
Balance Sheet
January 2, 2004

Assets:		
Cash		$30,000
Total Assets		$30,000
Liabilities:		$ 0
Liabilities and Stockholders' Equity:		
Common stock	$15,000	
Additional paid-in capital	15,000	
Total Stockholders' Equity		30,000
Total Liabilities and Stockholders' Equity		$30,000

On January 3, 2004, F&E sold 100 of its $1,000, five-year, 10% bonds. Interest is to be paid semiannually on July 2 and January 2. The bonds mature (must be repaid) on January 2, 2007.

Required:

a. Prepare a new balance sheet for F&E at January 3, 2004, to reflect the sale of the bonds, assuming they sold at their par value.
b. Calculate the amount of interest F&E must pay each July 2 and January 2.
c. How much would F&E have received from the sale of the bonds on January 3, 2004, assuming bonds sold at 98 (a discount)?
d. How much would F&E have received from the sale of the bonds on January 3, 2004, assuming bonds sold at 103 (a premium)?

LO 7
Bonds versus Notes

3-33   The two main instruments of debt financing are bonds and notes. Explain under what circumstances each instrument is generally used.

LO 8
Cost of Borrowing

3-34   Mills Company needs to borrow funds to modernize its plant facility. Mills decided to issue $50,000,000 worth of 8%, 30-year bonds in the primary bond market.

Required:

a. Explain why Mills Company would rather issue bonds than borrow money from a bank.
b. Compute the cost of borrowing over the life of the bonds if the bonds sell at par.
c. Compute the cost of borrowing over the life of the bonds if the bonds sell at 104.

LO 7, 8
Note Maturity and
Due Dates

3-35   The Weaver Company borrowed $20,000 from a bank. The note was a 90-day, 8% note.

Required:

a. Compute the amount due at maturity.
b. Calculate the due date of the note assuming the note was signed on the following dates:
   1. March 3
   2. April 20
   3. July 19
   4. October 5

LO 7, 8
Note Maturity and
Due Dates

3-36   The Schwartz Company borrowed $8,000 from a bank. The note was a 120-day, 7% note.
a. Compute the amount due at maturity.
b. Calculate the due date of the note assuming the note was signed on the following dates:
   1. March 7
   2. April 19
   3. May 5
   4. August 10

LO 7, 8
Note Maturity and
Due Dates

3-37   The Davis Company borrowed $5,000 from a bank. The note was a 60-day, 9% note.
a. Compute the amount due at maturity.
b. Calculate the due date of the note assuming the note was signed on the following dates:
   1. April 3
   2. May 19
   3. June 5
   4. July 10

LO 7, 8
Computation of
Effective Interest Rates

3-38   The Argo Bank discounted a $20,000, 10% loan to the Gail Company for a period of 120 days. The loan was signed on April 25.

Required:

a. What is the due date of the loan?
b. What are the loan proceeds Gail Company received?
c. How much should the bank should receive as repayment?
d. Compute the effective interest rate for the bank.

LO 7, 8
Computation of
Effective Interest Rates

3-39   The Mutual Bank discounted a $50,000, 9% loan to the Gail Company for a period of 120 days. The loan was signed on April 25.

Required:

a. What is the due date of the loan?
b. What is the net amount of loan proceeds that Gail will deposit to its account?
c. What is the total amount the bank should receive as repayment?
d. Compute the effective interest rate for the bank.

3-40   The Union Bank discounted a $50,000, 8% loan to the Aikman Company for a period of six months. The loan was signed on May 5.

LO 7, 8
Computation of
Effective Interest Rates

Required:

a. What is the due date of the loan?
b. What is the net amount of loan proceeds that Aikman will deposit to its account?
c. What is the total amount the bank should receive as repayment?
d. Compute the effective interest rate for the bank.

3-41   The Swift Bank loaned $100,000 at 12% to the Lett Company for a period of one year. The bank required Lett to maintain a compensating bank balance of $30,000. Lett's bank balance has averaged $5,000 for the past two years. The loan was signed on March 19.

LO 7, 8
Computation of
Effective Interest Rates

Required:

a. What is the due date of the loan?
b. What is the net amount of loan proceeds that Lett will deposit to its account?
c. What is the total amount the bank should receive as repayment?
d. Compute the effective interest rate for the bank.

3-42   Assume that Bailey, Inc. sells 6,500 five-year, 8%, $1,000 bonds at 96.

LO 7, 8
Cost of Borrowing for
Bonds

Required:

a. How much cash will Bailey receive from the sale?
b. How much cash will the investors buying the bonds receive each year as interest?
c. What is Bailey's cost of borrowing for the bond issue?
d. Is the effective interest rate less than, equal to, or greater than 8%? How can you determine this?
e. Using your calculator, determine the effective rate of the bonds.

3-43   Assume Adams Company sells 2,500 five-year, 12%, $1,000 bonds at 106.

LO 7, 8
Cost of Borrowing for
Bonds

Required:

a. How much cash will Adams receive from the sale?
b. How much cash will the investors buying the bonds receive each year as interest?
c. Compute Adams' cost of borrowing for the bonds.
d. Is the effective interest rate less than, equal to, or greater than 12%? How can you determine this?
e. Using your calculator, determine the effective rate of the bonds.

3-44   Assume that an investor pays $950 for a five-year, $1,000 bond paying 9% interest.

LO 7, 8
Cost of Borrowing for
Bonds

Required:

a. How much cash will the investor receive each year as interest?
b. Is the effective interest rate less than, equal to, or greater than 9%?
c. How can you determine this?
d. Using your calculator, determine the effective rate of the bonds.

LO 7, 8
Cost of Borrowing for Bonds

3-45   Assume an investor pays $1,040 for a five-year, $1,000 bond paying 8% interest.

Required:

a. How much cash will the person buying the bond receive each year as interest?
b. Is the effective interest rate less than, equal to, or greater than 8%?
c. How can you determine this?
d. Using your calculator, determine the effective rate of the bonds.

LO 7, 8
Computation of Interest

3-46   Alto, Inc. borrowed $10,000 on July 1, 2000, by signing a 10% note at ABC Bank due December 31, 2000.

Required:

a. Determine the total amount Alto will have to pay (principal and interest) on December 31, 2000.
b. How much interest will ABC Bank earn on this note?
c. How will the answer to question b differ if the note was signed on October 1, 2000?

LO 7, 8
Computation of Interest

3-47   The Lesa Company borrows $20,000 in 2003 to finance a piece of equipment. Calculate the interest and principal it would pay to the bank for the year 2003 if the loan is due December 31, 2003, and:

a. the loan is at 12%, signed on January 2, 2003
b. the loan is at 10%, signed on January 2, 2003
c. the loan is at 12%, signed on April 1, 2003
d. the loan is at 9%, signed on September 1, 2003

LO 7, 8
Computation of Interest

3-48   The Shannan Company borrows $100,000 to purchase a building. Calculate the interest it would pay to the bank for the year 2003 if the loan is due December 31, 2003, and:

a. the loan is at 6%, signed on January 2, 2003
b. the loan is at 8%, signed on January 2, 2003
c. the loan is at 6%, signed on April 1, 2003
d. the loan is at 8%, signed on September 1, 2003

LO 7, 8
Effect of Market Interest on Bond Selling Prices

3-49

a. Explain how an *increase* in the market rate of interest days before a corporation issues new bonds will impact a new issuance of bonds in terms of the selling price of the bonds.
b. Explain how a *decrease* in the market rate of interest will impact a new issuance of bonds in terms of the selling price of the bonds.

LO 7, 8, 9
Effect of Market Interest on Bond Selling Prices

3-50   King Corporation decides to sell bonds and is prepared to issue 5,000 10-year bonds with a par value of $1,000 paying interest of 6%. Assume the market rate of interest is currently 8%.

Required:

a. Would you expect the bonds to sell for par value, a premium, or a discount? Explain your answer.
b. Will these bonds sell in the primary or secondary bond market?
c. Compute the total cost of borrowing if the bonds sell at 103.
d. Using the calculator, determine the effective interest rate if the bonds sell at 103.

3-51 Tara Corporation decides to sell bonds. Tara is prepared to issue 9,000 5-year bonds with a par value of $1,000 paying interest of 8%. Assume the market rate of interest is currently 7%.

Required:

a. Would you expect the bonds to sell for par value, a premium, or a discount? Explain your answer.
b. Will these bonds sell in the primary or secondary bond market?
c. Compute the cost of borrowing if the bonds sell at 98.
d. Using a calculator, determine the effective interest rate if the bonds sell at 98.

LO 7, 8, 9
Effect of Market Interest on Bond Selling Prices

3-52 Geoffrey Corporation decides to sell bonds and is prepared to issue 7,000 10-year bonds with a par value of $1,000 paying interest of 9%. Assume the market rate of interest is currently 9%.

a. Would you expect the bonds to sell for par value, a premium, or a discount? Explain your answer.
b. Will these bonds sell in the primary or secondary bond market?
c. Using a calculator, determine the effective interest rate if the bonds sell at 100.

LO 7, 8, 9
Effect of Market Interest on Bond Selling Prices

3-53 Sam Layton decided to incorporate his business because his friend told him that a corporation would allow him to write off more of his personal expenses. He also told Sam that it would be easier for him to present financial statements to the bank that would allow him to borrow greater sums of money. As a CPA, you know that much of what Sam has been told is not correct. You would really like to have his business.

Ethics Case

Required:

a. Write a report to Sam detailing what you know about a corporation.
b. Would you allow Sam to go on believing these untruths if you thought that might help in getting him as a client? Why or why not?

FOR ADDITIONAL READING

"Eight Essentials for E-business." *Fortune* (Summer 2000):44–45.
Glover, Steven M., Stephen W. Liddle, and Douglas F. Prawitt. *eBusiness: Principles and Strategies for Accountants.* Upper Saddle River, NJ: Prentice Hall, 2001.
"Setting Up Shop." *Fortune* (Summer 2000):40–47.
"Tell Me How." *Fortune* (Summer 2000):49–54.

CHAPTER 4

LEARNING OBJECTIVES

After completing this chapter you should be able to:

1 Classify costs by cost objects and cost drivers and describe the characteristics of activity-based cost systems and standard cost systems.

2 Distinguish between product and period costs.

3 Differentiate between fixed and variable costs and classify costs by cost behavior.

4 Explain the concept of a relevant range and its effect on cost information.

5 Analyze cost information to construct a total cost formula for a business activity.

6 Conduct cost-volume-profit analysis to determine break-even points.

7 Perform sensitivity analysis.

8 Build initial operating and capital budgets.

Planning for and Predicting Performance

To launch Elevation Sports, Inc. in a fiscally responsible manner, Angie, Jon, Megan, and Rob need to spend time and energy preparing budgets to analyze their costs, revenues, equipment needs, and financing. They can accomplish this by preparing a capital budget and an operating budget. Budgets not only serve managers as a plan for their business activities, but they also provide a standard against which to measure the firm's performance. A **capital budget** outlines how a company intends to allocate its scarce resources to purchase major investments in long-lived assets for current and future years. An **operating budget** plans a company's routine business activities for one to five years.

In preparing for the summit meeting, Megan asked the others to determine their furniture, equipment, and technology needs to run the manufacturing, sales, and corporate offices. She asked Jon to determine the equipment required to manufacture, package, and ship the snowboards. Angie had to determine the type and quantity of computer equipment and software needed to operate the business, make sales, and support a Web site. Rob volunteered to help Angie on the sales and Web site, and to work with Jon on the graphics process needed for the snowboard production.

Megan agreed to research the type of accounting system needed to produce financial and management accounting information that would interface with the information system Angie would build. She reminded the others that many manufacturers have financing available for equipment purchases. The team needed

Visit the **www.prenhall.com/terrell** Web site to view the "It's Just Lunch" video.

● **capital budget**
A budget that outlines how a company intends to allocate its scarce resources to purchase major investments in long-lived assets for current and future years.

● **operating budget**
A budget that plans a company's routine business activities for one to five years.

to obtain details of the financing (interest rates, payment amounts, and number of payments) and any down payments required. With all this data, Megan was confident that she could prepare the preliminary capital budget. We will show you the results of her preliminary capital budget at the end of this chapter, and go through the details of the capital budgeting process for a functioning business in Chapter 11.

Classifying Costs

Businesses incur many operating costs, and the more clearly managers understand the nature and behavior of such costs, the better they can manage operations. The types of decisions management must make determines the types of cost information needed. For example, when Ford Motor Company wants to change the body style and performance characteristics of a car model, managers must investigate how that change will affect the cost of materials, equipment, and labor for each car of that model produced compared to its ultimate selling price. On the other hand, if Ford managers want to determine whether to increase or decrease the quantity produced for four truck models, they need information on past sales and projected future demand in addition to the established cost to produce each model. The information gathered can help to plot sales strategies to maximize profits or minimize losses.

We can describe costs in many ways, just as we might describe the cards in a deck of playing cards in different ways. For example, we can classify the 52 cards in the following manner:

1 whole deck of 52 cards
2 12 face cards and 40 number cards
3 26 red cards and 26 black cards
4 4 of each number 1–10, 4 jacks, 4 queens, and 4 kings
5 13 diamonds, 13 hearts, 13 spades, and 13 clubs.

Although a card may be described at least three ways, it is still only one card. Depending on the game we play with the cards, one or more of the designations matters to us. Business costs are similar in that their classification depends on the decision we need to make in a particular business situation.

Cost Objects

● **cost object**
An activity, product, service, project, geographic region, or business segment for which management wants separate cost measurement.

An efficient way to classify costs is by cost object. A **cost object** is an activity, product, service, project, geographic region, or business segment for which management wants separate cost measurement. The management of Old Navy might wish to determine the costs incurred by each of its stores. During the same time frame, they might wish to know the cost of transporting merchandise throughout the organization. The manager of the women's department in store 1202 needs the cost of labor in her department for the month. Each of these—the individual store, the transportation costs, and the employee cost of store 1202—is a cost object.

Although a cost only occurs once, we may wish to associate it with more than one cost object to provide information for different decisions. For example, the vice president of Manufacturing for La-Z-Boy Incorporated may need to know the cost and amount of wood used each year in production because he fears that fine woods may become scarce. The CEO of its Pennsylvania House division may need to analyze his total material cost (which includes wood) because his profit has declined. At the same time, he may need to analyze the cost of each product made in his furniture line to determine whether or not to discontinue certain styles. The same wood costs are included in all three studies, but their inclusion assists the manager in making distinct decisions. A well-designed accounting information system will allow management to retrieve specific cost information as needed.

Some costs, called **direct costs**, are easily traced to one cost object. The labor cost at one store in a chain is easily identifiable as a direct cost for that store. On the other hand, a marketing director in the home office outlines the advertising plan for the chain, which includes both national and local media advertising. The national marketing costs benefit each store in the chain, but cannot be attributed to any one store. **Common costs** are costs shared by a number of cost objects. The home office allocates a proportionate share of the common marketing costs to each store and the local advertising costs to the specific store(s) benefited. Unit managers frequently resist allocating common costs, because they seldom have any control over the decision to incur such costs. Omitting allocated common costs from the unit's expenses underestimates the real costs of one unit in a large organization.

● **direct costs**
Costs easily traced to one cost object.

● **common costs**
Costs shared by a number of cost objects.

What Do You Think?

For each of the following questions, assume that you are the plant manager of a plastics manufacturer with one location.

4-1 Would your salary be a direct cost or a common cost for the manufacturing plant? Explain your reasoning.

4-2 Would your salary be a direct cost or a common cost to the molding department in the plant? Explain your reasoning.

4-3 Would you expect to have part of the cost of the human resources payroll and benefits department staff salaries allocated to the plant? Why or why not?

Activity-Based Costing Systems

An **activity-based costing (ABC) system** identifies specific activities that cause costs to occur and uses those activities as bases for common cost allocation. Many managers believe that an ABC system provides them with better quality cost information because it better identifies the **cost driver**, the activity that causes the expense to occur. Prior to ABC systems, management relied on allocating common costs based on the dollar amount of manufacturing labor costs or the number of manufacturing labor hours. The assumption was that human effort defined the only measurable activity. The advent of robotics and other sophisticated manufacturing techniques made that assumption irrelevant. By taking the time to better identify the real cost drivers for any activity, cost accountants have developed more accurate costing methods.

Be mindful that the total amount of common costs incurred does not change with a different allocation method. Identifying the real cost drivers for different common costs, however, may enable management to make appropriate changes to operations to reduce future costs. Take, for example, the cost of gasoline for your automobile. If your miles per gallon suddenly drops, your fuel costs rise. To reduce those costs in the future, you must identify the problem that has caused your miles per gallon to fall. The following cost drivers affect gas mileage:

● **activity-based costing (ABC) system**
A cost system that identifies specific activities that cause costs to occur and uses those activities as the bases for common cost allocation.

● **cost driver**
The activity that causes an expense to occur.

- quality of the fuel,
- condition of the engine,
- carburetor efficiency,
- condition of the tires,
- type of driving.

Putting an expensive fuel additive into each tank of fuel adds expense to each tank, but may do nothing to raise the fuel efficiency. If you assume the fuel additive is the only appropriate solution, you may increase total future costs and do nothing to improve the problem. Until you find the correct cause of the problem, any changes may only increase the costs or the problem.

Management has the same problem in diagnosing manufacturing costs. If managers misallocate common costs, they will make decisions based on erroneous information. If they misunderstand the real cost of producing products, they may also make errors in pricing the products and predicting their profits.

Standard Cost Systems

● **standard**
A preestablished benchmark for desirable performance.

● **standard cost system**
A system in which management sets cost standards and uses them to evaluate actual performance.

When management and employees can establish excellent estimates of the material and labor cost of producing a unit of its product, they can employ a standard cost system. A **standard** is a preestablished benchmark for desirable performance. A **standard cost system** is one in which management, after careful analysis, sets cost standards and uses them to evaluate actual performance. Under standard costing, employees plan how factory resources will be acquired and used and strive to control costs so manufacturing goals can be met. The goals also provide management with a basis for performance evaluation when actual results are compared with goals to help find areas of weakness.

Costs in a standard cost system are divided into material costs, labor costs, and other manufacturing costs. Each of those costs consists of two components—price and quantity. By analyzing the actual costs incurred during production, the data can reveal the reasons for any deviation from the standard costs. In short, standard costing provides managers with a means to quickly focus their attention on the real problem areas.

Standard cost systems also simplify many accounting transactions because the accountants use the standard costs to value inventory and the cost of the goods sold. Ethical considerations prevent management from falsely portraying standard costs to manipulate reported net income. Therefore, any actual costs that vary from the standard are still considered to be part of the manufacturing costs. Standard costs must change over time as conditions of supply and manufacturing processes change.

Product Costs

● **product costs**
All costs of acquiring or manufacturing goods to make them available for sale to customers.

From a financial perspective, we must separate costs into two classifications so that financial statements separate the costs of the products sold to customers from the costs to sell the product and run the business. The first of these cost categories is **product costs,** which are all costs of acquiring or manufacturing goods to make them available for sale to customers. For completed goods purchased from a manufacturer or wholesaler, these encompass the purchase or invoice price, transportation to get the product to the selling location, packaging, storage, and any other make-ready costs to make the product available to the customer. In the case of manufactured goods, product costs include all the materials and costs to ship them to the plant, labor, other costs of running the production plant used to produce those goods, transportation to sales location, storage, packaging, and make-ready costs. Product costs begin as inventory assets on the balance sheet, and when sold to customers they move to the cost of goods sold on the income statement. As Exhibit 4-1 illustrates, all product costs represent an asset if unsold or a cost of goods sold expense when sold to a customer.

Period Costs

● **period costs**
The costs of operating a business that are not product costs.

● **selling costs**
Period costs related to advertising, selling, and delivering goods to customers.

The second type of cost is **period costs**, or costs of operating a business that are not product costs. These are classified into two main categories: selling costs and administrative costs. **Selling costs** are period costs related to advertising, selling, and delivering

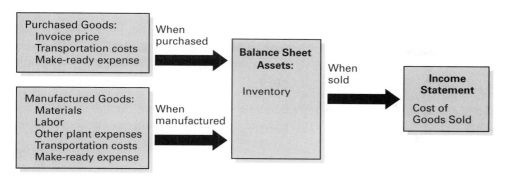

Exhibit 4-1
Product Costs

goods to customers. **Administrative costs** include all costs of operating a business that are not product and selling costs. These include support functions such as accounting, finance, executive, and human resources. Period costs are included on the income statement as operating expenses in the period when they help produce revenue, or in the period incurred if no clear association with revenue production exists. Revisit the income statement of Family Dollar Stores, Inc. in Exhibit 4-2. The cost of goods sold is product cost and the selling, administrative, and general expenses are period costs.

● **administrative costs**
All costs of operating a business that are not product and selling costs. Includes support functions such as accounting, finance, executive, and human resources.

Distinguishing Product and Period Costs

How can you distinguish between product and period costs? Look at the nature of the expense in question. Does this expense facilitate the product's reaching a saleable state? If so, the expense is a product expense. Once the product becomes available for sale, product expenses normally cease. Expenses beyond the point of a saleable product are normally period expenses.

If the expense is a period cost and is related to selling the product, it is a selling expense. Selling expenses include sales staff salaries, sales commissions, advertising, depreciation of sales fixtures, selling facilities costs, delivery of goods to customers, sacks or other packaging used by customers to carry products, and other sales supplies such as invoices, business cards, and sales staff's stationery. We include selling expenses on the income statement for the period in which the company receives the benefit, thus matching the expenses to the sales revenue. Supplies become an expense on the income statement when used. We recognize advertising as an expense when it is aired in the media, printed and distributed, or mailed to customers.

Exhibit 4-2
Income Statement for Family Dollar Stores, Inc.

Family Dollar Stores, Inc. and Subsidiaries Consolidated Income Statement For the Year Ended August 30, 2003 (in thousands)	
Net sales	$4,750,171
Costs and expenses:	
Cost of sales	3,145,788 ← Product Costs
Selling, general, and administrative	1,214,658 ← Period Costs
	4,360,446
Income before income taxes	389,725
Income taxes	142,250
Net income	$ 247,475

The accompanying notes are an integral part of the consolidated financial statements.

Administrative costs include facilities expenses for administrative offices; depreciation of administrative equipment and furniture; legal, accounting, finance, and human resources services; and executive officers. Administrative costs seldom have direct correlation to revenue production and are expenses of the time in which they occur. Some support functions represent common costs that product, selling, and administrative costs share. Examples are the costs of the human resources services or the accounting department. Say for example that expenses for the human resources department for the year are $250,000. Listed below are the number of employees who work in various departments:

Manufacturing	3,500
Sales	500
Administration	1,000

The company would determine the best cost driver to allocate the costs of the human resources department. Most would use the number of employees as the allocation base and make the following type of allocation:

Department	Number of Employees	Percent of Total	Cost Allocation
Manufacturing	3,500	70%	$175,000
Sales	500	10%	25,000
Administration	1,000	20%	50,000
Total	5,000	100%	$250,000

What Do You Think?

4-4   What might be the best cost driver to distribute the cost of the accounting department among manufacturing, sales, and administration? Support your choice.

4-5   If your company had a central warehouse for purchased goods for resale, four retail outlets, and a home office, what selling and administrative costs might be allocated to the warehouse and retail outlets, and what is likely to be the cost driver for each cost?

Cost Behavior

To prepare a budget for a new business, we must be able to predict the costs it will incur. Part of the difficulty in estimating the costs is that some costs may vary depending on the level of business activity—the number of units of product we sell or manufacture. So we find that another way to describe business costs is to separate each cost by how it behaves at various levels of activity. What we discover is that within a defined level of activity, some costs may remain constant, others vary proportionately to the amount of activity, and still others vary at a disproportional rate.

Fixed Costs

● **fixed cost**
A cost that remains the same regardless of the volume of sales or production.

A **fixed cost** remains the same regardless of the volume of sales or production. Examples of fixed costs are building rent or a fixed-premium insurance policy. If rent is $1,200 per month, a graph of its cost over time will look like the solid horizontal line in Exhibit 4-3. If the vertical axis represents dollars and the horizontal axis represents the number of units produced, the monthly cost of rents does not vary at any level of production. Therefore the graph line is the straight, horizontal line connected by small rectangles.

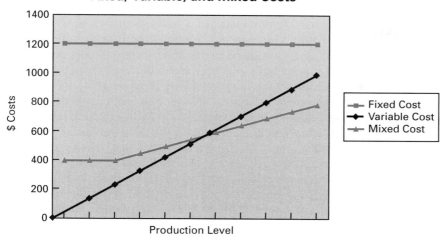

Fixed, Variable, and Mixed Costs

Exhibit 4-3
Graph of Fixed, Variable, and Mixed Costs

Variable Costs

A **variable cost** changes proportionately with the volume of sales or production. For example, if a company manufactures snowboards made of wood and the wood costs $10 per board, the material cost is $10 for one board and $1,000 for 100 boards. The total cost of wood varies directly with the volume of production. A graph line of the variable costs is an upward-sloping line that begins at zero, represented by the line connected by diamonds in Exhibit 4-3.

● **variable cost**
A cost that changes proportionately with the volume of sales or production.

Mixed Costs

A cost can have both a fixed component and a variable component. Such a cost is called a **mixed cost.** For example, suppose that Elevation Sports has a contract with the electric company to provide service to the manufacturing plant. The minimum monthly service fee is $400 with a constant usage charge per kilowatt-hour above a certain level of kilowatt-hours. The higher the number of snowboards produced, the higher the number of kilowatt-hours will be used. In Exhibit 4-3 the mixed cost is represented by the curve connected by triangles that starts as a horizontal line at the $400 level, the minimum charge, and then slopes upward as the usage increases for increased production.

● **mixed cost**
A cost that has both a fixed component and a variable component.

What Do You Think?

Base your answers to these questions on the information provided in Chapter 3 about Elevation Sports and what you have learned so far in Chapter 4.

4-6 What do you believe the fixed costs will be for the snowboard manufacturing and retail operations? Give amounts of each cost where possible.

4-7 What do you believe the variable cost components will be for the company?

4-8 What do you believe the mixed cost components will be for the company?

Relevant Range

Knowing the behavior pattern for each cost of a business allows us to predict with some degree of accuracy the future cost and potential profit or loss for a period of time. As the scale of a company's activity increases or decreases, cost behaviors may change. The study of cost behaviors indicates that individual costs behave in predictable patterns within a relevant range of activity.

A **relevant range** is a range of business activity in which cost-behavior patterns remain unchanged. Fixed, variable, and mixed costs can have a relevant range. Perhaps the easiest to illustrate is a relevant range for fixed costs, one in which the fixed costs remain unchanged. Consider a local Wonder Bread bakery that currently operates one eight-hour shift each day with annual fixed costs of $250,000 as illustrated in Exhibit 4-4. This activity level requires one warehouse supervisor, one plant manager, and two night guards. Regardless of the amount of daily production, these three costs remain constant. Likewise, the depreciation, taxes, and insurance for the plant building are fixed. What happens to all six costs if the company expands to two eight-hour shifts each day? Although depreciation, taxes, and insurance for the building remain unchanged, Wonder Bread will need two plant managers, two warehouse supervisors, but only one night guard. Total annual fixed manufacturing costs will increase to $350,000. If Wonder Bread increases to three shifts, total fixed costs will rise to $450,000 to pay for three plant managers and warehouse supervisors, with one guard to protect employees arriving and departing during nighttime hours. As you can see from Exhibit 4-4, fixed costs are stepped; they rise suddenly, then remain fixed for three million cases.

Relevant range is quite important in budgeting decisions because any decision that considers a situation in which the relevant range changes cannot be reliable without appropriate changes in the fixed costs.

Variable costs can also have a relevant range in per-unit terms. In other words, within one relevant range of variable costs, flour costs $0.05 per loaf of bread; in another relevant range, it costs $0.04 per loaf. Whereas total fixed costs tend to rise with increases in production, per-unit variable costs may decrease. Why is this so? If you think about it, the more flour a bakery buys, the more likely it might receive a quantity discount. Likewise, the more units workers produce, the more likely they might achieve efficiency and spend less time per unit produced. Economists describe

Exhibit 4-4
Relevant Ranges of Fixed Costs

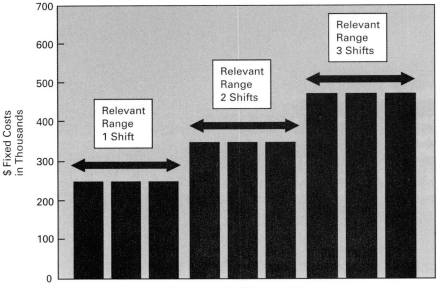

Relevant Ranges of Fixed Costs by Number of Shifts

these phenomena as economies of scale. Per-unit costs can also increase, however, if there are material shortages or if laborers have to work overtime at premium pay.

We care about the behavior of costs within a relevant range because we can use this information to develop a total cost formula for a business. This formula can help us to plan operations and predict the results of our performance.

Total Cost Formula

The total cost formula is simple:

$$\text{Total Cost} = \text{Fixed Costs} + \text{Variable Costs}$$
$$\text{TC} = \text{FC} + \text{VC}$$

Within a relevant range, both total fixed costs and the per-unit cost of variable costs remain stable. Because the total variable cost changes in proportion to the activity volume, we can also describe the variable costs as:

$$\text{Variable Costs} = \text{Unit Variable Cost} \times \text{Volume}$$
$$\text{VC} = \text{UVC} \times \text{V}$$

By means of mathematical substitution, we can arrive at an expanded total cost formula of:

$$\text{Total Cost} = \text{Fixed Costs} + (\text{Unit Variable Cost} \times \text{Volume})$$
$$\text{TC} = \text{FC} + (\text{UVC} \times \text{V})$$

Look at our example of the local Wonder Bread bakery. From past experience, its managers have determined the following costs for the bakery per shift:

Number of Shifts	Fixed Costs	Unit Variable Costs per Case
1	$250,000	$12.00
2	$350,000	$11.75
3	$450,000	$11.40

If the bakery manager wants to budget his costs for the next year, he can estimate them for annual production of 3 million cases, 6 million cases, and 9 million cases as follows:

3 million cases (employing 1 shift of workers)
$\text{TC} = \text{FC} + (\text{UVC} \times \text{V})$
$\text{TC} = \$250,000 + (\$12.00 \times 3,000,000)$
$\text{TC} = \$250,000 + \$36,000,000$
$\text{TC} = \$36,250,000 \qquad \text{per case} = \$12.08$

6 million cases (employing 2 shifts of workers)
$\text{TC} = \text{FC} + (\text{UVC} \times \text{V})$
$\text{TC} = \$350,000 + (\$11.75 \times 6,000,000)$
$\text{TC} = \$350,000 + \$70,500,000$
$\text{TC} = \$70,850,000 \qquad \text{per case} = \$11.81$

9 million cases (employing 3 shifts of workers)
$\text{TC} = \text{FC} + (\text{UVC} \times \text{V})$
$\text{TC} = \$450,000 + (\$11.40 \times 9,000,000)$
$\text{TC} = \$450,000 + \$102,600,000$
$\text{TC} = \$103,050,000 \qquad \text{per case} = \$11.45$

We took the projection one step further by computing the cost of one case in each relevant range by dividing the total cost by the number of cases. The cost to produce each case falls as production increases because the variable costs decrease and the fixed costs are spread over more cases. If the manager used the cost estimates for producing nine million cases and he was only planning to produce three million cases, he would underestimate his costs by $1,600,000 ($0.53 per case) computed as follows:

Using the correct range:
$$TC = FC + (UVC \times V)$$
$$TC = \$250,000 + (\$12.00 \times 3,000,000)$$
$$TC = \$250,000 + \$36,000,000$$
$$TC = \$36,250,000 \qquad \text{per case} = \$12.08$$
Using the incorrect range:
$$TC = FC + (UVC \times V)$$
$$TC = \$450,000 + (\$11.40 \times 3,000,000)$$
$$TC = \$450,000 + \$34,200,000$$
$$TC = \$34,650,000 \qquad \text{per case} = \$11.55$$

Few budgets could tolerate a $1,600,000 error. Knowing the total cost formula for a business can help to prevent such disasters.

Contribution Margin Income Statement

As you recall from Chapter 2, a financial income statement presents a report of revenues and expenses that result in net profit (or loss). Management accountants designed an income statement that classifies costs by behavior (fixed and variable) rather than by product costs and period costs. A **contribution income statement** is an income statement that classifies expenses by cost behavior. It allows managers to see a clear picture of the fixed and variable costs of operations that lead to other important decision-making tools. We will assume that all of the following analyses will occur within a relevant range of production or activity.

● **contribution income statement**
An income statement that classifies expenses by cost behavior.

Let's return to the financial income statement for Jason's Furniture Gallery, Inc., which we examined in Chapter 2 and which is partially reproduced in Exhibit 4-5. We will consider only the operating income for our analysis. We can convert this statement into a contribution income statement by separating the costs into fixed and variable components. Jason's accountant furnished the following information:

	Fixed	**Variable**
Cost of goods sold		$245,000
Selling expenses	$ 50,000	55,000
Administrative expenses	50,600	9,400
Totals	$100,600	$309,400

Exhibit 4-5
Jason's Furniture Gallery, Inc.
Operating Income

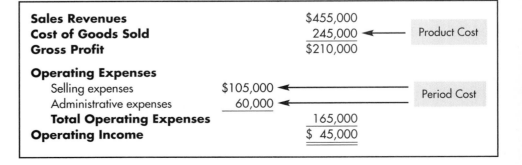

Jason's Furniture Gallery, Inc.
Income Statement
For the Year Ended December 31, 2004

Sales Revenues	$455,000	
Cost of Goods Sold	245,000 ◄— Product Cost	
Gross Profit	$210,000	
Operating Expenses		
Selling expenses	$105,000 ◄—	Period Cost
Administrative expenses	60,000 ◄—	
Total Operating Expenses	165,000	
Operating Income	$ 45,000	

Jason's Furniture Gallery, Inc.
Contribution Income Statement
For the Year Ended December 31, 2004

Revenues		$455,000
Variable Expenses		
Cost of goods sold	$245,000	
Selling expenses	55,000	
Administrative expenses	9,400	309,400
Contribution Margin		$145,600
Fixed Expenses		
Selling expenses	$ 50,000	
Administrative expenses	50,600	100,600
Operating Income		$ 45,000

We now have enough information to prepare a contribution income statement. We begin with sales and subtract from sales all variable costs. The **contribution margin** is the amount remaining after all variable costs are deducted from operating revenues. Both revenues and variable expenses vary with the volume of activity, whereas fixed costs remain the same regardless of volume. The contribution margin, therefore, is the amount available to contribute toward fixed costs and profits for the income statement period.

● **contribution margin**
The difference between operating revenues and variable costs, which measures the amount of revenues remaining after variable costs to contribute toward fixed costs and profits.

Consider the following contribution income statement format, prepared from the cost behavior information from Jason's Furniture Gallery, in Exhibit 4-6. Notice that the operating income is the same in both the financial income statement and the contribution income statement. The statements differ only in the association of costs (product/period versus variable/fixed) and gross profit versus contribution margin.

The contribution income statement allows us to perform a different type of management analysis than the financial income statement does. For example, assume that Jason's sole product is one style of sofa and that in 2004 the company sold 910 sofas. We can use that information to derive a unit selling price (USP), unit variable cost (UVC), and the unit contribution margin (UCM).

		Total		Per Unit
Sales	S	$455,000	USP	$500
Variable costs	VC	309,400	UVC	340
Contribution margin	CM	$145,600	UCM	$160
Fixed costs	FC	100,600		
Operating income	OI	$ 45,000		

The information contained in the contribution income statement combined with the per-unit information become the backbone of an important decision-making tool: cost-volume-profit (CVP) analysis.

Cost-Volume-Profit Analysis

Cost-volume-profit (CVP) analysis is the analysis of the relationships between cost and volume, and the effect of those relationships on profit. Let's explore the concepts of CVP analysis to see how it helps us budget for a new business or analyze an existing one. A CVP analysis allows us to determine the level of sales required to break even or attain a target profit—a powerful management and budgeting tool. It also

● **cost-volume-profit (CVP) analysis**
The analysis of the relationships between cost and volume, and the effect of those relationships on profit.

allows us to anticipate the effect that potential changes in price, volume, or cost will have on operating income to allow managers to make informed decisions. We will begin our discussion with break-even analysis.

Break-Even Analysis

● **breakeven**
Occurs when a company's operating income is zero.

● **break-even point**
The sales volume required to achieve breakeven.

Breakeven occurs when a company's operating income is zero. The sales volume required to achieve breakeven is the **break-even point**. The break-even point can be determined in terms of the sales dollars or the number of sales units required to achieve breakeven. Why would management, creditors, and investors care about break-even measurements? Because they wish to limit their risks. Knowing the amount of business revenue required to break even helps to establish a lower limit of risk. Let's begin our analysis by analyzing the contribution income statement.

By examining the contribution income statement, we can write its equation in much the same way we wrote the income statement equation in Chapter 2:

$$\begin{array}{ccccccc} (1) & \text{Sales} & - & \text{Variable Costs} & - & \text{Fixed Costs} & = & \text{Operating Income} \\ & \text{S} & - & \text{VC} & - & \text{FC} & = & \text{OI} \\ & \$455{,}000 & - & \$309{,}400 & - & \$100{,}600 & = & \$45{,}000 \end{array}$$

We can also separate this long equation in two parts:

$$\begin{array}{ccccc} (2) & \text{Sales} & - & \text{Variable Costs} & = & \text{Contribution Margin} \\ & \text{S} & - & \text{VC} & = & \text{CM} \\ & \$455{,}000 & - & \$309{,}400 & = & \$145{,}600 \end{array}$$

and

$$\begin{array}{ccccc} (3) & \text{Contribution Margin} & - & \text{Fixed Costs} & = & \text{Operating Income} \\ & \text{CM} & - & \text{FC} & = & \text{OI} \\ & \$145{,}600 & - & \$100{,}600 & = & \$45{,}000 \end{array}$$

The same relationship exists between sales and variable costs in equation 2 on a per-unit basis.

$$\begin{array}{ccccc} (4) & \text{Unit Selling Price} & - & \text{Unit Variable Cost} & = & \text{Unit Contribution Margin} \\ & \text{USP} & - & \text{UVC} & = & \text{UCM} \\ & \$500 & - & \$340 & = & \$160 \end{array}$$

Because we know that the unit selling price times the number of units sold equals the amount of the sales, we could also transform equation 2, with the help of equation 4, into:

$$\begin{array}{ccccc} (5) & (\text{USP} \times \text{V}) & - & (\text{UVC} \times \text{V}) & = & \text{UCM} \times \text{V} \\ & (\$500 \times 910) & - & (\$340 \times 910) & = & (\$160 \times 910) \\ & \$455{,}000 & - & \$309{,}400 & = & \$145{,}600 \end{array}$$

where *V* equals volume. These five formulas contain the core relationships between sales volume and costs we need to conduct break-even analysis.

Determining Break-Even Units

Breakeven (BE) occurs when operating income is zero. How many ways can we express breakeven using the prior five equations? Breakeven occurs when:

$$\begin{array}{ccccccc} (a) & \text{Sales} & - & \text{Variable Costs} & - & \text{Fixed Costs} & = & 0 \\ & \text{S} & - & \text{VC} & - & \text{FC} & = & 0 \end{array}$$

(b)   Contribution Margin − Fixed Costs = 0
                        CM   −   FC   = 0

(c)   Contribution Margin = Fixed Costs
                        CM   =   FC

So breakeven occurs when operating income is zero as shown in equations a and b and contribution margin equals the fixed costs in equation c. We can also rewrite equation c where contribution margin equals fixed costs with the substitution of the contribution margin from equation 5 as:

$$CM = FC$$
$$UCM \times V = FC \text{ (substitution from equation 5)}$$

If we divide both sides of the final equation by the UCM, we can solve for the volume of units required to break even:

(6) $$V_{BE} = \frac{FC}{UCM}$$

Using the facts of Jason's Furniture Gallery we can apply this equation to determine the company's break-even point (rounded to the next whole unit).

$$V_{BE} = \frac{FC}{UCM} = \frac{\$100,600}{\$160} = 628.75 \approx 629 \text{ sofas}$$

Therefore, if the company sells 629 sofas in a year, it will break even. If this is true, we should be able to verify our calculations with a simple contribution income statement:

		Total	Per Unit	
Sales (629 x $500)	S	$314,500	USP	$500
Variable costs (629 x $340)	VC	213,860	UVC	340
Contribution margin	CM	$100,640	UCM	$160
Fixed costs	FC	100,600		
Operating income	OI	$ 40		

The equation proves reliable and gives Jason the minimum number of sofas he must sell each year to break even. He currently sells 910 sofas and realizes a profit of $45,000. What if Jason's goal were to make $75,000 per year? Can this same type of analysis help us to determine the number of sofa sales required to meet his goal? Let's call his income goal a desired profit (DP) and substitute the desired profit for operating income in equation 2.

(3)   CM − FC = OI
        CM − FC = DP (Substitute DP for OI)

We can rewrite the equation by adding FC to both sides to arrive at equation 7.

(7)   CM − FC = DP
        CM − FC + FC = DP + FC
                CM = FC + DP

We can substitute part of equation 5 in equation 7 as we did to find the break-even volume, and derive the desired profit volume (V_{DP}).

(7)   CM = FC + DP
        UCM × V = FC + DP
        $$V_{DP} = \frac{FC + DP}{UCM}$$

When we use Jason's fixed costs and desired profit of $75,000 to apply the equation, we discover that Jason must sell 1,098 sofas to make a $75,000 operating profit.

$$V_{DP} = \frac{FC + DP}{UCM} = \frac{\$100,600 + \$75,000}{\$160} = 1,097.5 \approx 1,098$$

We can verify the results with the same contribution income statement computation:

	Total	Per Unit
Sales (1,098 x $500)	$549,000	USP $500
Variable costs (1,098 x $340)	373,320	UVC 340
Contribution margin	$175,680	UCM $160
Fixed costs	100,600	
Operating income	$ 75,080	

Once again the formula gives us the results we anticipated. Break-even analysis is a powerful management tool for strategic planning. It helps management set realistic performance goals and plan to achieve them.

In our example, we assumed that Jason only sold one type of sofa with a uniform price. What happens to our ability to use this analysis tool when a company sells many products with different prices? Does this mean we cannot use break-even analysis? Of course not because we have another way of looking at CVP to determine break-even sales in dollars.

Determining Break-Even Sales Dollars

Assume that Jason sells many types of furniture and accessories that retail from $25 to $1,000 each. He would still want to determine a break-even point or be able to determine his activity level to achieve a desired profit. We can develop the same type of CVP models that change the focus from units to the dollar amount of sales. Return to Jason's original contribution income statement, and let's compute the ratio of variable costs and contribution margin to sales.

		Total	Percent of Sales
Sales	S	$455,000	100%
Variable costs	VC	309,400	68%
Contribution margin	CM	$145,600	32%

● **contribution margin ratio (CMR)**
The contribution margin divided by sales.

The **contribution margin ratio (CMR)** is the contribution margin divided by sales. Assuming that Jason's contribution margin has a relatively stable relationship to sales, we can assume that the CMR represents the normal relationship between sales and contribution margin. Returning to equations 1, 2, and 3, we can develop a model to calculate break-even sales dollars.

We begin with the contribution margin income statement equation:

(1)   Sales   − Variable Costs − Fixed Costs = Operating Income
          S   −   VC   −   FC   =   OI
$455,000 − $309,400   − $100,600 = $45,000

We can also separate this long equation in two parts:

(2)   Sales   − Variable Costs = Contribution Margin
          S   −   VC   =   CM
    $455,000 − $309,400   = $145,600

and

(3)   Contribution Margin − Fixed Costs = Operating Income
               CM   −   FC   =   OI
         $145,600   − $100,600 = $45,000

We can compute the ratio of variable costs and contribution margin to sales in equation 2 by dividing both sides by sales.

(8) $\dfrac{\text{Sales}}{\text{Sales}} - \dfrac{\text{Variable Cost}}{\text{Sales}} = \dfrac{\text{Contribution Margin}}{\text{Sales}}$

$\dfrac{\$455,000}{\$455,000} - \dfrac{\$309,400}{\$455,000} = \dfrac{\$145,600}{\$455,000}$

100% −   68%   =   32%

100% − Variable Cost Ratio = Contribution Margin Ratio

100% −   VCR   =   CMR

We can extract equation 9 from the right side of equation 8. We can rearrange equation 9 by multiplying both sides of the equation by sales. Application of actual data from Jason's operations shows that the equation holds true:

(9) $\text{CMR} = \dfrac{\text{Contribution Margin}}{\text{Sales}}$

(10)   Contribution Margin = Sales   × CMR
          $100,600 = $455,000 × 32%

Breakeven occurs when contribution margin equals the fixed costs as described in equation c.

(c)   Contribution Margin = Fixed Costs
               CM = FC

We can rewrite equation c where contribution margin equals fixed costs by substituting the contribution margin from equation 10 as:

CM = FC
$S \times \text{CMR} = \text{FC}$ (substitution from equation 10)

If we divide both sides of the final equation by the CMR, we can solve for the volume of sales dollars required to break even (S_{BE}):

(11) $S_{BE} = \dfrac{\text{FC}}{\text{CMR}}$

Using the facts of Jason's Furniture Gallery we can determine his break-even point in sales dollars:

$$S_{BE} = \dfrac{\text{FC}}{\text{CMR}} = \dfrac{\$100,600}{0.32} = \$314,375$$

Therefore, if Jason has sales of $314,375 in a year with a 32 percent contribution margin, he will break even. We can verify our calculations with a contribution income statement:

Sales	$314,375	100%
Variable costs ($314,375 x 68%)	213,775	68%
Contribution margin	$100,600	32%
Fixed costs	100,600	
Operating income	$ 0	

Once again our formula has worked. Considering that most businesses offer a wide variety of products, the formula for break-even sales dollars is important to most managers.

Just as we were able to factor in a desired profit when computing break-even unit, we should be able to adjust our break-even sales dollars formula to plan for a desired profit. We will add the desired profit to the fixed cost in equation 11 just as we did in equation 7.

$$(11) \quad S_{DP} = \frac{FC + DP}{CMR} = \frac{\$100,600 + \$75,000}{0.32} = \$548,750$$

Therefore, Jason's sales must reach $548,750 with a stable contribution margin ratio of 32 percent to make a $75,000 operating profit. We should verify it with a contribution income statement:

Sales	$548,750	100%
Variable costs ($548,750 x 68%)	373,150	68%
Contribution margin	$175,600	32%
Fixed costs	100,600	
Operating income	$ 75,000	

Break-even analysis helps us to understand the cost behavior peculiar to a specific business. It is a simple but robust tool for business analysis, budgeting, and planning. Perhaps its most important and valuable use comes in sensitivity analysis.

Sensitivity Analysis

● **sensitivity analysis**
A technique used to determine the effect of changes on the CVP relationship.

Business is dynamic, and astute business people know that change is frequent and unpredictable. **Sensitivity analysis** is a technique used to determine the effect of changes on the CVP relationship. Sensitivity analysis helps us to solve what-if questions, such as:

- What if we raised the selling price?
- What if we increased our units sold by lowering the price?
- What if we could lower our variable or fixed costs?

Let's look at each of these questions for Jason's situation. If he raised the selling price of the sofas to $525 and kept the same volume of 910 sofas per year, how much would his profit change? The solution is simple. The contribution margin would increase by $25 to $185 and fixed costs would remain the same at $100,600, so his profit would increase by $22,750 ($25 x 910) to $67,750. But at $525 per sofa, how many sofas would he have to sell to make his desired profit of $75,000?

$$S_{DP} = \frac{FC + DP}{UCM} = \frac{\$100,600 + \$75,000}{\$185} = 949.2 \approx 950$$

With the increase in price, he can reach his goal by selling 950 sofas at $525 instead of 1,098 at the old price.

Jason might decide, on the other hand, that the secret to his success is to increase the volume of business by reducing his price. He decides that by reducing his selling price 10 percent, he can increase the volume of his sales by 20 percent. Although this sounds like a great strategy of trading 10 percent sales price to gain 20 percent in the number sold, what will it do to his business profits? A 10 percent decrease in price reduces his selling price to $450 (0.90 × $500) and his contribution margin to $110 ($160 − $50). A 20 percent increase in volume increases his sales to 1,092 (1.20 × 910). Look at the break-even units required and the units required to make his $75,000 desired profit:

$$V_{BE} = \frac{FC}{UCM} = \frac{\$100,600}{\$110} = 914.55 \approx 915$$

and

$$V_{DP} = \frac{FC + DP}{UCM} = \frac{\$100,600 + \$75,000}{\$110} = 1,596.4 \approx 1,597$$

His break-even units rise to 915, and to 1,597 to make a $75,000 profit. Look at his contribution income statement at a proposed sales volume of 1,092 and a reduced selling price of $450:

	Total	Per Unit	
Sales ($450 x 1,092)	$491,400	USP	$450
Variable costs ($340 x 1,092)	371,280	UVC	340
Contribution margin	$120,120	UCM	$110
Fixed costs	100,600		
Operating income	$ 19,520		

His 20 percent increase in units sold at the reduced price of $450 net him $19,520 for the year. Do you believe that Jason would be happy with these results? Two or three minutes of planning might save him a year's grief in lowered profits.

Suppose Jason finds a way to save 10 percent on his variable costs. Will this increase his profits 10 percent? By reducing his cost 10 percent, he lowers the UVC to $306 and raises his UCM to $194. Look at his break-even numbers:

$$V_{BE} = \frac{FC}{UCM} = \frac{\$100,600}{\$194} = 518.56 \approx 519$$

and

$$V_{DP} = \frac{FC + DP}{UCM} = \frac{\$100,600 + \$75,000}{\$194} = 905.15 \approx 906$$

Jason could reach his desired profit at 906 sofas by reducing his variable costs by 10 percent as verified in the following contribution income statement:

		Total	Per Unit	
Sales (906 x $500)	S	$453,000	USP	$500
Variable costs (906 x $306)	VC	277,236	UVC	306
Contribution margin	CM	$175,764	UCM	$194
Fixed costs	FC	100,600		
Operating income	OI	$ 75,164		

What Do You Think?

4-9   Did Jason's profits rise by more or less than 10% when he reduced his variable cost by 10%? Explain your answer.

4-10   What would happen to Jason's operating income if instead of lowering his variable costs by 10%, he lowered his fixed costs by 10%?

4-11   What conclusions about performance planning and CVP can you draw from these examples of sensitivity analysis?

As you have seen, any changes in CVP inputs can create some rather startling consequences for business profits. Managers must be very careful to examine those consequences before making such decisions. Although we did not illustrate it, sensitivity analysis is a versatile tool and can also be used with information based on sales dollars. Knowledge of cost behavior, CVP analysis, and sensitivity analysis are the tools that our entrepreneurs from Elevation Sports need to build their initial capital and operating budgets. Let's see the many ways they use these techniques.

Building an Initial Budget

For a new organization, building initial capital and operating budgets is easier because the operation is small. Because the operation is new, however, the budgets must be based on estimates instead of historical data, creating some difficulty. Initial budgets focus heavily on cost estimation whereas ongoing budgets begin with revenue estimation. To be practical, Megan began with the costs of operations, determined the capital needs, and computed break-even points to estimate sales. Let's look at her estimates of operating costs first.

Operating Costs

Elevation Sports will have a number of operating costs that we can classify as manufacturing, selling, and administrative. As the group gathered data, they found the following items:

1   Rent. The city of Vail offered a $20,000 per year, five-year lease for the plant, including office space and the retail space in the ski village. After researching comparable costs for space, Megan determined that 20 percent of costs should be allocated to retail space, 10 percent to administrative space, and 70 percent to manufacturing. The lease is for five years, but Elevation Sports will only pay for four and one-half years because the first six months are free. We compute the monthly expense as follows:

$$\frac{\$20,000 \times 4.5}{60 \text{ months}} = \frac{\$90,000}{60} = \$1,500 \text{ per month}$$

Megan will allocate the rent expense as follows:

Selling expense	($1,500 x .20)	$ 300
Administrative expense	($1,500 x .10)	150
Manufacturing costs	($1,500 x .70)	1,050
Total rent expense		$1,500

2   Insurance will cost $5,000 per year plus $1 per snowboard manufactured. Of the $5,000 base amount, $3,000 relates to overall corporate liability and $2,000 is for property insurance for the plant. The $1 per board is for product liability on the snowboards. Megan will allocate the insurance expense as follows:

	Annual	Monthly
Administrative expense	$3,000	$250
Fixed manufacturing costs	2,000	167
Variable manufacturing costs	$1/unit	$1/unit

3   Interest expense will be 10 percent of the long-term debt on the equipment loan. Elevation Sports will owe $60,000 during the first year, making the annual interest expense $6,000 or $500 per month for the production equipment. Because the computer equipment is less than $5,000, the group decided not to finance it.

4   The attorney will charge $2,000 to file all the incorporation papers, write employment contracts for the four officers, and draft other legal documents. The $2,000 is a one-time expense, but the attorney will charge $300 per month as a retainer for other legal services in the future. In addition, it will cost an estimated $12,000 to secure the patents, trademarks, and copyrights on the products and advertising.

5   Based on estimates from the utility companies, the utilities on the ski shop should average $250 per month, the plant should average $500 per month, and the administrative space about $75 per month. The utilities on the shop and administrative offices approximate fixed expenses. The utilities on the plant should be about $400 fixed and $0.50 per snowboard manufactured.

6   Rob researched advertising costs. After a fall blitz of local advertising that will cost $3,000, the company needs to spend about $1,000 per month on Internet and print media advertising. The four need to attend the winter USSA convention in November in Chicago. Annual USSA membership fees are $600 and the booth space and travel expenses will cost $9,000. They plan to attend this type of convention each year.

7   Angie estimates the monthly Internet Web site costs at $300. Initial costs to register the Web site and domain name will be $500.

8   After studying the engineering specifications Jon prepared for the snowboards and researching the materials and labor costs, the group estimated the following variable costs per unit of production:

Direct materials	$ 9
Other indirect materials	2
Labor per board	25
Other variable manufacturing costs	4

9   After studying all other estimated costs, the four estimated that other fixed manufacturing costs would be $2,000 per month; fixed administrative costs, $300; and fixed selling costs, $250.

10   During busy times, the group can hire salespersons for the ski shop on commission at $5 per snowboard sold.

11   They need to purchase the following furniture and fixtures:

Administrative furniture	$ 2,100
Selling fixtures	8,400
Factory furniture and fixtures	12,600

A local office supply store would finance the acquisition with a $2,000 down payment and the balance over 24 months ($880 per month) with no interest.

12   The following are the useful lives and residual values of the long-term assets:

	Useful Life	Residual Value
Factory equipment	5	$15,000
Computers	2	300
Furniture & fixtures	7	—0—

Exhibit 4-7
Elevation Sports, Inc. Summary
of Estimated Monthly Costs

Elevation Sports, Inc. Summary of Estimated Monthly Costs	VARIABLE COST PER UNIT	MONTHLY FIXED COSTS
Manufacturing Costs:		
Direct materials	$ 9.00	
Direct labor	25.00	
Other manufacturing costs:		
Indirect materials	2.00	
Rent		$ 1,050
Utilities	0.50	400
Insurance	1.00	167
Depreciation—equipment		1,000
Depreciation—fixtures		150
Other expenses	4.00	2,000
Payroll tax expense	2.50	
Employee benefits	2.00	
Selling Expenses:		
Rent		300
Utilities		250
Advertising		1,000
Depreciation—fixtures		100
Internet costs		300
Sales commissions	5.00	
Payroll taxes	0.50	
Employee benefits	0.40	
Convention expense		750
Other expenses		250
Administrative Expenses:		
Rent		150
Utilities		75
Insurance		250
Depreciation—computers		175
Depreciation—furniture		25
Amortization		67
Interest expense		500
Legal expense		300
Salaries		4,000
Payroll taxes		400
Employee benefits		320
USSA membership		50
Other expenses		300
Total Expenses	$51.90	$14,329

Elevation Sports will use straight-line depreciation. Monthly depreciation costs can be computed as follows:

	Cost	Life in Months	Residual Value	Monthly Depreciation
Production equipment	$75,000	60	$15,000	$1,000
Factory fixtures	12,600	84	—0—	150
Administrative furniture	2,100	84	—0—	25
Computers	4,500	24	300	175
Selling fixtures	8,400	84	—0—	100

13 Patents, trademarks, and copyrights are **intangible assets**, or assets consisting of contractual rights. They should have a life of at least 15 years. Patent and copyright legal costs are allocated over the useful life of the asset with no residual value. Allocation of costs of intangible assets to the time periods benefited is called **amortization**. Monthly amortization, computed like depreciation for tangible assets, would be $67 per month ($12,000/180 months).

14 Payroll taxes are approximately 10 percent of the salaries and wages. Employee benefits for insurance and other benefits are eight percent of salaries and wages.

15 The salaries for each of the four officers will start at $12,000 per year and will be considered administrative expenses.

⬤ **intangible assets**
Assets consisting of contractual rights.

⬤ **amortization**
Allocation of costs of intangible assets to the time periods benefited.

Exhibit 4-7 contains a summary of the estimated monthly costs previously listed in an organized format we can use to separate all the various costs into fixed and variable and into manufacturing, selling, and administrative. One-time costs will be included as a separate section of the capital budget.

Capital Costs and One-Time Expenses

After determining the monthly costs, Megan wanted to develop the initial capital budget, including some one-time start-up costs. She created the summary shown in Exhibit 4-8.

Megan was very concerned about whether or not the group would have enough cash to pay the capital items and one-time costs and survive the first year of operations. She prepared a quick check of the initial cash position and eased her mind.

Exhibit 4-8
Elevation Sports, Inc.
Summary of Capital Costs
and One-Time Expenses

Elevation Sports, Inc.
Summary of Capital Costs and One-Time Expenses

Capital Items:	
Factory equipment	$75,000
Computers	4,500
Furniture and fixtures down payment	2,000
Patents, trademarks, and copyrights	12,000
Total Capital Items	$93,500
One-Time Costs:	
Web site costs	$ 500
Legal costs for incorporation	2,000
Initial advertising	3,000
Total One-Time Costs	$5,500

Exhibit 4-9
Elevation Sports, Inc. Sources and Uses of Initial Cash

Elevation Sports, Inc. Sources and Uses of Initial Cash		
Sources of Cash:		
Investment in stock by owners		$100,000
Equipment loan		60,000
Total Sources of Cash		$160,000
Uses of Cash:		
Capital items	$93,500	
One-time costs	5,500	99,000
Remaining Initial Cash		$ 61,000

Exhibit 4-9 shows the initial sources and uses of cash for the capital items and one-time costs. With their initial investments and loan on the equipment, they could pay for the capital items and one-time costs with $61,000 to spare. Megan quickly determined that the remaining $61,000 would provide approximately four months fixed operating costs ($61,000/$14,329 = 4.26). She knew that they must guard their cash carefully, but they might survive if they could begin to sell boards quickly.

Break-Even Analysis

The final step in creating the initial budget was to perform break-even analyses to set sales and production goals. Based on their research into the market, the officers believe that their snowboards will retail at $135, selling well below the competitor's price of $160. Their wholesale price to retailers will be $90. They believe that in their first year most of their sales will be retail and that the wholesale market will develop after the USSA convention in Chicago. Let's compute their monthly break-even units, based on the retail selling price, using the unit variable costs and fixed costs developed in Exhibit 4-7.

$$USP = \$135.00 \text{ (Retail)}$$
$$UVC = \quad 51.90$$
$$UCM = \quad 83.10$$

$$V_{BE}(\text{Retail}) = \frac{FC}{UCM} = \frac{\$14,329}{\$83.10} = 162.64 \approx 163$$

If all the sales were retail, based on their estimated variable and fixed costs, they would reach breakeven at 163 boards per month. What would happen if all the sales were wholesale? How many boards would they need to manufacture and sell? We can recompute the break-even point as follows:

$$USP = \$90.00 \text{ (Wholesale)}$$
$$UVC = 51.90$$
$$UCM = 38.10$$

$$V_{BE}(\text{Wholesale}) = \frac{FC}{UCM} = \frac{\$14,329}{\$38.10} = 376.08 \approx 377$$

If all sales are wholesale, they would reach breakeven at 377 boards. In all likelihood, neither scenario will occur because they will generate a mixture of retail and wholesale sales. But what it does reveal is that two wholesale sales are equivalent to one retail sale in terms of the gross profit generated.

Jon raised the point that each of them was working for $12,000, about one-fourth of their desired salary of $48,000. He wanted to calculate a more realistic break-even point that would include their desired salaries. So Megan quickly figured that at Jon's desired salary, monthly fixed costs would increase by $3,540 per person as shown below. Recall that payroll taxes cost 10 percent and benefits cost 8 percent of salaries so that the total cost of salaries is 118 percent of the gross wage.

$$\frac{\$48,000}{12} = \$4,000 - \$1,000 \text{ (current)} = \$3,000 \text{ increase}$$

$$\$3,000 \times 1.18 = \$3,540$$

Total monthly fixed costs would rise by $14,160 ($3,540 × 4) and break-even units would increase to:

$$V_{BE} \text{ (Retail)} = \frac{FC}{UCM} = \frac{\$14,329 + \$14,160}{\$83.10} = 342.83 \approx 343$$

and

$$V_{BE} \text{ (Wholesale)} = \frac{FC}{UCM} = \frac{\$14,329 + \$14,160}{\$38.10} = 747.74 \approx 748$$

The increases in their salaries almost double the sales required to break even. Now they have sales goals.

Megan estimated that the firm would have to sell 5.76 (173/30) snowboards per day for a 30-day month to break even based on her original budget. She decided to prepare the budget based on selling seven boards per day at retail price. (A wholesale sale equals about one-half the contribution of a retail sale. So the combination of sales needs to equal the equivalent of seven retail boards per day in terms of revenue.) Megan prepared her final budget summary for Elevation Sports, shown in Exhibit 4-10. Based on the budgeted income statement, they can make a small profit selling an average of seven boards each day at retail.

The stage is set, and the four are eager to begin. In Chapters 5 and 6 we will examine the results of their first year of operations and learn how to record that data into an accounting system that can produce desirable financial and management information to help them effectively operate the business.

Exhibit 4-10
Elevation Sports, Inc. Initial Monthly Operating Budget

Elevation Sports, Inc. Initial Monthly Operating Budget	
Budgeted sales ($135.00 × 7 × 30)	$28,350
Budgeted variable expenses ($51.90 × 7 × 30)	10,899
Budgeted contribution margin ($83.10 × 7 × 30)	$17,451
Budgeted fixed expenses	14,329
Budgeted operating income	$ 3,122
Estimated income taxes (30%)	937
Budgeted net income	$ 2,185

CHAPTER SUMMARY

To predict and analyze performance we need to understand the different types of costs and how to classify them. Costs may be classified by cost object such as an activity, product, service, project, geographic region, or business segment. Direct costs are easily traced to one cost object, whereas common costs are shared by a number of cost objects. When using an activity-based costing (ABC) system, cost drivers form the basis for allocating cost objects. When a company has an excellent understanding of its costs, it may use a standard cost system to simplify the financial transactions to separate inventory costs from cost of goods sold.

From the financial perspective costs are divided into product costs and period costs. Product costs include the costs of acquiring or manufacturing goods for sale to customers, whereas period costs are the costs of operating a business and include selling and administrative costs.

A fixed cost remains the same regardless of the volume of sales or production, while a variable cost changes with the volume of sales or production. Mixed costs have both a fixed component and a variable component. Analysis of the behavior pattern for each cost a business incurs allows us to predict future cost and potential profit or loss. The cost behavior patterns remain unchanged over a relevant range. Management decisions are more often the result of analysis based on cost behaviors rather than on financial classification. A prime example of the analytical approach to management decision making is cost-volume-profit (CVP) analysis.

A contribution income statement classifies expenses by cost behavior instead of financial categories. The formula for a contribution income statement is revenue minus variable costs equals contribution margin minus fixed costs equals operating income. Breakeven is the point at which total sales equals the total of all costs. At this point the company has realized neither a profit nor a loss. Sensitivity analysis is a technique used to determine the effect of changes on the CVP relationship.

A new business should develop an initial operating budget and as well as an initial capital and one-time expense budget in the planning process.

Visit the Web site *www.prenhall.com/terrell* for additional study help with the Online Study Guide.

REVIEW OF CONCEPTS

A   Describe a cost object.

B   Distinguish between a *direct cost* and a *common cost*.

C   Describe a cost driver and distinguish between a *cost driver* and a *cost object*.

D   Compare and contrast an *ABC system* and a *standard cost system*.

E   Compare and contrast product costs and period costs.

F   Discuss why the cost of delivering merchandise to customers is included in selling expense.

G   Discuss why the cost of storing inventory that is ready to sell is part of product costs.

H   Distinguish between *selling costs* and *administrative costs*.

I   Explain why product costs are called *inventoriable costs*.

J   Discuss how understanding of cost behavior improves the quality of management's decisions.

K   Describe the effect of fixed costs on total cost as the level of activity increases.

L   Describe what happens to the fixed cost per unit, variable cost per unit, and total cost per unit as activity increases within a relevant range.

M   With respect to cost behavior, describe a relevant range and explain how it affects production planning.

N   Describe the effect of variable costs on total cost as the level of activity increases.

O   Compare and contrast a *fixed cost*, a *variable cost*, and a *mixed cost*.

P   Describe what happens to the fixed cost per unit, variable cost per unit, and total cost per unit as activity increases across relevant ranges.

Q   Discuss whether or not a relevant range pertains to fixed costs, variable costs, or both.

R   Describe the meaning and uses of *contribution margin*.

S   Describe *CVP analysis* and its use in planning and performance analysis.

T   Discuss the importance of break-even analysis in planning and performance analysis.

U   Define *sensitivity analysis* and explain how management uses it.

APPLICATION EXERCISES

4-12   Sandy operates five stores for children's shoes called KIDS. She employs a store manager and two salesclerks for each store. In addition, she rents office space, which houses her office, the human resources department, and the bookkeeping department for the chain.

LO 1
Direct Costs and Common Costs

Required:

For each of the following items, indicate which would describe a direct cost (D) for an individual store and which would describe a common cost (C) for an individual store.
   a. rent on the office building
   b. rent for a store
   c. Sandy's salary
   d. store manager's salary
   e. human resources manager's salary
   f. bookkeeper's salary
   g. maintenance cost for a store
   h. depreciation on sales equipment
   i. depreciation on bookkeeping computer
   j. salesclerk's salary
   k. cost of shoes
   l. advertising cost for the chain

4-13   Edwina is the president of Kiddy Care. The company operates four child-care centers in southern Florida. In addition to the four Kiddy Care locations, the company rents office space that the company's bookkeeper and Edwina use.

LO 1
Direct Costs and Common Costs

Required:

   a. List four costs that would be considered direct costs of one of the four child-care centers.
   b. List four costs that would be considered common costs of one of the four child-care centers.

4-14   OK Travel operates a chain of travel agent offices in the western United States. OK Travel's home office is in Tulsa. It has seven sales offices and a district office located in Texas.

LO 1
Direct Costs and Common Costs

Required:

If the cost object is one of the sales offices in Texas, indicate which of the following would describe a direct cost (D) and which would describe a common cost (C):

a. rent for the Texas district office building
b. rent for the home office building in Tulsa
c. rent for the sales office
d. the company president's salary
e. the salary of the vice president in charge of the Texas division
f. the salary of a sales office manager
g. the salary of a sales associate

LO 2
Cost Drivers

4-15 The following estimates are available for Hoffman Manufacturing for 2004:

Hoffman Manufacturing
Estimated Manufacturing Overhead
For the year ended December 31, 2004

Materials handling cost	$ 20,000
Product engineering	220,000
Production machine setup	100,000
Production machine depreciation	225,000
Quality testing	200,000
Other overhead cost	250,000
Total Manufacturing Overhead	$1,015,000

Hoffman Manufacturing
Estimated Overhead Activities
For the year ended December 31, 2004

Number of material movements	200,000
Number of product engineering hours	4,400
Number of machine setups	100
Number of machine hours	18,000
Number of tests performed	25,000
Number of direct labor hours	25,000

The following information is available for production runs for two products, the XX and the YY:

	XX	YY
Selling price	$ 23	$ 26
Number of units produced	5,000	500
Direct material cost	$60,000	$6,000
Direct labor cost	$14,400	$1,440
Number of material movements	10,000	1,000
Number of product engineering hours	100	100
Number of machine setups	1	1
Number of machine hours	200	20
Number of tests performed	1,250	125
Number of direct labor hours	800	80

Hoffman Manufacturing's sales manager has submitted a proposal that would shift the marketing focus to low-volume products such as product YY. The proposal is prompted by the higher markups that can be charged for these products without generating customer complaints. The company president is concerned that the company's cost per unit may be sending the wrong message. He recently learned about ABC systems and wonders if they might help.

Assume that you are part of a group that has been assigned to review the situation.

Required:

a. How would you assign cost drivers to the various items of overhead?

b. Discuss the marketing manager's proposal. What do you think would happen if the marketing manager's sales strategy were adopted?

4-16 The following estimates are available for ALF Manufacturing for 2005:

LO 2
Calculate ABC
Overhead Allocation

ALF Manufacturing
Estimated Manufacturing Overhead
For the year ended December 31, 2005

Production machine setup	$ 75,000
Production machine depreciation	240,000
Quality testing	25,000
Other overhead cost	150,000
Total Manufacturing Overhead	$490,000

ALF Manufacturing
Estimated Overhead Activities
For the year ended December 31, 2005

Number of machine setups	100
Number of machine hours	3,200
Number of tests performed	50,000
Number of direct labor hours	16,000

The following information is available for production runs for two products, the AA and the BB:

	AA	BB
Selling price	$ 2.40	$ 3.25
Number of units produced	10,000	500
Direct material cost	$ 5,000	$ 250
Direct labor cost	6,400	320
Number of machine setups	1	1
Number of machine hours	100	5
Number of tests performed	100	50
Number of direct labor hours	400	20

ALF Manufacturing's vice president has questioned why the company does not shift the marketing focus to low-volume/high-profit products such as the BB. The proposal is prompted by the higher markups and lack of competition, even at high selling prices.

The company president is concerned that the company's cost per unit may not be correct. One of his accountants mentioned ABC and wonders if it should be considered before a decision is made.

Required:

a. Determine the per-unit cost for AA and BB using ABC to allocate manufacturing overhead costs. (Note: Allocate other overhead cost based on direct labor hours.)

b. Discuss how the decision might change if ABC were not used to determine the per-unit costs.

LO 2
Cost Drivers

4-17   The following is a list of overhead items:
   a. utilities
   b. depreciation of factory machines
   c. indirect labor
   d. cost of handling raw materials
   e. factory machine setup
   f. other factory overhead

Required:
   For each of the preceding items of factory overhead, identify an appropriate cost driver.

LO 3
Types of Cost for a Manufacturer

4-18   Listed below are several representative costs a typical manufacturing company might incur. For each of the costs, indicate whether the cost is a product cost (PR) or a period cost (PE).
   a. _____ material incorporated into products
   b. _____ sales supplies
   c. _____ supplies used in the factory
   d. _____ wages of plant security guard
   e. _____ wages of security guard for the sales office
   f. _____ depreciation on a file cabinet used in the factory
   g. _____ depreciation on a file cabinet used in the general accounting office
   h. _____ president's salary
   i. _____ president's secretary's salary
   j. _____ wages paid to production-line workers
   k. _____ factory rent
   l. _____ accounting office rent
   m. _____ depreciation on a copy machine used in the sales department
   n. _____ depreciation on a copy machine used to copy work orders in the factory
   o. _____ salary of the plant supervisor

LO 3
Classifying Cost by Cost Behavior

4-19   Indicate whether the following costs are more likely to be fixed costs (F), variable costs (V), or mixed costs (M) with respect to the number of units produced:
   a. _____ direct material
   b. _____ direct labor
   c. _____ cost of a plant security guard
   d. _____ straight-line depreciation on production equipment
   e. _____ maintenance on production equipment
   f. _____ maintenance on a factory building
   g. _____ cost of cleaning supplies used in the factory
   h. _____ salary for two factory supervisors
   i. _____ units-of-production depreciation
   j. _____ cost of electricity used in the factory
   k. _____ cost of production machine lubricants
   l. _____ rent on the factory building

LO 3
Classifying Cost by Cost Behavior

4-20   Assume that you are trying to analyze the costs associated with driving your car. Indicate whether the following costs are more likely to be fixed costs (F), variable costs (V), or mixed costs (M) with respect to the number of miles driven:
   a. _____ cost of the car
   b. _____ insurance cost
   c. _____ maintenance cost

d. ____ cost of gasoline
e. ____ cost of a college parking permit
f. ____ cost of a AAA membership
g. ____ cost of new tires
h. ____ cost of a new CD player

4-21 Assume that you are planning a wedding. As you are trying to determine how much the wedding reception will cost, you decide to separate the costs according to cost behavior. Indicate whether the following costs are more likely to be fixed costs (F), variable costs (V), or mixed costs (M) with respect to the number of guests attending the event:

a. ____ rent for the reception hall
b. ____ cost of the band
c. ____ cost of caterer
d. ____ cost of food
e. ____ cost of table decorations
f. ____ cost of renting tables and chairs
g. ____ cost of wedding cakes
h. ____ cost of linen rental

LO 3
Classifying Cost by Cost Behavior

4-22 Discuss the meaning of the term *relevant range* as it applies to fixed cost and variable cost and provide an example of how the term is applied to each type of cost.

LO 3
Relevant Range

4-23 Styles Furniture Company has been in business for two years. When the business began, Styles established a delivery department with a small fleet of trucks. The delivery department was designed to be able to handle the substantial future growth of the company. As expected, sales for the first two years of business were low and activity in the delivery department has been minimal.

In an effort to control costs, Styles Furniture Company's store manager is considering a proposal from a delivery company to deliver the furniture for a flat fee of $30 per delivery. The following information is available regarding the cost of operating Styles' delivery department during its first two years of business.

LO 1, 3, 5, and 6
Analyzing a Situation Using Cost Behavior Concepts

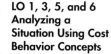

	2002	2003
Number of deliveries	600	700
Cost of operating the delivery department	$25,480	$26,480

Sales and the number of deliveries are expected to increase greatly in the coming years. For example, sales next year will require an estimated 1,250 deliveries, whereas in 2005, 1,775 deliveries are expected. Due to the high growth rate, the store manager is concerned that the delivery cost will increase greatly unless the proposal is accepted. He states that the cost per delivery was about $42.47 ($25,480/600) in 2002 and $37.83 ($26,480/700) in 2003. Even at the lower cost of $37.83, it seems the company can save about $7.83 ($30.00−$37.83) per delivery. For 2005, the store manager feels the proposal can save the company about $13,898.25 (1,775 × $7.83).

Required:

Assume that you have been assigned to analyze the delivery cost of Styles Furniture Company. Prepare a report that indicates the advantages or disadvantages of accepting the proposed delivery contract, including not only calculations to support your recommended course of action, but also addressing the nonmonetary considerations of contracting with an outside source for delivery services.

LO 3, 6, and 7
Analyzing a
Situation Using Cost
Behavior Concepts

4-24 Shannon Davis is considering opening a greeting card shop in a local mall. Shannon contacted the mall manager and determined that the store rent will be $550 per month. In addition, he called the telephone company and based on the information from the telephone company representative, he estimates that the cost of telephone service will be about $95 per month. Based on the size of the store, Shannon believes that cost of electricity will average about $200 per month. Shannon will be able to buy the greeting cards for $0.50 each and plans to sell them for $2 each. Salaries are expected to be $1,200 per month regardless of the number of cards sold. Shannon estimates that other miscellaneous fixed costs will total $150 per month and miscellaneous variable costs will be $0.10 per card. Shannon anticipates that he will be able to sell about 3,000 greeting cards per month. If Shannon opens the store, his first month of business will be November 2004.

Required:

a. Prepare a projected contribution income statement for November 2004.
b. Determine how many cards must be sold per hour to break even if the store is open from 10:00 A.M. to 9:00 P.M. each day, six days per week.
c. Compute the break-even sales volume and sales dollars for the card shop.
d. Determine how many cards he must sell to earn $40,000 per year. Is this feasible?

LO 3, 6, and 7
Analyzing a
Situation Using Cost
Behavior Concepts

4-25 Jon's Pretzel Stand is located in the Rose Bowl stadium and sells pretzels during sporting events. The following information is available:
1. selling price per pretzel, $2
2. cost of each pretzel, $0.25
3. cost of renting the pretzel stand, $12,000 per year
4. instead of an hourly wage, Jon pays college students $0.20 per pretzel sold to run the pretzel stand

Required:

a. Prepare a contribution income statement for 2004 assuming that 8,000 pretzels are sold.
b. Determine whether or not Jon should continue to operate the stand at the volume of 8,000 units. What are his opportunity costs?
c. Determine three ways that Jon might increase his profits.

LO 3, 6, and 7
Analyzing a
Situation Using Cost
Behavior Concepts

4-26 The following information is available for Medical Testing Corporation:

Amount charged for each test performed	$ 90
Annual fixed cost	$200,000
Variable cost per test	$ 25

Required:

a. Calculate how many tests Medical Testing must perform each year to break even.
b. Calculate how many tests Medical Testing must perform each year to earn a profit of $25,000.
c. Calculate how many tests per hour must be performed to break even.
d. Assuming that each test takes 15 minutes, what is the potential annual income of this business with one employee working 8 hours a day, 50 weeks per year?
e. What is the source of potential customers? How would you promote the business?

LO 3, 6, and 7
Analyzing a
Situation Using Cost
Behavior Concepts

4-27 Lucien Calendar Company is considering adding a new calendar design to its line. The following information is available:

Wholesale selling price	$ 3.97
Additional annual fixed cost	$ 4,558.00
Variable cost per calendar	$ 3.11

Required:

   a. Calculate how many calendars must be sold each year to break even.

   b. Calculate how many calendars must be sold each year to earn a profit of $5,000.

   c. With a national distribution potential of 2,500 stores, should Lucien produce the calendar?

4-28 Mercy Medical, Inc. is considering opening a new emergency care facility. The fees charged and costs of the new facility will be similar to that of the existing facility. The only exception is that the annual fixed cost for the new facility is expected to be $125,000 more than that of the existing facility. The following information is available for Mercy Medical's existing facility for 2004:

LO 3, 6, and 7
Analyzing a
Situation Using Cost
Behavior Concepts

Revenue	$1,250,000
Variable cost	600,000
Fixed cost	420,000

Required:

   a. Determine the revenues required for the new emergency care facility to break even.

   b. Determine the revenues required for the new emergency care facility to earn a profit of $120,000 per year.

4-29 Wendt Industries is considering opening a second school supply store. The annual fixed cost of the new store is expected to be $225,000 per year. Wendt expects the new store's contribution margin ratio to be similar to the existing store. The following information is available for Wendt's first school supply store for 2004:

LO 3, 6, and 7
Analyzing a
Situation Using Cost
Behavior Concepts

Revenue	$3,650,000
Variable cost	1,387,000

Required:

   a. Determine the required revenue for the second store to break even.

   b. Determine the required revenue for the second store to earn a profit of $125,000.

4-30 Bill Haddock wants to sell ice cream bars at school events. The vendor stand will cost $800, and the ice cream bars cost $0.65. In exchange for the right to sell the ice cream bars, Bill has agreed to donate $600 per year and $0.25 per ice cream bar to the school's booster club. Bill plans to sell the ice cream bars for $1.50 each. Bill intends to sell the ice cream bars for four years until he graduates.

LO 3, 6, and 7
Analyzing a
Situation Using Cost
Behavior Concepts

Required:

   a. Assuming the vendor stand can be used for only four years, calculate the cost per year for the vendor stand.

   b. Calculate the total fixed cost per year for Bill's ice cream business.

   c. Calculate the variable cost per ice cream bar.

   d. Calculate the annual break-even point in units and in dollars.

   e. Calculate how many ice cream bars Bill must sell to earn an annual profit of $3,000.

   f. Calculate the sales in dollars required to earn an annual profit of $3,000.

   g. Calculate Bill's profit if sales were $8,000 for this year.

LO 3, 6, and 7
Analyzing a Situation Using Cost Behavior Concepts

4-31 Tiffany is considering opening a gift shop. She has collected the following information:

Monthly rent	$2,800
Monthly sales salaries	$1,200

In addition to the sales salaries, Tiffany intends to pay a 5% sales commission to her sales staff. The cost of the merchandise sold is expected to be 40% of sales.

Required:
- a. Determine Tiffany's break-even point in monthly sales dollars.
- b. Determine the monthly sales dollars required to earn a profit of $2,000 per month.
- c. Determine Tiffany's break-even point if she is able to reduce rent by $200.

   Now assume that Tiffany has negotiated a 10% discount on all merchandise purchases. The new cost of merchandise will not change the selling price of product.

- d. Determine the new contribution margin ratio.
- e. Determine the new break-even point in monthly sales dollars.
- f. Determine the amount of sales necessary to earn a profit of $2,000 per month.

LO 3, 6, and 7
Analyzing a Situation Using Cost Behavior Concepts

4-32 Quality Instrument Company manufactures various industrial thermometers. Last year the company sold 600 model QI22 thermometers for $129 each. Managers are concerned that the profits from the QI22 were only $7,740 last year. Fixed costs for this product are $50,000 per year. In an effort to increase profits, the company raised the price of the QI22 to $148. Based on annual sales of 600 units, managers are confident that profits from the QI22 will be increased to $19,740 next year.

The sales manager is concerned about the price increase. He believes the company should move a little slower in making the pricing decision and has suggested that a group be formed to explore the ramifications of such a pricing move.

Required:

You have been assigned to evaluate the proposed price change. Prepare a report discussing the various ramifications of the price increase including its effect on projected sales and profits. Your report should make recommendations that are supported by calculations similar to those found in this chapter.

Ethics Case

4-33 Roger Craig has been asked to serve as a member of the board of directors of the Smersh Company. Roger has never held such a position, and he is not familiar with the responsibility he is being asked to assume. His first assignment is to review a proposal to change to a standard cost system.

Required:
- a. Explain to Roger the basic responsibilities of a board member.
- b. Should Roger have any misgivings about accepting this prestigious position?
- c. How should Roger handle his first assignment?

FOR ADDITIONAL READING

Bonsack, Robert A. "Does Activity-Based Costing Replace Standard Costing?" *Journal of Cost Management* 4 (Winter 1991):46ff.

Cheatham, Carole B., and Leo R. Cheatham. "Redesigning Cost Systems: Is Standard Costing Obsolete?" *Accounting Horizons* 10 (December 1996):23ff.

Holmes, Stanley. "Boeing's Secret." *Business Week* (May 20, 2002):110ff.

Kidwell, Linda A., Shib-Jen Kathy Ho, John Blake, and Philip Wraith. "New Management Techniques: An International Comparison." *CPA Journal* 72 (February 2001):63ff.

Lere, John C. "Selling Activity-Based Costing." *CPA Journal* 72 (March 2003):54ff.

CHAPTER 5

LEARNING OBJECTIVES

After completing this chapter you should be able to:

1 Identify and describe the eight steps of the accounting cycle.

2 Distinguish between debits and credits and apply them to the accounting equation.

3 Identify the normal balance of accounts and distinguish between permanent accounts and temporary accounts.

4 Describe accounts, charts of accounts, journals, ledgers, and worksheets.

5 Record transactions in journals.

6 Post transactions from the general journal to the general ledger.

7 Compute cash discounts and determine the implication of freight terms.

8 Prepare a trial balance.

Recording Accounting Data

Although financial statement readers often do not wish to participate in the details of accumulating data to prepare the financial statements, the better a user understands the accounting process, the more he or she can comprehend the implications of those numbers. When we grasp how the accounting system interprets the revenue recognition and the expense recognition principles, we appreciate the meaning of the income and expense numbers on the income statement. When we recognize the checks and balances inherent in the accounting system, we can appreciate the need for internal control to protect those checks and balances. When we grasp the concept of financial statement articulation, we notice when something is not right with a set of financial statements.

So where do we begin? We will walk through each step of the accounting process learning how to apply the accounting equation in each decision-making situation. We will apply the concepts discussed in Chapter 2 about revenue and expense recognition, accruals, and deferrals. In essence, we will utilize the decision-making skills we discussed in Chapter 2, applying accounting principles within an accounting system that transforms events and data into valuable accounting information.

The Accounting Cycle

● **accounting cycle**
The sequence of steps repeated in each accounting period to enable the company to analyze, record, classify, and summarize the transactions into financial statements.

The **accounting cycle** is the sequence of steps repeated in each accounting period to enable the company to analyze, record, classify, and summarize the transactions into financial statements. The steps are:

Step 1   Analyzing transactions
Step 2   Journalizing transactions
Step 3   Posting transactions to the general ledger
Step 4   Preparing the trial balance (and worksheet)
Step 5   Adjusting the accounts and reconciling the bank statement
Step 6   Preparing financial statements
Step 7   Preparing and posting closing entries
Step 8   Preparing the post-closing trial balance

The accounting process is a cycle because its events occur repeatedly: some daily, some monthly, and some annually. At the end of the annual cycle, the process begins anew. Exhibit 5-1 provides an overview of the dynamics of the accounting system. To understand this process, we will look at what happens in each step of the cycle and learn how to apply each step of the cycle to Elevation Sports, Inc. transactions.

Step 1: Analyzing Transactions

Analyzing transactions, the most important step in the accounting cycle, consists of two parts as illustrated in Exhibit 5-2. The first is deciding when a transaction occurs. The timing of the transaction is important because financial statements reflect only the transactions that occurred by the balance sheet date. The simple answer is that a transaction occurs when an accounting element changes. For example, if a customer pays the company for a purchase made last month, cash increases and accounts receivable

Exhibit 5-1
The Accounting Cycle:
A Dynamic System

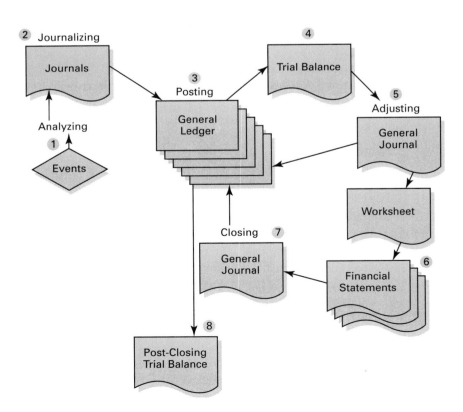

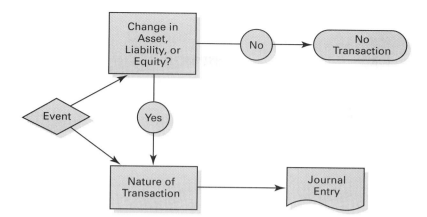

Exhibit 5-2
Step 1: Analyzing Transactions

decreases. Assets both increase and decrease, and a transaction occurs. What if a company orders merchandise that the vendor will deliver in three weeks? Has a transaction occurred? No. Neither assets, nor liabilities, nor equity has changed. When will this transaction occur? The transaction will occur when title to the merchandise passes from the vendor to the buyer during the shipping process. At that moment, the company will have new assets and a new liability.

The second part of analyzing transactions is identifying which accounts or accounting elements are changed. If we classify the merchandise purchased on credit as a long-term asset and reduce cash by that amount, we have created errors in four accounts. Inventory, long-term assets, accounts payable, and cash are either overstated or understated. As you can see, knowing when and how to record the transaction are critical to maintaining the integrity of the accounting records. We make the decision about transactions as frequently as we journalize transactions.

What Do You Think?

5-1   With the many accounting software packages for beginners on the market, why do we need accountants?

5-2   What is the difference between a bookkeeper and an accountant?

Step 2: Journalizing Transactions

Journalizing transactions is the act of recording accounting transactions into a journal. A **journal** is a book of original entry where a chronology of the business entity's transactions is recorded. In the days of pen and ink, the accountant or bookkeeper kept the journal in a book. Today, with computerization, a journal may be a listing of transactions on a computer printout or a file in the computer. Regardless of form, the journal lists transactions in order of occurrence. Employees, management, and auditors frequently use the journal's chronological listing of transactions to trace transactions and answer inquiries. For this reason, we record transactions formally into journals daily, weekly, or sometimes monthly for small businesses. Large companies use online, real-time processing techniques that create the journals as the transactions occur. Sophisticated cash register systems often create journals simultaneously as the cashier scans the items sold.

Businesses use several journals to capture details. The most common forms are sales journals, cash receipt journals, cash payment journals, purchases journals, and the general journal. All except the general journal are called **special journals**, which record a specific type of transaction such as sales. The sales journal, for instance, contains a record of the firm's sales to its customers but no other type of transaction. We use the **general journal** to record all transactions that cannot be recorded in a special

● **journalizing**
The act of recording accounting transactions into a journal.

● **journal**
A book of original entry where a chronology of the business entity's transactions is recorded.

● **special journals**
Journals that record a specific type of transaction such as sales.

● **general journal**
A journal for recording all transactions that cannot be recorded in a special journal.

Exhibit 5-3
Step 2: Journalizing
Transactions

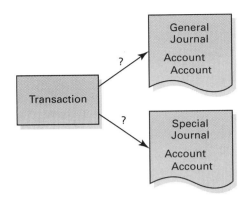

journal (see Exhibit 5-3). If a firm has no special journals, it records all transactions in the general journal. For example, Quicken® and QuickBooks® use only a general journal format. Why do we have special journals? Special journals save a great deal of time when a firm experiences many similar transactions during a period. The reason for this will become obvious when we discuss posting to the general ledger, the next step in the accounting cycle.

Journals have many uses in the business operation, but the long lists of data contained in them lack the quality of information. The next step in the cycle helps us to transform those data into usable information.

Step 3: Posting to the General Ledger

With the journals full of difficult-to-use data, we need a method of sorting or classifying the data into usable information. The information we desire is the amount of sales made, the amount of cash or inventory on hand, how much is owed for purchases, and so on. Each of the accounting elements provides us with information about the financial statements, so the elements become the classification system for accounting records.

Each accounting element has an **account**, which contains the history of all increases and decreases in that accounting element. A **chart of accounts** is a list of all the accounts used by a business entity. It lists each account with its account number (particularly important in computerized systems) in the balance sheet and income statement order of assets, liabilities, equity, revenue, and expense accounts. The chart of accounts becomes a reference tool for accountants and expands as needed to record new types of transactions. Each business entity should tailor its chart of accounts to its business activities. As an example, the Appendix to this chapter contains an annotated chart of accounts for Elevation Sports.

The entire group of accounts in an accounting system constitutes the **general ledger** in which each account is a page or a file. At the end of a month or a week, the bookkeeper posts, or records, each journal transaction into the general ledger account it changes—the process is known as **posting** (see Exhibit 5-4). In a computerized system, the software actually re-sorts the transactions from a date order to an account number order and accumulates all transactions with like account numbers into the proper account.

Then we have a record of what happened to each account as a result of these transactions. We add all increases and subtract all decreases to the previous balance of the account to arrive at a new account balance. We use the general ledger account balances to prepare financial statements after two additional steps in the accounting cycle.

● **account**
The history of all increases and decreases in an accounting element.

● **chart of accounts**
A list of all the accounts used by a business entity.

● **general ledger**
The entire group of accounts in an accounting system.

● **posting**
Recording each journal transaction into the general ledger account it changes.

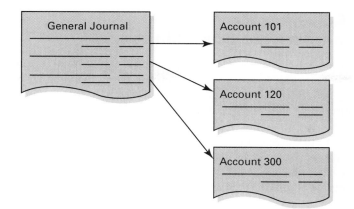

Exhibit 5-4
Step 3: Posting Transactions to
the General Ledger

Step 4: Preparing the Trial Balance (and Worksheet)

Each time we post a month's or a week's transactions from the journals, we need to make sure that the accounting equation remains in balance. To accomplish this, we prepare a trial balance. A **trial balance** is a listing of each general ledger account balance to verify that the general ledger, and therefore the accounting equation, is in balance (see Exhibit 5-5). Accounting software packages often print a trial balance after each processing session. Others automatically check to be sure that the system is in balance and alert the operator if it is not.

Frequently, accountants use a **worksheet** as a tool to accumulate the data required to prepare financial statements. The first two columns of the 10-column worksheet are the trial balance on the balance sheet date. Most firms prepare monthly financial statements and follow this step each time financial statements are prepared. (Some firms prepare financial statements weekly, quarterly, or semiannually.) The worksheet allows the accountant to examine each account and make appropriate adjustments necessary to prepare financial statements. We will examine the preparation of a trial balance and a worksheet as we apply the accounting cycle to actual transactions.

● **trial balance**
A listing of each general ledger account balance to verify that the general ledger, and therefore the accounting equation, is in balance.

● **worksheet**
A tool accountants use to accumulate the data required to prepare financial statements.

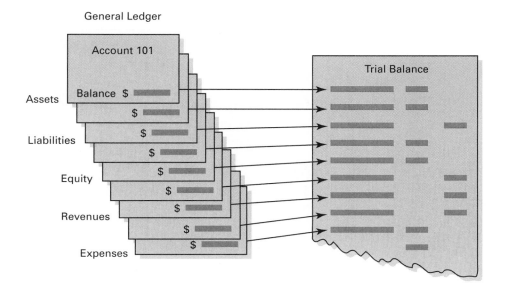

Exhibit 5-5
Step 4: Preparing the Trial Balance

Step 5: Adjusting the Accounts and Reconciling the Bank Statement

At the end of an accounting period, prior to preparing financial statements, accountants review the accounts to ensure each complies with the matching principle, properly matching the expenses of the period with the revenues that they helped to produce. They also make sure that the assets, liabilities, and equity accounts are properly stated and look for errors that might have been made in the posting process (see Exhibit 5-6). Five basic types of adjustments are made for these purposes, and they fall into three basic categories. Let's look at each one more closely.

The three basic categories of adjustments are accruals, deferrals, and error corrections. **Accruals** are adjustments made to recognize items that should be included in the income statement period but have not yet been recorded. For accruals, the receipt or payment of cash *follows* recognition of revenue or expense. The first two types of adjustments are accruals:

1   **Accrued revenue** is revenue earned and realizable during the financial statement period that has not yet been recognized or recorded. Because this revenue meets the revenue recognition criteria, it must be recognized as revenue even though the cash has not yet been received. Consider AT&T, which sends bills on the second of each month for services performed during the previous month. At the end of December, AT&T has a legal claim to payment for services it provided in that month. Revenues recognized should include the amount earned in December, even though the customers will not be billed until January 2 of the next year. Accrual of revenue always creates an account receivable asset.

2   An **accrued expense** is an expense incurred during the financial statement period that has not yet been recognized. Assume The Boeing Company pays its employees every two weeks for work performed in the previous two weeks. If part of the two-week pay period is in 2004 and part is in 2005, Boeing must make an adjustment at the end of 2004 to recognize the portion of wages expense incurred during that period. Accrual of an expense always creates a corresponding liability, usually called a *payable*.

Deferrals are postponements of the recognition of a revenue or expense even though the cash has been received or paid. They are adjustments of revenues for which the cash has been collected but not yet earned, and of expenses for which cash has

Margin glossary

● **accruals**
Adjustments made to recognize items that should be included in the income statement period but have not yet been recorded.

● **accrued revenue**
Revenue earned and realizable during the financial statement period that has not yet been recognized or recorded.

● **accrued expense**
Expense incurred during the financial statement period that has not yet been recognized.

● **deferrals**
Postponements of the recognition of a revenue or expense even though the cash has been received or paid.

Exhibit 5-6
Step 5: Adjusting the Accounts and Reconciling the Bank Statement

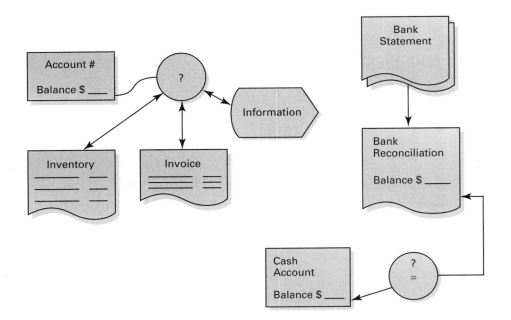

been paid but no benefit has yet been received. For deferrals, cash receipt or payment *precedes* recognition of revenue or expense. The next two types of adjustments are deferrals:

3 **Deferred revenue** is unearned revenue created when cash is received before the revenue is earned. For example, the *Wall Street Journal* (WSJ) sends a daily newspaper to the Bidlack family who on June 1 sent the paper an advance payment of $180 for the cost of a year's subscription. As of June 1, WSJ has not earned any revenue, even though it has received cash. In fact, receipt of unearned cash creates a liability. The company owes the Bidlack family either one year's newspaper service or their money back. The key here is who has legal claim to the cash. Because WSJ has no legal claim to the cash, it cannot account for it as earned revenue. By the time the month ends in June, however, the paper has earned one month's fees and recognizes $15 as revenue. The remaining $165, representing 11 months' fees, remains a deferred revenue. This amount represents a liability for the *Wall Street Journal* and will remain so until the company either performs the services required to attain a legal claim to the cash or returns the cash to the Bidlack family.

● **deferred revenue**
Unearned revenue created when cash is received before the revenue is earned.

4 A **deferred expense** is an asset created when cash is paid before an expense has been incurred. On January 2, 2004, Coldwater Creek purchased a three-year insurance policy for $24,000. By December 31, 2004, one-third of the insurance coverage has expired (one-third of the benefit has been received). Financial statements prepared for 2004 should reflect the fact that one-third of the cost of the policy ($8,000) is an expense for that year. The remaining portion of the policy, two years' worth of coverage, is an asset providing future benefits to the company. Even though the entire $24,000 was spent in 2004, two-thirds of the cost is a deferred expense, a $16,000 prepaid asset that will be recognized as an expense in future periods.

● **deferred expense**
An asset created when cash is paid before an expense has been incurred.

The final type of adjustment corrects random errors:

5 **Error corrections** are made through adjusting entries when the accountant reviews the trial balance and notices errors in the recording or posting process. Take, for example, the Einstein Corporation's trial balance that shows $4,000 in account #196, Land. When the accountant reviewed the trial balance, this looked unusual because the company does not own any land. Upon further investigation, the accountant discovered that the data entry clerk recorded the expenditure for advertising, account #691, and transposed the account numbers. The accountant will make a correcting entry to correct the posting.

● **error corrections**
Corrections made through adjusting entries when the accountant reviews the trial balance and notices errors in the recording or posting process.

The adjustment process requires the following steps:

1 Identify any accounts requiring adjustment;
2 Determine the correct balance in each account requiring adjustment; and
3 Prepare the necessary adjusting entry or entries to bring the accounts into agreement with the balances determined in the previous step.

Another major step in the adjusting process is reconciling the Cash in Bank account with the **bank statement**, a summary of the cash inflows and outflows processed by the bank. Because most transactions ultimately result in the receipt or the payment of cash, it is important to reconcile the bank statement with the Cash in Bank account as part of the firm's internal control structure. We will prepare a bank reconciliation as we apply these concepts later in the chapter.

● **bank statement**
A summary of the cash inflows and outflows processed by the bank.

Step 6: Preparing Financial Statements

When the accountant is satisfied that the bank accounts are reconciled and the accounts listed on the worksheet represent fair amounts, he or she will prepare the financial statements (see Exhibit 5-7). The accountant should verify that the financial statements articulate. Specifically, the net income or net loss figure for the period must agree with the net income or net loss on the statement of stockholders' equity or the statement of retained earnings, which must agree with total stockholders' equity and retained earnings on the balance sheet.

Exhibit 5-7
Step 6: Preparing Financial
Statements

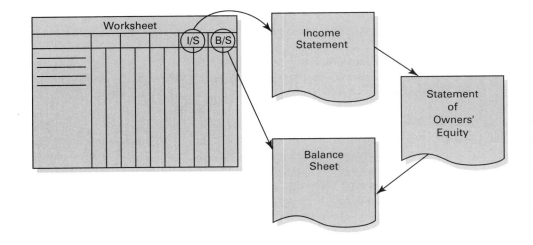

What Do You Think?

**5-3   How often should a company prepare its financial statements?
Explain your answer.**

Step 7: Preparing and Posting Closing Entries

At the end of each fiscal year, after the accounting staff adjusts all the accounts and the auditors have finished the audit, we close the books. The closing process resets the temporary accounts to zero and moves the net income to the appropriate equity accounts (see Exhibit 5-8). **Temporary accounts** are all revenue, expense, gain, and loss accounts that are part of net income plus the dividend account. We do not close permanent accounts in this process. **Permanent accounts** include all asset, liability, and equity accounts, except for the dividend account. The closing entries zero the temporary accounts much like a trip switch on an automobile odometer. The odometer (like permanent accounts) continues to record miles, but we reset the trip switch (like temporary accounts) to zero before each event (such as a new fiscal year). Each year we reset the temporary accounts to zero to accumulate the current year's net income. At the end of the year we close the net income into the equity accounts and start over again.

● **temporary accounts**
All revenue, expense, gain, and loss
accounts that are part of net income
plus the dividend account.

● **permanent accounts**
All asset, liability, and equity
accounts, except for the dividend
account.

The four closing entries are:

1   Close the revenue accounts to income summary;
2   Close the expense accounts to income summary;
3   Close the dividend accounts to retained earnings; and
4   Close income summary to retained earnings.

Step 8: Preparing the Post-Closing Trial Balance

● **post-closing trial balance**
A trial balance prepared after the
closing entries are posted to prove
that the closing entries zeroed the
temporary accounts and the
remaining accounts are in balance.

After we prepare the closing entries and post them to the general ledger, only the balance sheet accounts should have a balance remaining. In addition, the dividend account should have a zero balance. We prepare a **post-closing trial balance** after the closing entries have been posted to prove that the closing entries zeroed the temporary

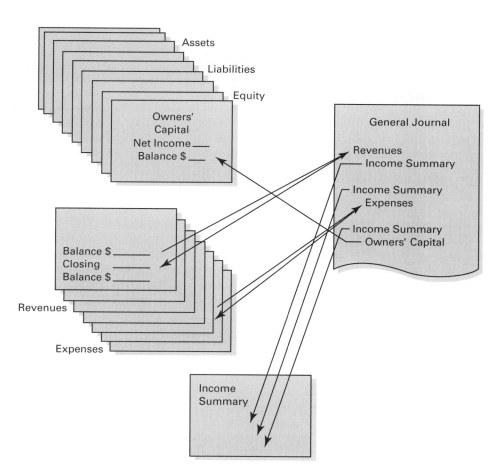

Exhibit 5-8
Step 7: Preparing and Posting Closing Entries

accounts and the remaining accounts are in balance (see Exhibit 5-9). In a computerized system, this step is crucial to verify the integrity of the closing process and to show that the accounting equation remains in balance.

Before we apply the steps of the accounting cycle to Elevation Sports, we need to discuss several topics necessary to begin the data accumulation.

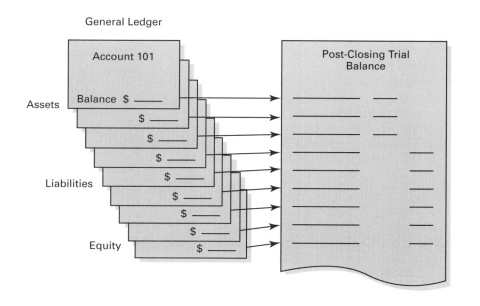

Exhibit 5-9
Step 8: Preparing the Post-Closing Trial Balance

An Accounting System of Debits and Credits

● **accounting system**
A system that gathers data from source transactions to create the books and records that transform the data into a manageable format and eventually produces useful information in the form of financial statements.

An **accounting system** gathers data from source transactions to create the books and records that transform the data into a manageable format and eventually produces useful information in the form of financial statements. The accounting system operates within the parameters of the basic accounting equation introduced in Chapter 2:

$$Assets\ =\ Liabilities\ +\ Equity$$

As we know from mathematics, a change on one side of the equation requires a change on the other side of the equation to keep the equation in balance. Each transaction is recorded to describe in a meaningful way the changes in the equation, thus requiring two entries to keep the equation in balance. Over the past 7,000 years, accountants have developed the accounting system and a system language to describe the process. In the accounting system **debit** means left and **credit** means right. Thus:

$$Assets = Liabilities + Equity$$
$$Left = Right$$
$$Debit = Credit$$

When our accounting system is in balance, the debits equal the credits; left equals right.

● **normal balance**
Defines the type of entry that increases the account; debits increase debit balance accounts and credits decrease debit balance accounts.

An account's **normal balance** defines the type of entry that increases the account; debits increase debit balance accounts and credits decrease debit balance accounts. Therefore, asset accounts have normal debit balances; liability and equity accounts have normal credit balances.

$$Assets\ =\ Liabilities\ +\ Equity$$
$$\text{Normal Balance:}\quad Debit\ =\quad Credit\quad +\ Credit$$

We also learned in Chapter 2 that equity has four components. We can expand the accounting equation to include the four components of equity as follows:

$$Assets = Liabilities + Owners'\ Investments - Dividends + Revenues - Expenses$$
$$Debit = Credit\ +\qquad Credit\qquad -\quad Debit\ +\ Credit\ -\quad Debit$$

With the expanded equation we can identify the normal balances of revenues, expenses, and dividends. Therefore, a debit:

- increases assets;
- decreases liabilities;
- decreases stockholders' equity,
  - decreases capital stock accounts,
  - increases the dividend account,
  - decreases revenues or gains, and
  - increases expenses or losses.

A credit:

- decreases assets;
- increases liabilities;
- increases stockholders' equity,
  - increases capital stock accounts,
  - decreases the dividend account,
  - increases revenues or gains, and
  - decreases expenses or losses.

Exhibit 5-10
Effect of Debits and Credits on
Accounting Elements

ACCOUNTING ELEMENT	DEBITS	CREDITS
Assets	Increase	Decrease
Liabilities	Decrease	Increase
Equity	Decrease	Increase
Revenues	Decrease	Increase
Expenses	Increase	Decrease
Owners' Investments	Decrease	Increase
Dividends	Increase	Decrease
Gains	Decrease	Increase
Losses	Increase	Decrease

(See also the summary in Exhibit 5-10.)

Every transaction requires at least one debit and one credit to describe its substantive change in the accounting equation.

The Account

Each account contains a summary of activity for one accounting element during the year. It includes the following important information:

- account name and number;
- date of each transaction;
- beginning balance;
- each posting from journals including the date, posting reference, and amount; and
- ending balance.

A typical account might look like the example in Exhibit 5-11.

When you read the account, you learn that on December 1, 2004, the company began with $34,589.26 in the bank. It collected $54,197.75, recorded on page 34 of the Cash Receipts Journal, and paid out $56,110.68, recorded on page 57 of the Cash Payments Journal. At month end, the company had $32,676.33 in the bank. Notice that the general ledger has no dollar signs. Dollar signs appear in financial statements and trial balance, but not on journals, ledgers, or worksheets.

To save time when analyzing an account, we often use an abbreviated general ledger account form called the **T-account**, which has only two columns and no explanations. The balance appears after a horizontal line. Exhibit 5-12 contains the T-account version of the cash account illustrated in Exhibit 5-11 (see p. 142).

● **T-account**
An abbreviated general ledger account that has only two columns and no explanations.

Exhibit 5-11
The Account Form

ACCOUNT NAME	Cash in Bank				ACCOUNT NUMBER	101	
2004		**POST**				**BALANCE**	
DATE	**DESCRIPTION**	**REF.**	**DEBIT**	**CREDIT**		**DEBIT**	**CREDIT**
Dec 1	Beginning Balance					34,589.26	
31		CR34	54,197.75			88,787.01	
31		CP57		56,110.68		32,676.33	

Exhibit 5-12
T-Account

CASH IN BANK 101			
2004			
12-1	34,589.26		
12-31	54,197.75	56,110.68	12-31
	32,676.33		

The Journal Entry

For simplicity, we will use only the General Journal in this chapter. Proper general journal entries contain the pertinent details of the transaction in an easy-to-read format. Exhibit 5-13 illustrates a general journal page containing a journal entry.

The journal entry provides us with the following information:

1 the date of the transaction;
2 the accounts affected by the transaction;
3 a description of the transaction with any important details; and
4 the amounts of the debit or credit to each account.

What Do You Think?

5-4   From the entry made into the General Journal in Exhibit 5-13, describe what happened in this transaction.

5-5   Where will this entry be posted in the General Ledger?

5-6   Can each journal entry have only one debit and one credit?

Notice that the debit equals the credit. Some transactions affect more than two accounts, such as when a manager buys office supplies and furniture at the same time and pays for them with one check. Both office supplies and equipment increase and cash decreases. Journal entries with more than two accounts listed are called **compound journal entries**. Regardless of the number of accounts, the total debits must equal the total credits for each transaction, or the system will be out of balance. Now that we know what to do and how to do it, we can apply the accounting cycle to actual transactions.

● **compound journal entries**
Journal entries with more than two accounts listed.

Exhibit 5-13
The General Journal

GENERAL JOURNAL				PAGE	423
DATE 2003		DESCRIPTION	POST REF.	DEBIT	CREDIT
Jan	24	Accounts Receivable	110	23,425.00	
		Sales	401		23,425.00
		To record the sale of 1500 units to			
		John George, Inc. Terms 2/10, n 30			

Accounting Cycle Application

To illustrate the accounting cycle, we will examine the transactions for the first month of operations for Elevation Sports during June 2003 listed in Exhibit 5-14. Read Exhibit 5-14 before you proceed. Note that each transaction is numbered for easy reference.

We will walk through the first two steps of the accounting cycle, analyzing and journalizing transactions, using these transactions.

Exhibit 5-14
Elevation Sports, Inc. Summary of June 2003 Transactions

		Elevation Sports, Inc. Summary of June 2003 Transactions
1.	June 1	Each of the four officers contributed $25,000 to receive 1,000 shares of $10 par value stock.
2.	1	Paid attorney Howard Schmidt $2,000 for preparing and filing the articles of incorporation and by-laws, and drafting other legal documents.
3.	1	Paid the city of Vail $10,000 for the first year's rent of $20,000, less the first six months free, and signed a five-year lease.
4.	1	Paid Vail National Bank $15,000 down to acquire the manufacturing equipment. The total purchase price is $75,000, and the company must pay interest at 10% each year plus another $15,000 in principal.
5.	1	Paid General Insurance Agency $5,000 for the first year's insurance premium; $3,000 represents corporate liability insurance and $2,000 covers property insurance for the plant and sales outlet. The agency will bill the company quarterly for additional product liability insurance at $1.00 per snowboard produced.
6.	2	Paid Dell $5,000 for the computer equipment. Of this amount, $2,000 of the cost was for manufacturing purposes and the remainder for general administrative use.
7.	2	Paid Mountain Cable $500 to register a secured Web site and domain name. Also paid $300 installation for high-speed cable modem access and the first month's Internet service.
8.	5	Paid High Country Office Supply a $2,000 down payment for furniture and fixtures. The total bill was $23,100: administrative furniture, $2,100; selling fixtures, $8,400; and factory furniture and fixtures, $12,600. Elevation Sports will pay $880 per month for 24 months.
9.	6	Ordered $1,800 of materials and supplies for production from Specialty Wood Source.
10.	6	Paid cash to High Country Office Supply for $350 office supplies and $650 drafting supplies.
11.	7	Ordered $3,500 of bindings and miscellaneous parts from National Ski Supply. Of these parts, $1,200 will be for sale in the shop and the remainder will go on the snowboards.
12.	9	Received the order from Specialty Wood Source, shipped FOB shipping, terms 2/10, net 30 days. The invoice dated June 8 included $75 of freight charges.
13.	10	Received the order from National Ski Supply, shipped FOB destination, terms net 30 days.
14.	10	Requisitioned $1,100 of raw materials for production.
15.	16	A salesperson from Nordic Ski Wear delivered $3,100 of summer ski apparel, goggles, sunglasses, and other miscellaneous items to stock the retail shop. He left an invoice with terms net 60 days.
16.	17	Paid the Specialty Wood Source invoice, less discount.
17.	23	Paid the *Vail Daily News* $65 for an ad to announce the opening of the retail shop on the 25th and paid $184 for refreshments for the grand opening.
18.	30	Paid $4,000 salaries to the officers less taxes of $800. Paid $1,000 in labor costs for the plant less taxes of $200.
19.	30	Sold 35 snowboards. Retail sales were $3,375 for 25 boards plus sales tax of $270. Wholesale sales were $900 for 10 boards. Retail sales of other merchandise was $1,840 plus sales tax of $92. Retail sales were all for cash and wholesale sales were on terms of 2/10, net 30 days.
20.	30	Received Colorado Power and Light bill for $654 due on July 20. The allocation was $25 for administrative offices, $153 for the retail space, and $476 for the factory, and received the telephone bill from Mountain Bell due by July 20. Shop phone was $85; administrative offices, $160; and factory phones, $235.
21.	30	Paid attorney Howard Schmidt a $6,000 retainer to secure the copyrights and patents. He estimates that $5,000 is for the patent, $400 for copyrights, and $600 for trademark registration.
22.	30	Received cash payment for half the wholesale sales less the discount.

Steps 1 and 2: Analyzing and Journalizing Transactions

● **posting reference column**
A column in the general journal that contains a reference to the general ledger account number affected by each transaction.

Before we begin to write transactions in the general journal, take time to examine the annotated chart of accounts for Elevation Sports contained in the Appendix. We will refer to those account numbers and descriptions as we make the journal entries. The **posting reference column** in the general journal contains a reference to the general ledger account number affected by each transaction. Journal entries for transactions 1 through 6 are illustrated in Exhibit 5-15.

Exhibit 5-15
Journalizing Transactions 1 through 6

	DATE 2003		DESCRIPTION	POST REF.	DEBIT	CREDIT
ELEVATION SPORTS, INC. **GENERAL JOURNAL** — PAGE 1						
#1	Jun	1	Cash in Bank	101	100,000	
			Common Stock	310		40,000
			Paid-in Capital – Common Stock	311		60,000
			To record issuance of 4,000 shares of $10 par			
			value common stock.			
#2			Legal Expense	730	2,000	
			Cash in Bank	101		2,000
			To record payment for incorporation.			
#3			Prepaid Rent	140	10,000	
			Cash in Bank	101		10,000
			To record prepayment of rent for first year.			
#4			Production Equipment	158	75,000	
			Cash in Bank	101		15,000
			Note Payable—Vail National Bank	250		60,000
			To record purchase of equipment with annual			
			payments of $15,000 each plus 10% interest.			
#5			Prepaid Insurance	141	5,000	
			Cash in Bank	101		5,000
			To record payment of annual insurance.			
#6		2	Production Equipment	158	2,000	
			Administrative Equipment and Furniture	154	3,000	
			Cash in Bank	101		5,000
			To record purchase of computer equipment.			

1   The officers contributed a total of $100,000 cash for 4,000 shares of common stock with a par value of $10 per share. Cash increased $100,000, Common Stock increased $40,000 (4,000 × $10), and Paid-in Capital—Common Stock increased $60,000, the amount paid for the stock in excess of par value. Debit Cash in Bank (#101) $100,000, credit Common Stock (#310) $40,000, and credit Paid-in Capital—Common Stock (#311) $60,000 to increase the asset and equity accounts.

2   The attorney fees for incorporation increase Legal Fees and decrease Cash. Debit Legal Expense (#730) and credit Cash in Bank (#101).

3   The first year's reduced rent on the five-year lease was paid in advance, thus creating a deferred asset. Debit Prepaid Rent (#140) and credit Cash in Bank (#101) $10,000.

4   The officers purchased the equipment from the Vail National Bank making a $15,000 down payment and signing a note for $60,000. This creates a Production Equipment increase, a Note Payable increase, and a decrease in Cash. Debit Production Equipment (#158) for the whole $75,000, and credit Cash in Bank (#101) for $15,000 and the Note Payable—Vail National Bank (#250) for $60,000.

5   Insurance policies are normally paid in advance, requiring deferral of the expense until the insurance expires. Increase (debit) the deferred asset, Prepaid Insurance (#141), and decrease (credit) Cash in Bank (#101) $5,000.

6   The computer equipment serves both manufacturing and administration. Separate the cost between Production Equipment and Administrative Equipment and Furniture. Debit Production Equipment (#158) $2,000 and Administrative Equipment and Furniture (#154) $3,000; credit Cash in Bank (#101) $5,000.

Transactions 7 through 13 are illustrated in Exhibit 5-16.

7   All charges for Internet services and Web site registration increase the Internet Expense. Debit Internet Expense (#640) $500 and credit Cash in Bank (#101) $500. Another company might wish to separate Internet service charges and Web site expense. The number of expense accounts depends on the kind of information the company wishes to capture.

8   Furniture and fixture purchases are separated into the areas in which they will be used as we discussed in Chapter 4. The cash down payment reduces Cash in Bank and the remainder increases Other Accounts Payable. Debit each long-lived asset account: Administrative Furniture and Fixtures (#154) $2,100, Sales Furniture and Fixtures (#156) $8,400, and Production Equipment (#158) $12,600. Credit Cash in Bank (#101) $2,000 and Other Accounts Payable (#205) $21,100.

9   Ordering raw materials, or any other asset, does not change any accounting element; therefore, no transaction occurs and an entry to the General Journal is not appropriate. Although you might think that this creates a liability, it does not because an entity does not have an obligation to pay for the order until the seller performs by shipping or delivering the merchandise. At the point the seller can recognize revenue according to the revenue recognition principle, a transaction takes place.

10 Purchase of supplies increases a Supplies Inventory account until used. As the supplies are used, the cost is transferred to the Office Supply Expense for office supplies used or to Work-in-Process for production supplies used. Debit Supplies Inventory (#134) and credit Cash in Bank (#101) $1,000.

11 Ordered items are not transactions as explained in transaction 9.

12 To understand the transactions involving wholesale purchases and sales, let's look at cash discounts and freight terms.

Cash Discounts and Freight Terms

Two issues arise for firms that purchase merchandise inventory—freight costs and cash discounts. Buying agents pay particular attention to these because careful negotiations of freight and payment terms can decrease the cost of purchasing merchandise.

Exhibit 5-16
Journalizing Transactions 7 Through 13

	DATE 2003		DESCRIPTION	POST REF.	DEBIT	CREDIT
#7	Jun	2	Internet Expenses	640	500	
			Cash in Bank	101		500
			To record cost of Internet service and Web site.			
#8		5	Administrative Equipment and Furniture	154	2,100	
			Selling Furniture and Fixtures	156	8,400	
			Production Equipment	158	12,600	
			Cash in Bank	101		2,000
			Other Accounts Payable	205		21,100
			To record purchase of furniture and			
			equipment. Balance to be paid in 24 monthly payments.			
#10		6	Supplies Inventory	134	1,000	
			Cash in Bank	101		1,000
			To record purchase of drafting and office			
			supplies.			
#12		9	Raw Materials Inventory	131	1,875	
			Accounts Payable	201		1,875
			To record purchase of raw materials from			
			Specialty Wood Source, terms 2/10, net			
			30 days.			
#13		10	Raw Materials Inventory	131	2,300	
			Merchandise Inventory	130	1,200	
			Accounts Payable	201		3,00
			To record purchase from National Ski			
			Supply, terms net 30 days.			

Cash Discounts. A firm frequently encourages its customers to pay invoices quickly, which improves the firm's cash flow, by offering a cash discount. The following represent commonly used payment terms and their meaning:

1 **2/10, net 30 days**—A 2 percent discount is allowed if payment is made within 10 days of the invoice date; otherwise, payment is due 30 days after the invoice date.

2 **Net 30 days**—The net amount is due 30 days after the invoice date with no cash discount offered.

3 **1/10, EOM, net 60 days**—A 1 percent discount is allowed if paid within 10 days after the end of the month (EOM); otherwise payment is due 60 days from the invoice date.

Return to transactions 9 and 12. If the purchase on June 8 has terms of 2/10, net 30, Elevation Sports would pay the invoice by June 18 to receive a 2 percent discount. Payment required by June 18 would be 98% of $1,800 or $1,764. (No discount is allowed on the shipping charges of $75.) The discount of $36 reduces the purchase cost to Elevation Sports, which is why good cash managers take advantage of cash discounts.

What Do You Think?

5-7   When would payment be due by Elevation Sports if the terms were net 30 days? 1/10 EOM, net 60 days?

5-8   What is the annual percentage rate of a 2 percent discount for payment in 10 days instead of 30 days?

Freight Terms. Freight terms define the point at which ownership of the goods, or title, passes between the seller and the purchaser. The **FOB point**, an old shipping term meaning free on board, defines the point where title passes and the purchase/sales transaction legally occurs. FOB shipping point indicates that the title passes when the merchandise leaves the seller's shipping dock. FOB destination indicates that the title passes when the merchandise arrives at the purchaser's loading dock. Transportation costs also transfer to the buyer when title passes at the FOB point. Therefore, if the terms are FOB shipping point, title passes at the sellers dock and the buyer bears the freight expense. If the terms are FOB destination, the seller owns the goods until delivery and bears the freight expense.

● **FOB point**
An old shipping term meaning free on board, which defines the point where title passes and the purchase/sales transaction legally occurs.

Returning to transaction 12, because the freight terms are FOB shipping point, the freight expense becomes part of the acquisition cost of the raw materials. Debit Raw Materials Inventory (#131) and credit Accounts Payable (#201) $1,875.

We now move on to the remaining transactions.

13 The National Ski Supply order included both raw materials for $2,300 and merchandise for resale for $1,200. Freight charges are the expense of the seller because the terms are FOB destination. Debit Raw Materials Inventory (#131) $2,300 and Merchandise Inventory (#130) $1,200, and credit Accounts Payable (#201) $3,500.

Transactions 14 through 19 are illustrated in Exhibit 5-17.

14 When the production department needs raw materials, the manager prepares a requisition for the needed items. This causes the personnel in charge of raw materials to physically transfer the requested items to the production floor. The cost of those items increases the Work-in-Process Inventory account and decreases Raw Materials Inventory. Debit Work-in-Process Inventory (#132) $1,100 and credit Raw Materials Inventory (#131) $1,100.

15 The delivery of merchandise by the Nordic Ski Wear salesperson increases the Merchandise Inventory and Accounts Payable. Because it was delivered, no freight expense is incurred. This invoice does not offer a cash discount. Debit Merchandise Inventory (#130) $3,100 and credit Accounts Payable (#201) $3,100.

16 Accounts Payable must be decreased by the amount of the invoice, $1,875. Cash will decrease by the payment amount calculated in the discussion of cash discounts, $1,839. The discount reduces the cost of the purchase recorded in transaction 12 by $36. Because the cost was recorded in Raw Materials

Exhibit 5-17
Journalizing Transactions 14 Through 19

	DATE 2003		DESCRIPTION	POST REF.	DEBIT	CREDIT
#14	Jun	10	Work-in-Process Inventory	132	1,100	
			Raw Materials Inventory	131		1,100
			To record transfer of materials to			
			production.			
#15		16	Merchandise Inventory	130	3,100	
			Accounts Payable	201		3,100
			To record purchase from Nordic Ski Wear			
			terms: net 60 days.			
#16		17	Accounts Payable	201	1,875	
			Cash in Bank	101		1,839
			Raw Materials Inventory	131		36
			To record payment of invoice less 2%			
			discount on $1,800.			
#17		23	Advertising Expense	600	249	
			Cash in Bank	101		249
			To record cost of ad and refreshments for			
			the grand opening.			
#18		30	Officers' Salaries Expense	740	4,000	
			Work-in-Process Inventory	132	1,000	
			Cash in Bank	101		4,000
			Payroll Taxes Payable	212		1,000
			To record payment of salaries and wages.			
#19			Cash in Bank	101	5,577	
			Accounts Receivable	110	900	
			Retail Sales—Snowboards	401		3,375
			Wholesale Sales—Snowboards	405		900
			Retail Sales—Other	410		1,840
			Sales Tax Payable	213		362
			To record payment of salaries and			
			wages.			

Table heading: ELEVATION SPORTS, INC. GENERAL JOURNAL — PAGE 3

Inventory, decrease it by the cash discount. Debit Accounts Payable (#201) $1,875, credit Cash in Bank (#101) $1,839, and credit Raw Materials Inventory (#131) $36.

17 Advertising costs normally are expensed when the advertising appears in the media. The ad ran in the paper on this date. Refreshments for a grand opening party can be considered advertising or promotion expense. We will use the advertising expense account for this item. Debit Advertising Expense (#600) and credit Cash in Bank (#101) $249.

18 Payment of salaries increases the appropriate salary expense and the withholding taxes decrease the amount of cash paid. Because the taxes withheld from the employee must be paid to the various government agencies, they represent a liability to the company. The gross salary amounts must be separated into the correct account. Officers' salaries increase Officers' Salaries Expense and the wages for direct labor costs increase the Work-in-Process Inventory account. Debit Officers' Salaries Expense (#740) $4,000 for the gross salaries, debit Work-in-Process Inventory (#132) $1,000 for gross wages, credit Payroll Taxes Payable (#212) $1,000 for combined withholdings, and credit Cash in Bank (#101) $4,000 for the total amount paid to employees.

19 Sales for the month will be separated into three categories for Elevation Sports: retail sales and wholesale sales of snowboards, and sales of other retail items. Retail sales are all cash or credit cards. Credit cards are deposited to the bank account much like checks and the credit card companies will decrease the bank account by a direct withdrawal for their charges once each month. Wholesale sales increase Accounts Receivable. The company also collects sales tax for the state of Colorado on retail sales. Sales taxes collected are held in trust for the state and are a liability to the company. The company will remit these funds to the state after month end. Debit Cash in Bank (#101) for the total of the retail sales and sales tax $5,577 ($3,375 + $1,840 + $362); debit Accounts Receivable (#101) $900; credit Retail Sales—Snowboards (#401) $3,375; credit Wholesale Sales—Snowboards (#405) $900; credit Retail Sales—Other (#410) $1,840; and credit Sales Tax Payable (#213) $362.

Transactions 20 through 22 are shown in Exhibit 5-18.

20 Utilities and telephone, like other expenses for Elevation Sports, must be divided among production, selling, and administrative costs. These bills will be paid in July but reflect expenses of June, so we will record the expense in the month of June. Debit Utilities Expense—Sales (#690) $153, Utilities Expense—Administrative (#790) $25, and Work-in-Process Inventory (#132) $476 for the production costs. Telephone expense will be handled much like the utilities. Debit Telephone Expense—Sales (#680) $85, Telephone Expense—Administrative (#680) $160, and Work-in-Process Inventory (#132) for the production cost $235. Credit Other Accounts Payable (#205) for the total $1,134.

21 The cost of intangible assets will be capitalized as assets to be amortized over the useful life of asset. Even though the amounts on the lawyer's bill are estimated, they are recorded as the asset amounts until the final bill is received. Debit Patents (#180) $5,000, Copyrights (#185) $400, and Trademarks (#190) $600; credit Cash in Bank (#101) $6,000.

22 One-half the accounts receivable for wholesale sales is $450. The terms allowed the customers to take a 2 percent discount for payment within 10 days. The discount amount increases the Sales Discounts account. The 2 percent discount is $9 ($450 × .02). Debit Cash in Bank (#101) $441 and Sales Discounts (#420) $9, and credit Accounts Receivable (#110) $450.

Assuming that these transactions represent all transactions for June, we can now post them to the general ledger in Step 3.

Exhibit 5-18
Journalizing Transactions 20 Through 22

	DATE 2003		DESCRIPTION	POST REF.	DEBIT	CREDIT
#20	Jun	30	Utilities Expense—Sales	690	153	
			Utilities Expense—Administrative	790	25	
			Work-in-Process Inventory	132	476	
			Telephone Expense—Sales	680	85	
			Telephone Expense—Administrative	780	160	
			Work-in-Process Inventory	132	235	
			Other Accounts Payable	205		1,134
			To record electric and telephone bills			
			for June, due July 20.			
#21			Patents	180	5,000	
			Copyrights	185	400	
			Trademarks	190	600	
			Cash in Bank	101		6,000
			To record estimated legal costs.			
#22			Cash in Bank	101	441	
			Sales Discounts	420	9	
			Accounts Receivable	110		450
			To record receipt of accounts receivable			
			less discount.			

The table header reads: **ELEVATION SPORTS, INC. GENERAL JOURNAL   PAGE 4**

Step 3: Posting to the General Ledger

Although time consuming, the posting process presents no serious challenge. Posting requires attention to detail in the following procedures:

1 Post to the general ledger each entry in the order that it appears in the general journal.
2 Record the date as the same date as the entry in the general journal.
3 There is no need to write any description unless you wish to indicate a special notation.
4 For the posting reference on the general ledger, use the page number of the journal page, such as GJ1 or GJ2, for General Journal pages 1 and 2.
5 Record the amount of the entry in the correct debit or credit column.

Exhibit 5-19
Posting Transactions 1 and 2 to the General Ledger

ACCOUNT NAME	Cash in Bank				ACCOUNT NUMBER		101
DATE		POST			BALANCE		
2003	DESCRIPTION	REF.	DEBIT	CREDIT	DEBIT	CREDIT	
Jun 1		GJ 1	100,000		100,000		
		GJ 1		2,000	98,000		

ACCOUNT NAME	Common Stock				ACCOUNT NUMBER		310
DATE		POST			BALANCE		
2003	DESCRIPTION	REF.	DEBIT	CREDIT	DEBIT	CREDIT	
Jun 1		GJ 1		40,000		40,000	

ACCOUNT NAME	Paid-in Capital—Common Stock				ACCOUNT NUMBER		311
DATE		POST			BALANCE		
2003	DESCRIPTION	REF.	DEBIT	CREDIT	DEBIT	CREDIT	
Jun 1		GJ 1		60,000		60,000	

ACCOUNT NAME	Legal Expense				ACCOUNT NUMBER		730
DATE		POST			BALANCE		
2003	DESCRIPTION	REF.	DEBIT	CREDIT	DEBIT	CREDIT	
Jun 1		GJ 1	2,000		2,000		

Exhibit 5-19 shows the postings of the first two general journal entries. Exhibit 5-20 presents the general ledger accounts for each account that has a balance after the monthly transactions were posted.

Step 4: Preparing the Trial Balance

To prepare the trial balance, simply list in order each general ledger account and its account balance. Put each debit balance in the debit column and each credit balance in the credit column. Total each column and verify that the total debits equal the total credits. The trial balance for Elevation Sports at June 30, 2003, appears in Exhibit 5-21 on page 159. Because the debits equal the credits in the trial balance, our general ledger balances.

What Do You Think?

5-9 If the debits equal the credits, does this mean that the general ledger is correct? If not, what might be wrong?

5-10 If the debits do not equal the credits, what are the most likely causes of the imbalance?

Exhibit 5-20
General Ledger at June 30, 2003

ACCOUNT NAME	Cash in Bank				ACCOUNT NUMBER	101
DATE		**POST**			**BALANCE**	
2003	**DESCRIPTION**	**REF.**	**DEBIT**	**CREDIT**	**DEBIT**	**CREDIT**
Jun 1		GJ 1	100,000		100,000	
		GJ 1		2,000	98,000	
		GJ 1		10,000	88,000	
		GJ 1		15,000	73,000	
		GJ 1		5,000	68,000	
2		GJ 1		5,000	63,000	
		GJ 1		500	62,500	
5		GJ 1		2,000	60,500	
6		GJ 1		1,000	59,500	
19		GJ 1		1,839	57,661	
23		GJ 1		249	57,412	
30		GJ 1		4,000	53,412	
		GJ 1	5,577		58,989	
		GJ 1		6,000	52,989	
		GJ 1	441		53,430	

ACCOUNT NAME	Accounts Receivable				ACCOUNT NUMBER	110
DATE		**POST**			**BALANCE**	
2003	**DESCRIPTION**	**REF.**	**DEBIT**	**CREDIT**	**DEBIT**	**CREDIT**
Jun 30		GJ 3	900		900	
		GJ 4		450	450	

ACCOUNT NAME	Merchandise Inventory				ACCOUNT NUMBER	130
DATE		**POST**			**BALANCE**	
2003	**DESCRIPTION**	**REF.**	**DEBIT**	**CREDIT**	**DEBIT**	**CREDIT**
Jun 10		GJ 2	1,200		1,200	
16		GJ 3	3,100		4,300	

Exhibit 5-20 *continued*

ACCOUNT NAME	Raw Materials Inventory				ACCOUNT NUMBER	131
DATE		**POST**			**BALANCE**	
2003	**DESCRIPTION**	**REF.**	**DEBIT**	**CREDIT**	**DEBIT**	**CREDIT**
Jun 9		GJ 2	1,875		1,875	
10		GJ 2	2,300		4,175	
		GJ 3		1,100	3,075	
19		GJ 3		36	3,039	

ACCOUNT NAME	Work-in-Process Inventory				ACCOUNT NUMBER	132
DATE		**POST**			**BALANCE**	
2003	**DESCRIPTION**	**REF.**	**DEBIT**	**CREDIT**	**DEBIT**	**CREDIT**
Jun 10	Raw Materials	GJ 3	1,100		1,100	
30	Direct Labor	GJ 3	1,000		2,100	
	Utilities & Telephone	GJ 4	711		2,811	

ACCOUNT NAME	Office Supplies Inventory				ACCOUNT NUMBER	134
DATE		**POST**			**BALANCE**	
2003	**DESCRIPTION**	**REF.**	**DEBIT**	**CREDIT**	**DEBIT**	**CREDIT**
Jun 6		GJ 2	1,000		1,000	

ACCOUNT NAME	Prepaid Rent				ACCOUNT NUMBER	140
DATE		**POST**			**BALANCE**	
2003	**DESCRIPTION**	**REF.**	**DEBIT**	**CREDIT**	**DEBIT**	**CREDIT**
Jun 1		GJ 1	10,000		10,000	

ACCOUNT NAME	Prepaid Insurance				ACCOUNT NUMBER	141
DATE		**POST**			**BALANCE**	
2003	**DESCRIPTION**	**REF.**	**DEBIT**	**CREDIT**	**DEBIT**	**CREDIT**
Jun 1		GJ 1	5,000		5,000	

continued

Exhibit 5-20 *continued*

ACCOUNT NAME	Administrative Equipment and Furniture				ACCOUNT NUMBER	154
DATE		**POST**			**BALANCE**	
2003	**DESCRIPTION**	**REF.**	**DEBIT**	**CREDIT**	**DEBIT**	**CREDIT**
Jun 2		GJ 1	3,000		3,000	
5		GJ 2	2,100		5,100	

ACCOUNT NAME	Selling Furniture and Fixtures				ACCOUNT NUMBER	156
DATE		**POST**			**BALANCE**	
2003	**DESCRIPTION**	**REF.**	**DEBIT**	**CREDIT**	**DEBIT**	**CREDIT**
Jun 5		GJ 2	8,400		8,400	

ACCOUNT NAME	Production Equipment				ACCOUNT NUMBER	158
DATE		**POST**			**BALANCE**	
2003	**DESCRIPTION**	**REF.**	**DEBIT**	**CREDIT**	**DEBIT**	**CREDIT**
Jun 1		GJ 1	75,000		75,000	
2		GJ 1	2,000		77,000	
5		GJ 2	12,600		89,600	

ACCOUNT NAME	Patents				ACCOUNT NUMBER	180
DATE		**POST**			**BALANCE**	
2003	**DESCRIPTION**	**REF.**	**DEBIT**	**CREDIT**	**DEBIT**	**CREDIT**
Jun 30		GJ 4	5,000		5,000	

ACCOUNT NAME	Copyrights				ACCOUNT NUMBER	185
DATE		**POST**			**BALANCE**	
2003	**DESCRIPTION**	**REF.**	**DEBIT**	**CREDIT**	**DEBIT**	**CREDIT**
Jun 30		GJ 4	400		400	

Exhibit 5-20 *continued*

ACCOUNT NAME	Trademarks				ACCOUNT NUMBER	190	
DATE		POST				BALANCE	
2003	DESCRIPTION	REF.	DEBIT	CREDIT	DEBIT	CREDIT	
Jun 30		GJ 4	600		600		

ACCOUNT NAME	Accounts Payable				ACCOUNT NUMBER	201	
DATE		POST				BALANCE	
2003	DESCRIPTION	REF.	DEBIT	CREDIT	DEBIT	CREDIT	
Jun 6		GJ 2		1,875		1,875	
10		GJ 2		3,500		5,375	
16		GJ 3		3,100		8,475	
17		GJ 3	1,875			6,600	

ACCOUNT NAME	Other Accounts Payable				ACCOUNT NUMBER	205	
DATE		POST				BALANCE	
2003	DESCRIPTION	REF.	DEBIT	CREDIT	DEBIT	CREDIT	
Jun 5		GJ 2		21,100		21,100	
30		GJ 4		1,134		22,234	

ACCOUNT NAME	Payroll Taxes Payable				ACCOUNT NUMBER	212	
DATE		POST				BALANCE	
2003	DESCRIPTION	REF.	DEBIT	CREDIT	DEBIT	CREDIT	
Jun 30		GJ 3		1,000		1,000	

ACCOUNT NAME	Sales Tax Payable				ACCOUNT NUMBER	213	
DATE		POST				BALANCE	
2003	DESCRIPTION	REF.	DEBIT	CREDIT	DEBIT	CREDIT	
Jun 30		GJ 3		362		362	

continued

Exhibit 5-20 *continued*

ACCOUNT NAME	Note Payable—Vail National Bank				ACCOUNT NUMBER	250
DATE		**POST**			**BALANCE**	
2003	**DESCRIPTION**	**REF.**	**DEBIT**	**CREDIT**	**DEBIT**	**CREDIT**
Jun 1		GJ 1		60,000		60,000

ACCOUNT NAME	Common Stock				ACCOUNT NUMBER	310
DATE		**POST**			**BALANCE**	
2003	**DESCRIPTION**	**REF.**	**DEBIT**	**CREDIT**	**DEBIT**	**CREDIT**
Jun 1		GJ 1		40,000		40,000

ACCOUNT NAME	Paid-in Capital—Common Stock				ACCOUNT NUMBER	311
DATE		**POST**			**BALANCE**	
2003	**DESCRIPTION**	**REF.**	**DEBIT**	**CREDIT**	**DEBIT**	**CREDIT**
Jun 1		GJ 1		60,000		60,000

ACCOUNT NAME	Retail Sales—Snowboards				ACCOUNT NUMBER	401
DATE		**POST**			**BALANCE**	
2003	**DESCRIPTION**	**REF.**	**DEBIT**	**CREDIT**	**DEBIT**	**CREDIT**
Jun 30		GJ 3		3,375		3,375

ACCOUNT NAME	Wholesale Sales—Snowboards				ACCOUNT NUMBER	405
DATE		**POST**			**BALANCE**	
2003	**DESCRIPTION**	**REF.**	**DEBIT**	**CREDIT**	**DEBIT**	**CREDIT**
Jun 30		GJ 3		900		900

Exhibit 5-20 *continued*

ACCOUNT NAME	Retail Sales—Other				ACCOUNT NUMBER	410
DATE		**POST**			**BALANCE**	
2003	**DESCRIPTION**	**REF.**	**DEBIT**	**CREDIT**	**DEBIT**	**CREDIT**
Jun 30		GJ 3		1,840		1,840

ACCOUNT NAME	Sales Discounts				ACCOUNT NUMBER	420
DATE		**POST**			**BALANCE**	
2003	**DESCRIPTION**	**REF.**	**DEBIT**	**CREDIT**	**DEBIT**	**CREDIT**
Jun 30		GJ 3	9		9	

ACCOUNT NAME	Advertising Expense				ACCOUNT NUMBER	600
DATE		**POST**			**BALANCE**	
2003	**DESCRIPTION**	**REF.**	**DEBIT**	**CREDIT**	**DEBIT**	**CREDIT**
Jun 23		GJ 3	249		249	

ACCOUNT NAME	Internet Expenses				ACCOUNT NUMBER	640
DATE		**POST**			**BALANCE**	
2003	**DESCRIPTION**	**REF.**	**DEBIT**	**CREDIT**	**DEBIT**	**CREDIT**
Jun 2		GJ 2	500		500	

ACCOUNT NAME	Telephone Expense—Sales				ACCOUNT NUMBER	680
DATE		**POST**			**BALANCE**	
2003	**DESCRIPTION**	**REF.**	**DEBIT**	**CREDIT**	**DEBIT**	**CREDIT**
Jun 30		GJ 4	85		85	

continued

Exhibit 5-20 *continued*

ACCOUNT NAME	Utilities Expense—Sales				ACCOUNT NUMBER	690
DATE		**POST**			**BALANCE**	
2003	**DESCRIPTION**	**REF.**	**DEBIT**	**CREDIT**	**DEBIT**	**CREDIT**
Jun 30		GJ 4	153		153	

ACCOUNT NAME	Legal Expense				ACCOUNT NUMBER	730
DATE		**POST**			**BALANCE**	
2003	**DESCRIPTION**	**REF.**	**DEBIT**	**CREDIT**	**DEBIT**	**CREDIT**
Jun 1		GJ 1	2,000		2,000	

ACCOUNT NAME	Officers' Salaries Expense				ACCOUNT NUMBER	740
DATE		**POST**			**BALANCE**	
2003	**DESCRIPTION**	**REF.**	**DEBIT**	**CREDIT**	**DEBIT**	**CREDIT**
Jun 15		GJ 3	4,000		4,000	

ACCOUNT NAME	Telephone Expense—Administrative				ACCOUNT NUMBER	780
DATE		**POST**			**BALANCE**	
2003	**DESCRIPTION**	**REF.**	**DEBIT**	**CREDIT**	**DEBIT**	**CREDIT**
Jun 30		GJ 4	160		160	

ACCOUNT NAME	Utilities Expense—Administrative				ACCOUNT NUMBER	790
DATE		**POST**			**BALANCE**	
2003	**DESCRIPTION**	**REF.**	**DEBIT**	**CREDIT**	**DEBIT**	**CREDIT**
Jun 30		GJ 4	25		25	

A trial balance guarantees only one thing: the debits equal the credits in the system. If the system is in balance, the accounts are more likely recorded correctly than if the system were out of balance. When it does not balance, we know that the system contains errors. Even when in balance, amounts may be incorrectly recorded or wrong accounts may have been used. Accountants look for the integrity of the results when they go through the adjusting process in step 5. We will begin that process and complete the accounting cycle in Chapter 6.

Exhibit 5-21
Trial Balance—Elevation
Sports, Inc. at June 30, 2003

Elevation Sports, Inc.
Trial Balance
June 30, 2003

		DEBIT	CREDIT
101	Cash in Bank	$ 53,430	
110	Accounts Receivable	450	
130	Merchandise Inventory	4,300	
131	Raw Materials Inventory	3,039	
132	Work-in-Process Inventory	2,811	
134	Office Supplies Inventory	1,000	
140	Prepaid Rent	10,000	
141	Prepaid Insurance	5,000	
154	Administrative Equipment and Furniture	5,100	
156	Selling Furniture and Fixtures	8,400	
158	Production Equipment	89,600	
180	Patents	5,000	
185	Copyrights	400	
190	Trademarks	600	
201	Accounts Payable		$ 6,600
205	Other Accounts Payable		22,234
212	Payroll Taxes Payable		1,000
213	Sales Tax Payable		362
250	Note Payable—Vail National Bank		60,000
310	Common Stock		40,000
311	Paid-in Capital—Common Stock		60,000
401	Retail Sales—Snowboards		3,375
405	Wholesale Sales—Snowboards		900
410	Retail Sales—Other		1,840
420	Sales Discounts	9	
600	Advertising Expense	249	
640	Internet Expense	500	
680	Telephone Expense—Sales	85	
690	Utilities Expense—Sales	153	
730	Legal Expense	2,000	
740	Officers' Salaries Expense	4,000	
780	Telephone Expense—Administrative	160	
790	Utilities Expense—Administrative	25	
	Totals	$196,311	$196,311

ANNOTATED CHART OF ACCOUNTS

The following chart of accounts describes each account used by Elevation Sports. Although the chart of accounts is for one company, it illustrates a common group of accounts. Any chart of accounts can be expanded or amended over time to reflect changes in the company structure or business activities.

Account Number	Account Name	Description
	Assets	
	Current Assets	Assets that are likely to be converted to cash or expected to be used within the longer of one year or operating cycle.
100	Petty Cash	Currency and coin on hand.
101	Cash in Bank	Cash in banks available for current use.
110	Accounts Receivable	Amounts due from customers who have acquired goods or services on credit and have agreed to pay within a specified period.
111	Allowance for Doubtful Accounts	Valuation account for accounts receivable to reduce the receivables to an amount assumed to be collectible.
115	Notes Receivable	Amounts due based on a signed written promise to pay.
120	Trading Securities	Investments in marketable stocks and bonds intended to be held for one year or less.
130	Merchandise Inventory	The cost of goods acquired from wholesalers that are ready for sale to customers.
131	Raw Materials Inventory	The cost of materials that will be used in the manufacture of the company's products.
132	Work-in-Process Inventory	The costs of materials, labor, and overhead for goods in the process of being completed and readied for sale.

Account Number	Account Name	Description
133	Finished Goods Inventory	The cost of goods manufactured for resale.
134	Supplies Inventory	Supplies purchased and unused.
140	Prepaid Rent	Amounts paid for rent in advance.
141	Prepaid Insurance	Amounts paid in advance for insurance coverage.
	Property, Plant, and Equipment	Assets expected to have a useful life longer than one year or operating cycle.
150	Land	Historical cost of land purchased for use in the business.
152	Buildings	Buildings the company owns and uses in the business.
154	Administrative Equipment and Furniture	Equipment and furniture administrative staff uses.
156	Selling Furniture and Fixtures	Furniture and fixtures used in a retail environment.
158	Production Equipment	Equipment and fixtures used in a manufacturing facility.
160	Accumulated Depreciation	The total cost of long-lived assets that have been allocated as expenses to date.
	Intangible Assets	Assets that give the entity contractual rights.
180	Patents	Legal costs to obtain an exclusive right to use a process developed by an entity or the purchase price of buying a patent from a patent holder.
185	Copyrights	Legal costs to obtain an exclusive right to reproduce artwork, written works, or music developed by an entity or the purchase price of buying a copyright.
190	Trademarks	Legal costs to obtain an exclusive right to use a symbol developed by an entity or the purchase price of an existing trademark.
	Current Liabilities	Debts an entity owes that are expected to be satisfied within one year or one operating cycle with cash, goods, or services.
201	Accounts Payable	Amounts owed to supplier for the purchase of raw materials or merchandise for resale on credit that will be satisfied within a specified time.
205	Other Accounts Payable	Amounts owed to creditors other than for raw materials or merchandise inventory.
210	Interest Payable	Interest earned by a creditor but not yet paid.
211	Wages Payable	Amounts earned by employees but not yet paid.
212	Payroll Taxes Payable	Amounts withheld from employees' paychecks for taxes plus the employer's share of payroll taxes.

Account Number	Account Name	Description
213	Sales Tax Payable	Amounts collected from customers for sales taxes but unpaid.
214	Income Taxes Payable	Amount of income taxes owed to IRS or states but unpaid.
220	Notes Payable	Principal amounts borrowed from banks or other creditors that must be repaid within the longer of one year or operating cycle.
	Long-Term Liabilities	Debts owed that are due after one year or operating cycle.
250	Notes Payable	Principal amounts borrowed from banks or other creditors that must be repaid after one year or operating cycle.
260	Bonds Payable	Principal amounts of bonds sold to investors.
	Stockholders' Equity	Amounts that represent the ownership interests of the entity.
300	Preferred Stock	Par value of preferred stock issued to shareholders.
301	Paid-in Capital—Preferred Stock	Amounts paid in excess of par value when preferred stock is originally issued.
310	Common Stock	Par value of common stock issued to shareholders.
311	Paid-in Capital—Common Stock	Amounts paid in excess of par value when common stock is originally issued.
320	Retained Earnings	Total of all earnings of an entity since inception minus all dividends declared.
321	Dividends	Total dividends declared during the current year.
	Revenues	Amount of equity increased by the normal business activities of the business.
401	Retail Sales—Snowboards	Amount of snowboard sales to retail customers.
405	Wholesale Sales—Snowboards	Amount of snowboard sales to wholesale customers.
410	Retail Sales—Other	Amount of sales of goods purchased for resale to retail customers.
415	Sales Returns	Amount of goods customers returned for refund or replacement.
420	Sales Discounts	Cash discounts given to wholesale customers for early payment.
	Cost of Goods Sold	Cost of product sales.
500	Cost of Snowboards Sold	Cost of manufactured goods sold to customers.
510	Cost of Other Goods Sold	Cost of purchased goods sold to customers.
	Selling Expenses	Period expenses to market the entity's products.
600	Advertising	Cost of advertisements placed in the media.
610	Convention Expense	Cost of attending the USSA convention.

Account Number	Account Name	Description
620	Credit Card Merchant Discount Expense	Fees credit card companies charge to a merchant.
630	Depreciation—Selling Fixtures	Depreciation expense for the current period for selling furniture and fixtures.
640	Internet Expenses	Cost of running the Web site and Internet connection.
650	Payroll Taxes— Sales Salaries	Employer's portion of payroll taxes for sales staff.
660	Rent—Retail Space	Cost of renting the retail space.
670	Sales Salaries	Payroll cost of the sales staff.
680	Telephone Expense—Sales	Cost of local and long-distance telephone for the retail shop.
690	Utilities Expense—Sales	Cost of utilities for the retail shop.
	Administrative Expenses	Period costs of running the organization.
700	Amortization of Intangibles	Amortization of patent, copyright, and trademark costs.
705	Bank Service Charges	Cost of using a bank checking account.
710	Depreciation— Administrative Assets	Cost of depreciation for the current period for administrative furniture and fixtures.
715	Doubtful Account Expense	Cost of bad debts anticipated from sales of the current period.
720	Employee Benefits	Cost of health, life, and disability insurance and 401(k) plan for employees.
725	Insurance Expense	Cost of general liability insurance.
730	Legal Expense	Cost of general legal expenses.
740	Officers' Salaries	Cost of corporate officers' salaries.
750	Office Supplies	Cost of office supplies consumed during the current period.
760	Payroll Taxes— Administrative Salaries	Employer's portion of payroll taxes for administrative staff.
770	Rent—Administrative Offices	Rent expense for the administrative offices.
780	Telephone Expense	Cost of local and long-distance services.
790	Utilities Expense	Cost of utilities for administrative offices.
	Other Revenues and Expenses	Increases or decreases in equity from ancillary activities of the entity.
800	Interest Revenue	Interest earned on investments and loaned funds.
810	Interest Expense	Cost of interest on borrowed funds.
820	Dividend Revenue	Dividends earned on investments.
830	Gains and Losses	Gains and losses on the sale of assets.
840	Income Tax Expense	Income tax on net income earned.
900	Income Summary	Account used to close the temporary accounts at year end.

● CHAPTER SUMMARY

The accounting system transforms events and data into valuable accounting information through a sequence of steps repeated each period known as the accounting cycle. The accounting cycle consists of the following steps:

Step 1 Analyzing transactions. Deciding whether a transaction has occurred and then determining the nature of such transaction.

Step 2 Journalizing transactions. Recording transactions into a book of original entry or journal.

Step 3 Posting to the general ledger. Sorting the transactions into the debits and credits for each accounting element and then posting from the journals into the appropriate accounts in the general ledger.

Step 4 Preparing the trial balance (and worksheet). Proving the integrity of the accounting equation by listing all debits and credits to prove that the general ledger and therefore the accounting equation is still in balance. A trial balance should be prepared each time transactions are posted to the general ledger. Worksheets are prepared each time financial statements are prepared.

Step 5 Adjusting the accounts and reconciling the bank statement (see, e.g., page 132). Reviewing the accounts before preparing the financial statements to ensure compliance with the matching principle. Expenses of the period must be properly matched with the revenues they helped to produce. The three basic categories of adjustments used for this purpose are accruals, deferrals, and error corrections. Accrual adjustments of revenues and expenses recognize items that should be included in the income statement period but have not yet been recorded. Deferral adjustments of revenues and expenses postpone the recognition of revenues and expenses even though the cash has been received or paid. A reconciliation of the firm's bank accounts with the cash account in the general ledger is a check on the internal control within the accounting system.

Step 6 Preparing financial statements. Preparing a set of financial statements once the accountant is satisfied that the bank accounts are reconciled and all accounts listed on the trial balance represent fair amounts.

Step 7 Preparing closing entries. Closing the temporary accounts at the end of each fiscal year after the accounts have been adjusted and the financial statements have been audited. The closing process resets the temporary accounts (all revenue, expense, gain, and loss accounts plus the dividend account) to zero and transfers the net income or loss to Retained Earnings. Permanent accounts (asset, liability, and equity accounts, except for dividends) are not closed in this process.

Step 8 Preparing the post-closing trial balance. Providing a check that after all the closing entries are posted, only the balance sheet accounts remain with any balances.

The accounting system bases the accounting cycle on the basic accounting equation and uses the terms debit and credit to indicate the normal balance of the various accounts. A summary of the normal balances of the accounts shows:

Assets	=	Liabilities	+	Owners' Investments	−	Dividends	+	Revenues	−	Expenses
Debit	=	Credit	+	Credit	−	Debit	+	Credit	−	Debit

The normal balance of an account defines the type of entry (debit or credit) that increases the balance in the account. Debits increase assets, expenses, and dividends. Credits increase liabilities, equity, and revenue accounts.

Freight terms determine when the title passes to goods purchased. FOB shipping point indicates that title passes when the goods leave the seller's shipping dock and the purchaser bears the cost of the freight. FOB destination indicates that title passes when the goods arrive at the buyer's loading dock and the seller bears the cost of the freight. Sellers offer cash discounts to customers for early payments. Discounts reduce net sales to the seller and the net cost of the purchase to the buyer.

Visit the Web site *www.prenhall.com/terrell* for additional study help with the Online Study Guide.

REVIEW OF CONCEPTS

A Describe the eight steps in the accounting cycle.

B Distinguish between *debits* and *credits* and explain how they relate to the accounting equation.

C Describe the differences between *an account*, *a journal*, *a ledger*, and *a worksheet*.

D Explain the purpose of a chart of accounts.

E Explain the purposes of the general journal and the special journals.

F Identify and discuss the important elements of a general journal entry.

G Describe how to post general journal entries to the general ledger.

H Discuss the purpose of the trial balance and the worksheet.

I Describe at least four causes of a trial balance failing to balance.

J Explain the difference between *FOB shipping point* and *FOB destination*.

K Discuss why a company should take cash discounts.

APPLICATION EXERCISES

5-11 Define the following terms:
  a. journal
  b. ledger
  c. post-closing trial balance
  d. trial balance
  e. bank reconciliation
  f. worksheet

LO 1
Terminology

5-12 Define the following terms:
  a. journalizing
  b. posting
  c. adjusting
  d. closing

LO 1
The Accounting Cycle

5-13 Indicate whether the normal balance of each account listed below is a debit or credit:
  a. Cash
  b. Accounts Payable
  c. Common Stock
  d. Revenues
  e. Prepaid Insurance
  f. Merchandise Inventory
  g. Rent Expense
  h. Income Tax Expense
  i. Income Taxes Payable
  j. Dividends

LO 2 and 3
Normal Account Balances

LO 3
Permanent or Temporary Accounts

5-14 Examine the following accounts. Indicate whether the type of account is permanent or temporary:
a. Cash
b. Accounts Payable
c. Common Stock
d. Revenues
e. Prepaid Insurance
f. Merchandise Inventory
g. Rent Expense
h. Wages Expense
i. Income Taxes Payable
j. Dividends

LO 3
Normal Account Balances

5-15 Indicate whether the normal balance of each account listed below is a debit or credit.
a. Accounts Receivable
b. Notes Payable
c. Preferred Stock
d. Sales
e. Prepaid Rent
f. Raw Materials Inventory
g. Insurance Expense
h. Wages Expense
i. Wages Payable
j. Retained Earnings

LO 3
Permanent or Temporary Accounts

5-16 Examine the following accounts. Indicate whether the type of account is permanent or temporary:
a. Accounts Receivable
b. Notes Payable
c. Preferred Stock
d. Sales
e. Prepaid Rent
f. Raw Materials Inventory
g. Insurance Expense
h. Wages Expense
i. Wages Payable
j. Retained Earnings

LO 3
Normal Account Balances

5-17 Indicate whether the normal balance of each account listed below is a debit or credit.
a. Patents
b. Advertising Expense
c. Accumulated Depreciation
d. Depreciation Expense
e. Rent Revenue
f. Automotive Equipment
g. Utilities Payable
h. Truck Expense
i. Gasoline Expense
j. Interest Receivable

LO 4
Account Classification

5-18 Classify each of the accounts listed below according to the following categories:
Asset
Liability
Revenue
Expense
Equity

a. Patents
b. Advertising Expense
c. Retained Earnings
d. Depreciation Expense
e. Rent Revenue
f. Automotive Equipment
g. Accounts Payable
h. Repairs Expense
i. Telephone Expense
j. Common Stock

5-19 Classify each of the accounts listed below according to the following categories:

LO 4
Account
Classification

   Asset
   Liability
   Revenue
   Expense
   Equity

a. Cash
b. Accounts Receivable
c. Common Stock
d. Sales
e. Prepaid Insurance
f. Work-in-Process Inventory
g. Warranty Expense
h. Insurance Expense
i. Income Taxes Payable
j. Preferred Stock

5-20 Classify each of the accounts listed below according to the following categories:

LO 4
Account
Classification

   Asset
   Liability
   Revenue
   Expense
   Equity

a. Copyrights
b. Bonds Payable
c. Dividends
d. Prepaid Insurance
e. Gain on Sale
f. Finished Goods Inventory
g. Internet Expense
h. Salaries Expense
i. Interest Payable
j. Paid-in Capital—Common Stock

5-21 On May 1, Ben Stout started a computer repair business, Stout's Computers, Inc. Stout opened a bank account for the business by depositing $7,000 for which he received 7,000 shares of no-par common stock. He paid two months rent in advance totaling $400. On May 3, Stout purchased computer repair supplies for $700 and three computers at a total cost of $4,500. He hired a student, agreeing to pay the student $1,000 per month, which he paid $500 on May 15 and $500 on May 31. On May 25, Stout paid $200 for a newspaper advertisement to announce the opening of the business. Stout earned $3,500 in fees in July, of which he collected $2,800 in cash.

LO 4, 5, 6, and 8
Transaction Analysis

Required:

   a. Prepare a chart of accounts for Stout's Computers, Inc.

   b. Prepare the journal entries for Stout's transactions.

   c. Post the transactions to the general ledger.

   d. Prepare a trial balance after completing the posting process.

LO 4, 5, 6, and 8
Transaction Analysis—Service Company

5-22   On July 1, Kelly Taylor began the Taylor Travel Agency, Inc. and paid $10,000 for 1,000 shares of no-par common stock. She paid $500 for one month's rent. On July 5, she purchased office supplies for $700 and three desks at a total cost of $1,500. Taylor hired a travel consultant, agreeing to pay her $20 per hour. The consultant worked 100 hours in July, which Taylor will pay on August 1. Taylor paid $100 on July 29 for a newspaper advertisement to announce the opening of the business. Taylor booked a cruise for her first customer and received a check from the cruise line for $800 on July 22. On July 31, she borrowed $12,000 from the bank for two years at 9%.

Required:

   a. Prepare a chart of accounts for the Taylor Travel Agency, Inc.

   b. Prepare the journal entries for the company's transactions.

   c. Post the transactions to the general ledger.

   d. Prepare a trial balance after completing the posting process.

LO 4, 5, 6, and 8
Recording Transactions— Service Company

5-23   On December 1, 2003, Tricia Braswell, CPA, incorporated her new professional practice. She paid $5,000 to the corporation for 500 shares of $10 par value common stock. She paid office rent for three months in advance, totaling $900. On December 2, she purchased a desk for cash of $500 and bought $1,200 worth of office supplies on account. Braswell also borrowed $1,500 from the First State Bank for three years at 6% to purchase computer equipment from a local dealer.

Required:

   a. Prepare a chart of accounts for Tricia Braswell, CPA.

   b. Prepare the journal entries for Braswell's transactions.

   c. Post the transactions to the general ledger.

   d. Prepare a trial balance after posting to the ledger.

LO 4, 5, 6, and 8
Recording Transactions— Service Company

5-24   The transactions for September 2004 for Parrish High Flight School, Inc. are as follows:

1	President Ralph Parrish paid the corporation $125,000 for 10,000 shares of $10 par value stock and deposited the check into the corporation's bank account.
1	Purchased an airplane for $80,000 cash.
2	Purchased fuel for the airplane costing $1,500 on account.
2	Paid $260 for a newspaper advertisement.
2	Paid rent on an airplane hangar for six months in advance totaling $3,000.
5	Collected $100 for a new student's first lesson.
5	Purchased a desk for $300 on account.
5	Borrowed $10,000 from the bank for two years at 8%.
6	Purchased office supplies for $450 cash.
8	Collected $100 for the second lesson of our student.
12	Paid Ralph Parrish $1,000 salary.
15	Paid the Yellow Pages advertising bill of $800.
20	Ordered $1,000 of repair parts for the airplane.
23	Received the parts ordered on the 20th paying cash.
29	Paid the utility bill received for $150.

Required:

   a. Prepare a chart of accounts for the flight school.

   b. Prepare the journal entries for the listed transactions.

   c. Post the transactions to the general ledger.

   d. Prepare a trial balance after completing the posting process.

5-25 The AAA Termite, Inc. transactions for October 2004 are as follows:

LO 4, 5, 6, 7, and 8
Recording
Transactions—
Service Company

1   CEO Helen Laws deposited $60,000 in the corporation's bank account in exchange for 5,000 shares of $5 par value stock.
1   Purchased a truck for $18,000 cash.
1   Borrowed $8,000 from the bank using the truck as collateral. Interest of 9% will be paid monthly on the first day of each month.
2   Purchased spraying equipment for the truck costing $3,500 plus $400 of chemicals with cash.
2   Paid $600 for a newspaper advertisement to run each week in October.
2   Paid rent on an office for three months in advance totaling $6,000.
4   Collected $300 for spraying a residence under construction.
6   Purchased a desk for $250 cash at a garage sale.
7   Billed a customer $1,500 for treating a house.
7   Purchased office supplies for $200 on account.
7   Collected $200 for a termite inspection.
8   Collected the $1,500 from the customer on October 5.
10 Declared and paid a $500 dividend.
11 Paid the telephone bill of $300 including installation.
12 Ordered $1,000 of chemicals.
15 Received the chemicals ordered on October 12 with payment terms of 2/10, net 30 from invoice date of October 14.
23 Paid the chemical bill less discount.
30 Collected $2,300 in termite inspections for a loan company and billed an apartment complex $1,800 for spraying 10 units.
31 Paid the $135 utility bill on the office.

Required:

a. Prepare a chart of accounts for AAA Termite, Inc.
b. Prepare the journal entries for AAA's transactions.
c. Post the transactions to the general ledger.
d. Prepare a trial balance after completing the posting process.

5-26 The transactions for December 2005 for Brady Janes Auto Repair Shop, Inc. are as follows:

LO 4, 5, 6, and 8
Recording
Transactions—
Service Company

1   President Brady Janes deposited $45,000 in the corporate bank account in exchange for 40,000 shares of no-par common stock.
1   Borrowed $30,000 at 8% interest from the bank to buy a wrecker, using it as collateral. Interest is payable monthly on the first day of the month and a semiannual principal payment of $5,000 is due the first day of June and December each year.
1   Purchased a wrecker for $30,000.
2   Purchased shop equipment costing $12,500 on account.
2   Paid $1,360 for a direct mail advertisement to announce the opening of his business.
2   Paid $1,400 rent on garage and office space for December.
3   Paid $4,200 for a one-year liability and fire insurance policy.
5   Signed a contract to perform maintenance service on all auto equipment of a car rental agency.
5   Purchased a desk and chair for $850 cash.
5   Billed a customer $2,500 for auto repairs.
6   Purchased office supplies for $750 on account.
8   Billed the rental agency $2,500 for work performed.
10 Collected the $2,500 from the customer on December 8.
15 Paid $2,000 salary to Brady Janes.
15 Paid the telephone and cable installation bill of $390.
18 Paid the local parts distributor $600 for parts used on jobs and ordered $1,300 of parts for inventory.
24 Received the parts ordered on December 18 and paid cash on delivery.
29 Paid the office and shop electric bill of $720.
31 Billed the rental agency $3,600 for services that used $680 of parts purchased on December 18.

Required:

a. Prepare a chart of accounts for Brady Janes Auto Repair Shop, Inc.
b. Prepare the journal entries for the corporation.
c. Post the transactions to the general ledger.
d. Prepare a trial balance after completing the posting process.

LO 4, 5, 6, 7, and 8
Recording
Transactions—
Manufacturing
Concern

5-27 The transactions for December 2005 for Hackler Manufacturing Corporation are as follows:

1	CEO Jim Hackler deposited $175,000 in the corporate bank account for 50,000 shares of $1 par value common stock.
1	Purchased a milling machine for $80,000 cash.
1	Borrowed $70,000 at 9% interest from the bank to pay for the milling machine, using it as collateral. Interest is payable monthly on the first day of the month and a semiannual principal payment of $5,000 is due the first day of June and December each year.
2	Purchased shop equipment costing $20,000 on account.
2	Paid $4,000 for an advertising campaign to announce the opening of his business.
2	Paid $12,000 for rent on the factory and office for December and the last two months of a two-year lease.
4	Purchased raw materials, on account, costing $20,000, terms 2/10, net 30.
4	Purchased office furniture for $2,500 on account.
5	Requisitioned $5,230 of raw material to put into process.
6	Purchased office supplies for $430.
8	Paid $3,000 for direct labor.
9	Sold manufactured products for $16,000 to a wholesale customer on account.
14	Collected the $16,000 from the customer on December 9.
15	Paid officer's salary of $2,500.
15	Paid for the raw materials purchased on December 4.
16	Paid $5,200 for direct labor.
19	Paid the telephone bill of $410 and utility bills of $698.
20	Sold manufactured products for $9,500 cash.
20	Purchased $13,000 of raw materials that were delivered and paid for with cash.
21	Requisitioned $19,430 of raw materials for transfer to work-in-process.
23	Paid the local parts distributor $600 for parts used to repair the milling machine, and ordered $1,300 of repair parts for inventory.
29	Ordered $15,000 of raw materials from a vendor, terms 1/15, net 30.
30	Received the order placed on December 29, the goods were shipped FOB shipping point.
30	Paid the freight bill of $225 on the order received on December 30.
31	Sold $22,500 of manufactured product on account.
31	Paid $6,500 in direct labor.
31	Paid officer's salary of $3,500.

Required:

a. Prepare a chart of accounts for Hackler Manufacturing Corporation.
b. Prepare the journal entries for Hackler's corporate transactions.
c. Post the transactions to the general ledger.
d. Prepare a trial balance after posting to the ledger.

LO 4, 5, 6, 7, and 8
Recording
Transactions—
Manufacturing
Concern

5-28 The transactions for December 2004 for Miles Manufacturing, Incorporated, are as follows:

1	Deposited $200,000 in the corporate bank account in exchange for 50,000 shares of $4 par value common stock.
1	Purchased production equipment for $100,000.
1	Borrowed $100,000 at 9% interest from the bank to pay for the equipment, using it as collateral. Interest is payable monthly on the first day of the month and a semiannual principal payment of $5,000 is due the first day of June and December each year.
2	Purchased shop equipment costing $20,000, paying cash.
2	Ordered $25,000 of raw materials, terms 1/15, net 30, FOB shipping point.

2	Paid $4,000 rent on shop and office for December.
5	Received the order placed on the December 2 for raw materials and paid $534 of freight on receipt.
5	Purchased raw materials costing $10,000, paying with cash.
5	Purchased office furniture for $2,650, paying with cash.
5	Requisitioned $17,065 of raw material to put into process.
6	Purchased office supplies of $506 and factory supplies of $1,893.
7	Paid direct labor of $6,000 less $1,495 of withholding taxes.
8	Requisitioned $16,753 of raw materials to put into process.
9	Sold manufactured products for $30,000 on account.
10	Collected the $30,000 from the customer on December 9.
10	Paid for the raw materials purchased on December 2.
14	Paid direct labor of $7,000 less $1,865 of withholding taxes.
15	Purchased $32,780 of raw materials, terms 3/10, net 15, FOB destination from a local supplier.
15	Paid officers' salaries of $5,000 less $1,680 of withholding taxes.
15	Paid withholding taxes to the government plus $1,440 in employer payroll taxes.
15	Requisitioned $12,672 of raw materials for the factory.
16	Sold manufactured products for $28,500 on account, terms 2/10, net 30.
16	Paid utilities for the factory of $1,535.
17	Purchased $273 of repair parts for the production equipment, and ordered $500 of repair parts for inventory.
17	Purchased $12,780 of raw materials, terms 3/10, net 15, FOB destination.
21	Paid $7,500 of direct labor less $1,980 in withholding taxes.
22	Requisitioned $23,765 of raw materials for the factory.
23	Sold manufactured products for $37,250 for cash.
24	Paid for the materials purchased on December 15.
26	Received payment for the sale on December 16.
28	Paid $7,000 of direct labor less $1,865 of withholding taxes.
29	Ordered $21,654 of raw materials from a vendor, terms 1/15, net 60, FOB destination.
30	Received the order placed on December 29.
30	Sold manufactured products for $37,920, terms 2/10, net 20 days.
30	Paid officers' salaries of $5,000 less $1,680 of withholding taxes.
30	Paid withholding taxes to the government plus $1,560 in employer payroll taxes.

Required:

a. Prepare a chart of accounts for Miles Manufacturing, Incorporated.
b. Prepare the journal entries for the company's transactions.
c. Post the transactions to the general ledger.
d. Prepare a trial balance after completing the posting process.

5-29   The Will Company made the following purchases from the Grace Company in August of the current year:

LO 7
Cash Discounts and Freight Terms

2	Purchased $5,000 of merchandise, terms 1/10, n/30, FOB shipping point. The goods were received on August 8 and the invoice dated August 7.
5	Purchased $2,000 of merchandise, terms 2/10, n/45, FOB shipping point. The goods were received on August 10 and the invoice dated August 10.
10	Purchased $4,000 of merchandise, terms 3/10, n/15, FOB shipping destination. The goods were received on August 18 and the invoice was dated August 19.

Required:

For each of the listed purchases, answer the following questions:
a. When is the payment due if the company takes advantage of the discount?
b. When is the payment due if the company does not take advantage of the discount?
c. What is the amount of the cash discount allowed?
d. Assume the freight charges are $250 on each purchase. Which company is responsible for the freight charges?
e. What is the total cost of inventory purchased during August if all discounts were taken?

LO 7
Cash Discounts and Freight Terms

5-30   The Gruber Company made the following purchases from the Belte Company in May of the current year:

2   Purchased $3,000 of merchandise, terms 2/10, n/30, FOB destination point. The goods were received on May 10 with an invoice dated May 9.

10   Purchased $2,800 of merchandise, terms 2/10, n/60, FOB shipping point. The invoice date was May 12 and the goods were received on May 15.

20   Purchased $6,000 of merchandise, terms 3/10, n/20, FOB shipping destination. The goods were received on May 23 and the invoice dated May 24.

Required:

For each of the listed purchases, answer the following questions:
a. When is the payment due if the company takes advantage of the discount?
b. When is the payment due if the company does not take advantage of the discount?
c. What is the amount of the cash discount allowed?
d. Assume the freight charges are $400 on each purchase. Which company is responsible for the freight charges?
e. What is the total cost of inventory purchased during May if all discounts were taken?

LO 7
Cash Discounts and Freight Terms

5-31   The Payne Company made the following purchases from the Ritz Company in July of the current year:

3   Purchased $7,000 of merchandise, terms 2/10, n/15, FOB shipping point. The invoice was dated July 9.

7   Purchased $1,700 of merchandise, terms 1/10, n/60, FOB shipping point. The goods were received on July 13 with the invoice dated July 15.

20   Purchased $9,000 of merchandise, terms 4/10, n/30, FOB destination. The goods were received on July 23 with the invoice dated July 21.

Required:

For each of the listed purchases, answer the following questions:
a. When is the payment due if the company takes advantage of the discount?
b. When is the payment due if the company does not take advantage of the discount?
c. What is the amount of the cash discount allowed?
d. Assume the freight charges are $400 on each purchase. Which company is responsible for the freight charges?
e. What is the total cost of inventory purchased during July if all discounts were taken?

LO 8
Trial Balance

5-32   The following is a list of the accounts of Tiffany's Floral, Inc. at December 31, 2004. All account balances are normal balances.

Required:

Prepare a trial balance in good form.

Accumulated Depreciation	$ 1,000
Cash	40,000
Common Stock	10,000
Fixtures	6,000
Merchandise Inventory	24,000
Note Payable, Bank	20,000
Paid-in Capital—Common Stock	15,000
Prepaid Rent	500
Retained Earnings	24,500

5-33 The following is a list of account balances for the Gleason, Inc. at June 30, 2004. All balances of accounts had normal balances.

LO 8
Trial Balance

Required:

Prepare a trial balance in good form.

Accounts Payable	$ 1,650
Accounts Receivable	33,650
Accumulated Depreciation	1,250
Automotive Equipment	14,000
Cash in Bank	76,500
Common Stock	100,000
Cost of Goods Sold	57,000
Depreciation Expense	1,250
Inventory	18,000
Notes Payable	10,000
Operating Expenses	22,500
Sales	110,000

5-34 The following is a trial balance for Bernstein Enterprises at September 30, 2004.

LO 8
Trial Balance

Required:

Determine the errors on the trial balance and offer probable causes for the errors.

Trial Balance
Bernstein Enterprises
For the year ended September 30, 2004

	Debit	Credit
Cash	$576,000	
Accounts Receivable		$ 253,000
Inventory	223,000	
Accounts Payable	22,000	
Notes Payable		61,000
Common Stock		200,000
Paid-in Capital— Common Stock		194,000
Retained Earnings		575,000
	$821,000	$1,283,000

5-35 Eloise Long is the chief accountant for Star Company, a furniture manufacturer. Eloise has known for quite a while that the company was in poor condition. Today, the CFO came into her office and closed the door. He told Eloise that he wanted her to make a journal entry to record a material amount of expenses as new additions to a building. Eloise argued that it was improper. He asked her if she thought she could replace her current salary elsewhere. Eloise is a single parent of a child with medical problems and does not know what to do.

Ethics

Required:

a. How would you advise Eloise?
b. Should Eloise be concerned about making the journal entry if she is only following orders?

CHAPTER 6

 LEARNING OBJECTIVES

After completing this chapter you should be able to:

1 Reconcile a bank statement.
2 Adjust the accounts to apply the matching principle.
3 Prepare classified income statements.
4 Compute basic earnings per share.
5 Prepare statements of equity.
6 Prepare classified balance sheets.
7 Close the temporary accounts.
8 Prepare a post-closing trial balance.

Completing the Accounting Cycle and Preparing Financial Statements

Continuing our discussion in Chapter 5 about the accounting cycle, we now turn to adjusting the accounts, preparing the financial statements, and closing the temporary accounts at year end. To accomplish this, we look into the future at the end of Elevation Sports, Inc.'s first year of operations. It is now May 31, 2004, and Megan has just created a trial balance for the first year of operations. To simplify her work, she used a worksheet to aid in adjusting the accounts and preparing the financial statements. Megan's worksheet, as shown in Exhibit 6-1 on page 176, begins with the trial balance at May 31, 2004, listed in the first two columns. That becomes the starting point for preparing the adjusting entries.

Step 5: Adjusting the Accounts

We examine each account to see whether the balance is reasonable and to determine whether we need any accrual, deferral, or correcting entry. As we examine each account, we have to think of other related accounts so that we can examine both accounts together for reasonableness. For example, when we record Sales, we normally also record either Cash or Accounts Receivable. Therefore, Sales is closely related to Accounts Receivable and Cash. When we examine Accounts Receivable and Cash, consequently, we see sales information. If the Cash and Accounts Receivable information give us an impression that Sales should be about $1,000,000, but the Sales account indicates $200,000, we assume a problem might exist.

Exhibit 6-1
Elevation Sports, Inc. Worksheet at May 31, 2004

Elevation Sports, Inc.
Worksheet
For the Year Ended May 31, 2004

ACCT. #	ACCOUNT NAME	TRIAL BALANCE		ADJUSTMENTS		ADJUSTED TRIAL BALANCE		INCOME STATEMENT		BALANCE SHEET	
		DEBIT	CREDIT	DEBIT	CREDIT	DEBIT	CREDIT	DEBIT	CREDIT	DEBIT	CREDIT
101	Cash in Bank	129,161									
110	Accounts Receivable	9,900									
111	Allowance for Doubtful Accounts										
130	Merchandise Inventory	35,287									
131	Raw Materials Inventory	2,315									
132	Work-in-Process Inventory	293,442									
133	Finished Goods Inventory										
134	Supplies Inventory	1,330									
140	Prepaid Rent	12,000									
141	Prepaid Insurance	5,000									
154	Administrative Equipment and Furniture	5,100									
156	Selling Furniture and Fixtures	8,400									
158	Production Equipment	89,600									
160	Accumulated Depreciation		17,800								
180	Patents	11,000									
185	Copyrights	600									
190	Trademarks	1,500									
201	Accounts Payable		6,942								
205	Other Accounts Payable		10,246								
210	Interest Payable										
211	Wages Payable										
212	Payroll Taxes Payable		1,400								
213	Sales Taxes Payable		560								
250	Notes Payable-Vail Bank		60,000								
310	Common Stock		40,000								
311	Paid-in Capital—Common Stock		60,000								
320	Retained Earnings										
321	Dividends	4,000									
401	Retail Sales—Snowboards		330,750								
405	Wholesale Sales—Snowboards		151,650								
410	Retail Sales—Other		52,385								

Exhibit 6-1 *continued*

ACCT. #	ACCOUNT NAME	TRIAL BALANCE		ADJUSTMENTS		ADJUSTED TRIAL BALANCE		INCOME STATEMENT		BALANCE SHEET	
		DEBIT	CREDIT	DEBIT	CREDIT	DEBIT	CREDIT	DEBIT	CREDIT	DEBIT	CREDIT
415	Sales Returns	5,213									
420	Sales Discounts	2,426									
500	Cost of Snowboards Sold										
510	Cost of Other Goods Sold	13,321									
600	Advertising	9,325									
610	Convention Expense										
620	Credit Card Merchant Discount	9,300									
630	Depreciation—Selling Fixtures	1,200									
640	Internet Expenses	3,350									
650	Payroll Taxes—Sales Salaries	270									
660	Rent—Retail Space	3,600									
670	Sales Salaries	3,000									
680	Telephone Expense—Sales	985									
690	Utilities Expense—Sales	2,113									
700	Amortization of Intangibles										
705	Bank Service Charges	400									
710	Depreciation—Administrative	1,800									
715	Doubtful Account Expense										
720	Employee Benefits	4,080									
725	Insurance Expense	3,000									
730	Legal Expense	5,200									
740	Officers' Salaries Expense	48,000									
750	Office Supplies										
760	Payroll Taxes—Administrative	3,520									
770	Rent—Administrative Offices	1,800									
780	Telephone Expense	1,413									
790	Utilities Expense	294									
800	Interest Revenue		512								
810	Interest Expense										
	Totals	732,245	732,245								
	Net Income										
840	Income Tax Expense										
214	Income Taxes Payable										

What Do You Think?

6-1   Which accounts are related to the following accounts?

(a) **Insurance Expense**
(b) **Interest Payable**
(c) **Depreciation Expense**
(d) **Wage Expense**
(e) **Notes Payable**

Try to associate accounts as we analyze the account balances on the trial balance. Let's begin with Cash in Bank, frequently the first account listed on the trial balance.

Cash in Bank

Relating the Cash in Bank account to any single account is difficult because the cash account is related to almost all other accounts. We can, however, relate cash inflows to revenues, borrowings, and stockholders' contributions of capital. Likewise, we can relate cash outflows to expenses, liability repayments, and dividends. In a practical sense, the best way to first examine the Cash in Bank account is to reconcile the bank statement. Each month the bank sends a statement that lists the beginning and ending account balance according to the bank's records. It also lists each check that cleared the bank and each deposit the bank received. Remember that the bank refers to debits and credits from *the bank's perspective*. Our bank account has a debit balance for us because it is an asset, but it is a liability to the bank, and a liability has a credit balance. On June 3, 2004, Elevation Sports received its bank statement from Vail National Bank with the following summary:

Vail National Bank	
Account Name: Elevation Sports, Inc. 500 North Aspen Street Vail, Colorado	Account Number: 105833842 Date: May 31, 2004
Previous statement balance 04-30-04	$ 105,452.00
15 Deposits or other credits totaling	129,579.00
42 Checks or other debits totaling	89,000.00
Bank Service Charge	45.00
Current balance as of statement date 05-31-04	$ 145,986.00

Reconciling the Bank Account

Exhibit 6-2 contains a standard bank reconciliation format. We will use it to reconcile Elevation Sports' bank statement and to verify the cash balance. Reconciling a bank statement relies on the process that follows.

1   Record the bank statement's ending balance ($145,986.00) on the first line.
2   Note any deposits recorded in the books that have not been included in the bank statement, called **deposits in transit**. These deposits should occur during the last few days of the month. If you find earlier deposits missing, notify the bank at once because the bank may have credited them to the wrong account. Most banks require that you notify them within 10 days of the bank statement date of any errors. Beyond that time, the bank assumes that the statement is correct.

● deposits in transit
Deposits recorded in the books that have not been included in the bank statement.

Exhibit 6-2
Standard Bank Reconciliation Format

Company Name
Bank Reconciliation
Date

Balance per Bank Statement $ _____

Add: Deposits in Transit

_____ _____
_____ _____
_____ _____
                                                              _____

Deduct: Checks Outstanding

#_____ _____   #_____ _____
#_____ _____   #_____ _____
#_____ _____   #_____ _____   _____

Corrected Bank Balance $ _____

Balance per Books $ _____
Add: _____
     _____
     _____   _____

Deduct: Service Charges $ _____
         _____
         _____   _____

Corrected Book Balance $ _____

---

3 Compare the list of checks that cleared the bank to those recorded in the general journal through the end of the month. Those that did not appear on the bank statement are **outstanding checks**.

4 Compute the corrected bank balance by adding deposits in transit and deducting outstanding checks from the balance on the bank statement. Write the balance per the general ledger on the appropriate line. If the corrected bank balance agrees with the general ledger, or book balance, the reconciliation is complete.

5 If the corrected bank balance and the book balance do not agree, you must find the reason for the difference. This can be a simple process or an aggravating one, depending on the number of adjustments or errors required to reconcile the amounts. The following are the most common problems that occur and helpful hints on how to discover them:

(a) Bank service charges. Banks charge for many services and do not notify the firm except on the bank statement. These charges include check printing charges, monthly service fees, overdraft charges, returned check fees, and special service fees.

(b) Checks or deposits recorded incorrectly in the journals. **Transposition errors** are number reversals that cause errors that are always evenly divisible by nine. For example, if a check was recorded as $257 instead of $275 the difference is $18, evenly divisible by nine. When the difference between the corrected bank balance and the book balance is divisible by nine, look for a transposition error.

(c) Other deductions by the bank. Banks deduct from the account nonsufficient funds (NSF) checks and other items that may not be included in the bookkeeping records. **NSF checks** are customers' checks that their banks dishonor for insufficient funds and return to the depositors' banks.

● **outstanding checks**
Checks that were written through the end of the month but did not appear on the bank statement.

● **transposition errors**
Number reversals that cause errors that are always divisible by nine.

● **NSF checks**
Customers' checks that their banks dishonor for insufficient funds and return to the depositors' banks.

Exhibit 6-3
Bank Encoding of Checks

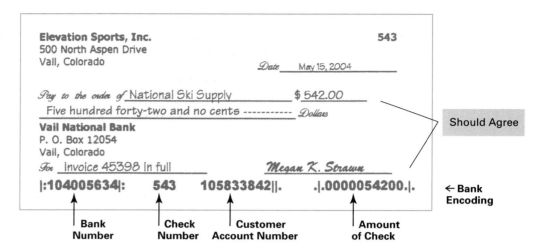

(d) If the balances still do not agree, the next step is to make sure the bank's encoding of the check and deposit amounts matches the actual amount of the deposit or check. The bank's encoding is in the bottom right corner of the check or deposit slip (see Exhibit 6-3). Banks seldom make errors, but can on occasion.

Exhibit 6-4 contains Elevation Sports' bank reconciliation with a number of reconciling items, which Megan completed on June 5, 2004. Three deposits were made on the last day of the month after bank hours, not in time to be included on the bank statement. Ten checks written during May had not cleared the bank by May 31. The bank deducted a merchant's fee from the credit card company and a service charge. Notice that the corrected bank balance and the corrected book balance agree.

Exhibit 6-4
Elevation
Sports, Inc.
Bank
Reconciliation

Elevation Sports, Inc.
Bank Reconciliation
May 31, 2004

Balance per bank statement					$145,986
Add: Deposits in transit					
5–31–02	$1,521				
5–31–02	2,452				
5–31–02	7,586				11,559
Deduct: Checks outstanding					
#651	$15,000	#687	$ 842		
#675	1,021	#688	842		
#682	250	#689	853		
#685	368	#690	853		
#686	87	#691	9,045		29,161
Corrected bank balance					$128,384
Balance per books					$129,161
Deduct: Service charges			$ 45		
Merchant's fee			732		777
Corrected book balance					$128,384

All changes in the book balance require adjusting journal entries. In this case, we must record the following entry to the general journal and post it to the Adjustments columns of the worksheet (see Exhibits 6-11 and 6-12):

Bank Service Charges	45	
Credit Card Merchant Discount	732	
Cash in Bank		777
To correct bank balance per bank reconciliation		

Now that we have corrected the Cash in Bank balance, we can proceed down the list of accounts looking for possible adjustments.

Accounts Receivable

Megan prepared a listing of accounts receivable by customer, called an **aged accounts receivable schedule**, to confirm the total of the receivables and determine the extent to which any accounts are past due (see Exhibit 6-5).

Uncollectible Accounts

After completing the aged accounts receivable schedule, Megan believes she will collect all the current accounts. She also determined that a small Utah retailer owes the firm for 10 snowboards purchased in January. After talking with the customer, she believes she will collect only one-half the amount he owes. She proposes to make the following entry to recognize a potential bad debt:

Doubtful Account Expense	450	
Allowance for Doubtful Accounts		450
To record potential doubtful accounts.		

To remain faithful to the matching principle, we must consider future losses from bad debts to be a current cost of making those sales. For this reason, a business that grants credit to its customers prepares an aging schedule to analyze its potential for losses and recognize the loss in current expenses. The offset to this account is a contra asset account, Allowance for Doubtful Accounts, which values the Accounts Receivable at the amount we expect to eventually collect. In this case, Megan expects to collect $9,900 minus $450, or $9,450, the amount reported on the balance sheet when we complete the financial statements.

Merchandise Inventory

We must adjust the Merchandise Inventory account to the amount on hand at the end of the period. After conducting a physical count of the purchased merchandise on hand and comparing that to its original cost, Angie provided an ending Merchandise

● **aged accounts receivable schedule**
A listing of accounts receivable by customer to confirm the total of receivables and determine the extent to which any accounts are past due.

Exhibit 6-5
Elevation Sports, Inc. Aged Accounts Receivable Schedule

	Elevation Sports, Inc. Aged Accounts Receivable Schedule May 31, 2004				
CUSTOMER NUMBER	AMOUNT	0–30 DAYS	30–60 DAYS	60–90 DAYS	OVER 90 DAYS
100548	$ 270	$ 270			
102453	2,700	2,700			
115487	3,600	3,600			
148921	900				$ 900
151647	1,800	1,800			
182229	630	630			
Totals	$9,900	$9,000			$ 900

Inventory balance from the information system of $4,397. The inventory system Angie installed included a program that keeps track of the cost of the purchased inventory items. Inventory is either gone or on hand. Those items that are gone are presumed sold and their cost becomes part of Cost of Other Goods Sold.

What Do You Think?

6-2 For what reasons would inventory be gone in addition to being sold?

6-3 How should an accountant deal with items that are gone but were not sold?

To make the necessary adjusting entry, Megan must correct the balance of inventory by making a debit entry to Cost of Other Goods Sold of $30,890 and a credit entry to Merchandise Inventory for $30,890, leaving $4,397 in Merchandise Inventory.

Cost of Other Goods Sold	30,890	
Merchandise Inventory		30,890
To record the cost of purchased merchandise sold.		

Manufacturing Inventories and Cost of Goods Manufactured Statement

Companies that manufacture products instead of purchasing them have no single invoice from which to extract a cost per item. In fact, they have three inventories to deal with: Raw Materials Inventory, Work-in-Process Inventory, and Finished Goods Inventory. To understand these inventories, we must look more closely at the manufacturing process discussed in Chapter 4.

Components of Manufacturing Costs

● **direct materials**
Raw materials and purchased components that are measurable in quantity and cost.

● **direct labor**
The wages of persons who transform direct materials into finished goods.

● **factory overhead**
All other manufacturing costs that are not direct materials or direct labor.

● **indirect materials**
Supply items used in manufacturing in small quantities that are impractical to measure.

● **indirect labor**
The cost of supervisory, janitorial, maintenance, security, and other personnel who do not work directly on production but assist direct laborers.

If you recall, manufacturing costs consist of three components: materials, labor, and factory overhead. **Direct materials** are raw materials and purchased components that are measurable in quantity and cost. **Direct labor** costs are the wages of persons who transform direct materials into finished goods. **Factory overhead** represents all other manufacturing costs that are not direct materials or direct labor. Factory overhead encompasses the costs of providing a space to manufacture, depreciation on production equipment, and other costs necessary to complete the manufacturing process including indirect materials and indirect labor. **Indirect materials** are supply items used in manufacturing in small quantities that are impractical to measure, such as staples, glue, paint, and nondecorative nails. **Indirect labor** includes the cost of supervisory, janitorial, maintenance, security, and other personnel who do not work directly on production but assist direct laborers.

The costs of manufacturing flow through the three inventories on the balance sheet until the final product is sold (see Exhibit 6-6). These inventories represent real physical locations, as well as cost centers. The Raw Materials Inventory is located in a secured warehouse or an area segregated from the rest of the factory. The Work-in-Process Inventory is located in the factory. The materials, labor, and overhead costs accumulate in the Work-in-Process account until completion. When completed, the finished goods are transferred to a separate secured area or warehouse for goods ready for sale, or to a sales showroom. Likewise, the final cost transfers to the Finished Goods Inventory. At the point of sale, the goods physically transfer to the buyer, and the cost of the items sold is transferred to the income statement through the Cost of Goods Sold account.

To organize the data, the accounting system keeps track of the costs on this journey from raw materials to cost of goods sold by preparing a Cost of Goods Manufactured

Exhibit 6-6
Flow of Manufacturing Costs

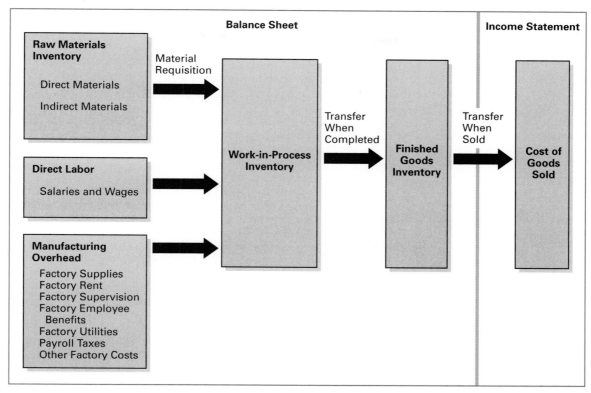

report as shown in Exhibit 6-7. To begin the process of preparing the Statement of Cost of Goods Manufactured, Angie had the accounting information system gather the following information for the period from June 1, 2003, to May 31, 2004:

Raw materials purchased	$ 38,655
Direct labor	101,250
Manufacturing overhead	155,852

Megan furnished the following inventory information:

	Beginning	Ending
Raw materials	—0—	$ 2,315
Work-in-process	—0—	14,864
Finished goods	—0—	13,634

With this information, we can work through the inventory cost process illustrated in Exhibit 6-6 to ultimately complete the Statement of Cost of Goods Manufactured. We begin with the Raw Materials Inventory.

Raw Materials Inventory

When discussing an inventory account, we use the following equation to determine the costs that leave the account:

	Beginning inventory
+	Cost added during the period
=	Cost of items available for use
−	Ending inventory
=	Cost of items used

When we add the beginning Raw Materials Inventory ($0) to the amount purchased during the year ($38,655), we derive the total raw materials ($38,655) we have available for use during the year. After subtracting the cost of the raw materials remaining in the inventory at year end ($2,315), we can determine the cost of raw materials used in the manufacturing process ($36,340).

	Beginning inventory	$ — 0 —
+	Cost added during the period	38,655
=	Cost of items available for use	$ 38,655
−	Ending inventory	2,315
=	Cost of items used	$ 36,340

Raw materials flow from the Raw Materials Inventory to the Work-in-Process Inventory when the factory manager requisitions them.

Work-in-Process Inventory

To compute the cost of goods manufactured, we analyze the Work-in-Process Inventory by adding all the costs of direct materials, direct labor, and manufacturing overhead incurred during the year. Because not all goods are finished during a period, we must make adjustments for the beginning and ending inventory amounts using the same formula we used for the Raw Materials Inventory:

	Beginning inventory	$ — 0 —
+	Cost added during the period	?
=	Cost of items available for use	$?
−	Ending inventory	14,864
=	Cost of items used	$?

Because we deal with more than material costs, the computation requires more space, so we use a Statement of Cost of Goods Manufactured as shown in Exhibit 6-7. Notice that it follows the basic inventory formula shown previously. We add the beginning

Exhibit 6-7
Elevation Sports, Inc. Statement of Cost of Goods Manufactured

Elevation Sports, Inc.
Statement of Cost of Goods Manufactured
For the Year Ended May 31, 2004

Direct materials:	
Beginning raw materials inventory	$ —0—
Add: Purchases	38,655
Direct materials available for use	$ 38,655
Less: Ending inventory	2,315
Direct materials used	$ 36,340
Direct labor:	101,250
Manufacturing overhead:	155,852
Total costs transferred to work-in-process	$293,442
Add: Beginning work-in-process inventory	—0—
Total work-in-process	$293,442
Less: Ending work-in-process inventory	14,864
Total Costs of Goods Manufactured and	
Transferred to Finished Goods	$278,578

Work-in-Process Inventory ($0) to the amount of materials, labor, and overhead added for the year ($293,442) to find the amount of costs in the Work-in-Process Inventory available to complete ($293,442), and subtract the cost of the ending Work-in-Process Inventory ($14,864). The ending Work-in-Process Inventory is the cost of the items not yet completed. The remainder is the cost of the goods completed ($278,578) during the period.

Now, to adjust these three inventories, compare the computed ending inventories as shown on the Cost of Goods Manufactured with amounts in the trial balance in Exhibit 6-1. The amount on the trial balance for the Raw Materials Inventory agrees with Megan's calculation of the ending raw materials on hand, so no adjustment is necessary.

The Work-in-Process Inventory account has $293,442, compared to the amount Megan determined on hand of $14,864. The difference is the amount transferred to the Finished Goods Inventory of $278,578, as shown in Exhibit 6-7. To make the proper adjusting entry, Megan needs to debit Finished Goods Inventory $278,578 and credit Work-in-Process Inventory $278,578:

Finished Goods Inventory	278,578	
Work-in-Process Inventory		278,578
To adjust per Statement of Cost of Goods Manufactured.		

Finished Goods Inventory and Cost of Goods Sold

The Finished Goods Inventory had no balance in Exhibit 6-1 before the last journal entry was made, but now has a balance of $278,578. According to Megan's information, the actual balance is $13,634. The items that were finished and transferred to the Finished Goods Inventory but are no longer on hand are presumed to be sold. If we use a similar formula to analyze finished goods as we did for raw materials and work-in-process, we can compute the cost of goods sold:

	Beginning finished goods inventory	$ — 0 –
+	Cost of goods manufactured	278,57
=	Goods available for sale	$278,57
−	Ending finished goods inventory	13,63
=	Cost of manufactured goods sold	$264,94

The entry to record cost of goods sold and adjust the ending Finished Goods Inventory debits Cost of Snowboards Sold and credits Finished Goods Inventory for $264,944.

Cost of Snowboards Sold	264,944	
Finished Goods Inventory		264,944
To record the cost of snowboards sold.		

Supplies Inventory

Megan counted the office supplies still on hand at May 31, 2004, and discovered that the company still had $593 of supplies. The account shows $1,330, so she must make an adjustment of $737 to show how many supplies were used during the year. She will decrease the Supplies Inventory and increase Office Supplies expense account by $737.

Office Supplies	737	
Supplies Inventory		737
To record office supplies used.		

Prepaid Rent

Prepaid accounts need to be analyzed to determine the nature of the amounts included. As you recall from Chapter 3, Elevation Sports officers signed a five-year lease with some unusual terms. The annual rent is $20,000, but the City of Vail gave the company the first six months rent free. We determined that the true annual rent is $18,000 because the company will pay a total of $90,000 in five years—the first year at $10,000 plus four years at full price of $20,000. It paid $10,000 for the first year's lease and has already paid $20,000 for the second year's lease. The following is Megan's analysis of the account:

Total amount paid	$30,000
Amount of rent used	18,000
Amount of rent prepaid	$12,000

According to her analysis, the amount in Prepaid Rent is correct and no adjustment is needed.

Prepaid Insurance

The insurance policy is $5,000 per year. Megan paid $5,000 in June 2003 and again in May 2004 for the next year. In addition, the May bill included an additional charge for $4,090, which she paid. If you recall from Chapter 3, the product liability insurance was $1 per snowboard manufactured, which Megan included in the manufacturing overhead costs recorded in the Work-in-Process Inventory. The company manufactured 4,090 snowboards during the first year according to information Angie provided. Because the liability insurance is part of product costs, it is absorbed into total manufacturing costs like the cost of materials or direct labor. Of the 4,090 manufactured, 3,890 were sold and 200 were on hand. The cost of manufacturing the 3,890 has been transferred to the Cost of Goods Sold and the cost of those on hand is included in the Finished Goods Inventory.

None of the $4,090 should be prepaid insurance, but the remainder of the business policy is prepaid for the next year. Therefore, the balance of the Prepaid Insurance account should be $5,000, and it needs no adjustment.

Furniture, Equipment, and Depreciation

We analyzed the estimated equipment and furniture and the estimated annual depreciation factors in Chapter 3. Megan has prepared a similar analysis based on actual figures shown in Exhibit 6-8.

Exhibit 6-8
Depreciation Schedule for Elevation Sports, Inc.

Elevation Sports, Inc. Depreciation Schedule For the Year Ended May 31, 2004							
ASSET	**LIFE**	**COST**	**RESIDUAL VALUE**	**DEPRECIATION EXPENSE**	**MFG. OVERHEAD**	**ADMIN.**	**SELLING**
Production Equip.	5 yr.	$ 75,000	$15,000	$12,000	$12,000		
Factory Fixtures	7 yr.	12,600	—0—	1,800	1,800		
Factory Computers	2 yr.	2,000	—0—	1,000	1,000		
Admin. Furniture	7 yr.	2,100	—0—	300		$ 300	
Admin. Computers	2 yr.	3,000	—0—	1,500		1,500	
Selling Fixtures	7 yr.	8,400	—0—	1,200			$1,200
Totals		$103,100		$17,800	$14,800	$1,800	$1,200

The only change in the estimated amounts from Chapter 3 to the actual amounts on the depreciation schedule in Exhibit 6-8 is the residual value of $300 on the computers. Angie rethought her position and decided that the computer equipment would have no residual value. Management can change the decision on residual value and life of the asset as circumstances change.

The Accumulated Depreciation account agrees with Megan's depreciation schedule. Because this is Elevation Sports' first year of operation, the depreciation expense and the accumulated depreciation will be the same. In future years the amount of the depreciation will not agree with the balance in the Accumulated Depreciation account because the Depreciation Expense is closed each year and the Accumulated Depreciation is not.

Next we need to see whether the Depreciation Expense accounts are correct. The Administrative Depreciation Expense is $1,800, which agrees with the depreciation schedule, as does the $1,200 for Selling Fixtures Depreciation Expense. The remainder was taken to the Manufacturing Overhead account. No adjustments are necessary.

Intangible Assets and Amortization

The patent, copyright, and trademark amounts differ from what the attorney originally estimated. He believes that the patent has a useful life of 12 years, and the copyrights and trademarks have a useful life of 20 years. Megan knows that accounting rules allow amortization of intangible assets with finite lives over the lesser of their remaining legal life or their useful life. She prepared a schedule of amortization shown in Exhibit 6-9.

On inspection of the trial balance, you will see no account for accumulated amortization of intangibles because amortization is normally subtracted directly from an intangible asset account. The Amortization of Intangibles expense has a zero balance, which indicates that Megan made no entries to amortize the cost. She needs to reduce each of the asset accounts by their annual amortization and increase the expense account by $1,022. She should make the following entry to adjust the accounts:

Amortization of Intangibles	1,022	
Patents		917
Copyrights		30
Trademarks		75

To record one year's amortization expense.

Elevation Sports, Inc.
Amortization Table
For the Year Ended May 31, 2004

INTANGIBLE ASSET	COST	USEFUL LIFE	ANNUAL AMORTIZATION
Patents	$11,000	12 years	$ 917
Copyrights	600	20 years	30
Trademarks	1,500	20 years	75
Totals	$13,100		$1,022

Exhibit 6-9
Elevation Sports, Inc. Amortization Schedule for Intangible Assets

Accounts Payable and Other Accounts Payable

Angie produced the computer-generated detail of Accounts Payable and Other Accounts Payable, and Megan verified that the account balances were correct at May 31, 2004. Megan, however, received the following bills after May 31 for May expenses:

Advertising	$983
Internet Expense	155
Employee Benefits	428

These bills will be paid in June. To apply the matching principle, the expenses should be accrued as follows:

Advertising	983	
Internet Expense	155	
Employee Benefits	428	
Other Accounts Payable		1,566
To record May expenses unpaid at year end.		

Interest Payable

The only interest-bearing debt the company has is the note to Vail National Bank, due on June 1. Interest for the year at 10 percent is $6,000 ($60,000 \times 10\%$). Megan needs to make the following adjusting entry:

Interest Expense	6,000	
Interest Payable		6,000
To accrue one year's interest due to Vail National Bank.		

Wages Payable

When an employee earns wages in one month and the employer pays them in the following month, the cost of the wages earned in the first month must be accrued in the month earned. All wages earned in May were paid by May 31.

Payroll Taxes Payable and Sales Taxes Payable

The amounts shown on the trial balance equal the amounts shown on the various government reports for May.

Income Taxes Payable

Corporate income taxes cannot be computed until the income statement has been completed and net income determined. The combined corporate income tax rate for Elevation Sports is 40 percent. The amount of the accrual for income taxes will have to wait until the financial statements are prepared.

The remaining note payable and equity accounts are correctly stated and require no adjustment. The Retained Earnings account will not have a balance until after the closing entries are made.

That completes the analysis for the adjusting entries. The next step is to record these adjusting entries in the general journal shown in Exhibit 6-10 and post them to the worksheet in Exhibit 6-11 to obtain the adjusted trial balance in the third set of columns. Notice that the total debits and credits of the first three pairs of columns are equal. If this were not the case, the worksheet would contain an error.

The final task of adjusting the accounts is to post the adjusting entries from the general journal to the general ledger accounts. After posting the adjusting entries, the general ledger will agree with the worksheet in Exhibit 6-11.

Exhibit 6-10
Adjusting Entries

		ELEVATION SPORTS, INC. GENERAL JOURNAL			PAGE 95
DATE 2004		**DESCRIPTION**	**POST REF.**	**DEBIT**	**CREDIT**
May	31	Bank Service Charges	705	45	
		Credit Card Merchant Discount	620	732	
		Cash in Bank	101		777
		To correct bank balance per bank reconciliation.			
		Doubtful Account Expense	715	450	
		Allowance for Doubtful Accounts	111		450
		To record potential doubtful account.			
		Cost of Other Goods Sold	510	30,890	
		Merchandise Inventory	130		30,890
		To record the cost of purchased merchandise sold.			
		Finished Goods Inventory	133	278,578	
		Work-in-Process Inventory	132		278,578
		To adjust per Statement of Cost of Goods Manufactured.			
		Cost of Snowboards Sold	500	264,944	
		Finished Goods Inventory	133		264,944
		To record the cost of snowboards sold.			
		Office Supplies	750	737	
		Supplies Inventory	134		737
		To record office supplies used.			
		Amortization of Intangibles	700	1,022	
		Patents	180		917
		Copyrights	185		30
		Trademarks	190		75
		To record one year's amortization.			
		Advertising Expense	600	983	
		Internet Expense	640	155	
		Employee Benefits	720	428	
		Other Accounts Payable	205		1,566
		To record May's expenses unpaid at year end.			
		Interest Expense	810	6,000	
		Interest Payable	210		6,000
		To accrue one year's interest due to Vail National Bank.			

Exhibit 6-11
Worksheet after Adjusting Entries

Elevation Sports, Inc.
Worksheet
For the Year Ended May 31, 2004

ACCT. #	ACCOUNT NAME	TRIAL BALANCE DEBIT	TRIAL BALANCE CREDIT	ADJUSTMENTS DEBIT	ADJUSTMENTS CREDIT	ADJUSTED TRIAL BALANCE DEBIT	ADJUSTED TRIAL BALANCE CREDIT	INCOME STATEMENT DEBIT	INCOME STATEMENT CREDIT	BALANCE SHEET DEBIT	BALANCE SHEET CREDIT
101	Cash in Bank	129,161			777	128,384					
110	Accounts Receivable	9,900				9,900					
111	Allowance for Doubtful Accounts				450		450				
130	Merchandise Inventory	35,287			30,890	4,397					
131	Raw Materials Inventory	2,315				2,315					
132	Work-in-Process Inventory	293,442		278,578	278,578	14,864					
133	Finished Goods Inventory				264,944	13,634					
134	Supplies Inventory	1,330			757	593					
140	Prepaid Rent	12,000				12,000					
141	Prepaid Insurance	5,000				5,000					
154	Administrative Equipment and Furniture	5,100				5,100					
156	Selling Furniture and Fixtures	8,400				8,400					
158	Production Equipment	89,600				89,600					
160	Accumulated Depreciation		17,800				17,800				
180	Patents	11,000			917	10,083					
185	Copyrights	600			30	570					
190	Trademarks	1,500			75	1,425					
201	Accounts Payable		6,942				6,942				
205	Other Accounts Payable		10,246		1,566		11,812				
210	Interest Payable				6000		6000				
211	Wages Payable										
212	Payroll Taxes Payable		1,400				1,400				
213	Sales Taxes Payable		560				560				
250	Notes Payable—Vail National Bank		60,000				60,000				
310	Common Stock		40,000				40,000				
311	Paid-in Capital—Common Stock		60,000				60,000				
320	Retained Earnings										
321	Dividends	4,000				4,000					
401	Retail Sales—Snowboards		330,750				330,750				
405	Wholesale Sales—Snowboards		151,650				151,650				
410	Retail Sales—Other		52,385				52,385				

Exhibit 6-11 *continued*

ACCT. #	ACCOUNT NAME	TRIAL BALANCE DEBIT	TRIAL BALANCE CREDIT	ADJUSTMENTS DEBIT	ADJUSTMENTS CREDIT	ADJUSTED TRIAL BALANCE DEBIT	ADJUSTED TRIAL BALANCE CREDIT	INCOME STATEMENT DEBIT	INCOME STATEMENT CREDIT	BALANCE SHEET DEBIT	BALANCE SHEET CREDIT
415	Sales Returns	5,213				5,213					
420	Sales Discounts	2,426				2,426					
500	Cost of Snowboards Sold			264,944		264,944					
510	Cost of Other Goods Sold			30,890		30,890					
600	Advertising	13,321		983		14,304					
610	Convention Expense	9,325				9,325					
620	Credit Card Merchant Discount	9,300		732		10,032					
630	Depreciation—Selling Fixtures	1,200				1,200					
640	Internet Expenses	3,350		155		3,505					
650	Payroll Taxes—Sales Salaries	270				270					
660	Rent—Retail Space	3,600				3,600					
670	Sales Salaries	3,000				3,000					
680	Telephone Expense—Sales	985				985					
690	Utilities Expense—Sales	2,113				2,113					
700	Amortization of Intangibles			1,022		1,022					
705	Bank Service Charges	400		45		445					
710	Depreciation—Administrative Assets	1,800				1,800					
715	Doubtful Account Expense			450		450					
720	Employee Benefits	4,080		428		4,508					
725	Insurance Expense	3,000				3,000					
730	Legal Expense	5,200				5,200					
740	Officers' Salaries Expense	48,000				48,000					
750	Office Supplies			737		737					
760	Payroll Taxes—Administrative	3,520				3,520					
770	Rent—Administrative Offices	1,800				1,800					
780	Telephone Expense	1,413				1,413					
790	Utilities Expense	294				294					
800	Interest Revenue		512				512				
810	Interest Expense			6,000		6,000					
	Totals	732,245	732,245	584,964	584,964	740,261	740,261				
	Net Income										
840	Income Tax Expense										
214	Income Taxes Payable										

Step 6: Preparing Financial Statements

Many computer software packages can prepare the financial statements after the adjusting entries are journalized. Most, however, also allow you to print a worksheet, post the adjusting entries by hand, and complete the worksheet before you enter the adjusting entries. Most accountants prefer to complete the worksheet by hand, as in Exhibit 6-12. To do so, decide whether each item on the worksheet, as shown in Exhibit 6-11, will be part of the income statement or balance sheet, and write the amount in the appropriate debit or credit column. Total the last four columns, and you will discover that the pairs of numbers in the two income statement and balance sheet columns are not equal, as they were in the first three pairs of columns. The difference between the column pairs is net income (or loss) before taxes, $105,301, and the amounts should equal one another.

To compute income taxes, multiply the before tax income by the tax rate ($105,301 × .40) to find the income tax expense of $42,120. This tax will be an expense on the income statement and a liability on the balance sheet. Write the income tax expense amount of $42,120 in the debit column of the income statement columns on the line labeled Income Tax Expense and in the credit column of the balance sheet columns on the line labeled Income Taxes Payable. Write the net income after tax ($105,301 − $42,120 = $63,181) in the debit column of the income statement columns and the credit column of the balance sheet columns on the line labeled net income. Total the income statement columns and the balance sheet columns. Now, the amounts for each pair will be equal. When the net income amounts are equal, you can complete the income statement, statement of equity, and balance sheet. Examine the completed worksheet in Exhibit 6-12 and the financial statements in Exhibits 6-13, 6-14, and 6-15. As you do so, notice the distinctive characteristics of each of the classified financial statements.

Income Statement

The classified income statement follows an organizational pattern illustrated in Chapter 2. Data to prepare the income statement comes directly from the income statement columns on the worksheet. Compare the completed income statement in Exhibit 6-13 to the worksheet in Exhibit 6-12. One additional disclosure of information is reported on the income statement called earnings per share.

● **earnings per share (EPS)**
A ratio that reveals how much of a company's net earnings is attributable to each share of common stock.

Earnings per share (EPS) is a ratio that reveals how much of a company's net earnings is attributable to each share of common stock. Many investors and other financial statement users rely on this statistic more than any other to measure a company's performance. To comply with GAAP, income statements must disclose the firm's EPS. We calculate EPS, in its simplest form, with the following formula:

$$EPS = \frac{net\ income}{number\ of\ shares\ of\ common\ stock\ outstanding}$$

To compute Elevation Sports' EPS, we use the net income from the income statement and the number of shares outstanding from the balance sheet, as follows:

$$EPS = \frac{net\ income}{number\ of\ shares\ OS} = \frac{\$63,181}{4,000} = \$15.79$$

Statement of Stockholders' Equity

Once we have prepared the income statement, we can prepare the statement of stockholders' equity. The income statement must come first because we need to determine net income to complete the statement of stockholders' equity. Once again, the format

Exhibit 6-12
Completed Worksheet

Elevation Sports, Inc.
Worksheet
For the Year Ended May 31, 2004

ACCT. #	ACCOUNT NAME	TRIAL BALANCE		ADJUSTMENTS		ADJUSTED TRIAL BALANCE		INCOME STATEMENT		BALANCE SHEET	
		DEBIT	CREDIT	DEBIT	CREDIT	DEBIT	CREDIT	DEBIT	CREDIT	DEBIT	CREDIT
101	Cash in Bank	129,161			777	128,384				128,384	
110	Accounts Receivable	9,900				9,900				9,900	
111	Allowance for Doubtful Accounts				450		450				450
130	Merchandise Inventory	35,287			30,890	4,397				4,397	
131	Raw Materials Inventory	2,315				2,315				2,315	
132	Work-in-Process Inventory	293,442			278,578	14,864				14,864	
133	Finished Goods Inventory			278,578	264,944	13,634				13,634	
134	Supplies Inventory	1,330			737	593				593	
140	Prepaid Rent	12,000				12,000				12,000	
141	Prepaid Insurance	5,000				5,000				5,000	
154	Administrative Equip. and Furniture	5,100				5,100				5,100	
156	Selling Furniture and Fixtures	8,400				8,400				8,400	
158	Production Equipment	89,600				89,600				89,600	
160	Accumulated Depreciation		17,800				17,800				17,800
180	Patents	11,000			917	10,083				10,083	
185	Copyrights	600			30	570				570	
190	Trademarks	1,500			75	1,425				1,425	
201	Accounts Payable		6,942				6,942				6,942
205	Other Accounts Payable		10,246		1,566		11,812				11,812
210	Interest Payable				6,000		6,000				6,000
211	Wages Payable										
212	Payroll Taxes Payable		1,400				1,400				1,400
213	Sales Taxes Payable		560				560				560
250	Notes Payable—Vail National Bank		60,000				60,000				60,000
310	Common Stock		40,000				40,000				40,000
311	Paid-in Capital—Common Stock		60,000				60,000				60,000
320	Retained Earnings										
321	Dividends	4,000				4,000				4,000	
401	Retail Sales—Snowboards		330,750				330,750		330,750		
405	Wholesale Sales—Snowboards		151,650				151,650		151,650		
410	Retail Sales—Other		52,385				52,385		52,385		

193

Exhibit 6-12 continued

ACCT. #	ACCOUNT NAME	TRIAL BALANCE DEBIT	TRIAL BALANCE CREDIT	ADJUSTMENTS DEBIT	ADJUSTMENTS CREDIT	ADJUSTED TRIAL BALANCE DEBIT	ADJUSTED TRIAL BALANCE CREDIT	INCOME STATEMENT DEBIT	INCOME STATEMENT CREDIT	BALANCE SHEET DEBIT	BALANCE SHEET CREDIT
415	Sales Returns	5,213				5,213		5,213			
420	Sales Discounts	2,426				2,426		2,426			
500	Cost of Snowboards Sold			264,944		264,944		264,944			
510	Cost of Other Goods Sold			30,890		30,890		30,890			
600	Advertising	13,321		983		14,304		14,304			
610	Convention Expense	9,325				9,325		9,325			
620	Credit Card Merchant Discount	9,300		732		10,032		10,032			
630	Depreciation—Selling Fixtures	1,200				1,200		1,200			
640	Internet Expenses	3,350		155		3,505		3,505			
650	Payroll Taxes—Sales Salaries	270				270		270			
660	Rent—Retail Space	3,600				3,600		3,600			
670	Sales Salaries	3,000				3,000		3,000			
680	Telephone Expense—Sales	985				985		985			
690	Utilities Expense—Sales	2,113				2,113		2,113			
700	Amortization of Intangibles			1,022		1,022		1,022			
705	Bank Service Charges	400		45		445		445			
710	Depreciation—Administrative Assets	1,800				1,800		1,800			
715	Doubtful Account Expense			450		450		450			
720	Employee Benefits	4,080		428		4,508		4,508			
725	Insurance Expense	3,000				3,000		3,000			
730	Legal Expense	5,200				5,200		5,200			
740	Officers' Salaries Expense	48,000				48,000		48,000			
750	Office Supplies			737		737		737			
760	Payroll Taxes—Administrative	3,520				3,520		3,520			
770	Rent—Administrative Offices	1,800				1,800		1,800			
780	Telephone Expense	1,413				1,413		1,413			
790	Utilities Expense	294				294		294			
800	Interest Revenue		512				512		512		
810	Interest Expense			6,000		6,000		6,000			
	Totals	732,245	732,245	584,964	584,964	740,261	740,261	429,996	535,297	310,265	204,964
	Net Income							**63,181			**63,181
840	Income Tax Expense							*42,120			
214	Income Taxes Payable										*42,120
								535,297	535,297	310,265	310,265

* $535,297 − $429,996 = $105,301 X 40% = $42,120

** $105,301 − $42,120 = $63,181

Exhibit 6-13
Income Statement

Elevation Sports, Inc.
Income Statement
For the Year Ended May 31, 2004

Sales			
Sales of snowboards			$ 482,400
Sales of other merchandise			52,385
Less: Sales returns		$ 5,213	
Sales discounts		2,426	(7,639)
Net Sales			$ 527,146
Cost of Goods Sold			
Cost of snowboards		$264,944	
Cost of other goods sold		30,890	295,834
Gross Profit			$ 231,312
Operating Expenses			
Selling Expenses			
Advertising	$14,304		
Convention expense	9,325		
Credit card merchant discount	10,032		
Depreciation—selling equipment	1,200		
Internet expenses	3,505		
Payroll taxes—sales salaries	270		
Rent—retail sales	3,600		
Sales salaries	3,000		
Telephone expense—sales	985		
Utilities expense—sales	2,113		
Total Selling Expenses		$ 48,334	
Administrative Expenses			
Amortization of intangibles	$ 1,022		
Bank service charges	445		
Depreciation—administrative	1,800		
Doubtful accounts expense	450		
Employee benefits	4,508		
Insurance expense	3,000		
Legal expense	5,200		
Officers' salaries	48,000		
Office supplies	737		
Payroll taxes—administrative	3,520		
Rent—administrative	1,800		
Telephone expense	1,413		
Utilities expense	294		
Total Administrative Expenses		72,189	
Total Operating Expenses			120,523
Operating Income			$ 110,789
Other Revenues and Expenses			
Interest revenue		$ 512	
Interest expense		(6,000)	
Total Other Revenues and Expenses			(5,488)
Income Before Income Taxes			$ 105,301
Income taxes			42,120
Net Income			$ 63,181
Earnings per Share			$ 15.79

Exhibit 6-14
Statement of Stockholders'
Equity

	Elevation Sports, Inc. Statement of Stockholders' Equity For the Year Ended May 31, 2004			
	COMMON STOCK	PAID-IN CAPITAL	RETAINED EARNINGS	TOTAL
Balance, June 1, 2003	$ —0—	$ —0—	$ —0—	$ —0—
Add: Sale of common stock	40,000	60,000		100,000
Net income			63,181	63,181
Deduct: Dividends declared			(4,000)	(4,000)
Balance, May 31, 2004	$40,000	$60,000	$59,181	$159,181

follows that shown in Chapter 2. The data comes from the balance sheet columns of the worksheet, which contain the beginning retained earnings balance for the year, the amount of dividends declared, and net income. The totals provide information that will be shown also on the stockholders' equity section of the balance sheet. Examine the completed statement shown in Exhibit 6-14.

Balance Sheet

The classified balance sheet shown in Exhibit 6-15 is more detailed than the balance sheets shown in Chapter 2. It follows the breakdown of accounts illustrated and defined in the Appendix to Chapter 5. We separate assets into current assets; property, plant, and equipment; and intangible assets. We divide liabilities between current liabilities and long-term liabilities. We section stockholders' equity into paid-in capital and earned capital. These classifications provide the statement user with more qualitative information about the timing for availability of assets or requirements to settle debts. Notice that the long-term liabilities are reduced by any principal payments due within the next year and include that same amount as a current liability. Elevation Sports owes a $15,000 payment to the bank on June 1, 2004.

The stockholders' equity section also includes information about the authorized, issued, and outstanding stock and the par value. Compare the stockholders' equity section in Exhibit 6-15 to the statement of stockholders' equity in Exhibit 6-14. The ending amounts of each account match in both statements.

Step 7: Closing the Accounts

● **fiscal year**
A year that differs from the calendar year but normally coincides with the end of the normal business cycle for its industry.

Elevation Sports chose a **fiscal year** that differs from the calendar year but normally coincides with the end of the normal business cycle for its industry. This choice simplifies inventory taking and year-end accounting procedures. To close Elevation Sports' books, we will zero the temporary or nominal accounts and close them to the Income Summary account. To zero an account, debit accounts with normal credit balances and credit accounts with normal debit balances with an amount equal to the account balance. Offset the resulting total amount with an entry-balancing amount to Income Summary. We can review the closing entries for a corporation discussed in Chapter 5:

1 Close the revenue and gain accounts to Income Summary.
2 Close the expense and loss accounts to Income Summary.
3 Close the Dividend account to the Retained Earnings.
4 Close the Income Summary account to Retained Earnings.

Exhibit 6-15
Balance Sheet

Elevation Sports, Inc.
Balance Sheet
May 31, 2004

Assets
Current Assets

Cash		$128,384
Accounts receivable	$ 9,900	
Less: Allowance for doubtful accounts	450	9,450
Merchandise inventory		4,397
Raw materials inventory		2,315
Work-in-process inventory		14,864
Finished goods inventory		13,634
Supplies inventory		593
Prepaid rent		12,000
Prepaid insurance		5,000
Total Current Assets		$190,637

Property, Plant, and Equipment

Administrative equipment	$ 5,100		
Selling furniture and fixtures	8,400		
Production equipment	89,600	$103,100	
Less: Accumulated depreciation		17,800	
Total Property, Plant, and Equipment			85,300

Intangible Assets

Patents	$ 10,083	
Copyrights	570	
Trademarks	1,425	
Total Intangible Assets		12,078
Total Assets		$288,015

Liabilities and Stockholders' Equity
Current Liabilities

Accounts payable	$ 6,942
Other accounts payable	11,812
Interest payable	6,000
Payroll taxes payable	1,400
Sales taxes payable	560
Income taxes payable	42,120
Current portion of long-term note payable	15,000
Total Current Liabilities	$ 83,834

Long-Term Liabilities

Note payable—Vail National Bank	$ 60,000	
Less: Current portion	15,000	
Total Long-Term Liabilities		45,000
Total Liabilities		$128,834

Stockholders' Equity
Paid-in Capital:

Common stock, $10 par value, 100,000 shares authorized, 4,000 shares issued and outstanding	$ 40,000	
Paid-in capital in excess of par—common stock	60,000	
Total Paid-in Capital	$100,000	
Retained earnings	59,181	
Total Stockholders' Equity		159,181
Total Liabilities and Stockholders' Equity		$288,015

Exhibit 6-16
Closing Entries

		ELEVATION SPORTS, INC. GENERAL JOURNAL			PAGE 96
DATE 2004		**DESCRIPTION**	**POST REF.**	**DEBIT**	**CREDIT**
May	31	Retail Sales—Snowboards	401	330,750	
		Wholesale Sales—Snowboards	405	151,650	
		Retail Sales—Other	410	52,385	
		Interest Revenue	800	512	
		Sales Returns	415		5,213
		Sales Discounts	420		2,426
		Income Summary	900		527,658
		To close revenue accounts.			
		Income Summary	900	464,477	
		Cost of Snowboards Sold	500		264,944
		Cost of Other Goods Sold	510		30,890
		Advertising	600		14,304
		Convention Expense	610		9,325
		Credit Card Merchant Discount	620		10,032
		Depreciation—Selling Fixtures	630		1,200
		Internet Expenses	640		3,505
		Payroll Taxes—Sales Salaries	650		270
		Rent—Retail Services	660		3,600
		Sales Salaries	670		3,000
		Telephone Expense—Sales	680		985
		Utilities Expense—Sales	690		2,113
		Amortization of Intangibles	700		1,022
		Bank Service Charges	705		445
		Depreciation—Administrative	710		1,800
		Doubtful Account Expense	715		450
		Employee Benefits	720		4,508
		Insurance Expense	725		3,000
		Legal Expense	730		5,200
		Officers' Salaries	740		48,000
		Office Supplies	750		737
		Payroll Taxes—Administrative	760		3,520
		Rent—Administrative Offices	770		1,800
		Telephone Expense	780		1,413
		Utilities Expense	790		294
		Interest Expense	810		6,000
		Income Tax Expense	840		42,120
		To close the expense accounts.			
		Retained Earnings	320	4,000	
		Dividends	321		4,000
		To close to retained earnings.			
		Income Summary	900	63,181	
		Retained Earnings	320		63,181
		To close income summary.			

Exhibit 6-17
General Ledger for Elevation Sports, Inc.

ACCOUNT NAME   Cash in Bank   **ACCOUNT NUMBER**   101

DATE		POST			BALANCE	
2004	DESCRIPTION	REF.	DEBIT	CREDIT	DEBIT	CREDIT
May 31					129,161	
		GJ95		777	128,384	

ACCOUNT NAME   Accounts Receivable   **ACCOUNT NUMBER**   110

DATE		POST			BALANCE	
2004	DESCRIPTION	REF.	DEBIT	CREDIT	DEBIT	CREDIT
May 31					9,900	

ACCOUNT NAME   Allowance for Doubtful Accounts   **ACCOUNT NUMBER**   111

DATE		POST			BALANCE	
2004	DESCRIPTION	REF.	DEBIT	CREDIT	DEBIT	CREDIT
May 31		GJ95				450

ACCOUNT NAME   Merchandise Inventory   **ACCOUNT NUMBER**   130

DATE		POST			BALANCE	
2004	DESCRIPTION	REF.	DEBIT	CREDIT	DEBIT	CREDIT
May 31					35,287	
		GJ95		30,890	4,397	

continued

Exhibit 6-17 *continued*

ACCOUNT NAME	Raw Materials Inventory				ACCOUNT NUMBER	131
DATE		**POST**			**BALANCE**	
2004	**DESCRIPTION**	**REF.**	**DEBIT**	**CREDIT**	**DEBIT**	**CREDIT**
May 31					2,315	

ACCOUNT NAME	Work-in-Process Inventory				ACCOUNT NUMBER	132
DATE		**POST**			**BALANCE**	
2004	**DESCRIPTION**	**REF.**	**DEBIT**	**CREDIT**	**DEBIT**	**CREDIT**
May 31					293,442	
		GJ95		278,578	14,864	

ACCOUNT NAME	Finished Goods Inventory				ACCOUNT NUMBER	133
DATE		**POST**			**BALANCE**	
2004	**DESCRIPTION**	**REF.**	**DEBIT**	**CREDIT**	**DEBIT**	**CREDIT**
May 31		GJ95	278,578		278,578	
		GJ95		264,944	13,634	

ACCOUNT NAME	Office Supplies Inventory				ACCOUNT NUMBER	134
DATE		**POST**			**BALANCE**	
2004	**DESCRIPTION**	**REF.**	**DEBIT**	**CREDIT**	**DEBIT**	**CREDIT**
May 31					1,330	
		GJ95		737	593	

ACCOUNT NAME	Prepaid Rent				ACCOUNT NUMBER	140
DATE		**POST**			**BALANCE**	
2004	**DESCRIPTION**	**REF.**	**DEBIT**	**CREDIT**	**DEBIT**	**CREDIT**
May 31					12,000	

Exhibit 6-17 *continued*

ACCOUNT NAME	Prepaid Insurance				ACCOUNT NUMBER	141
DATE		**POST**			**BALANCE**	
2004	**DESCRIPTION**	**REF.**	**DEBIT**	**CREDIT**	**DEBIT**	**CREDIT**
May 31					5,000	

ACCOUNT NAME	Administrative Equipment and Furniture				ACCOUNT NUMBER	154
DATE		**POST**			**BALANCE**	
2004	**DESCRIPTION**	**REF.**	**DEBIT**	**CREDIT**	**DEBIT**	**CREDIT**
May 31					5,100	

ACCOUNT NAME	Selling Furniture and Fixtures				ACCOUNT NUMBER	156
DATE		**POST**			**BALANCE**	
2004	**DESCRIPTION**	**REF.**	**DEBIT**	**CREDIT**	**DEBIT**	**CREDIT**
May 31					8,400	

ACCOUNT NAME	Production Equipment				ACCOUNT NUMBER	158
DATE		**POST**			**BALANCE**	
2004	**DESCRIPTION**	**REF.**	**DEBIT**	**CREDIT**	**DEBIT**	**CREDIT**
May 31					89,600	

ACCOUNT NAME	Accumulated Depreciation				ACCOUNT NUMBER	160
DATE		**POST**			**BALANCE**	
2004	**DESCRIPTION**	**REF.**	**DEBIT**	**CREDIT**	**DEBIT**	**CREDIT**
May 31						17,800

continued

Exhibit 6-17 *continued*

ACCOUNT NAME	Patents				ACCOUNT NUMBER	180
DATE		**POST**			**BALANCE**	
2004	**DESCRIPTION**	**REF.**	**DEBIT**	**CREDIT**	**DEBIT**	**CREDIT**
May 31					11,000	
		GJ95		917	10,083	

ACCOUNT NAME	Copyrights				ACCOUNT NUMBER	185
DATE		**POST**			**BALANCE**	
2004	**DESCRIPTION**	**REF.**	**DEBIT**	**CREDIT**	**DEBIT**	**CREDIT**
May 31					600	
		GJ95		30	570	

ACCOUNT NAME	Trademarks				ACCOUNT NUMBER	190
DATE		**POST**			**BALANCE**	
2004	**DESCRIPTION**	**REF.**	**DEBIT**	**CREDIT**	**DEBIT**	**CREDIT**
May 31					1,500	
		GJ95		75	1,425	

ACCOUNT NAME	Accounts Payable				ACCOUNT NUMBER	201
DATE		**POST**			**BALANCE**	
2004	**DESCRIPTION**	**REF.**	**DEBIT**	**CREDIT**	**DEBIT**	**CREDIT**
May 31						6,942

ACCOUNT NAME	Other Accounts Payable				ACCOUNT NUMBER	205
DATE		**POST**			**BALANCE**	
2004	**DESCRIPTION**	**REF.**	**DEBIT**	**CREDIT**	**DEBIT**	**CREDIT**
May 31						10,246
		GJ95		1,566		11,812

Exhibit 6-17 *continued*

ACCOUNT NAME	Interest Payable				ACCOUNT NUMBER	210
DATE		**POST**			**BALANCE**	
2004	**DESCRIPTION**	**REF.**	**DEBIT**	**CREDIT**	**DEBIT**	**CREDIT**
May 31		GJ95		6,000		6,000

ACCOUNT NAME	Payroll Taxes Payable				ACCOUNT NUMBER	212
DATE		**POST**			**BALANCE**	
2004	**DESCRIPTION**	**REF.**	**DEBIT**	**CREDIT**	**DEBIT**	**CREDIT**
May 31						1,400

ACCOUNT NAME	Sales Tax Payable				ACCOUNT NUMBER	213
DATE		**POST**			**BALANCE**	
2004	**DESCRIPTION**	**REF.**	**DEBIT**	**CREDIT**	**DEBIT**	**CREDIT**
May 31						560

ACCOUNT NAME	Income Taxes Payable				ACCOUNT NUMBER	214
DATE		**POST**			**BALANCE**	
2004	**DESCRIPTION**	**REF.**	**DEBIT**	**CREDIT**	**DEBIT**	**CREDIT**
May 31		GJ95		42,120		42,120

ACCOUNT NAME	Note Payable—Vail National Bank				ACCOUNT NUMBER	250
DATE		**POST**			**BALANCE**	
2004	**DESCRIPTION**	**REF.**	**DEBIT**	**CREDIT**	**DEBIT**	**CREDIT**
May 31						60,000

continued

Exhibit 6-17 *continued*

ACCOUNT NAME	Common Stock				ACCOUNT NUMBER	310
DATE		**POST**			**BALANCE**	
2004	**DESCRIPTION**	**REF.**	**DEBIT**	**CREDIT**	**DEBIT**	**CREDIT**
May 31						40,000

ACCOUNT NAME	Paid-in Capital—Common Stock				ACCOUNT NUMBER	311
DATE		**POST**			**BALANCE**	
2004	**DESCRIPTION**	**REF.**	**DEBIT**	**CREDIT**	**DEBIT**	**CREDIT**
May 31						60,000

ACCOUNT NAME	Retained Earnings				ACCOUNT NUMBER	320
DATE		**POST**			**BALANCE**	
2004	**DESCRIPTION**	**REF.**	**DEBIT**	**CREDIT**	**DEBIT**	**CREDIT**
May 31		GJ96	4,000		4,000	
		GJ96		63,181		59,181

ACCOUNT NAME	Dividends				ACCOUNT NUMBER	321
DATE		**POST**			**BALANCE**	
2004	**DESCRIPTION**	**REF.**	**DEBIT**	**CREDIT**	**DEBIT**	**CREDIT**
May 31					4,000	
	To close	GJ96		4,000	—0—	

Exhibit 6-17 *continued*

ACCOUNT NAME	Retail Sales—Snowboards				ACCOUNT NUMBER	401
DATE		**POST**			**BALANCE**	
2004	**DESCRIPTION**	**REF.**	**DEBIT**	**CREDIT**	**DEBIT**	**CREDIT**
May 31						330,750
	To close	GJ96	330,750			—0—

ACCOUNT NAME	Wholesale Sales—Snowboards				ACCOUNT NUMBER	405
DATE		**POST**			**BALANCE**	
2004	**DESCRIPTION**	**REF.**	**DEBIT**	**CREDIT**	**DEBIT**	**CREDIT**
May 31						151,650
	To close	GJ96	151,650			—0—

ACCOUNT NAME	Retail Sales—Other				ACCOUNT NUMBER	410
DATE		**POST**			**BALANCE**	
2004	**DESCRIPTION**	**REF.**	**DEBIT**	**CREDIT**	**DEBIT**	**CREDIT**
May 31						52,385
	To close	GJ96	52,385			—0—

ACCOUNT NAME	Sales Returns				ACCOUNT NUMBER	415
DATE		**POST**			**BALANCE**	
2004	**DESCRIPTION**	**REF.**	**DEBIT**	**CREDIT**	**DEBIT**	**CREDIT**
May 31					5,213	
	To close	GJ96		5,213	—0—	

continued

Exhibit 6-17 *continued*

ACCOUNT NAME	Sales Discounts				ACCOUNT NUMBER	420	
DATE		**POST**			**BALANCE**		
2004	**DESCRIPTION**	**REF.**	**DEBIT**	**CREDIT**	**DEBIT**	**CREDIT**	
May 31					2,426		
	To close	GJ96		2,426	—0—		

ACCOUNT NAME	Cost of Snowboards				ACCOUNT NUMBER	500	
DATE		**POST**			**BALANCE**		
2004	**DESCRIPTION**	**REF.**	**DEBIT**	**CREDIT**	**DEBIT**	**CREDIT**	
May 31					—0—		
		GJ95	264,944		264,944		
	To close	GJ96		264,944	—0—		

ACCOUNT NAME	Cost of Other Goods Sold				ACCOUNT NUMBER	510	
DATE		**POST**			**BALANCE**		
2004	**DESCRIPTION**	**REF.**	**DEBIT**	**CREDIT**	**DEBIT**	**CREDIT**	
May 31							
		GJ95	30,890		30,890		
	To close	GJ96		30,890	—0—		

ACCOUNT NAME	Advertising Expense				ACCOUNT NUMBER	600	
DATE		**POST**			**BALANCE**		
2004	**DESCRIPTION**	**REF.**	**DEBIT**	**CREDIT**	**DEBIT**	**CREDIT**	
May 31					13,321		
		GJ95	983		14,304		
	To close	GJ96		14,304	—0—		

Exhibit 6-17 *continued*

ACCOUNT NAME	Convention Expense				ACCOUNT NUMBER	610
DATE		**POST**			**BALANCE**	
2004	**DESCRIPTION**	**REF.**	**DEBIT**	**CREDIT**	**DEBIT**	**CREDIT**
May 31					9,325	
	To close	GJ96		9,325	—0—	

ACCOUNT NAME	Credit Card Merchant Expense				ACCOUNT NUMBER	620
DATE		**POST**			**BALANCE**	
2004	**DESCRIPTION**	**REF.**	**DEBIT**	**CREDIT**	**DEBIT**	**CREDIT**
May 31					9,300	
		GJ95	732		10,032	
	To close	GJ96		10,032	—0—	

ACCOUNT NAME	Depreciation—Selling Fixtures				ACCOUNT NUMBER	630
DATE		**POST**			**BALANCE**	
2004	**DESCRIPTION**	**REF.**	**DEBIT**	**CREDIT**	**DEBIT**	**CREDIT**
May 31					1,200	
	To close	GJ96		1,200	—0—	

ACCOUNT NAME	Internet Expenses				ACCOUNT NUMBER	640
DATE		**POST**			**BALANCE**	
2004	**DESCRIPTION**	**REF.**	**DEBIT**	**CREDIT**	**DEBIT**	**CREDIT**
May 31					3,350	
		GJ95	155		3,505	
	To close	GJ96		3,505	—0—	

continued

Exhibit 6-17   *continued*

ACCOUNT NAME	Payroll Taxes—Sales Salaries				ACCOUNT NUMBER	650
DATE		**POST**			**BALANCE**	
2004	**DESCRIPTION**	**REF.**	**DEBIT**	**CREDIT**	**DEBIT**	**CREDIT**
May 31					270	
	To close	GJ96		270	—0—	

ACCOUNT NAME	Rent—Retail Space				ACCOUNT NUMBER	660
DATE		**POST**			**BALANCE**	
2004	**DESCRIPTION**	**REF.**	**DEBIT**	**CREDIT**	**DEBIT**	**CREDIT**
May 31					3,600	
	To close	GJ96		3,600	—0—	

ACCOUNT NAME	Sales Salaries				ACCOUNT NUMBER	670
DATE		**POST**			**BALANCE**	
2004	**DESCRIPTION**	**REF.**	**DEBIT**	**CREDIT**	**DEBIT**	**CREDIT**
May 31					3,000	
	To close	GJ96		3,000	—0—	

ACCOUNT NAME	Telephone Expense—Sales				ACCOUNT NUMBER	680
DATE		**POST**			**BALANCE**	
2004	**DESCRIPTION**	**REF.**	**DEBIT**	**CREDIT**	**DEBIT**	**CREDIT**
May 31					985	
	To close	GJ96		985	—0—	

Exhibit 6-17 *continued*

ACCOUNT NAME	Utilities Expense—Sales				ACCOUNT NUMBER	690
DATE		**POST**			**BALANCE**	
2004	**DESCRIPTION**	**REF.**	**DEBIT**	**CREDIT**	**DEBIT**	**CREDIT**
May 31					2,113	
	To close	GJ96		2,113	—0—	

ACCOUNT NAME	Amortization of Intangibles				ACCOUNT NUMBER	700
DATE		**POST**			**BALANCE**	
2004	**DESCRIPTION**	**REF.**	**DEBIT**	**CREDIT**	**DEBIT**	**CREDIT**
May 31					—0—	
		GJ95	1,022		1,022	
	To close	GJ96		1,022	—0—	

ACCOUNT NAME	Bank Service Charges				ACCOUNT NUMBER	705
DATE		**POST**			**BALANCE**	
2004	**DESCRIPTION**	**REF.**	**DEBIT**	**CREDIT**	**DEBIT**	**CREDIT**
May 31					400	
		GJ95	45		445	
	To close	GJ96		445	—0—	

ACCOUNT NAME	Depreciation—Administrative				ACCOUNT NUMBER	710
DATE		**POST**			**BALANCE**	
2004	**DESCRIPTION**	**REF.**	**DEBIT**	**CREDIT**	**DEBIT**	**CREDIT**
May 31					1,800	
	To close	GJ96		1,800	—0—	

continued

Exhibit 6-17 *continued*

ACCOUNT NAME	Doubtful Accounts Expense				ACCOUNT NUMBER	715
DATE		**POST**			**BALANCE**	
2004	**DESCRIPTION**	**REF.**	**DEBIT**	**CREDIT**	**DEBIT**	**CREDIT**
May 31					—0—	
		GJ95	450		450	
	To close	GJ96		450	—0—	

ACCOUNT NAME	Employee Benefits				ACCOUNT NUMBER	720
DATE		**POST**			**BALANCE**	
2004	**DESCRIPTION**	**REF.**	**DEBIT**	**CREDIT**	**DEBIT**	**CREDIT**
May 31					4,080	
		GJ95	428		4,508	
	To close	GJ96		4,508	—0—	

ACCOUNT NAME	Insurance Expense				ACCOUNT NUMBER	725
DATE		**POST**			**BALANCE**	
2004	**DESCRIPTION**	**REF.**	**DEBIT**	**CREDIT**	**DEBIT**	**CREDIT**
May 31					3,000	
	To close	GJ96		3,000	—0—	

ACCOUNT NAME	Legal Expense				ACCOUNT NUMBER	730
DATE		**POST**			**BALANCE**	
2004	**DESCRIPTION**	**REF.**	**DEBIT**	**CREDIT**	**DEBIT**	**CREDIT**
May 31					5,200	
	To close	GJ96		5,200	—0—	

Exhibit 6-17 *continued*

ACCOUNT NAME	Officers' Salaries Expense				ACCOUNT NUMBER	740
DATE		**POST**			**BALANCE**	
2004	**DESCRIPTION**	**REF.**	**DEBIT**	**CREDIT**	**DEBIT**	**CREDIT**
May 31					48,000	
	To close	GJ96		48,000	—0—	

ACCOUNT NAME	Office Supplies				ACCOUNT NUMBER	750
DATE		**POST**			**BALANCE**	
2004	**DESCRIPTION**	**REF.**	**DEBIT**	**CREDIT**	**DEBIT**	**CREDIT**
May 31					—0—	
		GJ95	737		737	
	To close	GJ96		737	—0—	

ACCOUNT NAME	Payroll Taxes—Administrative				ACCOUNT NUMBER	760
DATE		**POST**			**BALANCE**	
2004	**DESCRIPTION**	**REF.**	**DEBIT**	**CREDIT**	**DEBIT**	**CREDIT**
May 31					3,520	
	To close	GJ96		3,520	—0—	

ACCOUNT NAME	Internet Expenses				ACCOUNT NUMBER	770
DATE		**POST**			**BALANCE**	
2004	**DESCRIPTION**	**REF.**	**DEBIT**	**CREDIT**	**DEBIT**	**CREDIT**
May 31					1,800	
	To close	GJ96		1,800	—0—	

continued

Exhibit 6-17 *continued*

ACCOUNT NAME	Telephone Expense—Administrative				ACCOUNT NUMBER	780
DATE		**POST**			**BALANCE**	
2004	**DESCRIPTION**	**REF.**	**DEBIT**	**CREDIT**	**DEBIT**	**CREDIT**
May 31					1,413	
	To close	GJ96		1,413	—0—	

ACCOUNT NAME	Utilities Expense—Administrative				ACCOUNT NUMBER	790
DATE		**POST**			**BALANCE**	
2004	**DESCRIPTION**	**REF.**	**DEBIT**	**CREDIT**	**DEBIT**	**CREDIT**
May 31					294	
	To close	GJ96		294	—0—	

ACCOUNT NAME	Interest Revenue				ACCOUNT NUMBER	800
DATE		**POST**			**BALANCE**	
2004	**DESCRIPTION**	**REF.**	**DEBIT**	**CREDIT**	**DEBIT**	**CREDIT**
May 31						512
	To close	GJ96	512			—0—

ACCOUNT NAME	Interest Expenses				ACCOUNT NUMBER	810
DATE		**POST**			**BALANCE**	
2004	**DESCRIPTION**	**REF.**	**DEBIT**	**CREDIT**	**DEBIT**	**CREDIT**
May 31					—0—	
		GJ95	6,000		6,000	
	To close	GJ96		6,000	—0—	

Exhibit 6-17 *continued*

ACCOUNT NAME	Income Tax Expenses				ACCOUNT NUMBER		840
DATE		**POST**			**BALANCE**		
2004	**DESCRIPTION**	**REF.**	**DEBIT**	**CREDIT**	**DEBIT**	**CREDIT**	
May 31					—0—		
		GJ95	42,120		42,120		
	To close	GJ96		42,120	—0—		

ACCOUNT NAME	Income Summary				ACCOUNT NUMBER		900
DATE		**POST**			**BALANCE**		
2004	**DESCRIPTION**	**REF.**	**DEBIT**	**CREDIT**	**DEBIT**	**CREDIT**	
May 31					—0—		
		GJ95		527,658	527,658		
		GJ95	464,497			63,181	
	To close	GJ96	63,181			—0—	

After consulting the worksheet, we determine that there are several revenue accounts, many expense accounts, and the corporation declared dividends during the year. Therefore, we must make all four closing entries as shown in Exhibit 6-16. If the company does not declare a dividend, we need make only three closing entries. These entries must be posted to the general ledger. At this point, with all adjusting and closing entries made, the general ledger should look like Exhibit 6-17.

Step 8: Preparing the Post-Closing Trial Balance

After posting the closing entries to the general ledger, we have reached the final step in the process. By preparing the post-closing trial balance from the general ledger shown in Exhibit 6-17, we verify that each temporary account is closed and the general ledger remains in balance. The account balances in the post-closing trial balance become the opening balances for the new fiscal year. Exhibit 6-18 contains Elevation Sports' post-closing trial balance at May 31, 2004.

We now have completed all the accounting cycle steps. This, however, is the beginning, not the end, of the usefulness of accounting information. In Chapter 7 we will explore the many ways to analyze the performance and financial position of the company from the financial information generated during the accounting cycle.

Exhibit 6-18
Post-Closing Trial Balance

	Elevation Sports, Inc. Post-Closing Trial Balance May 31, 2004		
ACCT. #	**ACCOUNT NAME**	**DEBIT**	**CREDIT**
101	Cash in bank	$128,384	
110	Accounts receivable	9,900	
111	Allowance for doubtful accounts		$ 450
130	Merchandise inventory	4,397	
131	Raw materials inventory	2,315	
132	Work-in-process inventory	14,864	
133	Finished goods inventory	13,634	
134	Supplies inventory	593	
140	Prepaid rent	12,000	
141	Prepaid insurance	5,000	
154	Administrative equipment and furniture	5,100	
156	Selling furniture and fixtures	8,400	
158	Production equipment	89,600	
160	Accumulated depreciation		17,800
180	Patents	10,083	
185	Copyrights	570	
190	Trademarks	1,425	
201	Accounts payable		6,942
205	Other accounts payable		11,812
210	Interest payable		6,000
212	Payroll taxes payable		1,400
213	Sales taxes payable		560
214	Income taxes payable		42,120
250	Notes payable—Vail National Bank		60,000
310	Common stock		40,000
311	Paid-in capital—common stock		60,000
320	Retained earnings		59,181
	Totals	$306,265	$306,265

CHAPTER SUMMARY

Chapter 6 continues the discussion of the accounting cycle beginning with adjusting the accounts and continuing through the post-closing trial balance. The adjustment process requires that each account balance be analyzed to determine whether it is reasonable and whether any adjustment is required to properly reflect each balance. The best approach to examining the cash account is to reconcile the balance each month using the standard bank reconciliation. Analyze the remaining accounts on the worksheet to determine the need for adjusting entries. Write the adjusting entries in the general journal and post them to the general ledger.

Use a worksheet to prepare the trial balance, adjusting entries, and adjusted trial balance, and gather the data for the income statement, statement of equity, and balance sheet. Once you have completed the worksheet, it is relatively easy to prepare the financial statements.

The classified income statement includes information about sales, cost of sales, gross profit, selling expenses, administrative expenses, other revenue and expenses, income taxes, net income, and EPS. The EPS reveals the amount of net income attributable to each share of common stock.

The statement of stockholders' equity shows how the beginning balance of the stockholders' equity changes during the year and reconciles with the ending balance. The classified balance sheet separates assets into current assets; plant, property, and equipment; and intangible assets. Liabilities are divided into current and long-term liabilities.

After completing the financial statements, the accountant must close all the temporary accounts through the Income Summary account. Closing the accounts transfers the income or loss for the year to the retained earnings account in a corporation. The closing process allows the measurement of income and expense to begin anew at the start of the next accounting period. Once the closing entries to the general ledger are posted, a post-closing trial balance is prepared to verify that each temporary account has been closed and the general ledger remains in balance.

Visit the Web site *www.prenhall.com/terrell* for additional study help with the Online Study Guide.

REVIEW OF CONCEPTS

A Describe the steps in reconciling a bank statement.

B Explain how the adjusting entries apply the matching principle.

C Discuss what a classified income statement shows the user.

D Describe how to compute basic earnings per share.

E Explain how to prepare a statement of equity.

F Describe how to prepare a classified balance sheet.

G Describe the purpose of closing the temporary accounts and how to accomplish it.

H Explain the purpose of the post-closing trial balance and how to prepare it.

APPLICATION EXERCISES

6-4 The Frazzle Company showed a cash balance of $2,522 on November 30, 2004. The bank statement for November 2004 showed a balance of $2,750. The other differences that appear between the company's book balance of cash and the bank statement include:

1. A $500 deposit made on November 30 that was not included on the bank statement.
2. Outstanding checks on November 30 were $1,280.
3. Bank service charges were $35.
4. The bank included a debit memo for an NSF check totaling $512.

Required:

a. Prepare a bank reconciliation for the Frazzle Company on November 30, 2004.

b. Prepare the general journal entries necessary to adjust the accounts.

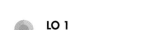
LO 1
Bank Reconciliation

LO 1
Bank Reconciliation

6-5 The Coyote Company received its bank statement for October 2005. The following information is available for the bank reconciliation of October 31, 2005:

Balance per general ledger	$7,500
Balance per bank statement	8,250
NSF check returned by customer's bank	1,000
Outstanding checks total	2,365
Deposits in transit	1,800
Bank charges	60
Credit memo for collection from a customer of amount owed on a note	1,245

Required:

a. Prepare a bank reconciliation for the Coyote Company on October 31, 2005.
b. Prepare the general journal entries necessary to adjust the accounts.

LO 1
Bank Reconciliation

6-6 The Goodwin Company received the bank statement for December 2004. The company showed a cash balance of $1,958 on December 31, 2004, but the bank statement showed a balance of $3,500. The other differences that appear between the company's book balance of cash and the bank statement include:

1. A $300 deposit made on December 31 that was not included in the bank statement.
2. Outstanding checks on December 31 were $1,280.
3. Bank service charges were $28.
4. The bank included a debit memo for VISA card discounts totaling $390.
5. Included in the bank statement was a credit memo for $1,590 for the collection of an outstanding account a customer owed to Goodwin.
6. The bookkeeper entered check number 482 for advertising in the general journal for $1,512. The check was actually for $1,152.

Required:

a. Prepare a bank reconciliation for the Goodwin Company on December 31, 2004.
b. Prepare the general journal entries necessary to adjust the accounts.

LO 2
Adjusting Entries

6-7 The Zephyr Company had the following accrual information available at year end 2004:

1. Unpaid wages to employees were $2,500.
2. Interest due on a loan to the bank was $1,000.
3. Sales taxes collected during December and unpaid to the state were $3,000.
4. A customer owed one year's interest on a note to Zephyr for $4,000.
5. One of Zephyr's renters failed to pay the December rent of $5,000 because she was out of the country. She will pay this when she returns on January 10.

Required:

Prepare the appropriate general journal entries with explanations to record the preceding adjustments.

LO 2
Adjusting Entries

6-8 The Halley Corporation had the following information available at year end 2004.

1. The accountant completed the 2004 depreciation schedule, which showed the depreciation expense as $10,520. The Depreciation Expense account has a balance of $8,500.
2. Commissions for December of $22,000 will be paid to Halley's sales staff on January 5. The Commissions Payable account has a zero balance.
3. Halley's Accounts Receivable account shows $64,500. After the accountant completed an analysis, he discovered that it should be $68,400. The difference is a sale made on December 31 that was not recorded.
4. A good customer borrowed $20,000 on July 1 for one year at 12% interest. The principal and interest will be paid on June 30, 2005.
5. On July 1 Halley paid $14,000 in rent for one year on a temporary warehouse. The accountant recorded this payment as rent expense.

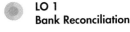

Required:

Prepare the appropriate general journal entries with explanations to record the preceding adjustments.

6-9 The Dow Company has the following information available at year end:

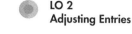

1. Wages earned by employees but not paid at year end are $4,000. The Wages Payable account shows a balance of $7,000.
2. A two-year insurance policy was paid for on October 1 for $2,000. The Prepaid Insurance account's balance is zero.
3. Service Fee Income earned but not collected at year end is $14,000. Accounts Receivable has a zero balance.
4. Real estate taxes payable at year end are $3,900 and the expense account has no balance.
5. Interest owed to the bank but not paid at year end is $2,200. The Interest Payable account shows $500, and this is the only loan the company owes.

Required:

Prepare the appropriate general journal entries with explanations to record the preceding adjustments.

6-10 The Edward Company's trial balance at June 30, its year end, has the following balances before adjustments:

LO 2
Adjusting Entries

Unearned Rental Income	$7,200
Prepaid Rent Expense	3,600
Prepaid Insurance	4,200
Supplies Inventory	1,200

1. On May 1 the company paid rent expense of $3,600 for one year.
2. On April 1 the company collected rental income of $14,400 on its only rental property in advance for the following 24 months.
3. On June 1 the company paid $4,200 for its only business insurance policy for the next 2 years.
4. At year end the physical count of the supplies inventory indicated that $295 of supplies were on hand.

Required:

Prepare the appropriate adjusting entries with explanations to record the preceding information.

6-11 The Abshere Company's trial balance at June 30, its year end, has the following balances before adjustments:

LO 2
Adjusting Entries

Unearned Rental Income	$7,200
Prepaid Rent	—0—
Prepaid Insurance	8,400
Supplies Inventory	200

1. On October 1 the company paid the rent expense of $9,600 for one year's rent in advance.
2. On March 1 the company collected rental income of $300 per month in advance, for the following 24 months.
3. On May 1 the company paid for a catastrophe insurance policy for the next 2 years at a rate of $4,200 per year. This was the only policy in force.
4. On June 30 the physical count of the supplies inventory on hand was $450.

Required:

Prepare the appropriate adjusting entries with explanations to record the preceding adjustments.

LO 2
Adjusting Entries

6-12   In 2005 *Elegant Entertaining* magazine sold 1,000 annual subscriptions to its monthly magazine for $16 each. It also sold 500 two-year subscriptions for $25 each and 250 three-year subscriptions for $32 each.

Required:

a. Prepare the appropriate adjusting entries with explanations to record the adjustments necessary at the end of years 1 and 2 if the subscriptions were all sold at the beginning of 2005 and were originally recorded as income.
b. Prepare the appropriate adjusting entries with explanations to record the adjustments necessary at the end of years 1 and 2 if the subscriptions were all sold at the beginning of 2005 and were originally recorded as a liability.

LO 2
Adjusting Entries—
Depreciation

6-13   At the beginning of the year the Shamrock Company purchased a copy machine for $2,000. Management believed the machine would have an estimated useful life of 6 years and a salvage value of $200. The company also purchased a delivery van costing $28,000 with an estimated useful life of 4 years and a salvage value of $4,000. The company decided to use straight-line depreciation for both assets.

Required:

a. Prepare the appropriate adjusting entries with explanations to record the depreciation expense at the end of year 1, assuming no entries had been made.
b. Prepare the appropriate adjusting entries with explanations to record the depreciation adjustment at the end of year 1 when the Accumulated Depreciation account had a balance of $4,500 and these were the only depreciable assets the company owned.

LO 2
Adjusting Entries—
Depreciation

6-14   At the beginning of the year the Walters Company purchased a copy machine for $3,000. Management believed the machine would have an estimated useful life of 4 years and a salvage value of $200. The firm also purchased a tractor costing $56,000 with an estimated useful life of 6 years and a salvage value of $2,000. The company decided to use straight-line depreciation for both assets.

Required:

a. Prepare the appropriate adjusting entries with explanations to record the depreciation adjustment at the end of year 1 assuming that the company recorded no depreciation in the first year.
b. Prepare the appropriate adjusting entries with explanations to record the depreciation adjustment at the end of year 1 assuming the Accumulated Depreciation account has a balance of $10,800 and these are the company's only depreciable assets.

LO 2
Adjusting Entries—
Depreciation

6-15   At the start of the year the Merkel Corporation purchased a piece of equipment for $36,000. The firm believed the machine would have an estimated useful life of 5 years and a salvage value of $6,000. The company also purchased a building costing $200,000 with an estimated useful life of 40 years and no residual value. The company uses straight-line depreciation.

Required:

a. Prepare the appropriate adjusting entries with explanations to record the depreciation adjustment at the end of year 1 assuming the company did not record any depreciation.
b. Prepare the appropriate adjusting entries with explanations to record the depreciation adjustment at the end of year 1 assuming that the Accumulated Depreciation account had a balance of $30,000 and these are the company's only depreciable assets.

6-16 At the beginning of the year the Lisa Antonelli Company purchased a computer for $3,000. Management believed the computer would last 3 years with a residual value of $200. The company also purchased a truck costing $56,000 with an estimated useful life of 4 years and a salvage value of $6,000. The company uses straight-line depreciation for both assets. At year end, the general ledger contains the following accounts and balances:

LO 2
Adjusting Entries

Office Equipment	$ 2,800	Debit
Accumulated Depreciation—Office Equip.	200	Credit
Automotive Equipment	56,000	Debit
Accumulated Depreciation—Auto Equip.	14,000	Credit
Depreciation Expense	14,200	Debit

Required:

Prepare the appropriate adjusting entries with explanations to record the depreciation adjustment at the end of year 1.

6-17 The following is a partial trial balance for the Dallas Company as of December 31, 2005.

LO 2
Adjustments from
Trial Balance
Accounts with
Supplemental
Information

The Dallas Company
Partial Trial Balance
December 31, 2005

	Debit	Credit
Prepaid Insurance	$12,000	
Prepaid Rent Expense	18,000	
Interest Receivable	—0—	
Wages Payable		$10,000
Unearned Fee Income		36,000
Interest Income		12,000

Additional information includes the following:
1. The insurance policy indicates that on December 31, 2005, 7 months remain on the 24-month policy that originally cost $18,000.
2. Dallas has a note receivable with $2,500 of interest due and payable on January 1, 2006.
3. The records show that two-thirds of the $36,000 service fees paid in advance by a customer on June 30 have now been earned.
4. The company prepaid rent of $2,000 per month for 9 months on July 1.
5. The wages payable on December 31 was $7,000. The amount in the Wages Payable account is from December 31, 2004.

Required:

Record in proper general journal form the adjustments required by the preceding information.

6-18 The following is a partial trial balance for the Reese Company as of December 31, 2005.

LO 2
Adjustments from
Trial Balance
Accounts with
Supplemental
Information

Reese Company
Partial Trial Balance
December 31, 2005

	Debit	Credit
Prepaid Insurance	$ 6,000	
Prepaid Rent Expense	10,000	
Wages Payable		—0—
Unearned Subscription Income		$72,000
Interest Payable		12,000

Additional information includes the following:
1. The company paid a $7,200 3-year premium for its only business insurance policy on July 1, 2004.
2. Reese borrowed $200,000 on January 2 and must pay 12% interest on January 2, 2006, for the entire year of 2005. The company has no other loans.
3. The books show that all but $12,000 of subscriptions have now been earned.
4. The company prepaid 10 months rent on November 1, 2005, to take advantage of a special discount that reduced the rent to $1,000 per month.
5. Wages for December 31 of $3,000 will be paid to employees on January 6, 2006.

Required:

Record in proper general journal form the adjustments required by the above information.

LO 2
Adjustments from Trial Balance Accounts with Supplemental Information

6-19 The following is a partial trial balance for the Marr Company as of December 31, 2005.

Marr Company
Partial Trial Balance
December 31, 2005

	Debit	Credit
Office Supply Expense	$ 36,000	
Cost of Goods Sold	122,000	
Merchandise Inventory	63,000	
Office Supply Inventory	400	
Wage Expense	41,500	
Wages Payable	4,000	

Additional information includes the following:
1. Office supplies on hand at year end were $1,230.
2. The ending merchandise inventory was $61,350. The cost of the goods sold during the year was $122,000.
3. The total payroll cost for the year 2005 was $50,000. At the end of last year, the company owed employees $4,000 for December wages and at December 31, 2005, the company owes employees $4,500 for December wages.

Required:

Record in proper general journal form the adjustments required by the preceding information.

LO 2
Adjustments and Impact on Financial Statements

6-20 The Thallberg Company has the following normal account balances at year end:

Prepaid Insurance	$6,000
Rental Income	4,800
Wages Expense	7,660
Taxes Payable	4,398
Interest Income	2,325

The company also has the following information available at year end:
1. $4,000 of the Prepaid Insurance has now expired.
2. $2,200 of the Rental Income has not yet been earned.
3. The company must accrue an additional $1,500 of Wages Expense.
4. The Taxes Payable account is overstated by $398.
5. The company has earned an additional $500 of Interest Income.

Required:

a. Prepare the journal entries necessary to adjust the accounts.

b. Use T-accounts to compute both the income statement and balance sheet account balances after the adjustments.

6-21 The Pat Gruber Company has the following normal account balances at year end:

Insurance Expense	$4,000
Unearned Rental Income	3,800
Wages Payable	5,550
Taxes Expense	4,000
Depreciation Expense	7,625

LO 2
Adjustments and Impact on Financial Statements

The company also has the following information available at year end:
1. $1,000 of the Insurance Expense has not yet expired.
2. $1,600 of the Unearned Rental Income has now been earned.
3. The company currently owes employees $1,200 of wages.
4. The company owes an additional $4,900 in real estate taxes.
5. Depreciation Expense for the year totals $8,743.

Required:

a. Prepare the journal entries necessary to adjust the accounts.

b. Use T-accounts to compute both the income statement and balance sheet account balances after the adjustments.

6-22 The Hinton Company has the following account balances at year end:

Insurance Expense	$5,400
Unearned Fee Income	3,525
Wages Payable	3,000
Advertising Expense	9,500
Depreciation Expense	3,850

LO 2
Adjustments and Impact on Financial Statements

The company also has the following information available at year end:
1. $3,200 of the Insurance Expense has not yet expired.
2. $1,200 of the Unearned Fee Income was earned in the last month of the year.
3. The company must accrue an additional $1,800 of Wages Expense.
4. The company paid for $1,900 of advertisements that will be aired next month.
5. Depreciation Expense for the year totals $8,625.

Required:

a. Prepare the journal entries necessary to adjust the accounts.

b. Use T-accounts to compute both the income statement and balance sheet account balances after the adjustments.

6-23 The Willys Company has the following account balances at year end:

Supplies Expense	$2,000
Supplies on Hand	230
Unearned Subscription Income	3,758
Prepaid Rent Expense	4,950
Taxes Expense	1,259
Accumulated Depreciation	8,964

LO 2
Adjustments and Impact on Financial Statements

The company also has the following information available at year end:
1. $500 of the Supplies are still on hand.
2. $1,785 of the Unearned Subscription Income has now been earned.
3. Two months of rent at $850 per month is still prepaid.
4. The Taxes Expense account is overstated by $189.
5. Depreciation Expense for the year is a total of $12,326.

Required:

a. Prepare the general journal entries necessary to adjust the accounts.
b. Use T-accounts to compute both the income statement and balance sheet account balances after the adjustments.

LO 3 and 4
Multistep Income Statement and Earnings Per Share

6-24   The following items relate to Fred Cole Company for the year ended December 31, 2004:

1. Sales for the year totaled $1,075,000.
2. Cost of goods sold for the year totaled $667,000.
3. Operating expenses for the year were $102,500 of which $45,900 were selling expenses.
4. Interest expense for the year was $43,000.
5. Interest income for the year totaled $12,700.
6. Cole's income tax rate is 40%.

Required:

a. Prepare Cole's income statement for the year ended December 31, 2004, using the multistep format presented in this chapter.
b. Compute EPS if Cole has 5,000 shares of common stock outstanding.

LO 3 and 4
Multistep Income Statement and Earnings Per Share

6-25   The following items relate to Toni Bradshaw, Inc. for the year ended December 31, 2005:

1. Sales for the year totaled $465,000.
2. Cost of goods sold for the year totaled $239,000.
3. Operating expenses for the year were $113,200, of which $34,560 was for administrative expenses.
4. Interest expense for the year was $11,000.
5. Bradshaw's income tax rate is 30%.

Required:

a. Prepare Bradshaw's income statement for the year ended December 31, 2005, using the expanded multistep format presented in this chapter.
b. Compute EPS if Bradshaw has 10,000 shares of common stock outstanding.

LO 6
Balance Sheet Accounts

6-26   Listed below are balance sheet classifications followed by a numbered list of balance sheet accounts.

a. Current assets   e. Long-term liabilities
b. Long-term assets   f. Contributed capital
c. Current liabilities   g. Earned capital
d. Intangible assets   h. Investments

1. _____ Accounts Payable
2. _____ Common Stock
3. _____ Franchises
4. _____ Accounts Receivable
5. _____ Note Payable (due within one year)
6. _____ Prepaid Expenses
7. _____ Preferred Stock
8. _____ Note Payable (due in two years)
9. _____ Retained Earnings
10. _____ Paid-in Capital—Common Stock
11. _____ Bond Investments (held for the interest to be earned)
12. _____ Land

13. ____ Investment in Subsidiary
14. ____ Wages Payable
15. ____ Vehicles
16. ____ Copyrights
17. ____ Cash
18. ____ Buildings
19. ____ Bonds Payable
20. ____ Trademarks

Required:

Indicate next to each numbered item where it should be shown on the classified balance sheet. The sections of the classified balance sheet may be used more than once.

6-27   The following items relate to the Dana Corporation at December 31, 2005:

LO 6
Preparation of Balance Sheet

Land	$210,000
Cash	14,600
Accounts Receivable	92,300
Accounts Payable	74,000
Common Stock (75,000 shares outstanding)	300,000
Bonds Payable	100,000
Additional Paid-in Capital—Common Stock	10,000
Inventory	118,000
Prepaid Expenses	11,200
Taxes Payable	17,000
Short-Term Note Payable	50,000
Buildings and Equipment	400,000
Accumulated Depreciation	142,000
Retained Earnings	?
Wages Payable	35,800

Required:

a. What is the par value of Dana Corporation's common stock? Explain how you determined your answer.
b. How much cash did Dana Corporation receive from the sale of its common stock? Explain how you determined your answer.
c. Prepare a classified balance sheet for Dana Corporation at December 31, 2005.

6-28   The following items relate to Wesnidge, Inc. at December 31, 2005:

LO 6
Preparation of Balance Sheet

Accounts Payable	$172,000
Common Stock ($2.00 Par Value)	400,000
Bonds Payable	307,700
Prepaid Expenses	9,800
Taxes Payable	47,000
Short-Term Note Payable	70,000
Buildings and Equipment	875,000
Accumulated Depreciation	271,000
Additional Paid-in Capital—Common Stock	240,000
Land	490,000
Cash	124,200
Accounts Receivable	212,000
Inventory	338,000
Retained Earnings	?
Wages Payable	77,600

Required:

a. How many shares of Wesnidge's common stock are outstanding at December 31, 2005? Explain how you determined your answer.
b. How much cash did Wesnidge, Inc. receive from the sale of its common stock? Explain how you determined your answer.
c. Prepare a classified balance sheet for Wesnidge, Inc. at December 31, 2005.

LO 6
Classified Balance Sheet

6-29 Assets and liabilities on the classified balance sheet are identified as either current or long-term.

Required:

a. What criterion is used to determine whether an asset or liability is classified as current or long-term?
b. Explain in your own words why the following parties would be interested in the separation of current and long-term assets and liabilities on a company's balance sheet:
    1. short-term creditors (other businesses from whom the company buys inventory, supplies, etc.)
    2. long-term creditors (banks and others from whom the company borrows money on a long-term basis)
    3. the company's stockholders
    4. the company's management

LO 6
Classified Balance Sheet

6-30 Stockholders' equity on the classified balance sheet of a corporation is divided into two major categories: contributed capital and retained earnings.

Required:

a. Explain in your own words what each of the two major categories under stockholders' equity represents.
b. Explain in your own words why the following parties would be interested in the relative amounts of contributed capital and retained earnings in the stockholders' equity section of a company's balance sheet:
    1. short-term creditors (other businesses from whom the company buys inventory, supplies, etc.)
    2. long-term creditors (banks and others from whom the company borrows money on a long-term basis)
    3. the company's stockholders
    4. the company's management

Comprehensive Merchandising Company

6-31 The Allen Home Decorating Center began operations on November 1, 2005. Transactions for November are as follows:

Day	Transaction
1	Hal Allen invested $45,000 in exchange for 5,000 shares of $5 par value common stock.
2	Allen signed a lease on a store and paid 6 months' rent in advance of $9,450.
2	Purchased $500 of office supplies from Mott's Office Supply on account.
2	Purchased $25,000 merchandise for resale from Associated Supply on account.
8	Paid $100 for the freight bill on the November 2 purchase.
8	Paid $575 for radio ads to announce the store opening.
9	Purchased a forklift to move merchandise for $5,000 cash.
12	Borrowed $5,000 from First National Bank. Signed a 9%, 90-day note with interest payable on the last day of each month.
14	Sold merchandise for cash of $4,000.
15	Sold $2,500 merchandise on a 30-day account to J. Adams.

Day	Transaction
16	Paid freight on Adams sale of $75.
17	Sold $3,000 merchandise on a 30-day account to A. Bear.
19	Purchased $10,000 merchandise from the Rider Company on account.
20	Made cash sales of $20,000.
21	Paid Mott's Office Supply.
23	Paid Associated Supply for the purchase on November 2.
24	Collected payment in full from A. Bear.
25	Paid Rider Company for the purchase on November 19.
25	Received payment in full from J. Adams.
28	Paid utilities for the month of $800.
29	Paid wages for the month of $4,000.
30	Paid Allen a salary of $1,000 for the month.

Required:

a. Journalize the transactions for November in the general journal.

b. Open the necessary accounts in the general ledger and post the November transactions to the appropriate accounts in the general ledger.

c. Prepare a trial balance on November 30, 2005.

d. Prepare adjusting entries and complete a worksheet using the following information in addition to that listed in the transactions:
   1. Allen depreciated the forklift for the entire month of November, assuming straight-line depreciation with no residual value and a 5-year estimated life.
   2. Allen accrued the interest on the bank loan for 18 days.
   3. Allen incurred payroll tax expense of $400 for the month.
   4. The ending Merchandise Inventory balance is $24,800.
   5. The corporate income tax rate is 30%.

e. Prepare a balance sheet as of November 30, 2005, and a statement of income and a statement of stockholder's equity for the month ended November 30, 2005.

f. Compute EPS.

g. Post the adjusting entries to the general ledger.

h. Assume that Allen decides to make November 30 his year end. Prepare and post the closing entries.

i. Prepare a post-closing trial balance.

6-32 John Robles began his retail clothing business Fineries, Inc. on November 1, 2004. The post-closing trial balance at November 30, 2004, appeared as follows:

Comprehensive
Merchandising
Company

Fineries, Inc.
Post-Closing Trial Balance
November 30, 2004

	Debits	Credits
Cash	$40,000	
Prepaid Rent	200	
Merchandise Inventory	24,000	
Fixtures	12,000	
Accumulated Depreciation		$ 200
Wages Payable		1,500
Common Stock, $1 Par		10,000
Paid-in Capital—Common Stock		60,000
Retained Earnings		4,500
Totals	$76,200	$76,200

The following transactions occurred in December 2004:

Day	Transaction
1	Robles invested an additional $100,000 cash in exchange for 20,000 shares of common stock.
1	Bought more store fixtures on account from the Acme Company for $13,600, terms n/30.
1	Paid three months rent in advance, $12,000.
2	Purchased $8,000 merchandise on account from Triad Company. The invoice date was December 3, terms 2/10, n/60.
3	Paid for a 24-month contents insurance policy for fire damage at a cost of $1,440.
4	Purchased merchandise for resale for $25,000 cash.
5	Returned damaged merchandise to Triad Company and received credit for $1,600.
10	Sold merchandise to Jean Peoples on account for $12,600. The terms of the sale were 1/10, n/30.
12	Paid the balance due to Triad Company.
15	Cash sales for the first half of the month totaled $27,500.
15	Sold merchandise to Janeal Foster on account for $10,000. The terms of the sale were 1/10, n/30.
15	Paid wages for the first half of the month totaling $5,500, including the balance due from November.
18	Purchased merchandise on account from Kerr Company for $9,500. The invoice date was December 20, and the terms were 2/10, n/30.
20	Purchased office supplies totaling $250.
20	Received merchandise returned by Janeal Foster. Issued a credit memo for $1,500.
20	Received a check from Jean Peoples for her invoice less discount.
24	Received a check from Janeal Foster for payment of invoice less discount.
28	Sold merchandise on account to Paul Larsen, $8,600. The terms were 1/10, n/30.
28	Paid utility bill of $490 for December.
28	Received telephone bill for $255 for December due on January 10.
28	Paid Kerr Company for the invoice of December 18, less discount.
31	Recorded cash sales for the second half of December totaling $44,900.
31	Paid wages for the second half of December, $4,500.
31	Received a bill for delivery services for December $250 due on January 5.

Required:

a. Journalize the transactions for December in the general journal assuming Robles selected November 30 as the company's year end.

b. Open the necessary accounts in the general ledger and post the December transactions to the general ledger.

c. Prepare a trial balance at December 31, 2004.

d. Prepare adjusting entries and complete a worksheet using the following information along with that found in the transactions:
1. Robles accrued payroll tax expense of $1,200 for the month.
2. Store fixtures have a 6-year life with no salvage value.
3. Ending Merchandise Inventory balance was $14,000.

e. Prepare a balance sheet as of December 31, 2004, a statement of income, and a statement of owner's equity for the month ended December 31, 2004.

f. Compute EPS.

g. Post the adjusting entries to the general ledger.

Comprehensive Merchandising Company

6-33 Jay Chambless started a retail hardware store, Chambless Home Haven, Inc. on December 1, 2004. The following transactions occurred in December:

Day	Transaction
1	Chambless invested $200,000 cash to purchase 100,000 shares of common stock of Chambless Home Haven. The stock had a par value of $1 per share, and 200,000 shares were authorized.
1	Bought store fixtures on account from the Ace Company for $22,000, terms n/30.
1	Paid $9,000 rent for December, January, and February.

Day	Transaction
3	Purchased merchandise on account from Taylor Company for $50,000. The invoice date was December 5, terms 2/10, n/30.
3	Paid for a 12-month umbrella business insurance policy at a cost of $1,200.
4	Returned damaged merchandise to Taylor Company and received credit for $16,000.
4	Sold merchandise to A. V. Hill on account, $24,000. The terms were 1/10, n/30.
5	Paid for store supplies of $630 for items received December 2.
5	Purchased merchandise for resale for $30,000 cash.
7	Recorded cash sales for the first week of $11,400.
10	Paid the balance due to Taylor Company.
14	Received a check from A. V. Hill for invoice less discount.
15	Cash sales for the second week totaled $18,600.
15	Paid wages for the first half of the month totaling $7,000 less 1,200 of withholding taxes.
16	Sold merchandise to Mel Hays on account, $5,000. The terms were 1/10, n/30.
16	Purchased merchandise on account from McGee Company for $18,000. The invoice date was December 17, terms 2/10, n/30.
17	Received merchandise returned by Mel Hays. Issued a credit memo for $700.
21	Sales for the third week totaled $18,200.
23	Received a check from Mel Hays for payment of invoice less discount.
23	Sold merchandise on account to Dennis Rhodes for $12,600, terms 1/10, n/30.
27	Paid McGee Company for the invoice of December 18 less discount.
31	Recorded cash sales for the last 10 days of December totaling $17,000.
31	Paid utility bill of $452 for December.
31	Received telephone bill for $320 for December due on January 12.
31	Paid wages for the second half of December, $7,500, less $1,450 of withholding taxes.
31	Received a bill for delivery services for December, $400, due January 10.
31	Chambless declared and paid a 10¢ per share cash dividend.

Required:

a. Journalize the transactions for December in the general journal.

b. Open the necessary accounts in the general ledger and post the December transactions to the appropriate accounts.

c. Prepare a trial balance at December 31, 2004.

d. Prepare adjusting entries, post them to the general ledger, and complete a worksheet using the following information:
   1. Chambless accrued payroll tax expense of $2,000 for the month.
   2. Fixtures are depreciated using the straight-line method, life of 4 years, with no salvage value.
   3. The ending Merchandise Inventory balance is $15,000.
   4. The combined corporate tax rate is 40%.

e. Prepare a balance sheet as of December 31, 2004, a statement of income, and a statement of stockholder's equity for the month ended December 31, 2004.

f. Assume that Chambless selects a calendar year as his fiscal year. Prepare the closing entries to close the year.

g. Prepare a post-closing trial balance at December 31, 2004.

6-34 The Blues Brothers began a management consulting business on October 1, 2004, called Blues Brothers Consulting, Inc. The following transactions occurred in October:

Comprehensive Service Company

Day	Transaction
1	John Blue invested $6,000 for 600 shares of $10 par value common stock and his brother Art invested $4,000 for 400 shares.
1	Purchased a computer for $3,000 and a copy machine for $2,000. Each piece of equipment had an expected life of 5 years with no residual value. The equipment was financed with a 3-year, 10% bank loan that requires monthly interest payments and $1,000 principal payments each September 30.

Day	Transaction
1	Paid $3,000 rent for October, November, and December.
2	Purchased on account from Spring Company office supplies for $700 and office furniture for $2,600. The invoice date was October 4, terms 2/10, n/30. The office furniture has a useful life of 10 years with no salvage value.
2	Paid for a 1-year business insurance policy at a cost of $650.
10	Performed consulting services and billed Sam Hall on account, $14,000.
11	Received $4,000 for cash consulting services performed.
12	Paid for the purchases from Spring Company on October 2.
15	Received $2,000 for cash consulting services performed.
15	Billed Gary Suter $5,000 for consulting fees.
16	Paid secretarial wages for the first half of the month totaling $1,000 less $125 of withholding taxes.
19	Purchased computer supplies on account from Dale Company, $400. The invoice date was October 19, terms 2/10, n/30.
20	Purchased office supplies for cash totaling $400.
20	Received payment from Sam Hall.
25	Received a check from Gary Suter for payment of his invoice.
28	Paid Dale Company for the invoice of October 19, less discount.
28	Provided services on account to Dan Lee for $21,600.
29	Paid the utility bill of $310 for October.
29	Received telephone bill for $325 for October. The payment is due November 6.
31	Paid wages for the second half of October, $1,500 less $160 withholding taxes.
31	Received and paid a bill for fax services for October, $100.
31	Paid $4,500 for officers' salaries less $1,300 in withholding taxes.

Required:

  a. Journalize the transactions for October in the general journal.

  b. Open the necessary accounts in the general ledger and post the October transactions to the appropriate accounts.

  c. Prepare a trial balance at October 31, 2004.

  d. Prepare and post adjusting entries and complete a worksheet using the following information along with that listed in the transactions:

    1. The employer payroll tax expense is $800 for the month.

    2. Office supplies of $100 were on hand at October 31.

    3. No computer supplies were left at month end.

    4. The corporate tax rate is 35%.

  e. Prepare a balance sheet as of October 31, 2004, a statement of income, and a statement of stockholders' equity for the month ended October 31, 2004.

Comprehensive Manufacturing Company

6-35   The transactions for December 2003 for Hackler Manufacturing Corporation are as follows:

Day	Transaction
1	CEO Jim Hackler deposited $175,000 in the corporate bank account for 50,000 shares of $1 par value common stock.
1	Purchased a milling machine for $80,000 cash.
1	Borrowed $70,000 at 9% interest from the bank to pay for the milling machine, using it as collateral. Interest is payable monthly on the first day of the month and a semiannual principal payment of $5,000 is due the first day of June and December each year.
2	Purchased shop equipment costing $20,000 on account.
2	Paid $4,000 for an advertising campaign to announce the opening of his business.
2	Paid $12,000 for rent on the factory and office for December and the last 2 months of a two-year lease.
4	Purchased raw materials, on account, costing $20,000, terms 2/10, net 30.
4	Purchased office furniture for $2,500 on account.
5	Requisitioned $5,230 of raw material to put into process.
6	Purchased office supplies for $430.

NOTE

This is the same data as in problem 5-27. Information is given to complete the accounting cycle for the month.

Day	Transaction
8	Paid $3,000 for direct labor.
9	Sold manufactured products for $16,000 to a wholesale customer on account.
14	Collected the $16,000 from the customer on December 9.
15	Paid officer's salary of $2,500.
15	Paid for the raw materials purchased on December 4.
16	Paid $5,200 for direct labor.
19	Paid the telephone bill of $410 and utility bills of $698.
20	Sold manufactured products for $9,500 cash.
20	Purchased $13,000 of raw materials that were delivered and paid for with cash.
21	Requisitioned $19,430 of raw materials for transfer to work-in-process.
23	Paid the local parts distributor $600 for parts used to repair the milling machine, and ordered $1,300 of repair parts for inventory.
29	Ordered $15,000 of raw materials from a vendor, terms 1/15, net 30.
30	Received the order placed on December 29, the goods were shipped FOB shipping point.
30	Paid the freight bill of $225 on the order received on December 30.
31	Sold $22,500 of manufactured product on account.
31	Paid $6,500 in direct labor.
31	Paid officer's salary of $3,500.

Required:

a. Prepare a chart of accounts for Jim Hackler's corporation.
b. Prepare the journal entries for Hackler's corporate transactions.
c. Post the transactions to the general ledger.
d. Prepare a trial balance after posting to the ledger.
e. Prepare adjusting entries, post them to the general ledger, and complete a worksheet using the following information:
   1. Hackler accrued payroll tax expense of $1,660 for the month.
   2. The company policy requires straight-line depreciation. Equipment has a life of 5 years with no salvage value and office furniture has a 10-year life with no salvage value.
   3. Factory rent is $3,600 of the total and the utilities allocated to the factory are $620 of the total.
   4. The ending inventory balances are as follows:

Office Supplies	$ 205
Raw Materials	13,340
Work-in-Process	4,500
Finished Goods	3,950

   5. The combined corporate tax rate is 40%.
f. Prepare a balance sheet as of December 31, 2003, a statement of income, and a statement of stockholder's equity for the month ended December 31, 2003.
g. Assume that Hackler selects a calendar year as his fiscal year. Prepare the closing entries to close the year.
h. Prepare a post-closing trial balance at December 31, 2003.

6-36 The transactions for December 2004 for Miles Manufacturing, Incorporated, are as follows:

Comprehensive Manufacturing Company

Day	Transaction
1	Deposited $200,000 in the corporate bank account in exchange for 50,000 shares of $4 par value common stock.
1	Purchased production equipment for $100,000.
1	Borrowed $100,000 at 9% interest from the bank to pay for the equipment, using it as collateral. Interest is payable monthly on the first day of the month and a semiannual principal payment of $5,000 is due the first day of June and December each year.

NOTE
This is the same data as in problem 5-28. Information is given to complete the accounting cycle for the month.

Day	Transaction
2	Purchased shop equipment costing $20,000 paying cash.
2	Ordered $25,000 of raw materials, terms 1/15, net 30, FOB shipping point.
2	Paid $4,000 rent on shop and office for December.
5	Received the order placed on December 2 for raw materials and paid $534 of freight on receipt.
5	Purchased raw materials costing $10,000 paying with cash.
5	Purchased office furniture for $2,650 paying with cash.
5	Requisitioned $17,065 of raw material to put into process.
6	Purchased office supplies of $506 and factory supplies of $1,893.
7	Paid direct labor of $6,000 less $1,495 of withholding taxes.
8	Requisitioned $16,753 of raw materials to put into process.
9	Sold manufactured products for $30,000 on account.
10	Collected the $30,000 from the customer on December 9.
10	Paid for the raw materials purchased on December 2.
14	Paid direct labor of $7,000 less $1,865 of withholding taxes.
15	Purchased $32,780 of raw materials, terms 3/10, net 15, FOB destination from a local supplier.
15	Paid officers' salaries of $5,000 less $1,680 of withholding taxes.
15	Paid withholding taxes to the government plus $1,440 in employer payroll taxes.
15	Requisitioned $12,672 of raw materials for the factory.
16	Sold manufactured products for $28,500 on account, terms 2/10, net 30.
16	Paid utilities for the factory of $1,535.
17	Purchased $273 of repair parts for the production equipment, and ordered $500 of repair parts for inventory.
17	Purchased $12,780 of raw materials, terms 3/10, net 15, FOB destination.
21	Paid $7,500 of direct labor less $1,980 in withholding taxes.
22	Requisitioned $23,765 of raw materials for the factory.
23	Sold manufactured products for $37,250 for cash.
24	Paid for the materials purchased on December 15.
26	Received payment for the sale on December 16.
28	Paid $7,000 of direct labor less $1,865 of withholding taxes.
29	Ordered $21,654 of raw materials from a vendor terms 1/15, net 60, FOB destination.
30	Received the order placed on December 29.
30	Sold manufactured products for $37,920, terms 2/10, net 20 days.
30	Paid officers' salaries of $5,000 less $1,680 of withholding taxes.
30	Paid withholding taxes to the government plus $1,560 in employer payroll taxes.

Required:

a. Prepare a chart of accounts for Miles Manufacturing, Incorporated.
b. Prepare the journal entries for the company's transactions.
c. Post the transactions to the general ledger.
d. Prepare a trial balance after completing the posting process.
e. Prepare adjusting entries, post them to the general ledger, and complete a worksheet using the following information:
   1. Shop rent is $3,300 of the total for the month.
   2. Direct labor wages unpaid at month end were $3,000.
   3. The company policy requires straight-line depreciation. Shop equipment and machinery have a life of 6 years with no salvage value and office furniture has a 12-year life with no salvage value.

4. The ending inventory balances are as follows:

Office Supplies	$ 920
Raw Materials	32,200
Work-in-Process	11,300
Finished Goods	14,725

5. The Combined corporate tax rate is 40%.

f. Prepare a balance sheet as of December 31, 2004, a statement of income, and a statement of stockholder's equity for the month ended December 31, 2004.

g. Assume that Miles selects a calendar year as his fiscal year. Prepare the closing entries to close the year.

h. Prepare a post-closing trial balance at December 31, 2004.

6-37 The CEO of the Viper Company was concerned because the company's profit levels have dropped over the past two years. The CEO asked the CFO how the company could improve its financial picture for the current year. The CEO reminded the CFO of the large increase in fixed assets acquired this year. The CEO told the CFO that it was crucial to increase the reported profitability.

 Ethics

Required:

a. Can the CFO do anything to please the CEO and remain both ethical and legal?

b. What would the impact on the financial statements be if the CFO changed the method of determining depreciation from double-declining-balance to straight-line on the new equipment? Would this action be ethical or legal?

CHAPTER 7

Using Analytical Review for Internal Financial Decisions and Cash Management

W ith the first year of operations completed at Elevation Sports, Inc., the officers had a nearly complete set of financial statements. Now what? Financial statements are not an end unto themselves; rather, they are the beginning of a financial information analysis process. As internal analysts, the four officers can file the financial statements and send a copy to their only external analyst at the time, the banker. The ostrich approach is to wait for the banker's comments. If the comments are good, the firm must be doing all right. If they are not, the banker will tell them what to do. Surprisingly, many small start-up companies take that approach. Our group, however, has the education and experience to make the most of their firm's financial information.

Both internal and external analysts employ a number of techniques to understand the financial information presented in the financial statements. Internal analysts have access to detailed financial information continuously during a year and can monitor activities monthly or weekly. In contrast, external analysts have access to aggregate information only a limited number of times each year. Consequently, both groups look back in time for their analyses, but external analysts have a much longer time lag in information. In Chapter 7 we will explore analytical review techniques for financial accounting information and the analysis of cash emphasizing internal financial management. Analytical review techniques are tools financial analysts use to identify relationships among financial data. Such relationships can become early warning signals to help managers discover impending problems or the beginning of negative trends. In Chapter 8 we

● **analytical review techniques**
Tools financial analysts use to identify relationships among financial data.

will complete the financial statement analysis process used by both internal and external analysts, with emphasis on profitability, liquidity, and solvency.

Internal Analysts of Financial Information

Management is responsible for a company's day-to-day operation. As financial decision makers, managers share some objectives of external analysts, but they also have distinctive objectives in performing financial statement analysis. Their first objective is to ensure the integrity of the financial statements. Managers naturally want the financial statements to present the financial results to external parties in the most favorable manner. The qualitative characteristic of accounting information of representational faithfulness, however, indicates that the statement should represent the true operations and resources of the company. Some people, however, believe that many managers emphasize managing the financial statements rather than managing the business. Financial scandals of the 21st century have revealed the consequences of misplaced management attention.

What Do You Think?

7-1   What do you think the phrase "managing the financial statements rather than managing the business" means?

7-2   Are there any ethical boundaries in managing the financial statements?

Managers' second objective in analyzing the company's financial statements is to monitor the overall performance of the business in much the same way that external parties do. Managers use analytical review techniques to discover the firm's positive and negative financial trends. Their ability to responsibly manage cash flow also plays a role in the survival of any business. Cash enables a company to operate and pay its bills. Without enough cash, an otherwise profitable company can go bankrupt. The most problematic issue of most growing companies is maintaining positive cash flow, a condition in which cash inflows exceed cash outflows.

Analyzing Information from Financial Statements

● **trend analysis**
A technique that indicates the amount of changes in key financial data over time.

● **common-size statement**
An analysis that converts each element of the balance sheet from dollar amounts to percentages of total assets and each element of an income statement from dollar amounts to percentages of sales.

In this chapter, we will explore two forms of analytical review—trend analysis and common-size statements. **Trend analysis** is a technique that indicates the amount of changes in key financial data over time. An analyst can view the changes in each balance sheet or income statement element to determine whether a pattern of change emerges. Are assets and equity growing over time and at the same rate or at different rates? Have sales increased over time and at a faster pace than expenses? Is net income increasing at a steady rate or erratically? These are some of the questions that trend analysis can help the analyst discern.

A **common-size statement** is an analysis that converts each element of the balance sheet from dollar amounts to percentages of total assets and each element of an income statement from dollar amounts to percentages of sales. Instead of dollars, a common-size statement expresses all elements in ratios, making it easier for the user to understand the relationships among the numbers. With a common-size statement, an analyst can examine the composition of assets or the composition of its capital structure.

We analyze the composition of the company's assets to determine whether the company has the best mix of assets. As an analogy, if you want to create a culinary masterpiece, once you have assembled the right ingredients, the percentage of each ingredient in the finished dish is the most critical factor in the success of the effort. Likewise, a firm needs the right mix of cash, inventory, and equipment to enable workers to conduct profitable operations. If a company has buildings full of equipment, but no cash to pay workers, no inventory can be produced or sold.

A common-size statement can help the analyst examine each element on the income statement as a percentage of net sales to determine when certain expenses are too high. When the analysis reveals that advertising expense is 20 percent of sales in an industry where 10 percent is normal, the analyst might conclude that the advertising is not effective. Such analysis helps managers run the company more profitably.

Because businesses do not operate in a vacuum, managers must also weigh a company's analytical reviews and all its financial information in the context of background information about a company's external environment. Conclusions drawn from analyses should also consider general economic conditions, the political climate, and the industry outlook. Is the company ahead of or behind the curve of the economy and its industry? Not knowing where the company stands can cause managers to make disastrous decisions. Consider the shock to the retail and travel industries in the last third of 2001.

What Do You Think?

7-3 What were the immediate and longer range effects of the events of 2001 for the retail and travel industries?

7-4 If you owned a retail business at the end of September 2001, would you have changed your normal purchasing practices for the next year? Why?

If we look at the general retail merchandise industry during 2001, it was plagued by extremes of success and failure. Wal-Mart Stores, Inc. claimed to be the undisputed sales leader in the industry with seemingly unstoppable momentum. Prior leaders in the industry such as the J. C. Penney Company, Montgomery Ward, and Kmart Corporation were in trouble. Both Montgomery Ward and Kmart filed for bankruptcy; Montgomery Ward chose to cease operations and Kmart attempted to survive. After September 2001, the whole industry was struggling to improve profit margins and stem fourth-quarter losses. Family Dollar Stores, Inc. is a very small player in the industry—much like Wal-Mart was in the early 1970s. As we analyze Family Dollar in these two chapters, we see how analysts might predict whether it would become a success story or another failure.

Limitations of Analytical Review Analysis

Analytical reviews give the internal or external analyst a useful tool for understanding the nature of the company. Along with the insight garnered during this process, any analyst should remember to view the information within the context of the economic, political, and industry environments. We also recognize the following limitations:

1 **Our ability to predict the future using past results depends on the predictive value of the information we use.** Changes in the general economy, in the economy of the particular industry being studied, and in the company's management are some of the uncertainties that can cause past results to be an unreliable predictor of the future.
2 **The financial statements used for the analysis are based on historical cost.** In a time of rapidly changing prices, comparison between years might be difficult.

With these limitations in mind, let's look first at trend analysis.

Trend Analysis

The technique for trend analysis is a simple method of time series analysis. We will plot a specific financial measure over time. A humorous axiom in statistics is, "If you torture the data sufficiently, it will confess something." Although humorous, it is often true. The study of financial measures over time provides information and sometimes insight into truths we might otherwise overlook. We will conduct a trend analysis for balance sheets, income statements, EPS, and cash flow statements.

First, we need data for a series of years. Elevation Sports has only completed one year of operation, so we will use Family Dollar Stores, the company we highlighted in Chapter 2. For the analysis to have the most predictive value, we must use the most recent consecutive years. Exhibit 7-1 shows financial statements for fiscal years 1996 through 2003. To compute the trend balance sheets, we set the oldest year as the base year so that we can see growth patterns more clearly. The base year values for each balance sheet item are denoted as 100. To compute subsequent years, for each item on the balance sheet, such as Cash or Accounts Payable, we divide the current year dollar amount by the base year dollar amount. For example, look at the following trend computation for Cash:

Use a worksheet program such as Microsoft Excel® to prepare your analyses.

Year	Computation		Trend Value
1996	$\dfrac{\$\ 18{,}845}{\$\ 18{,}845}$	=	100.00
1997	$\dfrac{\$\ 42{,}468}{\$\ 18{,}845}$	=	225.35
1998	$\dfrac{\$134{,}221}{\$\ 18{,}845}$	=	712.24
1999	$\dfrac{\$\ 95{,}301}{\$\ 18{,}845}$	=	505.71
2000	$\dfrac{\$\ 43{,}558}{\$\ 18{,}845}$	=	231.14
2001	$\dfrac{\$\ 21{,}753}{\$\ 18{,}845}$	=	115.43
2002	$\dfrac{\$220{,}265}{\$\ 18{,}845}$	=	1,168.82
2003	$\dfrac{\$206{,}731}{\$\ 18{,}845}$	=	1,097.01

We continue the process for each element in the balance sheet to arrive at the trend balance sheet in Exhibit 7-2 on page 238.

The Trend Balance Sheet

What can we learn from the trend balance sheet for Family Dollar? Consider the following items:

1 **What happened to total assets during this eight-year period?** Total assets almost tripled; you see that the 2003 trend amount is 284.97 percent of 1996. If you look at the total assets line in Exhibit 7-2, growth was spread over the eight years and each year had growth over the previous year. Normally, steady asset growth indicates a positive direction for a company.

Exhibit 7-1

Comparative Financial Statements for Family Dollar Stores, Inc. For years 1996 through 2003*

Family Dollar Stores, Inc. and Subsidiaries
Consolidated Balance Sheets

For the Year Ended (In Thousands)	AUGUST 30 2003	AUGUST 31 2002	SEPTEMBER 1 2001	AUGUST 26 2000	AUGUST 28 1999	AUGUST 29 1998	AUGUST 31 1997	AUGUST 31 1996
Assets								
Cash and cash equivalents	$ 206,731	$ 220,265	$ 21,753	$ 43,558	$ 95,301	$ 134,221	$ 42,468	$ 18,845
Merchandise inventories	854,370	766,631	721,560	644,614	568,781	465,556	467,946	462,840
Other current assets	95,391	68,963	63,952	62,500	55,873	46,852	34,289	26,215
Property and equipment (net)	812,123	685,617	580,879	487,585	371,141	291,760	231,235	184,607
Other assets	17,080	13,143	11,601	5,457	4,156	3,791	4,356	4,301
Total Assets	**$1,985,695**	**$1,754,619**	**$1,399,745**	**$1,243,714**	**$1,095,252**	**$942,180**	**$780,294**	**$696,808**
Liabilities and Shareholders' Equity								
Liabilities								
Accounts payable	$ 401,799	$ 381,164	$ 264,965	$ 277,265	$ 244,810	$ 214,099	$ 165,150	$ 157,012
Other current liabilities	193,532	149,616	125,329	134,752	133,737	129,176	96,077	77,194
Deferred income taxes	79,395	68,891	50,436	33,733	26,054	20,754	18,869	17,645
Total Liabilities	$ 674,726	$ 599,671	$ 440,730	$ 445,750	$ 404,601	$ 364,029	$ 280,096	$ 251,851
Shareholders' Equity	1,310,969	1,154,948	959,015	797,964	690,651	578,151	500,198	444,957
Total Liabilities and Equity	**$1,985,695**	**$1,754,619**	**$1,399,745**	**$1,243,714**	**$1,095,252**	**$942,180**	**$780,294**	**$696,808**

Accompanying notes are an integral part of the consolidated financial statements.

Family Dollar Stores, Inc. and Subsidiaries
Consolidated Income Statements

For the Year Ended (In Thousands)	AUGUST 30 2003	AUGUST 31 2002	SEPTEMBER 1 2001	AUGUST 26 2000	AUGUST 28 1999	AUGUST 29 1998	AUGUST 31 1997	AUGUST 31 1996
Net sales	$4,750,171	$4,162,652	$3,665,362	$3,132,639	$2,751,181	$2,361,930	$1,994,973	$1,714,627
Costs and expenses:								
Cost of sales	3,145,788	2,766,733	2,439,261	2,076,916	1,833,442	1,588,656	1,350,157	1,156,195
Selling, general & administrative	1,214,658	1,054,298	927,679	784,812	695,060	607,286	523,339	459,666
Total Expenses	4,360,446	3,821,031	3,366,940	2,861,728	2,528,502	2,195,942	1,873,496	1,615,861
Income before income taxes	389,725	341,621	298,422	270,911	222,679	165,988	121,477	98,766
Income taxes	142,250	124,692	108,917	98,894	82,600	62,700	46,800	38,178
Net income	$ 247,475	$ 216,929	$ 189,505	$ 172,017	$ 140,079	$ 103,288	$ 74,677	$ 60,588
Net income per common share	$1.44	$1.25	$1.10	$1.00	$0.81	$0.60	$0.44	$0.35

Accompanying notes are an integral part of the consolidated financial statements.

Family Dollar Stores, Inc. and Subsidiaries
Consolidated Statement of Cash Flows

For the Year Ended (In Thousands)	AUGUST 30 2003	AUGUST 31 2002	SEPTEMBER 1 2001	AUGUST 26 2000	AUGUST 28 1999	AUGUST 29 1998	AUGUST 31 1997	AUGUST 31 1996
Operating cash flows	$294,998	$402,603	$165,910	$183,556	$110,883	$211,538	$123,242	$81,241
Investing cash flows	(218,726)	(184,040)	(160,170)	(171,371)	(123,112)	(95,330)	(75,783)	(52,845)
Financing cash flows	(89,806)	(20,051)	(27,545)	(63,928)	(26,691)	(24,455)	(23,836)	(18,404)
Net change in cash	(13,534)	198,512	(21,805)	(51,743)	(38,920)	91,753	23,623	9,992
Cash, beginning of year	220,265	21,753	43,558	95,301	134,221	42,468	18,845	8,853
Cash, end of year	$206,731	$220,265	$ 21,753	$ 43,558	$ 95,301	$134,221	$ 42,468	$18,845

Accompanying notes are an integral part of the consolidated financial statements.

*These are abbreviated financial statements. The complete statements can be found on the company Web site at *www.familydollar.com*.

Exhibit 7-2
Trend Balance Sheet

Family Dollar Stores, Inc. and Subsidiaries Trend Consolidated Balance Sheets								
For the Year Ended	AUGUST 30 2003	AUGUST 31 2002	SEPTEMBER 1 2001	AUGUST 26 2000	AUGUST 28 1999	AUGUST 29 1998	AUGUST 31 1997	AUGUST 31 1996
Assets								
Cash and cash equivalents	1097.01	1168.82	115.43	231.14	505.71	712.24	225.35	100.00
Merchandise inventories	184.59	165.64	155.90	139.27	122.89	100.59	101.10	100.00
Other current assets	363.88	263.07	243.95	238.41	213.13	178.72	130.80	100.00
Property and equipment (net)	439.92	371.39	314.66	264.12	201.04	158.04	125.26	100.00
Other assets	397.12	305.58	269.73	126.88	96.63	88.14	101.28	100.00
Total Assets	284.97	251.81	200.88	178.49	157.18	135.21	111.98	100.00
Liabilities and Shareholders' Equity								
Liabilities								
Accounts payable	255.90	242.76	168.75	176.59	155.92	136.36	105.18	100.00
Other current liabilities	250.71	193.82	162.36	174.56	173.25	167.34	124.46	100.00
Deferred income taxes	449.96	390.43	285.84	191.18	147.66	117.62	106.94	100.00
Total Liabilities	267.91	238.11	175.00	176.99	160.65	144.54	111.21	100.00
Shareholders' Equity	294.63	259.56	215.53	179.34	155.22	129.93	112.41	100.00
Total Liabilities and Equity	284.97	251.81	200.88	178.49	157.18	135.21	111.98	100.00

● **supply-chain management**
The business process of ordering, handling, and managing inventory.

2 **Did each component of assets grow at the same rate as total assets?**
No, each element varied from total assets. Cash had both increases and decreases over the eight years. Inventory grew steadily but at a much slower rate than total assets. Both other current assets and property and equipment grew at a steady, but faster, rate than total assets. Other assets grew more than total assets but at inconsistent rates.

Taken as a whole, the company's assets grew during the eight years. The firm expanded its operations because, as Exhibit 7-2 shows, property and equipment grew at 1.54 times the rate of total assets (439.92 / 284.97 = 1.54). The company may have become more efficient with its **supply-chain management**, the business process of ordering, handling, and managing inventory. We speculate about that new efficiency because of the evidence that the inventory grew at a slower rate than total assets or property and equipment. We can confirm this supposition when we examine the income statement. Look at the graph in Exhibit 7-3 for a pictorial view of the growth of assets for Family Dollar.

3 **Did assets, liabilities, and stockholders' equity grow at the same rate?**
Liabilities grew 268 percent over eight years, whereas stockholders' equity grew 295 percent. Therefore, the company improved its equity position with profitable operations and decreased its relative debt position, a positive indicator for a growing company.

Notice that the amount of liabilities increased 268 percent, but the percentage of assets owed to creditors declined from 36.14 percent ($251,851/$696,808) in 1996 to 33.98 percent ($674,726/$1,985,695). Due to the small amount of debt and absence of long-term debt, Family Dollar has a conservative liability position, which reduces the relative risk of an investment in the company. The liabilities grew, however, in 2003 compared to 2002. Confirm these trends in Exhibit 7-4.

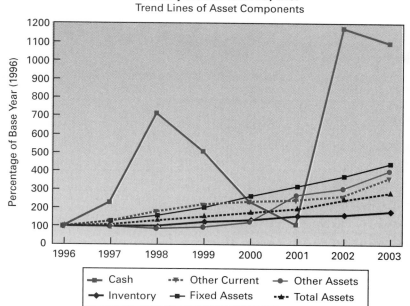

Family Dollar Stores, Inc.
Trend Lines of Asset Components

Exhibit 7-3
Trend Lines of Asset Components, Family Dollar Stores, Inc. 1996 through 2003

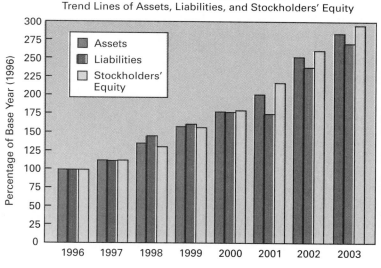

Family Dollar Stores, Inc.
Trend Lines of Assets, Liabilities, and Stockholders' Equity

Exhibit 7-4
Trend Lines for Family Dollar Stores, Inc. Assets, Liabilities, and Stockholders' Equity, 1996 through 2003

The Trend Income Statement

Turning our attention to the trend income statement, we can analyze the changes in revenues, expenses, and the resulting net income by computing the trend statistic in the same way we did for the balance sheet, using 1996 as the base year. Exhibit 7-5 illustrates the trend income statements for Family Dollar for the eight-year period from 1996 to 2003. We want to consider the following items:

1 Did sales, expenses, and net income increase steadily during the periods examined? Yes, each component of the income statement increased at a fairly steady rate over the eight years, as Exhibit 7-6 illustrates. The best news, however, is that while sales increased each year, expenses increased at a slower rate each year, resulting in higher profits before and after taxes. It is critical for managers to understand that increasing revenues does little good if it causes expenses to increase at a higher rate than the revenues. At some point, the increasing expenses

Exhibit 7-5
Trend Income Statements

	Family Dollar Stores, Inc. and Subsidiaries Trend Consolidated Income Statements							
For the Year Ended	AUGUST 30 2003	AUGUST 31 2002	SEPTEMBER 1 2001	AUGUST 26 2000	AUGUST 28 1999	AUGUST 29 1998	AUGUST 31 1997	AUGUST 31 1996
Net sales	277.04	242.77	213.77	182.70	160.45	137.75	116.35	100.00
Costs and expenses:								
Cost of sales	272.08	239.30	210.97	179.63	158.58	137.40	116.78	100.00
Selling, general & administrative	264.25	229.36	201.82	170.74	151.21	132.11	113.85	100.00
Total Expenses	269.85	236.47	208.37	177.10	156.48	135.90	115.94	100.00
Income before income taxes	394.59	345.89	302.15	274.30	225.46	168.06	122.99	100.00
Income taxes	372.60	326.61	285.29	259.03	216.35	164.23	122.58	100.00
Net income	408.46	358.04	312.78	283.91	231.20	170.48	123.25	100.00
Net income per common share	411.43	357.14	314.29	285.71	231.43	171.43	125.71	100.00

Exhibit 7-6
Trend Lines for Sales,
Expenses, and Net Income for
Family Dollar Stores, Inc.
1996 through 2003

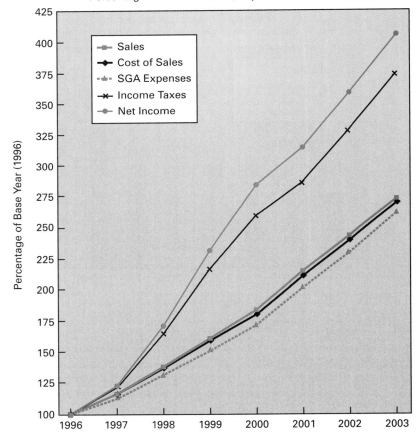

Family Dollar Stores, Inc.
Percentage Increase in Sales, Expenses, and Net Income

can overtake the revenue increases and cause losses to occur. For Family Dollar, a 277 percent increase in sales resulted in a 408 percent increase in net profit.

2   **Did the cost of sales increase or decrease relative to sales during the period?**   For a merchandising firm, the key factor to increasing profits is maintaining or decreasing the cost of sales. Sales increased 277 percent whereas cost of sales only increased 272 percent. Therefore, Family Dollar increased its

gross margin spread during this time. We suggested that management might have achieved some efficiency in their supply-chain management. This serves to confirm it. Sales increased 277 percent, but inventory only grew 185 percent and cost of sales increased 272 percent. The proportionate decrease in the amount of inventory on hand decreased the costs of managing it and increased the profitability.

Earnings per Share

A publicly traded company will carefully watch its EPS because shareholders and potential investors consider it a critical indicator of performance. We should address the following questions:

1 **Did EPS rise steadily each year during the period?** Investors do not like erratic EPS amounts; neither do they like declining trends in EPS. Family Dollar increased EPS at about 1.49 times the increase in sales.

2 **Did EPS rise in proportion to the increase in sales?** The answer here is no, and this time no is good. Increases in EPS outstripped the increase in sales each year indicating that profitability increased each year. Such news is the best news for investors and stockholders.

You can verify both these assumptions with Exhibit 7-7.

Trend Cash Flow Statement

The trend cash flow statement helps us to determine the sources and uses of cash for a company. Exhibit 7-8 contains the trend cash flow statements for 1996 through 2003.

With the information Exhibit 7-8 provides, we can answer the following questions:

1 **Are the operating cash flows positive for all years?** The answer is yes and in increasing amounts except for 1999 and 2003. Operating activities are the only renewable source of cash flows so it is imperative that cash flow from operations remains positive. We expect investing cash flows to be negative, more cash outflow than cash inflow, in a growing company because most company growth comes from investments made to expand the business. Negative financing cash flows arise from three basic sources—payment of dividends, repayment of debt, and purchase of treasury stock. Paying dividends and repaying debt are very worthwhile uses of cash and a positive sign of growing financial strength. Whether the purchase of treasury stock is a good or bad strategy depends on the personal beliefs of the analyst.

2 **Are the operating cash flows sufficient to cover any negative cash flows from investing and financing activities?** Here we have mixed answers. Operating cash flows easily covered investing and financing outflows

Family Dollar Stores, Inc.
Trend Lines for Sales and EPS

Exhibit 7-7
Trend Lines for Sales and EPS for Family Dollar Stores, Inc. 1996 through 2003

Exhibit 7-8
Trend Cash Flow Statements

	Family Dollar Stores, Inc. and Subsidiaries Trend Consolidated Statements of Cash Flow							
For the Year Ended	**AUGUST 30 2003**	**AUGUST 31 2002**	**SEPTEMBER 1 2001**	**AUGUST 26 2000**	**AUGUST 28 1999**	**AUGUST 29 1998**	**AUGUST 31 1997**	**AUGUST 31 1996**
Operating cash flows	363.11	495.57	204.22	225.94	136.49	260.38	151.70	100.00
Investing cash flows	413.90	348.26	303.09	324.29	232.97	180.40	143.41	100.00
Financing cash flows	487.97	108.95	149.67	347.36	145.03	132.88	129.52	100.00
Net change in cash	−135.45	1986.71	−218.22	−517.84	−389.51	918.26	236.42	100.00
Cash, beginning of year	2488.03	245.71	492.01	1076.48	1516.11	479.70	212.87	100.00
Cash, end of year	1097.01	1168.82	115.43	231.14	505.71	712.24	225.35	100.00

for 1997 and 1998, but not in years 1999 through 2001. Let's look for help to analyze this further in Exhibits 7-1 and 7-3, and for confirmation in Exhibit 7-9 that graphs the trend lines for the cash flows. Family Dollar began to build its investment in property and equipment in 1997 and by 2003 had quadrupled its 1996 investment. You can see that management paid for this expansion with operating dollars because no long-term debt appears on the financial statements. That is an amazing accomplishment in most businesses.

After further research into the complete financial statements, Family Dollar's financing outflows were for dividends and employee stock plans every year, except in 2000 and 2003. In those years, management made large purchases of treasury stock. Looking at Exhibit 7-9 you can see that in 2000 and 2003, investments, treasury stock purchases, and dividend payments created large investing and financing cash outflows. In spite of these transactions, cash remained above the level of cash in 1996 throughout the eight-year period. By 2001, Family Dollar appeared ominously low in cash and might have to slow its expansion. Operating cash flows, however, made a dramatic turnaround in 2002 restoring cash to ten times the amount of 1996. Even with the large cash outflows in 2003, cash decreased by a small amount in 2003.

Now let's turn our attention to common-size statements to see the type of information they provide.

Exhibit 7-9
Trend Lines for Operating, Investing, and Financing Cash Flows for Family Dollar Stores, Inc. 1996 through 2003

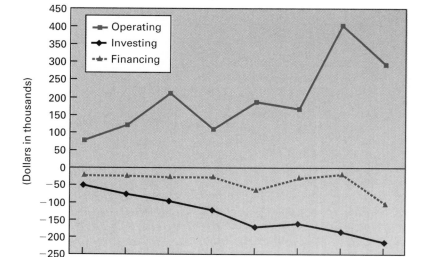

Family Dollar Stores, Inc.
Trend Lines of Cash Flows

Common-Size Statements

Common-size statements give us a different perspective of the business. Instead of looking at the changes in one element across time as we did in trend analysis, we look at the relationship of data within a fiscal period. (When we have comparative data, we get the bonus of being able to determine whether the composition of these relationships changes across time.) For this analysis, we will look at the balance sheet and income statement.

To compute the common-size balance sheet, each element on the balance sheet is shown as a percentage of total assets. For example, refer to the balance sheet in Exhibit 7-1. The following lists each account on the balance sheet as a percentage of total assets for 2003:

Account	Computation		Percentage of 2003 Total Assets
Cash	$\dfrac{\$\ 206{,}731}{\$1{,}985{,}695}$	=	10.41
Inventory	$\dfrac{\$\ 854{,}370}{\$1{,}985{,}695}$	=	43.03
Other current assets	$\dfrac{\$\ 95{,}391}{\$1{,}985{,}695}$	=	4.80
Property and equipment	$\dfrac{\$\ 812{,}123}{\$1{,}985{,}695}$	=	40.90
Other assets	$\dfrac{\$\ 17{,}080}{\$1{,}985{,}695}$	=	.86
Accounts payable	$\dfrac{\$\ 401{,}799}{\$1{,}985{,}695}$	=	20.23
Other current liabilities	$\dfrac{\$\ 193{,}532}{\$1{,}985{,}695}$	=	9.75
Deferred income taxes	$\dfrac{\$\ 79{,}395}{\$1{,}985{,}695}$	=	4.00
Shareholders' equity	$\dfrac{\$1{,}310{,}969}{\$1{,}985{,}695}$	=	66.02

Remember that each year is independent of the other years.

The Common-Size Balance Sheet

Exhibit 7-10 (see p. 244) contains the common-size balance sheet for Family Dollar. It tells us about the composition of the assets and capital structure of the corporation.

Let's answer the following questions:

1 **What is the composition of assets, and is it appropriate for the company?** Exhibit 7-11 (p. 244) features a graphic representation of the composition of assets. Cash ranges from 1.55 percent in 2001 to a high of 14.25 percent in 1998. Most companies try to keep about five percent of assets in cash. Family Dollar's cash position was thin in 2001 but was restored to high levels in 2002 and 2003. Inventories had leveled out at about 50 percent of total assets, but dropped sharply in 2002 and slightly again in 2003. Inventory is normally the largest asset of a merchandising company, and management has efficiently reduced the percentage of its assets tied up in inventory over the past six years.

Exhibit 7-10
Common-Size Balance Sheet

Family Dollar Stores, Inc. and Subsidiaries
Common-Size Consolidated Balance Sheets

	AUGUST 30 2003	AUGUST 31 2002	SEPTEMBER 1 2001	AUGUST 26 2000	AUGUST 28 1999	AUGUST 29 1998	AUGUST 31 1997	AUGUST 31 1996
Assets								
Cash and cash equivalents	10.41	12.55	1.55	3.50	8.70	14.25	5.44	2.70
Merchandise inventories	43.03	43.69	51.55	51.83	51.93	49.41	59.97	66.42
Other current assets	4.80	3.93	4.57	5.03	5.10	4.97	4.39	3.76
Property and equipment (net)	40.90	39.07	41.50	39.20	33.89	30.97	29.63	26.49
Other assets	0.86	0.75	0.83	0.44	0.38	0.40	0.56	0.62
Total Assets	100.00	100.00	100.00	100.00	100.00	100.00	100.00	100.00
Liabilities And Shareholders' Equity								
Liabilities								
Accounts payable	20.23	21.72	18.93	22.29	22.35	22.72	21.17	22.53
Other current liabilities	9.75	8.53	8.95	10.83	12.21	13.71	12.31	11.08
Deferred income taxes	4.00	3.93	3.60	2.71	2.38	2.20	2.42	2.53
Total Liabilities	33.98	34.18	31.49	35.84	36.94	38.64	35.90	36.14
Shareholders' Equity	66.02	65.82	68.51	64.16	63.06	61.36	64.10	63.86
Total Liabilities and Equity	100.00	100.00	100.00	100.00	100.00	100.00	100.00	100.00

Exhibit 7-11
Composition of Assets for Family Dollar Stores, Inc. 1996 through 2003

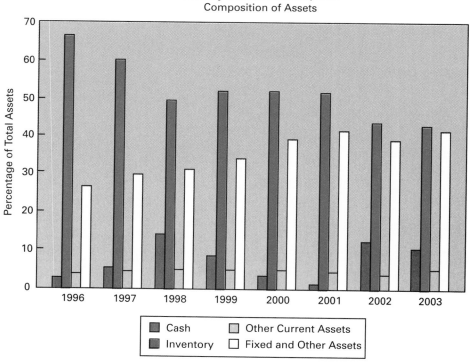

Family Dollar Stores, Inc.
Composition of Assets

Visit the company Web site at **www.familydollar.com.**

Other current assets are a small portion of the asset total. Property and equipment have expanded greatly in the past eight years. By visiting the company's Web site, you can learn about the company's expansion. In 1996 Family Dollar had 2,581 stores and 2 distribution centers. By August 30, 2003, it operated 5,000 stores and 7 distribution centers in 41 states. Rapid expansion creates risk because the business becomes more complex to manage. As you can see,

Family Dollar Stores, Inc.
Composition of Capital

Exhibit 7-12
Composition of Capital for
Family Dollar Stores, Inc.
1996 through 2003

the cash position was less than optimal in 2001, but rebounded in 2002 and 2003. An analyst has to recognize how the increased profitability in recent years improved its cash position.

2 Is the capital structure risky? Family Dollar has a very conservative capital structure comprised of 33.98 percent debt and 66.02 percent equity at 2003 year end. Most companies try to keep their debt between 40 and 60 percent of total assets. Forty percent is conservative and beyond 60 percent is aggressive. The more aggressive the debt structure, the higher the risk. With almost two-thirds of assets free and clear of outside claims, the company presents a low risk for investors and shareholders. Over the past eight years, even with the expansion, the equity of the company has risen from 63.86 percent to 66.02 percent. It fell during 1998 and 2002 when Family Dollar made some major expansions but rebounded in other years. It has remained consistently higher than 60 percent. See Exhibit 7-12 to confirm the steady nature of the capital structure.

The Common-Size Income Statement

A common-size income statement helps analysts to discern the components of profit each year. With comparative statements, we can see how these components change over time. Exhibit 7-13 depicts the Family Dollar common-size income statements for 1996 through 2003.

To compute the statements, set Sales as the denominator and compute percentage of sales for each expense item and net income. The computations for 2003 are as follows:

Component	Calculation		Percentage
Sales	$\dfrac{\$4,750,171}{\$4,750,171}$	=	100.00
Cost of sales	$\dfrac{\$3,145,788}{\$4,750,171}$	=	66.22
SGA Expenses	$\dfrac{\$1,214,658}{\$4,750,171}$	=	25.57
Income taxes	$\dfrac{\$\ \ 142,250}{\$4,750,171}$	=	2.99
Net Income	$\dfrac{\$\ \ 247,475}{\$4,750,171}$	=	5.21

Exhibit 7-13
Common-Size Income Statements

				Family Dollar Stores, Inc. and Subsidiaries Common-Size Consolidated Income Statements				
For the Year Ended	AUGUST 30 2003	AUGUST 31 2002	SEPTEMBER 1 2001	AUGUST 26 2000	AUGUST 28 1999	AUGUST 29 1998	AUGUST 31 1997	AUGUST 31 1996
Net sales	100.00	100.00	100.00	100.00	100.00	100.00	100.00	100.00
Costs and expenses:								
Cost of sales	66.22	66.47	66.55	66.30	66.64	67.26	67.68	67.43
Selling, general & administrative	25.57	25.33	25.31	25.05	25.26	25.71	26.23	26.81
Total Expenses	91.80	91.79	91.86	91.35	91.91	92.97	93.91	94.24
Income before income taxes	8.20	8.21	8.14	8.65	8.09	7.03	6.09	5.76
Income taxes	2.99	3.00	2.97	3.16	3.00	2.65	2.35	2.23
Net income	5.21	5.21	5.17	5.49	5.09	4.37	3.74	3.53

Using the preceding information, we can answer these questions:

1 **Has the net income percentage increased or decreased over time?** The net income percentage has increased steadily from 3.53 percent in 1996 to 5.21 percent in 2002 and 2003. It was highest in 2000 at 5.49 percent, before the economic downturn that started in 2001.

2 **What components of net income contributed to its increase or decrease?** Both the cost of sales and the selling, general, and administrative expenses show slow and steady declines from 1996 to 2000. Both expenses increased slightly in 2001, although cost of sales declined in 2002 and again in 2003. Income before taxes also rebounded in 2002 and remained constant in 2003.

Notice the change in the components of sales in Exhibit 7-14. The increase in income tax expense is a natural function of net income rising. Family Dollar should seriously consider any increase in expenses to prevent future erosion of net income.

Although the Elevation Sports officers cannot perform trend analysis, they still can prepare a common-size income statement that will set a base line for future trend analysis and give them a sense of the components of their costs and net income.

Exhibit 7-14
Components of Sales for Family Dollar Stores, Inc. 1996 through 2003

Family Dollar Stores, Inc.
Expenses and Net Income Compared to Sales

Elevation Sports, Inc. Common-Size Income Statement For the Year Ended May 31, 2004	
Net Sales	100.00
Cost of Goods Sold	
Cost of snowboards	50.26
Cost of other goods sold	5.86
Total Cost of Goods Sold	56.12
Gross Profit	43.88
Operating Expenses	
Selling expenses	9.17
Administrative expenses	13.69
Total Operating Expenses	22.86
Operating Income	21.02
Other Revenues and Expenses	(1.04)
Income Before Income Taxes	19.98
Income Taxes	7.99
Net Income	11.99

Exhibit 7-15

Common-Size Income Statement for Elevation Sports, Inc.

Exhibit 7-15 contains a common-size income statement for the year ended May 31, 2004. In Chapter 8 we will compare these results to the industry averages. Now let's turn our attention to the analysis of cash.

Analysis of Cash

To analyze cash we will look at the preparation of the statement of cash flows, how to use that information, how to compute and analyze cash ratios, and the importance of cash management.

The Statement of Cash Flows

In Chapter 6 Megan prepared the income statement, the statement of stockholders' equity, and the balance sheet for Elevation Sports on the accrual basis. Recall that accrual accounting employs accruals and deferrals of revenues and expenses to properly account for net income and the corporation's financial resources. Such adjustments cause net income to differ from the net change in cash. As we have discussed, cash flow is critical to the survival of any organization. By preparing a statement of cash flows and combining it with the information contained in the other three financial statements, decision makers gain a more complete picture of a company's financial health. The cash flow statement is basically an analysis of cash.

In addition to providing information about a company's cash receipts and cash payments during a specific period, the statement of cash flows helps internal and external parties to:

1 assess a company's ability to generate positive future net cash flows;
2 assess a company's need for external financing and its ability to pay its debts and pay dividends;
3 assess a company's overall financial health; and
4 reconcile the differences between net income and the change in cash.

As you recall from Chapter 2, a firm performs four functions: It operates to generate revenues, invests earnings to support operations, finances operating and investing activities, and makes decisions. To accomplish the disclosure objectives previously listed, we separate the cash inflows and outflows into three categories that conform to the first three functions of a firm—operating, investing, and financing. To help you distinguish among the functions, we will describe each type of activity in turn.

Operating Activities

● **operating activities**
Activities centered around the company's primary business activities.

Operating activities, those centered around the company's primary business activities, generate the company's operating revenues and expenses and utilize the company's current assets and current liabilities. Operating cash inflows come from the firm's customers or from interest or dividends the company receives from its investments. Some customers pay for sales at the time of sale and others charge their purchases and pay for them later. Operating cash outflows come from the many expenses a company incurs, whether paid for in cash as incurred or paid for later by paying accounts payable or other payables. How does the measurement of cash inflows and outflows differ from income measurement? It differs in that, for cash flow purposes, we measure only the cash inflows or outflows, not the revenues and expenses.

If you think about the items in the previous paragraph, you will see they are all items that are reported on the income statement. Therefore, when attempting to determine the cash inflow and cash outflow from operating activities, we start with the income statement for the period. We use the accrual basis of accounting, however, so the net income figure must be adjusted for any revenue item that did not provide cash during this income statement period and any expense item that did not use cash during this income statement period. You will discover that to determine the operating activities for the cash flow statement, you will analyze the income statement and the current assets and liabilities for items that represent accruals and deferrals of revenues and expenses.

Investing Activities

● **investing activities**
Activities that provide the resources that support operations.

Investing activities provide the resources that support operations. This support may take the form of either investments in assets necessary to the operation or investments outside the company to use excess cash wisely. When a company invests in noncurrent assets, it uses cash. When it sells these assets, it receives cash inflow.

Companies normally sell these types of assets when they are no longer useful to the firm. However, a company cannot logically sell assets it needs to run its operations because then cash generated through operating activities would eventually cease. An airline could generate cash by selling all its airplanes, but if it did so, it would no longer be able to transport passengers and would go out of business. In fact, a growing and healthy company will most likely use cash to acquire assets that can generate additional revenues. For this reason, it will frequently experience negative net cash flow from investing activities. In this case, negative cash flow represents economic health.

A company can use cash to purchase the stocks or bonds of other companies or to lend money to another company. Cash is generated when a company sells the investment or when the borrower repays the loan. If you think about the examples of investing activities in the previous two paragraphs, you will see they all involve items that are reported in the noncurrent asset sections of the balance sheet. The only exception to this rule is short-term cash loans made to other entities or individuals that are reported as current assets. All cash loans, whether current or long term, are considered to be investing activities. Current assets, other than cash, that represent accruals of revenue or deferrals of expenses are classified as operating activities. Therefore, when determining the cash inflow and cash outflow from investing activities, you must analyze the current and long-term asset section of the balance sheets at the start of the period and at the end of the period.

Financing Activities

● **financing activities**
Activities that involve the borrowing and repayment of cash and changes in equity from owners' transactions.

Financing activities involve the borrowing and repayment of cash and changes in equity from owners' transactions. Because internal financing is accomplished through operating activities, financing activities reported on the statement of cash flows deal only with external financing. A company obtains financing cash from two external sources: the sale of common or preferred stock (equity financing) or borrowing from lenders in the form of loans and/or corporate bonds (debt financing). A company uses cash for financing activities when it repays loan or bond principal, pays dividends to shareholders, and purchases treasury stock. Notice that we included only the principal on borrowed money. Cash paid for interest expense is an operating cash outflow.

To determine the items that are reported in the financing activities of the cash flow statement we will analyze the right side of the balance sheet, primarily the long-term liability and stockholders' equity section. Most of the current liabilities are considered operating activities, except for any liabilities representing cash borrowed from banks or other lenders. Any current liabilities that involve cash borrowed instead of expenses accrued are financing activities. Current liabilities that represent expense accruals or revenue deferrals are part of operating activities.

Exhibit 7-16 summarizes the three types of business activities as they are reported in the statement of cash flows. You should refer to this exhibit often as we discuss the

Operating Activities (Income Statement, Current Assets, and Current Liabilities Items)
  Cash inflows:
      From customers as a result of the sale of goods or services
      From interest earned on loans to others
      From dividends received from investment in the stock of other companies
      From the sale of trading securities

  Cash outflows:
      To suppliers for the purchase of inventory
      To employees for salaries and wages
      To governments for taxes
      To creditors for interest on loans
      To others for operating expenses
      To purchase trading securities

Investing Activities (Long-Term Asset Items)
  Cash inflows:
      From the sale of property, plant, and equipment
      From the sale of investments in debt or equity securities of other companies
      From the collection of monies loaned to others

  Cash outflows:
      To purchase property, plant, and equipment
      To purchase debt and equity investments in other companies or loan money to others

Financing Activities (Long-Term Liability and Stockholders' Equity Items)
  Cash inflows:
      From selling shares of common stock or preferred stock
      From selling treasury stock
      From loan proceeds or the sale of corporate bonds

  Cash outflows:
      To pay dividends to stockholders
      To reacquire shares of capital stock from stockholders
      To repay principal of loans or redeem corporate bonds

Exhibit 7-16
Types of Business Activities Reported on the Statement of Cash Flows

preparation and uses of the statement because every inflow and outflow of cash can be classified as a result of operating, investing, or financing activities. Before we begin to prepare the statement of cash flows, we must recognize that the FASB allows us to use two methods to present the operating cash flows.

Direct Method versus Indirect Method

The FASB allows two methods of preparing the operating section of the statement of cash flows: the direct method and the indirect method. Both arrive at exactly the same amount of cash flow from operations. The difference lies in how the information is presented. The **direct method** presents the amount of cash inflows from customers, interest earned on loans, and dividends received and the cash outflows for merchandise, wages, operating expenses, taxes, and interest. The **indirect method** begins with net income and adjusts it for all items that did not generate or use cash. Approximately 97 percent of firms use the indirect method, so we will concentrate on the indirect method in this chapter. Exhibit 7-17 contains the operating section of the cash flow statement for Jason's Furniture Gallery, Inc. prepared using both methods.

In keeping with the definitions, the direct method lists the cash received from customers ($455,000) and then deducts the cash paid for merchandise ($160,000), operating expenses ($150,000), and taxes ($21,000). The indirect method begins with net income of $41,000 and makes adjustments. Notice that the amount of operating cash flows of $124,000 is the same for both methods. For the indirect method, we must also disclose the amounts paid for interest and taxes at the bottom of the statement.

Let's look at how the preparer arrives at the adjustments amounts for the indirect method.

● **direct method**
A method of preparing the operating section of the cash flow statement that presents the amount of cash inflows from customers, interest earned on loans, and dividends received and the cash outflows for merchandise, wages, operating expenses, taxes, and interest.

● **indirect method**
A method of preparing the operating section of the cash flow statement that begins with net income and adjusts it for all items that did not generate or use cash.

Exhibit 7-17
Operating Cash Flows Prepared Using the Direct and Indirect Methods

Jason's Furniture Gallery, Inc.
Partial Statement of Cash Flows
For the Year Ended December 31, 2004

Direct Method:		
Operating Activities:		
Cash received from customers		$455,000
Cash paid for:		
Merchandise	$160,000	
Operating expenses	150,000	
Income taxes	21,000	331,000
Cash Provided by Operating Activities		$124,000
Indirect Method:		
Operating Activities:		
Net income		$ 41,000
Adjustments to reconcile net income to		
net cash provided by operating activities:		
Depreciation	$ 15,000	
Loss on sale of equipment	8,000	
Deduct: Gain on sale of securities	(25,000)	
Decrease in inventory	45,000	
Increase in accounts payable	40,000	83,000
Cash Provided by Operating Activities		$124,000
Amount paid for:		
Interest	$ —0—	
Taxes	$21,000	

Preparing the Statement of Cash Flows Using the Indirect Method

We need three financial statements to prepare a statement of cash flows: two consecutive balance sheets and the income statement that bridges them. We will analyze and account for each change in the balance sheet accounts by using the information in the income statement and balance sheets. If you think about it, all items on the left side of the balance sheet add together to equal the sum of all items on the right side of the balance sheet. If we explain the difference in each account other than cash from the beginning to the end of the year, we have successfully explained the difference in cash from the beginning to the end of the year. In equation form we can explain it as:

$$\text{Cash} + \text{Other Assets} = \text{Liabilities} + \text{Equity}$$

$$\Delta\,\text{Cash} + \Delta\,\text{Other Assets} = \Delta\,\text{Liabilities} + \Delta\,\text{Equity}$$

$$\Delta\,\text{Cash} = \Delta\,\text{Liabilities} + \Delta\,\text{Equity} - \Delta\,\text{Other Assets}$$

Now let's see how Megan prepared the cash flow statement for Elevation Sports at the end of the first year. She followed six logical steps:

1 Gather the information needed to prepare the statement:
   (a) consecutive, comparative balance sheets;
   (b) the income statement for the period between the two balance sheets; and
   (c) any information needed about noncash transactions.
2 Determine the net change in each account of the balance sheets.
3 Complete the operating activities section.
4 Complete the investing activities section.
5 Complete the financing activities section.
6 Add the operating, investing, and financing activities to derive the net change in cash. Add it to the beginning balance of cash to derive the ending balance of cash. Check to see whether it agrees with the balance sheet. If it does not, retrace steps 1–5.

This detailed explanation of the construction of this statement is not intended to make you an expert preparer, but rather to help you become a wise user of this financial tool. Knowing how the amounts on a statement of cash flows were determined will help you to assess their usefulness and impact your decision-making process and the quality of your decisions.

Step 1: Gather information—The comparative condensed balance sheets in Exhibit 7-18 (see p. 252) are reprinted from Chapter 6. The beginning balance was zero because this is the first year of operation. The income statement from Chapter 6 is condensed in Exhibit 7-19 (see p. 253).

Now we have all the necessary information to prepare Elevation Sports' statement of cash flows.

We begin by creating a format for Elevation Sports' statement of cash flows in Exhibit 7-20 (see p. 253) from the basic format presented in Chapter 2. You should note two things about this format. First, it is divided into the three broad types of activities that can either generate or use cash (operating, investing, and financing). Second, we have already put three amounts into the statement (the $128,384 increase in cash for the year, and the beginning and ending cash balances). The cash flow statement is one of the few accounting reports for which we know the result before we start to prepare it. In the case of Elevation Sports, we determined the change in cash by looking at the comparative balance sheets (Exhibit 7-18). Remember, the more important purpose of the statement of cash flows is not to disclose the amount of the change in cash, but to disclose what caused the change.

Exhibit 7-18
Elevation Sports, Inc. Condensed, Comparative Balance Sheets

	Elevation Sports, Inc. Balance Sheets May 31	
	2004	**2003**
Assets		
Current Assets		
Cash	$128,384	$ —0—
Accounts receivable (net)	9,450	—0—
Inventories	35,803	—0—
Prepaid expenses	17,000	—0—
Total Current Assets	$190,637	$ —0—
Property, Plant, and Equipment		
Equipment and furniture	$103,100	$ —0—
Less: Accumulated depreciation	17,800	—0—
Total Property, Plant and Equipment	$ 85,300	$ —0—
Intangible Assets	12,078	—0—
Total Assets	$288,015	$ —0—
Liabilities and Stockholders' Equity		
Current Liabilities		
Accounts payable	$ 6,942	$ —0—
Other accounts payable	13,772	—0—
Interest payable	6,000	—0—
Income taxes payable	42,120	—0—
Current portion of long-term note payable	15,000	—0—
Total Current Liabilities	$ 83,834	$ —0—
Long-Term Liabilities		
Note payable – Vail National Bank	$ 60,000	$ —0—
Less: Current portion	15,000	—0—
Total Long-Term Liabilities	$ 45,000	$ —0—
Total Liabilities	$128,834	$ —0—
Stockholders' Equity		
Paid-in capital:		
Common stock, $10 par value, 100,000 shares authorized, 4,000 shares issued and outstanding	$ 40,000	$ —0—
Paid-in capital in excess of par – common stock	60,000	—0—
Total paid-in capital	$100,000	$ —0—
Retained earnings	59,181	—0—
Total Stockholders' Equity	$159,181	$ —0—
Total Liabilities and Stockholders' Equity	$288,015	$ —0—

Exhibit 7-19
Elevation Sports, Inc. Condensed Income Statement

Elevation Sports, Inc. Income Statement For the Year Ended May 31, 2004			
Net Sales			$ 527,146
Cost of Goods Sold			
Cost of snowboards		$264,944	
Cost of other goods sold		30,890	295,834
Gross Profit			$ 231,312
Operating Expenses			
Selling Expenses			
Depreciation – selling equipment	$ 1,200		
Other selling expenses	47,134		
Total Selling Expenses		$ 48,334	
Administrative Expenses			
Amortization of intangibles	$ 1,022		
Depreciation – administration	1,800		
Other administrative expenses	69,367		
Total Administrative Expenses		72,189	
Total Operating Expenses			120,523
Operating Income			$ 110,789
Other Revenues and Expenses			
Interest revenue		$ 512	
Interest expense		(6,000)	
Total other revenues and expenses			(5,488)
Income Before Income Taxes			$ 105,301
Income Taxes			42,120
Net Income			$ 63,181

Elevation Sports, Inc. Statement of Cash Flows For the Year Ended May 31, 2004	
Cash Flows from Operating Activities:	
Net Cash Provided (Used) by Operating Activities	$?
Cash Flows from Investing Activities:	
Net Cash Provided (Used) by Investing Activities	?
Cash Flows from Financing Activities:	
Net Cash Provided (Used) by Financing Activities	?
Net Increase (Decrease) in Cash during the Year	$128,384
Beginning Cash Balance, May 31, 2003	—0—
Ending Cash Balance, May 31, 2004	$128,384

Exhibit 7-20
Elevation Sports, Inc. Basic Format for the Statement of Cash Flows

Step 2: Determine the net change in each account on the balance sheet—
The easiest way to determine the net change in each account is to add a difference column to the comparative balance sheets, which Exhibit 7-21 shows. For a new company such as Elevation Sports, this may seem unnecessary—but do not forget that zero is a

Exhibit 7-21
Elevation Sports, Inc. Condensed, Comparative Balance Sheets

Elevation Sports, Inc. Balance Sheets May 31			
	2004	**2003**	**INCREASE (DECREASE)**
Assets			
Current Assets			
Cash	$128,384	$ —0—	$128,384
Accounts receivable (net)	9,450	—0—	9,450
Inventories	35,803	—0—	35,803
Prepaid expenses	17,000	—0—	17,000
Total Current Assets	$190,637	$ —0—	$190,637
Property, Plant, and Equipment			
Equipment and furniture	$103,100	$ —0—	$103,100
Less: Accumulated depreciation	17,800	—0—	17,800
Total Property, Plant and Equipment	$ 85,300	$ —0—	$ 85,300
Intangible Assets	12,078	—0—	$ 12,078
Total Assets	$288,015	$ —0—	$288,015
Liabilities and Stockholders' Equity			
Current Liabilities			
Accounts payable	$ 6,942	$ —0—	$ 6,942
Other accounts payable	13,772	—0—	13,772
Interest payable	6,000	—0—	6,000
Income taxes payable	42,120	—0—	42,120
Current portion of long-term note payable	15,000	—0—	15,000
Total Current Liabilities	$ 83,834	$ —0—	$ 83,834
Long-Term Liabilities			
Note payable – Vail National Bank	$ 60,000	$ —0—	$ 60,000
Less: Current portion	15,000	—0—	15,000
Total Long-Term Liabilities	$ 45,000	$ —0—	$ 45,000
Total Liabilities	$128,834	$ —0—	$128,834
Stockholders' Equity			
Paid-in capital:			
Common stock, $10 par value, 100,000			
shares authorized, 4,000 shares issued and outstanding	$ 40,000	$ —0—	$ 40,000
Paid-in capital – common stock	60,000	—0—	60,000
Total paid-in capital	$100,000	$ —0—	$100,000
Retained earnings	59,181	—0—	59,181
Total Stockholders' Equity	$159,181	$ —0—	$159,181
Total Liabilities and Stockholders' Equity	$288,015	$ —0—	$288,015

real number that provides important information. Notice that the Increase (Decrease) column adds exactly like the balance sheet, and the net change in assets must equal the net change in liabilities and equity ($288,015 = $288,015).

Step 3: Complete the operating activities section—Megan used the indirect method to prepare the operating activities section of the cash flow statement. We make three basic types of adjustments to net income, listed in the following order, on the cash flow statement:

1 Add back depreciation and amortization.
2 Add back losses or subtract gains on the sale of assets or any other investing and financing event.
3 Add or subtract the adjustments for accrual accounting from current assets and current liabilities that represent operating activities. Remember not to include Notes Receivable and Notes Payable because these represent investing and financing activities.

Exhibit 7-22 shows a basic format of the indirect method.

We will use information primarily from the income statement, the current assets and current liabilities, and other information pertinent to preparing the report. We need to determine three groups of values:

1 **Depreciation and amortization**—Because depreciation and amortization represent a noncash expenditure of converting the cost of long-lived items (equipment and furniture in this case) from asset to expense, the deduction for them on the income statement reduces income but not cash. Therefore, we must add the amount of depreciation and amortization expense for the period to net income. Elevation Sports' income statement (Exhibit 7-19) shows depreciation expense for the year of $3,000 ($1,200 for selling equipment and $1,800 on administrative equipment). The change in accumulated depreciation, however, is $17,800, and we must explain the entire difference. Recall that much of the equipment purchased was for production. Production equipment depreciation is part of the cost of manufacturing shown, as recorded in the journal entries and detailed on the depreciation schedule in Exhibit 6-8 (see page 186). So the total depreciation is $17,800 including production depreciation of $14,800. Amortization of intangibles is $1,022.

When part or all the depreciation is included in cost of goods sold or combined with other expenses, we must use means other than the income statement to determine the amount of amortization or depreciation. Provided that no

Exhibit 7-22
Elevation Sports, Inc. Basic Format for the Indirect Method Operating Section

Elevation Sports, Inc.
Partial Statement of Cash Flows
For the Year Ended May 31, 2004

Cash Flows from Operating Activities:

Net income		$63,181
Adjustments to reconcile net income to net cash provided by operating activities:		
Depreciation expense	$17,800	
Amortization of intangibles	1,022	
Gain or loss on sale of assets	?	
Increase in ?	?	
Decrease in ?	?	?
Net Cash Provided (Used) by Operating Activities		$?

depreciable assets were disposed of, we can look at the change in the Accumulated Depreciation accounts to determine the amounts. If depreciable assets were sold, we would need more detailed information such as a depreciation schedule.

2 **Gains or losses on disposal of assets—** The income statement shows no gains or losses on disposal of assets. Another clue would be finding that the amount of long-lived assets decreased on the balance sheet or intangible assets decreased more than the amount of the amortization.

3 **Changes in current assets or current liabilities—** Changes in current assets and current liabilities are directly related to the difference between cash flows and accrual-basis statements. We will look at each account, reproduced in Exhibit 7-23.

  ○ **Accounts Receivable—**According to Elevation Sports' balance sheets, Accounts Receivable increased $9,450 during the year. The only way Accounts Receivable can increase is for the customers' payments to be less than current sales. Conversely, the only way Accounts Receivable can decrease is for customers' payments to exceed current sales. Therefore, we subtract increases in Accounts Receivable and add decreases in Accounts Receivable to convert from the accrual basis to the cash flows. We must subtract $9,450 as an adjustment to net income.

  ○ **Inventories—**The inventory accounts increased by $35,803 during the year according to Exhibit 7-23. The increase in inventory requires the use of cash resources.

    When inventory decreases, we use up inventory purchased in previous periods and conserve current cash. We add decreases and subtract increases in the Inventory accounts to net income. Therefore, we must subtract Elevation Sports' increase in the Inventory account.

Exhibit 7-23
Elevation Sports, Inc. Current Assets and Current Liabilities

Elevation Sports, Inc. Partial Balance Sheets May 31			
	2004	**2003**	**INCREASE (DECREASE)**
Assets			
Current Assets			
Cash	$128,384	$ —0—	$128,384
Accounts receivable (net)	9,450	—0—	9,450
Inventories	35,803	—0—	35,803
Prepaid expenses	17,000	—0—	17,000
Total Current Assets	$190,637	$ —0—	$190,637
Current Liabilities			
Accounts payable	$ 6,942	$ —0—	$ 6,942
Other accounts payable	13,772	—0—	13,772
Interest payable	6,000	—0—	6,000
Income taxes payable	42,120	—0—	42,120
Current portion of long-term note payable	15,000	—0—	15,000
Total Current Liabilities	$ 83,834	$ —0—	$ 83,834

○ **Prepaid Expenses**—Elevation Sports increased its Prepaid Expenses by $17,000 during the year. When the account increases, the cash payments must exceed the amount of the expense. If the account decreases, the cash payments must be less than the amount of the expense. Therefore, we must add decreases and subtract increases in the Prepaid Expenses account. Elevation Sports' increase in Prepaid Expenses should be subtracted from net income as part of the adjustments.

○ **Current Liabilities**—Each of the current liabilities increased during the current year. If the current liability accounts increase during a period, then the firm incurs more expense than it pays in cash. Conversely, if the company pays more cash on the liability than the corresponding expenses, the account balances will decrease. Therefore, we will add increases in the account and subtract decreases in the account as an adjustment to net income. Note that increases and decreases in liabilities take the *opposite* sign that increases and decreases to assets do.

○ **Note Payable**—Changes in the current portion of the Note Payable represent a financing activity even though it is a current liability.

With these determinations made, we can complete the operating section of the cash flow statement in Exhibit 7-24.

Step 4: Complete the investing activities section—Determining cash flow from investing activities requires analysis of the noncurrent assets plus additional information we collected. Exhibit 7-25 duplicates that section from the company's comparative balance sheets.

Elevation Sports, Inc. Partial Statement of Cash Flows For the Year Ended May 31, 2004		
Cash Flows from Operating Activities:		
Net income		$63,181
Adjustments to reconcile net income		
to net cash provided by operating activities:		
Depreciation expense	$17,800	
Amortization expense	1,022	
Increase in accounts receivable	(9,450)	
Increase in inventories	(35,803)	
Increase in prepaid expenses	(17,000)	
Increase in other accounts payable	6,942	
Increase in accounts payable	13,772	
Increase in interest payable	6,000	
Increase in taxes payable	42,120	25,403
Net Cash Provided by Operating Activities		$88,584

Exhibit 7-24
Elevation Sports, Inc. Operating Section of the Statement of Cash Flows

Exhibit 7-25
Elevation Sports, Inc. Long-Term Asset Section of Balance Sheets

	MAY 31, 2004	MAY 31, 2003	DIFFERENCE
Property, Plant, and Equipment			
Equipment and furniture	$103,100	$ —0—	$103,100
Less: Accumulated depreciation	17,800	—0—	17,800
Total Property, Plant and Equipment	$ 85,300	$ —0—	$ 85,300
Intangible Assets	$ 12,078	—0—	$ 12,078

Exhibit 7-26
Elevation Sports, Inc.
Operating and Investing
Sections of the Cash Flow
Statement

Elevation Sports, Inc. Partial Statement of Cash Flows For the Year Ended May 31, 2004		
Cash Flows from Operating Activities:		
Net income		$ 63,181
Adjustments to reconcile net income		
to net cash provided by operating activities:		
Depreciation expense	$ 17,800	
Amortization expense	1,022	
Increase in accounts receivable	(9,450)	
Increase in inventories	(35,803)	
Increase in prepaid expenses	(17,000)	
Increase in other accounts payable	6,942	
Increase in accounts payable	13,772	
Increase in interest payable	6,000	
Increase in taxes payable	42,120	25,403
Net Cash Provided by Operating Activities		$88,584
Cash Flows from Investing Activities:		
Purchase of equipment and furniture	$(43,100)	
Investment in intangible assets	(13,100)	
Net Cash Used by Operating Activities		(56,200)

The $103,100 increase in Equipment and Furniture represents all the investment made during the first year of Elevation Sports. We know from the transactions recorded in Chapter 5 that all the purchases were paid for in cash except for the production equipment. Megan paid the down payment of $15,000 and financed $60,000 with the bank. Consequently, the cash paid to acquire the long-term assets was $43,100 ($103,100 minus $60,000).

The company also acquired intangible assets for $13,100. Exhibit 6-9 (see p. 187) contains the amortization table that identifies both the cost of the intangibles and the amount of the amortization. Exhibit 7-26 adds the investing activities to the cash flow statement.

Step 5: Complete the financing activities section—By analyzing the liabilities and stockholders' equity sections of the balance sheet, we can determine the cash flows from Elevation Sports' financing activities. Refer to the Liabilities and Stockholders' Equity section of Elevation Sports' balance sheet in Exhibit 7-21. We must consider the changes in current notes payable, long-term liabilities, and equity accounts. Elevation Sports borrowed $60,000 toward the equipment, but did not receive the amount in cash. It sold $100,000 of common stock for cash. But, what about the $59,181 change in Retained Earnings? Look at the Statement of Stockholders' Equity in Exhibit 6-14 (see p. 196) to determine the amount of dividends declared. Because there is no Dividends Payable account, we know that the dividends were paid.

What Do You Think?

7-5 Why is Retained Earnings not equal to cash?

Exhibit 7-27
Elevation Sports, Inc. Statement of Cash Flows

Elevation Sports, Inc. Statement of Cash Flows For the Year Ended May 31, 2004		
Cash Flows from Operating Activities:		
Net income		$ 63,181
Adjustments to reconcile net income to net cash provided by operating activities:		
Depreciation expense	$ 17,800	
Amortization expense	1,022	
Increase in accounts receivable	(9,450)	
Increase in inventories	(35,803)	
Increase in prepaid expenses	(17,000)	
Increase in other accounts payable	6,942	
Increase in accounts payable	13,772	
Increase in interest payable	6,000	
Increase in taxes payable	42,120	25,403
Net Cash Provided by Operating Activities		$ 88,584
Cash Flows from Investing Activities:		
Purchase of equipment and furniture	$ (43,100)	
Investment in intangible assets	(13,100)	
Net Cash Used by Operating Activities		(56,200)
Cash Flows from Financing Activities:		
Sale of common stock	$100,000	
Payment of dividends	(4,000)	
Net Cash Provided (Used) by Financing Activities		96,000
Net Change in Cash		$128,384
Beginning Cash, June 1, 2003		—0—
Ending Cash, May 31, 2004		$128,384

Step 6: Complete the cash flow statement—We can now complete the statement of cash flows by totaling the net change in cash, adding the beginning cash balance of zero, and computing the ending cash balance. Exhibit 7-27 shows the completed statement. The final step is to ensure that the ending cash agrees with the balance sheet at May 31, 2004. This cash flow statement agrees with the balance sheet. If it did not, we would repeat the steps and ensure that we accounted for each change in the balance sheet amounts in Exhibit 7-21.

Elevation Sports' statement of cash flows was fairly simple to create, whereas statements of cash flows for actual companies can be complicated. But whether simple or complex, all statements of cash flows assume the basic format used for Elevation Sports.

Supplemental Schedules

To complete the disclosures for users, the statement of cash flows preparer must include two supplemental schedules. The first indicates the amount paid for interest and income taxes. Elevation Sports paid zero for interest and income taxes the first year. We can determine this by examining the transactions or the financial statements. The income statement indicates that Interest Expense was $6,000 and Income Tax

Expense was $42,120. The balance sheet shows Interest Payable of $6,000 and Income Taxes Payable of $42,120. Evidently these expenses were not paid because the full amount is still payable. A simple equation can help us determine the amount paid when it is not so obvious:

	Interest	Taxes
Payable at beginning of year	$ —0—	$ —0—
+ Amount of expense	+ 6,000	+ 42,120
	= 6,000	= 42,120
– Payable at the end of the year	– 6,000	– 42,120
= Amount paid during the year	$ —0—	$ —0—

The amount of zero should be reported because it provides significant information to the reader.

What Do You Think?

7-6 Think of at least three situations when the number zero is important information in your life. Why?

The second supplemental schedule should outline any significant noncash investing and financing activities. Examples of such transactions include trading an asset for a loan or stock, repaying a loan by issuing stock to the creditor, or trading one asset for another. In such transactions, no cash exchanges hands but the transaction may have future cash consequences. Look at a company that pays off a bond issue with common stock. The issuance of common stock removes the future cash outflow required to repay the bonds because common stocks have no maturity value or required repayment date. The issuance of common stock, however, will increase the amount of dividends required in the future. Both have future cash flow implications.

Elevation Sports had one noncash transaction when the equipment was purchased with $15,000 and signing a $60,000 note. The company must repay the loan, which will affect future cash outflows. The following supplemental schedules should complete the statement of cash flows:

Amount paid for:
Interest $ —0—
Income Taxes $ —0—

Significant noncash investing and financing activity:
Equipment purchased with a note payable $60,000

Exhibit 7-28 contains the completed statement of cash flows in good form.

Using Information from the Statement of Cash Flows

The statement of cash flows discloses the company's sources and uses of cash during a specific time period. One of the most important things the statement shows is what a company invested in during the period and how such investments were financed. Investments in long-lived productive assets create revenues and, eventually, cash. Operating and financing activities should provide the cash for investments. How investments were financed is presented in the top section of the statement (operating activities) and the bottom section of the statement (financing activities).

To demonstrate this concept, we have extracted the cash flow totals for the three types of activities from Elevation Sports' statement of cash flows in Exhibit 7-28.

Net cash provided by operating activities	$ 88,584
Net cash used by investing activities	$(56,200)
Net cash provided by financing activities	$ 96,000

> In the long run, all investments must be financed through operations because operations is the only renewable source of cash.

Elevation Sports invested $56,200 for equipment during 2003. The officers made the investment to enable the company to build and sell its product. The only two sources of cash available to Elevation Sports, or to any company, are to generate cash internally from profitable operations or to obtain cash from external sources by borrowing or selling stock. Elevation Sports generated more than 100 percent of the cash required for the investment internally from operating activities during the first year, after a generous capital contribution from the stockholders. A firm can only borrow a finite amount of

Exhibit 7-28
Elevation Sports, Inc. Completed Statement of Cash Flows

Elevation Sports, Inc.
Statement of Cash Flows
For the Year Ended May 31, 2004

Cash Flows from Operating Activities:		
Net income		$ 63,181
Adjustments to reconcile net income		
to net cash provided by operating activities:		
Depreciation expense	$ 17,800	
Amortization expense	1,022	
Increase in accounts receivable	(9,450)	
Increase in inventories	(35,803)	
Increase in prepaid expenses	(17,000)	
Increase in other accounts payable	6,942	
Increase in accounts payable	13,772	
Increase in interest payable	6,000	
Increase in taxes payable	42,120	25,403
Net Cash Provided by Operating Activities		$ 88,584
Cash Flows from Investing Activities:		
Purchase of equipment and furniture	$ (43,100)	
Investment in intangible assets	(13,100)	
Net Cash Used by Operating Activities		(56,200)
Cash Flows from Financing Activities:		
Sale of common stock	$100,000	
Payment of dividends	(4,000)	
Net Cash Provided (Used) by Financing Activities		96,000
Net Change in Cash		$128,384
Beginning Cash, June 1, 2003		—0—
Ending Cash, May 31, 2004		$128,384
Amount paid for:		
Interest	$ —0—	
Income taxes	$ —0—	

Significant noncash investing and financing activity:
Equipment purchased with a note payable $60,000

cash, can only sell a finite amount of stock, and can only sell a few of its assets or it would have none. But operations provide a renewable source of cash limited only by the company's ability to operate profitably.

Now you can see why the statement of cash flows is an economic decision maker's most valuable tool in determining how a company finances its investments. By carefully examining it, users can obtain insights into many aspects of a company's operations. The statement of cash flows, in combination with the other three financial statements, provides important information on which economic decision makers rely.

Cash Ratios

● **cash to total assets ratio**
A ratio that measures the percentage of total assets made up of cash.

Additional financial analysis tools exist to help manage cash. Let's look at four measures for cash that the internal analyst can use as evidence of a healthy or weak cash position. The first is the cash ratio. The **cash to total assets ratio** measures the percentage of total assets made up of cash. The formula is simple:

$$\text{Cash to Total Assets} = \frac{\text{Cash}}{\text{Total Assets}}$$

When we apply this to Elevation Sports, we find that its cash to total assets ratio is 44.58 percent.

$$\text{Cash to Total Assets} = \frac{\text{Cash}}{\text{Total Assets}} = \frac{\$128,384}{\$288,015} = 44.58\%$$

Is this good or bad? A company usually tries to maintain at least five percent of its assets in cash. So, should almost 45 percent be wonderful? Not really. Cash is the least productive asset, so companies try to not keep excess cash. Elevation Sports needed its cash to pay principal and interest due on its loan of $21,000 and income taxes of $42,120. After paying those two items, the cash will be reduced by $63,120. The officers are being very conservative with their cash because of the uncertainty of being new in the business.

If we look at Family Dollar Stores for the eight-year period, we can chart its cash to total assets ratio:

August 30 2003	August 31 2002	September 1 2001	August 26 2000	August 28 1999	August 29 1998	August 31 1997	August 31 1996
10.41%	12.55%	1.55%	3.50%	8.70%	14.25%	5.44%	2.70%

Family Dollar has a wide variation in its cash balance with five years higher than five percent and three years lower than five percent for the years shown.

● **free cash flows**
The operating cash flows remaining after capital expenditures and dividends.

A second measure of cash position is the computation of free cash flows. **Free cash flows** are the operating cash flows remaining after capital expenditures and dividends. They represent the cash available for strategic-planning goals such as special projects and expansion. If a company wishes to plan its own destiny, it must have cash available for strategic goals.

In its first year, Elevation Sports has a good amount of free cash flows:

$$\text{Free cash flows} = \text{Operating Cash Flows} - \text{Capital Expenditures} - \text{Dividends}$$
$$\$28,384 \quad = \quad \$88,584 \quad - \quad \$56,200 \quad - \quad \$4,000$$

The officers intended to have free cash flows to enable the company to expand the business.

Exhibit 7-29
Family Dollar Stores, Inc. Free Cash Flows

In thousands	AUGUST 30 2003	AUGUST 31 2002	SEPTEMBER 1 2001	AUGUST 26 2000	AUGUST 28 1999	AUGUST 29 1998	AUGUST 31 1997	AUGUST 31 1996
Operating cash flows	$294,998	$402,603	$165,910	$183,556	$110,883	$211,538	$123,242	$81,241
Capital expenditures	219,777	186,687	162,848	172,056	125,038	96,854	77,062	54,265
Dividends	48,242	43,161	39,443	36,084	32,769	29,235	26,849	23,858
Free Cash Flows	$ 26,979	$172,755	$ (36,381)	$ (24,584)	$ (46,924)	$ 85,449	$ 19,331	$ 3,118

Exhibit 7-29 calculates Family Dollar's free cash flows. The free cash flows in fiscal years 1996 through 1998 allowed the expansions to occur in years 1999 through 2001. By 2001, however, the cash and free cash flows were depleted, suggesting that management might slow down its expansion until cash reserves could be replaced. Cash increased in 2002 and 2003 due to high profits, reduced growth of inventory, and increases in accounts payable.

Both the third and fourth tools measure the ability of a firm to pay its current and total liabilities from its operating cash flows. As we emphasized, the only renewable source of cash is operating cash flows, so those flows must be capable of paying liabilities. When this ability is strained, borrowing capacity suffers. The third ratio is the **operating cash flows to average current liabilities ratio**, which measures the ability to pay current debt from operating cash flows. The higher this ratio, the more likely the company can borrow short-term funds. The formula applied to Elevation Sports is:

● **operating cash flows to average current liabilities ratio**
A ratio that measures the ability to pay current debt from operating cash flows.

$$\frac{\text{Operating Cash Flow}}{\text{Average Current Liabilities}} = \frac{\$88,584}{\$41,917} = 2.11 \text{ times}$$

The ratio indicates that Elevation Sports can pay its average current liabilities twice from operating cash flows, which is a healthy position. Average current liabilities can be found by adding the beginning and ending balance of current liabilities and dividing by two. For a new company, remember, the beginning balance is zero.

The final ratio is the **operating cash flows to average total liabilities ratio**, which measures the ability to pay total debt from operating cash flows. Closely related to the previous ratio, it describes a more stringent measure of the ability to pay debts from operating cash flows. The calculation for Elevation Sports and the formula are:

● **operating cash flows to average total liabilities ratio**
A ratio that measures the ability to pay total debt from operating cash flows.

$$\frac{\text{Operating Cash Flow}}{\text{Average Total Liabilities}} = \frac{\$88,584}{\$64,417} = 1.37 \text{ times}$$

With the ability to pay all debts from operating cash flows, the company exhibits strong solvency, which will help it with future expansion.

Now let's apply these ratios to Family Dollar. For current liabilities, the ratio results are:

August 30 2003	August 31 2002	September 1 2001	August 26 2000	August 28 1999	August 29 1998	August 31 1997	August 31 1996
0.52	0.87	0.41	0.46	0.31	0.70	0.50	0.35

For total liabilities, the ratios are:

August 30 2003	August 31 2002	September 1 2001	August 26 2000	August 28 1999	August 29 1998	August 31 1997	August 31 1996
0.46	0.77	0.37	0.43	0.29	0.66	0.46	0.32

Because Family Dollar has few long-term liabilities, the two ratios differ only slightly. We discussed that Family Dollar has a very conservative debt policy. In 2003 the company can repay all of its debt within 2.27 years, a remarkable accomplishment in an age of heavily indebted companies. It also affords the company a generous borrowing capacity.

These four analysis tools can help a cash manager track progress over time and maintain awareness of borrowing capacity. In addition, the manager can watch for predictors of cash problems as the ratios change over time. A business operates in a fast-paced, global economy that can change in a heartbeat. The more solvent the company, the more likely it can survive a sudden economic shock, which usually affects cash flow immediately. Cash management becomes an important daily activity.

Importance of Cash Management

A seemingly unbelievable truth is that a firm's financial health can change abruptly. Take the case of Gap Inc. Gap's earnings were $824 million in 1998, $1.127 billion in 1999, $878 million in 2000, and a loss of $7.8 million in 2001. Net income fell more than $1.2 billion in two years, while cash increased $585 million because debt increased from $3 billion to $4.7 billion. In the spring of 2002 its bond rating fell to junk bond status. Most people believe that this is what causes a company to file bankruptcy. They shake their heads and ask, "What happened?" What happened is that customers did not buy Gap clothes. The CEO went from being a hero to one scrambling to keep his job. The one thing the CEO did correctly was keep the cash flow positive to continue operations. He resigned in 2002. The new leadership increased net income by $485 million, increased cash by $2.35 billion, but also increased debt by $1.57 billion. Only time will tell how Gap survives.

Sometimes very profitable businesses go bankrupt because they run out of cash. A rapidly growing business needs a lot of cash—to replenish inventory, to buy new equipment, to build new stores, and to repay debt. When the company has a small amount of contributed capital from shareholders, cash flows undoubtedly suffer. So the company borrows cash on a short-term basis. Borrowed money, however, must be repaid quickly. During a rapid growth period, the need for cash continues to grow, leaving little to repay the debt. If the lender decides to recall the loan for any reason, the company may have few options—sell to a larger company, attract more investors, or file bankruptcy.

Both these examples represent extreme problems. What about the company that seems to get by each year without extremes of growth or contraction? Good cash management is vital to that type of company also. Improper cash management can reduce profits in several ways. First, the cash manager fails to take discounts on purchases. With 2/10 terms on purchases, the annual percentage rate amounts to 36 percent interest on the lost discount. Without available cash, management might have to pass up opportunities to lower operating costs by taking advantage of bargains on raw materials, equipment, and other operating expenses. The lack of cash can also cause the loss of future revenues because the firm fails to make needed investments to make growth possible or to keep the company current with cost-saving technology. Cash management must be proactive, not reactive. Mature firms will plan carefully for reliable cash flows with multiple contingency plans for economic shocks and other unexpected emergencies.

In Chapter 8 we will explore other methods of analyzing the financial statements to make decisions for and about a company's profitability, liquidity, and solvency.

CHAPTER SUMMARY

Managers serve as the primary internal analysts of the company and use trend analysis and common-size statements for analytical review. Trend analysis highlights changes in key financial indicators over time, whereas common-size statements convert each element of the balance sheet to percentages of total assets and each element of the income statement to percentages of sales. Analytical review is a useful tool for understanding the nature of the company, but it is subject to several limitations.

The statement of cash flows provides information about cash flows used by or provided by three major activities of the firm: operating, investing, and financing. Operating cash flows represent cash provided from revenue-producing activities. To compute the cash flow from operating activities, analyze the income statement, current assets, and current liabilities. Healthy companies have positive operating cash flows. Operating cash flows are the only renewable source of cash and should be large enough to provide investing and financing cash needs.

Investing cash flows represent cash inflows and outflows from the long-term assets the company buys and sells. Typical transactions classified as investing activities are the purchase and sale of property, plant, and equipment, as well as long-term investments in other companies. Growing companies normally have negative investing cash flows. The financing activities section of the statement of cash flows shows what types of external financing the company used to provide funds. Information showing the results of financing activities can be found in the long-term liability section and the stockholders' equity section of the balance sheet.

The statement of cash flows furnishes valuable information about the cash inflows and outflows of a business during a particular period. It provides an explanation of the changes in cash from the beginning to the end of a period. Therefore, the statement of cash flows can be considered a financial statement analysis tool as well as a financial statement.

Cash ratios are additional financial tools managers use to help manage cash. The cash to total assets ratio measures the percentage of total assets made up of cash. Free cash flow is the operating cash flows remaining after deducting capital expenditures and dividends. Free cash flow represents the remainder of cash available for strategic-planning goals such as expansion. The operating cash flows to average current liabilities ratio measures a firm's ability to pay current debt from operating cash flows. The operating cash flows to average total liabilities ratio measures the company's ability to pay total debt from operating cash flows. The cash ratios indicate the health of the firm's cash position and its ability to repay debt from operations.

Good cash management is extremely important to the financial health and well-being of a company. Cash management is vital to minimize operating expenses, provide alternatives to management during economic downturns, and furnish resources for investments in the company to produce growth and future revenues.

Visit the Web site *www.prenhall.com/terrell* for additional study help with the Online Study Guide.

REVIEW OF CONCEPTS

A Describe the internal users of analytical data review techniques.

B Describe the types of decision information the analytical review techniques provide.

C Describe the difference between *trend analysis* and *common-size statement techniques*.

D Discuss how the cash flow statement is a type of analysis.

E Explain the main purpose of the statement of cash flows.

F Compare and contrast the two methods of preparing the statement of cash flows. Identify the method that publicly traded companies more commonly use.

G Describe the three major classifications of activities presented on the statement of cash flows.

H Identify the only renewable source of cash and explain your choice.

I Identify the categories in which the cash flows related to interest and dividends received and dividends and interest paid are usually reported.

J Provide examples of an inflow of cash and an outflow of cash for each of the three categories of business activity shown on the statement of cash flows.

K Indicate where the items included in operating activities are reported in the financial statements.

L Indicate where the items included in investing activities are reported in the financial statements.

M Indicate where the items included in financing activities are reported in the financial statements.

APPLICATION EXERCISES

LO 3
Trend Analysis and Common-Size Statements

7-7 Go to the JCPenney Web site and locate the most recent annual report's financial statements.

Required:

a. Prepare a trend analysis of the company's balance sheets for the most recent three-year period.

b. Prepare common-size balance sheets and income statements for the most recent two-year period.

c. Prepare a brief analysis of your work in parts a and b.

LO 3
Trend Analysis and Common-Size Statements

7-8 Go to the Microsoft Corporation Web site and locate the most recent annual report's financial statements.

Required:

a. Prepare a trend analysis of the company's balance sheets for the most recent four-year period.

b. Prepare common-size balance sheets and income statements for the most recent three-year period.

c. Prepare a brief analysis of your work in parts a and b.

LO 3
Trend Analysis and Common-Size Statements

7-9 Go to the Nike Corporation Web site and locate the most recent annual report's financial statements.

Required:

a. Prepare a trend analysis of the company's balance sheets for the most recent five-year period.

b. Prepare common-size balance sheets and income statements for the most recent five-year period.

c. Prepare a brief analysis of your work in parts a and b.

7-10 Listed below are the three broad types of activities that can either generate or use cash in any business.

LO 4
Identification
of Activities

* Operating   * Investing   * Financing

Required:

Classify each of the items listed below by the appropriate activity category.

a. payment of dividends

b. adjustment for depreciation

c. purchase of merchandise inventory

d. purchase of vehicles

e. repayment of 90-day loans

f. issuing capital stock

g. payment of wages to employees

h. payment of taxes

i. cash from sale of property and equipment

j. loans to other companies

k. adjustments for changes in current asset and current liability items

l. cash from selling investments in other companies

7-11 Listed below are the three broad types of activities that can either generate or use cash in any business.

LO 4
Identification
of Activities

* Operating   * Investing   * Financing

Required:

Classify each of the items listed below by the appropriate activity category.

a. amortization expense

b. depreciation expense

c. sale of merchandise inventory

d. sale of treasury stock

e. repayment of 30-day loans

f. purchase of one's own stock

g. payment of rent on office space

h. payment of insurance on factory equipment

i. cash from sale of treasury stock

j. purchase of stock in other companies

k. cash from the sale of bonds held for investment

l. cash from the collection of accounts receivable

7-12 Some of Sam Cagle Company's assets, liabilities, and equities have changed from December 31, 2003, to December 31, 2004, as shown below. Cagle is in the process of preparing the operating activities section of its statement of cash flows for 2004. Some of the following items will be included and others will not.

LO 4
Identification of
Sources and Uses

Required:

Indicate whether each of items should be considered a **source** of cash in the operating activities section, a **use** of cash in the operating activities section, or **not included** in the operating activities section.

a. accounts payable decreased

b. property and equipment increased

c. accounts receivable increased

d. long-term notes payable decreased

e. prepaid expenses decreased

f. short-term notes payable increased

Continued

> g. taxes payable decreased
> h. common stock increased
> i. wages payable increased
> j. merchandise inventory decreased

LO 4
Operating Activities Section

7-13 Presented below are partial comparative balance sheets of Jackson Company at December 31, 2004 and 2003:

Jackson Company
Partial Balance Sheets
December 31, 2004, and December 31, 2003
(in thousands)

	2004	2003	Increase/ (Decrease)
Current Assets			
Cash	$ 3,400	$2,920	$480
Accounts receivable	1,825	2,212	(387)
Merchandise inventory	1,170	966	204
Prepaid expenses	240	270	(30)
Total Current Assets	$ 6,635	$6,368	$267
Current Liabilities			
Accounts payable	$ 2,321	$1,740	$581
Notes payable	3,100	3,300	(200)
Total Current Liabilities	$ 5,421	$5,040	$381

Additional Information: Net income for 2004 was $406,000. Included in the operating expenses for the year was depreciation expense of $175,000.

Required:

Prepare the operating activities section of Jackson Company's statement of cash flows for 2004.

LO 4
Operating Activities Section

7-14 Presented below are partial comparative balance sheets of Scotia Company at December 31, 2004 and 2003:

Scotia Company
Partial Balance Sheets
December 31, 2004, and December 31, 2003
(in thousands)

	2004	2003	Increase/ (Decrease)
Current Assets			
Cash	$2,110	$2,650	$ (540)
Accounts receivable	1,254	977	277
Merchandise inventory	730	856	(126)
Prepaid expenses	127	114	13
Total Current Assets	$4,221	$4,597	$ (376)
Current Liabilities			
Accounts payable	$1,054	$1,330	$ (276)
Notes payable	2,100	1,750	350
Total Current Liabilities	$3,154	$3,080	$ 74

Additional Information: Net income for 2004 was $86,900. Included in the operating expenses for the year was depreciation expense of $99,000 and amortization expense of $3,000.

Required:

Prepare the operating activities section of Scotia Company's statement of cash flows for 2004.

7-15 The Powers Corporation worksheet for 2005 included the following:

	January 1	December 31
Cash	$54,000	$29,000
Accounts receivable (net)	74,000	69,000
Prepaid insurance	48,000	36,000
Inventory	56,000	75,000
Accounts payable	23,000	34,000
Notes payable	35,000	50,000

LO 4
Operating Activities
Section

Additional Information: Powers Corporation reported net income of $450,000 for the year and amortization and depreciation expense of $38,000.

Required:

Prepare the operating activities section of Powers Corporation's statement of cash flows for 2005.

7-16 Mavis Company gathered the following data for the year ended December 31, 2004:

LO 4
Investing Activities
Section

Gain on sale of machinery	$ 18,000
Proceeds from sale of machinery	60,000
Purchase of Fred, Inc. bonds	80,000
Purchase of inventory for resale	195,000
Purchase of new building	250,000
Dividends declared	75,000
Dividends paid	40,000
Proceeds from the sale of treasury stock	50,000

Required:

Prepare the investing section of the statement of cash flows for Mavis Company.

7-17 Nash Company gathered the following data for the year ended December 31, 2004:

LO 4
Investing Activities
Section

Loss on sale of machinery	$ 24,000
Proceeds from sale of machinery	40,000
Purchase of Alco, Inc. bonds	180,000
Purchase of equipment with treasury stock	120,000
Proceeds of loan to purchase bonds	60,000
Dividends paid	96,000
Resale of treasury stock	80,000

Required:

Prepare the investing section of the statement of cash flows for Nash Company.

7-18 Rambler, Inc. gathered the following data for the year ended December 31, 2004:

LO 4
Investing Activities
Section

Loss on sale of equipment	$ 4,000
Proceeds from sale of equipment	20,000
Purchase of equipment	980,000
Proceeds of loan for equipment	600,000
Purchase of stock in subsidiary company	240,000
Dividends received from investments	10,000
Purchase of treasury stock	60,000

Required:

Prepare the investing section of the statement of cash flows for Rambler Inc.

LO 4
Financing Activities Section

7-19 Reo Company gathered the following data for the year ended December 31, 2005:

Proceeds from sale of equipment	$300,000
Proceeds from sale of common stock	890,000
Dividends declared	35,000
Dividends paid	28,000
Purchase of treasury stock	60,000
Proceeds from bank loan	200,000
Repayment of mortgage	10,000
Payment of interest on loans	30,000

Required:

Prepare the financing section of the statement of cash flows for Reo Company.

LO 4
Financing Activities Section

7-20 Diamond Company gathered the following data for the year ended December 31, 2004:

Loss on sale of equipment	$ 54,000
Proceeds from sale of equipment	230,000
Proceeds from sale of preferred stock	200,000
Dividends declared	95,000
Dividends paid	80,000
Proceeds from sale of treasury stock	160,000
Proceeds from bank loan	300,000
Repayment of bank loan (interest)	20,000
Repayment of bank loan (principal)	120,000

Required:

Prepare the financing section of the statement of cash flows for Diamond Company.

LO 4
Financing Activities Section

7-21 Cirrus Company gathered the following data for the year ended December 31, 2005:

Proceeds from sale of equipment	$300,000
Proceeds from sale of common stock	890,000
Dividends declared	35,000
Dividends paid	28,000
Purchase of treasury stock	60,000
Proceeds from bank loan	200,000
Repayment of mortgage	10,000
Payment of interest on loans	30,000

Required:

Prepare the financing section of the statement of cash flows for Cirrus Company.

LO 5
Concepts of Cash Flow Statements

7-22 Examine Rock Company's statement of cash flows for the year ended December 31, 2004:

Required:

Respond to the following questions:
a. For which of the three types of activities did Rock Company use the majority of its cash during 2004?
b. What does your answer to part a tell you about Rock?
c. From which of the three types of activities did Rock obtain the majority of its cash during 2004?
d. Is the activity you identified in part c an appropriate source of cash in the long run? Explain your reasoning.

Rock Company
Statement of Cash Flows
For the Year Ended December 31, 2004
(in thousands)

Cash Flows from Operating Activities:		
Net Income		$ 389
Adjustments to reconcile net income		
to net cash provided by operating activities:		
Depreciation expense	$ 131	
Increase in accounts receivable	(287)	
Increase in merchandise inventory	(104)	
Increase in prepaid expense	(70)	
Decrease in accounts payable	(4)	(334)
Net Cash Provided by Operating Activities		$ 55
Cash Flows from Investing Activities:		
Purchase of building	$(1,255)	
Purchase of equipment	(304)	
Net Cash Used by Investing Activities		(1,559)
Cash Flows from Financing Activities:		
Proceeds from long-term loan	$ 800	
Proceeds from sale of common stock	300	
Payment of cash dividends	(100)	
Net Cash Provided by Financing Activities		1,000
Net Decrease in Cash During 2004		$ (504)
Cash Balance, January 1, 2004		1,000
Cash Balance, December 31, 2004		$ 496

7-23 McDaniel, Inc.'s statement of cash flows for the year ended December 31, 2005, follows.

LO 5
Concepts of Cash Flow Statements

McDaniel, Inc.
Statement of Cash Flows
For the Year Ended December 31, 2005
(in thousands)

Cash Flows from Operating Activities:		
Net Income		$ 1,608
Adjustments to reconcile net income		
to net cash provided by operating activities:		
Depreciation expense	$ 218	
Increase in accounts receivable	(341)	
Decrease in merchandise inventory	81	
Increase in prepaid expense	(100)	
Increase in accounts payable	154	12
Net Cash Provided by Operating Activities		$ 1,620
Cash Flows from Investing Activities:		
Purchase of building	$ (1,000)	
Purchase of equipment	(200)	
Net Cash Used by Investing Activities		(1,200)
Cash Flows from Financing Activities:		
Repayment of long-term loan	$ (350)	
Proceeds from sale of common stock	350	
Payment of cash dividends	(100)	
Net Cash Used by Financing Activities		(100)
Net Increase in Cash During 2005		$ 320
Cash Balance, January 1, 2005		430
Cash Balance, December 31, 2005		$ 750

Required:

a. For which of the three types of activities did McDaniel use the majority of its cash during 2005?
b. What does your answer to part a tell you about McDaniel?
c. From which of the three types of activities did McDaniel obtain the majority of its cash during 2005?
d. Is the activity you identified in part c an appropriate source of cash in the long run? Explain your reasoning.

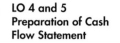

LO 4 and 5
Preparation of Cash Flow Statement

7-24 Use the following balance sheets, income statement, and the additional information to complete this problem.

Hubble Company
Balance Sheets
At December 31

(in thousands)	2005	2004
Assets		
Current Assets		
Cash	$ 1,618	$1,220
Accounts receivable	1,925	2,112
Merchandise inventory	1,070	966
Prepaid expenses	188	149
Total Current Assets	$ 4,801	$4,447
Plant and Equipment		
Buildings and equipment	$ 6,252	$4,437
Less: Accumulated depreciation	(502)	(400)
Total Plant and Equipment	$ 5,750	$4,037
Total Assets	$10,551	$8,484
Liabilities and Stockholders' Equity		
Current Liabilities		
Accounts payable	$ 1,818	$1,686
Notes payable	900	1,100
Total Current Liabilities	$ 2,718	$2,786
Long-Term Liabilities	2,500	2,000
Total Liabilities	$ 5,218	$4,786
Stockholders' Equity		
Common stock, no par value	$ 3,390	$2,041
Retained earnings	1,943	1,657
Total Stockholders' Equity	$ 5,333	$3,698
Total Liabilities		
and Stockholders' Equity	$10,551	$8,484

Hubble Company
Income Statement
For the Year Ending December 31, 2005
(in thousands)

Net Sales		$11,228
Cost of goods sold		7,751
Gross Profit		$ 3,477
Operating Expenses		
Depreciation—buildings and equipment	$ 102	
Other selling and administrative	2,667	
Total Expenses		(2,769)
Operating Income		$ 708
Interest expense		(168)
Income before Taxes		$ 540
Income taxes		(114)
Net Income		$ 426

Additional Information: There were no sales of plant and equipment during the year, and the company paid dividends to stockholders during the year of $140,000.

Required:

a. Prepare Hubble's statement of cash flows for the year ended December 31, 2005, using the indirect method for operating activities.

b. In which of the three categories of activities did Hubble use the majority of its cash during 2005?

c. What does your answer to part b tell you about Hubble?

d. From which of the three types of activities did Hubble obtain the majority of its cash during 2005?

e. Is the activity you identified in part d an appropriate source of cash in the long run? Explain your reasoning.

7-25   Use the following balance sheets, income statement, and additional information to complete this problem.

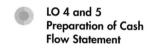

LO 4 and 5
Preparation of Cash Flow Statement

Jeff Brown Company
Balance Sheets
At December 31

(in thousands)	2004	2003
Assets		
Current Assets		
Cash	$ 529	$ 660
Accounts receivable	1,006	1,011
Merchandise inventory	396	452
Prepaid expenses	38	62
Total Current Assets	$1,969	$2,185
Plant and Equipment		
Buildings	$2,000	$1,681
Less: Accumulated depreciation	(176)	(146)
Buildings, net	$ 1,824	$1,535
Equipment	$ 809	$ 609
Less: Accumulated depreciation	(76)	(61)
Equipment, net	$ 733	$ 548
Total Plant and Equipment	$2,557	$2,083
Total Assets	$4,526	$4,268
Liabilities and Stockholders' Equity		
Current Liabilities		
Accounts payable	$ 726	$ 809
Notes payable	750	600
Total Current Liabilities	$1,476	$1,409
Long-Term Liabilities	1,500	1,200
Total Liabilities	$2,976	$2,609
Stockholders' Equity		
Common stock, no par value	$1,300	$1,000
Retained earnings	250	659
Total Stockholders' Equity	$1,550	$1,659
Total Liabilities and Stockholders' Equity	$4,526	$4,268

Additional Information: There were no sales of plant and equipment during the year, and the company paid dividends to stockholders during the year of $70,000.

Jeff Brown Company
Income Statement
For the Year Ended December 31, 2004
(in thousands)

Sales		$6,391
Cost of goods sold		4,474
Gross Profit		$1,917
Operating Expenses		
Depreciation—buildings and equipment	$ 45	
Other selling and administrative	2,066	
Total Expenses		2,111
Operating Income		$ (194)
Interest expense		145
Income Before Taxes		$ (339)
Income taxes		—0—
Net Loss		$ (339)

Required:

a. Prepare Brown Company's statement of cash flows for the year ended December 31, 2004, using the indirect method for operating activities.

b. In which of the broad activities did Brown use the majority of its cash during 2004?

c. What does your answer to part b tell you about Brown?

d. In which of the three activities did Brown obtain the majority of its cash during 2004?

e. Is the activity you identified in part d an appropriate source of cash in the long run? Explain your reasoning.

LO 5
Analysis of Cash Flow Information

7-26 Following are the totals from the main three sections of Kay Coleman and Company's most recent statement of cash flows:

Net cash used by operating activities	$ (835,000)
Net cash used by investing activities	(1,280,000)
Net cash provided by financing activities	2,153,000

Required:

a. What does this information tell you about Coleman?

b. What additional information would you want to see before you analyze Coleman's ability to generate positive cash flow in the future?

c. Did Coleman have a net income or loss for the period? What additional information would you want before trying to predict the company's net income for next period?

LO 5
Analysis of Cash Flow Information

7-27 Following are the totals from the main sections of Glenn Eddleman and Company's most recent statement of cash flows:

Net cash used by operating activities	$(1,409,000)
Net cash provided by investing activities	1,980,000
Net cash used by financing activities	(303,000)

Required:

a. What do these totals tell you about Eddleman?

b. What additional information would you want to see before you analyze Eddleman's ability to generate positive cash flow in the future?

c. Did Eddleman have a net income or loss for the period? What additional information would you want before trying to predict the company's net income for next period?

7-28   Compare the two methods for preparing the statement of cash flows, the direct method and the indirect method.

LO 5
Direct Method versus Indirect Method

  a. Which sections are different and which sections are the same?
  b. Discuss the quality of the information that each provides.
  c. Which method do you prefer? Explain your answer.

7-29   The Skaggs Company is preparing a statement of cash flows for the year ended December 31, 2005. Selected beginning and ending account balances are:

LO 5
Depreciation and Purchases of Equipment

	Beginning	Ending
Machinery	$450,000	$475,500
Accumulated depreciation—machinery	95,000	129,000
Loss on sale of machinery		2,000

During the year, the company received $44,500 for a machine that cost $49,500 and purchased other items of machinery.

Required:

  a. Compute the depreciation on machinery for the year.
  b. Compute the amount of machinery purchases for the year.

7-30   The Miles Company is preparing a statement of cash flows for the year ended December 31, 2005. Selected beginning and ending account balances are:

LO 5
Depreciation and Purchases of Equipment

	Beginning	Ending
Equipment	$250,000	$280,000
Accumulated depreciation—equipment	65,000	89,000
Gain on sale of machinery		2,000

During the year, the company received $50,000 for equipment that cost $65,000 and purchased other items of equipment.

Required:

  a. Compute the depreciation on equipment for the year.
  b. Compute the amount of equipment purchases for the year.

7-31   The Foster Company gathered the following information from its accounting records for the year ended December 31, 2005:

LO 4
Operating Activities—Direct Method

Collections from customers	$450,000
Payments to suppliers	150,000
Payments for income taxes	75,000
Interest received from investments	5,000
Payments to employees	64,000
Payments for interest	85,000
Depreciation expense	50,000

Required:

  Prepare the operating section of the cash flow statement for the Foster Company using the direct method.

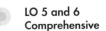

LO 4
Operating
Activities—Direct
Method

7-32 The Galway Company gathered the following information from its accounting records for the year ended June 30, 2005:

Collections of accounts receivable	$350,000
Cash sales	85,000
Payments to suppliers	260,000
Payments for income taxes	45,000
Interest received from investments	15,000
Payments to employees	95,000
Payments for interest	68,000
Depreciation expense	25,000

Required:

Prepare the operating section of the cash flow statement for the Galway Company using the direct method.

LO 4
Operating
Activities—Direct
Method

7-33 The Porter Company gathered the following information from its accounting records for the year ended September 30, 2006:

Payment for treasury stock	$200,000
Payments for dividends	100,000
Collections of accounts receivable	870,000
Cash sales	385,000
Payments to suppliers on account	738,000
Cash purchases	250,000
Payments for income taxes	245,000
Interest received from investments	95,000
Payments to employees	460,000
Payments for interest	35,000
Depreciation expense	125,000

Required:

Prepare the operating section of the cash flow statement for the Porter Company using the direct method.

LO 5 and 6
Comprehensive

7-34 Visit the Coca-Cola Company Web site and find its latest statement of cash flows and do the following.

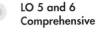

Required:

a. List the total for operating, financing, and investing cash flows for each of the years shown in the report's statement of cash flows.
b. Does the company use the direct or indirect method of preparing the statement of cash flows?
c. Have the operating cash flows been positive?
d. Identify the transactions that affect the cash flow for financing activities.
e. Compute the following items:
  1. cash to total assets ratio
  2. free cash flow
  3. operating cash flows to average current liabilities ratio
  4. operating cash flows to average total liabilities ratio
f. Analyze Coke's cash position based on the information you gathered.

LO 5 and 6
Comprehensive

7-35 Visit the Southwest Airlines Web site and find the statement of cash flows to answer the following questions:

Required:

a. List the total for operating, financing, and investing cash flows for each of the years shown in the report's statement of cash flows.
b. Does the company use the direct or indirect method of preparing the statement of cash flows?

c. Have the operating cash flows been positive?

d. Identify each of the transactions that affect cash flow from investing activities.

e. Compute the following items:
   1. cash to total assets ratio
   2. free cash flow
   3. operating cash flows to average current liabilities ratio
   4. operating cash flows to average total liabilities ratio

f. Analyze Southwest Airlines' cash position based on the information you gathered.

7-36

a. Calculate the following for the Jeff Brown Company in exercise 7-25:
   1. cash to total assets ratio
   2. free cash flow
   3. operating cash flows to average current liabilities ratio
   4. operating cash flows to average total liabilities ratio

b. Analyze the cash position of Brown based on the ratios.

LO 6
Cash Ratios

7-37

a. Calculate the following for the Hubble Company in exercise 7-24.
   1. cash to total assets ratio
   2. free cash flow
   3. operating cash flows to average current liabilities ratio
   4. operating cash flows to average total liabilities ratio

b. Analyze the cash position of Hubble based on the ratios.

LO 6
Cash Ratios

7-38   While preparing a preliminary cash flow statement for the CFO, you realize that the cash flow from operations section of the statement is reporting a material outflow of cash. At the same time you see that cash flow from investing activities is again showing a positive inflow of a large amount of cash. On further examination, the cash inflow from investing is largely the result of the sale of fixed assets that are vital to production. When you confront the CFO with the information, she asks you to remain quiet about the situation, assuring you that she will remedy the situation. Her comment makes you wonder.

Ethics

Required:

a. What are the long-term implications for the company if this cash flow situation is allowed to continue?

b. Can the CFO remedy this situation? If so, how would she go about it?

FOR ADDITIONAL READING

Algeri, Salvatore, "Cash Is King." *www.deloitte.com/dtt/article/0,2297,sid%253 D9465%2526cid% 253D22357,00.html.*

Fraser, Jill Andresky, "The Art of Cash Management." *Inc. Magazine* (October, 1998) *www.inc.com/magazine/19981001/1019.html.*

Lowe, Keith, "Managing Your Cash Flow." Entrepreneur®.com *www.entrepreneur. com/article/ 0,4621,295043,00.html.*

CHAPTER 8

LEARNING OBJECTIVES

After completing this chapter you should be able to:

1 **Distinguish among profitability, liquidity, and solvency.**

2 **Calculate financial ratios designed to measure a company's profitability, liquidity, and solvency.**

3 **Locate industry averages.**

4 **Evaluate a company's ratios using a comparison to industry averages.**

5 **Use ratio values from consecutive time periods to evaluate the profitability, liquidity, and solvency of a business.**

6 **Draw conclusions about the creditworthiness and investment-attractiveness of a company.**

7 **State the limitations of ratio analysis.**

Analyzing Financial Statements for Profitability, Liquidity, and Solvency

T he financial and cash analyses performed in Chapter 7 provided a good start to understanding the financial anatomy of a firm. Financial reporting is an essential source of information for internal and external decision makers, and financial statements are a central component of financial reporting. A publicly held company is required to submit financial statements to the SEC both quarterly and annually, which gives its stakeholders regular access to financial information. Both internal and external analysts should combine these financial reports with industry and economic information to understand fully the results of any financial analysis.

Financial statement analysis is the process of looking beyond the face of the financial statements to gain additional insight into a company's financial health. Financial statement analysis uses many tools including trend analysis, common-size statements, and ratio analysis. You learned how to prepare and use both trend analysis and common-size statements in Chapter 7. In this chapter, we will focus on ratio analysis.

Ratio analysis is a technique for analyzing the relationship between two items from a company's financial statements for a given period. These items may be on the same financial statement, or they may come from different financial statements. The ratios we discuss in this chapter are based on items from the balance sheet and the income statement, although you frequently must also look at the Notes to the Financial Statements to get the details necessary to compute the ratios. We will look at the ratio analysis for two companies—Elevation Sports,

Visit **www.prenhall.com/terrell** to view the video entitled "Financial Statement Analysis."

● **financial statement analysis**
The process of looking beyond the face of the financial statements to gain additional insight into a company's financial health.

● **ratio analysis**
A technique for analyzing the relationship between two items from a company's financial statements for a given period.

Inc., a private (fictional) company, and Family Dollar Stores, Inc., a public company. We cannot compare the two companies directly because they operate in different industries, and we will examine Elevation Sports for only one year, its first. We can, however, examine Family Dollar over an eight-year period. With a financial history of its ratios, we can also perform a trend analysis.

In Chapter 3, we discussed how to find background information about companies. Anyone who wants to conduct a thorough analysis of a company's financial statements should consult the sources suggested in Chapter 3 and gather enough background information about the company to put its financial statement information in proper context. Chapter 3 also explains how to analyze a firm's internal and external environment. We expanded this discussion in Chapter 7 and stressed the importance of understanding the economic, political, and industry context in which to judge the results of your analysis. The FASB warns financial statement users to understand that context before interpreting the results of financial performance. The best sources of economic and political information are respected business periodicals such as the *Wall Street Journal, Business Week, Forbes*, and *Fortune*. They inform readers about current economic conditions, economic trends, political events and trends that may shape the national and global economy, and industry information. Other good sources of industry information are *U.S. Industry & Trade Outlook* and *Mergent Industry Review*. With an understanding of the importance of context, we can now look at ratio analysis.

Visit *Fortune* at ***www.fortune.com*** and *Forbes* at ***www.forbes.com*** for free search for articles with print capability.

Ratio Analysis

Before we compute any ratios, you need to understand that the absolute numbers resulting from the calculations are of little value in themselves. The analysis and interpretation of the numbers—the art of ratio analysis—produce the desired information. To be truly useful to economic decision makers, a company's ratios need to be compared to other information, such as the ratio values for industry averages or the company's ratios in past years. So after introducing all the ratios in this section of the chapter, we will make these comparisons and interpret the findings in the next.

As we introduce each ratio, we will explore what information it offers and show how it is calculated. We selected 13 ratios found in the *Almanac of Business and Industrial Financial Ratios*, a widely used source of financial ratio data, because they give us a means of comparing company information to industry averages. Later in the chapter, we will compare Elevation Sports' ratios to its industry averages and Family Dollar's ratios to its industry averages.

Decision makers compute a variety of ratios when analyzing financial statements. These ratios are used to glean information about a company's past performance and current financial position that will help the decision maker predict future results of business activity. Analysts are not consistent in the way they calculate various ratios, however, even when they use the same ratio name. This inconsistency often makes it very difficult to compare ratios calculated by different analysts or financial publications. Descriptions of the ratios in this chapter follow those provided in the *Almanac of Business and Industrial Financial Ratios*. We will illustrate computations of each ratio using the Elevation Sports financial statements presented in Chapters 6 and 7 and reproduced in Exhibits 8-1 through 8-4 for your convenience. Be certain you understand how

Exhibit 8-1
Elevation Sports, Inc. Balance Sheet

Elevation Sports, Inc. Balance Sheet May 31, 2004			
Assets			
Current Assets			
Cash			$128,384
Accounts receivable		$ 9,900	
Less: Allowance for doubtful accounts		450	9,450
Merchandise inventory			4,397
Raw materials inventory			2,315
Work-in-process inventory			14,864
Finished goods inventory			13,634
Supplies inventory			593
Prepaid rent			12,000
Prepaid insurance			5,000
Total Current Assets			$190,637
Property, Plant, and Equipment			
Administrative equipment	$ 5,100		
Selling furniture and fixtures	8,400		
Production equipment	89,600	$103,100	
Less: Accumulated depreciation		17,800	
Total Property, Plant, and Equipment			85,300
Intangible Assets			
Patents		$ 10,083	
Copyrights		570	
Trademarks		1,425	
Total Intangible Assets			12,078
Total Assets			$288,015
Liabilities and Stockholders' Equity			
Current Liabilities			
Accounts payable			$ 6,942
Other accounts payable			11,812
Interest payable			6,000
Payroll taxes payable			1,400
Sales taxes payable			560
Income taxes payable			42,120
Current portion of long-term note payable			15,000
Total Current Liabilities			$ 83,834
Long-Term Liabilities			
Note payable – Vail National Bank		$ 60,000	
Less: Current portion		15,000	
Total Long-Term Liabilities			45,000
Total Liabilities			$128,834
Stockholders' Equity			
Paid-in capital:			
Common stock, $10 par value, 100,000 shares			
authorized, 4,000 shares issued and outstanding		$ 40,000	
Paid-in capital in excess of par – common stock		60,000	
Total paid-in capital		$100,000	
Retained earnings		59,181	
Total Stockholders' Equity			159,181
Total Liabilities and Stockholders' Equity			$288,015

Exhibit 8-2
Elevation Sports, Inc.
Income Statement

Elevation Sports, Inc. Income Statement For the Year Ended May 31, 2004			
Sales			
Sales of snowboards			$482,400
Sales of other merchandise			52,385
Less: Sales returns		$ 5,213	
Sales discounts		2,426	(7,639)
Net Sales			$527,146
Cost of Goods Sold			
Cost of snowboards		$264,944	
Cost of other goods sold		30,890	295,834
Gross Profit			$231,312
Operating Expenses			
Selling Expenses			
Advertising	$14,304		
Convention expense	9,325		
Credit card merchant discount	10,032		
Depreciation – selling equipment	1,200		
Internet expenses	3,505		
Payroll taxes – sales salaries	270		
Rent – retail sales	3,600		
Sales salaries	3,000		
Telephone expense – sales	985		
Utilities expense – sales	2,113		
Total Selling Expenses		$ 48,334	
Administrative Expenses			
Amortization of intangibles	$ 1,022		
Bank service charges	445		
Depreciation – administration	1,800		
Doubtful account expense	450		
Employee benefits	4,508		
Insurance expense	3,000		
Legal expense	5,200		
Officers' salaries	48,000		
Office supplies	737		
Payroll taxes – administration	3,520		
Rent – administration	1,800		
Telephone expense	1,413		
Utilities expense	294		
Total Administrative Expenses		72,189	
Total Operating Expenses			120,523
Operating Income			$110,789
Other Revenues and Expenses			
Interest revenue		$ 512	
Interest expense		(6,000)	
Total Other Revenues and Expenses			(5,488)
Income Before Income Taxes			$105,301
Income Taxes			42,120
Net Income			$ 63,181
Earnings Per Share			$ 15.79

Exhibit 8-3
Elevation Sports, Inc. Statement of Stockholders' Equity

Elevation Sports, Inc. Statement of Stockholders' Equity For the Year Ended May 31, 2004				
	COMMON STOCK	PAID-IN CAPITAL	RETAINED EARNINGS	TOTAL
Balance, June 1, 2003	$ —0—	$ —0—	$ —0—	$ —0—
Add: Sale of common stock	40,000	60,000		100,000
Net income			63,181	63,181
Deduct: Dividends declared			(4,000)	(4,000)
Balance, May 31, 2004	$40,000	$60,000	$59,181	$159,181

Exhibit 8-4
Elevation Sports, Inc.
Statement of Cash Flows

Elevation Sports, Inc. Statement of Cash Flows For the Year Ended May 31, 2004		
Cash Flows from Operating Activities:		
Net income		$ 63,181
Adjustments to reconcile net income to net cash provided by operating activities:		
Depreciation expense	$ 17,800	
Amortization expense	1,022	
Increase in accounts receivable	(9,450)	
Increase in inventories	(35,803)	
Increase in prepaid expenses	(17,000)	
Increase in other accounts payable	6,942	
Increase in accounts payable	13,772	
Increase in interest payable	6,000	
Increase in taxes payable	42,120	25,403
Net Cash Provided by Operating Activities		$ 88,584
Cash Flows from Investing Activities:		
Purchase of equipment and furniture	$ (43,100)	
Investment in intangible assets	(13,100)	
Net Cash Used by Operating Activities		(56,200)
Cash Flows from Financing Activities:		
Sale of common stock	$100,000	
Payment of dividends	(4,000)	
Net Cash Provided (Used) by Financing Activities		96,000
Net Change in Cash		$128,384
Beginning Cash, June 1, 2003		—0—
Ending Cash, May 31, 2004		$128,384

we determined which figures from Elevation Sports' balance sheet and income statement to use for each ratio.

The 13 ratios presented in this chapter are used to measure either profitability, liquidity, or solvency—three characteristics important to those assessing a company's well-being. As each characteristic is described, we will discuss which users are most interested in it and why it is of concern to them.

Profitability

● **profitability**
The ease with which a company generates income.

Profitability is the ease with which a company generates income. If a company generates a high level of income very easily, it is said to have high profitability. All companies must maintain at least a minimum level of profitability to meet their obligations, such as servicing long-term debt and paying dividends to stockholders.

● **profitability ratios**
Ratios that measure a firm's past performance and help predict its future profitability level.

Profitability ratios measure a firm's past performance and help predict its future profitability level. Present and potential stockholders and long-term creditors, therefore, use these ratios to evaluate investments. Similarly, managers use them to monitor and evaluate their company's performance.

Analysts must interpret profitability ratios carefully, knowing that managers have two potential reasons to enhance these ratios. First, the market judges the value of stocks based in part on the company's profitability. Second, managers' compensation may include bonuses based on the level of profitability the company achieves. Managers, therefore, may take a short-term view of profitability. Stockholders and creditors generally take a longer-term view of the company's financial health than can be measured by short-term profitability alone. As you examine the profitability ratios in this section, consider that profitability of a particular year is less important than a trend of profitability over a period of years.

What Do You Think?

8-1 In the 1980s, Honda, a Japanese firm, looked at the profitability of its automobile division with a long-term perspective and chose quality over current profits. At the same time, U.S. carmakers focused on current profits. Discuss how Honda's approach affected the automobile industry in the 1990s.

8-2 Think of another example of a management decision that would be made differently depending on whether the decision is considering the short-term or long-term well-being of the company. Explain the impact of the two perspectives on the outcome of the decision.

Return on Assets Ratio

● **return on assets ratio**
A ratio that measures how efficiently a company uses its assets to produce profits. Also called return on **total assets**.

The **return on assets ratio** (sometimes called the **return on total assets**) measures how efficiently a company uses its assets to produce profits. After all, the reason companies invest in assets is to produce revenue and ultimately profit (net income). Delta Airlines, for example, invests in aircraft and other assets for the express purpose of producing income. Delta's creditors (particularly long-term creditors), stockholders, and management are all interested in knowing how efficiently the aircraft and other assets are being used to produce the company's income. The return on assets ratio is one approach to measuring that efficiency. It is computed as follows:

$$\text{Return on assets} = \frac{\text{Net income before taxes}}{\text{Total assets}}$$

The numerator comes from the income statement and represents the total return (pretax) on the company's assets. The denominator is drawn from the balance sheet and indicates the company's level of investment in assets. We calculate Elevation Sports' return on assets for fiscal 2004:

$$\text{Return on assets} = \frac{\$105,301}{\$288,015} = .3656 \text{ or } 36.56\%$$

If a company has a low return on its assets, how would its managers determine the cause of the problem and improve the situation? The answer to that question lies in the next two profitability ratios we will examine because the return on assets ratio can be deconstructed into two components.

Profit Margin before Income Tax Ratio

The **profit margin before income tax ratio** measures the percentage of income before income taxes produced by a given level of revenue. It has the same numerator as the return on assets ratio. The denominator for this ratio is net sales for the period. We calculate the profit margin before income tax as follows:

● **profit margin before income tax ratio**
A ratio that measures the profitability of sales before income taxes.

$$\text{Profit margin before income tax} = \frac{\text{Net income before taxes}}{\text{Sales}}$$

Both components of the profit margin before tax are drawn from the income statement. This ratio indicates the contribution of sales to the overall profitability of the company. Elevation Sports' profit margin before income taxes for fiscal 2004 is:

$$\text{Profit margin before income tax} = \frac{\$105,301}{\$527,146} = 19.98\%$$

What Do You Think?

8-3 What situations might cause a company to have a low profit margin before income tax?

8-4 Why would a manager, knowing that income taxes are not optional, care to measure profit margin before income taxes?

Profit margin before income tax is just one component of the return on assets ratio; the second component—total asset turnover—is equally important.

Total Asset Turnover Ratio

The **total asset turnover ratio** calculates the amount of sales produced for a given level of assets used. The purpose of this ratio is similar to that of the return on total assets ratio except that it indicates how effectively the company uses its total assets to generate sales or revenue, rather than income before taxes. Total asset turnover has the same denominator as the return on assets ratio, but the numerator is total sales for the period. We calculate total asset turnover as follows:

● **total asset turnover ratio**
A ratio that calculates the amount of sales produced for a given level of assets used.

$$\text{Total asset turnover} = \frac{\text{Sales}}{\text{Total assets}}$$

The numerator is found on the income statement and the denominator on the balance sheet. We calculate the total asset turnover ratio for Elevation Sports for fiscal 2004 as:

$$\text{Total asset turnover} = \frac{\$527,146}{\$288,015} = 1.83 \text{ times}$$

Our calculation indicates that Elevation Sports produced 1.83 times as many dollars in sales as it had invested in assets. Now that we have explored both components of the return on assets ratio, we can look more closely at the relationship among the three ratios:

$$\text{Return on assets} = \text{Profit margin before income tax} \times \text{Total asset turnover}$$

$$\frac{\text{Net income before taxes}}{\text{Total assets}} = \frac{\text{Net income before taxes}}{\text{Sales}} \times \frac{\text{Sales}}{\text{Total assets}}$$

If a company's return on assets is low, both its profit margin before income tax and its total asset turnover should be investigated—separately—to determine the source of the problem. After managers have analyzed each component, they can focus the company on areas needing improvement.

What Do You Think?

8-5 Suggest two ways a company can make its total asset turnover ratio higher.

8-6 A company wishing to boost its return on assets ratio could focus its efforts on either the profit margin before income tax ratio or the total asset turnover ratio. Which ratio do you think would be easier to improve? Explain your reasoning.

Rather than relying on any single measure of profitability, wise financial statement users turn to several ratios to make sure that a single ratio is not an anomaly. We will explore three more profitability ratios.

Profit Margin after Income Tax Ratio

● **profit margin after income tax ratio**
A ratio that measures the after-tax net income each sales dollar generates.

As its name suggests, this ratio is only slightly different from the profit margin measure already discussed. The **profit margin after income tax ratio** measures the after-tax net income each sales dollar generates. This is a subtle difference, but it may be important in some analyses.

The profit margin after income tax ratio is calculated as follows:

$$\text{Profit margin after income tax} = \frac{\text{Net income after taxes}}{\text{Sales}}$$

Both components of this ratio are drawn from the income statement. The calculation of Elevation Sports' profit margin after income tax for fiscal 2004 is:

$$\text{Profit margin after income tax} = \frac{\$\ 63{,}181}{\$527{,}126} = 11.98\%$$

Whether profit margin is computed before or after taxes, the result is a useful measure of profitability. Executives can manage two components of net income—revenues and expenses. Effective managers will attempt to maximize revenues and minimize costs to produce the highest income. Realistically, competitive forces hinder their ability to maximize revenues and scarcity limits their abilities to minimize costs. Seldom does a low profit margin result from just one element of revenues or expenses. Managers, therefore, remain vigilant in carefully analyzing *all* revenue and expense components to create additional profit margins.

Just as profit margin after tax is very similar to profit margin before tax, the final two profitability ratios we examine next are very similar to one another.

Return on Equity after Taxes Ratio

The **return on equity after taxes ratio** indicates how much after-tax income was generated for a given level of equity. Return on equity demonstrates profitability by comparing a company's after-tax net income to the amount of investment by the company's owners. We calculate the return on equity ratio as follows:

$$\text{Return on equity after taxes} = \frac{\text{Net income after taxes}}{\text{Equity}}$$

● **return on equity after taxes ratio**
A ratio that indicates how much after-tax income was generated for a given level of equity.

The numerator of this ratio is drawn from the income statement and the denominator is taken from the balance sheet. The calculation of Elevation Sports' return on equity for fiscal 2004 is:

$$\text{Return on equity after taxes} = \frac{\$\,63,181}{\$159,181} = 39.69\%$$

The final profitability ratio we will examine is only slightly different from the return on equity after income taxes ratio.

Return on Equity before Taxes Ratio

As its name suggests, the **return on equity before taxes ratio** calculates how much before-tax income was generated for a given level of equity. To calculate net income before income taxes, we add the income tax expense for the period to the net income. This addition of income tax expense to the numerator is the only difference between return on equity before income taxes and return on equity after income taxes. The denominator, total shareholders' equity, remains the same.

● **return on equity before taxes ratio**
A ratio that calculates how much before-tax income was generated for a given level of equity.

$$\frac{\text{Return on equity}}{\text{before taxes}} = \frac{\text{Net income after taxes} + \text{Income taxes}}{\text{Equity}}$$

Elevation Sports' income statement indicates the amount of income before income taxes. Many publicly traded companies do likewise so we can use that amount directly from the income statement for the numerator.

The calculation of Elevation Sports' return before interest on equity for fiscal 2004 is:

$$\frac{\text{Return on equity}}{\text{before taxes}} = \frac{\$105,301}{\$159,181} = 66.15\%$$

By the nature of the calculation, as long as a company has at least some income tax expense, its return before income taxes on equity will be higher than its return on equity after taxes.

Liquidity

An asset's **liquidity** describes the ease with which it can be converted to cash. A company's liquidity refers to its ability to generate the cash needed to meet its short-term obligations. Clearly, all economic decision makers must consider a firm's liquidity because if a company cannot meet its current obligations, it may not be around long enough to be profitable in the long run. Short-term creditors and a company's management pay careful attention to liquidity. Over time many ratios have been developed specifically to measure liquidity. We selected five **liquidity ratios** that evaluate a company's ability to generate sufficient cash to meet its short-term obligations. Naturally, these ratios focus on current assets and current liabilities.

● **liquidity**
The ease with which an asset can be converted to cash.

● **liquidity ratios**
Ratios that evaluate a company's ability to generate sufficient cash to meet its short-term obligations.

Current Ratio

● **current ratio**
A ratio that measures a company's ability to meet its current liabilities with cash generated from current assets.

The **current ratio** measures a company's ability to meet its current liabilities with cash generated from current assets. It is probably the most commonly used gauge of a company's liquidity. The current ratio is calculated as follows:

$$\text{Current ratio} = \frac{\text{Current assets}}{\text{Current liabilities}}$$

This ratio reflects the amount of current assets for each dollar of current liabilities. The fiscal 2004 current ratio for Elevation Sports is:

$$\text{Current Ratio} = \frac{\$190,637}{\$83,834} = 2.27 \text{ to } 1$$

The ratio indicates that Elevation Sports had $2.27 of current assets for every $1.00 of current liabilities at the end of fiscal 2004.

Many experts believe that companies should maintain a ratio of $2 of current assets to every $1 of current liabilities because of the uncertain nature of some of the current assets. For example, some accounts receivable may not be collectible and some inventory may not be saleable. Some companies choose to exceed this recommendation and maintain more than twice as many current assets as current liabilities. However, companies whose sales are predominately cash have found that a current ratio slightly lower than 2:1 is adequate. You will learn how to interpret Elevation Sports' current ratio of 2.27:1 later in this chapter.

What Do You Think?

8-7 If Elevation Sports were to borrow money to retire current liabilities, it would have to pay interest on the borrowed funds. What effect (if any) would the additional interest expense have on the following ratios?

(a) **profit margin before income tax**
(b) **profit margin after income tax**
(c) **return on assets**
(d) **return on equity**
(e) **total asset turnover**

Quick Ratio

● **quick ratio**
A stringent test of liquidity that compares highly liquid current assets to current liabilities. Also called the **acid-test ratio**.

The **quick ratio** is a stringent test of liquidity that compares highly liquid current assets to current liabilities. It is sometimes called the **acid-test ratio**. Some variation exists with regard to what assets are included in the quick ratio calculation because the definition of *highly liquid* is subjective. We will calculate the quick ratio as:

$$\text{Quick ratio} = \frac{\text{Cash} + \text{Receivables} + \text{Trading securities}}{\text{Current liabilities}}$$

In the numerator of our equation, cash is obviously liquid. We also assume accounts receivable and notes receivable will be converted to cash within the shorter of an operating cycle or one year. If, however, management knows that any account receivable or note receivable will not be quickly converted, they should exclude that item in the calculation of this ratio. Marketable securities held in a company's trading portfolio are highly liquid and often represent excess cash that the company plans to use in the near future. The denominator of the quick ratio is identical to the one used for the current ratio.

We can compute the fiscal 2004 quick ratio for Elevation Sports as follows:

$$\text{Quick ratio} = \frac{\$128,384 + \$9,450 + \$0}{\$83,834} = 1.64 \text{ to } 1$$

This figure suggests that Elevation Sports has $1.64 of quick assets for each $1.00 of current liabilities. Note that Elevation Sports' quick ratio (1.64:1) is lower than its current ratio (2.27:1). That is normally the case because we have removed assets that are not highly liquid from the numerator, leaving the denominator unchanged. Some experts believe that a company should maintain a ratio of $1 of quick assets to every $1 of current liabilities. As our calculation shows, Elevation Sports' quick ratio exceeds that benchmark.

What Do You Think?

8-8   How would holding an excessive amount of inventory affect the following ratios?

   (a) profit margin before income tax
   (b) profit margin after income tax
   (c) return on assets
   (d) return on equity
   (e) current ratio
   (f) quick ratio
   (g) total asset turnover

The liquidity ratios we have examined thus far have focused on the proportion of current assets to current liabilities. The next liquidity ratio considers the dollar difference between current assets and current liabilities.

Net Sales to Working Capital Ratio

Recall that liquidity refers to a company's ability to generate sufficient cash to meet its short-term obligations. Our discussion of the current ratio suggested that to maintain their liquidity, companies should have more current assets than current liabilities. The difference between current assets and current liabilities is called **working capital**. Some decision makers use working capital to evaluate a company's liquidity. The **net sales to working capital ratio** goes one step further: It indicates the level of sales generated for a given level of working capital, and it is calculated as follows:

$$\frac{\text{Net sales to}}{\text{working capital}} = \frac{\text{Sales}}{\text{Current assets} - \text{Current liabilities}}$$

● **working capital**
The difference between current assets and current liabilities.

● **net sales to working capital ratio**
A ratio that indicates the level of sales generated for a given level of working capital.

This ratio indicates the amount of sales generated for each dollar of working capital. The fiscal net sales to working capital ratio for Elevation Sports is:

$$\frac{\text{Net sales to}}{\text{working capital}} = \frac{\$527,146}{\$190,637 - \$83,834} = 4.94 \text{ times}$$

This figure suggests that in fiscal 2004 Elevation Sports generated $4.94 in sales for every $1.00 of working capital it had at the end of fiscal 2004.

The net sales to working capital ratio is not the only liquidity ratio to focus on the generation of sales. Receivables turnover does as well.

Receivables Turnover Ratio

The **receivables turnover ratio** measures how quickly a company collects its accounts receivable. Accounts receivable is often a sizable current asset, and companies need to convert it to cash as quickly as possible because it represents interest-free loans to customers.

● **receivables turnover ratio**
A ratio that measures the liquidity of accounts receivable.

Most companies routinely sell to their business customers on a credit basis. Because Elevation Sports' retail sales are cash sales, it has few receivables from its wholesale customers. This increases the timing of Elevation Sports' cash flow and shortens its operating cycle. To make the ratio more meaningful, we should only include its wholesale sales in the computation. The calculation for receivables turnover is:

$$\text{Receivables turnover} = \frac{\text{Net credit sales}}{\text{Accounts receivable}}$$

The sales figure is usually drawn from the income statement and accounts receivable is found on the balance sheet. To calculate net credit sales in this instance, we can go to the final worksheet for the year in Chapter 6 to find the wholesale sales of $151,650 less the sales discounts of $2,426. The fiscal 2004 receivables turnover ratio for Elevation Sports is computed as follows:

$$\text{Receivables turnover} = \frac{\$151,650 - \$2,426}{\$9,450} = 15.79 \text{ times}$$

It's easier to interpret a company's turning over its accounts receivable 15.79 times per year if we determine the average collection period for its accounts receivable. We can do that by dividing the receivables turnover into 365 (the number of days in a year).

$$\text{Average collection period} = \frac{365}{15.79} = 23.12 \text{ days}$$

Our calculation shows that the company takes an average of 23.12 days from the time it makes a credit sale to the time it collects cash from the customer. Is that good or bad? Once again, there is no way to tell from the absolute number. This figure becomes meaningful only when it is compared to a company's results for other years and the average for the industry in which it operates.

The final liquidity ratio we present is very similar in nature to the receivables turnover.

Inventory Turnover Ratio

● inventory turnover ratio
A ratio that indicates the number of times total merchandise inventory is purchased (or finished goods inventory is produced) and sold during a period.

The **inventory turnover ratio** indicates the number of times total merchandise inventory is purchased (or finished goods inventory is produced) and sold during a period. The calculation of inventory turnover is as follows:

$$\text{Inventory turnover} = \frac{\text{Cost of sales}}{\text{Inventory}}$$

We normally find the cost of sales expense on the income statement and the inventory asset on the balance sheet. But Elevation Sports' balance sheet inventories amount includes raw materials inventory and work-in-process inventory. This will give us a less-than-desirable measure of the inventory turnover. We can look on the general ledger (or worksheet) on May 31, 2004, to find the merchandise inventory of $4,397 and the final finished goods inventory amount of $13,634. As we discussed, analysts sometimes have to find the information they need in the Notes to the Financial Statements and other information. The note on inventory will normally present a breakdown between the three inventories for a manufacturing company. The fiscal 2004 inventory turnover ratio for Elevation Sports is:

$$\text{Inventory turnover} = \frac{\$295,834}{\$4,397 + \$13,634} = 16.41 \text{ times}$$

This means Elevation Sports turns its inventory over often, an average of 16.41 times per year. The high number suggests that the company requires a low investment in inventory to support its sales.

We might find the information that Elevation Sports turns over its inventory 16.41 times per year easier to interpret if we extend it to determine the average number of days Elevation Sports holds its inventory. We can do that by dividing the inventory turnover into 365 (the number of days in a year).

$$\frac{365}{16.41} = 22.24 \text{ days}$$

Our calculation shows that, on average, only 22.24 days pass between the time Elevation Sports purchases or manufactures inventory and the time it sells that inventory. Is that good or bad? As was the case with receivables turnover, there is no way to tell from the absolute number. This figure becomes useful only when it is compared to Elevation Sports' results for other years and the average for the industry in which Elevation Sports operates. It may be less for this company because it manufactures the majority of products sold.

Solvency

Solvency is the third important characteristic that decision makers use as an indication of companies' financial well-being. **Solvency** is a company's ability to meet the obligations created by its long-term debt. Obligations resulting from debt include both paying back the amount borrowed and paying interest on the debt. Solvency ratios are of most interest to stockholders, long-term creditors, and, of course, company management. There are numerous solvency ratios; we will look at two of the ones most widely used.

● **solvency**
A company's ability to meet the obligations created by its long-term debt.

Debt Ratio

The **debt ratio** measures what proportion of a company's assets is financed by debt. All assets are claimed by either creditors or owners. You can see this by looking once again at the accounting equation:

● **debt ratio**
A ratio that measures what proportion of a company's assets is financed by debt.

Assets	=	Liabilities	+	Owners' Equity
100%	=	Some %	+	Some %

Creditors and stockholders watch the debt ratio from their individual perspectives and tend to get nervous if they perceive it to be out of balance. We will calculate the debt ratio as follows:

$$\text{Debt ratio} = \frac{\text{Total liabilities}}{\text{Total assets}}$$

Both the items necessary to calculate the debt ratio exist on the balance sheet. Elevation Sports, Inc.'s fiscal 2004 debt ratio is:

$$\text{Debt ratio} = \frac{\$128,834}{\$288,015} = 44.73\%$$

This ratio indicates that 44.73 percent of Elevation Sports' assets are supported by debt, leaving 55.27 percent of the company's assets for the shareholders to claim. There is no absolute rule concerning what amount of a company's assets should be financed through debt, although a rule of thumb ranges from 40 to 60 percent debt financing. A company's debt ratio must be evaluated in light of the industry in which the company operates, how mature the company is (new businesses tend to have more debt relative to equity), and management's philosophy concerning the proper balance between debt financing and equity financing. Elevation Sports has proven to be a very conservative company.

The debt ratio indicates the relationship between the amount of liabilities and the assets a company holds. It reminds us of the percentage of assets against which creditors have claims. The last solvency ratio we will examine indicates a company's ability to meet the interest obligations associated with its debt.

Coverage Ratio

● **coverage ratio**
A ratio that indicates a company's ability to make its periodic interest payments. Also called the times **interest earned ratio**.

The **coverage ratio**, also called the **times interest earned ratio**, indicates a company's ability to make its periodic interest payments. It compares the amount of income available for interest payments to the interest requirements. Creditors use this ratio to assess the risk associated with lending money to a business. The formula we used to calculate this ratio is:

$$\text{Coverage ratio} \;=\; \frac{\text{Earnings before interest expense and income taxes}}{\text{Interest expense}}$$

The numerator consists of earnings before interest and tax expense because this figure represents the amount of earnings available to pay periodic interest payments. To arrive at this amount, we need to add interest expense to earnings before taxes on the income statement. Not all publicly traded companies indicate the amount of interest on their income statements.

What Do You Think?

8-9 Can we always find the amount of interest expense for the reporting period in the annual report? Why or why not?

8-10 Name at least three places the interest expense might be found in an annual report.

Another place to discover the amount of interest paid is the statement of cash flows. There is a difference between the interest expense and the interest paid as evidenced in the Elevation Sports' financial statements. A simple conversion from the cash perspective to the accrual can be made by adding the net change in interest payable to the interest paid:

Interest paid	$ —0—
Increase in interest payable	6,000
Interest expense	$ 6,000

Elevation Sports' fiscal 2004 coverage ratio is:

$$\text{Coverage ratio} = \frac{\$105,301 \;+\; \$6,000}{\$6,000} = 18.55 \text{ times}$$

Some experts believe a coverage ratio of at least four provides an appropriate degree of safety for creditors. This means a company's earnings before interest and taxes should be at least four times as great as its interest expense. Elevation Sports' figure far exceeds that level.

To arrive at a valid assessment of a company's solvency, financial statement users should evaluate ratios that indicate the level of debt the company carries (debt ratio) as well as those indicating the company's ability to meet its obligations associated with the debt (coverage ratio). In fact, when evaluating any of the three characteristics indicative of a company's well-being, analysts usually consider more than one approach.

Analysts use ratio analysis to evaluate the company's current levels of profitability, liquidity, and solvency. Unsatisfactory ratios can send up red flags that warn management, creditors, and investors of trouble ahead. An unprofitable company becomes illiquid because it cannot generate profits and cash, which eventually leads to insolvency. Insolvency then leads to bankruptcy. When these red flags appear, however, an alert management can initiate corrective action to prevent future troubles. Exhibit 8-5 summarizes the calculations and purpose of the profitability, liquidity, and solvency ratios discussed in this chapter.

Exhibit 8-5
Summary of Key Ratios

RATIO	CALCULATION	PURPOSE OF RATIO
PROFITABILITY RATIOS		
1. Return on assets	$\dfrac{\text{Net income before taxes}}{\text{Total assets}}$	Measures the return earned on investment in assets
2. Profit margin before income tax	$\dfrac{\text{Net income before taxes}}{\text{Sales}}$	Measures the pretax earnings produced from a given level of revenues
3. Total asset turnover	$\dfrac{\text{Sales}}{\text{Total assets}}$	Indicates the firm's ability to generate revenues from a given level of assets
4. Profit margin after income tax	$\dfrac{\text{Net income after taxes}}{\text{Sales}}$	Measures the amount of after-tax net income generated by a dollar of sales
5. Return on equity after taxes	$\dfrac{\text{Net income after taxes}}{\text{Equity}}$	Measures the after-tax income generated from a given level of equity
6. Return on equity before taxes	$\dfrac{\text{Net income before taxes}}{\text{Equity}}$	Measures the return on equity before the cost of income taxes
LIQUIDITY RATIOS		
7. Current ratio	$\dfrac{\text{Current assets}}{\text{Current liabilities}}$	Indicates a company's ability to meet short-term obligations
8. Quick ratio	$\dfrac{\text{Cash + Receivables + Trading securities}}{\text{Current liabilities}}$	Measures short-term liquidity more stringently than the current ratio does
9. Net sales to working capital	$\dfrac{\text{Sales}}{\text{Current assets} - \text{Current liabilities}}$	Measures the level of sales generated from a given level of working capital
10. Receivables turnover	$\dfrac{\text{Sales}}{\text{Accounts receivable}}$	Indicates how quickly a company collects its receivables
11. Inventory turnover	$\dfrac{\text{Cost of sales}}{\text{Inventory}}$	Indicates how long a company holds its inventory
SOLVENCY RATIOS		
12. Debt ratio	$\dfrac{\text{Total liabilities}}{\text{Total assets}}$	Measures the proportion of assets financed by debt
13. Coverage ratio	$\dfrac{\text{Earnings before interest expense and income taxes}}{\text{Interest expense}}$	Indicates a company's ability to make its periodic interest expense payments

What Do You Think?

8-11 Assume you had to decide to invest in one of two companies with no information other than values of four of their financial ratios. Which four would you want to know? Explain the reasons for your choices.

Industry Comparisons

We have calculated 13 ratios based on the financial statements included in Elevation Sports' fiscal 2004 financial statements. What now? How do we use these ratios to evaluate the profitability, liquidity, and solvency of the business? Financial ratios are bits of data that become valuable information when used to compare to prior years' ratios or to industry averages. Because this is the first year for Elevation Sports, we cannot compare ratios to prior years. We can, however, compare the results to industry averages.

In Chapter 3, Rob identified the recreation industry under the NAICS as 339920. The *Almanac of Business and Industrial Financial Ratios*, however, uses the IRS codes. The *Almanac* has only two appropriate groupings of companies—sporting goods, hobby, book and music stores, and miscellaneous manufacturers. Which should we use? The majority of the company sales were retail sales, yet the company is a manufacturer. In addition, the IRS has no number for recreational retail sales. So the closest industry is the sporting goods industry. One of the reasons we selected the *Almanac* as a reference is that it includes all companies, public and private. Other sources include only publicly held companies. Elevation Sports is a private company and may be more comparable to all companies rather than to publicly held companies. If we were using another source of industry information, such as *RMA Annual Statement Studies* or *Industry Norms & Key Business Ratios*, we could find data for the specific NAICS industry. Remember, however, that the ratios these two sources use will differ from the ratio formulas we provided and that the companies included in the data are publicly held firms.

Information provided in the *Almanac* for each industry takes up four pages and consists of two tables. Table I provides an analysis of all companies in the particular industry, regardless of whether they had any net income for the year. Table II provides the same information items as Table I, but considers only companies that showed a net income for the year. Exhibit 8-6 is a portion of Table II for IRS classification 451000. Looking down the left column of the exhibit, you will see the 13 key financial ratios we presented earlier in this chapter. They are not in the same order as we covered them and are included in the items numbered from 30 to 50. We did not compare items 1 through 29 because we are interested only in the ratios.

Also included in the portion of Table II reproduced in Exhibit 8-6 are 13 columns of data. Looking at the column headings, we discover that the first column ("Total") provides averages for all companies in the industry. The other columns provide averages for companies of different size within the industry. As we compare Elevation Sports' ratios to industry averages, we will be interested in the first column and the fifth column: the first because we want to see how Elevation Sports compares with the entire industry, and the fifth because Elevation Sports is comparable in size to companies with total assets between $250,000 and $500,000.

Exhibit 8-7 compares the 13 ratios to the total industry and to companies with assets from $250,000 to $500,000. The ratios we calculated earlier in the chapter are rounded to the nearest tenth in Exhibit 8-7 to correspond with the data listed in the *Almanac*. We will use this information as we analyze Elevation Sports in the following segment.

Exhibit 8-6

TABLE II

Corporations with Net Income

SPORTING GOODS, HOBBY, BOOK, AND MUSIC STORES

MONEY AMOUNTS AND SIZE OF ASSETS IN THOUSANDS OF DOLLARS

Item Description for Accounting Period 7/99 6/00	#	Total	Zero Assets	Under 100	100 to 250	251 to 500	501 to 1,000	1,001 to 5,000	5,001 to 10,000	10,001 to 25,000	25,001 to 50,000	50,001 to 100,000	100,001 to 250,000	250,001 and over
Number of Enterprises	1	17992	872	6862	5221	1784	1795	1247	117	43	16	14	7	14
Revenues ($ in thousands)														
Net Sales	2	41208093	357199	891997	2570346	1394402	2842173	6053594	1875193	1516829	998803	2163348	2750791	17793417
Interest	3	66429	100	0	2063	1223	3346	10556	697	1554	2329	3160	2910	38492
Rents	4	24883	1261	0	83	709	1876	1414	565	597	542	1160	1430	15245
Royalties	5	9870	0	0	0	0	0	667	0	115	473	0	0	8616
Other Portfolio Income	6	150250	35253	0	0	758	175	5552	430	693	971	1686	5	104726
Other Receipts	7	435666	45144	5686	40683	14467	21396	53857	19174	21223	51202	9583	20042	133208
Total Receipts	8	41895191	438957	897683	2613175	1411559	2868966	6125640	1896059	1541011	1054320	2178937	2775178	18093704
Average Total Receipts	9	2329	503	131	501	791	1598	4912	16206	35837	65895	155638	396454	1292407
Operating Costs/Operating Income (%)														
Cost of Operations	10	61.1	78.4	53.0	54.7	59.3	62.3	64.6	67.5	63.4	64.4	62.1	61.3	59.7
Salaries and Wages	11	11.9	9.1	5.2	10.4	8.5	11.0	11.5	10.6	11.3	14.6	12.4	12.0	12.9
Taxes Paid	12	2.2	1.1	4.1	2.9	3.1	2.0	1.8	1.7	1.7	2.0	1.9	2.4	2.2
Interest Paid	13	1.0	1.0	0.4	0.8	1.1	0.8	0.8	0.7	1.0	0.8	0.5	1.9	1.1
Depreciation	14	1.9	0.8	0.9	1.1	1.6	2.3	1.2	0.8	1.1	1.3	1.6	1.7	2.6
Amortization and Depletion	15	0.1	0.4	0.0	0.0	0.0	0.0	0.0	0.1	0.1	0.0	0.1	0.4	0.1
Pensions and Other Deferred Comp.	16	0.2	0.0	*	0.5	0.1	0.3	0.3	0.0	0.2	0.5	0.1	0.2	0.2
Employee Benefits	17	0.5	0.4	0.2	0.4	0.3	0.2	0.3	0.2	0.5	0.8	0.3	0.8	0.6
Advertising	18	2.1	0.9	1.0	2.0	2.2	2.6	2.5	1.1	2.4	2.1	4.1	3.6	1.6
Other Expenses	19	14.6	15.9	19.9	19.2	12.8	11.2	11.6	11.0	13.9	13.0	11.9	13.8	16.2
Officers' Compensation	20	1.9	1.1	7.3	5.2	6.2	3.2	3.0	1.9	1.6	1.6	1.0	0.4	0.6
Operating Margin	21	2.6	*	7.9	2.9	4.8	4.0	2.3	4.2	2.9	*	3.9	1.6	2.2
Operating Margin Before Officers' Comp.	22	4.4	*	15.2	8.0	11.0	7.2	5.3	6.1	4.5	0.6	4.9	1.9	2.7
Selected Average Balance Sheet ($ in Thousands)														
Net Receivables	23	81	0	1	16	23	49	220	1479	2735	5065	6874	6277	432048
Inventories	24	565	0	18	63	216	298	1160	3292	7135	18129	37891	114606	395747
Net Property, Plant and Equipment	25	225	0	4	29	60	111	219	943	2150	5092	13123	43936	179758
Total Assets	26	1188		33	155	345	661	1886	6450	15440	34777	67570	198202	848195
Notes and Loans Payable	27	279		31	83	118	167	447	1456	4299	7179	12294	87097	146860

*Information not available.

continued

Exhibit 8-6 *continued*

296

Item Description for Accounting Period 7/99 Through 6/00		Total	Zero Assets	Under 100	100 to 250	251 to 500	501 to 1,000	1,001 to 5,000	5,001 to 10,000	10,001 to 25,000	25,001 to 50,000	50,001 to 100,000	100,001 to 250,000	250,001 and over
All Other Liabilities	28	503	0	5	27	117	211	700	2591	5409	17559	20214	68802	416085
Net Worth	29	406	0	-3	45	110	283	740	2404	5732	10040	35062	42303	285250
Selected Financial Ratios (Times to 1)														
Current Ratio	30	1.6	*	3.7	3.6	1.9	1.9	1.8	1.5	1.7	1.7	2.1	1.9	1.4
Quick Ratio	31	0.4	*	1.1	1.5	0.5	0.6	0.5	0.6	0.5	0.6	0.5	0.2	0.2
Net Sales to Working Capital	32	7.3	*	6.9	5.6	5.9	7.0	6.7	9.1	7.2	5.8	5.9	6.1	8.4
Coverage Ratio	33	5.3	14.7	20.2	6.7	6.7	7.3	5.1	8.6	5.7	6.8	9.8	2.3	4.5
Total Asset Turnover	34	1.9	*	4.0	3.2	2.3	2.4	2.6	2.5	2.3	1.8	2.3	2.0	1.5
Inventory Turnover	35	2.5	*	3.7	4.3	2.1	3.3	2.7	3.3	3.1	2.2	2.5	2.1	1.9
Receivables Turnover	36	28.6	*	76.4	38.8	31.7	30.3	20.4	10.9	11.1	8.7	29.7	125.2	79.3
Total Liabilities to Net Worth	37	1.9	*	.	2.4	2.1	1.3	1.5	1.7	1.7	2.5	0.9	3.7	2.0
Current Assets to Working Capital	38	2.7	*	1.4	1.4	2.1	2.1	2.2	2.9	2.5	2.4	1.9	2.1	
Current Liabilities to Working Capital	39	1.7	*	0.4	0.4	1.1	1.1	1.2	1.9	1.5	1.4	0.9	1.1	2.7
Working Capital to Net Sales	40	0.1	*	0.1	0.2	0.2	0.1	0.1	0.1	0.1	0.2	0.2	0.2	0.1
Inventory to Working Capital	41	1.9	*	1.0	0.8	1.5	1.3	1.5	1.6	1.5	1.5	1.3	1.8	2.6
Total Receipts to Cash Flow	42	8.8	8.4	4.4	6.4	7.1	8.6	9.8	8.0	7.3	7.9	10.0	10.3	9.7
Cost of Goods to Cash Flow	43	5.4	6.6	2.3	3.5	4.2	5.4	6.3	5.4	4.6	5.1	6.2	6.3	5.8
Cash Flow to Total Debt	44	0.3	*	0.8	0.7	0.5	0.5	0.4	0.5	0.5	0.3	0.5	0.2	0.2
Selected Financial Factors (in Percentages)														
Debt Ratio	45	65.8	*	110.7	71.0	68.2	57.2	60.8	62.7	62.9	71.1	48.1	78.7	66.4
Return on Total Assets	46	10.1	*	35.8	16.9	16.1	13.8	11.2	14.9	12.5	9.4	11.7	8.6	7.4
Return on Equity Before Income Taxes	47	23.9	*	*	49.5	43.1	27.7	22.9	35.4	27.8	27.7	20.3	22.7	17.2
Return on Equity After Income Taxes	48	19.3	*	*	48.7	40.5	25.0	20.2	32.3	24.5	22.9	15.9	16.1	11.6
Profit Margin (Before Income Tax)	49	4.2	13.8	8.5	4.5	6.1	5.0	3.5	5.3	4.5	4.5	4.6	2.4	3.8
Profit Margin (After Income Tax)	50	3.4	12.9	8.5	4.5	5.7	4.5	3.1	4.8	4.0	3.7	3.6	1.7	2.6

Source: Leo Troy, Ph.D., *Almanac of Business and Industrial Financial Ratios* © 2003. Reprinted by permission of Aspen Publishers, New York City, NY.

Exhibit 8-7
Comparison of Elevation
Sports, Inc. to Industry
Averages

RATIO	ELEVATION SPORTS, INC.	TOTAL INDUSTRY[1]	INDUSTRY WITH $250,000 TO ASSETS $500,000[2]
Return on assets	36.6%	10.1%	16.1%
Profit margin before taxes	20.0%	4.2%	6.1%
Total asset turnover	1.8 times	1.9 times	2.3 times
Profit margin after taxes	12.0%	3.4%	5.7%
Return on equity after taxes	39.7%	19.3%	40.5%
Return on equity before taxes	66.2%	23.9%	43.1%
Current ratio	2.3 to 1	1.6 to 1	1.9 to 1
Quick ratio	1.6 to 1	0.4 to 1	0.5 to 1
Net sales to working capital	4.9 times	7.3 times	5.9 times
Receivables turnover	15.8 times	28.6 times	31.7 times
Inventory turnover	16.4 times	2.5 times	2.1 times
Debt ratio	44.7%	65.8%	68.2%
Coverage ratio	18.6 times	5.3 times	6.7 times

1. Leo Troy, *Almanac of Business and Industrial Financial Ratios* (New York: Aspen Publishers, 2003):228.
2. Leo Troy, *Almanac of Business and Industrial Financial Ratios* (New York: Aspen Publishers, 2003):230.

Company Analysis

To best understand a company, we will use a four-step company analysis process. First, compare the company's ratios to the industry statistics. Second, look for trends in the company's ratios over a multiyear period. Third, gather industry information and economic projections to consider the industry environment. Finally, synthesize all the information to draw conclusions about the profitability, liquidity, solvency, and investment potential of the company. We will perform this analysis for both Elevation Sports and Family Dollar to let you become familiar with the technique. We cannot perform the second step for Elevation Sports, however, because it is a new company.

Analyzing a Fictional Company

Step 1: Compare Ratios to the Industry Averages

To organize our study of Elevation Sports, we will first compare Elevation Sports' profitability ratios to the industry averages shown in Exhibit 8-7 and recapped below:

Ratio	Elevation Sports, Inc.	Total Industry	Industry with Assets $250,000 to $500,000
Return on assets	36.6%	10.1%	16.1%
Profit margin before income taxes	20.0%	4.2%	6.1%
Total asset turnover	1.8 times	1.9 times	2.3 times
Profit margin after income tax	12.0%	3.4%	5.7%
Return on equity after income taxes	39.7%	19.3%	40.5%
Return on equity before income taxes	66.2%	23.9%	43.1%

Elevation Sports exceeds every industry profitability ratio but one for the total industry and all but two for companies with assets between $250,000 and $500,000. Is the comparison fair? If you remember, the officers of Elevation Sports elected to take considerably lower salaries than desirable for their level of expertise and responsibility to allow the business to get a head start. Had they taken more reasonable salaries, the net income would be much lower than the amount presented.

How does this affect our analysis? Instead of thinking that the company is unbelievably profitable, we recognize that the results of profitability are inflated and were carefully designed to produce maximum results. With that basic fact in mind, we can look at the profitability comparison between Elevation Sports and companies of its same size within the industry.

Elevation Sports' return on assets is more than twice the industry average even though the total asset turnover is about 78 percent of the industry average. The profit margin before tax is more than three times the industry average and profit margin after tax is more than twice the industry average. Return on equity before taxes is much higher than the industry average, whereas the return on equity after taxes is slightly lower than the industry average. Although Elevation Sports generally outperformed the industry, we will have to see future results with more realistic officers' salaries included to judge how consistently the company can maintain so profitable a performance.

What Do You Think?

8-12 Elevation Sports' return on assets is 2.3 times the industry average but the return after taxes on equity is only 98 percent of the industry average. How can this happen?

8-13 Elevation Sports' profit margin before income taxes is 3.3 times the industry average but the return before taxes on equity is only 1.53 times the industry average. How can this happen?

Next, we can examine the following liquidity ratios from Exhibit 8-7:

Ratio	Elevation Sports, Inc.	Total Industry	Industry with Assets $250,000 to $500,000
Current ratio	2.3 to 1	1.6 to 1	1.9 to 1
Quick ratio	1.6 to 1	0.4 to 1	0.5 to 1
Net sales to working capital	4.9 times	7.3 times	5.9 times
Receivables turnover	15.8 times	28.6 times	31.7 times
Inventory turnover	16.4 times	2.5 times	2.1 times

Elevation Sports has a strong current ratio that is 20 percent higher than the industry. Its quick ratio is 3.4 times the industry average. The net sales to working capital is only 83 percent of the industry. Elevation Sports has a receivables turnover that is only half the industry average, probably because it has wholesale customers and the rest of the industry may be geared more to retail customers. Elevation Sports' inventory turnover is about eight times the industry average. This may be due to its small scale of operation or management's decision to keep inventory levels as low as possible. With consideration we might conclude that Elevation Sports' managers have maintained strong liquidity through the first year.

What Do You Think?

8-14 The computation of Elevation Sports' inventory turnover included only the finished goods inventory and the purchased merchandise inventory. Would adding the raw materials and work-in-process inventories to the computation raise or lower the inventory turnover?

8-15 Could the industry averages in a wholesale trade group include the raw materials and work-in-process inventories? How could you determine this?

Finally, we look at Elevation Sports' solvency ratios from Exhibit 8-7:

Ratio	Elevation Sports, Inc.	Total Industry	Industry with Assets $250,000 to $500,000
Debt Ratio	44.7%	65.8%	68.2%
Coverage Ratio	18.6 times	5.3 times	6.7 times

As we stated, Elevation Sports has a conservative debt ratio that is only two-thirds the industry average. Likewise, Elevation Sports' coverage ratio is 2.8 times the industry average. The large coverage ratio occurs because Elevation Sports incurs little interest expense. Compared to the industry, Elevation Sports has much better than average solvency ratios.

What Do You Think?

8-16 If Elevation Sports' coverage ratio were 1.86 instead of 18.6 and you were its banker, would you be concerned? Why or why not?

8-17 When a company has a low debt ratio, what is the effect on the return on stockholders' equity? Explain your reasoning.

Step 2: Look for Company Trends

Because Elevation Sports is a new company, we cannot analyze company trends. We will return to this topic when we examine Family Dollar.

Step 3: Consider the Industry Environment

The industry outlook will change frequently. Any sudden change in political or economic forecasts will have a ripple effect in most industries. Elevation Sports participates in a leisure industry that is more subject to economic downturns than a necessity industry. When researching the industry outlook, you cannot find the outlook for NAICS number 339920 because information sources consider broad groups of related industries for its industry outlooks. Look for the most appropriate industry classification. *Standard & Poor's Industry Surveys* contains information on the leisure products industry, which we detailed in Chapter 3. It predicts a declining population base of young people for the next 10 years, but an increasing share of snowboarding activity in relationship to snow skiing. With snowboarding sports included in the Winter Olympics, it also predicts continuation of the popularity of snowboarding. Standard & Poor's suggests that success will require continuous product innovation and quality.

The U.S. and world economy will also have significant influence on the leisure industry. The level of discretionary income available to families dictates the level of demand for leisure products. Children and young adults comprise the majority of snowboard users, and they have more discretionary money each year. A severe economic downturn, however, can dramatically reduce discretionary income.

Now that we have all this information, what do we do with it? Look at the important pieces of information for Elevation Sports:

1 Growth in this industry will depend on continuous innovation and quality.
2 Short-term sales may be good because of the growing popularity of snowboarding as a winter sport, but long-term growth will depend on the ability to sell to a declining youth segment of the U.S. population.

Armed with this information, we can now draw our conclusions.

Step 4: Draw Conclusions

The evaluation process depends on individual perception. Remember that the industry information we gathered is only good for the time period during which we did our research. By the time you read this material it will undoubtedly have changed. But we might, however, draw the following conclusions about the process:

1   In its first year, Elevation Sports indicates strong profitability, liquidity, and solvency, especially because the officers accepted unusually low salaries.
2   If Elevation Sports can maintain its profitability, hold down its debt, and produce a quality, innovative product, it might be a survivor in the tough competitive industry in which it operates.
3   If we choose to invest in a leisure industry stock and Elevation Sports were a real company, it might be one to consider as a speculative investment.

Analyzing a Real Company

Step 1: Compare Ratios to the Industry Averages

One of the rewards and challenges of analyzing a real company is that a few years into the future, you can review your analysis and determine where you were right, where you were wrong, and where you completely missed the clues. The more frequently you review your past work, the more likely that you will learn to pay attention to the right details and become better at analysis techniques.

Exhibit 8-8 contains the comparison of Family Dollar's fiscal year 2003 ratios to the retail trade, general merchandise stores, IRS code 452000, from the *Almanac*. Let's examine each group closely.

The following profitability ratios are from Exhibit 8-8:

Ratio	Family Dollar Stores, Inc.	Total Industry	Industry with Assets over $250,000,000
Return on assets	19.6%	9.1%	8.9%
Profit margin before income taxes	8.2%	4.0%	4.0%
Total asset turnover	2.4 times	1.5 times	1.5 times
Profit margin after income tax	5.2%	2.7%	2.7%
Return before taxes on equity	29.7%	17.5%	17.1%
Return after taxes on equity	18.8%	11.8%	11.4%

Clearly, all of Family Dollar's profitability ratios are almost twice the industry averages. Notice that the industry average debt ratio is more than twice Family Dollar's debt ratio. Family Dollar saves a lot of expense by not having interest payments on long-term debt because most of its debt is non-interest-bearing short-term debt.

What Do You Think?

8-18   Which ratio do you think is more important to a stockholder, the return after taxes on equity or the return before taxes on equity? Explain your reasoning.

8-19   Ignoring interest expense, which operates more profitably, Family Dollar or the theoretically average large company in the industry? Explain your reasoning.

Exhibit 8-8

Comparison of Family Dollar Stores, Inc. to Industry Averages

RATIO	FAMILY DOLLAR STORES, INC.	TOTAL INDUSTRY[1]	INDUSTRY WITH ASSETS ASSETS OVER $250,000,000[2]
Return on assets	19.6%	9.1%	8.9%
Profit margin before taxes	8.2%	4.0%	4.0%
Total asset turnover	2.4 times	1.5 times	1.5 times
Profit margin after taxes	5.2%	2.7%	2.7%
Return before taxes on equity	29.7%	17.5%	17.1%
Return after taxes on equity	18.8%	11.8%	11.4%
Current ratio	1.9 to 1	1.1 to 1	1.1 to 1
Quick ratio	0.4 to 1	.5 to 1	.5 to 1
Net sales to working capital	8.5 times	32.5 times	36.3 times
Receivables turnover	*	8.4 times	8.1 times
Inventory turnover	3.7 times	5.1 times	5.1 times
Debt ratio	34.0%	64.2%	64.5%
Coverage ratio	**	3.2 times	3.2 times

*No receivables

**No interest, cannot be computed.

1. Leo Troy, *Almanac of Business and Industrial Financial Ratios* (New York: Aspen Publishers, 2003): 228.

2. Leo Troy, *Almanac of Business and Industrial Financial Ratios* (New York: Aspen Publishers, 2003): 230.

We can turn now to the following liquidity ratios from Exhibit 8-8:

Ratio	Family Dollar Stores, Inc.	Total Industry	Industry with Assets above $250,000,000
Current ratio	1.9 to 1	1.1 to 1	1.1 to 1
Quick ratio	0.4 to 1	.5 to 1	.5 to 1
Net sales to working capital	8.5 times	32.5 times	36.3 times
Receivables turnover	*	8.4 times	8.1 times
Inventory turnover	3.7 times	5.1 times	5.1 times

*No receivables

Family Dollar's liquidity presents mixed results. Its current ratio is almost twice the industry average, but its quick ratio is only 80 percent of the industry average. Family Dollar's current ratio is almost equal to the benchmark of 2:1, but the industry average is much closer to the quick ratio benchmark of 1:1. Sales to working capital ratio is less than one-fourth of the industry average because Family Dollar has such a large working capital. Family Dollar's business is cash only so it has no receivables and we cannot, therefore, compute a receivables turnover. A cash-only business policy puts the company in a more liquid position.

The inventory turnover is only 70 percent of the industry average. This is the most troubling ratio of the group. When we compute the average day's inventory, the company holds its inventory 99 days on average compared to 72 days for the industry. That seems to be a very long time. *Standard & Poor's Industry Surveys* warns that cost of goods sold includes occupancy costs, an important cost component in the retail business. This distorts the inventory turnover and the average day's inventory computation by decreasing the turnover and increasing the days in inventory. It does not, however, distort the comparison between companies. In this case, Family Dollar's turnover is less than the average for the industry, which puts the company at a distinct disadvantage by lengthening the operating cycle and creating more possibility of price markdowns to clear slow-moving inventory items. Family Dollar's inventory consists of more staple items than its competitors such as Target or Wal-Mart. Family Dollar's inventory has decreased since they increased the number of distribution centers, and the inventory turnover has slowly increased from 2.5 to 3.7 from 1996 to 2003.

Finally, we consider the following solvency ratios from Exhibit 8-5:

Ratio	Family Dollar Stores, Inc.	Total Industry	Industry with Assets over $250,000,000
Debt Ratio	34.0%	64.2%	64.5%
Coverage Ratio	**	3.2 times	3.2 times

**No interest, cannot be computed.

As can be easily seen, the Family Dollar debt picture is dramatically better than the remainder of the industry. With only one-half the debt level of its competitors, Family Dollar should have a strong coverage ratio. On the contrary, we indicated that it cannot be computed. The reason is that when the amount of interest is zero, the mathematical computation is impossible. Look in the trend analysis in Step 2 to see how high Family Dollar's coverage ratio is for the years it actually had interest expense.

Family Dollar exhibits very strong profitability and solvency, and overall good liquidity with a question mark about inventory turnover. Let's look at its ratio pattern over the past eight years.

Step 2: Look for Company Trends

Exhibit 8-9 presents the ratios for Family Dollar for the fiscal years 1996 through 2003. As you inspect the ratios, you see that most of its ratios have improved over the eight-year period. A few, such as the quick ratio and the coverage ratio, have bounced around during the time period. Remember the debt ratio has steadily declined, which shows improvement because, unlike the case for most ratios, in this instance the lower the amount, the better the ratio.

We have also prepared a trend analysis of each ratio over the past seven years, using 1996 for the base year, shown in Exhibit 8-10. This helps you to evaluate the magnitude of the change over time. Let's examine more closely any troubling indicators as we look at Exhibit 8-10.

1   The total asset turnover rose steadily over six years but fell in 2002 and then rebounded slightly in 2003. The remaining profitability ratios rose steadily over the first

Exhibit 8-9
Family Dollar Stores, Inc. Ratios, 1996 through 2003

	2003	2002	2001	2000	1999	1998	1997	1996
Return on assets	19.6%	19.5%	21.3%	21.8%	20.3%	17.6%	15.6%	14.2%
Profit margin before taxes	8.2%	8.2%	8.1%	8.6%	8.1%	7.0%	6.1%	5.8%
Total asset turnover	2.4 times	2.4 times	2.6 times	2.5 times	2.5 times	2.5 times	2.6 times	2.5 times
Profit margin after taxes	5.2%	5.2%	5.2%	5.5%	5.1%	4.4%	3.7%	3.5%
Return on equity after taxes	18.9%	18.8%	19.8%	21.6%	20.3%	17.9%	14.9%	13.6%
Return on equity before taxes	29.7%	29.6%	31.1%	34.0%	32.2%	28.7%	24.3%	22.2%
Current ratio	1.9 to 1	2.0 to 1	2.1 to 1	1.8 to 1	1.9 to 1	1.9 to 1	2.1 to 1	2.2 to 1
Quick ratio	0.4 to 1	0.4 to 1	0.1 to 1	0.1 to 1	0.3 to 1	0.4 to 1	0.2 to 1	0.1 to 1
Net sales to working capital	8.5 times	7.9 times	8.8 times	9.3 times	8.1 times	7.8 times	7.0 times	6.3 times
Receivables turnover	*	*	*	*	*	*	*	*
Inventory turnover	3.7 times	3.6 times	3.4 times	3.2 times	3.2 times	3.4 times	2.9 times	2.5 times
Debt ratio	34.0%	34.2%	31.4%	35.8%	36.9%	38.6%	35.9%	36.1%
Coverage ratio	*	2163.2 times	539.7 times	*	*	12769.3 times	379.4 times	172.2 times

*Not calculable

Exhibit 8-10
Trend Analysis of the Ratios for Family Dollar Stores, Inc. 1996 through 2003

	2003	**2002**	**2001**	**2000**	**1999**	**1998**	**1997**	**1996**
Return on assets	138.5	137.4	150.4	153.7	143.4	124.3	109.8	100.00
Profit margin before taxes	142.4	142.5	141.3	150.1	140.5	122.0	105.7	100.00
Total asset turnover	97.2	96.4	106.4	102.4	102.1	101.9	103.9	100.00
Profit margin after tax	147.4	147.5	146.3	155.4	144.1	123.8	105.9	100.00
Return on equity after taxes	138.6	137.9	145.1	158.3	149.0	123.8	105.9	100.00
Return on equity before taxes	133.9	136.7	144.2	156.8	147.5	130.0	109.1	100.00
Current ratio	89.6	91.7	95.4	84.0	87.7	86.9	96.2	100.00
Quick ratio	431.6	515.8	69.3	131.4	312.9	486.0	202.1	100.00
Net sales to working capital	135.1	126.5	140.3	147.7	128.6	124.3	112.3	100.00
Receivables turnover	0	0	0	0	0	0	0	0
Inventory turnover	147.4	144.5	135.3	129.0	129.0	136.6	115.5	100.00
Debt ratio	94.0	94.6	87.1	99.2	102.2	106.91	99.3	100.00
Coverage ratio	0	1256.4	313.4	0	0	7416.6	220.4	100.00

five years and fell slightly in 2002 and rose slightly in 2003. The profit margins before and after taxes rose steadily over the eight years except for an unusual peak in 2000. Only the return on equity after taxes and the return before taxes on equity continued below the 1999 ratios. With the substantial growth in numbers of stores and distribution centers, this is not unusual. It cannot be dismissed, however, because it may be a sign of impending profit problems or a temporary reduction caused by rapid expansion. Profit margins have continued to rise since 2001, however, the results of the profitability ratios over the next few years will clue us to the cause of this decrease in profitability.

2 We have seen an erratic but small decline in the current ratio over the eight years. As we saw with the actual ratios, the current ratio still exceeds the industry average and the normal benchmark of 2:1. More troubling was the change in the quick ratio, although it increased dramatically in 2002 and 2003. The strain of the rapid expansion without increasing debt is more visible with the quick ratio; it is about 80 percent of the industry average. Creditors and lenders will watch this ratio closely to see if the 2002 and 2003 rebound continues. Family Dollar has primarily financed its expansion internally from operations. Although this indicates a strong financial structure, it plays havoc with the cash position and the quick ratio. The cash position should remain at the current level or improve for management to avoid borrowing long-term funds.

3 Net sales to working capital rose steadily until 2000 and then fell in 2001 and 2002. It rose in 2003. Because sales have continued to increase, this is probably associated with the increase in the level of working capital, which is a positive indicator.

4 As we noted, we need to look at the inventory turnover over time. Except for a spike in 1998, it has risen over the eight years. This suggests that the increased number of distribution centers is helping to increase the inventory turnover. Although the inventory turnover ratio continues to lag far behind the industry average, the condition is improving, not worsening. It does not appear to be a harbinger of trouble ahead such as occurred for Gap Inc. in 1998, yet it bears close monitoring by creditors and investors alike.

5 The solvency ratios show steady improvement over the eight years with slight decreases in 1998 and 1999, a time of distribution centers expansion.

To read about the dramatic decline in Gap Inc.'s income, go to **www.fortune.com** and read the article from the March 18, 2002, issue.

Step 3: Consider the Industry Environment

The industry outlook normally changes frequently. Any sudden change in political or economic forecasts will have a ripple effect in most industries. Consumer confidence, for example, changed from an index level of 114 in August 2001 to 85.5 in October 2001. Disposable personal income in 2002 slowed to a 3.8 percent growth rate after

Standard & Poor's Industry Surveys contains a segment on "How to Analyze a Retail Company." Check it out in your library.

two years of five percent to six percent gains. Although personal disposable income drives this industry, the discounters often profit in slower economies because higher income households shop in the discount stores more often than during strong economic times. Growth among discounters depends on their level of technology in their supply-chain management to move their goods from supplier to customer in the shortest possible time. Consumer behavior experts indicate that consumers no longer choose where to shop for the pleasure of the experience, but choose instead those retailers who offer them greater timesavings. They demand value as defined by price, value for the price, and the least time required to obtain the goods.[1]

Family Dollar made the 2002 *Fortune* 500 list,[2] coming in at number 443 and moved up to 388 in 2003. Although Family Dollar outlets are small in comparison to giants such as Wal-Mart and Target, the company has more stores than either. In 2003, Family Dollar ranked ninth in its industry in dollar profits, eighth in growth of profits, sixth in growth of earnings per share for the past decade, third in return to investors for the past decade, third in profit percentage on sales, fourth in return on equity, and first in profit percentage to assets. Among the *Fortune* 500 in 2003, Family Dollar ranked 46th in return to shareholders over the past five years and 20th in profits as a percentage of assets.[3]

Now that we have all this information, what do we do with it? Look at the important pieces of information for Family Dollar:

1 Growth in this industry will depend on value, price, convenience, and service.
2 Supply-chain management is a crucial component of success for discounters.
3 Family Dollar is a leader in profitability in both the industry and the *Fortune* 500 in both return on assets and return to shareholders.

Armed with this information, we can now draw our conclusions.

Step 4: Draw Conclusions

The evaluation process depends on individual perception. Remember that the industry information we gathered is only good for the time period during which we conducted the research. By the time you read this material it will undoubtedly have changed. To complete the process, however, we might draw the following conclusions:

1 Family Dollar is an industry leader in profitability and solvency.
2 Family Dollar has improved the distribution element of its supply chain.
3 Part of Family Dollar's profitability and liquidity will depend on its increasing the inventory turnover ratio to lower its dependence on discounted sales prices to turn inventory.
4 If we choose to invest in a general merchandise discounter, Family Dollar might be one to consider.

Limitations of Ratio Analysis

Ratio analysis is an excellent tool for gathering additional information about a company, but it does have its limitations:

1 **Attempting to predict the future using past results depends on the predictive value of the information we use.** Changes in the general economy, in the economy of the particular industry being studied, and in the company's management can cause past results to be an unreliable predictor of the future.
2 **The financial statements used to compute the ratios are based on historical cost.** Although the growth of prices has been relatively slower in the past few years, in times of faster changing prices, comparison between years may be difficult.

1. "Retailing: General," *Standard & Poor's Industry Surveys* (November 29, 2001):9–20.
2. "*Fortune* 500 Largest U.S. Corporations," *Fortune* 145 (April 15, 2002):F–26.
3. "*Fortune* 1,000 Ranked within Industries," *Fortune* 147 (April 14, 2003):F–53.

3 Figures from the balance sheet used to calculate the ratios are year-end numbers. Because most businesses have their fiscal year-end in the slowest part of the year, the balances in accounts such as receivables, payables, and inventory at year end may not be representative of the rest of the year.

4 Industry peculiarities create difficulty in comparing the ratios of a company in one industry with those of a company in another industry. Even comparison of companies within an industry may not be reasonable at times because not all companies use the same accounting methods.

5 Lack of uniformity concerning what is to be included in the numerators and denominators of specific ratios makes comparison to published industry averages extremely difficult. Perhaps the greatest single limitation of ratio analysis is that people tend to place too much reliance on the ratios. Financial ratios should not be viewed as a magical checklist in the evaluation process. Ratio analysis only enriches all the other information decision makers should consider when making credit, investment, and similar types of decisions.

CHAPTER SUMMARY

In response to the need to reduce uncertainty in the decision-making process, analysts have developed several techniques to assist economic decision makers as they evaluate financial statement information. Creditors, present and potential equity investors, and company management comprise the three major categories of financial statement users. Because the objectives of users may vary, their perspectives on the results of financial statement analysis will differ. Three external factors—general economic conditions and expectations, political events and political climate, and industry outlook—affect business performance and should be considered when evaluating results of any type of financial statement analysis.

One important method of financial statement analysis is ratio analysis, a technique for analyzing the relationship between two items from a company's financial statements for a given period. We compute ratios by dividing the dollar amount of one item from the financial statements by the dollar amount of the other item from the statements. Analysts have developed a great many ratios over time to help economic decision makers assess a company's financial health. Because not all ratios are relevant in a given decision situation, decision makers must carefully select appropriate ratios to analyze. Ratio values in and of themselves have very little meaning. They become meaningful only when compared to other relevant information, such as industry averages or the company's ratio values from other years.

We broadly classify financial ratios as profitability ratios, liquidity ratios, and solvency ratios. Profitability ratios attempt to measure the ease with which companies generate income. Liquidity ratios measure a company's ability to generate positive cash flow in the short run to pay off short-term liabilities. Solvency ratios attempt to measure a company's ability to meet the obligations created by its long-term debt. Exhibit 8-5 lists individual ratios. Each of the profitability, liquidity, and solvency ratios provides valuable information for both internal and external decision makers.

Ratio analysis does have its limitations. Placing too much reliance on the financial statements and the ratios derived from them without putting the information in the proper political, economic, and industry perspective can lead to poor decisions. Ratio analysis is an important financial analysis technique that must be used wisely and in the proper context.

Visit the Web site *www.prenhall.com/terrell* for additional study help with the Online Study Guide.

REVIEW OF CONCEPTS

A Explain the purpose of financial statement analysis.

B Define *profitability*. List the six profitability ratios discussed in the chapter. For each ratio, describe the calculation used and the purpose of the ratio.

C Describe the two component ratios of the return on assets. Explain how an analyst can use these to make a better prediction of profitability.

D Define *liquidity*. List the five liquidity ratios discussed in the chapter. For each ratio, describe the calculation used and the purpose of the ratio.

E Describe the difference between the current ratio and the quick ratio. Explain the analyst's purpose in examining both.

F Define *solvency*. List the two solvency ratios discussed in the chapter. For each ratio, describe the calculation used and the purpose of the ratio.

G Explain how to judge whether a company has a conservative or aggressive debt structure and how the debt structure correlates to investment risk.

H Describe the information that can be gained from calculating a company's coverage ratio.

I Explain the purpose of conducting a comparison among a company's ratio values from several recent years.

J Describe what additional information can be gleaned from an industry comparison of a company's ratios.

K Describe the limitations of ratio analysis discussed in the chapter.

APPLICATION EXERCISES

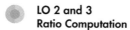

LO 2 and 3
Ratio Computation

8-20 Presented below are partial comparative balance sheets of Mikey Company at December 31, 2004, and December 31, 2003:

Mikey Company
Partial Balance Sheets
December 31, 2004, and December 31, 2003
Current Assets and Current Liabilities Only
(in thousands)

	2004	2003
Current Assets		
Cash	$3,400	$2,920
Accounts receivable	1,825	2,212
Merchandise inventory	1,170	966
Prepaid expenses	240	270
Total Current Assets	$6,635	$6,368
Current Liabilities		
Accounts payable	$2,321	$1,740
Notes payable	3,100	3,300
Total Current Liabilities	$5,421	$5,040

Required:

a. Calculate Mikey's current ratios for 2004 and 2003.
b. Calculate Mikey's quick ratios for 2004 and 2003.
c. Which financial statement users are most interested in these two sets of ratios? Explain why the ratios are considered important to these users.
d. Assume that the average company in Mikey's industry has a current ratio of 2:1 and a quick ratio of 1.25:1. If you were evaluating Mikey's liquidity, what could you learn by comparing Mikey's ratios to the industry averages?

8-21 Presented below are partial comparative balance sheets of Harold's Company at December 31, 2005, and December 31, 2004.

LO 2 and 3
Ratio Computation

Harold Company
Partial Balance Sheets
December 31, 2005, and December 31, 2004
Current Assets and Current Liabilities Only
(in thousands)

	2005	2004
Current Assets		
Cash	$2,110	$2,650
Accounts receivable	1,254	977
Merchandise inventory	730	856
Prepaid expenses	127	114
Total Current Assets	$4,221	$4,597
Current Liabilities		
Accounts payable	$1,054	$1,330
Notes payable	2,100	1,750
Total Current Liabilities	$3,154	$3,080

Required:

a. Calculate Harold's current ratios for 2005 and 2004.
b. Calculate Harold's quick ratios for 2005 and 2004.
c. Which financial statement users are most interested in these two sets of ratios? Explain why the ratios are considered important to these users.
d. Assume that the average company in Harold's industry has a current ratio of 2.5:1 and a quick ratio of 1:1. If you were evaluating Harold's liquidity, what could you learn by comparing Harold's ratios to those of the industry averages?
e. What if anything could you determine by comparing Harold's current ratio and quick ratio for 2004 with the same ratios for 2005? Explain your reasoning.

8-22 A five-year comparative analysis of Steven Sagal Company's current ratio and quick ratio is presented below:

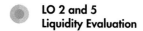

LO 2 and 5
Liquidity Evaluation

	2000	2001	2002	2003	2004
Current ratio	1.24 to 1	1.95 to 1	2.55 to 1	3.68 to 1	4.13 to 1
Quick ratio	1.20 to 1	1.06 to 1	.96 to 1	.77 to 1	.51 to 1

Required:

a. What does this analysis tell you about the overall liquidity of Sagal Company over the five-year period?
b. What does this analysis tell you about what has happened to the composition of Sagal's current assets over the five-year period?

LO 2 and 5
Liquidity Evaluation

8-23   A five-year comparative analysis of Carnegie Company's current ratio and quick ratio is presented below:

	2000	2001	2002	2003	2004
Current ratio	4.24 to 1	3.95 to 1	2.95 to 1	2.68 to 1	1.93 to 1
Quick ratio	.51 to 1	.86 to 1	1.03 to 1	1.33 to 1	1.68 to 1

Required:

a. What does this analysis tell you about the overall liquidity of Carnegie over the five-year period?
b. What does this analysis tell you about what has happened to the composition of Carnegie's current assets over the five-year period?

LO 2 and 5
Profitability Evaluation

8-24   Following is a five-year comparative analysis of "Buggsey" Moron Company's profit margin before tax and profit margin after tax:

	2000	2001	2002	2003	2004
Profit margin before tax	3.68%	4.61%	6.88%	7.96%	9.87%
Profit margin after tax	2.22%	4.95%	4.41%	5.27%	7.09%

Required:

a. What does this analysis indicate about Moron's performance over the five-year period?
b. Which of the following would be interested in this analysis and how do you think each would interpret this analysis?
   1. trade creditors
   2. long-term creditors
   3. stockholders

LO 2 and 5
Profitability Evaluation

8-25   Following is a five-year comparative analysis of Dexter Manley Company's profit margin before tax and profit margin after tax:

	2000	2001	2002	2003	2004
Profit margin before tax	11.28%	9.16%	8.48%	7.01%	5.78%
Profit margin after tax	9.33%	8.59%	6.14%	5.72%	3.89%

Required:

a. What does this analysis indicate about Manley's profitability over the five-year period?
b. Which of the following would be interested in this analysis and how do you think each would interpret this analysis?
   1. trade creditors
   2. long-term creditors
   3. stockholders

LO 2 and 5
Capital Structure Evaluation

8-26   Following is a five-year comparative analysis of Cibyll Smythe Company's coverage ratio and debt ratio:

	2000	2001	2002	2003	2004
Coverage ratio	2.75 times	3.50 times	4.25 times	5.50 times	6.00 times
Debt ratio	73.33%	71.43%	69.23%	60.00%	50.00%

Required:

a. What does this analysis indicate about Smythe's capital structure over the five-year period?

b. Which of the following would be interested in this analysis, and how do you think each would interpret this analysis?
   1. trade creditors
   2. long-term creditors
   3. stockholders

8-27 Following is a five-year comparative analysis of Peggy Bausch Company's coverage ratio and debt ratio:

LO 2 and 5
Capital Structure
Evaluation

	2000	2001	2002	2003	2004
Coverage ratio	6.50 times	7.15 times	4.65 times	5.25 times	5.90 times
Debt ratio	60.00%	53.49%	72.60%	69.23%	65.52%

Required:

a. What does this analysis indicate about Bausch's capital structure over the five-year period?
b. Which of the following would be interested in this analysis, and how do you think each would interpret this analysis?
   1. trade creditors
   2. long-term creditors
   3. stockholders

8-28 Presented below are the comparative balance sheets for Whipple Company at December 31, 2005, and December 31, 2004. Also included is Whipple's income statement for the year ended December 31, 2005.

LO 2
Ratio Computation

Whipple Company
Balance Sheets
December 31, 2005 and December 31, 2004
(in thousands)

	2005	2004
ASSETS		
Current Assets		
Cash	$ 1,618	$1,220
Accounts receivable	1,925	2,112
Merchandise inventory	1,070	966
Prepaid expenses	188	149
Total Current Assets	$ 4,801	$4,447
Plant and Equipment		
Buildings, net	$ 4,457	$2,992
Equipment, net	1,293	1,045
Total Plant and Equipment	$ 5,750	$4,037
TOTAL ASSETS	$10,551	$8,484
LIABILITIES AND STOCKHOLDERS' EQUITY		
Current Liabilities		
Accounts payable	$ 1,818	$1,686
Notes payable	900	1,100
Total Current Liabilities	$ 2,718	$2,786
Long-Term Liabilities	2,500	2,000
Total Liabilities	$ 5,218	$4,786
Stockholders' Equity		
Common stock, no par value	$3,390	$2,041
Retained earnings	1,943	1,657
Total Stockholders' Equity	$ 5,333	$3,698
TOTAL LIABILITIES AND STOCKHOLDERS' EQUITY	$10,551	$8,484

Whipple Company
Income Statement
For the Year Ended December 31, 2005
(in thousands)

Sales Revenue		$11,228
Cost of goods sold		7,751
Gross Profit on Sales		$ 3,477
Operating Expenses		
Depreciation—buildings and equipment	$ 102	
Other selling and administrative	2,667	
Total Expenses		2,769
Income before Interest and Taxes		$ 708
Interest expense		168
Income before Taxes		$ 540
Income taxes		114
Net Income		$ 426

Required:

Calculate the following ratios for 2005:
a. return on assets
b. profit margin before income tax
c. total asset turnover
d. profit margin after income tax
e. return after tax on equity
f. return before tax on equity
g. current ratio
h. quick ratio
i. net sales to working capital
j. receivables turnover
k. inventory turnover
l. debt ratio
m. coverage ratio

LO 2, 4, and 5
Ratio Computation

8-29 Presented below are the comparative balance sheets for Earlywine Company at December 31, 2005, and December 31, 2004, and the income statements for the years ended December 31, 2005, and December 31, 2004.

Required:

a. Calculate the following ratios for 2005 and 2004:
1. return on assets
2. profit margin before income tax
3. total asset turnover
4. profit margin after income tax
5. return after tax on equity
6. return before tax on equity
7. current ratio
8. quick ratio
9. net sales to working capital
10. receivables turnover
11. inventory turnover
12. debt ratio
13. coverage ratio

Earlywine Company
Balance Sheets
December 31, 2005 and December 31, 2004
(in thousands)

	2005	2004
ASSETS		
Current Assets		
Cash	$1,292	$ 980
Accounts receivable	1,068	1,112
Merchandise inventory	970	906
Prepaid expenses	88	109
Total Current Assets	$3,418	$3,107
Plant and Equipment		
Buildings, net	$3,457	$2,442
Equipment, net	993	945
Total Plant and Equipment	$4,450	$3,387
TOTAL ASSETS	$7,868	$6,494
LIABILITIES AND STOCKHOLDERS' EQUITY		
Current Liabilities		
Accounts payable	$ 998	$ 786
Notes payable	600	500
Total Current Liabilities	$1,598	$1,286
Long-Term Liabilities	837	467
Total Liabilities	$2,435	$1,753
Stockholders' Equity		
Common stock, no par value	$2,490	$2,000
Retained earnings	2,943	2,741
Total Stockholders' Equity	$5,433	$4,741
TOTAL LIABILITIES AND STOCKHOLDERS' EQUITY	$7,868	$6,494

Earlywine Company
Income Statements
For the Years Ended December 31, 2005 and 2004
(in thousands)

	2005	2004
Sales Revenue	$9,228	$8,765
Cost of goods sold	6,751	6,097
Gross Profit on Sales	$2,477	$2,668
Operating Expenses		
Depreciation—buildings and equipment	$ 80	$ 56
Other selling and administrative	1,667	1,442
Total Expenses	$1,747	$1,498
Income before Interest and Taxes	$ 730	$1,170
Interest expense	98	89
Income before Taxes	$ 632	$1,081
Income taxes	190	357
Net Income	$ 442	$ 724

	Total Industry	Assets between $5 million and $10 million	Earlywine
Current ratio	1.46	1.95	
Quick ratio	.93	1.11	
Net sales to working capital	6.42	5.78	
Coverage ratio	5.63	5.16	
Total asset turnover	1.76	1.42	
Inventory turnover	5.73	5.47	
Receivables turnover	7.83	6.54	
Debt ratio	65.99	65.87	
Return on assets	9.30	10.40	
Return after tax on equity	6.12	5.85	
Return before tax on equity	8.92	9.73	
Profit margin before tax	6.27	5.88	
Profit margin after tax	4.99	4.61	

b. Using the ratios you calculated in part a, complete the comparison of Earlywine Company's ratios to those of its entire industry and companies of comparable asset size for 2005.

c. Analyze the industry comparison you completed in part b as follows:
1. Identify any ratios you think do not warrant further analysis. Explain why any particular ratio is not going to be analyzed further.
2. For those ratios you felt deserved further analysis, assess whether Earlywine's ratios are better or worse relative to both the entire industry and companies of comparable asset size.

LO 5
Ratio Analysis

8-30 Following is a comparison of Dirty Harry Company's ratios for the years 2002 through 2006.

	2002	2003	2004	2005	2006
Current ratio	1.77	1.91	2.93	2.41	3.12
Quick ratio	1.40	1.26	1.08	.94	.79
Net sales to working capital	10.33	9.89	9.43	7.67	5.19
Coverage ratio	6.90	6.91	5.76	5.24	3.49
Total asset turnover	1.46	1.40	1.17	1.08	.99
Inventory turnover	8.88	8.24	8.11	6.46	4.45
Receivables turnover	8.93	7.41	6.52	5.87	5.34
Debt ratio	.49	.55	.66	.69	.72
Return on assets	9.28	8.44	8.20	7.68	6.21
Return after tax on equity	8.31	8.06	7.22	6.38	4.77
Return before tax on equity	9.98	9.56	8.80	8.43	5.71
Profit margin before tax	10.00	9.45	8.27	7.78	4.12
Profit margin after tax	8.66	7.90	7.14	6.52	2.28

Required:

Analyze the five-year company comparison as follows:

a. Identify any ratios you think do not warrant further analysis. Explain why any particular ratio is not going to be analyzed further.

b. For each ratio you felt deserved further analysis, assess whether it has improved or worsened over the five-year period.

c. Based on your analysis of the five-year company comparison, comment briefly on the trend of Dirty Harry's performance over the five-year period.

8-31   Exercises 8-31 through 8-35 are based on the following comparative financial statements of Glenn Eddleman and Company:

LO 2 and 5
Calculating Ratios

Glenn Eddleman and Company
Balance Sheets
December 31, 2005, and December 31, 2004
(in thousands)

	2005	2004
ASSETS		
Current Assets		
Cash	$ 2,240	$1,936
Accounts receivable	2,340	2,490
Merchandise inventory	776	693
Prepaid expenses	200	160
Total Current Assets	$ 5,556	$5,279
Plant and Equipment		
Buildings	$ 7,723	$6,423
Less: Accumulated depreciation	3,677	3,534
Buildings, net	$ 4,046	$2,889
Equipment	$ 2,687	$2,387
Less: Accumulated depreciation	1,564	1,523
Equipment, net	$ 1,123	$ 864
Total Plant and Equipment	$ 5,169	$3,753
TOTAL ASSETS	$10,725	$9,032
LIABILITIES AND STOCKHOLDERS' EQUITY		
Current Liabilities		
Accounts payable	$ 1,616	$1,080
Notes payable	2,720	2,920
Total Current Liabilities	$ 4,336	$4,000
Long-Term Liabilities	2,000	1,600
Total Liabilities	$ 6,336	$5,600
Stockholders' Equity		
Common stock, no par value	$ 3,000	$2,400
Retained earnings	1,389	1,032
Total Stockholders' Equity	$ 4,389	$3,432
TOTAL LIABILITIES AND STOCKHOLDER'S EQUITY	$10,725	$9,032

Glenn Eddleman and Company
Income Statements
For the Years Ended December 31, 2005, and December 31, 2004
(in thousands)

	2005	2004
Sales Revenue	$14,745	$12,908
Cost of goods sold	10,213	8,761
Gross Profit on Sales	$ 4,532	$ 4,147
Operating Expenses		
Advertising and sales commissions	$ 1,022	$ 546
General and administrative	2,721	2,451
Total Expenses	$ 3,743	$ 2,997
Income before Interest and Taxes	$ 789	$ 1,150
Interest expense	172	137
Income before Taxes	$ 617	$ 1,013
Income taxes	123	355
Net Income	$ 494	$ 658

Required:

Using the Glenn Eddleman and Company financial statements, calculate the following ratios for 2005 and 2004:
  a. return on assets
  b. profit margin before income tax
  c. total asset turnover
  d. profit margin after income tax
  e. return after tax on equity
  f. return before tax on equity
  g. current ratio
  h. quick ratio
  i. net sales to working capital
  j. receivables turnover
  k. inventory turnover
  l. debt ratio
  m. coverage ratio

LO 4
Comparing Ratios to Industry Averages

8-32 Presented below is a partially completed comparison of Eddleman's ratios to those of its entire industry and companies of comparable asset size for 2005:

	Total Industry	Assets between $10 million and $25 million	Eddleman
Current ratio	2.24	1.95	
Quick ratio	1.33	1.31	
Net sales to working capital	7.22	9.38	
Coverage ratio	5.43	3.16	
Total asset turnover	1.76	1.42	
Inventory turnover	5.78	5.77	
Receivables turnover	7.83	6.54	
Debt ratio	69.51	65.99	
Return on assets	9.30	10.40	
Return after tax on equity	16.12	15.85	
Return before tax on equity	11.11	11.73	
Profit margin before tax	6.67	3.88	
Profit margin after tax	4.49	2.61	

Required:

a. Complete the industry comparison by calculating each of Eddleman's ratios for 2005 and recording them in the space provided. Note: If you have completed Application Exercise 8-31, you have already done the calculations and may include them here.

b. Analyze the industry comparison you completed in part a as follows:
  1. Identify any ratios you think do not warrant further analysis. Explain why any particular ratio is not going to be analyzed further.
  2. For those ratios you felt deserved further analysis, assess whether Eddleman's ratios are better or worse relative to both the entire industry and companies of comparable asset size.
  3. Based on your analysis of the industry comparison, comment briefly on how you think Eddleman and Company compares to other companies in its industry.

LO 2 and 5
Calculating Ratios

8-33 Presented below is a partially completed comparison of Eddleman's ratios for the years 2001 through 2005:

Required:

a. Complete the five-year company comparison by calculating each of Eddleman's ratios for 2004 and 2005 and recording them in the space provided. Note: If you have completed Application Exercise 8-31, you have already done the calculations and may include them here.

	2001	2002	2003	2004	2005
Current ratio	2.07	2.62	1.79		
Quick ratio	1.00	1.09	1.01		
Net sales to working capital	9.33	8.41	9.97		
Coverage ratio	6.31	5.44	4.48		
Total asset turnover	1.11	1.86	1.34		
Inventory turnover	10.88	11.37	11.81		
Receivables turnover	4.80	4.99	5.10		
Debt ratio	54.95	62.26	61.69		
Return on assets	5.22	6.11	5.34		
Return after tax on equity	10.98	11.62	11.05		
Return before tax on equity	14.48	13.77	15.43		
Profit margin before tax	4.68	4.12	4.44		
Profit margin after tax	3.06	3.16	3.31		

b. Analyze the five-year company comparison you completed in part a as follows:
   1. Identify any ratios you think do not warrant further analysis. Explain why any particular ratio is not going to be analyzed further.
   2. For each ratio you felt deserved further analysis, assess whether it has improved or worsened over the five-year period.
   3. Based on your analysis of the five-year company comparison, comment briefly on the trend of Eddleman and Company's performance over the five-year period.

8-34 This chapter focused on ratio analysis performed on the income statement and the balance sheet. For this reason, the financial statements for Eddleman did not include a statement of cash flows. To assess the company's overall performance in 2005, however, you should also look at its statement of cash flows.

Comprehensive

Required:

a. Using the 2004 and 2005 comparative balance sheets and the income statement for 2005, prepare Eddleman's 2005 statement of cash flows.
b. Which of the three broad activities (operating, investing, and financing) provided Eddleman with the majority of its cash during 2005?
c. Briefly discuss whether the activity you identified in the previous requirement is an appropriate source of cash in the long run.
d. In which of the three broad activities (operating, investing, and financing) did Eddleman use most of its cash during 2005?
e. Briefly discuss what your answer to the previous requirement reveals about Eddleman.

8-35 This chapter focused on ratio analysis performed on the income statement and the balance sheet. For this reason, the financial statements for Eddleman did not include a statement of stockholders' equity. To assess the company's overall performance in 2005, however, you should also look at the company's statement of stockholders' equity.

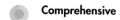

Comprehensive

Required:

a. Using the 2004 and 2005 comparative balance sheets and the income statement for 2005, prepare Eddleman's 2005 statement of stockholders' equity.
b. Briefly discuss how the statement of stockholders' equity demonstrates articulation among Eddleman's financial statements.

8-36 The chapter discussed several limitations of ratio analysis. They were:
   a. using past results to predict future performance
   b. using historical cost as a basis for ratios
   c. using year-end balances as either the numerator or denominator for many ratios

LO 6
Limitations of Ratio Analysis

d. industry peculiarities

e. lack of uniformity in defining the numerators and denominators used in calculating ratios

Required:

Explain why each of the items listed above limits the usefulness of ratio analysis.

Comprehensive Financial reporting Cases

8-37 Select two companies in the same industry in which you are interested.

Required:

a. Calculate the 13 basic ratios presented in the chapter for the most current year for each of the companies.

b. Based on the ratios that you have computed and the information learned in the chapter, how do these companies compare with each other and the industry averages? Industry averages may be obtained from the sources identified in the text, and these are usually found in the reference section of the library.

Comprehensive

8-38 Visit the Web sites for Dollar Tree Stores, Inc., and Target Corporation.

Required:

a. Using the corporations' latest financial statements, calculate the following ratios for the last year presented. (Assume minority interest is part of stockholders' equity.)

 1. return on assets
 2. profit margin before income tax
 3. total asset turnover
 4. profit margin after income tax
 5. return after tax on equity
 6. return before tax on equity
 7. current ratio
 8. quick ratio
 9. net sales to working capital
 10. receivables turnover
 11. inventory turnover
 12. debt ratio
 13. coverage ratio

b. Compare the profitability, liquidity, and solvency of the two companies. Determine which of the two you would invest in if you had to select one of them. Explain the reasons for your choice.

Comprehensive

8-39 Visit the Web site for Dillard's, Inc.

Required:

a. Using the financial statements and the financial summary of Dillard's, complete the following five-year company ratio analysis. If you find calculating a particular ratio impossible, put an asterisk (*) where the ratio would go. (Assume any minority interest is part of stockholders' equity.)

 1. current ratio
 2. quick ratio
 3. net sales to working capital
 4. coverage ratio
 5. total asset turnover
 6. inventory turnover
 7. receivables turnover
 8. debt ratio
 9. return on assets

10. return after tax on equity
11. return before tax on equity
12. profit margin before tax
13. profit margin after tax

b. Analyze the five-year company comparison you completed in part a as follows:

1. Identify any ratios you think do not warrant further analysis. Explain why any particular ratio is not going to be analyzed further.

2. For each ratio you felt deserved further analysis, assess whether it has improved or worsened over the five-year period.

3. Based on your analysis of the five-year company comparison, comment briefly on the trend of Dillard's performance over the five-year period.

8-40 As the chief accountant for the company, the CFO asks you to prepare a schedule of ratios for the current year. The CFO tells you he is concerned that the company will not meet the bank's loan requirement of maintaining a 2:1 current ratio. He tells you that if the company fails to meet the ratio again this year, the bank will call the loan and that the company has no way to pay off the loan.

Ethics

Required:

What would you advise the CFO if the ratio actually falls below the 2:1 current ratio?

FOR ADDITIONAL READING

Creswell, Julie. "Gap Got Junked—Now What?" *Fortune* 145 (March 18, 2002):93–96.

CHAPTER 9

LEARNING OBJECTIVES

After completing this chapter you should be able to:

1 Determine the fixed and variable components of a cost element using the high-low method and results of regression analysis.

2 Identify the characteristics of a relevant cost or revenue.

3 Demonstrate why sunk costs and costs that do not differ between alternatives are irrelevant costs.

4 Discuss several major qualitative factors that should be considered when making a business decision.

5 Use accounting information to determine the relevant cost of various decisions.

6 Interpret the effects of fixed costs and opportunity costs on various decisions.

Using Relevant Information for Internal Operations

In Chapter 4 you learned about cost behavior and how to use cost information to compute breakeven and plan for desired profits. You studied the internal analysis of a company to judge its profitability, liquidity, and solvency in Chapters 7 and 8. Now we can turn our attention to using accounting information for the internal analysis of operations and business decision making. In this chapter we will look at how to compute the fixed and variable components of a cost and how to determine whether or not information is relevant.

Visit the Web site *www.prenhall.com/terrell* to view the "Grand Canyon Railway" video.

Following the determination of relevance, we can examine how to use analysis techniques to help managers make important internal decisions about whether or not to replace equipment, accept special orders, outsource component production or services, and add or close divisions. Modern business managers often make these types of decisions. The quality of their decisions frequently defines the quality of the firm's earnings and its ultimate market value.

Let's begin with computing the fixed and variable components of a cost element within a relevant range of production volume.

Computing the Fixed and Variable Components of a Cost Element

Understanding the company's cost components and determining cost formulas are basic analysis techniques for planning and budgeting. After a company has been in business for a few years, its management can use sophisticated analysis techniques rather than simply estimating such cost components. The history of production costs, considered within a relevant range of production volume, can provide managers with enriched information to determine the behavior of a cost element.

How do we know whether a cost is fixed, variable, or mixed? Some costs are intuitively easy to determine. We know rent on a warehouse is fixed because it is the same amount per month regardless of whether we produce zero goods or a million goods. We can sometimes determine future costs by examining a contract for goods or services and predicting its fixed and variable components. Many cost elements, however, are mixed costs with both a fixed and variable portion. Mathematical models provide a method to compute the fixed and variable components of a particular cost using historical accounting data. First we will discuss the high-low method to approximate a cost formula, and second we will discuss the use of data from regression analysis to find a precise cost formula.

Using the High-Low Method to Find the Total Cost Formula

Although our ongoing illustration, Elevation Sports, Inc., is a manufacturing company, a merchandising or service firm can use the same applications. The only difference among the types of companies is the identity of the cost drivers. Instead of units produced, merchandisers might consider units sold and service providers might use the number of clients served.

Recall the total cost formula from Chapter 4:

$$\text{Total Cost} = \text{Fixed Costs} + (\text{Unit Variable Cost} \times \text{Volume})$$
$$\text{TC} = \text{FC} + (\text{UVC} \times \text{V})$$

● **high-low method**
A model that separates the fixed and variable components of a cost element by using the mathematical differences between the highest and lowest levels of activity within a relevant range of production volume.

Managers use the total cost formula in budgeting and planning, and the more precise the formula, the better the information. The **high-low method** is a model that separates the fixed and variable components of a cost element by using the mathematical differences between the highest and lowest levels of activity within a relevant range of production volume. Consider the five years of historical data from a bicycle shop:

Year	Units Sold	Rent	Cost of Goods Sold	Store Supplies	
1998	5,400	$12,000	$432,000	$30,000	
1999	5,200	12,000	416,000	33,000	
2000	5,000	12,000	400,000	32,000	**Low**
2001	6,000	12,000	480,000	35,000	
2002	6,400	12,000	512,000	38,000	**High**

Year 2002 has the highest cost and units sold and 2000 has the lowest units sold. The number of bicycles sold is our cost object because we believe the number sold causes the expenses to rise or fall. We will compare each expense to the number of bicycles sold. The high-low method employs the following four steps to determine the cost formula of a particular expense or cost element.

1 Select the highest and lowest unit observations in the data set. We have highlighted the high and low units in the data set as years 2002 and 2000.

2 Find the differences in the units and costs to determine the variable cost per unit. The difference between the cost at the high and low levels of production divided by the difference in the number of units gives us the variation per unit in the costs—hence, the variable cost per unit.

3 Solve the total cost equation to compute the fixed cost portion of the cost element. If we use the total cost formula and substitute the variable cost per unit, the units produced at the high level, and the total expense at the high level, we can solve for the fixed-cost component. The method also gives us the same answer for fixed costs if we substitute the equivalent information for the low level of production.

4 State the total cost formula for the cost element. After computing the unit variable cost and the fixed cost, we can state the total cost formula for the cost element and predict total costs at any production level within the relevant range.

Now let's examine the behavior of rent expense compared to bicycles sold.

Step 1 **Compare the high and low values to find the difference.**

	Units Sold	Rent
High	6,400	$12,000
Low	5,000	12,000
Difference	1,400	$ —0—

Step 2 **Compute the variable change in value per unit.**

$$\frac{\$\ 0}{1,400} = \$0 \text{ variable cost}$$

Step 3 **Solve the total cost formula to compute the fixed costs.**
You may use either the high values or the low values in the formula. In this instance, we use the low values.

$$TC = FC + (UVC \times Sales\ V)$$
$$\$12,000 = FC + (\$0 \times 5,000)$$
$$\$12,000 = FC + \$0$$

By rearranging the formula we arrive at:

$$FC = \$12,000 - \$0$$
$$FC = \$12,000$$

Step 4 **Write the total cost formula using the data from steps 1 through 3.**
The cost formula for rent:

$$TC = \$12,000 + (\$0 \times Sales\ V)$$

Determining that rent is a fixed cost is not too difficult because we can see that the rent does not change when sales change.

Now consider the cost of goods sold.

Step 1 **Compare the high and low values to find the difference.**

	Units Sold	Cost of Goods Sold
High	6,400	$512,000
Low	5,000	400,000
Difference	1,400	$112,000

Step 2 **Compute the variable change in value per unit.**

$$\frac{\$112,000}{1,400} = \$80 \text{ variable cost per unit sold}$$

Step 3 **Solve the total cost formula to compute the fixed costs.**
This time use the high costs to solve:

$$TC = FC + (UVC \times Sales\ V)$$
$$\$512,000 = FC + (\$80 \times 6,400)$$
$$\$512,000 = FC + \$512,000$$

By rearranging the formula we arrive at:

$$FC = \$512,000 - \$512,000$$
$$FC = \$0$$

Step 4 **Write the total cost formula using the data from steps 1 through 3.**
The cost formula for cost of goods sold:

$$TC = \$0 + (\$80 \times Sales\ V)$$

Because the fixed costs are zero, cost of goods sold is a variable cost of $80 per unit. Consider finally the cost of store supplies.

Step 1   **Compare the high and low values to find the difference.**

	Units Sold	Store Supplies
High	6,400	$38,000
Low	5,000	32,000
Difference	1,400	$ 6,000

Step 2   **Compute the variable change in value per unit.**

$$\frac{\$6,000}{1,400} = \$4.2857 \text{ variable cost per unit sold}$$

Step 3   **Solve the total cost formula to compute the fixed costs.**
This time use the high values to compute the cost formula.

$$\text{TC} = \text{FC} + (\text{UVC} \times \text{V})$$
$$\$38,000 = \text{FC} + (\$4.2857 \times 6,400)$$
$$\$38,000 = \text{FC} + \$27,428.48$$

By rearranging the formula we arrive at:

$$\text{FC} = \$38,000 - \$27,428.48$$
$$\text{FC} = \$10,571.52$$

Step 4   **Write the total cost formula using the data from steps 1 through 3.**
The cost formula for store supplies:

$$\text{TC} = \$10,571.52 + (\$4.28571 \times \text{Sales V})$$

Now, management knows the cost formula for three major expenses of its operation. The cost formula can be applied to any volume within the relevant range for budgeting and planning purposes. If you do not know the relevant range, you can always assume that it includes any volume between the high and low volume in a situation defined as being within a relevant range.

Assume these three expenses comprised all the costs of the organization. We could add the fixed costs and unit variable costs of each and derive a total cost formula for operations as follows:

Expense	Fixed Cost	Unit Variable Cost
Rent	$12,000.00	$00.00
Cost of goods sold	00.00	80.00
Store supplies	10,571.52	4.2857
Total	$22,571.52	$84.2857

$$\text{TC} = \$22,571.52 + (\$84.2857 \times \text{Units Sold})$$

As long as we stay within a relevant range, we can use the formula to predict future costs. For example, if management predicts it will sell 5,800 units in 2003, what would the formula predict the costs to be?

Rent	$\text{TC} = \$12,000$
Cost of goods sold	$\text{TC} = \$80 \times 5,800$
Store supplies	$\text{TC} = \$10,571.52 + (\$4.2857 \times 5,800)$
Total costs	$\text{TC} = \$22,571.52 + (\$84.2857 \times 5,800)$

Rent	$ 12,000.00
Cost of goods sold	464,000.00
Store supplies	35,428.58
Total costs	$511,428.58

This prediction can be a vital part of the budgeting process for management.

The high-low method is an easy method that approximates the total cost formula. Its major weakness is that it considers only two data points, the high point and the low point, instead of all the items in the data set. The appendix to this chapter contains a mathematical tool that can give us a more precise prediction.

Now let's turn our attention to relevant costs.

Relevant Versus Irrelevant Cost Concepts

It is critically important that managers base their decisions on relevant information and that they disregard all irrelevant information. To be relevant, the information must be pertinent to the decision at hand. In accounting, **relevant costing** is the process of determining which dollar inflows and outflows pertain to a particular management decision.

Why would managers not consider all information that might be available for a decision? Because not all information matters in the decision process and some may actually divert managers' attention. Past expenditures, for example, are irrelevant. Past costs are called **sunk costs**; current or future actions cannot change them.

Sunk costs are irrelevant, and managers should not consider them when evaluating current decision alternatives. For example, if the officers of Elevation Sports were deciding whether to replace the old production equipment they purchased from the bank with new digital equipment, the cost of the old equipment would be irrelevant. Why? The firm purchased and paid for the old equipment and the purchase of the new equipment cannot change the cost of either the old or new equipment. Sunk costs include both amounts paid in the past and past commitments to pay. That is, once a binding commitment to pay cash or otherwise transfer resources is made, the cost associated with that commitment is a sunk cost.

A **relevant cost** is a future cost that is pertinent to a particular decision and differs between two decision alternatives. A relevant cost must be a future cost because current decisions can have no effect on a past expenditure. A relevant cost must differ between decision alternatives. If a cost remains the same regardless of the decision alternative we choose, it is irrelevant. Again, focus on the decision to buy new equipment or to keep the old. If the new equipment requires fewer labor dollars to make snowboards than the old, future labor costs are relevant. If it requires the same amount of labor dollars as the existing equipment, future labor costs are irrelevant regardless of the dollar cost of labor.

In addition to relevant costs, we must also consider relevant revenues. A **relevant revenue** is a future revenue that differs between two decision alternatives. As you will see in our decision models, we look for the *net* relevant costs considering both relevant costs and relevant revenues.

● **relevant costing**
The process of determining which dollar inflows and outflows pertain to a particular management decision.

● **sunk costs**
Past expenditures that current or future actions cannot change.

● **relevant cost**
A future cost that is pertinent to a particular decision and differs between two decision alternatives.

● **relevant revenue**
A future revenue that differs between two decision alternatives.

What Do You Think?

9-1 Using the definition of a *relevant cost*, list the relevant costs of attending college.

9-2 Have you ever made a decision and later found that you mistakenly let irrelevant factors sway your choice? Explain.

Exhibit 9-1 (see p. 324) contains a decision model to determine if a factor is a relevant cost or revenue.

Relevant costs and revenues are **quantitative factors** that affect business decisions, that is, they are factors represented by numbers. Almost all accounting information is quantitative, including relevant costs and revenues. Managers, however, should also consider additional factors that cannot be quantified. **Qualitative factors** are nonnumerical attributes that affect decision alternatives. Some of these factors are customer satisfaction, product quality, employee morale, and customer perceptions. For example, when Wal-Mart, Target, or The Home Depot announces a new store will

● **quantitative factors**
Factors that affect business decisions and are represented by numbers.

● **qualitative factors**
Nonnumerical attributes that affect decision alternatives.

Exhibit 9-1
Decision Model to Determine
Relevant Costs and Revenues

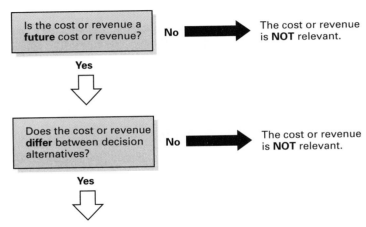

open in a small town, not everyone in the community is happy. Residents may save money on their purchases and have new job opportunities, but existing competitors face the loss of their businesses. Sales tax revenue will increase and help the town, but civic morale may suffer from the displacement of established businesses. Some town councils enthusiastically welcome a national chain and others refuse to allow a chain to open. The management of the national chain must assess all these qualitative factors in making the final decision whether to pursue the location or select another.

When managers consider purchasing new equipment or software, employees should test alternatives to see whether they prefer one over the others for comfort, safety, and stress. Employee morale can suffer quickly when managers make unpopular or unwise decisions, thereby causing lower productivity and sometimes outright sabotage. Remember that after the purchase, the costs are sunk costs. When making a decision, a manager should determine what factors are relevant and should evaluate all relevant quantitative *and* qualitative factors.

Throughout the remainder of this chapter, we will follow the officers of Elevation Sports as they encounter common business situations that require them to determine relevant costs and revenues using appropriate decision models. Each situation will help you to gather all costs associated with the decision, determine the relevant cost of each decision alternative, compare the relevant costs of each alternative, and determine the preferred alternative. The first example we will explore is an equipment replacement decision.

Equipment Replacement

After three years of operations, Jon called a meeting of Elevation Sports' officers to discuss replacing the production equipment. Although the equipment still operated well, Jon discovered some new technology at the last ski sports industry show that would allow more versatility for their products. Jon gathered and presented all the information about the replacement and existing equipment to the team.

Step 1: Gather All Decision Information

The three-year-old equipment cost $75,000 with a residual value of $15,000 and an estimated life of five years. Jon believes, however, that this equipment will last three years beyond the original estimated life. The firm recognizes $12,000 of straight-line depreciation each year but has only $24,000 left to depreciate. Operating this equipment requires employing two operators at $25,000 per year and costs $3,000 for maintenance each year. Jon believes he can sell this equipment now for $20,000.

	EXISTING EQUIPMENT	REPLACEMENT EQUIPMENT
Start-up costs		
Cost of equipment	$ 75,000	$100,000
Operating costs		
Annual depreciation	$ 12,000	$ 18,000
Total depreciation—5 years	60,000	90,000
Annual labor cost	50,000	30,000
Total labor cost—5 years	250,000	150,000
Annual maintenance cost	3,000	1,500
Total maintenance cost—5 years	15,000	7,500
Shutdown costs		
Residual value of equipment	$ 15,000	$ 10,000
Current sale price existing equipment		20,000

Exhibit 9-2
Elevation Sports, Inc.
Equipment Replacement
Cost Summary

The replacement equipment will cost $100,000 and has an estimated useful life of five years with a $10,000 residual value. Annual straight-line depreciation would be $18,000. Because the equipment is digital and faster, the new equipment will require only one operator with a $30,000 salary, because the person would need a higher level of training. A maintenance contract on the replacement equipment will cost $1,500 per year and will be cancellable at any time. Exhibit 9-2 summarizes the facts for each system. These costs are generally classified as start-up costs, operating costs, and shutdown costs.

To make an informed decision, Jon must consider the total cost of each alternative. This includes all the costs that would be incurred over the remaining five-year life of each alternative. To find the total cost of the equipment, multiply the annual costs associated with each alternative by the number of years the equipment will be used.

Step 2: Determine the Relevant Cost of Each Alternative

Next, Jon determines the relevant cost of each decision alternative. For each cost, return to the two primary questions: Is the cost a future cost, and does the cost differ between alternatives? Consider the costs associated with the existing equipment first.

Relevant Costs of the Existing Equipment

- The $75,000 cost of the existing equipment represents a sunk cost, so Jon's decision whether or not to purchase the replacement equipment cannot change the past expenditure for the existing equipment.
- Although depreciation appears to be a future cost, it is merely an allocation of an asset's original cost. The existing equipment's depreciation is not relevant because the depreciation is an allocation of the purchase price, which is a sunk cost.
- The total cost of $250,000 to pay for two operators is relevant because it is a future cost and it differs between alternatives. The existing equipment requires two operators, each costing $25,000 per year. Over the five-year remaining life of the old equipment, that totals $250,000 (2 operators × $25,000 × 5 years).
- The $15,000 total cost of maintenance for the existing equipment is relevant because it differs between decision alternatives.
- The $15,000 residual value of the existing equipment is relevant because it is a future revenue and it differs between alternatives. If Jon keeps the existing equipment, he will be able to sell it at the end of its useful life for $15,000. If, however, he buys the replacement equipment, he will sell the existing equipment

now for $20,000, and therefore he will be unable to sell it for its residual value in five years.

- The $20,000 Jon could get if he sells the existing equipment now is a future revenue that differs between alternatives. Therefore, it is relevant. If Jon buys the replacement equipment, he can sell the existing equipment for $20,000, but if he does not buy the replacement equipment, he will need to keep the existing equipment.

Relevant Costs of the Replacement Equipment

- The only start-up cost for the replacement equipment is the $100,000 to purchase and install it. This is a relevant cost because it is a future cost, and it differs between alternatives.
- The $90,000 in total depreciation on the replacement equipment is an allocation of its cost. To avoid double counting, Jon excludes its depreciation expense from the analysis of relevant costs.
- The $150,000 ($30,000 × 5 years) total labor cost for the replacement equipment's one operator is relevant because it is a future cost that is less than labor cost for the existing equipment.
- The total cost of the maintenance contract on the replacement equipment is $7,500, which is less than the maintenance cost for the existing equipment.
- The $10,000 residual value for the replacement equipment is relevant because it is a future revenue that differs between alternatives. If Jon replaces his existing equipment with the new, he can sell the replacement equipment for $10,000 at the end of its useful life. If he does not buy the new equipment, he obviously cannot sell it.

Step 3: Compare the Relevant Costs and Select an Alternative

After Jon determined which costs were relevant, he compared them to see which alternative was best for the firm, as Exhibit 9-3 illustrates. Parentheses indicate relevant outflows.

Exhibit 9-3
Elevation Sports, Inc.
Relevant Cost Comparison for
Replacement of Equipment

	KEEP EXISTING EQUIPMENT	PURCHASE REPLACEMENT EQUIPMENT
Start-up costs		
Cost of new equipment		$(100,000)
Operating costs		
Labor cost:		
Old equipment (2 X 5 X $25,000)	$(250,000)	
New equipment (1 X 5 X $30,000)		(150,000)
Maintenance cost:		
Old equipment (5 x $3,000)	(15,000)	
New equipment (5 x $1,500)		(7,500)
Shutdown costs		
Residual value of existing equipment	15,000	
Sale price if existing equipment sold now		20,000
Residual value of replacement equipment		10,000
Total relevant costs	$(250,000)	$(227,500)

Difference in relevant costs is $22,500 in favor of buying the replacement equipment.

As this analysis shows, by replacing the equipment Jon would save $22,500 over the next five years. Although this seems to be the obvious choice, Elevation Sports must have the cash or borrowing capacity to pay for the equipment. Considering only relevant costs in decision making will lead to better business decisions, but it does not necessarily enable managers to take advantage of what they learn in the process.

What Do You Think?

9-3 Assuming all purchases and sales of equipment are cash transactions, how much cash would Jon need to buy the new system?

9-4 Now that we know the relevant costs associated with the equipment replacement, what qualitative factors should Jon consider before he makes his final decision?

The Time Value of Money

New equipment purchase decisions generally have long-term effects because the associated cash inflows and outflows will occur over many years. Therefore, decision makers should consider the interest-earning potential of the cash flows associated with equipment acquisitions. The interest-earning potential of cash over time is called the **time value of money**. Chapter 11 covers special techniques developed to incorporate the effect of interest and the timing of cash flows.

● **time value of money**
The interest-earning potential of cash over time.

Special Orders

A manufacturing business must often consider whether to accept a **special order**, an order that is outside the normal scope of business activity. As you will see, proper treatment of fixed costs is critical in making sound special-order decisions. After a few years in operation, Elevation Sports begins to attract the attention of the snow sports world. A representative of a Swiss ski resort approaches Megan with an interesting proposition. He would like to purchase 2,000 snowboards labeled with the resort's logo for $70 each. The largest order the company has received to date was for 200 snowboards, so this order requires special consideration.

● **special order**
An order that is outside the normal scope of business activity.

Step 1: Gather All Decision Information

The $70 per board offer from the resort is considerably less than Elevation Sports' normal wholesale selling price of $95 per board. In fact, the snowboards cost $70 each to produce, so you might conclude they would make no profit if they accept the $70 offer. As Megan discusses the order with the Swiss representative, she tells him that she would be willing to sell the snowboards to them at a discounted price of $80 each because of the large quantity of snowboards they need. The Swiss representative will not negotiate and gives her five days to accept or reject the offer.

Megan gathers all the information necessary to make a wise decision. She develops a report detailing production costs to analyze the firm's normal cost per unit in more detail. Using expected total sales (excluding this special order) and production costs for the year, she prepares the report shown in Exhibit 9-4.

Megan must determine the potential effect on Elevation Sports' revenues and expenses of accepting the order. Which costs shown in Exhibit 9-4 would be affected by the decision to accept the special order? To determine which costs are relevant, she asks the two primary questions: Is the cost a future cost, and does the cost differ between alternatives?

Exhibit 9-4
Per Unit Cost Report for
Elevation Sports, Inc.

Expected wholesale sales (5,000 units at $95 each)		$475,000
Less: Cost of goods sold (see detail following)		350,000
Expected gross margin		$125,000

Detailed calculation for cost of goods sold:	Per Unit	Total
Number of units	1	5,000
Direct material costs	$ 10	$ 50,000
Direct labor costs	25	125,000
Variable production costs	15	75,000
Fixed production costs	20	100,000
Total cost of goods sold	$ 70	$350,000

Step 2: Determine the Relevant Costs of Each Alternative

Next, Megan must determine which costs are relevant. In this situation, the alternatives are to accept the order or reject it. No cost is associated with rejecting the order, so Megan's analysis focuses on the alternative to accept. If the company accepts the order, sales will increase by $140,000 (2,000 snowboards × $70 per board). The increase in sales due to the special order is relevant because it will happen in the future and it differs between alternatives.

All variable costs are relevant because they are future costs that differ between alternatives. If Megan accepts the special order, the company will incur the variable costs to produce the 2,000 snowboards. In this example, variable costs include direct material, direct labor, and variable production costs.

Depending on the decision situation, fixed cost may or may not be relevant. Often, fixed production costs are not relevant costs because they will not change with an increase in production volume. This holds true unless the special order creates an additional fixed cost, or the order is so substantial that production would exceed the relevant range if the company accepts the order. As Exhibit 9-4 indicates, Megan expects total fixed costs to be $100,000. Megan believes the decision to accept or reject the special order would not affect total fixed cost. Therefore, in this case, the fixed cost does not differ between alternatives and is irrelevant to the special-order decision.

Step 3: Compare the Relevant Costs and Select an Alternative

Armed with information about relevant costs, Megan can make an informed decision about the Swiss order. Exhibit 9-5 presents a schedule of relevant costs for this special order. The schedule excludes fixed costs because they are irrelevant.

Elevation Sports' income would increase by $40,000 if it accepted the special order. The reasoning in this example may seem logical, but managers often reject special orders they believe will not increase profits because they do not understand

Exhibit 9-5
Elevation Sports, Inc.
Relevant Costs for Special
Order of 2,000 Snowboards

	Per Unit	Total
Sales from special order	$ 70	$140,000
Direct material costs	$ 10	$ 20,000
Direct labor costs	25	50,000
Variable production costs	15	30,000
Total relevant production costs	$ 50	$100,000
Total increase in income	$ 20	$ 40,000

the concept of relevant cost as it pertains to fixed cost. To avoid making poor decisions, managers must carefully consider how a special order will affect fixed cost. If Megan had rejected the order, she would have foregone an additional $40,000 in profits. If you remember, the four officers had sacrificed salaries to begin this business. An additional $40,000 in profits could increase each of their salaries by about $10,000 each.

What Do You Think?

9-5 **What would happen if a manager treated every order as a special order and routinely disregarded fixed cost considerations from his or her pricing decisions?**

9-6 **Assume that Jon claims the company will exceed its capacity with this order. What implications does this information have on the decision to accept the special order?**

9-7 **What factors other than increased profits should Megan consider when accepting an order to sell snowboards for less than the price she charges her regular customers? For example, what would her regular wholesale customers think if they found that the Swiss ski resort was buying the same boards from Elevation Sports at a lower cost?**

What happens when you learn that another business makes something your company does, and offers to sell it to you at a price that is lower than your cost? Should you automatically discontinue production and buy that item? Let's look at the situation of whether to make or buy in the future.

Make-or-Buy Decisions

Often, companies purchase subcomponents used to manufacture their products instead of making them in their in-house manufacturing facilities. Buying services, products, or components of products from outside vendors instead of producing them is called **outsourcing**. Decision makers considering a make-or-buy decision must pay close attention to fixed costs and opportunity costs.

Elevation Sports has always purchased its bindings from a vendor. The vendor now indicates that the price of the bindings will increase from $5 each to $6. Jon wants Megan to prepare an analysis to see whether manufacturing the bindings themselves would be less expensive than continuing to buy them after the price increase. He will help her gather the information.

● **outsourcing**
Buying services, products, or components of products from outside vendors instead of producing them.

Step 1: Gather All Decision Information

Jon discovered he could purchase a machine to make the bindings. The plant has room for the equipment, which requires no special installation construction. The machine costs $20,000 and should last for five years with no salvage value. Annual depreciation will increase the fixed costs by $4,000 per year. The materials for the bindings cost approximately $2 per board. Each board still requires $1 of special hardware that must be purchased. Jon believes the labor will cost $1 or less per binding using people currently working on an hourly basis. Variable overhead cost will increase $0.50 per board and the only change in fixed overhead costs is the cost of the binding machine. Elevation Sports buys roughly 10,000 bindings each year. Megan details these facts in Exhibit 9-6 (see p. 330).

Exhibit 9-6
Elevation Sports, Inc.
Cost of Producing Snowboard
Bindings

Number of bindings produced each year		10,000
	Per Unit	**Total**
Direct material	$3.00	$30,000
Direct labor	1.00	10,000
Variable manufacturing overhead	0.50	5,000
Fixed manufacturing overhead	0.40	4,000
Total	$4.90	$49,000

Exhibit 9-7
Elevation Sports, Inc.
Selecting Relevant Costs
of Producing Bindings

	Future?	**Differs?**	**Relevant?**
Direct material	Yes	Yes	Yes
Direct labor	Yes	Yes	Yes
Variable manufacturing overhead	Yes	Yes	Yes
Fixed manufacturing overhead related only to new machine	Yes	Yes	Yes

Step 2: Determine the Relevant Costs of Each Alternative

Once more, Megan will assess whether each cost is relevant by asking the primary questions: Is the cost a future cost, and does the cost differ between alternatives? Exhibit 9-7 offers the answers.

By definition, *fixed* manufacturing overhead remains constant *in total* regardless of the level of activity described as the number of units produced. The fixed costs in Exhibit 9-8 are not an allocation of the fixed overhead cost of the whole factory, but rather the increase in depreciation for the new equipment required to make the bindings. If the company continues to buy the bindings, the existing fixed cost for the manufacturing plant will not change. The normal fixed cost is irrelevant, and the increased depreciation is relevant.

Step 3: Compare the Relevant Costs and Select an Alternative

Megan compared the relevant costs of the make-or-buy decision in Exhibit 9-8.

As Exhibit 9-8 indicates, Elevation Sports can save $21,000, or $2.10 per binding, compared to the cost after the vendor's price increase. Much to Jon's surprise, the cost of making each binding is $1.10 less than the current vendor price. In a meeting with the other officers, Rob declares that he does not believe this is true because the allocation does not include a proportionate amount of fixed costs. Megan acknowledges that an overhead allocation of $15,000 is proper for the bindings. In addition, Rob still

Exhibit 9-8
Elevation Sports, Inc.
Relevant Costs of Make-or-Buy
Decision for Bindings

	Make	**Buy**
Cost to purchase (10,000 × $7)		$70,000
Direct material	$30,000	
Direct labor	10,000	
Variable manufacturing overhead	5,000	
Fixed manufacturing overhead	4,000	
Total relevant cost	$49,000	$70,000

Difference in relevant costs is $21,000 in favor of making the bindings.

	Make	Buy
Cost to purchase (10,000 × $7)		$70,000
Direct material	$30,000	
Direct labor	10,000	
Variable manufacturing overhead	5,000	
Additional fixed overhead		
from the equipment	4,000	
Fixed manufacturing overhead	15,000	15,000
Total relevant cost	$64,000	$85,000

Difference in relevant costs is $21,000 in favor of making the bindings.

Exhibit 9-9
Elevation Sports, Inc.
Relevant Costs of Make-or-Buy
Decision for Bindings with
Fixed Costs Shown

believes it is better to buy from someone else and not have the hassle of producing them inside. Jon argues they can sell bindings in the retail shop and save money on those also. The investment in the new equipment also gives the company the ability to develop new styles of bindings. Rob insists the real problem is leaving out the allocated fixed costs. Megan agrees to include an allocation of fixed costs on the analysis and prepares the comparison in Exhibit 9-9.

Megan explains why the fixed manufacturing overhead is irrelevant. Although Rob argues that fixed manufacturing overhead is a very real part of business cost because it remains a cost whether the company purchases or produces the bindings, Exhibit 9-9 shows that fixed manufacturing overhead remains the same for the two alternatives, and the outcome remains the same as that in Exhibit 9-8. Elevation Sports can save $11,000 over the current price and $21,000 over the future projected price.

What Do You Think?

9-8 What will happen to the cost of producing other Elevation Sports products if the company decides to begin making the bindings? Explain your answer.

9-9 What qualitative factors should the officers consider with this decision?

Special Relevant Cost Considerations for Fixed Costs

Fixed costs normally are irrelevant in make-or-buy decisions. As you observed in the previous example, sometimes selecting the alternative affects fixed costs, such as the additional depreciation for the new equipment. When deciding to outsource a product line or service, a manager needs to analyze fixed costs and sort them into two categories: those that can change with a decrease of activities and those that cannot. Consider the following costs:

- **Building rent or depreciation**—When the company has a finite amount of space and cannot reduce its rent or depreciation by using less space or subletting space, its fixed costs will not be affected by the outsourcing decision.
- **Supervisory personnel**—When the firm can eliminate a supervisory position by outsourcing, fixed costs will decrease with the decision.

- **Equipment**—If the company rents equipment by the month or can sell the equipment, an outsourcing decision that makes the equipment unnecessary will decrease fixed costs. When the equipment can be used elsewhere in the factory, the fixed overhead for the company will not change.

Not all outsourcing decisions involve the cost of products. Services can also be outsourced.

Decisions to Outsource Services

Some companies are either too small to perform certain services within the company or grow too large to perform all the services required for a particular function. Common services that management often outsources include janitorial services, advertising, maintenance, and accounting functions. One example of an accounting function that might be outsourced is the payroll function. A company can hire a CPA firm or payroll specialty firm to create payroll checks, prepare payroll tax forms, and maintain employee payroll records.

Let's look at how Fast Track Delivery Service makes such a decision about whether or not to outsource its payroll preparation.

Step 1: Gather All Decision Information

Fast Track Delivery Service operates a small auto repair facility to service its fleet of 350 delivery vehicles. Fast Track's repair facility occupies space in an industrial area close to the home office. Fast Track is considering using a local CPA firm to prepare the weekly payroll for its 50 employees. It currently pays $1,500 per week plus benefits and payroll taxes of $525 per week. The $1,000 weekly administrative costs of the human resources department for these 50 employees will not change. A dependable CPA firm has offered to provide weekly payroll services at a cost of $2,000 per week. If Fast Track accepts the offer, they could reduce the weekly wages by $1,250, benefits by $450, and save supplies costs of $125 per week.

Step 2: Determine the Relevant Costs of Each Alternative

The following lists contains the relevant costs for the decision:

	Continue In-house	Outsource
Salary costs	$1,500	$ 250
Benefits & payroll taxes	525	75
Costs of CPA firm		2,000
Supplies	125	0
Total Relevant Costs	$2,150	$2,325

Step 3: Compare the Relevant Costs and Select an Alternative

From the information provided, outsourcing the payroll services appears to cost more than providing them in-house. The difference amounts to only $175 per week. Be careful not to make a decision based on weekly information, because $175 per week equals $9,100 per year. The more prudent decision seems to be to continue to perform the payroll function within the company.

Keep in mind how to determine the relevance of fixed overhead costs as we look at another common business decision.

Decisions to Add or Close Divisions

Elevation Sports has not used all its manufacturing space and Vail has lots of summer tourists. Rob suggests that they consider adding a line of mountain boards—skateboards with knobby tires instead of hard wheels. He believes that mountain boards will have year-round product appeal for people who live outside snow areas and those who live in suburban and rural areas with little concrete. The mountain board production is synergistic with snowboards, requiring only replacement of bindings with wheels and tires. Mountain boarding has become popular in the Rockies, and the sale of mountain boards would improve their summer retail sales and make their business less seasonal. The officers decide to seriously consider the possibilities.

When a firm has excess capacity, expanding to produce new product lines or adding new divisions can be profitable because the firm does not have to add capacity-related fixed costs. The costs for the new product are usually lower than if the firm produced only the new product and adds to the company's overall profitability. Conversely, when a company decides to eliminate a product or division, management is often mystified when the closure does not result in increased profits. The reason, of course, is that the firm eliminated only variable costs and unavoidable fixed costs remained. For that reason, as long as a product or division is producing contribution margin toward unavoidable fixed costs, continuing its operation is usually more profitable.

Be sure you understand the difference between avoidable and unavoidable fixed costs. Avoidable fixed costs are things such as a lease that could easily be sublet, equipment that has a realistic sales value, equipment with alternative uses, and manufacturing space with alternative uses. Look at the following example:

Austin Products has three product lines—A, B, and C—that it considers losers. These incur the following costs:

	A	B	C
Sales	$340,000	$210,000	$500,000
Variable costs	300,000	215,000	300,000
Unavoidable fixed costs	130,000	50,000	250,000
Avoidable fixed costs	20,000	75,000	50,000
Loss	$110,000	$130,000	$100,000

Let's look at each product from a different perspective:

	A	B	C
Current loss	$110,000	$130,000	$100,000
Unavoidable fixed costs	$130,000	$ 50,000	$250,000
Decision choice	Continue	Close	Continue

If the firm closes a division, the new loss becomes the amount of the unavoidable fixed costs. Management should choose the lesser of the two losses to maximize profits. For product A, the company nets $20,000 more profit by leaving the division open. Management should watch this closely because further deterioration might change the decision. For product B, the company saves $80,000 by eliminating the product line. For product C, the firm saves $150,000 by continuing to operate.

Let's look at Elevation Sports' situation to consider adding mountain boards to the product line.

Step 1: Gather All Decision Information

Megan and Jon compiled the following information:

Potential sales price per unit:		
Wholesale		$ 120
Retail		200
Variable costs per unit:		
Materials	$30	
Labor	20	
Variable overhead	30	
Total variable cost per unit	$80	
Allocated unavoidable fixed costs		
(part of current fixed costs)		20,000
Added new fixed costs		3,000

Step 2: Determine the Relevant Costs of Each Alternative

Megan computed break-even units for both retail and wholesale sales under two assumptions. The first assumption considers the fixed costs to include both avoidable ($3,000) and unavoidable ($20,000) fixed costs. The second assumption ignores the unavoidable fixed costs and considers only the added new fixed costs ($3,000).

Retail Sales:

$$1.\ BE_{Units} = \frac{FC}{UCM} = \frac{\$23,000}{\$200 - \$80} = 192\ units$$

$$2.\ BE_{Units} = \frac{FC}{UCM} = \frac{\$3,000}{\$200 - \$80} = 25\ units$$

Wholesale Sales:

$$1.\ BE_{Units} = \frac{FC}{UCM} = \frac{\$23,000}{\$120 - \$80} = 575\ units$$

$$2.\ BE_{Units} = \frac{FC}{UCM} = \frac{\$3,000}{\$120 - \$80} = 75\ units$$

According to the models of relevant costs you have examined, the unavoidable fixed costs are not relevant. Megan insists that the only items that matter are the second assumptions, which suggest that breakeven can be achieved if they sold 25 mountain boards at retail or 75 at wholesale prices. Rob insists that they should only look at the need to sell 575 mountain boards at wholesale price to break even.

Megan and Rob discussed the likelihood of achieving break-even sales. Rob insists that she use the full amount of the fixed costs because he believes they are deceiving themselves if the product cannot make its own way without subsidy from regular production. Megan concludes that selling only at wholesale prices under assumption one, recognizing both avoidable and unavoidable fixed costs, is the worst-case scenario. She also asserts that selling at retail prices under the second assumption, considering only additional (avoidable) fixed costs, is the best-case scenario. She prepared the following schedule:

		Worst Case	Best Case
Added sales	(A)	$69,000	$5,000
Additional variable costs	(B)	46,000	2,000
Additional contribution margin		$23,000	$3,000
Added fixed costs		3,000	3,000
Addition to net income		$20,000	$—0—

(A) $120 wholesale price × 575 units = $69,000
      $200 retail price × 25 units = $5,000

(B) $80 variable costs × 575 units = $46,000
      $80 variable costs × 25 units = $2,000

Rob laughs and asks Megan how she can turn the best case into the worst, and the worst case into the best. She explains that when dealing with risk of failing to break even after introducing a new product, the best-case scenario ends up being the one with the least risk of loss. In our example, the sale of only 25 units at retail affords the least risk of not recovering the additional $3,000 of fixed costs. Rob believes that needing to sell 575 units at wholesale is the most frightening because he is not sure they can sell that many mountain boards. Megan further explains that although Rob is most afraid of not making 575 sales, they actually make money at that level because $20,000 of fixed costs are irrelevant; they are already spent regardless of whether or not the company ventures into mountain boards. A more realistic version of the worst-case scenario is selling only 75 mountain boards at wholesale prices. The officers must decide whether this is the right time to take what appears to be a low risk to venture into mountain boards.

What Do You Think?

9-10   Do you agree with Megan or with Rob? Explain your rationale.

9-11   What decision would you make regarding adding mountain boards? Explain your reasoning.

Step 3: Compare the Relevant Costs and Select an Alternative

When we compare the relevant costs in an addition of a product situation, we have sometimes three alternatives: (1) do nothing; (2) choose the described alternative; and (3) pursue alternative opportunities. Other alternatives can be as easy as investing the cash in interest-bearing accounts.

Considering Opportunity Costs

An **opportunity cost** is the value of what is relinquished because of choosing one alternative over another. For example, the opportunity cost of attending college rather than working full time is the salary you would have received by working instead of going to college.

● **opportunity cost**
The value of what is relinquished because of choosing one alternative over another.

Return to the example of Elevation Sports making or buying its bindings. Say, for example, the excess capacity in the plant could be used to make the bindings or produce mountain boards, but not both. Further assume that the officers believe they can sell at least 200 mountain boards at retail. In this case, the decision whether to make the bindings has an opportunity cost of the lost contribution margin from the mountain boards. If they sell 200 boards at retail prices, the contribution margin after added fixed costs is as follows:

Sales ($200 × 200)	$40,000
Less: variable costs ($80 × 200)	(16,000)
added fixed costs	(3,000)
Net contribution margin	$21,000

The foregone $21,000 contribution margin on the mountain boards is an opportunity cost of making the bindings.

Let's revisit the decision on the bindings and add the opportunity costs of *not* making the mountain boards to Exhibit 9-10 (see p. 336).

The result in Exhibit 9-10 leaves our officers with a very real business dilemma. Remember that qualitative factors also must be considered in any business situation. In addition, the group has more alternatives to explore. If, for example, Jon can find another

Exhibit 9-10
Elevation Sports, Inc.
Relevant Cost of Make-or-Buy
Decision for Bindings

	MAKE	BUY
Cost to purchase (10,000 × $7)		$70,000
Direct material	$30,000	
Direct labor	10,000	
Variable manufacturing overhead	5,000	
Fixed manufacturing overhead	4,000	
Opportunity costs of mountain boards	21,000	
Total relevant cost	$70,000	$70,000

Difference in relevant costs is zero.

binding supplier who can match the current cost of $6 each, the company will be better off continuing to buy the bindings and adding the production of mountain boards.

Relevant cost concepts apply to almost every business decision and are also helpful with personal decisions, such as whether to attend summer school or work to save money for next year. In business as in life, an array of quantitative and qualitative considerations exist for every decision alternative. As a decision maker, you must be able to seek out the relevant considerations and disregard the irrelevant ones.

USING THE RESULTS OF REGRESSION ANALYSIS TO FIND THE TOTAL COST FORMULA

Regression analysis is a mathematical model that uses all the items in the data set to compute a least squares regression line that equals the total cost formula. Regression analysis derives a statistically accurate total cost formula provided that the historical accounting information is a reliable predictor of future costs. If a major change in the amounts of a particular expense has occurred, we use historical data only from the time since the change in the cost occurred. We are not going to learn the regression mathematics in this section because generic computer worksheet programs can calculate the regression data. Instead, we will use the computer output to determine the total cost formulas. The regression analysis provides the equation:

$$Y = a + bX \quad \text{where}$$
$$Y = \text{total costs}$$
$$a = \text{fixed costs}$$
$$b = \text{unit variable cost}$$
$$X = \text{the activity level}$$

This formula corresponds to

$$TC = FC + (UVC \times V)$$

Many advanced business calculators and any computer worksheet program can provide these statistics.

Exhibit 9-11 contains abbreviated regression output from a Microsoft Excel® spreadsheet for the data we previously used in the high-low method. We entered the data into columns labeled to identify the information. By selecting Data Analysis and then Regression in the Tools menu, you can generate the regression output data. First, identify the "input X range" by highlighting the data under Units Sold. Second, identify the "input Y range" by highlighting the data under Rent. Finally, select the "output range" by selecting a cell for the program to write the "summary output." Repeat this process for Cost of Goods Sold and Supplies, substituting each column in turn for the Rent column. Be sure to leave enough room for the summary.

Using the Summary Output for each cost, we can write the total cost formula the computer program generates. The intercept is the fixed costs and the X variable is the unit variable costs. Each expense has its own summary output.

Expense	Intercept	X Variable
Rent	12,000.00	0.00
Cost of goods sold	0.00	80.00
Store supplies	8,894.12	4.41

● **regression analysis**
A mathematical model that uses all the items in the data set to compute a least squares regression line that equals the total cost formula.

Exhibit 9-11
Microsoft Excel® Regression
Analysis Data Output

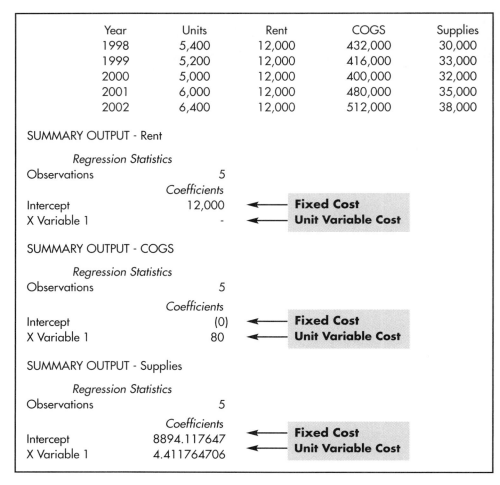

Year	Units	Rent	COGS	Supplies
1998	5,400	12,000	432,000	30,000
1999	5,200	12,000	416,000	33,000
2000	5,000	12,000	400,000	32,000
2001	6,000	12,000	480,000	35,000
2002	6,400	12,000	512,000	38,000

SUMMARY OUTPUT - Rent

Regression Statistics

Observations	5
	Coefficients
Intercept	12,000 ◄──── **Fixed Cost**
X Variable 1	- ◄──── **Unit Variable Cost**

SUMMARY OUTPUT - COGS

Regression Statistics

Observations	5
	Coefficients
Intercept	(0) ◄──── **Fixed Cost**
X Variable 1	80 ◄──── **Unit Variable Cost**

SUMMARY OUTPUT - Supplies

Regression Statistics

Observations	5
	Coefficients
Intercept	8894.117647 ◄──── **Fixed Cost**
X Variable 1	4.411764706 ◄──── **Unit Variable Cost**

We can convert the output into equations as follows:

Rent	TC = $12,000 + ($0 × units sold)
Cost of goods sold	TC = $0 + (80 × units sold)
Store supplies	TC = $8,894.12 + ($4.41 × units sold)
Total costs	TC = $20,894.12 + ($84.41 × units sold)

When you compare these formulas to those produced by the high-low method on page 322, the only one that is different is the mixed cost of store supplies. Applying the newly computed formula to the estimated sales of 5,800 units for 2003, we find the total estimated cost to be:

$$TC = \$20,894.12 + (\$84.41 \times \text{units sold})$$
$$TC = \$20,894.12 + \$489,578$$
$$TC = \$510,472$$

Rent	$ 12,000
Cost of goods sold	464,000
Store supplies	34,472
Total costs	$510,472

Comparing the results from the regression information of $510,472, to the results from the high-low method of $511,429, you can see that the high-low method results are within $1,000 of the regression results. Regression analysis will always provide more accuracy, and it is a more robust estimate because it considers all the data points instead of just two data points. Both methods, however, provide useful information for management.

CHAPTER SUMMARY

All management decision making entails choosing between or among alternatives. A valuable tool in making such decisions is determining the actual variable and fixed cost elements of a firm's expenses. The actual costs provide the best information for decision making.

To make the best decision in a given situation, a manager must consider only relevant information. Relevant information is a cost or revenue that makes a difference in a given decision situation. What is relevant in one situation may not be in another. Relevant costs are also always future costs because current or future actions cannot change past costs. Furthermore, a relevant future cost must differ between or among alternatives. Relevant revenues are future revenues that differ between alternatives. Managers should consider relevant opportunity costs when making decisions. An opportunity cost is the value of benefits foregone because one alternative is chosen over another.

In addition to quantitative information, when making decisions managers must consider qualitative information, such as customer satisfaction, product quality, and employee morale. Sometimes the qualitative considerations outweigh quantitative considerations. Many applications of relevant costing can be found in management decision making. The major types of decisions are whether to keep or replace a piece of equipment, whether to make or buy a component part, and whether to add or eliminate a product or business division. Careful application of relevant costing techniques can help managers to make appropriate decisions in these and other similar situations.

Visit the Web site *www.prenhall.com/terrell* for additional study help with the Online Study Guide.

REVIEW OF CONCEPTS

A   Distinguish between the quality of information obtained using the high-low method and using the results of regression analysis.

B   Describe two important characteristics that all relevant information possesses. Explain why the characteristics are important for decision making.

C   Explain the meaning of the term *sunk cost* and provide examples not included in the text.

D   Describe the difference between qualitative and quantitative factors and provide examples of each.

E   Describe how a manager determines the weight of qualitative and quantitative factors. Determine which of the two should prevail in decisions.

F   Explain why the depreciation for existing assets is considered irrelevant for equipment replacement decisions.

G   Define the term *time value of money* and explain its usefulness in accounting.

H   Discuss why the time value of money is important for decisions involving the purchase of long-lived assets.

I   Explain what would cause a fixed cost to be relevant for a special-order decision.

J   Define the term *outsourcing* and explain the relevant information considerations in making an outsourcing decision.

K   Define *opportunity cost* and provide several examples.

L   Describe the relevant costs/revenues important to a business decision to close a business.

M   Distinguish between an avoidable and unavoidable fixed cost. Describe why the distinction is important.

APPLICATION EXERCISES

LO 1
Determining Cost Behavior Using the High-Low Method

9-12 The inspection department at the Rose Garcia Company inspects every third unit produced. The following information is available for the inspection department:

	2002	2003
Number of inspections	41,950	48,600
Inspection cost	$77,273	$83,190

Required:

Using the high-low method, determine the following:
a. the variable-cost element for inspection cost
b. the fixed inspection cost
c. the inspection cost that can be expected if 45,000 units are inspected in 2004

LO 1
Determining Cost Behavior Using the High-Low Method

9-13 The transportation manager has asked you to estimate the operating cost that can be expected for the company jet for 2004. The following is information for 2002 and 2003:

	2002	2003
Flight time in hours	1,250	1,875
Aircraft operating cost	$1,563,750	$2,148,125

Required:

Estimate the cost of operating the company jet for 2004 assuming that flight time will be 1,500 hours.

LO 1
Determining Cost Behavior Using the High-Low Method

9-14 Charlie Nibarger, owner of Nibarger Fishing Guide Service, wants to estimate the cost of operating his fishing service next year. He expects to have 220 charters during 2004. The following information is available:

	2002	2003
Number of charters	150	230
Operating cost	$15,250	$22,000

Required:

a. Determine the estimated operating cost for 2004.
b. Assume that Charlie needs to make $50,000 before taxes to support his family. What must he charge for each charter to meet his needs?
c. What constraints might prevent him from charging the amount determined in part b?
d. How should Charlie determine his price?

LO 1
Determining Cost Behavior Using Regression Analysis Output

9-15 The following information pertains to Pioneer Manufacturing's purchasing department for 2002 and 2003:

	Number of Purchase Orders Issued	Cost of Operating the Purchasing Department
Fourth quarter 2002	2,500	$130,000
First quarter 2003	1,000	80,000
Second quarter 2003	1,500	110,000
Third quarter 2003	2,000	115,000
Fourth quarter 2003	3,000	140,000

A regression analysis on this information yields the following output:
Regression Statistics

		Coefficients	
Observations		Intercept	X Variable 1
5		59000.0000000000001	28

Required:

Using the regression output, determine the following:
a. the regression equation
b. the variable cost per purchase order
c. the fixed cost of operating the purchasing department for one quarter
d. the estimated cost of operating the purchasing department next year assuming that 8,000 purchase orders will be issued (Hint: Remember that the fixed cost for one year is four times the amount of fixed cost for one quarter.)

9-16 The following information pertains to the invoicing department of the Tessy Soda Company:

LO 1
Determining Cost Behavior Using Regression Analysis Output

	Number of Sales Invoices Processed	Cost of Operating the Invoicing Department
Fourth quarter 2002	10,500	$50,574.65
First quarter 2003	11,000	52,711.12
Second quarter 2003	15,000	58,231.51
Third quarter 2003	12,000	59,439.73
Fourth quarter 2003	9,000	46,299.73

A regression analysis on this information yields the following output:

Regression Statistics

Observations	Coefficients	
	Intercept	X Variable 1
5	29962.2443750000001	2.04253074999999999

Required:

Using the regression output, determine the following:
a. the regression equation
b. the variable cost per invoice processed
c. the fixed cost of operating the invoicing department for one quarter
d. the estimated cost of operating the invoicing department next year assuming that 52,000 invoices will be processed (Hint: Remember that the fixed cost for one year is four times the amount of fixed cost for one quarter.)

9-17 The following information pertains to Tao Tao & Associates:

LO 1
Determining Cost Behavior Using Regression Analysis Output

	Number of Computers Repaired	Cost of Operating the Repair Department
Fourth quarter 2002	125	$26,100.91
First quarter 2003	130	26,529.16
Second quarter 2003	110	25,400.65
Third quarter 2003	105	25,212.91
Fourth quarter 2003	115	25,799.88

A regression analysis on this information yields the following output:

Regression Statistics

Observations	Coefficients	
	Intercept	X Variable 1
5	19898.2674418604652	50.513953488372092

Required:

Using the regression analysis output, determine the following:
a. the regression equation
b. the variable cost per computer repair
c. the fixed cost of operating the repair department for one quarter
d. the estimated cost of operating the repair department next year assuming that 450 invoices will be processed (Hint: Remember that the fixed cost for one year is four times the amount of fixed cost for one quarter.)

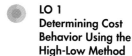

LO 1
Determining Cost Behavior Using Regression Analysis Output

9-18 The following information is from Calzone Manufacturing Company:

	Number of Calzones Produced	Total Production Cost
January	9,800	$17,100
February	7,000	15,000
March	8,000	16,000
April	7,500	15,500
May	10,100	17,200
June	9,000	17,000
July	10,500	19,000
August	11,600	20,000
September	10,600	18,200
October	8,500	16,800
November	12,100	20,500
December	11,000	18,000

A regression analysis on the data yields the following:

Regression Statistics

		Coefficients	
Observations	Intercept	X Variable 1
12	8017.47542738051652	0.986087250401329323

Required:

Using the regression analysis output, determine the following:
a. the regression equation
b. the variable cost per calzone
c. the fixed cost of operating the manufacturing plant for one year
d. the estimated cost of operating the manufacturing plant next month assuming that 10,800 calzones will be made

LO 1
Determining Cost Behavior Using the High-Low Method

9-19 Ace Computer Training offers short computer courses. The number of course sessions offered depends on student demand. The following information pertains to 2003:

	Number of Sessions	Cost
First quarter	30	$ 75,000
Second quarter	35	78,000
Third quarter	15	42,000
Fourth quarter	20	48,000
Total	100	$ 243,000

Required:

Using the high-low method, determine the following:
a. the variable cost per session
b. the total fixed cost of operating the company for one year
c. the expected quarter cost for 25 sessions

9-20 The following information is from Montana Avionics Testing Service:

LO 1
Determining Cost
Behavior Using
Regression Analysis
Output

	Number of Tests Performed	Total Cost of Testing
January	61,000	$1,420,000
February	55,000	1,340,000
March	50,000	1,290,000
April	72,000	1,430,000
May	78,000	1,440,000
June	81,000	1,540,000
July	90,000	1,590,000
August	108,000	1,610,000
September	111,000	1,700,000
October	128,000	1,720,000
November	140,000	1,860,000
December	132,000	1,810,000

A regression analysis on the data yields the following:

Regression Statistics

	Coefficients	
Observations	Intercept	X Variable 1
12	1026101.26979150337	5.81987772378115692

Required:

Using the regression analysis output, determine the following:
a. the regression equation
b. the variable cost per test
c. the fixed cost of operating for one month
d. the estimated cost of operating for one month assuming that 125,000 tests are performed

9-21 The following information pertains to the Palmer Supply Company:

LO 1
Determining Cost
Behavior Using the
High-Low Method

	2003	2004
Sales	$1,000,000	$1,150,000
Costs:		
Cost of goods sold	800,000	920,000
Sales commissions	15,000	17,250
Store rent	3,000	3,000
Depreciation	20,000	20,000
Maintenance cost	3,800	4,100
Office salaries	34,000	35,500

Required:

Assuming sales is the activity base, use the high-low method to determine the variable-cost element and the fixed-cost component of each of the preceding costs.

9-22 The following information pertains to the General Production Company:

LO 1
Determining Cost
Behavior Using the
High-Low Method

	2002	2003
Units produced	257,000	326,000
Costs:		
Direct material	$ 611,660	$ 775,880
Direct labor	1,662,790	2,109,220
Other manufacturing costs	1,781,820	1,868,760

Required:

Assuming units produced is the activity base, use the high-low method to determine the variable-cost element and fixed-cost component of each of the preceding costs.

LO 2
Determining Relevant Costs

9-23 The production manager at Armer Manufacturing contemplates several factors of whether he should upgrade some existing production equipment.

Required:

Indicate whether each of the following items is relevant or irrelevant and explain why.
 a. cost of existing equipment
 b. cost of replacement equipment
 c. depreciation on existing equipment
 d. depreciation on replacement equipment
 e. trade-in value of existing equipment
 f. salvage value of existing equipment
 g. salvage value of replacement equipment

LO 2 and 4
Quantitative and Qualitative Factors

9-24 Joe Birley is considering a purchase of a laptop computer. He has a computer at home, but the laptop would allow him to work during his frequent business trips. Joe is trying to convince his boss that the computer would save the company some money. Joe hopes that his company will pay at least part of the computer's purchase price and the monthly fee for an e-mail service. Joe asks you to help him think of all the advantages of buying the computer.

Required:

 a. Prepare an informal schedule of the costs associated with the computer purchase.
 b. Make a two-column list of the quantitative benefits the company will gain if Joe buys the computer (column 1) and those Joe will gain if he buys the laptop computer (column 2).
 c. Make a two-column list of the qualitative benefits the company will gain if Joe buys the laptop computer (column 1) and those Joe will gain if he buys the laptop (column 2).
 d. How much of the computer's cost do you think Joe should pay? How much should Joe's employer pay?

LO 2, 3, and 4
Relevant Cost Schedule

9-25 Marnie Wilkinson is thinking about trading her car for a new one. Her current car is only three years old, completely paid for, but out of warranty. The car's original cost was $22,000. Lately, the car has been somewhat undependable and the repair bills have been quite high. In the last three months, Marnie paid more than $1,200 for repairs. She intends to use her trade-in as the down payment and finance the balance. She is looking at a new Toyota, which she can get for about $23,000, less her trade. Marnie asks you to think of all the relevant advantages and disadvantages of purchasing the new car.

Required:

 a. Prepare an informal schedule listing the relevant quantitative factors Marnie should consider. Do not limit your answer to the items found in the problem. Where possible, try to include estimated dollar amounts in your schedule.
 b. Prepare an informal schedule listing the relevant qualitative factors Marnie should consider.

c. From a quantitative point of view, do you think Marnie should buy the new car?

d. Considering both quantitative and qualitative factors, do you think Marnie should buy the new car?

9-26 Shalisa Buley is a salesperson for Alamo Food Products, Inc. She is considering a 250-mile trip to visit a potential customer, Super Saver. She ponders some factors of that decision.

LO 2, 3, and 4
Relevant Cost
Schedule

Required:

Indicate whether each of the following factors is relevant or irrelevant and explain why:

a. cost of traveling 250 miles to Super Saver

b. time she will spend on the road

c. time she will spend meeting with Super Saver executives

d. time already devoted to the Super Saver account

e. revenue potential from Super Saver

f. cost of her last visit to Super Saver

g. probability that her visit will result in new sales

h. cost of lunch for herself if she visits Super Saver

i. cost of the lunch she would buy for Super Saver's executives

9-27 Managers at Beavers Manufacturing are considering upgrading some production equipment.

LO 2, 3, and 4
Relevant Cost
Schedule

Required:

Indicate whether each of the following factors is a quantitative or qualitative factor:

a. maintenance cost

b. potentially low employee morale because of the possible reduction in the labor force

c. changes in product quality

d. salvage value of the existing equipment

e. cost of replacement equipment

f. difficulty of training employees to use replacement equipment

g. salvage value of the replacement equipment

9-28 Assume that you are deciding whether to live in a campus dormitory room or an off-campus apartment.

LO 2, 3, and 4
Relevant Cost
Schedule

Required:

a. List all the costs that come to mind as you think about this decision.

b. Review your list and indicate which costs are relevant and which are irrelevant to the decision.

c. What are some qualitative factors that you should consider when making this decision?

9-29 Assume that you are considering two alternatives for next summer: attending summer school or touring Europe.

LO 2, 3, and 4
Relevant Cost
Schedule

Required:

a. List all the costs that come to mind as you think about this decision.

b. Review your list and indicate which costs are relevant and which are irrelevant to your decision.

c. What are some qualitative factors that you would consider when making this decision?

LO 5
Determining
Relevant Cost for
Equipment
Replacement

9-30 The managers at Nikolai Manufacturing Company are considering replacing the industrial mixer used in the company's factory.

Information about the existing mixer:

Cost	$28,000
Estimated useful life	10 years
Estimated salvage value	$ 0
Current age	5 years
Estimated current fair value	$ 8,000
Annual operating cost	$15,000

Information about the replacement mixer:

Cost	$40,000
Estimated useful life	5 years
Estimated salvage value	$ 0
Annual operating cost	$12,000

Required:

Prepare a relevant cost schedule showing the benefit of keeping the existing mixer or buying the new one.

LO 5
Determining
Relevant Cost for
Equipment
Replacement

9-31 The managers at Pham-Dang Manufacturing Company are considering replacing the industrial lathe used in the company's factory.

Information about the existing lathe:

Cost	$60,000
Estimated useful life	8 years
Estimated salvage value	$ 0
Current age	2 years
Estimated current fair value	$32,000
Annual operating cost	$32,000

Information about the replacement lathe:

Cost	$60,000
Estimated useful life	6 years
Estimated salvage value	$ 0
Annual operating cost	$24,000

Required:

Prepare a relevant cost schedule showing the benefit of keeping the existing lathe or buying the new one.

LO 5
Determining
Relevant Cost for
Equipment
Replacement

9-32 Jonathan Small, president of Small's Boat Hauling, is considering replacing the company's industrial lift used to haul boats. The new lift would allow the company to lift larger boats out of the water.

Information about the existing lift:

Cost	$ 94,000
Estimated useful life	12 years
Estimated salvage value	$ 10,000
Current age	6 years
Estimated current fair value	$ 48,000
Annual contribution margin	$ 50,000

Information about the replacement lift:

Cost	$120,000
Estimated useful life	6 years
Estimated salvage value	$ 25,000
Annual contribution margin	$ 63,000

Required:

Prepare a relevant cost schedule showing the benefit of keeping the existing lift or buying the new one.

9-33 The managers at Kelly Manufacturing are considering replacing a drill press with a new, high-speed model.

LO 5
Determining
Relevant Cost for
Equipment
Replacement

Information about the existing drill press:

Cost	$260,000
Estimated useful life	10 years
Estimated salvage value	$ 30,000
Annual depreciation	$ 23,000
Current age	3 years
Accumulated depreciation to date	$184,000
Estimated current fair value	$150,000
Annual contribution margin	$110,000

Information about the replacement drill press:

Cost	$540,000
Estimated useful life	7 years
Estimated salvage value	$ 50,000
Annual depreciation	$ 70,000
Annual contribution margin	$160,000

Required:

Prepare a relevant cost schedule showing the benefit of keeping the existing drill press or buying the new one.

9-34 Pipkin Photo Service operates a small camera store in Edmond, Oklahoma. The store has two departments, camera sales and photo finishing. Rent, utilities, and other operating expenses are allocated to the departments based on the square footage they occupy. Currently, the camera sales department occupies 3,000 square feet, and the photo finishing department occupies 2,000 square feet.

LO 5
Determining
Relevant Cost for a
New Department

Pipkin Photo Service's President, Peggy Grace, is thinking about buying a computer system to produce poster prints. The poster print system would occupy 200 square feet of the store's floor space.

Budgeted monthly information for the store:

Store rent	$ 5,000
Salaries and wages	10,500
Utilities	750
Other operating expenses	3,000
Sales	125,000
Cost of goods sold	95,000

Information about the poster print system:

Cost of the poster system	$ 25,700
Estimated useful life	5 years
Estimated salvage value	$ 500
Floor space required	200 square feet
Monthly cost of electricity used by poster system	$ 50

Budgeted monthly amounts:

Poster sales revenue	$ 1,200
Poster supplies	200
Added wages for poster operation	250
Store rent	200
Utilities	32
Other operating expenses	120

After reviewing the preceding information, Peggy believes the company should not buy the poster system because it will show a loss every month. However, she is not sure, so she asks for your advice.

Required:

a. Would the poster system show a loss every month as Grace suggests? Prepare a schedule to substantiate your answer.
b. Would the company's overall monthly profits increase or decrease as a result of buying the poster system? Prepare a schedule to substantiate your answer.
c. Prepare a relevant cost schedule showing the advantage or disadvantage of buying the poster system.

LO 5
Determining Relevant Cost for a New Product

9-35 The Mission Bay Gift Shop operates a small souvenir shop in San Diego, California. The shop has two departments, retail sales and mail order. Rent, utilities, and other operating expenses are allocated to the departments based on the square footage the department occupies. Currently, retail sales occupies 5,000 square feet and mail order occupies 1,000 square feet.

President Aman Vij is considering buying a silk-screen machine to make souvenir T-shirts. The silk-screen machine would occupy 500 square feet of the souvenir shop's floor space.

Budgeted monthly information for the store:	
Store rent	$ 5,100
Salaries and wages	8,500
Utilities	1,000
Other operating expenses	3,000
Sales	80,000
Cost of goods sold	57,000
Information about the silk-screen machine:	
Cost	$ 9,640
Estimated useful life	5 years
Estimated salvage value	$ 400
Floor space required	500 square feet
Monthly cost of electricity used	$ 20
Budgeted monthly amounts:	
T-shirt sales revenue	$ 1,700
Cost of T-shirts	450
Cost of T-shirt supplies	100
Added wages for the T-shirt operation	250
Store rent	425
Utilities	85
Other operating expenses	250

After reviewing the preceding information, Aman believes he should not buy the silk-screen machine because it will show a loss every month. Because he is unsure, he seeks your advice.

Required:

a. Would the silk-screen machine show a loss every month as Aman suggests? Prepare a schedule to substantiate your answer.
b. Would the company's overall monthly profits increase or decrease as a result of buying the silk-screen machine? Prepare a schedule to substantiate your answer.
c. Prepare a relevant cost schedule showing the advantage or disadvantage of buying the silk-screen machine.

LO 5
Determining Relevant Cost for Equipment Replacement

9-36 Yang's Auto Parts purchased a forklift five years ago for $15,000. When it was purchased the forklift had an estimated useful life of 10 years and a salvage value of $3,000. The forklift can be sold now for $6,000. The operating cost for the forklift is

$4,500 per year. Yang is thinking about buying a replacement forklift. It would cost $20,000. The newer model would have an estimated useful life of 5 years and a salvage value of $7,000. The operating cost for the newer forklift would be $3,000 per year.

Required:

a. What are the relevant costs associated with the decision to replace the forklift?
b. Prepare a relevant cost schedule showing the advantage or disadvantage of buying the forklift.

9-37 Eric Swenton of Swenton Engineering is considering whether to purchase a new copy machine. He purchased the existing machine 2 years ago for $8,500. When it was purchased, it had an estimated useful life of 8 years and a salvage value of $500. The operating cost of the existing machine is $3,000 per year, and it can be sold today for $2,000. A replacement machine can be bought today for $10,000 and would have an estimated useful life of 6 years with a salvage value of $1,000. The operating cost of the replacement copy machine is expected to be $1,500 per year.

LO 5
Determining Relevant Cost for Equipment Replacement

Required:

a. Prepare a schedule showing all the costs associated with the existing copy machine.
b. Prepare a schedule showing all the costs associated with the replacement copy machine.
c. Prepare a schedule showing the relevant cost of the copy machine replacement decision and the favored alternative.
d. Discuss the qualitative factors Eric should consider.
e. Would you buy the replacement copy machine? Explain your reasoning.

9-38 Joe Anzelmo is considering whether to replace one of his delivery trucks. He purchased the existing delivery truck 4 years ago for $24,000, and it came with a 3-year, 75,000-mile warranty. When purchased, the current truck had an estimated useful life of 5 years and a salvage value of $2,000. Joe uses the straight-line method for depreciation. The replacement truck would be identical to the current truck, except it would be new and would have the new-truck warranty. The operating cost for the current truck is $4,000 for fuel, $23,200 for the driver's salary, and maintenance cost is about $5,000 per year. If Joe keeps the old truck, it will last another 5 years, but would require the $5,000 in maintenance each year. The existing truck can be sold now for $4,000, or it can be sold in 5 years for $1,000. The replacement truck would cost $25,500, has an estimated useful life of 5 years, and can be sold at the end of the 5 years for $4,000. At the end of the warranty period, the replacement truck will require maintenance of $5,000 per year.

LO 5
Determining Relevant Cost for Equipment Replacement

Required:

a. Prepare a schedule showing all the costs associated with the existing truck.
b. Prepare a schedule showing all the costs associated with the replacement truck.
c. Prepare a schedule showing the relevant cost of the truck replacement decision and the favored alternative.
d. Discuss the qualitative factors that Joe should consider.
e. If the old truck had an estimated useful life of 5 years when it was purchased and it has already been used for 4 years, discuss the ramifications of using the truck for another 5 years.
f. Would you buy the new truck? Why or why not?

9-39 Jack Gordy is considering whether to replace a piece of production equipment with a new model. The replacement machine would cost $170,000, have an 8-year life, and no salvage value. The variable cost of operating the machine would be $180,000 per year. The existing machine was purchased one year ago and could be used for the next 8 years. When it was purchased, the existing machine had an estimated useful life

LO 5
Determining Relevant Cost for Equipment Replacement

of 9 years and no salvage value. The existing machine can be sold now for $28,000, but will have no salvage value in 8 years. The variable cost of operating the existing machine is $200,000.

Required:

   a. Prepare a schedule showing the costs associated with the existing machine.
   b. Prepare a schedule showing the costs associated with the replacement machine.
   c. Prepare a schedule showing the relevant cost of the equipment replacement decision and the favored alternative.
   d. Discuss the qualitative factors that Jack should consider.

LO 5
Relevant Cost of a Purchase Decision

9-40 David Strawn is in the process of buying a house. He is interested in two houses: an urban house 2 miles from his work and a rural house 34 miles from work. Surprisingly, the houses are nearly identical, except the closer house is more expensive. The urban house is $127,000, while the rural house is only $109,000. Maintenance, taxes, insurance, and other costs would be the same for both houses.

David goes to work about 250 days each year. He has just traded his old car for a new one. Each time his car reaches 80,000 miles, David trades it for a new model. Generally, he expects to pay about $20,000 when he trades for a new car. His cars usually get about 20 miles per gallon of regular, $1.50-per-gallon gasoline. Maintenance on his car runs about $0.05 per mile on average. In addition to driving to and from work, David drives about 15,000 miles each year.

Regardless of which house David buys, he expects that he will be transferred to another state in 5 years. He is about to buy the less expensive house when he seeks your advice.

Required:

   a. Which house should David choose?
   b. How much will David save if he follows your advice? (Disregard the time value of money.)
   c. What qualitative factors should David consider?

LO 5
Relevant Cost of a Make-or-Buy Decision

9-41 Universal Products is considering buying the casters it uses in the manufacture of office chairs from an outside vendor. Currently, Universal makes the casters in its own manufacturing facility. Universal can buy the casters for $1.15 each. The company uses 450,000 casters each year. Information about Universal's cost to manufacture the 450,000 casters follows:

	Per Unit	Total
Direct material	$ .50	$225,000
Direct labor	.10	45,000
Variable overhead	.40	180,000
Fixed overhead	.25	112,500
Total	$1.25	$562,500

Fixed costs for Universal would not change if the company stopped making the casters.

Required:

Prepare a relevant cost schedule indicating whether Universal Products should buy the casters or continue to make them.

9-42 Smokey Bear Manufacturing is considering buying the mounting brackets it uses with its fire extinguishers from an outside supplier. Currently, Smokey Bear makes the brackets in its manufacturing facility. Smokey Bear can buy the brackets for $0.75 each. The company uses 700,000 brackets each year.

Information about Smokey Bear's cost to manufacture the 700,000 brackets follows:

LO 5
Relevant Cost of a Make-or-Buy Decision

	Per Unit	Total
Direct material	$0.30	$210,000
Direct labor	0.10	70,000
Variable overhead	0.40	280,000
Fixed overhead	0.14	98,000
Total	$ .94	$658,000

Fixed costs for Smokey Bear would not change if the company stopped making the brackets.

Required:

Prepare a relevant cost schedule indicating whether Smokey Bear Manufacturing should buy the brackets or continue to make them.

9-43 Jumbo Chinese Restaurants operates a small laundry facility to launder the uniforms, tablecloths, and other linens its restaurant chain uses. Jumbo's laundry operation occupies space in an industrial area near the company's home office and largest restaurant. Jumbo is considering outsourcing its laundry service. Jumbo's $180,000 administrative expense is allocated based on the number of employees. Jumbo employs 90 people. Information about the laundry facilities follows:

LO 5
Relevant Cost of an Outsourcing Decision

Direct cost information:

Wages for 2 employees	$38,000
Cost of equipment	$ 7,500
Scrap value of the equipment	500
Building rent per year	3,000
Utilities	2,000
Miscellaneous cost	1,500
Original estimated useful life of equipment	5 years
Estimated remaining equipment life	1 year

Indirect cost information:

Administrative expense	$ 4,000

An outside laundry service has offered to provide Jumbo's laundering services for $50,000 per year. The fee is guaranteed for one year. If the offer is accepted, Jumbo will scrap the laundry equipment and close down its laundry operation completely.

Required:

The president of Jumbo has asked you to prepare a report that details the qualitative and quantitative factors that should be considered in deciding whether or not to close the laundry operation. Your report should discuss the relevant qualitative and quantitative factors for each alternative and include a relevant cost schedule. Your report should conclude with a well-supported recommended course of action.

LO 5
Relevant Cost of an Outsourcing Decision

9-44　Daniel's Delivery Service operates a small auto repair facility to service its fleet of 35 delivery vehicles. Daniel's repair facility occupies space in an industrial area close to the company's home office. Daniel is considering using a local repair shop to service its vehicles. The $120,000 administrative expense is allocated based on the number of employees, which is 50. Information about the repair facility follows:

Direct cost information:	
Wages for 3 employees	$64,000
Cost of equipment used	33,500
Building rent per year	6,000
Utilities	2,000
Cost of automobile parts	30,000
Miscellaneous cost	1,500
Original estimated useful life of equipment	12 years
Estimated remaining useful life of equipment	9 years
Indirect cost information:	
Administrative expense	$ 7,200

A dependable automotive service center has offered to provide maintenance contracts on each vehicle for $3,000 per vehicle per year. If Daniel accepts the offer, he would close the maintenance facility. The company estimates that it can sell the maintenance equipment for $10,000.

Required:

Daniel has asked you to prepare a report detailing the qualitative and quantitative factors he should considered in making the decision about whether to close the maintenance facility. Your report should discuss the relevant qualitative and quantitative factors for each alternative, include a relevant cost schedule, and conclude with a well-supported recommendation.

LO 4, 5, and 6
Relevant Cost and Qualitative Factors of a Special-Order Decision

9-45　Gulick Manufacturing produces 22,000 rubber engine mounts each year for use in its electric cart manufacturing plant. The engine mounts have an excellent reputation for strength and durability. At a production level of 22,000, the per-unit cost is as follows:

Direct material	$ .53
Direct labor	1.45
Variable overhead	.92
Fixed overhead	1.27
Total	$4.17

A competitor, Ngozi Cart Company, is interested in purchasing 14,000 rubber engine mounts from Gulick. Ngozi has offered to pay $4.17 each for the engine mounts. Gulick Manufacturing has the capacity and can easily manufacture the engine mounts for Ngozi. Several Gulick managers are concerned, however, that Gulick would receive no financial benefit if the engine mounts are sold at cost.

Required:

a. Prepare a schedule detailing the advantage or disadvantage of selling the 14,000 engine mounts to Ngozi.
b. Discuss the qualitative aspects of selling the parts to Ngozi.

9-46 Lee Gas Grill Company produces 300,000 RV22 propane gas regulator and valve assemblies each year for use in its gas grill factory. The company's gas grills are known for quality and have a reputation of lasting a lifetime. At 300,000 units per year, the per-unit cost is as follows:

LO 4, 5, and 6
Relevant Cost and Qualitative Factors of a Special-Order Decision

Direct material	$ 3.02
Direct labor	2.44
Variable overhead	1.20
Fixed overhead	5.60
Total	$12.26

A competitor, Econo Grill, is interested in purchasing 80,000 RV22 assemblies from Lee. Econo Grill has offered to pay $12.30 per unit. Lee has the capacity and can easily manufacture the parts for Econo Grill. Several Lee managers are concerned that Lee would receive little if any financial benefit if the RV22 assemblies are sold for $12.30 each.

Required:

a. Prepare a schedule detailing the advantage or disadvantage of selling the 80,000 RV22 assemblies to Econo Grill.
b. Discuss the qualitative aspects of selling the parts to Econo Grill.

9-47 Stewart Marine Cable Company produces 400,000 feet of SS316 cable each year. At 400,000 feet per year, the cost per foot is as follows:

LO 4, 5, and 6
Relevant Cost and Qualitative Factors of a Special-Order Decision

Direct material	$ .32
Direct labor	.14
Variable overhead	.08
Fixed overhead	.73
Total	$1.27

A new customer, Garcia Marine, is interested in purchasing 175,000 feet of SS316 cable from Stewart. Garcia has offered to pay $0.92 per foot for the cable. Stewart has the capacity and can easily manufacture the cable for Garcia. Kyle Stewart, president of Stewart Marine Cable, does not understand how the sales manager can expect him to accept this losing offer.

Required:

a. Prepare a schedule that details the advantage or disadvantage of selling the 175,000 feet of cable to Garcia Marine.
b. What if Stewart could produce the order, but it would require purchasing a $20,000 machine that would last 5 years with no salvage value. Should Stewart accept the order?

9-48 Davenport Corporation manufactures camping equipment. One of Davenport's most popular products is its T1012 tent, which the company sells for $30 each. Davenport sells about 9,000 T1012 tents each year through its mail order business. Another camping equipment company, TreeClimb Corporation, has approached Davenport about purchasing 2,000 T1012 tents. The tents would be the same as the T1012 except they would bear the TreeClimb brand. TreeClimb is willing to pay $20 per tent. Although Davenport has plenty of plant capacity to produce the additional 2,000 tents, the company's manufacturing cost is $20 per unit.

LO 4, 5, and 6
Relevant Cost and Qualitative Factors of a Special-Order Decision

The following per-unit information pertains to Davenport's cost to produce 9,000 T1012 tents.

Direct material	$ 9
Direct labor	4
Variable manufacturing overhead	2
Fixed manufacturing overhead	5
Total	$20

Required:

a. By what amount would Davenport's operating income increase or decrease if the company accepts the special order?
b. Discuss the qualitative aspects of this special-order decision.

LO 4, 5, and 6
Relevant Cost and Qualitative Factors of a Special-Order Decision

9-49   Refer to Exercise 9-48. Assume that Davenport would have to purchase an additional sewing machine to accept the special order from TreeClimb. The cost of the new sewing machine is $2,500, and it would last for two years.

Required:

By what amount would Davenport's operating income increase or decrease if the company accepts the special order under these circumstances?

LO 5
Relevant Cost of a Special-Order Decision

9-50   Hi-Cast Corporation manufactures fishing rods. Part of Hi-Cast's sales success comes from a patented material, tuflex, used to make the fishing rods. Tuflex allows the fishing rods to be very flexible, yet nearly unbreakable. Hi-Cast sells about 150,000 fishing rods annually to wholesalers for $18 each. A major chain, Pro Trout, is interested in purchasing 30,000 fishing rods that would bear the Pro Trout brand name. Pro Trout is willing to pay $9 per fishing rod, half of the normal selling price. Although Hi-Cast has plenty of plant capacity available to make the additional 30,000 fishing rods, the company's manufacturing cost is $11 per fishing rod, or $2 more per rod than Pro Trout is willing to pay. Pro Trout has indicated that the 30,000 fishing rods do not have to be as flexible and tough as the regular Hi-Cast rods.

The following per unit information pertains to Hi-Cast's cost to product 150,000 fishing rods:

Direct Materials:	
Tuflex	$ 4
Other material	1
Direct labor	3
Variable manufacturing overhead	1
Fixed manufacturing overhead	2
Total	$11

If fiberglass is used in place of tuflex, the direct material cost can be reduced by $2 per rod.

Required:

By what amount would Hi-Cast's operating income increase or decrease if the company accepts the special order?

9-51 Ace Equipment Company makes high-pressure pumps. Ace makes 10,000 V1 valve assemblies per year for use in production. The manufacturing facilities used to make the V1 valves are used to produce a variety of other subassemblies and products. Accordingly, no special production equipment is needed to make the V1 valves. The production cost for V1 valve assemblies is as follows:

LO 4, 5, and 6
Relevant Cost and Qualitative Factors of a Make-or-Buy Decision

Direct material	$ 55,000
Direct labor	140,000
Variable manufacturing overhead	70,000
Fixed manufacturing overhead	210,000
Total	$475,000

Sure Flow Valve Company has offered to supply the V1 valve assemblies to Ace for $32 each.

Required:

a. Prepare a schedule that shows whether Ace should buy the valves from Sure Flow, or continue to make them.

b. Discuss the qualitative factors that Ace should consider in this make-or-buy decision.

9-52 Refer to Exercise 9-51. Assume Ace could use the manufacturing facilities that are no longer needed to make the V1 valves to produce a new line of small pumps. The small pumps would provide a contribution margin of $60,000.

LO 4, 5, and 6
Relevant Cost and Qualitative Factors of an Outsourcing Decision

Required:

a. Prepare a schedule that shows whether Ace should buy the valves from Sure Flow or continue to make them.

b. Discuss the qualitative factors that Ace should consider in this make-or-buy decision.

9-53 General Manufacturing Company makes residential aluminum windows. A company can supply General with the window-crank assembly it needs for $3.50 each. General uses 50,000 crank assemblies each year. The machinery used to make the window cranks is used to produce a variety of other subassemblies and products.

LO 4, 5, and 6
Relevant Cost and Qualitative Factors of a Make-or-Buy Decision

The following details the production cost for the window-crank assemblies:

Direct material	$ 70,000
Direct labor	40,000
Variable manufacturing overhead	55,000
Fixed manufacturing overhead	35,000
Total	$200,000

Required:

a. Prepare a schedule that shows the relevant cost and the preferred alternative of this make-or-buy decision.

b. Discuss the qualitative factors that General should consider when deciding whether to buy the window cranks from an outside supplier.

9-54 Hutchens Electric produces electric fans. Hutchens manufactures 19,000 small electric fan motors each year. Dalta Motor Company has offered to supply Hutchens with the small electric motors for $12.50 each. The facility that Hutchens uses to make

LO 4, 5, and 6
Relevant Cost and Qualitative Factors of an Outsourcing Decision

the small motors is also used to make larger motors and other components. Following are Hutchens' production costs for the small electric fan motors:

Direct material	$132,000
Direct labor	26,500
Variable manufacturing overhead	43,500
Fixed manufacturing overhead	77,500
Total	$279,500

Required:

a. Prepare a schedule that shows whether Hutchens Electric should outsource the electric fan motors or continue to make them.

b. Discuss the qualitative factors that Hutchens should consider when making this make-or-buy decision.

LO 4, 5, and 6
Relevant Cost and Qualitative Factors of an Outsourcing Decision

9-55   Refer to Exercise 9-54. Assume that Hutchens Electric can use the facilities freed up by purchasing the electric motors from Dalta Motor Company to produce a new model fan that would have a contribution margin of $95,000.

Required:

a. Prepare a relevant cost schedule that shows whether Hutchens Electric should buy the electric fan motors or continue to make them.

b. Discuss the qualitative factors that Hutchens should consider when making this make-or-buy decision.

LO 4, 5, and 6
Relevant Cost and Qualitative Factors of an Outsourcing Decision

9-56   Nunez Inc. requires 12,000 units of part X45 per year. At the current level of production, the cost per unit is as follows:

Direct material	$ 3
Direct labor	1
Variable overhead	2
Fixed overhead	4
Total	$ 10

JLW Inc. has offered to sell Nunez 12,000 units of X45 for $8 each. If Nunez is no longer required to produce the X45s, a supervisor's position can be eliminated. The supervisor's salary of $24,000 is part of fixed overhead cost. Other fixed overhead costs would remain the same.

Required:

a. Prepare a schedule detailing the advantage or disadvantage of buying the 12,000 units of X45 from JLW Inc.

b. Discuss the qualitative aspects of purchasing the parts from JLW Inc.

LO 4, 5, and 6
Relevant Cost and Qualitative Factors of an Outsourcing Decision

9-57   Cox Inc. requires 300 spindles per year. At the current level of production, the cost per unit is as follows:

Direct material	$ 38
Direct labor	12
Variable overhead	14
Fixed overhead	44
Total	$ 108

AMW Inc. has offered to sell Cox the 300 spindles for $100 each. If Cox no longer has to produce the spindles, a supervisor's position can be eliminated. The supervisor's salary of $36,000 is part of fixed overhead cost. Other fixed overhead costs would remain the same.

Required:

a. Prepare a schedule that details the advantage or disadvantage of buying the 300 spindles from AMW Inc.

b. Discuss the qualitative aspects of purchasing the parts from AMW Inc.

9-58 Adcox Inc. requires 4,000 switch assemblies per year. At the current level of production, the cost per unit is as follows:

LO 4, 5, and 6
Relevant Cost and
Qualitative Factors
of an Outsourcing
Decision

Direct material	$ 3
Direct labor	3
Variable overhead	2
Fixed overhead	$ 2
Total	$ 10

Camron Inc. has offered to sell Adcox the 4,000 switch assemblies for $9 each. If Adcox no longer has to produce the switch assemblies, part of the building can be leased to another company for $10,000 per year. Other fixed overhead costs would remain the same.

Required:

a. Prepare a schedule detailing the advantage or disadvantage of buying the 4,000 switch assemblies from Camron.

b. Discuss the qualitative aspects of purchasing the parts from Camron.

9-59 Ed Smart is preparing a schedule of relevant costs relating to the acquisition of a replacement machine. Ed properly shows the cost of the existing machine as a sunk cost and treats it as irrelevant to the decision. On reviewing the schedule, Ed's boss wants Ed to treat the cost of the existing equipment as an additional operating cost of the existing equipment when comparing relevant costs of the existing and the replacement equipment. If Ed reports the information in this manner it will change the decision to benefit the purchase of the replacement equipment.

Ethics Case

Required:

Can you identify one reason why Ed's boss would make such a request? (Hint: Why might Ed's boss want to be certain of the new purchase?)

CHAPTER 10

LEARNING OBJECTIVES

After completing this chapter you should be able to:

1 Discuss some of the benefits of the operating budget.

2 Compare and contrast various approaches to preparing and using the operating budget.

3 Construct the three budgeted financial statements contained in the operating budget and the other budget schedules that support the budgeted financial statements.

4 Demonstrate the role of the sales forecast in the budgeting process.

5 Prepare the budgets included in the operating budget.

6 Integrate the operating budget into the overall management process.

7 Analyze budget variances.

Internal Planning and Measurement Tools

In Chapter 3, Megan prepared a preliminary budget to gather information about Elevation Sports, Inc. and to perform break-even analysis so that the investors could make investment decisions. As a business continues, management uses this kind of budgeting process to chart the organization's success. Managers in *Fortune* 500 companies such as Motorola Company and General Motors recognize that they achieve better results by involving all managers and employees in the budgeting process. Although your position may be far removed from the accounting department, you will very likely be involved in the budgeting process early in your career.

The operating budget, or master budget, is the plan for a firm's operating activities for a specified period of time. The budget process begins with sales forecasts, which lead to production and purchasing budgets, selling and administrative budgets, and a cash budget, all of which culminate in forecasted financial statements. Unlike the actual financial statements you have prepared and analyzed, forecasted or pro forma financial statements estimate what may happen in the future instead of what actually happened from past transactions. Because they forecast the future, the forecasted financial statements become the target of the planning and budgeting process.

Visit the ***www.prenhall.com/terrell*** Web site to view the "McDonald's Flexible Budgets" video.

● **operating budget**
The plan for a firm's operating activities for a specified period of time. Also called a **master budget**.

● **forecasted financial statements**
Financial statements that estimate what may happen in the future instead of what actually happened from past transactions. Also called **pro forma financial statements**.

Benefits of Budgeting

A well-prepared operating budget can create four benefits for the company. First, budgeting serves as a guide. Second, it assists the organization in its resource allocation. Third, it encourages communication and coordination within the organization. Fourth, it sets performance standards, or benchmarks, for achievement.

Let's explore each of these in greater detail.

Serves as a Guide

The operating budget should serve as a guide for a company to follow during the budget period. Notice that we used the term *guide*. A business is dynamic and change occurs rapidly at times. A business must remain flexible and open to opportunities—therefore, management should adjust its budget when desirable or necessary.

To illustrate, suppose Elevation Sports budgeted for forecasted sales revenue of $250,000 for the first three months of 2004. Business was better than expected and sales for January and February were $270,000. Should the company close the retail shop or the factory during March, historically its best month of the first quarter, because it made more than expected? Of course not. Or suppose Jon has the opportunity to purchase 500 sets of bindings at a bargain price because the company who makes them wants to increase its sales. This will lower the company's cost of production by $2 per board. Should Jon bypass this opportunity because the special purchase is not in the budget? As long as the company has the money to buy the bindings and will use them in the near future, Jon should take advantage of this opportunity.

In many organizations, especially government and not-for-profit organizations, management views the budget as static or unchangeable. In some organizations meeting the budget becomes the primary business objective. An unwillingness to adjust a budget based on new information is often detrimental to the company because management misses opportunities and makes poor decisions.

Assists in Resource Allocation

All organizations have scarce resources. No company can afford to do everything it desires, or even everything it needs to do, within a given time period. A budget can help management decide where to allocate its limited resources. The budgeting process may uncover potential bottlenecks and allow managers to address these issues as the budget is being prepared rather than as problems occur during the year. Suppose that the production increases in Jon's plant to the point where he is having problems getting everything produced on time. In the budgeting process, Jon produces Exhibit 10-1 to outline the problem.

As you can see from Exhibit 10-1, each snowboard requires three processes. The maximum number of finished units of product the company can produce per day is 20 because it can decorate only 20 boards per day in Process B. Jon could increase the capacity of Process A from 50 boards per day to 150 per day and the company still could produce only 20 finished units per day because of the restriction caused by Process B. Process B is the bottleneck in the company's production process.

Exhibit 10-1
Elevation Sports, Inc. Example of Production Bottleneck

Process A: Cutting and Sanding Board	
Maximum per day	50
Process B: Decorating Board	
Maximum per day	20
Process C: Final Assembly with Bindings	
Maximum per day	150

Process A: Cutting and Sanding Board	
Maximum per day	50
Process B: Decorating Board	
Maximum per day	20
Plus transfer from Process C	30
Maximum per day	50
Process C: Final Assembly with Bindings	
Maximum per day	150
Less transfer to Process B	(75)
Maximum per day	75

Suppose that Jon can move some people and a particular piece of equipment from Process C to Process B. That change will reduce the capacity of Process C by 75 units per day, but the capacity of Process B will increase by 30 units per day as reflected in Exhibit 10-2. As you can see by looking at Exhibit 10-2, Elevation Sports has increased its capacity to produce finished units by 250 percent (from 20 units to 50 units) without adding any additional machinery to its operation. This is a cost-efficient use of equipment and labor to both increase productivity and reduce the per-unit cost of the product.

The issue of resource allocation is important for a merchandising business as well. For example, December, January, and March are the busiest months for the retail outlet in Vail. Rob will be so busy that he will need extra workers. During the slower months, the officers can help in the retail shop during peak hours. In these three months, however, they are very busy filling Internet and wholesale orders and operating the production plant. If Rob knows this in advance, he will have time to hire the needed workers at the least cost so he can offer quality service and sell more products. In contrast, if Rob does not plan for the busy months, he will find himself understaffed and unable to provide quality, timely service. The budgeting process helps Rob make good decisions about how to allocate company resources.

Fosters Communication and Coordination

As managers from different functional areas in an organization work together to prepare the budget, they gain a better understanding of the entire business. When managers from all areas of the company learn of difficulties facing others and spot duplication of effort, the firm can both solve problems and coordinate efforts more effectively. With our small snowboard company, the coordination and cooperation improves somewhat when the officers work together during the budgeting process. In a large manufacturing operation, however, managers of departments, who otherwise interact infrequently, work together during the budgeting process. In learning about each other's needs for resources and costs of operations, they gain a broader perspective of the company's overall production process rather than continuing to focus only on their part of the process. Managers are forced to communicate with one another and to better coordinate their efforts.

Establishes Performance Standards

As managers prepare budgets for their companies, they must estimate performance levels they both desire and can attain. If a company's actual sales, for example, are less than its budgeted sales for a particular period, the sales manager should review the deficit and determine why the variance occurred. Performance standards introduce accountability into all levels of an organization and become benchmarks against which firms can compare the actual results. Standard costs are a perfect example of

● **budget variances**
Differences between the actual
results and the budget.

benchmarks or performance standards. Differences between the actual results and the budget are called **budget variances**. When variances occur, managers can explore reasons for the variances and make improvements. The improvements may focus on individual or group performance, the budgeting process, or both.

Now let's turn our attention to different approaches to budgeting.

Different Approaches to Budgeting

Not all companies or industries use the same approach to the budget process. The approach depends on the needs of the business and its managerial philosophy. Because it is so highly influenced by the managerial style of its top leaders and its accounting system software, the budgeting process is unique to each business entity. We will investigate seven of the most common budgeting approaches: perpetual, incremental, zero-based, top-down, bottom-up, imposed, and participative.

Perpetual Budgeting

● **perpetual budgeting**
A budgeting approach management
uses so that as one month ends,
another month's budget is added to
the end of the budget so that, at any
time, the budget projects 12 months
into the future. Also called **rolling
budgeting**.

Some companies continually update their operating budgets. When management uses **perpetual budgeting**, or **rolling budgeting**, as one month ends, another month's budget is added to the end of the budget so that, at any given time, the budget projects 12 months into the future.

The main advantage of perpetual budgeting is that it spreads the workload for budget preparation evenly over the year, allowing employees to incorporate budgeting into their normal monthly work schedule. Another advantage is that the budget always extends 12 months into the future, instead of decreasing from 12 months to 1 month at the end of each budget cycle.

One disadvantage of perpetual budgeting may be that the budget preparation process becomes so routine that employees lose the creativity required to look for better ways to operate. Another disadvantage is that many managers feel overburdened with daily responsibilities. Adding the responsibility of preparing a perpetual budget to a heavy workload can lead to ineffective budgeting.

Incremental Budgeting

● **incremental budgeting**
The process of using the prior year's
budget or the company's actual
results to build the new operating
budget.

Incremental budgeting is the process of using the prior year's budget or the company's actual results to build the new operating budget. If, for example, a company's 2002 budget included $100,000 for maintenance and repairs on the equipment in its plant, $100,000 becomes the starting point for this item in preparing the 2003 budget. The only question to be answered is whether the company needs to include more or less than $100,000 for repairs and maintenance in 2003. Government entities, such as the federal government, and many companies use this budgeting approach. One way to implement the new budget is to mandate a 10 percent decrease or 5 percent increase in last year's budget. Therefore, the new budget amount totals $90,000 (a 10 percent decrease) or $105,000 (a 5 percent increase)—regardless of the actual amount needed for 2003.

The trouble with the incremental budgeting approach is that if the prior year's budget included unnecessary costs, or items that did not optimize performance, this waste may be simply rolled over into the next year's budget. Some managers feel obligated to spend the current budget, regardless of whether the expense is necessary, because if the manager does not spend the current budget, he fears superiors will reduce next year's budget. This is the "use it or lose it" philosophy. The advantage to this approach is its simplicity. Some practitioners and many experts, however, believe the disadvantages greatly outweigh the advantages.

What Do You Think?

10-1 Why would a manager feel obligated to spend the full amount of a budgeted expense regardless of its necessity?

10-2 In what ways, if any, do you think the federal government's use of incremental budgeting contributes to the national debt?

Zero-Based Budgeting

An alternative to the incremental budgeting approach is zero-based budgeting. Managers using **zero-based budgeting** start from zero when preparing a new budget, and they must justify each item on the budget every year as though it were a new budget item. Zero-based budgeting requires more effort than incremental budgeting, but many organizations believe the results are worth that time and effort because managers are forced to reexamine the items included in the budget and justify their continuation.

● **zero-based budgeting**
An approach to budgeting where managers start from zero when preparing a new budget, and they must justify each item on the budget every year as though it were a new budget item.

Top-Down and Bottom-Up Budgeting

Budget information for a firm can flow either from the upper level managers down to managers and employees at lower levels, or the other way around. For obvious reasons, the former approach is known as top-down budgeting and the latter approach is known as bottom-up budgeting. Each of these two approaches has distinct advantages and disadvantages.

Top-Down Budgeting

In **top-down budgeting** senior executives prepare the budget, and lower level managers and employees work to meet that budget. The top-down approach has several advantages. The company's senior executives know the most about the firm's overall operations, strategic planning, and goals, so they will prepare the budget with company goals in mind. The top-down budgeting approach involves fewer people, so it causes fewer disruptions, takes less time, and is more efficient than the bottom-up approach. The top-down approach to budgeting, however, also has two disadvantages. First, lower level managers and employees are less accepting of budgets when they have no part in setting them. Second, top managers may know the goals and strategic plans for the enterprise, but they do not always have the working knowledge of daily activities needed to prepare the detailed budgets for all company activities.

● **top-down budgeting**
An approach to budgeting in which senior executives prepare the budget, and lower level managers and employees work to meet that budget.

A typical publicly traded company in the United States uses some element of top-down budgeting. Why? The firm's top management has a responsibility to maximize returns for stockholders in the form of increased market prices of the stock even more than dividends. Company profits have the greatest influence on the selling price of a company's stock. To ensure maximum stock appreciation, therefore, senior executives must manage the company to perform at its peak profitability. In top-down budgeting, the target profit figures become the starting and ending points of the budgeting process.

Traditionally, most firms that used top-down budgeting also used an imposed budgeting process. An **imposed budget** is one for which upper management sets amounts for all operating activities with little possibility of negotiation. No matter how unreasonable the budget numbers are, senior management expects all other managers to abide by them. This type of budgeting process can do more harm than good because different groups in the organization may be working at cross purposes. Today, however, not all top-down budgets are imposed budgets.

● **imposed budget**
A budget for which upper management sets budget amounts for all operating activities with little possibility of negotiation.

Bottom-Up Budgeting

● **bottom-up budgeting**
An approach to budgeting for which lower level managers and employees prepare the initial budget.

In **bottom-up budgeting**, lower level managers and employees prepare the initial budget. For example, members of the sales force prepare the sales schedule for their own sales territories. The sales manager then reviews these sales schedules, makes any necessary changes, and combines them to form the overall company sales schedule. Likewise, employees in the production facility prepare schedules for production, including schedules for direct material, direct labor, and manufacturing overhead. All the budget data flows upward from each segment of the company to the accounting or budget department where budget specialists compile the data into usable information.

Bottom-up budgeting has three main advantages. First, the budget may be more realistic than if senior managers prepared it. If lower level managers and employees take the process seriously, they are more likely to create an operating budget based on accurate, realistic information. Second, lower level managers and employees are more likely to work toward budgeted performance standards because they helped to set those standards. Third, as employees prepare the budget, they envision the company's goals, consider how various activities may affect the future, and assess their own participation. In short, they begin to think long term.

Bottom-up budgeting, however, has two disadvantages. First, employees at every level must make time to prepare, review, revise, and approve the budget. Employees may perceive this as an unwanted interruption in their daily activities. Second, some employees may be tempted to prepare a budget that underestimates performance and overestimates costs so that the department will easily outperform the budget.

Participative and Imposed Budgeting

● **participative budget**
A budget approach in which managers and employees at many levels of the company are engaged in setting performance standards and preparing the budget.

● **empower**
To give employees the authority to make decisions concerning their job responsibilities, including decisions about items in the operating budget.

Bottom-up budgeting is always a participative budgeting process. A **participative budget** approach is one in which managers and employees at many levels of the company are engaged in setting performance standards and preparing the budget. Although a bottom-up budget process will always be participative, a top-down budget can be either imposed or participative. In recent years, top executives discovered they could empower employees by allowing them more participation in the budgeting process. To **empower** employees means to give them the authority to make decisions concerning their job responsibilities, including decisions about items in the operating budget.

A company committed to both top-down budgeting and empowering employees must combine the top-down and bottom-up approaches to budgeting. Rather than having all budget information flow from the top down, senior managers provide profit targets to lower level managers. The lower level managers prepare the operating budget for their functional areas using the profit targets provided by senior management.

What Do You Think?

10-3   What positive results do you think come from more employee empowerment:

    (a) for the firm as a whole? Explain your reasoning.
    (b) for managers and employees? Explain your reasoning.

10-4   What negative results do you think come from more employee empowerment:

    (a) for the firm as a whole? Explain your reasoning.
    (b) for managers and employees? Explain your reasoning.

When the lower level managers cannot meet the profit requirements of senior managers, we see the real distinction between participative and imposed budget approaches. If the profit requirement is negotiable, the process is participative. When the profit requirement is nonnegotiable, the process is imposed. The key to making a top-down budget a participative budget is upper management's ability and willingness to negotiate and compromise.

What Do You Think?

10-5 If you were the CEO of your company, would you prefer a top-down or bottom-up budgeting process? Why?

10-6 If you were in middle management, would you prefer a top-down or bottom-up budgeting process? Why?

10-7 If you were the CEO, do you think it would be wise for you to spend time tending to the details of the various budgets, given all your other responsibilities?

The overall approach a company takes to preparing its operating budget may actually be a combination of several of the approaches discussed here. For example, one company may have a top-down, participative, zero-based budgeting approach. Another company may be committed to an incremental, participative, bottom-up, perpetual budgeting philosophy. The object is not to select one particular approach from a laundry list. Rather, managers must approach the preparation of the operating budget in a way that makes sense in their circumstances.

Building the Operations Budget

Far more complex than the simple budget of cash inflows and outflows we prepare personally, the business operating budget is a set of forecasted financial statements that includes the balance sheet, income statement, and statement of cash flows. This is true regardless of whether the business is a manufacturer, a merchandiser, or a service company. The budget, however, includes several supporting schedules that provide the necessary information to complete the budgeted financial statements.

The Sales Forecast

The **sales forecast** is the prediction of sales for the budget period. It is the cornerstone of the budgeting process because all other budgets depend on the amount of forecasted sales. Sales become the basis for the cost of goods sold, the amount of purchases or production required, the amount of the selling and administrative expenses, and ultimately net income. If the sales forecast is unrealistic, the budget will be unrealistic.

● **sales forecast**
The prediction of sales for the budget period.

Even with the most careful predictions, however, many factors can influence the accuracy of the sales forecast as a year or more progresses. It is critical for managers to scan the external environment during strategic planning to help protect the company against four factors that most influence sales: the general economy, industry conditions, competitors' actions, and technological developments. Changes in any of these factors can affect the accuracy of the sales forecast. For that reason, managers should disseminate economic, industrial, and technological information throughout the sales organization.

Polaroid Corporation is a perfect example of a company that lost its market due to technology and competitive pressures. Polaroid pictures were the only type that could be developed instantly from the 1950s to 1975. Its technology was unique and used by both consumers for personal pictures and professional photographers to check lighting and to get previews. Around 1975 Eastman Kodak Company decided to challenge Polaroid and created its own instant picture camera and film. The challenge cost both Polaroid and Kodak a lot of money, but Polaroid prevailed and once again was the king of instant pictures. Consumers, however, were not happy about using a Polaroid camera for all pictures because they were difficult and expensive to reproduce. You got an instant picture, but you only got one copy. Polaroid sales continued to slide. The advent of digital cameras in the 1990s rang the death knell of the company. Technological advances in computerization allowed consumers to see pictures instantly and reproduce them at will. Perhaps Polaroid should have spent its resources on solving the shortcomings of its products or developing new products, instead of protecting its niche in instant pictures.

In the past few years, many states have reduced their budgets because state revenues have fallen short of predictions. State agencies find it impossible to stop their activities midyear. Public schools, state universities, welfare agencies, and others have struggled to maintain minimal service levels as they put a number of employees on indefinite leave. States, like businesses, depend on revenue streams to fund their budgets. Some states can trace their budget woes back to the economic slowdown in the late 1990s. For many others, the abrupt change can be traced back to political events in 2001. Sales tax, income tax, and transportation tax revenues all experienced dramatic decreases during the last quarter of that year. Could anyone have predicted this disruption? Only a very few people in the world knew what might happen.

As you can see, the sales force must listen to its customers, stay abreast of technological advances, and pay close attention to industrial, economic, and political information to estimate reasonably accurate sales forecasts.

Sales Budget

● **sales budget**
A budget that details the expected sales revenue from a company's primary operating activities during the budget period.

The sales budget drives the budgeting process because all expenses are related to the level of sales. The **sales budget** details the expected sales revenue from a company's primary operating activities during the budget period. For manufacturing and merchandising firms, such as Ford and Sears, the sales budget details the number of units of each product the firm expects to sell at its anticipated sales price. The sales budget for a service firm, such as H&R Block, details the dollar amount of services the company expects to render. Because sales revenue is an income statement item, we use the information the sales budget provides to construct the budgeted income statement.

Production or Purchases Budget

● **production budget**
A budget which plans for the cost and number of units that must be manufactured to meet the sales forecast and the desired quantity of ending finished goods inventory.

● **purchases budget**
A budget which plans for the cost and number of units that must be purchased to meet the sales forecast and the desired quantity of ending finished goods inventory.

For manufacturers, the **production budget** plans for the cost and number of units that must be manufactured to meet the sales forecast and the desired quantity of ending finished goods inventory. Although merchandisers, such as JCPenney, call this budget the **purchases budget**, the two are functionally equivalent. The production budget and the purchases budget are the pro forma cost of goods manufactured schedule and the pro forma cost of purchases schedule we discussed in Chapter 6. A production budget includes schedules for materials, labor, and manufacturing overhead. An operating budget for a service business does not include a production budget or purchases budget because a service company does not sell tangible products.

A manufacturer or merchandiser intends to sell some of the product scheduled to be produced or purchased during the budget period and to retain the balance in inventory. The projected ending inventory is classified as an asset, so some of the information provided by the production budget or purchases budget is used to construct the budgeted balance sheet. The product projected to be sold during the budget period is classified as an expense item and will be shown on the budgeted income statement as cost of goods sold. The cost of goods sold information needed to construct the budgeted income statement comes from the cost of goods sold budget.

Cost of Goods Sold or Cost of Services Budget

A **cost of goods sold budget** calculates the total cost of all the products a company estimates it will sell during the budget period. This budget differs from the production or purchases budget because the cost of goods sold budget includes only the cost of goods anticipated to be sold during the budget period and the other two may be more or less depending on whether management plans to increase or decrease the amount of inventory on hand. For a service type business, this budget is called the **cost of services budget**.

● **cost of goods sold budget**
A budget that calculates the total cost of all the products a company estimates it will sell during the budget period. Also called a **cost of services budget** for a service business.

Selling and Administrative Expense Budget

After managers prepare the sales forecast and estimate the product or service cost, they can estimate all other costs needed to support that level of sales. A **selling and administrative expense budget** calculates all costs other than the cost of products or services required to support a company's forecasted sales. The kinds of items included in this budget are exactly the same as those included in the income statements, and those we described as period costs in Chapter 4, including items such as advertising, sales salaries, rent, and utilities.

● **selling and administrative expense budget**
A budget that calculates all costs other than the cost of products or services required to support a company's forecasted sales.

Cash Budget

A **cash budget** shows whether the expected amount of cash operating activities generate will be sufficient to pay anticipated expenses during the budget period. It also reveals whether a company should expect a need for short-term external financing during the budget period. Be careful not to confuse the cash budget with the budgeted statement of cash flows that we will discuss later. The budgeted statement of cash flows is more comprehensive than a simple cash budget.

● **cash budget**
A budget that shows whether the expected amount of cash operating activities generate will be sufficient to pay anticipated expenses during the budget period.

Budgeted Financial Statements

A **budgeted income statement** shows the expected net income for the budget period. It subtracts all estimated product or service cost and period cost from estimated sales revenue. This budget is prepared using information from the sales budget, the cost of goods sold (or cost of services) budget, and the selling and administrative expense budget.

A **budgeted balance sheet** is a presentation of estimated assets, liabilities, and owners' equity at the end of the budget period. It is created exactly the way a balance sheet based on actual historical results is prepared. At the start of the budget period, a company has a balance sheet that presents its assets, liabilities, and owners' equity. Most of the company's asset, liability, and equity items will be changed by the forecasted results of the budgeted income statement, the production or purchases budget, and the cash budget. A service-type company has no production or purchases budget, so the budgeted balance sheet is prepared using information from the actual balance sheet at the beginning of the budget period, the budgeted income statement, and the cash budget. The result is an estimated balance sheet at the end of the budget period.

A **budgeted cash flow statement** is a statement of a company's expected sources and uses of cash during the budget period. Manufacturers, merchandisers, and service companies create the budgeted statement of cash flows similar to the way they create the budgeted balance sheet. At the start of the period being budgeted, they report their cash balance. Based on the estimated results of the budgeted income statement and other business activities that either generate or use cash, they estimate the cash balance at the end of the budget period. The purpose of the budgeted statement of cash flows is to explain how that change in cash is to happen.

● **budgeted income statement**
A pro forma income statement that shows the expected net income for the budget period.

● **budgeted balance sheet**
A presentation of estimated assets, liabilities, and owners' equity at the end of the budget period.

● **budgeted cash flow statement**
A statement of a company's expected sources and uses of cash during the budget period.

Exhibit 10-3
Interrelationship Among
the Budgets

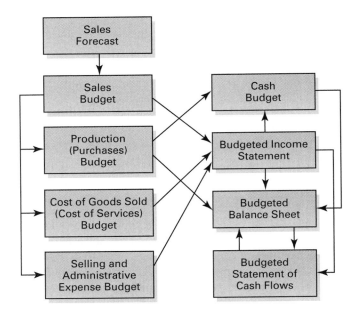

Interrelationship Among the Budgets

The budgets we presented are closely interrelated. Exhibit 10-3 shows the extent of this interrelationship. Arrows indicate the flow of information among the budgets. Notice that the flow is not linear from the sales forecast forward. Rather, once information feeds to the financial statements, information flows back and forth among the individual statements for their completion.

What Do You Think?

10-8   From what you have learned so far about the operating budget, which of the budgets do you think will be affected by the sales forecast? Explain how each is affected.

10-9   A change in which of the budgets will affect the least number of other budgets? Explain your reasoning.

A change in any one of the various budgets contained in the operating budget will cause a ripple effect throughout all the others. Because these budgets are so closely tied together, the preparation of the operating budget in most organizations is time consuming and complicated. Depending on the size of the company, preparing the operating budget may take several months. For example a manufacturer such as La-Z-Boy, Inc. or merchandiser like Gap Inc. prepares a sales budget for each product the company sells. If the company sells 80 products, it must prepare 80 sales budgets. If the company sells 10,000 products, it must prepare 10,000 sales budgets. Some large companies have budget departments that work year-round on budgets. Let's see how they do it.

Preparing a Master Operating Budget

Megan is coordinating the budget process for Elevation Sports for the year ending May 31, 2006. Because the business is seasonal, she is gathering data on a quarterly basis. Some companies budget by the year, others by the quarter, and some monthly. We start with Megan's budgeted income statement and the budgets that provide information used to construct that budgeted financial statement. Next, she will prepare the budgeted balance sheet with all its contributing schedules and, finally, the budgeted statement of cash flows.

Budgeted Income Statement

To prepare the budgeted income statement, Megan needs information about sales, cost of goods sold, and selling and administrative expenses for the budget period. Therefore, she must prepare a budget for each of those items before she can construct the budgeted income statement.

Sales Budget

The first information Megan needs to build the budgeted income statement is found in the sales budget. The starting point, of course, is the sales forecast. Rob agrees to analyze the past two years' sales to see whether he can spot a trend. He will also investigate information from industry analysts, economic forecasts, and new technology in snowboards and mountain boards. After doing his research, he prepares the forecast shown in Exhibit 10-4. All the manufactured products are given in units. The purchased merchandise is given in dollars because the company uses a standard markup for all purchased items.

Based on this forecast, Megan can prepare Elevation Sports' sales budget for the year, which Exhibit 10-5 shows. Notice that the schedule is not difficult to prepare. Each product has its estimated per-unit price, which can change. A price increase on retail snowboards occurs in the second quarter.

Cost of Goods Sold Budget

Once we know how many units Elevation Sports plans to sell and the cost per unit, we can prepare a cost of goods sold budget. This budget is used to determine how much cost of goods sold should be based on forecasted sales. Megan simply multiplied the estimated unit sales by the cost to produce or purchase. Retail sales of other products have an average gross profit of 40 percent, so the cost of goods sold averages 60 percent. The cost of goods sold budget for Elevation Sports Inc. is presented in Exhibit 10-6. The cost of goods sold budget provides the forecasted product cost information that is used to prepare the budgeted income statement.

Realistically, Elevation Sports will need to purchase and produce more units of product than just the ones it expects to sell in the first and second quarter. This means Megan will need to prepare a production budget and a purchases budget. She will prepare these after she completes the budgeted income statement. The only other budget she needs to prepare the budgeted income statement is the selling and administrative expense budget.

Exhibit 10-4

Elevation Sports, Inc. Sales Forecast

Elevation Sports, Inc. Sales Forecast For the Year Ended May 31, 2006					
QUARTER	**FIRST**	**SECOND**	**THIRD**	**FOURTH**	**TOTAL**
Budgeted Sales in Units:					
Wholesale snowboards	50	250	1,000	600	1,900
Retail snowboards	80	300	1,500	1,200	3,080
Wholesale mountain boards	500	300	200	250	1,250
Retail mountain boards	550	400	225	400	1,575
Budgeted Sales in Dollars:					
Retail merchandise	$10,500	$18,300	$34,600	$13,700	$77,100

Exhibit 10-5
Elevation Sports, Inc. Sales Budget

Elevation Sports, Inc.					
Sales Budget					
For the Year Ended May 31, 2006					
QUARTER	**FIRST**	**SECOND**	**THIRD**	**FOURTH**	**TOTAL**
Budgeted Sales in Units:					
Wholesale snowboards	50	250	1,000	600	
Selling price	$ 95	$ 95	$ 95	$ 95	
Subtotal	$ 4,750	$ 23,750	$ 95,000	$ 57,000	$ 180,500
Retail snowboards	80	300	1,500	1,200	
Selling price	$ 135	$ 140	$ 140	$ 140	
Subtotal	$ 10,800	$ 42,000	$210,000	$168,000	430,800
Wholesale mountain boards	500	300	200	250	
Selling price	$ 120	$ 120	$ 120	$ 120	
Subtotal	$ 60,000	$ 36,000	$ 24,000	$ 30,000	150,000
Retail mountain boards	550	400	225	400	
Selling price	$ 180	$ 180	$ 180	$ 180	
Subtotal	$ 99,000	$ 72,000	$ 40,500	$ 72,000	283,500
Budgeted Sales in Dollars:					
Retail merchandise	$ 10,500	$ 18,300	$ 34,600	$ 13,700	77,100
Total	$185,050	$192,050	$404,100	$340,700	$1,121,900

Exhibit 10-6
Elevation Sports, Inc. Cost of Goods Sold Budget

Elevation Sports, Inc.					
Cost of Goods Sold Budget					
For the Year Ended May 31, 2006					
QUARTER	**FIRST**	**SECOND**	**THIRD**	**FOURTH**	**TOTAL**
Budgeted sales in units:					
Wholesale snowboards	50	250	1,000	600	
Retail snowboards	80	300	1,500	1,200	
Total snowboards	130	550	2,500	1,800	
Cost to manufacture	65	65	65	65	
Subtotal	$ 8,450	$ 35,750	$162,500	$117,000	$ 323,700
Wholesale mountain boards	500	300	200	250	
Retail mountain boards	550	400	225	400	
Total mountain boards	1,050	700	425	650	
Cost to manufacture	$ 90	$ 90	$ 90	$ 90	
Subtotal	$ 94,500	$ 63,000	$ 38,250	$ 58,500	254,250
Budgeted sales in dollars:					
Retail merchandise	$ 10,500	$ 18,300	$ 34,600	$ 13,700	
Cost to purchase	60%	60%	60%	60%	
Subtotal	$ 6,300	$ 10,980	$ 20,760	$ 8,220	46,260
Total	$109,250	$109,730	$221,510	$183,720	$ 624,210

Exhibit 10-7
Elevation Sports, Inc. Selling and Administrative Expense Budget

Elevation Sports, Inc. **Selling and Administrative Expense Budget** **For the Year Ended May 31, 2006**					
QUARTER	**FIRST**	**SECOND**	**THIRD**	**FOURTH**	**TOTAL**
Selling Expenses:					
Advertising	$ 8,300	$17,000	$18,000	$12,000	$ 55,300
Merchant discounts	2,800	2,400	5,300	3,900	14,400
Rent	900	900	900	900	3,600
Sales salaries	7,500	11,500	15,000	11,800	45,800
Internet expenses	900	900	900	900	3,600
Utilities	1,000	1,000	1,000	1,000	4,000
Depreciation	300	300	300	300	1,200
Other selling expenses	600	920	1,200	944	3,664
Total	$22,300	$34,920	$42,600	$31,744	$131,564
Administrative Expenses:					
Officers' salaries	$48,000	$48,000	$48,000	$48,000	$192,000
Employee benefits	6,000	6,000	6,000	6,000	24,000
Insurance	2,050	2,050	2,050	2,050	8,200
Utilities	600	600	600	600	2,400
Depreciation and amortization	706	706	706	706	2,824
Other administrative expenses	6,350	6,350	6,350	6,350	25,400
Total	$63,706	$63,706	$63,706	$63,706	$254,824

Selling and Administrative Expense Budget

The various expenses associated with the selling and administrative functions are estimated and used to prepare this budget. Selling and administrative expenses include salaries, advertising, rent, utilities, and so forth. Exhibit 10-7 presents the selling and administrative expenses budget for Elevation Sports.

Building the Budgeted Income Statement

To prepare the budgeted income statement, Megan uses information from the sales, cost of goods sold, and selling and administrative expense budgets. The budgeted income statement depicts the amount of profit or loss a business can expect from its budgeted operating activities. First, Megan takes the total forecasted sales revenue from the sales budget and subtracts the forecasted cost of goods sold from the cost of goods sold budget. The result is a forecasted gross profit. She then subtracts the total selling and administrative expense from the selling and administrative expense budget. After including income taxes, she finds the company's budgeted net income for the budget year. Exhibit 10-8 presents the finished budgeted income statement for Elevation Sports.

You can see from Exhibit 10-8 that Elevation Sports is projecting a $6,124 net loss for the first quarter and a $9,783 net loss for the second quarter. Notice that the income tax is calculated for each quarter and shown as negative because the net losses in those quarters will reduce the profits of the third and fourth quarter, and therefore, the company's total taxes for the year. Megan ends up with $66,781 in net income projected for the year.

Exhibit 10-8
Elevation Sports, Inc. Budgeted Income Statement

Elevation Sports, Inc. **Budgeted Income Statement** **For the Year Ended May 31, 2006**					
QUARTER	**FIRST**	**SECOND**	**THIRD**	**FOURTH**	**TOTAL**
Sales	$185,050	$192,050	$404,100	$340,700	$1,121,900
Cost of Goods Sold	109,250	109,730	221,510	183,720	624,210
Gross Profit	$ 75,800	$ 82,320	$182,590	$156,980	$ 497,690
Selling expense	22,300	34,920	42,600	31,744	131,564
Administrative expense	63,706	63,706	63,706	63,706	254,824
Taxable Income	$ (10,206)	$ (16,306)	$ 76,284	$ 61,530	$ 111,302
Income taxes (40%)	(4,082)	(6,523)	30,514	24,612	44,521
Net Income	$ (6,124)	$ (9,783)	$ 45,770	$ 36,918	$ 66,781

After Megan has prepared the budgeted income statement, her fellow officers may want to change the company's plans so that it meets its profit goals more effectively. The main reason losses occur in the first and second quarters is that the officers are taking salary every month, including their slow period. If you remember, each of them accepted a minimal salary the first year. After profitable operations, they increased their salaries to reach a more optimal range. They must now decide whether the reduced cash flow is worth their individual desires for a level monthly salary.

At this point in the process, the officers may decide to make further adjustments in the budget or accept Megan's budget. The most important consideration, however, should be that the budgeted income statement be realistic and achievable. If they properly use the budget, they have an opportunity to see trouble spots in advance and make adjustments in the operations.

Budgeted Balance Sheet

Now that Megan has prepared the budgeted income statement, she has much of the information she needs to prepare the budgeted balance sheet. First, however, she must prepare three more budgets—the production budget, the purchases budget, and the cash budget.

Production Budget

The cost of goods sold budget Megan prepared accounts only for the units projected to be sold during the budget period. Because she knows that they will have beginning and ending finished goods inventory and merchandise inventory, she must prepare both a production budget and a purchases budget.

Megan begins with the production budget. Jon wants to use the slow time of the year to make design adjustments to improve the products and increase inventory in anticipation of the busy season. To accomplish both goals, he plans to end each quarter with 40 percent of the next quarter's estimated sales units in the ending inventory. Megan prepares the production budget in Exhibit 10-9 for Jon's approval.

As you can see by looking at Exhibit 10-9, the production budget, even for a small company like Elevation Sports, can seem rather complicated. A line-by-line analysis of this budget, however, reveals that much of its information comes from budgets

Exhibit 10-9
Elevation Sports, Inc. Production Budget

Elevation Sports, Inc.
Production Budget
For the Year Ended May 31, 2006

QUARTER	FIRST	SECOND	THIRD	FOURTH	TOTAL	
Snowboards:						
Forecasted unit sales	130	550	2,500	1,800	4,980	(a)
Desired ending inventory*	220	1,000	480	60	60	(b)
Total units needed	350	1,550	2,980	1,860	5,040	(c)
Beginning inventory	(80)	(220)	(1,000)	(480)	(80)	(d)
Units to be produced	270	1,330	1,980	1,380	4,960	(e)
Cost per unit	$ 65	$ 65	$ 65	$ 65	$ 65	(f)
Cost of production	$ 17,550	$ 86,450	$128,700	$ 89,700	$322,400	(g)
Mountain Boards:						
Forecasted unit sales	1,050	700	425	650	2,825	(a)
Desired ending inventory*	280	170	260	440	440	(b)
Total units needed	1,330	870	685	1,090	3,265	(c)
Beginning inventory	(150)	(280)	(170)	(260)	(150)	(d)
Units to be produced	1,180	590	515	830	3,115	(e)
Cost per unit	$ 90	$ 90	$ 90	$ 90	$ 90	(f)
Cost of production	$106,200	$ 53,100	$ 46,350	$ 74,700	$280,350	(g)
Total Cost of Production	$123,750	$139,550	$175,050	$164,400	$602,750	(h)

* 40% of the next quarter's sales requirements

Megan already prepared. The following explanations correspond to the letter codes at the end of each line of information in Exhibit 10-9:

(a) Forecasted Unit Sales. These numbers come from the sales budget and the cost of goods sold budget in Exhibits 10-5 and 10-6.

(b) Desired Ending Inventory. These numbers represent the number of units of product the company feels it needs on hand at the end of a given period to support sales in the early days of the next period. As the asterisk note in Exhibit 10-9 explains, Jon believes they should have inventory of product on hand at the end of any given quarter equal to 40 percent of the next quarter's forecasted sales. At the end of the first quarter, for example, Jon desires an ending inventory of 220 units, 40 percent of the second quarter's forecasted sales of 550 units (550 × 40% = 220 units). To complete the last quarter, Rob predicted that the first quarter sales of the following year would be 150 snowboards and 1,100 mountain boards, resulting in desired ending inventories of 60 snowboards and 440 mountain boards.

Managers consider at least two factors when determining the amount of desired ending inventory. First, how long does it usually take to produce the product? The plant manager can supply this information. Second, how many units of product will it sell in the early days of each quarter? This information comes from historical sales records and discussions with sales personnel.

(c) Total Units Needed. Add (a) and (b).

(d) Beginning Inventory. Because the purpose of the production budget is to determine how many units of inventory must be produced during each quarter, any inventory forecasted to be on hand at the beginning of each quarter must be subtracted from the total units needed to determine how many units must be produced during the quarter.

The beginning inventory for any period is the ending inventory for the previous period. You will note in the production budget in Exhibit 10-9 that the beginning inventory for the second quarter (220 units) is the same as the desired ending inventory for the first quarter, and the beginning inventory for the third quarter (1,000 units) is the same as the desired ending inventory for the second quarter. You should also note that the beginning inventory in the total column (80 units) is the same as the beginning inventory for the first quarter. This is so because the total column is for the entire year and the year begins with the first quarter.

(e) Units to Be Purchased. This is simply (c) minus (d) and tells us the number of snowboards that must be produced in each quarter and the total for the year.

(f) Cost per Unit. The cost per unit is the company's cost of goods sold as presented in Exhibit 10-6.

(g) Cost of Production. Multiply (e) by (f).

(h) Total Production Cost. Add both (g) amounts for both products made.

Purchases Budget

The purchases budget will be similar to the production budget, except that Megan will use the percentage of sales instead of units of product. Megan's completed purchases budget is shown in Exhibit 10-10. Much like the production budget, line by line this budget comes from the budgets Megan already prepared. The following explanations correspond to the letter codes at the end of each line of information.

(a) Forecasted Sales. Forecasted sales transfer from the sales budget in Exhibit 10-5.

(b) Cost of Forecasted Sales. Megan already computed the cost of sales on the cost of goods sold budget in Exhibit 10-6.

(c) Desired Ending Inventory. Rob believes the inventory should always be 40 percent of the cost of the next quarter's projected sales. He bases this decision on how long it takes to get inventory from his suppliers. For the first quarter, multiply the cost of the second quarter's sales by 40 percent ($10,980 \times 40\% = $4,392$). To calculate the last quarter's ending inventory, Rob estimates the cost of sales for the first quarter of the following year at $6,500 to obtain an ending inventory of $2,600 ($6,500 \times 40\%$).

Exhibit 10-10
Elevation Sports, Inc. Purchases Budget

QUARTER	FIRST	SECOND	THIRD	FOURTH	TOTAL	
Elevation Sports, Inc. Purchases Budget For the Year Ended May 31, 2006						
Forecasted sales	$10,500	$18,300	$34,600	$13,700	$77,100	(a)
Cost of forecasted sales*	$ 6,300	$10,980	$20,760	$ 8,220	$46,260	(b)
Desired ending inventory**	4,392	8,304	3,288	2,600	2,600	(c)
Total inventory needed	$10,692	$19,284	$24,048	$10,820	$48,860	(d)
Beginning inventory	5,600	4,392	8,304	3,288	5,600	(e)
Inventory to be purchased	$ 5,092	$14,892	$15,744	$ 7,532	$43,260	(f)

* 60% of the quarter's forecasted sales
** 40% of the cost of next quarter's sales requirements

(d) **Total Inventory Needed.** Add (b) and (c).

(e) **Beginning Inventory.** The beginning inventory is always the ending inventory from the prior period.

(f) **Inventory to Be Purchased.** Subtract (e) from (d).

With this information, we can now examine the cash budget.

Cash Budget

When a company uses accrual accounting, management recognizes revenue when it is earned rather than when it collects the cash associated with that revenue, and expenses when it receives the benefit rather than when it pays the cash associated with the expenses. What this means, of course, is that whereas the budgeted income statement (including the sales budget, cost of goods sold budget, and the selling and administrative expense budget) provides information about Elevation Sports' projected earnings for the budget period, it does not provide direct information about what is projected to happen during that period in terms of cash. Also, unless Megan pays cash for the materials and inventory, the production and purchases budgets suffer from the same limitation.

Before Megan can prepare the budgeted balance sheet, she must determine the effect on cash of the budgets she has prepared so far. She can do that by preparing a cash budget, which is composed of a cash receipts schedule and a cash payments schedule.

Cash Receipts Schedule. The **cash receipts schedule** details the amount of cash a company expects to collect during the budget period from the sales of its product. Before Megan can prepare her cash receipts schedule, she must make certain assumptions about the composition of the company's sales (cash or credit) and the pattern of collecting the accounts receivable created by the credit sales. Megan knows that 70 percent of the sales are for cash or credit cards and the remaining 30 percent are on account (credit sales). Of the sales on account, 80 percent are collected within the quarter of sale and 20 percent in the quarter following the sale. Therefore, Megan needs to know the prior quarter's credit sales, which were $80,000. Using the credit sales figures from the prior quarter and our assumptions about when cash is collected, she can prepare the cash receipts schedule for the year as shown in Exhibit 10-11.

The cash receipts schedule in Exhibit 10-11 is divided into two major parts. The first lists the amount of forecasted sales and separates them into cash sales and credit sales, (a) through (c). The second indicates when the cash from the credit sales will be received, (d) and (e). The following provides details of both sections.

● **cash receipts schedule**
A schedule that details the amount of cash a company expects to collect during the budget period from the sales of its product.

(a) **Total Forecasted Sales.** The amount of forecasted sales from the sales budget in Exhibit 10-5.

(b) **Credit Sales.** This amount is calculated at 30 percent of total sales, based on Megan's estimation.

(c) **Cash Sales.** Subtract (b) from (a).

(d) **Credit Sales Collected.** This section schedules the amount of cash collected from credit sales during the budget period. According to Megan's information, 80 percent of the credit sales are collected during the quarter they are sold. The remaining 20 percent of the credit sales are collected in the following quarter. The first amount collected during the first quarter is from the fourth quarter of the prior year. Fourth quarter 2005 credit sales of $80,000 multiplied by 20 percent equals $16,000. The first quarter credit sales are collected 80 percent ($55,515 80% = $44,412) in the first quarter and 20 percent ($55,515 $\times$ 20% = $11,103) in the second quarter. Follow the amounts through to the fourth quarter and notice that only the 80 percent collected in the fourth quarter are listed. The remaining collections will take place in the following budget year.

(e) **Budgeted Receipts from Credit Sales.** Total the amounts in the columns in the credit sales collections part of the schedule.

(f) **Total Budgeted Cash Receipts.** Add (c) and (e) to calculate the total forecasted cash receipts.

Exhibit 10-11
Elevation Sports, Inc. Cash Receipts Schedule

		Elevation Sports, Inc. Cash Receipts Schedule For the Year Ended May 31, 2006					
QUARTER	PRIOR	FIRST	SECOND	THIRD	FOURTH	TOTAL	
Total Forecasted Sales		$185,050	$192,050	$404,100	$340,700	$1,121,900	(a)
Credit sales (30%)	$80,000	55,515	57,615	121,230	102,210	336,570	(b)
Forecasted Cash Sales (70%)		$129,535	$134,435	$282,870	$238,490	$ 785,330	(c)
Credit Sales Collected: From Accounts Receivable at 5/31/05: (20% of $80,000)		$ 16,000				$ 16,000	
From New Credit Sales:							
First quarter credit sales:							
Collected-first quarter (80%)		44,412				44,412	
Collected-second quarter (20%)			$ 11,103			11,103	
Second quarter credit sales:							
Collected-second quarter (80%)			46,092			46,092	(d)
Collected-third quarter (20%)				$ 11,523		11,523	
Third quarter credit sales:							
Collected-third quarter (80%)				96,984		96,984	
Collected-fourth quarter (20%)					$ 24,246	24,246	
Fourth quarter credit sales:							
Collected-fourth quarter (80%)					81,768	81,768	
Budgeted Receipts from Credit Sales		$ 60,412	$ 57,195	$108,507	$106,014	$ 332,128	(e)
Total Budgeted Cash Receipts		$189,947	$191,630	$391,377	$344,504	$1,117,458	(f)

● **cash payments schedule**
A schedule that details the amount of cash a company expects to pay out during the budget period.

Cash Payments Schedule. The **cash payments schedule** details the amount of cash a company expects to pay out during the budget period. Megan analyzed the company's pattern of cash payments. She knows that purchases of materials and inventory are paid 30 days after purchase. For a normal quarter, 65 percent of the quarter's purchases and production costs are paid during that quarter and 35 percent are paid in the following quarter. She must detail the amount of the fourth quarter 2005 to know how much should be paid in the first quarter of 2006. All cash selling and administrative expenses are paid during the quarter incurred. Using these assumptions about when cash is paid and information from the production budget in Exhibit 10-9, the purchases budget in Exhibit 10-10, and the selling and administrative expense budget in Exhibit 10-7, Megan prepares the cash payments schedule shown in Exhibit 10-12.

As you can see from Exhibit 10-12, the cash payments schedule looks much like the cash receipts schedule. Not every business will have the same situation with cash inflows and outflows. All budget schedules, especially these two cash schedules, must be tailored for the situation of each business.

(a) Production Costs and Purchases. Production costs and purchases are paid for according to the assumption that 65 percent are paid within the quarter and

Exhibit 10-12
Elevation Sports, Inc. Cash Payments Schedule

QUARTER		PRIOR	FIRST	SECOND	THIRD	FOURTH	TOTAL	
Elevation Sports, Inc. **Cash Payments Schedule** **For the Year Ended May 31, 2006**								
Purchases		$ 6,500	$ 5,092	$ 14,892	$ 15,744	$ 7,532	$ 43,260	
Production costs		150,000	123,750	139,550	175,050	164,400	602,750	
Total		$156,500	$128,842	$154,442	$190,794	$171,932	$ 646,010	(a)
Amount paid:								
Fourth quarter 2005 (35%)			$ 54,775				$ 54,775	
First quarter:								
Paid in first quarter (65%)			83,747				83,747	
Paid in second quarter (35%)				$ 45,095			45,095	
Second quarter:								
Paid in second quarter (65%)				100,387			100,387	
Paid in third quarter (35%)					$ 54,055		54,055	
Third quarter:								
Paid in third quarter (65%)					124,016		124,016	
Paid in fourth quarter (35%)						$ 66,778	66,778	
Fourth quarter:								
Paid in fourth quarter (65%)						111,756	111,756	
Less: Depreciation			(3,700)	(3,700)	(3,700)	(3,700)	(14,800)	
Total paid for production costs and purchases			$134,822	$141,782	$174,371	$174,834	$ 625,809	(b)
Selling and Administrative Payments:								
Selling expenses			$ 22,300	$ 34,920	$ 42,600	$ 31,744	$ 131,564	
Less: Depreciation			(300)	(300)	(300)	(300)	(1,200)	
Administrative expenses			63,706	63,706	63,706	63,706	254,824	
Less: Amortization and depreciation			(706)	(706)	(706)	(706)	(2,824)	
Total paid for selling and administrative expenses			$ 85,000	$ 97,620	$105,300	$ 94,444	$ 382,364	(c)
Other Payments:								
Income taxes			$ —0—	$ —0—	$ 19,909	$ 24,612	$ 44,521	
Equipment purchase						120,000	120,000	
Loan payment			15,000				15,000	(d)
Dividend payment						10,000	10,000	
Total other payments			$ 15,000	$ —0—	$ 19,909	$154,612	$ 189,521	
Budgeted Cash Payments			$234,822	$239,402	$299,580	$423,890	$1,197,694	(e)

35 percent are paid during the next quarter. Megan computes the amount paid the same way she calculated the cash receipts. Remember that the only costs on this schedule are for cash payments. The depreciation included in production costs, from Chapter 6, has no cash outflow and must be removed.

(b) **Total Paid for Production Costs and Purchases.** After distributing the amounts paid for production costs and purchases to the various quarters, Megan totaled the amounts for each quarter.

(c) **Selling and Administrative Payments.** Megan took amounts for the selling and administrative expenses directly from the selling and administrative expense budget. According to her information, the cash expenses are paid during each quarter. Notice it says "cash" expenses. You recall that depreciation and amortization do not represent cash payments. The easiest way to compute the cash expenses is simply to subtract the amounts of amortization and depreciation.

(d) **Other Payments.** Megan realized that other items required cash payments including the annual note payment to the bank of $15,000, a planned purchase of new equipment for $120,000, and a long-awaited payment of dividends to the four owners of $10,000. The note payment is due on June 1 each year and Megan plans to buy the equipment and pay the dividends after their busy season when cash is most plentiful.

(e) **Total Cash Payments.** Megan added the three totals from each section of the report to find the total of cash payments.

Building the Cash Budget. Now that Megan has prepared the cash receipts schedule and the cash payments schedule, she can prepare the cash budget. As she did with the schedules, she must make some assumptions for the cash budget. First, she determines that Elevation Sports will have a cash balance of $124,000 on June 1, 2005. Second, Megan wants to maintain a cash balance of at least $50,000 at all times. If cash falls below $40,000, she has a $50,000 line of credit with the Vail National Bank for a temporary loan. Finally, she ignores any interest required to be paid on any temporary borrowing from the bank.

Using her assumption about the desired minimum cash balance and the information from the cash receipts schedule and the cash payments schedule, Megan prepares the cash budget shown in Exhibit 10-13.

Although the cash budget is fairly straightforward, let's review the source of the numbers.

(a) **Beginning Cash Balance.** The beginning cash balance for the first quarter comes from Megan's estimate of the May 31, 2005, balance of $124,000. The second quarter beginning balance is the ending balance from the first quarter. The third and fourth quarters' beginning balance come from the prior month's ending balance.

(b) **Cash Receipts.** Cash receipts come directly from the cash receipts schedule.

Exhibit 10-13
Elevation Sports, Inc. Cash Budget

Elevation Sports, Inc. Cash Budget For the Year Ended May 31, 2006						
QUARTER	**FIRST**	**SECOND**	**THIRD**	**FOURTH**	**TOTAL**	
Beginning cash balance	$124,000	$ 79,125	$ 40,000	$123,150	$ 124,000	(a)
Add: Cash receipts	189,947	191,630	391,377	344,504	1,117,458	(b)
Cash available	$313,947	$270,755	$431,377	$467,654	$1,241,458	(c)
Less: Cash payments	234,822	239,402	299,580	423,890	1,197,694	(d)
Balance Before borrowing	$ 79,125	$ 31,353	$131,797	$ 43,764	$ 43,764	(e)
Borrowing/(repayment)	—0—	8,647	(8,647)	—0—	—0—	(f)
Ending Cash Balance	$ 79,125	$ 40,000	$123,150	$ 43,764	$ 43,764	(g)

(c) **Cash Available.**   Add (a) and (b).

(d) **Cash Payments.**   Cash payments come directly from the cash payments schedule.

(e) **Balance before Borrowing.**   Subtract (d) from (c).

(f) **Borrowing/(Repayment).**   This line requires a decision. Megan does not want her cash balance to dip below $40,000. If line (e) is less than $40,000, line (f) equals $40,000 minus line (e). If a previous borrowing exists and has not been repaid and line (e) is more than $40,000, line (f) will be the greater of the excess of line (e) over $40,000 or the amount of the borrowing not repaid. For example, in the second quarter line (e) is less than $40,000. Line (f) is $40,000 minus $ 31,353, or $8,647. To keep her bank balance at $40,000, Megan needs to borrow $8,647. In the third quarter, line (e) is $131,797, well in excess of $40,000. In fact, Megan could repay $108,006. Her loan, however, is only $8,647, so that amount will be subtracted from the bank balance and be repaid. In fact, Megan may choose to repay the loan as soon as her balance exceeds $40,000 during the third quarter.

(g) **Ending Cash Balance.**   If line (f) is positive, add (e) to (f). If line (f) is negative, subtract (f) from line (e).

Now Megan can use the information from the cash budget and other budgets to prepare the budgeted balance sheet.

Building the Budgeted Balance Sheet

You already know how to construct a balance sheet—from the adjusted trial balance or worksheet taken from the general ledger and adjusted. Budgeted amounts, however, are not recorded in the general ledger. So, we will focus on how to determine the various asset, liability, and equity items and forecasted dollar amounts for these items. Although some of the amounts needed to prepare the budgeted balance sheet come directly from the budgets already prepared, many amounts are not specifically included in any of those budgets. For example, we have not prepared a budget or schedule that shows the ending balances for Accounts Receivable; Inventory; Property, Plant, and Equipment; Accumulated Depreciation; Accounts Payable; Notes Payable; Common Stock; Additional Paid-in Capital; or Retained Earnings. For each of these items, we will present a brief discussion and a schedule to show how to calculate the amounts that should appear on the budgeted balance sheet.

You will find as you examine each of these items that we calculate the budgeted ending balance by taking the beginning balance and adding or subtracting the changes that are expected to occur during the budget period. So, for each of these items, the beginning balance is our starting point, and the beginning balance is the May 31, 2005, ending balance sheet. In reality, Megan may not have the ending balance sheet at May 31, 2005, until July. What she will do is prepare a preliminary budgeted balance sheet and revise it after she finalizes the May 31, 2005, balance sheet. For study purposes here, we will use Megan's estimated balance sheet for May 31, 2005, in Exhibit 10-14.

Using the May 31, 2005, balance sheet in Exhibit 10-14 and information from the previously completed budgets, Megan can prepare a budgeted balance sheet for each quarter included in the budget period, which Exhibit 10-15 shows.

The balance sheets in Exhibit 10-15 are similar to the other balance sheets you have seen throughout your studies. The essential difference is not the format, but rather the time frame. These are *projected* balance sheets, whereas the others have presented past results. This budget has no total column because each column is a financial snapshot of the business taken at the end of a period.

Let's take a closer look at each of the items on the balance sheet.

(a) **Cash.**   Megan takes the Cash amount directly from the ending cash balance line of the cash budget in Exhibit 10-13. For example, she transfers the amount shown as the ending cash balance of $79,125 in the first quarter column of the cash budget to the Cash line in the August 31, 2005, column of the budgeted balance sheet.

Exhibit 10-14
Elevation Sports, Inc. Balance Sheet as of May 31, 2005

Elevation Sports, Inc.
Balance Sheet
May 31, 2005

ASSETS
Current Assets

Cash		$ 124,000
Accounts receivable		16,000
Merchandise inventory		5,600
Manufacturing inventories		38,700
Prepaid expenses		45,000
Total Current Assets		$ 229,300
Property, Plant, and Equipment		
Equipment and furniture	$103,100	
Less: Accumulated depreciation	71,200	
Total Property, Plant, and Equipment		31,900
Intangible Assets		9,012
Total Assets		$ 270,212
LIABILITIES AND STOCKHOLDERS' EQUITY		
Current Liabilities		
Accounts payable		$ 54,775
Note payable		15,000
Total Current Liabilities		$ 69,775
Stockholders' Equity		
Paid-in capital:		
Common stock, $10 par value, 100,000 shares authorized,		
4,000 shares issued and outstanding	$ 40,000	
Paid-in capital in excess of par—common stock	60,000	
Total Paid-in Capital	$100,000	
Retained earnings	100,437	
Total Stockholders' Equity		200,437
Total Liabilities and Stockholders' Equity		$ 270,212

(b) Accounts Receivable. To determine the ending Accounts Receivable balance for each quarter shown in Exhibit 10-15, Megan takes the beginning Accounts Receivable balance, adds budgeted credit sales for that quarter, and subtracts the budgeted collections for that quarter.

Quarter	First	Second	Third	Fourth
Beginning balance	$ 16,000	$ 11,103	$ 11,523	$ 24,246
Credit sales	55,515	57,615	121,230	102,210
Collections	60,412	57,195	108,507	106,014
Ending balance	$ 11,103	$ 11,523	$ 24,246	$ 20,442

Exhibit 10-15
Elevation Sports, Inc. Budgeted Balance Sheets

Elevation Sports, Inc.
Budgeted Balance Sheets

	AUGUST 31, 2005	NOVEMBER 30, 2005	FEBRUARY 28, 2006	MAY 31, 2006	
ASSETS					
Current Assets					
Cash	$ 79,125	$ 40,000	$123,150	$ 43,764	(a)
Accounts receivable	11,103	11,523	24,246	20,442	(b)
Merchandise inventory	4,392	8,304	3,288	2,600	(c)
Manufacturing inventories	59,500	100,300	74,600	63,500	(d)
Tax refund due	4,082	10,605	—0—	—0—	(e)
Prepaid expenses	45,000	45,000	45,000	45,000	(f)
Total Current Assets	$203,202	$215,732	$270,284	$175,306	
Equipment					
Equipment and furniture	$103,100	$103,100	$103,100	$223,100	(g)
Less: Accumulated depreciation	75,650	80,100	84,550	89,000	(h)
Total Equipment	$ 27,450	$ 23,000	$ 18,550	$134,100	
Intangible Assets	$ 8,756	$ 8,500	$ 8,244	$ 7,988	(i)
Total Assets	$239,408	$247,232	$297,078	$317,394	
LIABILITIES AND STOCKHOLDERS' EQUITY					
Current Liabilities					
Accounts payable	$ 45,095	$ 54,055	$ 66,778	$ 60,176	(j)
Note payable	—0—	8,647	—0—	—0—	(k)
Total Current Liabilities	$ 45,095	$ 62,702	$ 66,778	$ 60,176	
Stockholders' Equity					
Paid-in capital:					
Common stock	$ 40,000	$ 40,000	$ 40,000	$ 40,000	
Paid-in capital	60,000	60,000	60,000	60,000	
Total Paid-in Capital	$100,000	$100,000	$100,000	$100,000	(i)
Retained earnings	94,313	84,530	130,300	157,218	(j)
Total Stockholders' Equity	$194,313	$184,530	$230,300	$257,218	
Total Liabilities and Stockholders' Equity	$239,408	$247,232	$297,078	$317,394	

Megan uses the May 31, 2005, balance for the beginning balance of Accounts Receivable. For the first quarter, the cash receipts budget shows credit sales of $55,515 and a total of $60,412 collected from credit sales. After adding the credit sales of $55,515 to the beginning balance of $16,000, Megan subtracts the collections of $60,412 to arrive at the ending Accounts Receivable balance of $11,103. This amount is shown on the budgeted balance sheet for August 31, 2005, and becomes the beginning balance for the second quarter. She calculated the ending Accounts Receivable amounts for other quarters the same way.

(c) Merchandise Inventory. To determine the ending inventory balance for each quarter shown in Exhibit 10-15, Megan takes the beginning merchandise inventory balance from the May 31, 2005, balance sheet, adds purchases made during the quarter from the purchases budget, and subtracts that quarter's cost of goods sold from the cost of goods sold budget.

Quarter	First	Second	Third	Fourth
Beginning balance	$ 5,600	$ 4,392	$ 8,304	$ 3,288
Purchases	5,092	14,892	15,744	7,532
Cost of goods sold	6,300	10,980	20,760	8,220
Ending balance	$ 4,392	$ 8,304	$ 3,288	$ 2,600

Megan takes the beginning merchandise inventory balance for June 1, 2005, of $5,600 from the May 31, 2005, balance sheet in Exhibit 10-14. She finds the expected purchases for the first quarter of $5,092 on the purchases budget in Exhibit 10-9, and the cost of goods sold of $6,300 on the cost of goods sold budget in Exhibit 10-6. After adding the purchases of $5,092 to the beginning balance of $5,600, she subtracts the cost of goods sold of $6,300 to arrive at the ending merchandise inventory balance of $4,392. Megan shows this amount on the budgeted balance sheet for August 31, 2005. She calculates the ending inventory amounts for other quarters the same way.

(d) **Manufacturing Inventories.**   To determine the ending inventory balance for each quarter in Exhibit 10-15, Megan simply takes the beginning manufacturing inventory balance from the May 31, 2005, balance sheet, adds the cost of production during the quarter from the production cost budget, and subtracts that quarter's cost of manufactured goods sold from the cost of goods sold budget. The manufacturing inventories include raw materials inventory and work-in-process inventory, in addition to the finished goods inventory. For simplicity, Megan assumes that the raw materials inventory and work-in-process inventory remain a constant $20,000 throughout the year and are included in the beginning inventory:

Quarter	First	Second	Third	Fourth
Beginning balance	$ 38,700	$ 59,500	$100,300	$ 74,600
Cost of Production	123,750	139,550	175,050	164,400
COGS—Snowboards	8,450	35,750	162,500	117,000
COGS—Mountain boards	94,500	63,000	38,250	58,500
Ending Balance	$ 59,500	$ 100,300	$ 74,600	$ 63,500

Megan begins with the May 31, 2005, manufacturing inventories balance of $38,700. The cost of production of $123,700 comes from the last line of the production budget. The cost of goods sold budget provides her the cost of goods sold amounts in two lines—one for snowboards, $8,450, and another for mountain boards, $94,500. To find the ending manufacturing inventories total she adds $38,700 to the production costs of $123,750 and then subtracts the cost of goods sold of $8,450 for snowboards and $94,500 for mountain boards. The ending balance of $59,500 becomes the beginning balance for the second quarter. Megan calculates remaining quarters in the same way.

(e) **Tax Refund Due.**   During the first two quarters, the slow time of the year, the company shows a loss. This creates a negative income tax expense and if this were the only income for the entire year, it would produce a tax refund. As you can see, the refund goes away once the company shows a profit for the third quarter that exceeds the losses of the previous two quarters. The amounts come from the budgeted income statement.

(f) **Prepaid Expenses.**   For simplicity, Megan assumed that prepaid expenses would remain the same throughout the year.

(g) **Equipment.**   The officers have not bought any new equipment since the company started. Megan planned to buy new equipment at the end of May 2006 for

$120,000. She took the information from the cash payments schedule in the fourth quarter.

(h) **Accumulated Depreciation.**   Megan added the quarterly depreciation to the beginning balance of $71,200. She scheduled no equipment purchases or sales until the last day of the year, so depreciation remains unchanged. She calculated the amount of the depreciation by adding the amount found on the cash payments schedule of $3,700 per quarter to the amounts on the selling and administrative expense budget of $300 and $706. The only problem is that the administrative expenses include amortization of intangible assets. By referring to Chapter 6 adjustments, she separates the amount of amortization of $256 per quarter. The final total is $3,700, plus $300, plus $706, minus $256 to equal $4,450. The first quarter adds $4,450 to the beginning balance of $71,200 to total $75,650. Each quarter increases by $4,450.

(i) **Intangible Assets.**   Megan anticipated that no new intangible assets would be added in the new budget year. Therefore, each quarter she reduces the intangible assets balance by the $256 of amortization described in (h). The beginning balance from the May 31, 2005, is $9,012 less $256 to equal an August 31, 2005, balance of $8,756. She reduces each quarter by another $256.

(j) **Accounts Payable.**   To determine the ending Accounts Payable balance for each month shown in Exhibit 10-15, Megan finds the beginning Accounts Payable balance, adds budgeted production costs and purchases for that quarter, and subtracts budgeted payments for that quarter:

Quarter	First	Second	Third	Fourth
Beginning balance	$ 54,775	$ 45,095	$ 54,055	$ 66,778
Cost of production	123,750	139,550	175,050	164,400
Purchases	5,092	14,892	15,744	7,532
Less: Depreciation	(3,700)	(3,700)	(3,700)	(3,700)
Cash payments	(134,822)	(141,782)	(174,371)	(174,834)
Ending balance	$ 45,095	$ 54,055	$ 66,778	$ 60,176

The beginning Accounts Payable balance for the first quarter of $54,775 comes from the May 31, 2005, balance sheet in Exhibit 10-14. By looking at the production budget in Exhibit 10-9, the purchases budget in Exhibit 10-10, and the cash payments budget in Exhibit 10-12, Megan finds that expected production costs are $123,750 less depreciation of $3,700, purchases for the first quarter are $5,092, and cash payments are expected be $134,822. After adding the production costs of $123,750 and purchases of $5,092 to the beginning balance of $54,775, she subtracts the depreciation of $3,700 and cash payments of $134,822 to arrive at the ending Accounts Payable balance of $45,095. This amount is shown on the budgeted balance sheet for August 31, 2005. She calculates the ending Accounts Payable amounts for other quarters the same way.

(k) **Note Payable.**   To determine the ending Note Payable balance for each month in Exhibit 10-15, Megan takes the beginning Note Payable balance, adds the budgeted borrowing for that quarter, and subtracts budgeted payments for that quarter:

Quarter	First	Second	Third	Fourth
Beginning balance	$15,000	$ —0—	$8,647	$ —0—
Borrowing	—0—	8,647	—0—	—0—
Repayments	15,000	—0—	8,647	—0—
Ending balance	$ —0—	$ 8,647	$ —0—	$ —0—

The beginning Note Payable balance for the first quarter comes from the May 31, 2005, balance sheet in Exhibit 10-14. Megan was able to pay two additional loan payments in the prior year, leaving only one remaining payment. Megan uses the cash payment schedule in Exhibit 10-12 to discover the $15,000 note payment scheduled for the first quarter. In looking at the cash budget in Exhibit 10-13, she finds an expected borrowing of $8,647 in the second quarter with repayment in full expected in the third quarter.

(l) Common Stock and Additional Paid-in Capital. Megan expects no Common Stock or Additional Paid-in Capital transactions during the budget period. Therefore, the beginning first quarter balance for these items found on the May 31, 2005, balance sheet in Exhibit 10-14 remains unchanged during the budget period.

(m) Retained Earnings. To determine the ending Retained Earnings balance, Megan adds the income for the period or, if the company has a loss, subtracts the loss and deducts dividends, if they exist, from the beginning Retained Earnings balance.

Quarter	First	Second	Third	Fourth
Beginning balance	$100,437	$ 94,313	$ 84,530	$ 130,300
Income (loss)	(6,124)	(9,783)	45,770	36,918
Dividends	—0—	—0—	—0—	10,000
Ending balance	$ 94,313	$ 84,530	$ 130,300	$ 157,218

Megan begins with the $100,437 beginning balance of Retained Earnings found on the May 31, 2005, balance sheet shown in Exhibit 10-14. She calculates the ending Retained Earnings for the first quarter by deducting the budgeted loss for the first quarter of $6,124 and the dividends of zero from the beginning Retained Earnings balance of $100,437. That becomes the beginning balance of the second quarter. She continues in the same manner for each quarter.

Now that the budgeted balance sheet balances, the total assets equals the total liabilities and stockholders' equity each quarter, we can finish with the budgeted statement of cash flows.

Budgeted Statement of Cash Flows

Now that Megan has prepared all the other budgets, she can prepare the budgeted statement of cash flows. This must be the final budget prepared because, as you recall from your earlier study of this financial statement, it is a form of financial statement analysis. A statement of cash flows prepared on historical results analyzes the income statement and the balance sheet to explain what caused cash to change from the beginning of a period to the end of the period. The budgeted statement of cash flows does exactly the same thing, except that it analyzes the budgeted income statement and the budgeted balance sheet to explain what will cause the projected change in cash from the start to the end of the budget period. Exhibit 10-16 is a budgeted statement of cash flows for Elevation Sports.

We will not do a line-by-line analysis of Exhibit 10-16 because we have explained all the items elsewhere in this chapter as we have constructed the other budgets. Discussing what this budget reveals in overall terms, however, is important. In the normal course of business, a company can obtain cash from only three sources: borrowing, owner contributions, and profitable operations. Ultimately, the only renewable source of cash for any company, including Elevation Sports, is the profitable operation of the business. If a company does not generate enough cash from operations to run the business, it must seek outside financing (by borrowing or from owner contributions).

The budgeted statement of cash flows in Exhibit 10-16 reveals that for the four quarters the budget covers, Megan does not anticipate generating enough cash through operations in the first and second quarters to run the business and must borrow the money. Due to the seasonal nature of the business, Megan should not expect the cash flow to be as good then as in the third and fourth quarters. The solution is to always end the year with a surplus of cash to carry the company through until the third quarter. Operations will provide sufficient cash to last throughout the year.

Exhibit 10-16
Elevation Sports, Inc. Budgeted Statement of Cash Flows

Elevation Sports, Inc.				
Budgeted Statement of Cash Flows				
For the Year Ended May 31, 2006				
QUARTER	**FIRST**	**SECOND**	**THIRD**	**FOURTH**
Cash Flows from Operating Activities:				
Net income	$ (6,124)	$ (9,783)	$ 45,770	$ 36,918
Add: Depreciation	4,450	4,450	4,450	4,450
Amortization	256	256	256	256
Changes in working capital:				
Accounts receivable	4,897	(420)	(12,723)	3,804
Merchandise inventory	1,208	(3,912)	5,016	688
Manufacturing inventories	(20,800)	(40,800)	25,700	11,100
Tax refunds due	(4,082)	(6,523)	10,605	—0—
Accounts payable	(9,680)	8,960	12,723	(6,602)
Net Cash Flow from Operating Activities	$(29,875)	$(47,772)	$ 91,797	$ 50,614
Cash Flow from Investing Activities:				
Cash paid for equipment				$(120,000)
Net Cash Used by Investing Activities				$(120,000)
Cash Flow from Financing Activities:				
Borrowing		$ 8,647		
Loan payments	$(15,000)		$ (8,647)	
Dividends paid				$ (10,000)
Net Cash Flow from Financing Activities	$(15,000)	$ 8,647	$ (8,647)	$ (10,000)
Increase/(decrease) in cash	$(44,875)	$(39,125)	$ 83,150	$ (79,386)
Budgeted Beginning Cash Balance	124,000	79,125	40,000	123,150
Budgeted Ending Cash Balance	$ 79,125	$ 40,000	$123,150	$ 43,764

If the officers, however, decide to buy the new equipment in the last month of the year, the ending cash balance will be far below the beginning cash balance. They may decide to finance part of the equipment purchase or keep their line of credit available for temporary borrowing. Should Megan find the budget prospects unacceptable, she may want to start the whole budgeting process over again and allow the officers to make adjustments in their operations.

Connecting the Budget to the Strategic Plan

One of the most important budgeting functions is for top management to ensure that each budget aligns with the goals and objectives of the strategic plan. In Chapter 3 our four-some prepared a strategic plan to direct the course of their business over the next few years. At least annually, the board of directors and officers of a firm should review the strategic plan to see how well the company has followed the plan, how well the company achieved its goals, and what changes might be necessary in the plan. The strategic plan and the master budget control the allocation of resources. They must, therefore, conform with one another. They are, however, living and dynamic documents. They can function together to make sure that the board of directors sets achievable goals and remains accountable for their attainment. Investors require such behavior, and they express their approval or disapproval by their willingness to buy the company's stock at any given price.

What Do You Think?

10-10   Examine the strategic plan in Chapter 3. List and discuss the goals the officers of Elevation Sports have attained by the budget year 2006.

10-11   Which goals have not been attained by the budget year 2006? Should the officers adjust their operations to achieve these goals or adjust the strategic plan? Why or why not?

Analyzing Budget Variances

We have seen that the operating budget can serve as a guide for managers to follow, assist managers in allocating the firm's scarce resources, and foster communication and coordination among managers from functional areas across the company. It can also establish performance standards, or benchmarks, against which the company can compare the actual results. This fourth application, however, presents some serious challenges to managers.

Most of the challenges arise because managers consider the budget to be an authority to spend, or their bonuses or promotions are based on their ability to beat the budget, or they prepare inflated budgets to guarantee that they can come in under budget. This behavior does not improve the company's operations in the long run. Using the budget for these purposes encourages managers to make bad decisions and discourages them from making good decisions.

Budget Performance Report

● **budget performance report**
A report that compares the actual amounts spent against the budgeted amounts for a budget category.

● **budget variance**
The difference between the actual and budgeted amounts for a budget category.

Most firms require managers to prepare or review a **budget performance report**, which compares the actual amounts spent against the budgeted amounts for a budget category. The difference between the actual and budgeted amounts for a budget category is known as a **budget variance**. A typical budget performance report has four columns as shown for Elevation Sports in Exhibit 10-17. As you can see from Exhibit 10-17, the report is not complicated. For each area of responsibility, it gives the budgeted amount, the actual amount, and the difference. A positive variance means the actual exceeded the budget and a negative amount indicates that the actual was less than the budgeted amount.

Exhibit 10-17
Elevation Sports, Inc. Budget Performance Report

Elevation Sports, Inc. Budget Performance Report for Sales For the Year Ended May 31, 2005			
DESCRIPTION	**BUDGET**	**ACTUAL**	**VARIANCE**
Snowboard sales – retail	$350,000	$372,600	$22,600
Snowboard sales – wholesale	180,000	170,100	(9,900)
Mountain board sales – retail	240,000	225,000	(15,000)
Mountain board sales – wholesale	150,000	120,000	(30,000)
Other merchandise	60,000	63,400	3,400

When we discuss revenues, positive variances are favorable because they indicate sales in excess of the budget and negative variances are unfavorable because they represent underachievement. The opposite is true for expenses. Negative variances are favorable because they indicate cost savings, and positive variances are unfavorable because they represent cost overruns.

The budget performance report can provide data, but its information value is limited without further investigation. What caused the variance? Was the variance a factor of price or of quantity? The following are the possible causes of variances:

1 The number of units of product remained the same but the price increased or decreased. The sales forecast was accurate, but due to competitive forces, Rob lowered or raised the price of snowboards or mountain boards.

2 The price remained the same, but due to uncontrollable forces, such as the weather or the economy, the number of units sold varied from the budgeted amounts. Say, for example, that Colorado experienced a long, cold, and snowy winter followed by a short, unseasonably cool summer, while snow resorts in the Northeast experienced a warm, dry winter. The Colorado winter would have improved retail snowboard sales and other merchandise sales and would have reduced the mountain board sales because the summer season was shortened. Likewise, if the Northeast resorts had a poor season, wholesale snowboard sales would be reduced. Weather conditions cannot be predicted with a high degree of accuracy.

When we look at costs, the same types of questions are important. Did the quantity of units of an expense increase or did the price per unit of the expense increase? Quantity increases may indicate waste and quantity decreases may indicate frugal use. Switching suppliers can sometimes control price per unit increases, but frequently they are caused by imbalances in the economy.

Should managers investigate all variances, favorable or unfavorable, regardless of amount? Some firms look at variances only over a certain amount. The better management understands the firm's revenues and expenses and learns from the budgeting process, the less likely it will be caught short of information. When favorable budget variances mean that management will automatically reduce next year's budget, some managers seek to keep the actual amounts as close as possible to the budget amounts, somehow believing they will be losing something if the next budget is reduced. Instead of being rewarded for savings, they believe they are being punished. When an expense decreases, it no longer requires funding at the previous level. The manager loses nothing. When the manager wishes to use that saved amount for another purpose, he or she should request a new budget item. A firm that has a clear strategic plan, mission, values, and goals can achieve better overall performance when the budget process is an extension of its corporate strategy, instead of a territorial fight.

Regardless of the care taken with the budget process, variances will occur. Because of the interrelationships among the budgets, if the sales forecast is inaccurate, the operating budget will be inaccurate. The sales forecast will always be inaccurate because it is always an estimate. Therefore, the operating budget will always be inaccurate so variances will always exist. Inaccuracy is not bad—but variances should always be investigated. The focus of this analysis, however, should be on how to improve the budgeting process rather than how to eliminate the inevitable variances that have occurred.

ANALYSIS OF VARIANCE FOR STANDARD COST SYSTEMS

Manufacturing companies frequently use a standard cost system. Managers carefully analyze their cost experience to set standards for direct material, direct labor, variable manufacturing overhead, and fixed manufacturing overhead. Costs will vary from standards due to variances in quantity used and price paid. The first step in the process, of course, is determining the standard costs.

Determining Standard Costs

● **direct material quantity standard**
The amount of direct material required to make one unit of product.

● **bill of material**
A listing of the quantity and description of each direct material item used to produce one unit.

● **direct material price standard**
The anticipated price to be paid for each direct material item.

● **standard direct material cost**
The total expected cost of each material used to produce one unit, calculated by multiplying the standard quantity of direct material by the standard price.

● **direct labor efficiency standard**
The estimated number of direct labor hours required to produce one unit.

● **direct labor rate standard**
The expected hourly wage paid to production workers.

● **standard direct labor cost**
The total expected cost of labor used to produce one unit, calculated by multiplying the direct labor efficiency standard by the direct labor rate standard.

To determine realistic standard costs, managers compute the following:

1 The **direct material quantity standard** is the amount of direct material required to make one unit of product. Most products require more than one type of material so the manager creates a **bill of material**, which is a listing of the quantity and description of each direct material item used to produce one unit.
2 The **direct material price standard** is the anticipated price to be paid for each direct material item.
3 The **standard direct material cost** is the total expected cost of each material used to produce one unit, calculated by multiplying the standard quantity of direct material by the standard price.

Standard Direct Materials Cost = Standard Quantity × Standard Price

4 The **direct labor efficiency standard** is the estimated number of direct labor hours required to produce one unit. If the product requires different types of labor, each type of labor should have its own time estimate.
5 The **direct labor rate standard** is the expected hourly wage paid to production workers. Each type of labor may have a different rate.
6 The **standard direct labor cost** is the total expected cost of labor used to produce one unit, calculated by multiplying the direct labor efficiency standard by the direct labor rate standard.

Standard Direct Labor Cost = Standard Hours × Standard Labor Rate

7 The **standard variable manufacturing overhead rate** is an overhead rate calculated by dividing the budgeted variable manufacturing overhead cost by the budgeted direct labor hours.

$$\text{Standard Variable Manufacturing Overhead Rate} = \frac{\text{Budgeted Variable Manufacturing Overhead}}{\text{Budgeted Direct Labor Hours}}$$

8 The **standard variable overhead cost** is the expected variable overhead cost to produce one unit, calculated by multiplying the standard variable manufacturing overhead rate by the direct labor efficiency standard.

$$\text{Standard Variable Overhead Cost} = \text{Standard Variable Overhead Rate} \times \text{Standard Direct Labor Hours}$$

9 The **standard fixed manufacturing overhead rate** is an overhead rate calculated by dividing the budgeted fixed manufacturing overhead cost by the appropriate cost driver. For purposes of this chapter, we will use standard direct labor hours.

$$\text{Standard Fixed Manufacturing Overhead Rate} = \frac{\text{Budgeted Fixed Manufacturing Overhead}}{\text{Budgeted Direct Labor Hours}}$$

10 The **standard fixed overhead cost** is the expected fixed overhead cost to produce one unit, calculated by multiplying the standard fixed manufacturing overhead rate by the direct labor efficiency standard.

$$\text{Standard Fixed Overhead Cost} = \text{Standard Overhead Rate} \times \text{Standard Direct Labor Hours}$$

Megan and Jon analyzed costs for several years of production and updated amounts for known changes in costs. (For simplicity, we assumed that Elevation Sports was only producing snowboards.) They developed the following data for snowboard production:

Direct Materials

	Quantity	Price
Wood	3.00 sq. ft	$2/sq. ft.
Binding set	1.00	$4 each
Direct labor	2.5 hours	$10/hour
Budgeted monthly units produced	400	
Budgeted monthly variable overhead costs		$6,200
Budgeted monthly fixed overhead costs		$7,800
Budgeted monthly direct labor hours	1,000	

Using this information, Megan calculated the standard costs as follows:

1 Standard material costs:

	Unit Standard Material Quantity	×	Unit Standard Material Price	=	Unit Standard Material Cost
Wood	3	×	$2	=	$6.00
Bindings	1	×	$4	=	4.00

2 Standard labor costs:

Unit Standard Direct Labor Hours	×	Unit Standard Direct Labor Rate	=	Unit Standard Direct Labor Cost
2.5	×	$10	=	$25.00

3 Variable overhead rate:

Budgeted Variable Manufacturing Overhead	/	Budgeted Direct Labor Hours	=	Standard Variable Manufacturing Overhead Rate
$6,200	/	1,000	=	$6.20

● standard variable manufacturing overhead rate
An overhead rate calculated by dividing the budgeted variable manufacturing overhead cost by the budgeted direct labor hours.

● standard variable overhead cost
The expected variable overhead cost to produce one unit, calculated by multiplying the standard variable manufacturing overhead rate by the direct labor efficiency standard.

● standard fixed manufacturing overhead rate
An overhead rate calculated by dividing the budgeted fixed manufacturing overhead cost by the appropriate cost driver.

● standard fixed overhead cost
The expected fixed overhead cost to produce one unit, calculated by multiplying the standard fixed manufacturing overhead rate by the direct labor efficiency standard.

4   Standard variable overhead cost:

Unit Standard Variable Overhead Rate	×	Unit Standard Direct Labor Hours	=	Unit Standard Variable Overhead Cost
$6.20	×	2.5	=	$15.50

5   Standard fixed overhead rate:

Budgeted Fixed Manufacturing Overhead	/	Budgeted Direct Labor Hours	=	Standard Fixed Manufacturing Overhead Rate
$7,800	/	1,000	=	$7.80

6   Standard fixed overhead cost:

Unit Standard Fixed Overhead Rate	×	Unit Standard Direct Labor Hours	=	Unit Standard Fixed Overhead Cost
$7.80	×	2.5	=	$19.50

Megan calculated the final standard unit costs for an Elevation Sports snowboard as:

	Unit Standard Cost
Material	$10.00
Labor	25.00
Variable overhead	15.50
Fixed overhead	19.50
Total	$ 70.00

Megan and Jon understand, as you might also, that the *actual* cost of producing a snowboard will seldom equal the *standard* cost. She and Jon are determined to search for the cause of any variance between the two so they can take any warranted corrective action.

Calculating and Analyzing Material Variances

When actual total production costs exceed the standard costs, a manager must be able to pinpoint the true cause of the problem. By analyzing the various components of standard costs, the manager may be able to isolate the exact cause or causes of the problem to take proper corrective actions. If a manager, for example, assumes that the purchasing agent is paying too much for the materials, the purchasing agent may buy lower grade material at a cheaper cost. The manager may find, in reality, poor grade materials were the true source of the problem, and the cost overruns escalate because of the incorrect diagnosis of the problem.

To begin the variance analysis, let's look at the month of October 2005 for Elevation Sports. It was a disappointing month because the average temperature was 45°F and it did not have significant snowfall until the last week of the month. Exhibit 10-18 contains the October information necessary to analyze variances.

Direct material variances provide information for the managers to determine whether the company used more or less material than standard, paid more or less than standard for the material, and the dollar value of the differences.

First, let's consider the material usage.

The **direct material quantity variance** measures the difference between the standard and actual consumption of direct material for the number of units actually

● **direct material quantity variance**
The difference between the standard and actual consumption of direct material for the number of units actually manufactured.

Elevation Sports, Inc. Summary of Production Costs October 2005			
	QUANTITY	ACTUAL COST	STANDARD COST
Units produced	250		
Materials used			
Wood	600 sq. ft.	$ 1,200	$ 1,500
Bindings	252	756	1,000
Direct labor	750 hours	7,500	6,250
Variable overhead		3,600	3,875
Fixed overhead		7,800	4,875
Total		$20,856	$17,500

Exhibit 10-18
Elevation Sports, Inc.
October 2005 Information

manufactured. Megan followed three steps to calculate the direct material quantity variances. First, she calculated the standard quantity of direct material that should have been used for the actual units produced:

	Standard Quantity Per Unit	×	Number of Units Produced	=	Standard Quantity of Direct Material Allowed
Wood	3 sq. ft	×	250	=	750 sq. ft.
Bindings	1	×	250	=	250 Bindings

For 250 units, the production department should have used 750 square feet of wood and 250 sets of bindings.

Second, Megan calculated the variance in units of direct material:

	Standard Quantity of Direct Material Allowed	−	Actual Quantity Used	=	Quantity Variance in Square feet
Wood	750	−	600	=	150 Favorable
Bindings	250	−	252	=	2 Unfavorable

Finally, Megan calculated the dollar value of the variances:

	Quantity Variance in Square Foot	×	Standard Price per Square Foot	=	Quantity Variance in Dollars
Wood	150 Favorable	×	$2	=	$300 Favorable
Bindings	2 Unfavorable	×	$4	=	$ 8 Unfavorable

The production department used much less wood in making snowboards in October. Jon explained that because they were not rushed, they were able to cut the boards more carefully, which saved a significant amount of wood. They also ruined two sets of bindings and suspected that something was defective in those two sets.

Overall, the company netted $292 in savings. Jon will investigate the bindings, but he does not advocate slowing down production to save wood.

The **direct material price variance** measures the difference between the amount the company *expected* to pay for direct material and the amount it *actually* paid.

● **direct material price variance**
The difference between the amount the company expected to pay for direct material and the amount it actually paid.

Megan used two steps to compute the direct material price variance. First, she determined the amount the company should have paid for the actual direct material used:

	Actual Quantity Used	×	Direct Material Standard Price	=	Actual Quantity Used at Standard Price
Wood	600	×	$2	=	$1,200
Bindings	252	×	$4	=	$1,008

Second, Megan calculated the dollar amount of the direct material variance by subtracting the actual cost of direct material from the standard cost of the direct material purchased:

	Actual Quantity Used Priced at Standard	−	Actual Direct Material Cost	=	Direct Material Price Variance
Wood	$1,200	−	$1,200	=	$ 0
Bindings	$1,008	−	$ 756	=	$252 Favorable

Jon purchased the wood at the standard cost and had no price variance. He purchased the bindings, however, for $3 each instead of $4 each and created a favorable price variance of $252. Jon explained that he was able to purchase the bindings at a special price because of the warm fall season.

Next let's turn our attention to labor variances.

Calculating and Analyzing Labor Variances

Direct labor variances provide information for the managers to determine whether the company used more or fewer labor hours than standard, paid more or less than the standard rate, and the dollar value of the differences. First, let's consider the material usage.

The **direct labor efficiency variance** measures whether production consumed more or fewer than the standard direct labor hours to manufacture the actual quantity produced during the month. Megan used three steps to calculate the direct labor efficiency variance. First, she determined the standard number of direct labor hours allowed for production. Each board should require 2.5 hours, and they manufactured 250 snowboards. The total direct labor hours allowed should have been 625 hours. Second, Megan calculated the direct labor efficiency variance in hours by subtracting the actual number of direct labor hours worked from the standard direct labor hours allowed.

● **direct labor efficiency variance**
A variance that measures whether production consumed more or fewer than the standard direct labor hours to manufacture the actual quantity produced during the month.

Standard Direct Labor Hours Allowed	−	Actual Direct labor Hours	=	Efficiency Variance in Hours
625 Hours	−	750 Hours	=	125 Hours Unfavorable

The unfavorable variance correlates to Jon's report that they slowed down production in cutting out the snowboards. Megan then calculated the direct labor efficiency variance in dollars by multiplying the variance in hours by the standard direct labor rate as follows:

Direct Labor Efficiency Variance in Hours	×	Standard Direct Labor Rate	=	Direct labor Efficiency Variance in Dollars
125 Hours	×	$10	=	$1,250 Unfavorable

A manager should assess the variance and, when necessary, take corrective action. The unusually warm October allowed Jon to experiment with production time and materials.

The **direct labor rate variance** measures the effect of unanticipated wage rate changes by calculating the difference between the actual wage rate paid to employees and the direct labor rate standard. Elevation Sports' direct labor rate standard is $10 per hour. Megan computed the amount that should have been paid for the actual direct labor hours worked according to the direct labor rate standard as follows:

$$
\begin{array}{ccccc}
\text{Actual} & & \text{Direct Labor} & & \text{Actual Direct labor} \\
\text{Direct Labor} & & \text{Rate} & & \text{Hours at the} \\
\underline{\text{Hours}} & \times & \underline{\text{Standard}} & = & \underline{\text{Standard Rate}} \\
750 \text{ Hours} & \times & \$10 & = & \$7,500
\end{array}
$$

● **direct labor rate variance**
A variance that measures the effect of unanticipated wage rate changes by calculating the difference between the actual wage rate paid to employees and the direct labor rate standard.

Megan compared what the company should have paid according to the standard to the amount actually paid to determine the direct labor rate variance as follows:

$$
\begin{array}{ccccc}
\text{Actual Direct Labor} & & \text{Actual} & & \text{Direct labor} \\
\text{Hours at the} & & \text{Direct labor} & & \text{Rate} \\
\underline{\text{Standard}} & - & \underline{\text{Cost}} & = & \underline{\text{Variance}} \\
\$7,500 & - & \$7,500 & = & \$0
\end{array}
$$

Jon did not change the wage rate he paid the workers. Had the rate changed, the officers would have needed to investigate and determine what actions to take.

Calculating and Analyzing Manufacturing Overhead Variances

Manufacturing overhead variances help managers answer two important questions. First, did the company spend more or less on overhead items than the standard amounts? Second, did the company utilize its production facility efficiently? To answer these questions, we will examine four manufacturing overhead variances, two relating to variable manufacturing overhead and two corresponding to fixed manufacturing overhead.

The **variable manufacturing overhead efficiency variance** measures the difference between the variable manufacturing overhead cost attributable to planned and actual direct labor hours worked. This variance directly correlates to the efficiency of direct labor because the more direct labor hours worked, the higher the consumption of utilities, supplies, equipment, and factory resources. To compute this variance, Megan multiplied the direct labor efficiency variance in hours by the standard variable manufacturing overhead rate. Megan had already calculated these amounts to be 125 hours of unfavorable direct labor efficiency variance and the standard variable overhead rate of $6.20 per direct labor hour:

● **variable manufacturing overhead efficiency variance**
A variance that measures the difference between the variable manufacturing overhead cost attributable to planned and actual direct labor hours worked.

$$
\begin{array}{ccccc}
\text{Direct Labor Efficiency} & & \text{Standard} & & \text{Variable Overhead} \\
\text{Variance} & & \text{Variable} & & \text{Efficiency} \\
\underline{\text{in Hours}} & \times & \underline{\text{Overhead Rate}} & = & \underline{\text{Variance}} \\
125 \text{ Hours} & \times & \$6.20 & = & \$775 \text{ Unfavorable}
\end{array}
$$

Armed with this information, Megan can show Jon how using the extra production hours cost more than the wages paid to the workers. This variance will improve if Jon restricts any future unfavorable direct labor efficiency variances.

The **variable manufacturing overhead spending variance** measures the difference between what was actually spent on variable manufacturing overhead and what should have been spent based on the actual direct labor hours worked. This variance helps a manager determine if the dollar amount of the variable manufacturing overhead is appropriate for the amount of actual direct labor hours worked. Megan first determined the standard variable manufacturing overhead for the actual number of

● **variable manufacturing overhead spending variance**
A variance that measures the difference between what was actually spent on variable manufacturing overhead and what should have been spent, based on the actual direct labor hours worked.

hours worked by multiplying the standard variable manufacturing overhead rate by the actual number of direct labor hours:

$$
\frac{\begin{array}{c}\text{Actual}\\\text{Direct Labor}\\\text{Hours}\end{array}}{750 \text{ Hours}} \times \frac{\begin{array}{c}\text{Standard}\\\text{Variable}\\\text{Overhead Rate}\end{array}}{\$6.20} = \frac{\begin{array}{c}\text{Standard Variable}\\\text{Overhead For Actual}\\\text{Direct Labor Hours}\end{array}}{\$4,650}
$$

Now we know how much Elevation Sports' variable manufacturing overhead should have been, we can compare it to the actual variable manufacturing overhead amount to determine the amount of the variance as follows:

$$
\frac{\begin{array}{c}\text{Standard Variable}\\\text{Overhead for Actual}\\\text{Direct Labor Hours}\end{array}}{\$4,650} - \frac{\begin{array}{c}\text{Actual}\\\text{Variable}\\\text{Overhead}\end{array}}{\$3,600} = \frac{\begin{array}{c}\text{Variable}\\\text{Overhead Spending}\\\text{Variance}\end{array}}{\$1,050 \text{ Favorable}}
$$

The variable manufacturing overhead spending variance consists of many overhead expenditures. In practice, most companies break down the variable manufacturing overhead spending variance into separate variances for each variable manufacturing overhead item, such as electricity, water, and supplies.

● **fixed manufacturing overhead budget variance**
A variance that measures the difference between actual total fixed manufacturing overhead and budgeted fixed manufacturing overhead.

The **fixed manufacturing overhead budget variance** measures the difference between actual total fixed manufacturing overhead and budgeted fixed manufacturing overhead. Megan compared the actual fixed overhead of $7,800 to the budgeted fixed overhead of $7,800 as follows:

$$
\frac{\begin{array}{c}\text{Budgeted}\\\text{Fixed Overhead}\end{array}}{\$7,800} - \frac{\begin{array}{c}\text{Actual Fixed}\\\text{Fixed Overhead}\end{array}}{\$7,800} = \frac{\begin{array}{c}\text{Fixed Overhead}\\\text{Budget Variance}\end{array}}{\$0 \text{ Unfavorable}}
$$

As you can see, the lack of snow, in October did not change the amount of fixed manufacturing overhead. As with variable manufacturing overhead, fixed manufacturing overhead comprises many items and managers frequently calculate separate variances for each fixed manufacturing overhead item.

● **fixed manufacturing overhead volume variance**
A variance that measures utilization of plant capacity.

The **fixed manufacturing overhead volume variance** measures utilization of plant capacity. A variance is caused by the manufacture of more or less product during a particular production period than planned. When a manufacturer invests in expensive production machinery, it does so in anticipation of producing a given amount of product. The fixed manufacturing overhead volume variance focuses on this relationship between production capacity and the actual volume produced.

Elevation Sports has the capacity to produce 400 snowboards each month. Megan followed three steps to calculate the fixed manufacturing overhead volume variance. First, she found the difference between expected and actual production as follows:

$$
\frac{\begin{array}{c}\text{Plant}\\\text{Production}\\\text{Capacity}\end{array}}{400 \text{ Units}} - \frac{\begin{array}{c}\text{Actual}\\\text{Units}\\\text{Produced}\end{array}}{250 \text{ Units}} = \frac{\begin{array}{c}\text{Units of Under-}\\\text{or Overproduction}\end{array}}{150 \text{ Units Underproduction}}
$$

Second, she determined the standard number of direct labor hours associated with the underproduction because she allocates fixed manufacturing overhead based on direct labor hours. To determine the standard number of direct labor hours associated with the under- or overproduction, Megan multiplied the under- or overproduction by the direct labor efficiency standard.

$$
\frac{\begin{array}{c}\text{Amount of}\\\text{Under- or Overproduction}\end{array}}{150 \text{ Underproduction}} \times \frac{\begin{array}{c}\text{Direct Labor}\\\text{Efficiency}\\\text{Standard}\end{array}}{2.5 \text{ Hours/Unit}} = \frac{\begin{array}{c}\text{Standard Direct labor}\\\text{Hours for Under- or}\\\text{Overproduction}\end{array}}{375 \text{ Hours Underproduction}}
$$

Finally, she calculated the dollar amount of the fixed manufacturing overhead volume variance by multiplying the standard number of direct labor hours associated with the under- or overproduction by the standard fixed manufacturing overhead rate per direct labor hour:

Standard Direct Labor Hours for Over- or Underproduction		Standard Fixed Overhead Rate		Fixed Overhead Volume Variance
375 Hours	×	$7.80	=	$2,925 Unfavorable

Once Megan calculated the fixed manufacturing overhead volume variance, she and Jon can attempt to determine what caused it. In this case, Jon reduced the production because of the warm October weather, knowing that the lost demand would probably not be made up later in the winter. Marketing and sales activities often cause fixed manufacturing overhead volume variances. Generally, production occurs in response to sales demand. If the product is selling poorly, production volume will be low because little product is needed to fulfill demand. Conversely, if sales demand is high, production volume is likely to be large to meet demand.

Now that we have examined how to compute all the variances, let's explore how managers use this information to improve their profitability.

Using Standard Cost Variances to Manage by Exception

Once Megan calculates all the standard cost variances, she prepares a performance report that lists each variance. Then the officers can use management by exception to address the problems associated with the unfavorable variances, beginning with the largest. Exhibit 10-19 contains Megan's performance report for October 2005. The more frequently Megan and Jon review such reports, the more information they can glean from them. They must be careful to separate the correlation among some of the variances and factors over which they have no control from those factors for which they should implement corrective actions.

Elevation Sports, Inc. **Performance Report** **For October 2005**		
VARIANCE	**AMOUNT**	**FAVORABLE/ UNFAVORABLE**
Direct material quantity variance		
Wood	$ 300	Favorable
Bindings	8	Unfavorable
Direct material price variance		
Wood	—0—	
Bindings	252	Favorable
Direct labor efficiency variance	1,250	Unfavorable
Direct labor rate variance	—0—	
Variable overhead efficiency variance	775	Unfavorable
Variable overhead spending variance	1,050	Favorable
Fixed overhead budget variance	—0—	
Fixed overhead volume variance	2,925	Unfavorable
Total	$3,356	Unfavorable

Exhibit 10-19
Elevation Sports, Inc.
October Performance Report

CHAPTER SUMMARY

The operating budget is an integral part of the overall planning process for any company. Besides serving as a guide for the business throughout the period covered by the budget, the operating budget can assist management in allocating resources, fostering communication and coordination among various segments of the company, and establishing performance standards.

The operating budget is a set of estimated financial statements. These are the budgeted income statement, the budgeted balance sheet, and the budgeted statement of cash flows. Besides the budgeted financial statements, the operating budget includes several other budgets prepared to support the budgeted financial statements. These are the sales budget, the production (or purchases) budget, the cost of goods sold (or cost of services) budget, the selling and administrative expense budget, and the cash budget (including the cash receipts schedule and the cash payments schedule).

Several approaches exist when preparing the operating budget. Perpetual, incremental, zero-based, top-down, bottom-up, imposed, and participative budgets are just some of the approaches that have been developed. Each approach has advantages and disadvantages relative to the other approaches.

All the budgets included in the operating budget are dependent on the sales forecast. Indeed, the accuracy of the entire budget is dependent on the accuracy of the forecast. Many factors, including the state of the general economy, the condition of the company's industry, competitors' actions, and technological developments all influence a company's ability to forecast its sales reasonably. Management should analyze budget variances to improve the budget process.

A standard cost system contains estimates for the costs of direct materials, direct labor, and manufacturing overhead. Refined estimates become standard costs, which generally include a direct material quantity standard, a direct material price standard, a direct labor efficiency standard, a direct labor rate standard, a standard variable manufacturing overhead rate, and a standard fixed manufacturing overhead rate.

To use standard costs effectively, managers compare the standard costs for manufacturing to the actual costs to see whether a variance exists. They investigate any variances to see when to initiate corrective measures. The most common variances include the direct material quantity variance, the direct material price variance, the direct labor efficiency variance, the direct labor rate variance, the variable manufacturing overhead efficiency variance, the variable manufacturing overhead spending variance, the fixed manufacturing overhead budget variance, and the fixed manufacturing overhead volume variance.

Visit the Web site *www.prenhall.com/Terrell* for additional study help with the Online Study Guide.

REVIEW OF CONCEPTS

A   Define the term *operating budget* and explain how the budget is used.

B   Describe the master budget and identify its components.

C   Determine which budgeted financial statements are part of the operating budget.

D   Describe the difference between the financial statements included in the operating budget and the other financial statements you learned about in this course.

E   Describe the main benefits of budgeting.

F   Determine what circumstances cause one company to use a production budget and another to use a purchases budget.

G   Discuss two advantages and the disadvantage of perpetual budgeting.

H   Discuss the advantages and disadvantages of incremental budgeting.

I   Discuss the advantages and disadvantages of zero-based budgeting.

J   Describe the differences between top-down and bottom-up budgeting.

K   Describe the differences between an imposed budget and a participative budget.

L   Discuss why the sales forecast is often the cornerstone of budgeting.

M   Discuss three external factors that should be considered when preparing the sales forecast.

N   Discuss why the number of units budgeted to be purchased differs from the number of units budgeted to be sold.

O   When preparing the purchases budget, discuss what two factors should be considered when determining the budgeted ending inventory.

P   Describe what is presented on the cash receipts schedule and how the information is used.

Q   For a particular budget period, explain why the budgeted cash collection amount from customers does not equal budgeted sales.

R   In the normal course of business, describe the three sources from which a company can obtain cash. Discuss and describe which of the three is renewable.

S   Describe a performance budget analysis and a budget variance.

T   Discuss the importance of variance analysis and describe how the analysis is performed.

U   Describe how to set the various standard cost elements.

V   Discuss how a manager can use management by exception in a standard cost system.

W   Compare and contrast the difference between controllable and noncontrollable causes of variances.

APPLICATION EXERCISES

10-12   During the budgeting process, not all budgets are prepared at the same time.

LO 1 and 2
Determine Order of Operating Budget Preparation

Required:

Put the following operating budgets in a logical sequence for the preparation of the operating budget.
  a. cash budget
  b. budgeted financial statements
  c. purchases budget
  d. sales budget
  e. administrative expense budget
  f. selling expense budget

10-13   The master budget can be prepared using either the top-down or bottom-up approach.

LO 2
Advantages and Disadvantages of Top-Down, Bottom-Up Approaches

Required:

For each item listed, indicate whether it is associated with a top-down or a bottom-up approach, and whether it is an advantage or disadvantage.
  a. Budgeting process forces managers at various levels to think about future activities.
  b. Top manager is more knowledgeable.

c. Employees at various levels must take time from their schedules to work on the budget.
d. Employees will be more eager to work toward goals they helped set.
e. Employees feel more like part of the company team.
f. Top manager is more aware of company goals.
g. Employees may try to pad the budget.
h. Employees are less accepting of budgeted goals if they had no part in setting them.
i. Top manager lacks detailed knowledge required to prepare budgets.

LO 5
Prepare a Sales Budget

10-14   For 2005, David's Computer Game Company expects to sell 6,000 games in the first quarter, 7,000 games in the second quarter, 9,000 games in the third quarter, and 12,000 games in the fourth quarter. Each game sells for $11 in the first two quarters and $12 in the last two quarters.

Required:

Prepare the 2005 sales budget for David's Computer Game Company.

LO 5
Prepare a Sales Budget

10-15   For 2005, Paul Larsen's Barber Supply Company expects to sell 100 hair dryers in the first quarter, 90 hair dryers in the second quarter, 130 hair dryers in the third quarter, and 150 hair dryers in the fourth quarter. Each hair dryer sells for $67.

Required:

a. Prepare the 2005 sales budget for hair dryers for Paul Larsen's Barber Supply Company.
b. The company considers raising its price in the third quarter to $75. How much difference would this make in budgeted sales?

LO 5
Prepare a Sales Budget

10-16   For 2006, Irina Company expects to sell 20,000 units in January, 25,000 units in February, and 30,000 units in March. Half the units each quarter sell for $1.20 and the remaining units sell for $1.80.

Required:

Prepare the sales budget for Irina Company for the first quarter of 2006.

LO 5
Prepare a Sales Budget

10-17   The CEO of the Golden Bird Cage Company intends to sell 11,500 bird cages during 2005. The budgeted selling price per cage is $88.

The following unit sales forecast is available:

First quarter	2,500
Second quarter	2,100
Third quarter	3,800
Fourth quarter	3,100

Required:

a. Prepare the 2005 sales budget for Golden Bird Cage Company.
b. If sales in the fourth quarter of 2004 are slow, the CEO will reduce the selling price for the first quarter of 2005 to $80. How much would that reduce the total sales for the year?

LO 5
Prepare a Sales Budget

10-18   Easy-Glide Strollers intends to sell 73,000 baby strollers in the first quarter of 2005. The budgeted selling price per stroller is $59. The following unit sales forecast is available:

January	22,500
February	22,500
March	28,000

Required:

Prepare the sales budget for Easy-Glide Strollers for the first quarter of 2005.

10-19   Theresa's Hat Shop plans to sell the following quantity of hats during the first four months of 2005:

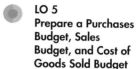

LO 5
Prepare a Purchases Budget, Sales Budget, and Cost of Goods Sold Budget

January	200
February	250
March	300
April	320

Theresa pays $6 for each hat, which she sells for $15. At the beginning of January, Theresa plans to have 40 hats on hand, and hopes to maintain an ending inventory equal to 20% of next month's sales.

Required:

a. Prepare a purchases budget for the first quarter of 2005 for Theresa's Hat Shop.
b. Prepare a sales budget for the first quarter of 2005 for Theresa's Hat Shop.
c. Prepare a cost of goods sold budget for the first quarter of 2005 for Theresa's Hat Shop.

10-20   Elane's Art Supplies plans to sell the following quantity of model AB222 airbrush during the first four months of 2005:

LO 5
Prepare a Sales Budget, Cost of Goods Sold Budget, and Purchases Budget

January	40
February	26
March	22
April	20

Elane pays $44 for each airbrush and sells them for $65. At the beginning of January, Elane plans to have 6 airbrushes on hand, and hopes to maintain an ending inventory equal to 15% of next month's sales.

Required:

a. Prepare a purchases budget for the first quarter of 2005 for Elane's Art Supplies.
b. Prepare a sales budget for the first quarter of 2005 for Elane's Art Supplies.
c. Prepare a cost of goods sold budget for the first quarter of 2005 for Elane's Art Supplies.

10-21   Duncan Lumber plans to sell the following quantity of A Grade 3/4-inch plywood sheets during the first four months of 2006:

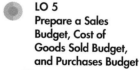

LO 5
Prepare a Sales Budget, Cost of Goods Sold Budget, and Purchases Budget

January	220
February	250
March	200
April	300

Duncan pays $9 for each sheet of plywood and sells it for $15. At the beginning of January, Duncan plans to have 66 sheets of plywood on hand and hopes to maintain an ending inventory equal to 30% of next month's sales.

Required:

a. Prepare a sales budget for the first quarter of 2006 for Duncan Lumber.

b. Prepare a cost of goods sold budget for the first quarter of 2006 for Duncan Lumber.

c. Prepare a purchases budget for the first quarter of 2006 for Duncan Lumber.

LO 5
Prepare a Budgeted Income Statement

10-22   Swenton Manufacturing has prepared the following budgeted information for January 2007.

Swenton Manufacturing
Sales Budget
For January 31, 2007

Budgeted sales in units	3,300
× Budgeted sales price	$ 200
= Budgeted Sales Dollars	$660,000

Swenton Manufacturing
Cost of Goods Sold Budget
For January 31, 2007

Budgeted sales in units	3,300
× Budgeted cost per unit	$ 110
= Budgeted Cost of Goods Sold	$363,000

Swenton Manufacturing
Selling and Administrative Expense Budget
For January 31, 2007

Salaries and wages	$101,500
Rent	64,000
Depreciation	53,200
Other	2,300
Budgeted Selling and Administrative Expense	$221,000

Required:

Prepare a budgeted income statement for January 2007 for Swenton Manufacturing.

LO 5
Prepare a Budgeted Income Statement

10-23   Gulick Sales Company has prepared the following budgeted information for March 2006.

Gulick Sales Company
Sales Budget
For March 31, 2006

Budgeted sales in units	110,000
× Budgeted sales price	$ 4.95
= Budgeted Sales Dollars	$544,500

Gulick Sales Company
Cost of Goods Sold Budget
For March 31, 2006

Budgeted sales in units	110,000
× Budgeted cost per unit	$ 3.35
= Budgeted Cost of Goods Sold	$368,500

Gulick Sales Company
Selling and Administrative Expense Budget
For March 31, 2006

Sales salaries	$ 51,500
Sales commission	11,000
Other salaries and wages	35,000
Store rent	24,000
Other expenses	10,500
Budgeted Selling and Administrative Expense	$132,000

Required:

Prepare a budgeted income statement for March 2006 for Gulick Sales Company.

10-24 Copas Company has prepared the following budgeted information for December 2005.

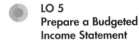
LO 5
Prepare a Budgeted Income Statement

Copas Company
Sales Budget
For December 31, 2005

Budgeted sales in units	10,000
× Budgeted sales price	$ 12
= Budgeted Sales Dollars	$120,000

Copas Company
Cost of Goods Sold Budget
For December 31, 2005

Budgeted sales in units	10,000
× Budgeted cost per unit	$ 8
= Budgeted Cost of Goods Sold	$ 80,000

Copas Company
Selling and Administrative Expense Budget
For December 31, 2005

Sales salaries	$18,500
Sales commission	3,000
Store rent	9,000
Other expenses	1,500
Budgeted Selling and Administrative Expense	$32,000

Required:

Prepare a budgeted income statement for December 2005 for Copas Company.

10-25 For the first quarter of 2006, Philip's Sales Corporation has budgeted sales of $390,000 and budgeted cost of goods sold of $280,000. In addition, the budget for the first quarter of 2006 includes wages and salaries of $42,000, rent of $9,000, utilities of $2,000, maintenance of $1,000, and other expenses of $3,000.

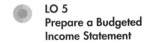
LO 5
Prepare a Budgeted Income Statement

Required:

Prepare a budgeted income statement for the first quarter of 2006 for Philip's Sales Corporation.

LO 5
Prepare a Budgeted Income Statement

10-26   For January 2005, Steiferman Manufacturing has budgeted sales of $1,200,000 and budgeted cost of goods sold of $980,000. In addition, the budget for January 2005 includes sales salaries of $98,000, administrative salaries of $54,000, rent of $24,000, utilities of $8,000, and other expenses of $9,000.

Required:

   Prepare a budgeted income statement for January of 2005 for Steiferman Manufacturing.

LO 5
Prepare a Budgeted Income Statement

10-27   For 2006, Martin Sales Corporation has budgeted sales of $3,500,000 and budgeted cost of goods sold of $2,800,000. In addition, the budget for 2006 includes sales salaries of $220,000, administrative salaries of $130,000, depreciation of $180,000, utilities of $38,000, and other expenses of $22,000.

Required:

   Prepare a budgeted income statement for 2006 for Martin Sales Corporation.

LO 5
Prepare a Budgeted Income Statement

10-28   The following budgets were prepared for Denson's Jean Store.

Denson's Jean Store
Sales Budget
For the Quarter Ended June 30, 2005

	April	May	June	Total
Budgeted sales in units	300	350	400	1,050
× Budgeted sales price	$ 27	$ 27	$ 27	$ 27
= Budgeted Sales Dollars	$8,100	$9,450	$10,800	$28,350

Denson's Jean Store
Cost of Goods Sold Budget
For the Quarter Ended June 30, 2005

	April	May	June	Total
Budgeted sales in units	300	350	400	1,050
× Budgeted cost per unit	$ 14	$ 14	$ 14	$ 14
= Budgeted Cost of Goods Sold	$4,200	$4,900	$5,600	$14,700

Denson's Jean Store
Selling and Administrative Expense Budget
For the Quarter Ended June 30, 2005

	April	May	June	Total
Salaries and wages	$1,800	$2,200	$1,900	$ 5,900
Rent	500	500	500	1,500
Depreciation	100	100	100	300
Other expenses	600	900	800	2,300
Budgeted Selling and Administrative Expense	$3,000	$3,700	$3,300	$10,000

Required:

   Prepare a budgeted income statement for the second quarter of 2005 for Denson's Jean Store.

10-29 Wilkinson's Cart Company manufactures small carts that are designed to be pulled behind a small tractor or riding lawn mower. Management prepared the following budgets for Wilkinson's Cart Company:

LO 5
**Prepare a Budgeted
Income Statement**

Wilkinson's Cart Company
Sales Budget
For the Quarter Ended March 31, 2006

	January	February	March	Total
Budgeted sales in units	1,300	1,450	1,700	4,450
× Budgeted sales price	$ 186	$ 186	$ 186	$ 186
= Budgeted Sales Dollars	$241,800	$269,700	$316,200	$827,700

Wilkinson's Cart Company
Cost of Goods Sold Budget
For the Quarter Ended March 31, 2006

	January	February	March	Total
Budgeted sales in units	1,300	1,450	1,700	4,450
× Budgeted cost per unit	$ 154	$ 154	$ 154	$ 154
= Budgeted Cost of Goods Sold	$200,200	$223,300	$261,800	$685,300

Wilkinson's Cart Company
Selling and Administrative Expense Budget
For the Quarter Ended March 31, 2006

	January	February	March	Total
Salaries and wages	$21,950	$22,200	$23,600	$67,750
Rent	4,000	4,500	4,500	13,000
Depreciation	3,200	3,200	3,200	9,600
Other expenses	2,300	2,500	2,800	7,600
Budgeted Selling and Administrative Expense	$31,450	$ 32,400	$34,100	$97,950

Required:

Prepare a budgeted income statement for the first quarter of 2006 for Wilkinson's Cart Company.

10-30 Management prepared the following budgets for Parrish Manufacturing:

LO 5
**Prepare a Budgeted
Income Statement**

Parrish Manufacturing
Sales Budget
For the Quarter Ended September 30, 2006

	July	August	September	Total
Budgeted unit sales	900	1,100	1,300	3,300
× Budgeted sales price	$ 225	$ 225	$ 225	$ 225
= Budgeted Sales Dollars	$202,500	$247,500	$292,500	$742,500

Parrish Manufacturing
Cost of Goods Sold Budget
For the Quarter Ended September 30, 2006

	July	August	September	Total
Budgeted unit sales	900	1,100	1,300	3,300
× Budgeted cost per unit	$ 204	$ 204	$ 204	$ 204
= Budgeted Cost of Goods Sold	$183,600	$224,400	$265,200	$673,200

Parrish Manufacturing
Selling and Administrative Expense Budget
For the Quarter Ended September 30, 2006

	July	August	September	Total
Salaries and wages	$ 4,800	$ 5,200	$ 5,800	$15,800
Rent	2,400	2,400	2,400	7,200
Depreciation	1,150	1,150	1,150	3,450
Other expenses	1,800	2,000	2,200	6,000
Budgeted Selling and Administrative Expense	$10,150	$10,750	$11,550	$32,450

Required:

Prepare a budgeted income statement for the third quarter of 2006 for Parrish Manufacturing.

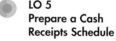
LO 5
Prepare a Cash Receipts Schedule

10-31   The Calvert Company is preparing a cash receipts schedule for the first quarter of 2006. Sales for November and December 2005 are expected to be $180,000 and $200,000, respectively. Budgeted sales for the first quarter of 2006 are:

The Calvert Company
Sales Budget
For the Quarter Ended March 31, 2006

	January	February	March	Total
Budgeted sales	$220,000	$240,000	$260,000	$720,000

For each month, 20% of sales is for cash, the remaining 80% is on account. Ten percent the sales on account is collected in the month of the sale, 60% is collected in the month following the sale, and the remaining 30% is collected in the second month following the sale. The company has no uncollectible accounts receivable.

Required:

Prepare a cash receipts schedule for the first quarter of 2006.

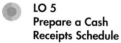
LO 5
Prepare a Cash Receipts Schedule

10-32   The Pursifull Company is preparing a cash receipts schedule for the first quarter of 2006. Sales for November and December 2005 are expected to be $300,000 and $310,000, respectively. Budgeted sales for the first quarter of 2006 are:

The Pursifull Company
Sales Budget
For the Quarter Ended March 31, 2006

	January	February	March	Total
Budgeted sales	$220,000	$290,000	$340,000	$850,000

For each month, 10% of sales is for cash, the remaining 90% is on account. Twenty percent of the sales on account is collected in the month of the sale, 70% is collected in the month following the sale, and the remaining 10% is collected in the second month following the sale. The company has no uncollectible accounts receivable.

Required:

Prepare a cash receipts schedule for the first quarter of 2006.

10-33   The Miller Company is preparing a cash receipts schedule for the first quarter of 2006. Sales for November and December 2005 are expected to be $30,000 and $50,000, respectively. Budgeted sales for the first quarter of 2006 are:

The Miller Company
Sales Budget
For the Quarter Ended March 31, 2006

	January	February	March	Total
Budgeted sales	$20,000	$25,000	$40,000	$85,000

For each month, 15% of sales is for cash, the remaining 85% is on account. Twenty percent of the sales on account is collected in the month of the sale, 50% is collected in the month following the sale, and the remaining 30% is collected in the second month following the sale. The company has no uncollectible accounts receivable.

Required:

Prepare a cash receipts schedule for the first quarter of 2006.

10-34   The Stumbaugh Company is preparing a cash receipts schedule for the first quarter of 2006. Sales for November and December 2005 are expected to be $33,000 and $55,000, respectively. Budgeted sales for the first quarter of 2006 are:

The Stumbaugh Company
Sales Budget
For the Quarter Ended March 31, 2006

	January	February	March	Total
Budgeted sales	$20,000	$30,000	$45,000	$95,000

For each month, 15% of sales is for cash, the remaining 85% is on account. Twenty percent of the sales on account is collected in the month of the sale, 50% is collected in the month following the sale, 30% is collected in the second month following the sale. The company has no uncollectible accounts receivable.

Required:

Prepare a cash receipts schedule for the first quarter of 2006.

10-35   The Mayes Company is preparing a cash receipts schedule for the first quarter of 2006. Sales for November and December 2005 are expected to be $40,000 and $80,000, respectively. Budgeted sales for the first quarter of 2006 are:

The Mayes Company
Sales Budget
For the Quarter Ended March 31, 2006

	January	February	March	Total
Budgeted sales	$30,000	$40,000	$50,000	$120,000

For each month, 10% of sales is for cash, the remaining 90% is on account. Fifteen percent of the sales on account is collected in the month of the sale, 60% is collected in the month following the sale, 25% is collected in the second month following the sale. The company has no uncollectible accounts receivable.

Required:

Prepare a cash receipts schedule for the first quarter of 2006.

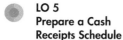

10-36 The Haskin Company is preparing a cash receipts schedule for the first quarter of 2005. Sales on account for November and December 2004 are expected to be $500,000 and $750,000, respectively. Budgeted sales for the first quarter of 2005 are presented below.

The Haskin Company
Sales Budget
For the Quarter Ended March 31, 2005

	January	February	March	Total
Budgeted cash sales	$ 40,000	$ 45,000	$ 55,000	$ 140,000
Budgeted sales on account	400,000	450,000	550,000	1,400,000
Total Sales	$440,000	$495,000	$605,000	$1,540,000

Expected collection pattern for sales on account:

15% in the month of sale
60% in the month following the sale
25% in the second month following the sale
0% uncollectible

Required:

Prepare a cash receipts schedule for the first quarter of 2005.

10-37 The Beavers Company is preparing a cash receipts schedule for the first quarter of 2006. Sales on account for November and December 2005 are expected to be $200,000 and $400,000, respectively. Budgeted sales for the first quarter of 2006 are presented below.

The Beavers Company
Sales Budget
For the Quarter Ended March 31, 2006

	January	February	March	Total
Budgeted cash sales	$ 20,000	$ 25,000	$ 27,000	$ 72,000
Budgeted sales on account	180,000	210,000	250,000	640,000
Total Sales	$ 200,000	$ 235,000	$ 277,000	$ 712,000

Expected collection pattern for sales on account:

10% in the month of sale
70% in the month following the sale
20% in the second month following the sale
0% uncollectible

Required:

Prepare a cash receipts schedule for the first quarter of 2006.

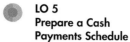

10-38 Jane Wesley and Company has prepared the following budgets for the first quarter of 2006:

Jane Wesley and Company
Selling and Administrative Expense Budget
For the Quarter Ended March 31, 2006

	January	February	March	Total
Salaries and wages	$ 1,700	$ 2,200	$ 1,900	$ 5,800
Rent	300	300	300	900
Depreciation	200	200	200	600
Other expenses	900	1,200	1,000	3,100
Budgeted Selling and Administrative Expense	$ 3,100	$ 3,900	$ 3,400	$ 10,400

Jane Wesley and Company
Purchases Budget
For the Quarter Ended March 31, 2006

	January	February	March	Total
Forecasted unit sales	50	60	70	180
+ Desired ending inventory	12	14	16	16
= Total units needed	62	74	86	196
− Beginning inventory	(10)	(12)	(14)	(10)
= Units to be purchased	52	62	72	186
× Cost per unit	$ 220	$ 220	$ 220	$ 220
= Cost of Purchases	$ 11,440	$ 13,640	$ 15,840	$ 40,920

Selling and administrative expenses are paid in the month incurred, and purchases are paid in the month following the purchase. Purchases for December 2005 are $10,500. No equipment purchases or additional expenditures are made during the quarter.

Required:

Prepare a cash payments schedule for the first quarter of 2006.

10-39 Jackson Sales Company has prepared the following budgets for the first quarter of 2006:

Jackson Sales Company
Selling and Administrative Expense Budget
For the Quarter Ended June 30, 2006

	April	May	June	Total
Salaries	$ 1,000	$ 1,200	$ 1,300	$ 3,500
Rent	200	200	200	600
Utilities	120	180	220	520
Depreciation	80	80	80	240
Other expenses	500	600	650	1,750
Budgeted Selling and Administrative Expense	$ 1,900	$ 2,260	$ 2,450	$ 6,610

Jackson Sales Company
Purchases Budget
For the Quarter Ended June 30, 2006

	April	May	June	Total
Forecasted unit sales	70	80	90	240
+ Desired ending inventory	16	18	19	19
= Total units needed	86	98	109	259
− Beginning inventory	(15)	(16)	(18)	(15)
= Units to be purchased	71	82	91	244
× Cost per unit	$ 100	$ 100	$ 100	$ 100
= Cost of Purchases	$ 7,100	$ 8,200	$ 9,100	$ 24,400

Selling and administrative expenses are paid in the month incurred, and purchases are paid in the month following the purchase. Purchases for March 2006 are $6,800. No equipment purchases or additional expenditures are made during the quarter.

Required:

Prepare a cash payments schedule for the second quarter of 2006.

LO 5
Prepare a Cash
Payments Schedule

10-40 The following budgeted information is available for the Top Coat Clothing Company for January 2006:

Salaries	$120,000
Rent	9,000
Utilities	1,200
Depreciation	3,200
Other expenses	1,500
Purchases	380,000

Selling and administrative expenses are paid in the month incurred, and purchases are paid in the month following the purchase. Purchases for December 2005 are $350,000. No equipment purchases or additional expenditures are made during the month.

Required:

Prepare a cash payments schedule for January 2006.

LO 5
Prepare a Cash
Payments Schedule

10-41 The following budgeted information is available for the Jack's Feed Store for June 2006:

Salaries	$12,000
Rent	600
Electricity	140
Depreciation	800
Other expenses	700
Purchases	80,000

Selling and administrative expenses are paid in the month incurred, and purchases are paid in the month following the purchase. Purchases for May 2006 are $75,000. No equipment purchases or additional expenditures are made during the month.

Required:

Prepare a cash payments schedule for June 2006.

10-42   The following information is available for the Wells Company for the first quarter of 2006:

LO 5
Prepare a Cash
Budget

	January	February	March
Budgeted receipts from credit sales	$5,000	$5,500	$5,800
Budgeted cash sales	1,200	1,250	1.300
Budgeted cash payments	6,300	7,185	6,520

Beginning cash balance for January 2006 is expected to be $1,500. The company intends to maintain a cash balance of at least $1,000, and has made arrangements to borrow from a local bank if necessary.

Required:

Prepare a cash budget for the first quarter of 2006.

10-43   The following information is available for the Bizé Company for the second quarter of 2006:

LO 5
Prepare a Cash
Budget

	April	May	June
Budgeted receipts from credit sales	$500,000	$520,000	$550,000
Budgeted cash sales	100,000	105,000	112,000
Budgeted cash payments	670,000	615,000	627,000

Beginning cash balance for April 2006 is expected to be $90,000. The company intends to maintain a cash balance of at least $50,000 and has made arrangements to borrow from the bank if necessary.

Required:

Prepare a cash budget for the second quarter of 2006.

10-44   The following information is available for the Ortega Company for the first quarter of 2005:

LO 5
Prepare a Cash
Budget

	January	February	March
Budgeted receipts from credit sales	$100,000	$110,000	$115,000
Budgeted cash sales	80,000	95,000	98,000
Budgeted cash payments	178,000	215,000	206,000

Beginning cash balance for January 2005 is expected to be $20,000. The company intends to maintain a cash balance of at least $15,000 and has made arrangements to borrow from a local bank if necessary.

Required:

Prepare a cash budget for the first quarter of 2005.

LO 5
Prepare a Cash Budget

10-45 The following information is available for November 2006:

Budgeted receipts from credit sales	$25,100
Budgeted cash sales	5,900
Budgeted cash payments	32,000

Beginning cash balance for November is expected to be $5,800. The Sheets Company intends to maintain a cash balance of at least $5,000 and has made arrangements to borrow from a local bank if necessary.

Required:

Prepare a cash budget for November of 2006.

LO 5
Prepare a Cash Budget

10-46 The following information is available for October 2006:

Budgeted receipts from credit sales	$300,000
Budgeted cash sales	80,000
Budgeted cash payments	410,000

Beginning cash balance for October is expected to be $60,000. The company intends to maintain a cash balance of at least $50,000 and has made arrangements to borrow from a local bank if necessary.

Required:

Prepare a cash budget for October 2006.

LO 5
Prepare a Cash Budget

10-47 The following information is available for July 2006:

Budgeted receipts from credit sales	$500,000
Budgeted cash sales	40,000
Budgeted cash payments	577,000

Beginning cash balance for July is expected to be $95,000. The company intends to maintain a cash balance of at least $75,000 and has made arrangements to borrow from a local bank if necessary.

Required:

Prepare a cash budget for July 2006.

LO 5
Prepare a Budgeted Balance Sheet and Budgeted Statement of Cash Flows for Three Months

10-48 The following information is available for the Price Printing Supply Company:

Price Printing Supply Company
Sales Budget
For the Quarter Ended September 30, 2005

	July	August	September
Budgeted sales dollars	$90,000	$80,000	$70,000

Price Printing Supply Company
Cost of Goods Sold Budget
For the Quarter Ended September 30, 2005

	July	August	September
Budgeted cost of good sold	$54,000	$48,000	$42,000

Price Printing Supply Company
Selling and Administrative Expense Budget
For the Quarter Ended September 30, 2005

	July	August	September
Salaries and wages	$12,600	$12,000	$11,800
Rent	1,000	1,000	1,000
Depreciation	1,800	1,800	1,800
Other expenses	$ 3,800	$ 3,000	$ 2,900
Total Selling and Administrative Expense	$19,200	$17,800	$17,500

Price Printing Supply Company
Purchases Budget
For the Quarter Ended September 30, 2005

	July	August	September
Cost of purchases	$52,000	$46,000	$41,000

Price Printing Supply Company
Budgeted Income Statement
For the Quarter Ended September 30, 2005

	July	August	September
Sales	$90,000	$80,000	$70,000
Cost of goods sold	54,000	48,000	42,000
Gross profit	36,000	32,000	28,000
Selling and administrative expense	19,200	17,800	17,500
Net Income	16,800	14,200	10,500

Price Printing Supply
Company Cash Receipts Schedule
For the Quarter Ended September 30, 2005

	July	August	September
Budgeted receipts— credit sales	$78,000	$76,000	$68,000
Budgeted cash sales	9,000	8,000	7,000
Total Cash Receipts	87,000	84,000	75,000

Price Printing Supply Company
Cash Payments Schedule
For the Quarter Ended September 30, 2005

	July	August	September
Purchases	$56,000	$52,000	$46,000
Selling and administrative expense			
Salaries and wages	12,600	12,000	11,800
Rent	1,000	1,000	1,000
Other expenses	3,800	3,000	2,900
Budgeted Cash Payments	$73,400	$68,000	$61,700

Price Printing Supply Company
Cash Budget
For the Quarter Ended September 30, 2005

		July	August	September
Beginning cash balance		$ 18,500	$ 32,100	$ 48,100
+	Cash receipts	87,000	84,000	75,000
=	Cash available	$105,000	$116,100	$123,100
−	Cash payments	(73,400)	(68,000)	(61,700)
=	Balance before borrowing	$ 32,100	$ 48,100	$ 61,400
+/−	Borrowing/(repayment)	—0—	—0—	—0—
=	Ending cash balance	$ 32,100	$ 48,100	$ 61,400

Price Printing Supply Company
Balance Sheet
June 30, 2005

Assets
Current Assets

Cash		$ 18,500
Accounts receivable		20,000
Inventory		16,000
Total Current Assets		$ 54,500

Property Plant and Equipment

Equipment	$ 108,000	
Less: Accumulated depreciation	(43,200)	
Equipment, net		64,800

Total Assets — $ 119,300

Liabilities and Stockholders' Equity
Current Liabilities

Accounts payable		$ 56,000
Total Current Liabilities		$ 56,000

Stockholders' Equity
Paid-in Capital:

Common stock	$ 1,000	
Additional paid-in capital	10,000	
Total Paid-in Capital	11,000	
Retained Earnings	52,300	
Total Stockholders' Equity		63,300

Total Liabilities and Stockholders' Equity — $ 119,300

Required:

a. Prepare budgeted balance sheets for July, August, and September 2005.

b. Prepare budgeted statements of cash flows for July, August, and September 2005.

LO 7
Direct Material
Variances

10-49 The Porter Company purchased 8,000 pounds of direct material at $5.20 per pound. It used 5,400 pounds to make 10,000 finished units. The standard cost for direct material is $5 per pound and the quantity standard is 1 pound per finished unit.

Required:

a. According to the appropriate standard, how much should the company have paid for the 8,000 pounds of direct material purchased?

b. Determine the direct material price variance based on the amount of direct material purchased.

c. According to the appropriate standard, how many pounds of direct material should have been used to make the 10,000 finished units?
d. Determine the direct material quantity variance in pounds of direct material.
e. Determine the direct material quantity variance in dollars.

10-50 The Nibarger Manufacturing Company purchased 30,000 pounds of direct material at $1.30 per pound. It used 29,400 pounds to make 10,000 finished units. The standard cost for direct material is $1.35 per pound and the quantity standard is 6 pounds per finished unit.

LO 7
Direct Material Variances

Required:

a. According to the appropriate standard, how much should the company have paid for the 30,000 pounds of direct material purchased?
b. Determine the direct material price variance based on the amount of direct material purchased.
c. According to the appropriate standard, how many pounds of direct material should have been used to make the 10,000 finished units?
d. Determine the direct material quantity variance in pounds of direct material.
e. Determine the direct material quantity variance in dollars.

10-51 The Miles-Scott Company purchased 5,000 square feet of direct material at $6.30 per square foot. It used 4,110 square feet of material to make 1,000 finished units. The standard cost for direct material is $6.15 per square foot and the quantity standard is 4 square feet per finished unit.

LO 7
Direct Material Variances

Required:

a. According to the appropriate standard, how much should the company have paid for the 5,000 square feet of direct material purchased?
b. Determine the direct material price variance based on the amount of direct material purchased.
c. According to the appropriate standard, how many square feet of direct material should have been used to make the 1,000 finished units?
d. Determine the direct material quantity variance in square feet of direct material.
e. Determine the direct material quantity variance in dollars.

10-52 Econo Manufacturing purchased 20,000 square feet of direct material at $0.54 per square foot. It used 12,625 square feet to make 1,250 finished units. The standard cost for direct material is $0.55 per square foot and the quantity standard is 10 square feet per finished unit.

LO 7
Direct Material Variances

Required:

a. According to the appropriate standard, how much should the company have paid for the 20,000 square feet of direct material purchased?
b. Determine the direct material price variance based on the amount of direct material purchased.
c. According to the appropriate standard, how many square feet of direct material should have been used to make the 1,250 finished units?
d. Determine the direct material quantity variance in square feet of direct material.
e. Determine the direct material quantity variance in dollars.

10-53 The direct labor rate standard for Pursifull Manufacturing is $24 per direct labor hour. The direct labor efficiency standard is 4 hours per finished unit. Last month, the company completed 4,000 units of product using 16,350 direct labor hours at an actual cost of $394,565.

LO 7
Direct Labor Variances

Required:

a. According to the appropriate standard, how much should the company have paid for the 16,350 actual direct labor hours?
b. Determine the direct labor rate variance.
c. According to the appropriate standard, how many hours of direct labor should workers have taken to produce the 4,000 units?
d. Determine the direct labor efficiency variance in hours.
e. Determine the direct labor efficiency variance in dollars.

LO 7
Direct Labor Variances

10-54   The direct labor rate standard for Osgood Manufacturing is $18.50 per direct labor hour. The direct labor efficiency standard is 6 minutes or one-tenth of one hour per finished unit. Last month, the company completed 105,650 units of product using 10,400 direct labor hours at an actual cost of $191,360.

Required:

a. According to the appropriate standard, how much should the company have paid for the 10,400 actual direct labor hours?
b. Determine the direct labor rate variance.
c. According to the appropriate standard, how many hours of direct labor should workers have taken to produce the 105,650 units?
d. Determine the direct labor efficiency variance in hours.
e. Determine the direct labor efficiency variance in dollars.

LO 7
Direct Labor Variances

10-55   The direct labor rate standard for Grand River Manufacturing is $10 per direct labor hour. The direct labor efficiency standard is 3 hours per finished unit. Last month, the company completed 5,600 units of product using 17,240 direct labor hours at an actual cost of $176,710.

Required:

a. According to the appropriate standard, how much should the company have paid for the 17,240 actual direct labor hours?
b. Determine the direct labor rate variance.
c. According to the appropriate standard, how many hours of direct labor should workers have taken to produce the 5,600 units?
d. Determine the direct labor efficiency variance in hours.
e. Determine the direct labor efficiency variance in dollars.

LO 7
Variable Manufacturing Overhead Variances

10-56   Beppo Manufacturing applies variable manufacturing overhead to production based on $13 per direct labor hour. The labor efficiency standard is 4 hours per finished unit. Last month the company produced 3,000 units and used 11,700 direct labor hours. Actual variable overhead cost incurred totaled $157,200.

Required:

a. Determine the variable manufacturing overhead spending variance.
b. Determine the variable manufacturing overhead efficiency variance in dollars.

LO 7
Variable Manufacturing Overhead Variances

10-57   The Adler Manufacturing Company applies variable manufacturing overhead to production based on $22 per direct labor hour. The labor efficiency standard is one-half hour per finished unit. Last month the company produced 14,500 units and used 7,300 direct labor hours. Actual variable overhead cost incurred totaled $162,000.

Required:

  a. Determine the variable manufacturing overhead spending variance.
  b. Determine the variable manufacturing overhead efficiency variance in dollars.

10-58 The following information is for the Austin Powers Manufacturing Company:

  Standard variable manufacturing overhead rate: $3.50 per direct labor hour
  Direct labor efficiency standard: 3 hours per finished unit
  Budgeted production: 810 finished units
  Production required: 2,370 direct labor hours
  Variable manufacturing overhead cost: $8,500
  Finished units of product produced: 775

Required:

  a. Determine the variable manufacturing overhead spending variance.
  b. Determine the variable manufacturing overhead efficiency variance in dollars.

10-59 The Denson Manufacturing Company applies fixed manufacturing overhead at the rate of $5.50 per direct labor hour. Fixed manufacturing overhead is budgeted to be $330,000 per month. The direct labor efficiency standard is 5 hours per finished unit. Although budgeted production for the month was 12,000, the company only produced 11,800 units. Production required actual direct labor hours of 60,000 and actual fixed manufacturing overhead cost incurred was $325,000.

Required:

  a. Determine the fixed overhead budget variance.
  b. What is the difference between the planned number of units and the number of units actually produced?
  c. Determine the fixed manufacturing overhead volume variance.

10-60 The Randy Ice Manufacturing Company applies fixed manufacturing overhead at the rate of $4.60 per direct labor hour. Fixed manufacturing overhead is budgeted to be $910,800 per month. The direct labor efficiency standard is 3 hours per finished unit. Although budgeted production for the month was 66,000, the company produced 67,800 units. Production required actual direct labor hours of 203,000 and actual fixed manufacturing overhead cost incurred was $920,000.

Required:

  a. Determine the fixed manufacturing overhead budget variance.
  b. What is the difference between the planned number of units and the number of units actually produced?
  c. Determine the fixed manufacturing overhead volume variance.

10-61 The Oddo Manufacturing Company applies fixed manufacturing overhead at the rate of $7 per direct labor hour. Fixed manufacturing overhead is budgeted to be $336,000 per month. The direct labor efficiency standard is 3 hours per finished unit. Although budgeted production for the month was 16,000, the company only produced 15,500 units. Production required actual direct labor hours of 60,000 and actual fixed manufacturing overhead cost incurred was $344,000.

LO 7
Variable Manufacturing Overhead Variances

LO 7
Fixed Manufacturing Overhead Variances

LO 7
Fixed Manufacturing Overhead Variances

LO 7
Fixed Manufacturing Overhead Variances

Required:

a. Determine the fixed manufacturing overhead budget variance.
b. Did the company produce as many units as it had planned? What is the difference between the planned number of units and the number of units actually produced?
c. Determine the fixed manufacturing overhead volume variance.

LO 7
Variance Analysis

10-62   Information from the Adair Company is as follows:

Actual costs and amounts

Actual production	3,800 units
Actual cost of 23,000 lbs. of direct material purchased	$89,700
Actual amount of direct material used	22,950 lbs.
Actual direct labor cost	$23,205
Actual direct labor hours	1,950 hours
Actual variable overhead cost	$12,000
Actual fixed overhead cost	$18,000

Standards and other budgeted amounts

Budgeted production	4,000 units
Direct material price standard	$3.85
Direct material quantity standard	6 lbs. per unit
Direct labor rate standard	$11 per hour
Direct labor efficiency standard per unit	0.5 hours
Standard variable manufacturing overhead rate	$5.50/direct labor hour
Standard fixed manufacturing overhead rate	$10/direct labor hour
Budgeted fixed manufacturing overhead	$20,000

Required:

a. Determine the following variances:
  1. direct material price variance
  2. direct material quantity variance in dollars
  3. direct labor rate variance
  4. direct labor efficiency variance in dollars
  5. variable manufacturing overhead spending variance
  6. variable manufacturing overhead efficiency variance in dollars
  7. fixed manufacturing overhead budget variance
  8. fixed manufacturing overhead volume variance in dollars
b. Prepare a final analysis indicating which variances need to be investigated further and why.

LO 7
Variance Analysis

10-63   Information from the Keath Company is as follows:

Actual costs and amounts

Actual production	6,300 units
Actual cost of 20,000 lbs. of direct material purchased	$40,000
Actual amount of direct material used	19,100 lbs.
Actual direct labor cost	$386,100
Actual direct labor hours	26,000 hours
Actual variable overhead cost	$165,000
Actual fixed overhead cost	$310,000

Standards and other budgeted amounts

Budgeted production	6,000 units
Direct material price standard	$2.10
Direct material quantity standard	3 lbs. per unit
Direct labor rate standard	$15.00/hour
Direct labor efficiency standard per unit	4 hours
Standard variable manufacturing overhead rate	$6.50/direct labor hour
Standard fixed manufacturing overhead rate	$12.75 direct labor hour
Budgeted fixed manufacturing overhead	$306,000

Required:

a. Determine the following variances:
   1. direct material price variance
   2. direct material quantity variance in dollars
   3. direct labor rate variance
   4. direct labor efficiency variance in dollars
   5. variable manufacturing overhead spending variance
   6. variable manufacturing overhead efficiency variance in dollars
   7. fixed manufacturing overhead budget variance
   8. fixed manufacturing overhead volume variance in dollars
b. Prepare a final analysis indicating which variances need to be investigated further and why.

10-64   Al Jones prepares the operating budget for his company. The past three years the company's sales have grown at a rate of 10% to 12% per year. Al is asked to increase the budget this year based on a projected 25% increase in sales volume.

Ethics

Required:

a. What steps do you think Al should take before preparing this budget?
b. Should he question the decision to increase the budget by the 25%? If yes, what actions should he take?

FOR ADDITIONAL READING

Banham, Russ, "Management Accounting, Better Budgets," *Journal of Accountancy* (February 2000):37–40.

Hunt, Stephen, "Budgets Roll with the Times," *Optimize* (August 1, 2003): 85ff.

Kaplan, Robert S., "Variance Analysis and Flexible Budgeting," *Harvard Business School Cases* (October 1, 2000):1–11.

Klock, Josef, and Ulf Schiller, "Marginal Costing: Cost Budgeting and Cost Variance Analysis," *Management Accounting Research* 8 (September 1997):299–324.

Mak, Y. T., and Melvin L. Roush, "Managing Activity Costs with Flexible Budgeting and Variance Analysis," *Accounting Horizons* 10 (September 1996):141–147.

Schmidt, Jeffrey A. "Management Accounting, Is It Time to Replace Traditional Budgeting?" *Journal of Accountancy* (October 1992):103ff.

"Should Your Company Do Away with Its Budget Process?" *Financial Analysis, Planning & Reporting* (August 2003):1ff.

CHAPTER 11

LEARNING OBJECTIVES

After completing this chapter, you should be able to:

1. Explain the process of capital budgeting.

2. Delineate the four shared characteristics of all capital projects.

3. Describe the cost of capital and the concept of scarce resources.

4. Determine the information relevant to a capital budgeting decision.

5. Evaluate potential capital investments using three capital budgeting decision models: payback method, net present value, and the internal rate of return.

6. Explain the concept of simple interest and compound interest and describe the concept of an annuity.

7. Determine present and future values using present value and future value tables.

Internal Allocation of Scarce Resources

Managers make business expenditures to further the goals of the firm's strategic plan and to increase its profits. Such expenditures are really investments by which the company hopes to earn both a return *of* its investment and a return *on* the investment. Business expenditures made to acquire expensive assets that will be used for more than one year are called **capital investments** or **capital projects**. Because of the cost and extended useful life of these assets, companies devote tremendous time and energy to evaluating potential capital investments. Family Dollar Stores, Inc., for example, invested the following amounts in the past few years:

2003	$219,777,000
2002	186,687,000
2001	162,848,000
2000	172,056,000
1999	125,038,000
1998	99,854,000
1997	77,062,000
1996	54,265,000

These investments exceed $1 billion. If you recall from Chapter 7, Family Dollar Stores added about 2,419 stores and 5 distribution centers with these investment dollars. Certainly, an investment of this magnitude required serious analysis by strategic managers before they committed to the various projects those dollars represent.

Visit the *www.prenhall.com/terrell* Web site to view the "Deer Valley Resort" video.

● **capital investments**
Business expenditures made to acquire expensive assets that will be used for more than one year. Also called **capital projects**.

Generally, capital investments are investments in property, plant, and equipment. Examples include investments in computer equipment, production equipment, another factory building, a new wing of a hospital, or a new campus dormitory. **Capital budgeting** is the planning and decision process for making investments in capital projects. Although we focus on business firms in our discussion, all types of organizations can use capital budgeting techniques: for-profit, not-for-profit, and social organizations. Two of the techniques used to evaluate potential capital projects rely heavily on knowledge of the time value of money. For this reason, the appendix to this chapter discusses this concept in detail.

● **capital budgeting**
The planning and decision process for making Investments in capital projects.

The Capital Budget

● **capital budget**
The budget that outlines how a firm intends to allocate its scarce resources over a 5-year, 10-year, or even longer time period.

● **capital assets**
Long-lived assets such as land, buildings, machinery, and equipment.

The **capital budget** is the budget that outlines how a firm intends to allocate its scarce resources over a 5-year, 10-year, or even longer time period. The capital budget lays out plans for the acquisition and replacement of long-lived expensive assets, called **capital assets**, such as land, buildings, machinery, and equipment. During the capital budgeting process, managers decide whether items should be purchased, how much should be spent, and how much profit the items promise to generate. No decisions made in the capital budgeting process, however, should conflict with the company's strategic plan or organizational goals.

Capitalizing Assets

By definition capital assets are long-lived assets. The firm only uses capital budgeting techniques for large dollar amounts of long-lived expenditures. (Recall that expenditures that offer economic benefits only for the current year are reflected as an expense on the company's income statement for the year of purchase.) We capitalize a long-lived asset by recording its purchase as an asset on the balance sheet.

When determining whether a purchased item should be capitalized or expensed, managers use their judgment. Recall that the cost-benefit constraint plays an important role in such decisions. For example, should the cost of a $150 file cabinet with an estimated useful life of 10 years be capitalized? Theoretically, the 10-year useful life requires that the cabinet be capitalized and depreciated over its estimated useful life. From a practical standpoint, however, it does not make sense to expend the additional accounting cost to capitalize and then depreciate the cabinet over 10 years. In addition, the accountant must consider the materiality constraint. Whether the file cabinet is capitalized and depreciated over its estimated useful life or expensed immediately, the effect on a company's financial statements would be so immaterial that no economic decision maker would be influenced by the alternative selected.

Company policy usually sets a cost threshold that determines the appropriate accounting treatment for capitalizing long-lived items. For example, when company policy indicates that any long-lived item costing less than $3,000 will be expensed when purchased, those costing $3,000 or more will be capitalized. There are no absolute rules for setting the capitalization threshold, but most companies choose an amount between $500 and $5,000 as their capitalization threshold, depending on the size of the company and its operating income.

Characteristics of Capital Projects

Although the capitalization amount and the evaluation process for capital assets vary among companies, all capital projects share certain characteristics. The four main shared characteristics are:

1 **Long Life.**   A capital project is expected to benefit the company for at least two years. Usually, the kinds of purchases discussed in this chapter benefit the company for 5 to 10 years or longer.

2 **High Cost.**   Technically, the purchase of any long-lived item for which the cost exceeds a company's capitalization amount is considered a capital project. In reality, however, most capital projects cost from tens of thousands to billions of dollars. Family Dollar Stores spent $220 million in 2003 to open 494 stores. Each of those 494 projects was carefully evaluated. By comparison, Wal-Mart Stores, Inc. spent $10.1 billion on capital projects in fiscal year 2003 and Target Corporation spent $3.2 billion on capital projects in fiscal 2002.

3 **Sunk Cost.**   Costs that cannot be recovered are called **sunk costs**. A capital project usually requires a company to incur substantial cost in the early stages of the project that normally cannot be recovered. For example, consider the case of a manufacturer that purchases new computerized production equipment at a cost of $250,000 that should last eight years. After using the equipment for two years, the company finds that new equipment has become available that will reduce the time and cost of production. Its competition has decided to use the new equipment. The cost of the two-year-old equipment is sunk and probably cannot be recovered. Who will want to purchase technologically obsolete equipment?

4 **High Degree of Risk.**   A capital project has a high degree of business risk because it involves high sunk costs and the future, which is always uncertain. The long time frame of the project requires the firm to estimate the returns from those projects in the years to come. Inevitable errors in the estimates affect the decision quality.

● **sunk costs**
Costs that cannot be recovered.

Such capital projects have risk and opportunity costs. Should they also have a minimum rate of return to the company, and if so, how can management determine the rate?

Cost of Capital

When you put money into a savings account, you expect to earn interest. This interest is the return on your investment. Like most people, you would like the return to be as high as possible. If you were going to deposit $5,000 in a savings account, you would probably shop for a secure bank offering the highest return. A company shops for capital projects the same way you would shop for a bank in which to deposit your $5,000. But even if a capital project appears that it will be profitable, how does a company determine whether it will be profitable *enough* to warrant investing its money? The answer is that a proposed project should promise a return that is equal to or exceeds the firm's minimum required rate of return.

In evaluating potential capital projects, management must determine a benchmark rate of return to help select which capital project or projects to undertake. The benchmark return rate for selecting projects is usually the company's **cost of capital**, which is the cost of obtaining financing from all available financing sources. Cost of capital is also referred to as the **required rate of return** or the **hurdle rate**.

As you may recall from Chapter 3, a company can obtain financing from two sources, borrowing from creditors (debt financing) and investments by owners (equity financing). When a company invests in a capital project, the money must come from one or both of these sources. Both creditors and owners require a return on the funding they provide to the company, and the company must seek investments that provide a return at least equal to the cost of obtaining funding from debt and equity sources. If a

● **cost of capital**
The cost of obtaining financing from all available financing sources. Also called the **required rate of return** or the **hurdle rate**.

company borrows funds at a 9 percent interest rate, then the expected return on a capital project must be at least 9 percent. Similarly, if a company's owners provide the financing and expect a return of 20 percent on their investment, then the expected return from a capital project should be at least 20 percent to be acceptable.

Blended Cost of Capital

● **blended cost of capital**
The combined cost of debt and equity financing.

● **cost of debt capital**
The interest a company pays to its creditors.

● **cost of equity capital**
The return equity investors expect to earn, combining dividends received and the appreciation in the market value of the stock.

Funding for a company's capital projects usually comes from a combination of debt and equity financing. The combined cost of debt and equity financing is called the **blended cost of capital**. The rate for the blended cost of capital represents the combined rate of the cost of both debt and equity financing.

The **cost of debt capital** is the interest a company pays to its creditors. The interest rate, say eight percent, is agreed on when a company borrows from either the bank or the bond market. The amount of interest a company incurs is easy to determine because it is reported on the company's income statement as interest expense.

The cost of a company's equity financing is more challenging to determine. This is so because the **cost of equity capital** is the return equity investors expect to earn, combining dividends received and the appreciation in the market value of the stock. Management must try to determine what percentage return equity investors can generally expect on their investments and use that percentage as the cost of equity capital. Unlike the debt financing cost of interest expense that is found on the income statement, the cost of equity financing is not reported in financial statements. Firms do report profit distributions to stockholders in the form of dividends. But the larger part of the cost of equity capital is the appreciation in the market value of stockholders' ownership interest. This market value is not reported on financial statements.

To determine the full cost of equity capital, we must examine how stocks appreciate in value. We assume first that rational investors would desire a return on an investment in an individual company at least equal to the return they could receive from investing in other, similar publicly traded companies. If all companies whose stock are traded on recognized stock markets (NYSE, AMEX, NASDAQ, and so on) were separated based on the percentage return they provide their stockholders, the breakdown might appear as shown in Exhibit 11-1. The high-return companies in Exhibit 11-1 represent one-fourth of all the publicly traded firms. The medium-return companies

Exhibit 11-1
Returns Provided by the Stock Market

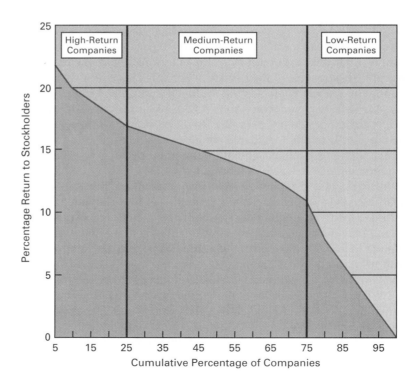

comprise one-half of the firms, and the low-return companies represent one-fourth of the total. Most investors want to own stock in high-return companies because they want their investment to earn the highest possible return. High-return companies give their stockholders annual yields of 17 to 20 percent. The issue is not whether investors can actually earn 20 percent on their investment—they only need to *expect* they can earn such a high return. Publicly traded companies usually consider their cost of equity financing to be as high as 20 percent and commonly use that rate to compute the company's blended cost of capital.

Computing the Blended Cost of Capital

To illustrate the calculation of the blended cost of capital, let's consider the case of Wreath Enterprises, which has $4,000,000 in assets. Of these assets, $2,400,000 (60 percent) were obtained using 7.5 percent debt financing. The remaining $1,600,000 (40 percent) of assets were financed with equity capital and the company uses a 20 percent cost of equity financing. We use the following model to find Wreath's blended cost of capital:

Method of Financing	Proportion of Financing Provided		Cost of Financing		Weighted Cost of Financing
Debt	60%	×	7.5%	=	4.5%
Equity	40%	×	20.0%	=	8.0%
Blended Cost of Capital					12.5%

Wreath's weighted cost of debt financing is the proportion of debt financing (60 percent) multiplied by the cost of that financing (7.5 percent). The company's weighted cost of equity financing is the proportion of equity financing (40 percent) times the cost of the equity financing (20 percent). Its blended cost of capital is 12.5 percent, the sum of the weighted cost of each type of financing.

Firms use their blended cost of capital as a benchmark rate of return to evaluate capital projects. For example, suppose Wreath is considering a capital project that requires an investment of $200,000. If it decides to undertake this project, the company must obtain $200,000 to fund it. Recall that Wreath's blended cost of capital is 12.5 percent. Unless the expected rate of return on the project is 12.5 percent or higher, Wreath's management will probably reject the project. Otherwise, funding the project would cost more than the project could earn.

What Do You Think?

11-1 When you consider that companies are in business to earn a profit, why might it be acceptable to select a capital project that promises a return that is just equal to the blended cost of capital?

11-2 Under what circumstances do you think a company might accept one capital project over another even though the project selected promises a lower return?

11-3 Do you think a situation would ever occur where a company should proceed with a capital project even though the project promises a return lower than the cost of capital? Explain your reasoning.

11-4 What do you think might cause a company to reject a proposed capital project even though it promises a return significantly higher than the cost of capital?

Scarce Resources

● **scarce resources**
The limited amount of funding available to spend on capital projects.

Just as you have limited funds to spend on a home or car, a company can undertake only a limited number of capital projects because it has **scarce resources**, a limited amount of funding available to spend on capital projects. Managers must carefully evaluate the alternative capital projects available so they can select the projects consistent with the firm's strategic plans that promise the highest return.

Evaluating Potential Capital Projects

A typical capital project evaluation process includes the following four steps:

1. Identify possible capital projects.
2. Determine the relevant cash flows for alternative projects.
3. Select a method of evaluating the alternatives.
4. Evaluate the alternatives and select the capital project or projects to be funded.

Let's investigate each of these steps from the manager's point of view.

Step 1: Identify Capital Projects

A company makes a capital investment to maximize profits by increasing revenue, reducing costs, or some combination of the two. A project that satisfies the company's desire to maximize profits will be identified as a potential capital expenditure.

Firms often invest in projects that increase capacity or draw more customers to increase revenues. A hotel chain might build additional rooms if management believes it can attract more convention business. A hospital might add high-tech equipment to add a specialty service, such as a heart transplant center or a neonatal unit to increase revenues.

Not all projects increase income. Reducing cost has exactly the same effect on net income, however, as increasing revenue. Benjamin Franklin knew this more than 250 years ago when he declared, "A penny saved is a penny earned." From an accounting standpoint, he is absolutely correct. Net income is an equation:

$$\text{Revenues} - \text{Expenses} = \text{Net Income}$$

Assume that you earn $100, which costs you $70 and leaves you with $30 net income.

$$\$100 - \$70 = \$30$$

Now assume that you earn an extra $5. This changes your net income to $35.

$$\text{Additional Income: } \$100 + \$5 - \$70 = \$35$$

What if you cannot earn an extra $5 but you have the opportunity to save $5 in expenses. That also changes your net income to $35, again proving Franklin's adage.

$$\text{Cost Savings: } \$100 - (\$70 - \$5) = \$35$$

To reduce operating costs a manufacturer might upgrade production equipment that requires less direct labor or less electricity. An accounting office could purchase a new copier that uses less toner and has a drum that lasts twice as long as the current model.

Although the majority of potential capital projects are intended either to increase revenue or to reduce costs, occasionally a company must make a capital expenditure that will result in neither. These projects are usually concerned with safety or environmental issues and ensure compliance with regulatory requirements or union contracts, or help the company maintain its image as a good corporate citizen. In any event, alternatives to achieve such goals may be evaluated using the same criteria as those projects that do promise increased profits. The techniques we will introduce can be used for both purposes.

As the need for increasing revenue or reducing costs presents itself, managers should seek all reasonable alternative courses of action. Brainstorming sessions and input from multiple sources both within and outside a company can help generate ideas for alternative options.

Step 2: Determine Relevant Cash Flows

We have discussed capital projects that promise to increase a company's profits either by increasing revenue or by reducing expenses. Recall, however, that if we are using accrual accounting, revenue on the income statement is not the same as cash inflows on the statement of cash flows. Neither is expense measured on the income statement the same as cash outflows on the statement of cash flows. Financial statements are produced in short time periods of a year. From the inception of a company to the end of its life, however, revenue and expenses measured using accrual accounting *are* the same as cash inflow and cash outflow.

Because capital projects usually are long-lived, most managers feel it is appropriate to analyze an alternative using cash inflow and cash outflow over the life of the project. They do this by determining the **net cash flow** of a project—the project's expected cash inflows minus its cash outflows for a specific period. For example, if a manager estimates that investing in a new production machine will yield $40,000 in cash inflows during the useful life of the machine but will require spending $30,000 for the same period, the net cash flow would be $10,000 ($40,000 – $30,000).

Only relevant net cash flows should be considered in a capital budgeting decision. **Relevant net cash flows** are future cash flows that differ among decision alternatives. Note that the definition has two criteria: (1) cash flows must be in the future, and (2) a difference must exist between the cash flows among the alternative choices. Past cash flows, or cash flows that will not change as a result of the investment decision, are irrelevant and should not be considered in the decision process. The concept of relevant costs follows the guidelines explored in Chapter 9.

Once a company assesses the relevant cash flows for each alternative project, the next step is to choose a method to measure the value of each project.

● **net cash flow**
The project's expected cash inflows minus its cash outflows for a specific period.

● **relevant net cash flows**
Future cash flows that differ among decision alternatives.

Step 3: Select Method of Evaluation

Over time, many capital budgeting decision models have been developed to evaluate potential capital projects. Some companies have even developed their own methods, many of which are adaptations of traditional methods. Most methods offer different ways to measure a project's value, and sometimes the different methods render conflicting rankings. In such a case, managers should recognize the strengths and weaknesses of each capital budgeting method to improve the decision process.

Step 4: Evaluate Alternatives

To select a capital budgeting project, firms decide first whether to accept or reject a project using one or more capital budgeting techniques to measure the project's value. If the project does not meet the decision criteria, it will probably be rejected. Furthermore, any proposed capital project that is inconsistent with a company's strategic plans should be rejected, even if the promised return on that project is higher than another potential project. Once managers accept a project as viable, they can rank the project with other acceptable projects based on expected performance.

The following section explores three capital budgeting methods: payback, net present value, and internal rate of return.

Capital Budgeting Decision Methods

We selected three traditional methods for evaluating capital projects to illustrate. The first method, payback, considers all cash inflows and outflows as equivalent dollars, regardless of the timing of receipt or payment.

Payback Period Method

● payback period method
A capital budgeting technique that measures the length of time a capital project must generate positive net cash flows that equal, or "pay back," the original investment in the project.

As its name implies, the **payback period method** is a capital budgeting technique that measures the length of time a capital project must generate positive net cash flows that equal, or "pay back," the original investment in the project. For instance, assume that a project's estimated initial outlay is $40,000. Assume further that the project is expected to generate a net cash inflow of $12,500 per year. When net cash inflows are equal from one year to the next, we determine the payback period by dividing the required initial investment by the annual cash inflows. In our example, we find that the payback period is 3.2 years. The calculation follows:

$$\text{Payback Period} = \frac{\text{Required Initial Investment}}{\text{Annual Net Cash Inflow}} = \frac{\$40,000}{\$12,500} = 3.2 \text{ Years}$$

The payback period of 3.2 years for this project will be compared against the payback of other projects. Generally, the lower the payback period, the more attractive the project.

If a project has uneven cash flows, we can determine the payback period by adding the cash inflows year by year until the total equals the required initial investment. For example, suppose a project requires an initial investment of $50,000 and is expected to generate the following net cash inflows:

2004	$12,000
2005	$15,000
2006	$18,000
2007	$15,000
2008	$12,000

We find the payback period by totaling the net cash inflows until we reach $50,000 as shown in Exhibit 11-2.

As Exhibit 11-2 shows, the project repays the initial investment after the third year, but before the end of the fourth year. By the end of the third year, the project proposal estimates that $45,000, or all but $5,000 of the initial $50,000 investment will be recovered. The project recovers the remaining $5,000 during the fourth year as part of the $15,000 net cash inflows anticipated for that year. About one-third

Exhibit 11-2
Payback Period with Uneven Cash Flows

YEAR	CASH RECEIVED IN PRIOR YEARS		CASH RECEIVED IN CURRENT YEAR		ACCUMULATED CASH RECEIVED
1	—0—	+	$12,000	=	$12,000
2	$12,000	+	15,000	=	27,000
3	27,000	+	18,000	=	45,000
4	45,000	+	15,000	=	60,000
5	60,000	+	12,000	=	72,000

($5,000/$15,000) of the fourth year will be needed to collect the final $5,000 to recover the $50,000 initial investment. Therefore, the payback period is approximately 3.33 years.

The payback period method highlights the liquidity of an investment and acts as a screening device to reject projects with unreasonably low cash flow expectations. This method is simple to use, is easily understood, and offers insight into a project's liquidity. Few managers, however, utilize the payback period to make final capital investment decisions because it does not consider three crucial elements: (1) the expected returns of a project after the payback period; (2) how the returns will compare to the firm's cost of capital; and (3) the time value of money. Considering these limitations, most managers use the payback method as a screening device after establishing a maximum payback period for potential projects. If the maximum payback period considered were three years, the project illustrated in Exhibit 11-2 would be eliminated from further consideration.

Management can also use the payback method as additional information to choose between two projects that promise the same return potential. For example, assume a company is considering two equipment manufacturers to supply new production equipment. If both projects promise the same return on investment, the payback period might favor one project over the other because it is shorter.

Discounted Cash Flow Methods

The final two capital budgeting decision methods, known as discounted cash flow methods, are used more frequently in business because they include the concept of the time value of money. What does that mean? You probably recall that a dollar received at some point in the future does not have the same value as a dollar received today. The reason for the difference in value is that if cash is available now, it can be invested now and earn a return as time passes. This increase in the value of cash over time due to the accumulation of investment income is the **time value of money**. We use the concept of the time value of money to determine either the future value of money invested today or the present value of money to be received at some point in the future.

In the following discussion of net present value and internal rate of return, we assume you have a working knowledge of the time value of money, which is discussed in detail in the appendix to this chapter. Refer to it now if you need to refresh your understanding. Capital projects deal with cash flows that begin in the present and extend into the future, sometimes for many years. Therefore, the evaluation of these kinds of projects requires the application of present value.

Determining the present value of cash to be received in future periods is called **discounting cash flows**. Business managers use two discounted cash flow methods to evaluate potential capital projects: net present value and the internal rate of return.

Net Present Value

The **net present value (NPV)** of a proposed capital project is the present value of cash inflows minus the present value of cash outflows associated with a capital budgeting project. Note that the *net* present value of a project differs from the *present value* of the project. The *net present value* is the difference between the present value of a capital project's net cash flows. The **present value (PV)** of a project is the amount the future cash inflows is worth today when discounted at the appropriate discount rate. We use the net present value method to determine whether a proposed capital project's return is higher or lower than the blended cost of capital.

A manager calculates the net present value of a capital project by discounting the net cash flows for all years of the project using the firm's blended cost of capital as the discount rate. A positive net present value indicates that the expected return on a proposed project exceeds the company's cost of capital. A negative net present value indicates that the expected return on a proposed project fails to meet the company's

● **time value of money**
The increase in the value of cash over time due to the accumulation of investment income.

● **discounting cash flows**
Determining the present value of cash to be received in future periods.

● **net present value (NPV)**
The present value of cash inflows minus the present value of cash outflows associated with a capital budgeting project.

● **present value (PV) of a project**
The amount the future cash inflows is worth today when discounted at the appropriate discount rate.

Exhibit 11-3
Elevation Sports, Inc. Expected
Cash Flows for Equipment
Upgrade

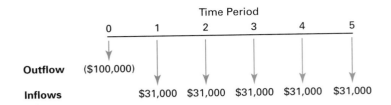

required cost of capital. A net present value of zero shows that the expected return on a project exactly equals the firm's cost of capital.

So that we can illustrate the net present value calculations, assume Elevation Sports considers purchasing new manufacturing equipment that will require a $100,000 investment. Assume further that the new equipment will save $31,000 annually in production salaries. Remember, this reduction of cash outflow is a cash inflow in net present value analysis. The equipment has an estimated useful life of five years with no residual value. Exhibit 11-3 contains the cash flows associated with the equipment upgrade. Notice in Exhibit 11-3 the initial cash outlay of $100,000 occurs at time period 0. When we are working with present values, we consider time period 0 to be today, or the present. Unless otherwise specified, we assume all other cash flows for this project will occur at the end of each period.

Elevation Sports uses a 14 percent blended cost of capital, so Megan will use 14 percent as the discount rate to evaluate whether the company should accept the computer upgrade project. In this case, the project's $100,000 cash outflow occurs today (time period 0). Therefore, the outflow is already stated in present value terms. Next, Megan must find the present value of the project's cash inflows, which occur at the end of each of the next five years. Because the stream of $31,000 positive cash flows every year constitutes an annuity, Megan will use the *Present Value of an Annuity of $1 Table*, reproduced as Exhibit 11-15 on page 441, to find the present value factor of a five-year annuity at a discount rate of 14 percent. We have reproduced a portion of the table as Exhibit 11-4. As you can see from the highlighted portion in Exhibit 11-4, the factor for five years with a discount rate of 14 percent is 3.4331.

Megan multiplies $31,000, the amount of the annuity, by the 3.4331 present value interest factor of an annuity PVIFA and finds that the present value of the annuity is $106,426 ($31,000 × 3.4331 = $106,426). Finally, Megan finds the net present value of the project by subtracting the present value of cash outflows from the present value of cash inflows. Exhibit 11-5 details her calculations.

As Exhibit 11-5 shows, the positive net present value of $6,426 indicates that the project's expected return exceeds Elevation Sports' 14 percent blended cost of capital. Be careful as you look at the net present value of the project. A net present value of $6,426 does not mean that the project's return is only $6,426. Rather, it means that the project's return *exceeds* the company's 14 percent cost of capital by $6,426.

The Elevation Sports example was relatively easy to calculate because the project's expected cash flows were the same each year. When the expected cash flows are uneven, we find the present value of each year's cash flow and then add those amounts. To demonstrate, assume that Elevation Sports' equipment upgrade has expected

Exhibit 11-4
Partial Present Value of an Annuity of $1 Table

TABLE 4 - The Present Value of an Annuity of $1 for *n* Payments

n	1%	2%	3%	4%	5%	6%	7%	8%	9%	10%	12%	14%
1	0.9901	0.9804	0.9709	0.9615	0.9524	0.9434	0.9346	0.9259	0.9174	0.9091	0.8929	0.8772
2	1.9704	1.9416	1.9135	1.8861	1.8594	1.8334	1.8080	1.7833	1.7591	1.7355	1.6901	1.6467
3	2.9410	2.8839	2.8286	2.7751	2.7232	2.6730	2.6243	2.5771	2.5313	2.4869	2.4018	2.3216
4	3.9820	3.8077	3.7171	3.6299	3.5460	3.4651	3.3872	3.3121	3.2397	3.1699	3.0373	2.9137
5	4.8884	4.7135	4.5797	4.4518	4.3295	4.2124	4.1002	3.9927	3.8897	3.7908	3.6048	3.4331

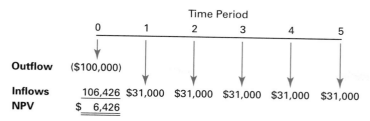

Time Period

| | 0 | 1 | 2 | 3 | 4 | 5 |

Outflow ($100,000)

Inflows 106,426 $31,000 $31,000 $31,000 $31,000 $31,000
NPV $ 6,426

NPV = **Present value of project's expected returns – initial cash outlay**
NPV = **$106,426 – $100,000**
NPV = **$6,426**

Exhibit 11-5
Elevation Sports, Inc.
Expected Cash Flows
for Equipment Upgrade

What Do You Think?

11-5   Should a business accept or reject a project with an NPV of zero? Explain your reasoning.

11-6   Compare a $100,000 project with an NPV of $6,426 to a $250,000 project with an NPV of $12,900. Is the larger project twice as profitable as the smaller project?

---

annual returns of $31,000, but in time period 3 the production equipment will require $12,000 in maintenance, and at the end of the time period 5, the system can be sold for $6,000. Exhibit 11-6 offers a timeline depicting these additional cash flows.

We can discount each of the amounts for the five years shown in Exhibit 11-6 to present value using the *Present Value of $1 Table*, reproduced as Exhibit 11-13 on page 439, a portion of which is reproduced as Exhibit 11-7. The calculation of the present values, using the highlighted factors in the 14 percent discount rate column, appears in Exhibit 11-8.

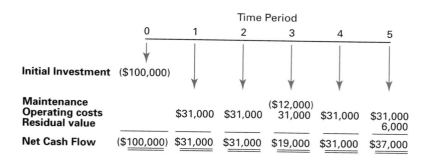

Time Period

| | 0 | 1 | 2 | 3 | 4 | 5 |

Initial Investment   ($100,000)

Maintenance
Operating costs $31,000 $31,000 ($12,000) 31,000 $31,000 $31,000
Residual value   6,000

Net Cash Flow   ($100,000) $31,000 $31,000 $19,000 $31,000 $37,000

Exhibit 11-6
Elevation Sports, Inc.
Uneven Expected Cash Flows
for Equipment Upgrade

Exhibit 11-7
Partial Present Value of $1 Table

Table 3 - The Present Value of $1 Due in *n* Periods

n	1%	2%	3%	4%	5%	6%	7%	8%	9%	10%	12%	14%
1	0.9901	0.9804	0.9709	0.9615	0.9524	0.9434	0.9346	0.9259	0.9174	0.9091	0.8929	0.8772
2	0.9803	0.9612	0.9426	0.9246	0.9070	0.8900	0.8734	0.8573	0.8417	0.8264	0.7972	0.7695
3	0.9706	0.9423	0.9151	0.8890	0.8638	0.8396	0.8163	0.7938	0.7722	0.7513	0.7118	0.6750
4	0.9610	0.9238	0.8885	0.8548	0.8227	0.7921	0.7629	0.7350	0.7084	0.6830	0.6355	0.5921
5	0.9515	0.9057	0.8626	0.8219	0.7835	0.7473	0.7130	0.6806	0.6499	0.6209	0.5674	0.5194
6	0.9420	0.8880	0.8375	0.7903	0.7462	0.7050	0.6663	0.6302	0.5963	0.5645	0.5066	0.4556
7	0.9327	0.8706	0.8131	0.7599	0.7107	0.6651	0.6227	0.5835	0.5470	0.5132	0.4523	0.3996
8	0.9235	0.8535	0.7894	0.7307	0.6768	0.6274	0.5820	0.5403	0.5019	0.4665	0.4039	0.3506
9	0.9143	0.8368	0.7664	0.7026	0.6446	0.5919	0.5439	0.5002	0.4604	0.4241	0.3606	0.3075

Exhibit 11-8
Net Present Value Calculations
with Uneven Cash Flows

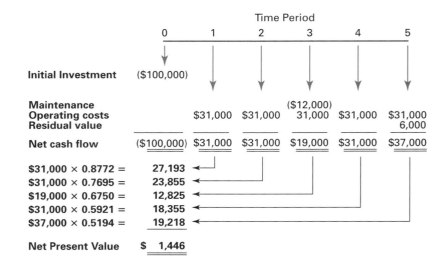

As Exhibit 11-8 demonstrates, the positive $1,446 net present value indicates the computer upgrade exceeds the 14 percent blended cost of capital for Elevation Sports and is thus an acceptable project for management to consider.

Although the net present value method indicates whether a proposed capital project is acceptable, it does have limitations as a ranking method to compare competing projects. A direct comparison of the net present values of various projects may lead to poor decisions regarding project selection because the net present value is measured in dollars rather than percentages. For example, assume that management intends to select one of two projects, project A or project B. Calculations indicate that the net present value of project A is $5,000, whereas the net present value of project B is $6,000.

Although choosing the project with the higher net present value seems wise, this is not always a good idea because NPV analysis does not consider the relative investments the projects require. For example, assume the present value of project A's cash inflows was $105,000 and the present value of its cash outflows was $100,000. Further assume the present value of project B's cash inflows was $206,000 and the present value of its cash outflows was $200,000. Project A requires a $100,000 investment, whereas project B requires double the investment amount. In firms with scarce funds, the relatively small increase in the net present value from $5,000 to $6,000 may not justify selecting a project that requires double the amount of investment. How then can we use the net present value method when ranking competing projects? We use a profitability index to help choose among projects.

Profitability Index

● **profitability index**
An index of the values of alternative but acceptable capital budgeting projects, whose index values we calculate by dividing the present value of the project's cash inflows by the present value of its cash outflows.

The **profitability index** is an index of the values of alternative but acceptable capital budgeting projects, whose index values we calculate by dividing the present value of the project's cash inflows by the present value of its cash outflows.

$$\text{Profitability Index (PI)} = \frac{\text{PV of Cash Inflows}}{\text{PV of Cash Outflows}}$$

To illustrate, let us return to the example. Projects A and B have positive NPVs and are acceptable projects, but we want to rank the projects in order of preference.

		Project A	**Project B**
PI =	PV of Inflows	$105,000 = 1.05	$206,000 = 1.03
	PV of Outflows	$100,000	$200,000

We find that the profitability index for project A is 1.05 and for project B is 1.03. We would rank project A higher than project B because project A's index value is 1.05 compared to project B's lower index value of 1.03. The profitability index thus allows firms to rank competing projects.

Although the net present value method indicates whether a project's return is lower or higher than the required rate of return, it does not show the project's expected percentage return. Many managers feel it is helpful to know the expected rate of return of projects when making capital budgeting decisions. The internal rate of return method is a capital budgeting method that provides this information.

Internal Rate of Return

The **internal rate of return (IRR)** of a proposed capital project is the calculated expected percentage return promised by the project. Just like the net present value method, the internal rate of return method considers all cash flows for a proposed project adjusted for the time value of money. The internal rate of return results, however, are expressed as a percentage rate, not a dollar amount. The internal rate of return computation determines the discount rate that makes the present value of a project's cash inflows and the present value of a project's outflows exactly the same. Computing the internal rate of return normally requires the use of a computer or a programmable calculator. A special case of internal rate of return, when the investment has no residual value, requires nothing more than a simple calculator and the present value tables. The following discussion assumes that special case. In this application, we consult the tables to determine a discount rate, rather than using present value amounts.

● **internal rate of return (IRR)** The calculated expected percentage return promised by the project.

Assume that project C requires an initial investment of $300,000 and will provide cash inflows of $56,232 per year for eight years. Because this project is an annuity, to determine the internal rate of return we use the *Present Value of an Annuity of $1 Table*, reproduced as Exhibit 11-15 on page 441, a portion of which is reproduced as Exhibit 11-9. Recall the equation to determine the present value of an annuity:

NOTE
Consult the directions on your financial calculator to determine how to enter the factors on your particular calculator.

$$PV = \text{Annual Payments} \times PVIFA$$

Also recall the following statement in the beginning of this section: "The internal rate of return computation determines the discount rate that makes the present value of a project's cash inflows and the present value of a project's outflows exactly the same." To interpret this sentence differently, the present value of the inflows will

Exhibit 11-9
Partial Present Value of an Annuity of $1 Table

TABLE 4 - The Present Value of an Annuity of $1 for *n* Payments

n	1%	2%	3%	4%	5%	6%	7%	8%	9%	10%	12%
1	0.9901	0.9804	0.9709	0.9615	0.9524	0.9434	0.9346	0.9259	0.9174	0.9091	0.8929
2	1.9704	1.9416	1.9135	1.8861	1.8594	1.8334	1.8080	1.7833	1.7591	1.7355	1.6901
3	2.9410	2.8839	2.8286	2.7751	2.7232	2.6730	2.6243	2.5771	2.5313	2.4869	2.4018
4	3.9820	3.8077	3.7171	3.6299	3.5460	3.4651	3.3872	3.3121	3.2397	3.1699	3.0373
5	4.8884	4.7135	4.5797	4.4518	4.3295	4.2124	4.1002	3.9927	3.8897	3.7908	3.6048
6	5.7985	5.6014	5.4172	5.2421	5.0757	4.9173	4.7665	4.6229	4.4859	4.3553	4.1114
7	6.7282	6.4720	6.2303	6.0021	5.7864	5.5824	5.3893	5.2064	5.0330	4.8684	4.5638
8	7.6517	7.3255	7.0197	6.7327	6.4632	6.2098	5.9713	5.7466	5.5348	5.3349	4.9676
9	8.5660	8.1622	7.7861	7.4353	7.1078	6.8017	6.5152	6.2469	5.9952	5.7590	5.3282

equal the initial investment. We could, therefore, substitute the initial investment for the present value as follows:

$$\text{Initial Investment} = \text{Annual Payments} \times \text{PVIFA}$$

With the information given in the example, we know the following:

$$\$300,000 = \$56,232 \times \text{PVIFA}$$

Solve the equation for the unknown:

$$\text{PVIFA} = \frac{\$300,000}{\$\ 56,232}$$

This provides us with a reusable equation as follows:

$$\text{PVIFA} = \frac{\text{Initial Investment}}{\text{Expected Annual Return}}$$

In the case of project C, the present value factor is:

$$\text{PVIFA} = \frac{\$300,000}{\$\ 56,232} = 5.335$$

Now that we know the present value factor, we can find project C's internal rate of return in the present value of an annuity table. To do this, move down the time period column in Exhibit 11-9 to eight periods because that is the life of the project. Next, follow across the row corresponding to eight periods until you find a factor that is close to the one calculated (5.335). As you follow across the row for eight periods, you find a factor that is not just close but matches exactly. The factor of 5.3349 is in the 10 percent column, which indicates the internal rate of return for project C is 10 percent. Now we can compare this internal rate of return to the cost of capital to gauge the project's acceptability. An internal rate of return that exceeds the firm's cost of capital indicates an acceptable project. For example, if the company's cost of capital is 9 percent, project C's 10 percent internal rate of return shows that the project analyst would find the project acceptable.

In the example for project C, we contrived the dollar amounts so that the PVIFA equaled one of the factors in the present value table. In a real-life situation, the calculated factor will usually fall between two factors on the present value table. For example, assume project D would require an investment of $330,000 and would generate estimated annual returns of $64,900 for eight years. The PVIFA for this project is 5.0847, determined as follows:

$$\frac{\text{Initial Investment}}{\text{Annual Return}} = \frac{\$330,000}{\$\ 64,900} = 5.0847 \text{ PVIFA}$$

Returning to Exhibit 11-9 and following across the period 8 row, we find that our calculated 5.0847 factor is between the factors 5.3349 (the 10 percent column) and 4.9676 (the 12 percent column), but is much closer to 4.9676. Therefore, the project's return would fall between 10 percent and 12 percent, but would be much closer to 12 percent. We then estimate that the internal rate of return for project D is less than 12 percent.

You can use a financial calculator to determine the exact rate of return in this special case of internal rate of return. Input the following items into your calculator:

PV	=	initial investment:	$330,000
FV	=	zero (no residual value)	
n	=	number of years:	8
PMT	=	annual return:	$64,900
CPT	=	compute	
$\%i$	=	interest rate	

The result the calculator gives is 11.33762 percent, which is consistent with the results in the previous paragraph.

Comparing Projects Using the Internal Rate of Return Method

Managers can use the internal rate of return method to rank projects. For example, they can compare the internal rate of return of project C (10 percent), to the approximate internal rate of return of project D (11.34 percent). Assuming both projects were acceptable, project D ranks higher than project C because it promises a higher internal rate of return.

Comparing the Net Present Value and Internal Rate of Return Methods

Both the net present value method and the internal rate of return method are well-respected techniques for determining the acceptability of a proposed capital project for two reasons. First, they are based on cash flows, not accounting income. Second, both methods consider the time value of money.

The net present value method determines whether the promised return from a proposed capital project meets the minimum required rate of return. A disadvantage of this method is that the calculated net present value is stated in dollars rather than percentages. Because of this, comparison between projects requiring different size investments is difficult. The profitability index overcomes this difficulty. The internal rate of return method calculates a proposed capital project's actual expected rate of return. Because this method uses percentages rather than dollars, it makes possible a direct comparison of various proposed projects requiring different size investments.

Avoiding Poor Capital Budgeting Decisions

Regardless of the rate of return a particular project promises, managers should accept only projects with the following four characteristics:

1 The project must be compatible with the strategic plans and goals of the company. If a project promises high returns but is not congruent with organizational goals, either the project will fail or it will lead the firm away from its committed strategies and might lead to its eventual failure.
2 Within a reasonable time, the majority of the employees the project affects must accept it. If a firm installs new equipment that the operators dislike or cannot use effectively, the costs become sunk quickly and may cause production disruption instead of saving costs.
3 Participants who propose projects must submit realistic estimates of cost, revenues, and potential savings. Projects with falsified data engender erroneous decisions that may prove to be very costly.
4 Firms may want to avoid project competitions that give monetary rewards to the project initiators. Such competitions may encourage participants to unethically manipulate the data to make the project seem more attractive. The individual gets a reward, but the company suffers a loss because it made a decision based on manipulated data.

A firm that uses a sound capital budgeting process and avoids these pitfalls should reap the rewards of making informed and appropriate use of its scarce resources.

THE TIME VALUE OF MONEY

The Concept of Interest

A dollar received at some point in the future does not have the same value as a dollar received today. If you were asked why this is so, you might think the change in value is due to inflation. But even if inflation did not exist, a dollar received in the future still would not have the same value as a dollar received today because if cash is available now, it can be invested now and earn a return as time passes. This increase in the value of cash over time due to investment income is the time value of money. The concept of the time value of money is used to determine either the future value of money invested today or the present value of money to be received at some point in the future.

Future Value

● **future value**
The value of a payment, or series of payments, at a future point in time, calculated with an interest rate.

Future value is the value of a payment, or series of payments, at a future point in time, calculated with an interest rate. For example, if you were to invest $2,000 at an annual interest rate of 10 percent, you can calculate that your investment would grow to $2,200 in one year by applying the interest formula you learned in Chapter 3:

$$\text{Principal} \times \text{Rate} \times \text{Time} = \text{Interest}$$
$$\$2,000 \quad \times 10\% \times 1 \quad = \$200$$

The $200 of interest added to the $2,000 investment produces a total of $2,200. Suppose you left the investment untouched for three years. What would its total value be at the end of the three years? The answer depends on whether the interest is calculated as simple interest or as compound interest.

● **simple interest**
Interest calculated only on the original principal.

Simple interest is interest calculated only on the original principal. The amount of interest earned at 10 percent per year for three years on a $2,000 principal using simple interest is:

$$\text{Principal} \times \text{Rate} \times \text{Time} = \text{Interest}$$
$$\$2,000 \quad \times 10\% \times 3 \quad = \$600$$

At the end of three years you would receive your $2,000 (return of your principal) and $600 interest (return on your investment).

● **compound interest**
Interest calculated on the investment principal plus all previously earned interest at the end of each compounding period.

● **compounding period**
The frequency that interest is calculated and added to the principal, such as annually, semiannually, quarterly, monthly, or daily.

Compound interest is interest calculated on the investment principal *plus* all previously earned interest at the end of each compounding period. The **compounding period** is the frequency that interest is calculated and added to the

	YEAR 1	YEAR 2	YEAR 3	TOTAL
Principal at beginning of year	$2,000	$2,200	$2,420	
Interest added at 10%	200	220	242	$662
Principal at end of year	$2,200	$2,420	$2,662	

Exhibit 11-10
Compound Interest
Calculations

principal, such as annually, semiannually, quarterly, monthly, or daily. Exhibit 11-10 illustrates the computation for principal of $2,000 that earns 10 percent interest compounded annually for three years. At the end of three years you would receive your $2,000 back (return of principal) and $662 interest (return on your investment). The difference of $62 between the interest earned using compound interest ($662) and the interest earned using simple interest ($600) is interest earned on your previously earned interest.

The power of compounding is tremendous. To demonstrate, let's extend our example of the $2,000 investment. Suppose Trevor Shipley invests $2,000 at 10 percent interest compounded annually when he is 25 years old and leaves it untouched until he is 65 years old and ready to retire. Using the simple interest calculation, Trevor's investment will earn interest of $8,000 ($2,000 × 10% × 40 years). If, however, the interest over that same 40 years is compounded, the total interest earned would be $88,518. The $80,518 difference in interest earned is due entirely to interest earnings on previously earned interest. If you had a lot of time, you could calculate the amount of compound interest on Trevor's investment by extending the three-year example in Exhibit 11-10 for another 37 years. Fortunately, future value tables and financial calculators greatly simplify the calculation of compound interest.

We use the *Future Value of $1* table in Exhibit 11-11 to determine the future value of a single amount deposited today. Using the information from the *Future Value of $1* table you can quickly determine the future value of Shipley's $2,000 investment at a 10 percent interest rate compounded annually. Locate the row for year 40 and go across to the 10 percent column to find the 45.2690 future value interest factor (FVIF). The following equation allows you to compute the future value:

$$\text{Future Value (FV)} = \text{Investment} \times \text{FVIF}$$
$$\text{FV} = \quad \$2,000 \quad \times 45.2590 = \$90,518$$

If you subtract his initial investment of $2,000, the amount of interest he will earn is $88,518.

The information in the *Future Value of an Annuity of $1* table in Exhibit 11-12 is used to determine the future value of a stream of cash flows when the stream of cash flows constitutes an annuity. An **annuity** is a stream of cash flows where the dollar amount of each payment and the time interval between each payment are uniform. To illustrate how to use the table in Exhibit 11-12, assume Shipley intends to deposit $2,000 in an account at the end of each year for 40 years at 10 percent compound annually. Using the table, you find the future value interest factor of an annuity (FVIFA) for 40 years at 10 percent is 442.5926. The following equation allows you to compute the future value:

● **annuity**
A stream of cash flows where the dollar amount of each payment and the time interval between each payment are uniform.

$$\text{FV} = \text{Annual Investment} \times \text{FVIFA}$$
$$\text{FV} = \quad \$2,000 \quad \times 442.5926 = \$885,185.20$$

Accordingly, if Shipley deposits $2,000 at the end of the each year for 40 years at 10 percent the account balance will be $885,185.20 at the end of 40 years. He will deposit $80,000 and earn $805,185.20 in interest. This demonstrates the power of a retirement savings account for a disciplined saver. You can also see why determining the future value of an amount invested today is called **compounding**.

● **compounding**
Determining the future value of an amount invested today.

Exhibit 11-11
Future Value of $1 Table

TABLE 1 - Future Value of $1 Due in *n* Periods

n	1%	2%	3%	4%	5%	6%	7%	8%	9%	10%	12%	14%	16%	18%	20%
1	1.0100	1.0200	1.0300	1.0400	1.0500	1.0600	1.0700	1.0800	1.0900	1.1000	1.1200	1.1400	1.1600	1.1800	1.2000
2	1.0201	1.0404	1.0609	1.0816	1.1025	1.1236	1.1449	1.1664	1.1881	1.2100	1.2544	1.2996	1.3456	1.3924	1.4400
3	1.0303	1.0612	1.0927	1.1249	1.1576	1.1910	1.2250	1.2597	1.2950	1.3310	1.4049	1.4815	1.5609	1.6430	1.7280
4	1.0406	1.0824	1.1255	1.1699	1.2155	1.2625	1.3108	1.3605	1.4116	1.4641	1.5735	1.6890	1.8106	1.9388	2.0736
5	1.0510	1.1041	1.1593	1.2167	1.2763	1.3382	1.4026	1.4693	1.5386	1.6105	1.7623	1.9254	2.1003	2.2878	2.4883
6	1.0615	1.1262	1.1941	1.2653	1.3401	1.4185	1.5007	1.5869	1.6771	1.7716	1.9738	2.1950	2.4364	2.6996	2.9860
7	1.0721	1.1487	1.2299	1.3159	1.4071	1.5036	1.6058	1.7138	1.8280	1.9487	2.2107	2.5023	2.8262	3.1855	3.5832
8	1.0829	1.1717	1.2668	1.3686	1.4775	1.5938	1.7182	1.8509	1.9926	2.1436	2.4760	2.8526	3.2784	3.7589	4.2998
9	1.0937	1.1951	1.3048	1.4233	1.5513	1.6895	1.8385	1.9990	2.1719	2.3579	2.7731	3.2519	3.8030	4.4355	5.1598
10	1.1046	1.2190	1.3439	1.4802	1.6289	1.7908	1.9672	2.1589	2.3674	2.5937	3.1058	3.7072	4.4114	5.2338	6.1917
11	1.1157	1.2434	1.3842	1.5395	1.7103	1.8983	2.1049	2.3316	2.5804	2.8531	3.4785	4.2262	5.1173	6.1759	7.4031
12	1.1268	1.2682	1.4258	1.6010	1.7959	2.0122	2.2522	2.5182	2.8127	3.1384	3.8960	4.8179	5.9360	7.2876	8.9161
13	1.1381	1.2936	1.4685	1.6651	1.8856	2.1329	2.4098	2.7196	3.0658	3.4523	4.3635	5.4924	6.8858	8.5994	10.6990
14	1.1495	1.3195	1.5126	1.7317	1.9799	2.2609	2.5785	2.9372	3.3417	3.7975	4.8871	6.2613	7.9875	10.1470	12.8390
15	1.1610	1.3459	1.5580	1.8009	2.0789	2.3966	2.7590	3.1722	3.6425	4.1772	5.4736	7.1379	9.2655	11.9730	15.4070
16	1.1726	1.3728	1.6047	1.8730	2.1829	2.5404	2.9522	3.4259	3.9703	4.5950	6.1304	8.1372	10.7480	14.1290	18.4880
17	1.1843	1.4002	1.6528	1.9479	2.2920	2.6928	3.1588	3.7000	4.3276	5.0545	6.8660	9.2765	12.4670	16.6720	22.1860
18	1.1961	1.4282	1.7024	2.0258	2.4066	2.8543	3.3799	3.9960	4.7171	5.5599	7.6900	10.5750	14.4620	19.6730	26.6230
19	1.2081	1.4568	1.7535	2.1068	2.5270	3.0256	3.6165	4.3157	5.1417	6.1159	8.6128	12.0560	16.7760	23.2140	31.9480
20	1.2202	1.4859	1.8061	2.1911	2.6533	3.2071	3.8697	4.6610	5.6044	6.7275	9.6463	13.7430	19.4600	27.3930	38.3370
30	1.3478	1.8114	2.4273	3.2434	4.3219	5.7435	7.6123	10.0620	13.2670	17.4490	29.9590	50.9500	85.8490	143.3700	237.3700
40	1.4889	2.2080	3.2620	4.8010	7.0400	10.2850	14.9740	21.7240	31.4090	45.2590	93.0500	188.8800	378.7200	750.3700	1,469.7000

Exhibit 11-12
Future Value of an Annuity of $1 Table

TABLE 2 - Future Value of an Annuity of $1 per _n_ Payments

n	1%	2%	3%	4%	5%	6%	7%	8%	9%	10%	12%	14%	16%	18%	20%
1	1.0000	1.0000	1.0000	1.0000	1.0000	1.0000	1.0000	1.0000	1.0000	1.0000	1.0000	1.0000	1.0000	1.0000	1.0000
2	2.0100	2.0200	2.0300	2.0400	2.0500	2.0600	2.0700	2.0800	2.0900	2.1000	2.1200	2.1400	2.1600	2.1800	2.2000
3	3.0301	3.0604	3.0909	3.1216	3.1525	3.1836	3.2149	3.2464	3.2781	3.3100	3.3744	3.4396	3.5056	3.5724	3.6400
4	4.0604	4.1216	4.1836	4.2465	4.3101	4.3746	4.4399	4.5061	4.5731	4.6410	4.7793	4.9211	5.0665	5.2154	5.3680
5	5.1010	5.2040	5.3091	5.4163	5.5256	5.6371	5.7507	5.8666	5.9847	6.1051	6.3528	6.6101	6.8771	7.1542	7.4416
6	6.1520	6.3081	6.4684	6.6330	6.8019	6.9753	7.1533	7.3359	7.5233	7.7156	8.1152	8.5355	8.9775	9.4420	9.9299
7	7.2135	7.4343	7.6625	7.8983	8.1420	8.3938	8.6540	8.9228	9.2004	9.4872	10.0890	10.7305	11.4139	12.1415	12.9159
8	8.2857	8.5830	8.8923	9.2142	9.5491	9.8975	10.2598	10.6366	11.0285	11.4359	12.2997	13.2328	14.2401	15.3270	16.4991
9	9.3685	9.7546	10.1591	10.5828	11.0266	11.4913	11.9780	12.4876	13.0210	13.5795	14.7757	16.0853	17.5185	19.0859	20.7989
10	10.4622	10.9497	11.4639	12.0061	12.5779	13.1808	13.8164	14.4866	15.1929	15.9374	17.5487	19.3373	21.3215	23.5213	25.9587
11	11.5668	12.1687	12.8078	13.4864	14.2068	14.9716	15.7836	16.6455	17.5603	18.5312	20.6546	23.0445	25.7329	28.7551	32.1504
12	12.6825	13.4121	14.1920	15.0258	15.9171	16.8699	17.8885	18.9771	20.1407	21.2843	24.1331	27.2707	30.8502	34.9311	39.5805
13	13.8093	14.6803	15.6178	16.6268	17.7130	18.8821	20.1406	21.4953	22.9534	24.5227	28.0291	32.0887	36.7862	42.2187	48.4966
14	14.9474	15.9739	17.0863	18.2919	19.5986	21.0151	22.5505	24.2149	26.0192	27.9750	32.3926	37.5811	43.6720	50.8180	59.1959
15	16.0969	17.2934	18.5989	20.0236	21.5786	23.2760	25.1290	27.1521	29.3609	31.7725	37.2797	43.8424	51.6595	60.9653	72.0351
16	17.2579	18.6393	20.1569	21.8248	23.6575	25.6725	27.8881	30.3243	33.0034	35.9497	42.7535	50.9804	60.9250	72.9390	87.4421
17	18.4304	20.0121	21.7616	23.6975	25.8404	28.2129	30.8402	33.7502	36.9737	40.5447	48.8837	59.1176	71.6730	87.0680	105.9306
18	19.6147	21.4123	23.4144	25.6454	28.1324	30.9057	33.9990	37.4502	41.3013	45.5992	55.7497	68.3941	84.1407	103.7403	128.1167
19	20.8190	22.8406	25.1169	27.6712	30.5390	33.7600	37.3790	41.4463	46.0185	51.1591	63.4397	78.9692	98.6032	123.4135	154.7400
20	22.0190	24.2974	26.8704	29.7781	33.0660	36.7856	40.9955	45.7620	51.1601	57.2750	72.0524	91.0249	115.3797	146.6280	186.6880
30	34.7849	40.5681	47.5754	56.0849	66.4388	79.0582	94.4608	113.2832	136.3075	164.4940	241.3327	356.7868	530.3117	490.9480	1,181.8816
40	48.8864	60.4020	75.4013	95.0255	120.7998	154.7620	199.6351	259.0565	337.8824	442.5926	767.0914	1,342.0251	2,360.7572	4,163.2130	7,343.8578

437

Present Value

The basic premise of the present value of money is that it is more valuable to receive cash today so it can be invested to receive interest, than to receive the cash later. The question is, just *how* valuable is it to receive cash sooner rather than later? If you know the expected rate of return, you can calculate the value of receiving cash sooner rather than later. For example, if you are offered the option of receiving $1,000 today or $1,000 one year from now, how much more valuable is it to receive the $1,000 today? If the $1,000 received today can be invested in a savings account earning 6 percent interest, it will grow by $60 during the year. At the end of one year, it will be worth $1,060 and you would be $60 richer than if you had opted to receive the $1,000 one year from now. The $60 growth in value over time exemplifies the time value of money. Clearly, if money is available and invested, it grows as time passes.

If cash can be invested at 6 percent, $1,000 received today is equivalent to receiving $1,060 one year from now. The amount an investment is worth today evaluated at the appropriate interest rate is the investment's **present value**. Determining the present value of an amount of cash to be received in the future is called **discounting**.

Present value tables greatly simplify the calculation of discounting to find the present value of a single amount or an annuity. The information in the *Present Value of $1* table in Exhibit 11-13 can be used to determine the present value of a single amount to be received at some point in the future.

To see how you use this information, suppose you visited your rich Aunt Virginia and helped her clean out her attic. Your aunt was so touched by your kindness, she offers to give you a gift of $1,000 in one year. Her only request is that you tell her how much to deposit in a 6 percent savings account today so that the account will equal $1,000 one year from now. You can use the *Present Value of $1* table in Exhibit 11-13. Find the point of intersection between the 6 percent interest rate column and the number of time periods row, which is 1. The point of intersection, the present value interest factor (PVIF), is 0.9434. Using the following equation, you can determine the present value:

$$PV = \text{Future Value} \times PVIF$$
$$PV = \quad \$1,000 \quad \times .9434 = \$943.40$$

If your Aunt Virginia deposits $943.40 today and earns 6 percent interest for one year of $56.60 ($943.40 × .06 × 1), she will have $1,000 to give you in one year.

During your visit with Aunt Virginia, she discovers that you will be going to college for two more years. Being an advocate of graduate education, she offers to give you $1,000 at the end of each of the next four years if you keep up your grades and promise to go to graduate school. She needs to know how much to set aside to ensure that you receive your money. Exhibit 11-14 contains a timeline outlining her offer.

Aunt Virginia can place $3,465.10 in an account today to guarantee that you can withdraw $1,000 each year for four years. To eliminate the cumbersome calculations, you can use the *Present Value of an Annuity of $1* table in Exhibit 11-15 to find the present value. Find the intersection of 4 periods and 6 percent, which yields a present value interest factor of an annuity (PVIFA) of 3.4651. Using the following equation, you can compute the present value of the annuity of four payments:

$$PV = \text{Amount of Payment} \times PVIFA$$
$$PV = \quad \$1,000 \quad \times 3.4651 = \$3,465.10$$

The annuity table in Exhibit 11-15 provides the same result as the timeline calculation with less effort.

In the business world, most managers rely on calculators and computers to calculate future and present values. The secret to using a financial calculator is to enter

● **present value (PV) of an investment**
The amount an investment is worth today evaluated at the appropriate interest rate.

● **discounting**
Determining the present value of an amount of cash to be received in the future.

Exhibit 11-13
Present Value of $1 Table

TABLE 3 - The Present Value of $1 Due in _n_ Periods

n	1%	2%	3%	4%	5%	6%	7%	8%	9%	10%	12%	14%	16%	18%	20%
1	0.9901	0.9804	0.9709	0.9615	0.9524	0.9434	0.9346	0.9259	0.9174	0.9091	0.8929	0.8772	0.8621	0.8475	0.8333
2	0.9803	0.9612	0.9426	0.9246	0.9070	0.8900	0.8734	0.8573	0.8417	0.8264	0.7972	0.7695	0.7432	0.7182	0.6944
3	0.9706	0.9423	0.9151	0.8890	0.8638	0.8396	0.8163	0.7938	0.7722	0.7513	0.7118	0.6750	0.6407	0.6086	0.5787
4	0.9610	0.9238	0.8885	0.8548	0.8227	0.7921	0.7629	0.7350	0.7084	0.6830	0.6355	0.5921	0.5523	0.5158	0.4823
5	0.9515	0.9057	0.8626	0.8219	0.7835	0.7473	0.7130	0.6806	0.6499	0.6209	0.5674	0.5194	0.4761	0.4371	0.4019
6	0.9420	0.8880	0.8375	0.7903	0.7462	0.7050	0.6663	0.6302	0.5963	0.5645	0.5066	0.4556	0.4104	0.3704	0.3349
7	0.9327	0.8706	0.8131	0.7599	0.7107	0.6651	0.6227	0.5835	0.5470	0.5132	0.4523	0.3996	0.3538	0.3139	0.2791
8	0.9235	0.8535	0.7894	0.7307	0.6768	0.6274	0.5820	0.5403	0.5019	0.4665	0.4039	0.3506	0.3050	0.2660	0.2326
9	0.9143	0.8368	0.7664	0.7026	0.6446	0.5919	0.5439	0.5002	0.4604	0.4241	0.3606	0.3075	0.2630	0.2255	0.1938
10	0.9053	0.8203	0.7441	0.6756	0.6139	0.5584	0.5083	0.4632	0.4224	0.3855	0.3220	0.2697	0.2267	0.1911	0.1615
11	0.8963	0.8043	0.7224	0.6496	0.5847	0.5268	0.4751	0.4289	0.3875	0.3503	0.2875	0.2366	0.1954	0.1619	0.1346
12	0.8874	0.7885	0.7014	0.6246	0.5568	0.4970	0.4440	0.3971	0.3555	0.3186	0.2567	0.2076	0.1685	0.1372	0.1122
13	0.8787	0.7730	0.6810	0.6006	0.5303	0.4688	0.4150	0.3677	0.3262	0.2897	0.2292	0.1821	0.1452	0.1163	0.0935
14	0.8700	0.7579	0.6611	0.5775	0.5051	0.4423	0.3878	0.3405	0.2992	0.2633	0.2046	0.1597	0.1252	0.0985	0.0779
15	0.8613	0.7430	0.6419	0.5553	0.4810	0.4173	0.3624	0.3152	0.2745	0.2394	0.1827	0.1401	0.1079	0.0835	0.0649
16	0.8528	0.7284	0.6232	0.5339	0.4581	0.3936	0.3387	0.2919	0.2519	0.2176	0.1631	0.1229	0.0930	0.0708	0.0541
17	0.8444	0.7142	0.6050	0.5134	0.4363	0.3714	0.3166	0.2703	0.2311	0.1978	0.1456	0.1078	0.0802	0.0600	0.0451
18	0.8360	0.7002	0.5874	0.4936	0.4155	0.3503	0.2959	0.2502	0.2120	0.1799	0.1300	0.0946	0.0691	0.0508	0.0376
19	0.8277	0.6864	0.5703	0.4746	0.3957	0.3305	0.2765	0.2317	0.1945	0.1635	0.1161	0.0829	0.0596	0.0431	0.0313
20	0.8195	0.6730	0.5537	0.4564	0.3769	0.3118	0.2584	0.2145	0.1784	0.1486	0.1037	0.0728	0.0514	0.0365	0.0261
25	0.7798	0.6095	0.4776	0.3751	0.2953	0.2330	0.1842	0.1460	0.1160	0.0923	0.0588	0.0378	0.0245	0.0160	0.0105
30	0.7419	0.5521	0.4120	0.3083	0.2314	0.1741	0.1314	0.0994	0.0754	0.0573	0.0334	0.0196	0.0116	0.0070	0.0042
40	0.6717	0.4529	0.3066	0.2083	0.1420	0.0972	0.0668	0.0460	0.0318	0.0221	0.0107	0.0053	0.0026	0.0013	0.0007

Exhibit 11-14
Present Value Calculation
for Four Payments

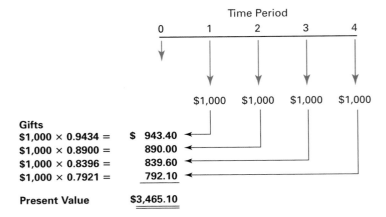

Gifts	
$1,000 × 0.9434 =	$ 943.40
$1,000 × 0.8900 =	890.00
$1,000 × 0.8396 =	839.60
$1,000 × 0.7921 =	792.10
Present Value	**$3,465.10**

all of the factors you know and have it compute the unknown factor. For example, each of the computations we made in this appendix can be solved using a calculator as follows:

1 Future value of $2,000 in 40 years at 10 percent interest compounded annually:

$$PV = 2,000$$
$$i = 10$$
$$n = 40$$
$$CPT, \ FV = \text{Result is } \$90,518.51$$

2 Future value of annual payments of $2,000 at the end of each of the next 40 years at 10 percent interest compounded annually:

$$PV = 0$$
$$i = 10$$
$$n = 40$$
$$CPT, \ FV = \text{Result is } \$885,185.11$$

3 Present value of $1,000 in 1 year discounted at 6 percent interest compounded annually:

$$FV = 1,000$$
$$i = 6$$
$$n = 1$$
$$CPT, \ FV = \text{Result is } \$943.40$$

4 Present value of a 4-year $1,000 annuity discounted at 6 percent interest compounded annually:

$$FV = 0$$
$$i = 6$$
$$n = 4$$
$$PMT = 1,000$$
$$CPT, \ FV = \text{Result is } \$3,465.10$$

Amounts from a calculator will vary slightly from amounts computed with the tables. The calculator amounts are more accurate because they carry out the computations to an infinite number of decimal points.

Exhibit 11-15
Present Value of an Annuity of $1 Table

TABLE 4 - The Present Value of an Annuity of $1 for *n* Payments

n	1%	2%	3%	4%	5%	6%	7%	8%	9%	10%	12%	14%	16%	18%	20%
1	0.9901	0.9804	0.9709	0.9615	0.9524	0.9434	0.9346	0.9259	0.9174	0.9091	0.8929	0.8772	0.8621	0.8475	0.8333
2	1.9704	1.9416	1.9135	1.8861	1.8594	1.8334	1.8080	1.7833	1.7591	1.7355	1.6901	1.6467	1.6052	1.5656	1.5278
3	2.9410	2.8839	2.8286	2.7751	2.7232	2.6730	2.6243	2.5771	2.5313	2.4869	2.4018	2.3216	2.2459	2.1743	2.1065
4	3.9820	3.8077	3.7171	3.6299	3.5460	3.4651	3.3872	3.3121	3.2397	3.1699	3.0373	2.9137	2.7982	2.6901	2.5887
5	4.8884	4.7135	4.5797	4.4518	4.3295	4.2124	4.1002	3.9927	3.8897	3.7908	3.6048	3.4331	3.2743	3.1272	2.9906
6	5.7985	5.6014	5.4172	5.2421	5.0757	4.9173	4.7665	4.6229	4.4859	4.3553	4.1114	3.8887	3.6847	3.4976	3.3255
7	6.7282	6.4720	6.2303	6.0021	5.7864	5.5824	5.3893	5.2064	5.0330	4.8684	4.5638	4.2883	4.0386	3.8115	3.6046
8	7.6517	7.3255	7.0197	6.7327	6.4632	6.2098	5.9713	5.7466	5.5348	5.3349	4.9676	4.6389	4.3436	4.0776	3.8372
9	8.5660	8.1622	7.7861	7.4353	7.1078	6.8017	6.5152	6.2469	5.9952	5.7590	5.3282	4.9464	4.6065	4.3030	4.0310
10	9.4713	8.9826	8.5302	8.1109	7.7217	7.3601	7.0236	6.7101	6.4177	6.1446	5.6502	5.2161	4.8332	4.4941	4.1925
11	10.3676	9.7868	9.2526	8.7605	8.3064	7.8869	7.4987	7.1390	6.8052	6.4951	5.9377	5.4527	5.0286	4.6560	4.3271
12	11.2551	10.5733	9.9540	9.3851	8.8633	8.3838	7.9427	7.5361	7.1607	6.8137	6.1944	5.6603	5.1971	4.7932	4.4392
13	12.1337	11.3484	10.6350	9.9856	9.3936	8.8527	8.3577	7.9038	7.4869	7.1034	6.4235	5.8424	5.3423	4.9095	4.5327
14	13.0037	12.1062	11.2961	10.5631	9.8986	9.2950	8.7455	8.2442	7.7862	7.3667	6.6282	6.0021	5.4675	5.0081	4.6106
15	13.8651	12.8493	11.9379	11.1184	10.3797	9.7122	9.1079	8.5595	8.0607	7.6061	6.8109	6.1422	5.5755	5.0916	4.6755
16	14.7179	13.5777	12.5611	11.6523	10.8378	10.1059	9.4466	8.8514	8.3126	7.8237	6.9740	6.2651	5.6685	5.1624	4.7296
17	15.5623	14.2919	13.1661	12.1657	11.2741	10.4773	9.7632	9.1216	8.5436	8.0216	7.1196	6.3729	5.7487	5.2223	4.7746
18	16.3983	14.9920	13.7535	12.6593	11.6896	10.8276	10.0591	9.3719	8.7556	8.2014	7.2497	6.4674	5.8178	5.2732	4.8122
19	17.2260	15.6785	14.3238	13.1339	12.0853	11.1581	10.3356	9.6036	8.9501	8.3649	7.3658	6.5504	5.8775	5.3162	4.8435
20	18.0456	16.3514	14.8775	13.5903	12.4622	11.4699	10.5940	9.8181	9.1285	8.5136	7.4694	6.6231	5.9288	5.3527	4.8696
25	22.0232	19.5235	17.4131	15.6221	14.0939	12.7834	11.6536	10.6748	9.8226	9.0770	7.8431	6.8729	6.0971	5.4669	4.9476
30	25.8077	22.3965	19.6004	17.2920	15.3725	13.7648	12.4090	11.2578	10.2737	9.4269	8.0552	7.0027	6.1772	5.5168	4.9789
40	32.8347	27.3555	23.1148	19.7928	17.1591	15.0463	13.3317	11.9246	10.7574	9.7791	8.2438	7.1050	6.2335	5.5482	4.9966

Changes in the Compounding Periods

Any time interest rates are quoted, the percentage rate is an annual rate. What happens if you can find a financial institution that will compound your investment more frequently than annually? You must do two things to adjust for a difference in the number of compounding periods:

1   Divide the quoted interest rate by the number of compounding times per year.
2   Multiply the number of periods by the number of compounding times per year.

For example, if you want to deposit $2,000 today at 8 percent for 4 years compounded annually, you look up the FVIF for 4 periods at 8 percent, which shows a FVIF of 1.3605 and a future value of $2,721. If you can compound the interest quarterly, you look up 2 percent for 16 periods, which shows a FVIF of 1.3728 and a future value of $2,745.60. The additional compounding periods increase the interest earned by $24.60.

Knowledge of present and future value concepts will be important to you in your college course work, your professional career, and your life. As you consider the purchases of homes and cars, as well as saving for retirement or college for children and grandchildren, these concepts will help you to make more intelligent decisions.

CHAPTER SUMMARY

The capital budgeting process outlines how a company will allocate its scarce resources over the next 5, 10, or even 20 years. All capital projects have at least four shared characteristics. Such projects are usually long-lived, have a high cost, have costs that become sunk almost immediately, and have a high degree of risk associated with the project.

In the long run, the capital projects a company undertakes must earn at least the cost of the company's capital. The cost of capital is the cost of obtaining financing from both debt and equity sources. The combination of the cost of debt financing and equity financing is referred to as the blended cost of capital.

Several methods allow managers to evaluate potential capital projects. Among these are the payback period method, the net present value method, and the internal rate of return method. Each of these methods has certain advantages and disadvantages relative to the other methods. The net present value and internal rate of return methods are generally considered to be superior to the payback method because they incorporate the time value of money in their approach to evaluating potential capital projects. The payback method is easy to calculate and addresses liquidity issues. No project should be undertaken, however, unless it furthers the strategic plans and goals of the organization.

Visit the Web site *www.prenhall.com/terrell* for additional study help with the Online Study Guide.

REVIEW OF CONCEPTS

A   Describe the purpose of a capital budget and how it relates to the firm's strategic plan and goals.
B   Compare and contrast a capital investment and a capital project.
C   Differentiate between capitalizing and expensing a purchased item.

D Discuss the four characteristics virtually all capital projects share.

E Describe what the net present value of an investment means.

F Discuss the advantage of calculating the profitability index when analyzing the net present value of an investment.

G Describe the difference between the internal rate of return and the net present value of an investment.

H Describe the payback method.

I Discuss the factors that contribute to poor capital project selection.

J Differentiate between simple interest and compound interest.

K Discuss the difference between an annuity and a single sum.

APPLICATION EXERCISES

11-7 The CFO of Margene, Inc. is determining a return rate to use for its cost of capital. After reviewing the financial statements, he determined that the total interest-bearing debt is $1,400,000 and total stockholders equity is $1,000,000. He computed the cost of debt financing at 8% and the cost of equity financing is 18%.

LO 3
Cost of Capital

Required:

a. What percentage of Margene's total financing comes from debt?
b. What percentage of Margene's total financing comes from equity?
c. Calculate Margene's blended cost of capital rate.

11-8 The Burns Company CFO needs to determine a return rate to use for its cost of capital. The total interest-bearing debt is $4,800,000 and total stockholders equity is $14,400,000. She determined that the cost of debt financing is 7% and the cost of equity financing is 22%.

LO 3
Cost of Capital

Required:

a. What proportion of Burns' total financing comes from debt?
b. What proportion of Burns' total financing comes from equity?
c. Calculate Burns' blended cost of capital rate.

11-9 The Cunningham Company has the following debt:

LO 3
Cost of Capital

Debt	Interest Rate
$300,000	6%
400,000	10%
200,000	12%

Total stockholders equity is $1,700,000 and the board of directors established the cost of equity financing at 20%.

Required:

Calculate the Cunningham Company's blended cost of capital rate.

11-10 Claudia Wade is contemplating the purchase of a machine for her business. The following estimates are available:

LO 5
Payback Period

Initial outlay	$5,826.50
Annual cash inflow	1,355.00

Required:

Determine the payback period for the machine purchase.

LO 5
Payback Period

11-11   Ted Rogers owns Discount Hardware. He is contemplating the purchase of a copy machine that would be used to make copies to sell to customers for $0.05 each. The following estimates are available:

Initial outlay	$4,500
Annual cash inflow	1,800

Required:
Determine the payback period for the copy machine purchase.

LO 5
Payback Period

11-12   Regina Brown owns You Can Do Magic Manufacturing. She is contemplating the purchase of a machine that will produce various products to sell to magic shops. The following estimates are available:

Initial outlay	$23,539.20
Annual cash inflow	7,356.00

Required:
Determine the payback period for the machine purchase.

LO 5
Payback Period

11-13   Tyler Strawn wants to purchase a new, technologically advanced machine for his business. The following estimates are available:

Initial outlay	$323,400.00
Annual cash inflow	33,000.00

Required:
Determine the payback period for the machine purchase.

LO 5
Payback Period

11-14   Christopher Wyont is considering the purchase of a fuel truck that he would use to sell gasoline at motor sport racing events. He found a used truck for $13,000. He believes that the cash inflows would grow each year as he acquires new customers. He has made the following cash inflow estimates:

First year	$3,000
Second year	4,500
Third and subsequent years	5,000

Required:
Determine the payback period for the fuel truck purchase.

LO 5
Payback Period

11-15   Veronica Torres wants to open an art studio with an investment of $15,000. She believes that the cash inflows would grow each year as follows:

First year	$2,000
Second year	4,000
Third and subsequent years	5,000

Required:
Determine the payback period for the art studio.

LO 5
Payback Period

11-16   Karen Harwood is considering adding a new style of gym shorts to her product line. With investment of $23,000, she believes that the cash inflows would grow each year as follows:

First year	$4,000
Second year	7,000
Third and subsequent years	10,000

Required:
Determine the payback period for the new style of gym shorts.

11-17 Jessica Miller, the owner of Discount Fashions, wants to purchase a soda machine to sell soft drinks to customers for $0.75 each. The following estimates are available:

Initial outlay	$3,500
Annual cash inflow	$1,000
Cost of capital	10%
Estimated life of the soda machine	5 years
Estimated residual value of the soda machine	$—0—

LO 5
Net Present Value

Required:

Determine the net present value of the soda machine purchase.

11-18 Anna Garcia is ready to sign a purchase agreement for an ice cream vending machine to sell ice cream treats to customers for $2 each. The following estimates are available:

Initial outlay	$4,000
Annual cash inflow	$1,200
Cost of capital	12%
Estimated life of the ice cream machine	5 years
Estimated residual value of the ice cream machine	$—0—

LO 5
Net Present Value

Required:

Compute the net present value of the ice cream machine purchase.

11-19 Joe Anzelmo is investigating the purchase of a machine that will automate the production of baseball bats in his factory. The sales representative has given him the following estimates:

Initial outlay	$97,000
Annual reduction in manufacturing labor cost	$22,500
Cost of capital	14%
Estimated life of the baseball bat machine	8 years
Estimated residual value of the baseball bat machine	$ —0—

LO 5
Net Present Value

Required:

Calculate the net present value of the machine purchase.

11-20 Debbie Gay is investigating the purchase of an automated hosiery machine for her factory. The following estimates are available:

Initial outlay	$112,000
Annual reduction in manufacturing labor cost	$ 22,500
Cost of capital	12%
Estimated life of the hosiery machine	8 years
Estimated residual value of the hosiery machine	$ —0—

LO 5
Net Present Value

Required:

Determine the net present value of the hosiery machine purchase.

11-21 Michael Dietz Sporting Goods is considering the purchase of a $265,000 machine that will cut leather to make baseball gloves. The machine will last 8 years, with no residual value. Currently, the company leases a similar machine for $50,000 per year. If the new machine were purchased, the company's cost of labor would be reduced by $12,000 per year.

LO 5
Net Present Value and Profitability Index

Required:

Determine the net present value and the profitability index of the machine under each of the following assumptions:
   a. the cost of capital is 12%
   b. the cost of capital is 14%
   c. the cost of capital is 16%

LO 5
Payback Period, Net Present Value, and Profitability Index

11-22   The CEO of Carl Smythe Manufacturing is considering the purchase of a $3,600,000 computer controlled manufacturing machine for its factory. The machine has an estimated useful life of 10 years with no residual value. The new machine should reduce the company's cost of labor by $650,000 per year.

Required:

   a. Compute the payback period.
   b. Determine the net present value and the profitability index of the machine under each of the following assumptions:
      1. the cost of capital is 14%
      2. the cost of capital is 16%
      3. the cost of capital is 18%

LO 5
Payback Period and Net Present Value

11-23   Frank Naifeh wants to purchase an engine lift for his marine repair business. He found a used lift for $5,500 that has an estimated useful life of 8 years and a residual value of zero. Currently, Naifeh rents engine lifts as needed at an annual rental cost of $1,400. The cost of capital is 16%.

Required:

Calculate the payback period and the net present value of the engine lift purchase.

LO 5
Payback Period and Net Present Value

11-24   Alfred Newman has located a $25,800 industrial glass-cutting machine for use in his business. The cutter has a useful life of 10 years and a residual value of zero. Currently, Newman rents an industrial cutter for $4,400 annually. The cost of capital is 14%.

Required:

Calculate the payback period and the net present value of the industrial glass cutter.

LO 5
Net Present Value

11-25   Serina Wynn, the owner of Wynn Sports Cards, wants to automate the production of her baseball cards. The sales representative provided the following estimates:

Initial outlay	$35,000
Annual reduction in manufacturing labor cost	$ 8,500
Cost of capital	14%
Estimated life of the card machine	5 years
Estimated residual value of the card machine	$ 2,000

Required:

Determine the net present value of the baseball card machine purchase.

LO 5
Net Present Value

11-26   Richard Petty owns Discount Auto Parts. He is contemplating the purchase of a revolutionary new brake lathe that could be used to refurbish brake parts for customers at great savings. The following estimates are available:

Initial outlay	$6,500
Annual cash inflow	$1,500
Cost of capital	18%
Estimated life of the brake lathe	6 years
Estimated residual value of the brake lathe	$1,000

Required:

Determine the net present value of the brake lathe purchase.

11-27 Jane Wesley, the owner of Jane's Skin Care Products, is contemplating the purchase of an industrial mixer to mix cosmetics in her factory. The following estimates are available:

Initial outlay	$78,500
Annual cash inflow	$19,500
Cost of capital	16%
Estimated life of the industrial mixer	7 years
Estimated residual value of the mixer	$ 4,000

LO 5
Net Present Value

Required:

Determine the net present value of the industrial mixer purchase.

11-28 Edie Vero wants to purchase a cutting machine to make shoes in her factory. The following estimates are available:

Initial outlay	$58,000
Annual cash inflow from reduced labor cost	$11,500
Cost of capital	12%
Estimated life of the cutter	8 years
Estimated residual value of the cutter	$ 2,000

LO 5
Net Present Value

Required:

Determine the net present value of the cutting machine purchase.

11-29 The George Gonzalez Construction Company is considering the purchase of a new road grader. The company has two options:

Option 1: The cost is $68,000 with a useful life of 7 years and an estimated residual value of $5,000.

Option 2: The cost is $90,000 with a useful life of 7 years and a salvage value of $10,000.

Currently, the company rents road graders as needed. If the road grader were purchased, annual rental payments of $17,000 would be saved. Additionally, option 2 would save $2,000 in labor costs each year.

LO 5
Payback Period, Net Present Value, and Profitability Index for Two Projects

Required:

a. Compute the payback period of each option.
b. Calculate the net present value of each option assuming a cost of capital of 16%.
c. Determine the profitability index for each option.
d. Which machine should the company purchase? Justify your answer.

11-30 The Wesley Parks Pencil Company is considering the purchase of one of two automated pencil machines. The first is a $248,000 machine with a useful life of 8 years and a residual value of $25,000. The cost of the second machine is $195,000 with a useful life of 8 years and a residual value of $5,000. Currently, the company leases a similar machine for $45,000 per year. The first machine can save $5,000 in supply costs over the leased machine and the second can save $2,500 in labor costs over the leased machine.

LO 5
Payback Period, Net Present Value, and Profitability Index

Required:

a. Compute the payback period for each machine.
b. Determine the net present value and the profitability index of each machine purchase with an 18% cost of capital.
c. Which machine should the company purchase? Justify your choice.

LO 5
Net Present Value and Profitability Index

11-31   Jandra Hahne's Catering Service is considering the purchase of new energy-efficient cooking equipment. The cost of the new equipment is $78,000. The equipment has an estimated useful life of 8 years and an estimated residual value of $5,000. Currently, the company leases similar cooking equipment for $10,000 per year. If the new cooking equipment were purchased, the company's cost of electricity would be reduced by $8,000 per year.

Required:

a. Determine the net present value of the cooking equipment if the cost of capital is 16%.
b. Determine the profitability index if the cost of capital is 16%.

LO 5
Internal Rate of Return

11-32   Lesa Leverett has decided to purchase a new computer system for Leverett Manufacturing, which will reduce energy costs and save overtime costs. Engineers made the following estimates:

Initial outlay	$18,023.88
Annual cash savings	$ 5,000.00
Estimated life of the computer	5 years
Estimated residual value of the computer	$ —0—

Required:

a. Determine the internal rate of return for the computer purchase.
b. Indicate whether the computer purchase should be accepted under each of the following assumptions:
   1. the cost of capital is 9%
   2. the cost of capital is 11%
   3. the cost of capital is 13%
   4. the cost of capital is 15%

LO 5
Internal Rate of Return

11-33   Valdez Moving and Storage needs to add another truck to its fleet. The following estimates are available:

Initial Investment	$48,966.44
Annual contribution margin from the truck	$14,000.00
Estimated life of the truck	6 years
Estimated residual value of the truck	$ —0—

Required:

a. Determine the internal rate of return for the truck purchase.
b. Indicate whether the truck purchase should be accepted under each of the following assumptions:
   1. the cost of capital is 16%
   2. the cost of capital is 18%
   3. the cost of capital is 20%

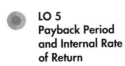

LO 5
Payback Period and Internal Rate of Return

11-34   John Henry & Company is in the process of replacing its existing computer system. The following three proposals are being considered:

	System A	System B	System C
Initial outlay	$18,023.88	$22,744.72	$24,031.57
Annual cash savings	$ 5,000.00	$ 6,000.00	$ 7,000.00
Residual value	—0—	—0—	—0—
Estimated useful life	5 years	5 years	5 years

Required:

a. Compute the payback period for each proposal.
b. Determine the internal rate of return for each of the proposed computer systems.
c. Which computer system would you recommend? Explain your reasoning.

11-35 The David Wilson Equipment Company is in the process of selecting some new manufacturing equipment. The following three proposals are being considered:

LO 5
Payback Period
and Internal Rate
of Return

	Equipment A	Equipment B	Equipment C
Initial outlay	$14,902.92	$18,555.46	$26,674.63
Annual cash savings	$ 3,000.00	$ 4,000.00	$ 5,000.00
Residual value	—0—	—0—	—0—
Estimated useful life	8 years	8 years	8 years

Required:

  a. Compute the payback period for each project.
  b. Determine the internal rate of return for each of the proposed pieces of equipment.
  c. Which piece of equipment would you recommend? Explain your reasoning.

11-36 Davis Manufacturing Company is working on a proposal to purchase a factory that makes valves. The company would use these valves to manufacture water pumps. The purchase would require an initial outlay of $1,449,968.24. The factory would have an estimated life of 10 years and no residual value. Currently, the company buys 500,000 valves per year at a cost of $1.50 each. If the factory were purchased, the valves could be manufactured for $.90 each.

LO 5
Net Present Value,
Profitability Index,
and Internal Rate

Required:

  a. Compute the payback period for the project.
  b. Determine the net present value and profitability index of the proposed project and whether it should be accepted under each of the following assumptions:
    1. the cost of capital is 14%
    2. the cost of capital is 16%
    3. the cost of capital is 18%
  c. Determine the profitability index under each of the following assumptions:
    1. the cost of capital is 14%
    2. the cost of capital is 16%
    3. the cost of capital is 18%
  d. Determine the internal rate of return of the proposed project and indicate whether it should be accepted under each of the following assumptions:
    1. the cost of capital is 14%
    2. the cost of capital is 16%
    3. the cost of capital is 18%

11-37 Frank's Marine Service purchased a forklift 5 years ago for $16,000. When it was purchased, the forklift had an estimated useful life of 10 years and a salvage value of $4,000. The forklift can be sold now for $6,000. The operating cost for the forklift is $4,500 per year. The company is considering buying a newer forklift for $17,000. The newer forklift would have an estimated useful life of 5 years and a salvage value of $7,000. The operating cost for the newer forklift would be 3,000 per year. The company's cost of capital is 10%.

LO 4 and 5
Relevant Information
and Net Present
Value

Required:

  a. Prepare a relevant cost schedule showing the benefits of buying the new forklift. (For this requirement, ignore the time value of money.)
  b. How much must the company invest today to replace the old forklift?
  c. If the company replaces the old forklift, what is the increase in the company's annual contribution margin?
  d. Calculate the net present value of replacing the old forklift.
  e. Do you think the company should replace the old forklift? Explain your reasoning.

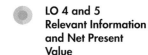

LO 4 and 5
Relevant Information and Net Present Value

11-38   Al Hart of Hart Engineering is considering the purchase of a new copy machine. He purchased the old machine 2 years ago for $8,500. When it was purchased, the old machine had an estimated useful life of 8 years and a salvage value of $500. The operating cost of the old machine is $3,000 per year, and it can be sold today for $2,000. A new machine can be bought today for $10,000 and would have an estimated useful life of 6 years with a salvage value of $1,000. The operating cost of the new copy machine is expected to be $1,500 per year. The company's cost of capital is 8%.

Required:

a. Prepare a relevant cost schedule showing the benefit of buying the new copy machine. (For this requirement, ignore the time value of money.)
b. How much must the company invest today to replace the old copy machine?
c. If the company replaces the old copy machine, what is the increase in the company's annual contribution margin?
d. Calculate the net present value of replacing the old copy machine.
e. Do you think the company should replace the old copy machine? Explain your reasoning.

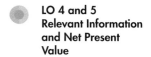

LO 4 and 5
Relevant Information and Net Present Value

11-39   The managers at AAA Manufacturing Company are considering replacing an industrial mixer used in the company's factory. The company's cost of capital is 10%.

Information about the old mixer:

Cost	$28,000
Estimated useful life	10 years
Estimated salvage value	$ —0—
Current age	5 years
Estimated current fair value	$ 8,000
Annual operating cost	$18,000

Information about the new mixer:

Cost	$34,000
Estimated useful life	5 years
Estimated salvage value	$ —0—
Annual operating cost	$12,000

Required:

a. Prepare a relevant cost schedule showing the benefit of buying the new mixer.
b. How much must the company invest today to replace the industrial mixer?
c. If the new mixer were purchased, how much would be saved in operating costs each year?
d. How much would the company receive at the end of the 5-year useful life of the new mixer?
e. Calculate the net present value of replacing the old mixer.
f. Do you think the company should replace the old mixer? Explain your reasoning.

LO 4 and 5
Relevant Information and Net Present Value

11-40   The managers at General Manufacturing Company are considering replacing the industrial lathe used in the company's factory. The company's cost of capital is 12%.

Information about the old lathe:

Cost	$57,000
Estimated useful life	8 years
Estimated salvage value	$ —0—
Current age	2 years
Estimated current fair value	$32,000
Annual operating cost	$32,000

Information about the new lathe:

Cost	$61,000
Estimated useful life	6 years
Estimated salvage value	$ —0—
Annual operating cost	$24,000

Required:

a. Prepare a relevant cost schedule showing the benefit of buying the new lathe. (For this requirement, ignore the time value of money.)
b. How much must the company invest today to replace the old lathe?
c. If the company replaces the old lathe, how much will be saved in operating costs each year?
d. Calculate the net present value of replacing the old lathe.
e. Do you think the company should replace the old lathe? Explain your reasoning.

11-41   John Paul Jones, president of Jones Marine, is considering replacing the company's industrial lift used to haul boats. The new lift would allow the company to lift larger boats out of the water. The company's cost of capital is 14%.

LO 4 and 5
Relevant Information and Net Present Value

Information about the old lift:

Cost	$94,000
Estimated useful life	12 years
Estimated salvage value	$10,000
Current age	4 years
Estimated current fair value	$48,000
Annual contribution margin	$50,000

Information about the new lift:

Cost	$128,000
Estimated useful life	8 years
Estimated salvage value	$ 25,000
Annual contribution margin	$ 65,000

Required:

a. Prepare a relevant cost schedule showing the benefit of buying the new lift. (For this requirement, ignore the time value of money.)
b. How much must the company invest today to replace the old lift?
c. If the company replaces the old lift, what is the increase in the company's annual contribution margin?
d. Calculate the net present value of replacing the old lift.
e. Do you think the company should replace the old lift? Explain your reasoning.

11-42   The managers at Wilma Printing are considering replacing a printing press with a new, high-speed model.

LO 4 and 5
Relevant Information and Net Present Value

Information about the old printing press:

Cost	$255,000
Estimated useful life	10 years
Estimated salvage value	$ 25,000
Annual depreciation	$ 23,000
Current age	3 years
Accumulated depreciation to date	$184,000
Estimated current fair value	$150,000
Annual contribution margin	$110,000

Information about the new printing press:

Cost	$535,000
Estimated useful life	7 years
Estimated salvage value	$ 45,000
Annual depreciation	$ 70,000
Annual contribution margin	$150,000

Required:

a. Prepare a relevant cost schedule showing the benefit of buying the new printing press. (For this requirement, ignore the time value of money.)

b. How much must the company invest today to replace the old printing press?

c. If the company replaces the old printing press, what is the increase in the company's annual contribution margin?

d. Calculate the net present value of replacing the old printing press.

e. Do you think the company should replace the old printing press? Explain your reasoning.

LO 6
Calculate Simple and Compound Interest

11-43   On January 1, 2006, Robin's Marine Repair Service borrowed $5,000 from First National Bank for three years.

Required:

a. Assuming 9% simple interest is charged, calculate interest for 2006, 2007, and 2008.

b. Assuming 9% compound interest is charged, calculate interest for 2006, 2007, and 2008.

LO 6
Calculate Simple and Compound Interest

11-44   On January 1, 2005, Gary Le Bron borrowed $8,000 from Orlando National Bank for four years.

Required:

a. Assuming 8% simple interest is charged, calculate interest for 2005, 2006, 2007, and 2008.

b. Assuming 8% compound interest is charged, calculate interest for 2005, 2006, 2007, and 2008.

LO 6
Calculate Simple and Compound Interest

11-45   On January 1, 2004, Cameron Browning borrowed $2,000 from Edmond National Bank due in three years.

Required:

a. Assuming 6% simple interest is charged, calculate interest for 2004, 2005, and 2006.

b. Assuming 6% compound interest is charged, calculate interest for 2004, 2005, and 2006.

LO 6
Future Value

11-46   Russell Jones made the following investments on January 1, 2005:

1.	$2,000 at 10% for 5 years
2.	$12,000 at 4% for 8 years
3.	$9,000 at 14% for 15 years

Assume the interest on each investment is compounded annually.

Required:

Calculate the value of each of Jones's investments at maturity.

LO 6
Future Value

11-47   Ivan Zhang made the following investments on January 1, 2006:

1.	$3,000 at 8% for 6 years
2.	$4,000 at 6% for 8 years
3.	$5,000 at 10% for 5 years

Assume the interest on each investment is compounded annually.

Required:

Calculate the future value of each of Zhang's investments at maturity.

11-48 Orlando Gonzalez made the following investments on January 1, 2006:

LO 6
Future Value

1.	$1,000 at 12% for 3 years
2.	$2,000 at 16% for 5 years
3.	$4,000 at 8% for 4 years

Required:

Calculate the value of each of Gonzalez's investments at maturity assuming the interest is compounded:
a. annually
b. semiannually
c. quarterly

11-49 Consider the following investments:
1. $2,000 at the end of each of the next 5 years at 10% interest compounded annually
2. $12,000 at the end of each of the next 8 years at 4% interest compounded annually
3. $9,000 at the end of each of the next 15 years at 14% interest compounded annually

LO 6
Future Value

Required:

Calculate the value of each of the investments listed above at maturity.

11-50 Consider the following investments.
1. $12,000 at the end of each of the next 3 years at 12% interest compounded annually
2. $16,000 at the end of each of the next 5 years at 10% interest compounded annually.
3. $20,000 at the end of each of the next 10 years at 8% interest compounded annually.

LO 6
Future Value

Required:

Calculate the future value of each of the investments listed above at their maturity.

11-51 Consider the following investments:
1. $1,000 at the end of each of the next 5 years at 6% interest compounded annually
2. $1,000 at the end of each of the next 5 years at 8% interest compounded annually
3. $1,000 at the end of each of the next 5 years at 10% interest compounded annually

LO 6
Future Value

Required:

Calculate the value of each of the investments listed above at maturity.

11-52 James Jones wants to buy a new car when he graduates from college in 5 years. His grandfather would like to invest a single amount now to have the $25,000 to give James as a graduation present.

LO 6
Present Value

Required:

Calculate the amount his grandfather must invest today earning 6% interest compounded quarterly to have $25,000 in five years.

11-53 John Peoples needs to have $50,000 at the end of five years. Peoples would like to invest a single amount now at 8% to have the $50,000 in five years.

LO 6
Present Value

Required:

Calculate the amount Peoples must invest today if it is compounded semiannually.

11-54 Lori Bourke is planning to buy a house for her daughter when she graduates from college in 20 years and wants to have $20,000 for the down payment. She wants to make a single investment today that will give her the $20,000.

LO 6
Present Value

Required:

Calculate the amount Lori must invest today to have $20,000 in 20 years assuming her investment will earn:
a. 6% compounded annually
b. 10% compounded semiannually
c. 8% compounded annually

LO 6
Present Value

11-55   Linda Chidister is planning to send her son, Edward, to college. While he is in college, Chidister intends to give him $3,000 at the end of each year.

Required:

How much must Chidister invest today so she will have enough to give Edward $3,000 at the end of each of the next four years assuming the investment will earn 6% interest?

LO 6
Present Value

11-56   Lisa Miller won the lottery yesterday and must select a payout option from the following:
1. $1,000,000 today and $1,000,000 at the end of each year for 20 years
2. $11,000,000 today
3. $5,000,000 today and $1,000,000 at the end of each year for 12 years

Required:

Which option should Miller accept if she believes she can earn 6% interest on her investment?

LO 6
Present Value and
Future Value

11-57   Charles Pursifull wants to retire at the end of 20 years. He wants to put the same amount in his retirement account each year for 20 years and be able to withdraw $12,000 per year at the end of each year for 14 years.

Required:

How much must he deposit each year for the next 20 years if he can earn:
a. 6% interest compounded annually
b. 8% interest compounded annually
c. 10% interest compounded annually

Ethics

11-58   Fred Armitage works as a capital budget analyst for Steel Works, Inc. Fred is a very driven employee and always wants to see his projects accepted. He is not above manipulating data and using improper tables to calculate the present values of his projects. Fred believes he is doing what is best for the company by ensuring that the company is always innovative with the newest technology and equipment, which he believes will lead to the company's long-term success.

Required:

Do you agree with Armitage's thought process regarding his approach to his job? Explain your answer.

FOR ADDITIONAL READING

Bartholdy, Jan, and Paula Peare. "Unbiased Estimation of Expected Return Using CAPM," *International Review of Financial-Analysis* 12 (2003):69–82.

Burgess, Deanna Oxender. "Consulting, Buy or Lease: The Eternal Question," *Journal of Accountancy* (April 1999):25ff.

"IRR and NPV Remain Chief Capital Budgeting Tools," *Financial Executives News* 3 (January 2003):2.

Jagannathan, Ravi, and Iwan Meier. "Do We Need CAPM for Capital Budgeting?" *Financial Management* 31 (Winter 2002):55–78.

Pawlina, Grzegorz, and Peter M. Kort. "Strategic Capital Budgeting: Asset Replacement under Market Uncertainty," *Operations Research Spektrum* 25 (October 2003): 443–480.

Ryan, Patricia A., and Glenn P. Ryan. "Capital Budgeting Practices of the *Fortune* 1000: How Have Things Changed?" *Journal of Business & Management* 8 (Fall 2002):355–365.

"Why CFOs Use Different Tools for Capital Budget Analysis," *Financial Analysis, Planning & Reporting* 2 (December 2002):1–5.

CHAPTER 12

External Financial Reporting

T he overarching objective of accounting is to provide information that is useful in making investment and credit decisions, assessing future cash flows, and identifying enterprise resources, claims to resources, and changes in them. Users who are external to the firm frequently make economic decisions about the firm after performing some type of financial statement analysis. Because users' objectives vary, their perspectives on the results of that analysis will differ. In this chapter, we will focus on external users of financial statements and the specific information they need to obtain from the financial information released to external parties.

Visit the *www.prenhall.com/terrell* Web site to view the "America West" video.

External Reporting Issues

To how much information should external users have access? Just as you as an individual have privacy rights, so does a firm have rights to protect proprietary information. Different classes of external decision makers have varied rights to obtain financial information. Independent auditors and government agencies may have virtually unlimited access to a company's financial transactions and other information. Independent auditors have a contractual right to examine what they need to form an opinion on the financial statements. Government agents have a legal right, within certain parameters, to examine everything appropriate to a specific inquiry.

What rights do creditors, present and potential equity investors, prospective employees, and curious people have to a company's financial records and statements? Creditors have a right to ask for information they believe is necessary to judge the creditworthiness of the borrower. The loan documents may give them the right to know about a limited number of specific future transactions and to receive financial

Visit *www.bigcharts.com* for a stock price history, news items, plus links to SEC filings and an annual report service.

Visit *www.prars.com* to find many annual reports. This reporting service will send you reports free of charge for as many companies as you wish to examine.

Visit *www.freeedgar.com* to find publicly held companies' SEC filings and links to their Web sites.

statements at regular intervals. For example, a loan agreement may specify that the lender cannot declare and pay cash dividends until the loan has been repaid. Creditors would thus have the right to notification of a declaration of cash dividends. The agreement may also specify that the borrower must send monthly or quarterly financial statements. This allows the creditor to monitor the borrower's activities to ensure the collectibility of the loan. As you can see, the creditor has limited access to the borrower's financial information.

Current and potential investors, present and potential employees, and curious people have a right to examine public information. The SEC requires publicly held companies to file quarterly (10-Q) and annual (10-K) financial statements. Those filings are public records that are available on the Internet at the SEC's Web site, on most individual companies' Web sites, by mail through investor relations departments in most companies, and in many libraries through various publications and database information services such as *Disclosure*.

Companies understand the needs of investors to acquire information and SEC requirements to make the information available.

Importance of External Information to Shareholders

Shareholders and potential investors expect safety for their investment and a return on the investment. First, they want to feel confident that their investment will be returned at some future point. Analysis of profitability ratios over several years indicates the volatility of the company's earnings. The more volatile the earnings, the more risky the investment. Analysis of liquidity ratios signals the ease or difficulty the company has in meeting current obligations. Analysis of solvency ratios indicates the long-term viability of an investment. Any evidence of unprofitability, illiquidity, or insolvency should be a red flag to the shareholder or investor. Exhibit 12-1 illustrates the road to bankruptcy, which usually begins with unprofitability, then leads to illiquidity and ends with insolvency.

What Do You Think?

12-1 Describe whether you believe the road to bankruptcy is accurately portrayed in Exhibit 12-1. Explain your reasoning.

12-2 List the corrective action you believe a company can take at each stop on the road to bankruptcy that will redirect it to financial health.

Exhibit 12-1
The Road to Bankruptcy

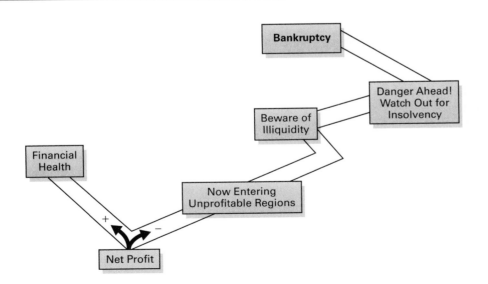

As we discussed in Chapter 3, the return on investment for a corporate shareholder has two components:

1 dividends, which represent a share of the profits; and
2 stock appreciation, which equals the difference between the current market price of one share in the secondary stock market and the purchase price of the share.

Present shareholders and potential investors analyze financial statements to determine whether the company can earn enough profits and have sufficient positive cash flow to distribute dividends in the future. Cash dividends can be paid only if a company has sufficient cash and adequate retained earnings, both of which depend on future generation of earnings. Furthermore, generation of earnings is widely considered to be the single most important factor affecting a company's stock appreciation over time.

A healthy company also has positive operating cash flows over a long time period to meet its investing and financing needs. In addition to analysis of profitability, liquidity, and solvency, careful analysis of the cash flow statement reveals the history of operating cash flows and dividend distributions. When combined with a history of the stock prices, past performance may help to predict future stock prices.

What Do You Think?

12-3   Does the past performance always predict future profitability? Why or why not?

12-4   List the possible internal and external factors that can change performance. For each, think of the possible warning signs, if any, that might signal a future company downturn.

Do investors always have ample warning about a downturn in a company's performance? Not always. Investigate the history of companies such as Sears, JCPenney, Kmart, and Gap, Inc. Investors in the stock market react quickly to announced earnings. Can a serious investor learn to find signs of trouble before they happen? If you watch the financial news, you might not believe so. Frequently, however, the signs are there, but are ignored or considered anomalies. Look, for example, at the charts of these four companies in Exhibits 12-2 and 12-3, which compare the reported annual earnings to the closing stock prices on the last day of the fiscal year.

What Do You Think?

Consider the information in Exhibits 12-2 and 12-3 for each of the following questions. For a weekly chart of the stock prices for these companies, go to the Big Charts Web site at *www.bigcharts.com*. The ticker symbols for each company are: S (Sears); JCP (JCPenney); KM (Kmart); and GPS (The Gap).

12-5   Describe the similarities and differences in earnings among these four companies.

12-6   Describe the similarities and differences in stock prices among these four companies. Is it fair to compare the stock prices of different companies, or should you compare the relative rise and fall of their individual prices? Why or why not?

12-7   Describe how closely the stock prices follow the earnings for each company.

12-8   What political and economic events occurred or climates existed during this decade? How did those events or climates affect stock market prices in general?

Exhibit 12-2
Comparison of Annual
Earnings and Closing
Stock Prices

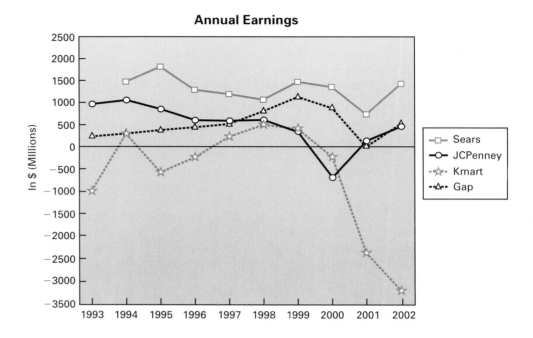

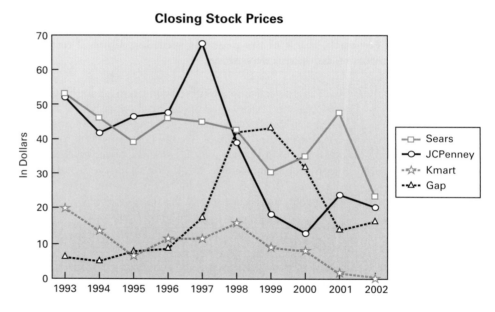

After you think about the answers to these questions, you will realize that many factors affect the stock prices including the company's earnings and stability, political and economic climate, and political and economic world events. When you look at Exhibit 12-2, you see some consistency between the stock price of each company and its earnings. You also see some roller coaster effect in the decade due to market forces. In 2001, JCPenney and Kmart go against the trend. Recall that the end of 2001 was politically unstable and economically tenuous.

With the exception of JCPenney, all the companies experienced a reduction in earnings. If you ignore its 2000 loss, however, JCPenney's 2001 income was still lower in 2001 than its 1999 earnings. After investigating its financial statements and company history, you learn that JCPenney purchased Eckerd Drugs in 1997. Although the 1997 retail sales rose from $22.6 billion in 1996 to $29.6 billion in 1997, the net income remained about the same at $565 million in 1996 and $566 million in 1997. Sales were flat in 1998 but income rose slightly to $594 million.

Visit the JCPenney Web site at **www.JCPenney.com** to learn more about the company. To visit the Web sites of the other companies go to **www.Sears.com**, **www.Kmart.com**, and **www.Gap.com**.

Exhibit 12-3

Comparison of Annual Earnings and Stock Prices by Company

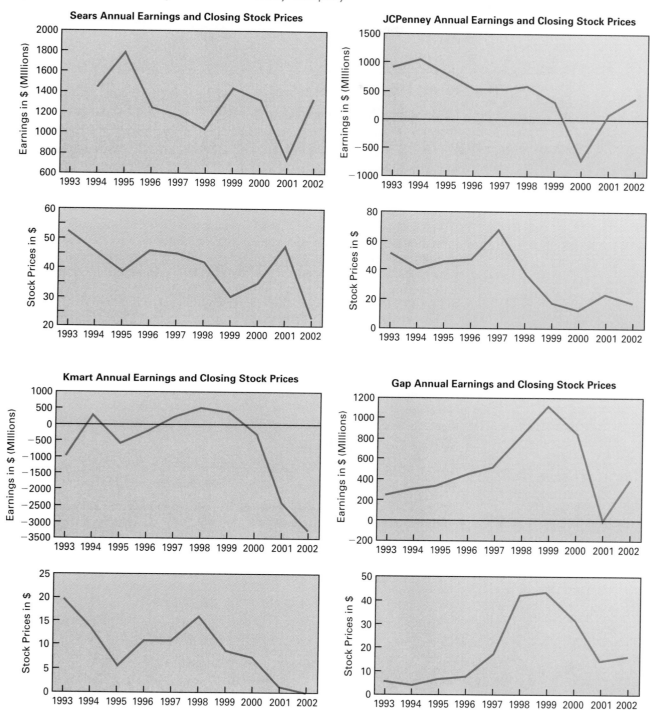

Many financial analysts believed that JCPenney was struggling under the debt burden assumed when it purchased Eckerds. Its cash position fell in 1998. From 1999 to 2001, sales flattened at near $32 billion and operating income fell to $174 million in 1999, a loss of $568 million in 2000, income of $114 million in 2001, and a much improved income of $371 million in 2002. Between 1999 and 2002, the company improved its cash position by $2.4 billion. In 2002, JCPenney celebrated its 100th anniversary as a company that was financially healthier than it had been in the previous five years.

Notice that its stock price, although 2002 stock market prices were depressed, was about 40 percent of its price in 1993.

During this decade, the Dow Jones Industrial Average rose from slightly higher than 3,000 in 1993 to almost 12,000 at the beginning of 2000, and fell to 8,300 by the end of 2002.

What Do You Think?

12-9 Using the information in Exhibits 12-2 and 12-3, which company's stock performed best over this decade? Explain your choice.

12-10 Had you been a stockholder of each of these four companies, would you have sold your stock? If so, when would you have sold each company's stock?

A stakeholder continuously looks for new ways to search for more meaningful information in the company's externally reported information. The stakeholder will find a different type of retailer information by looking at its sales per square foot of selling space. Exhibit 12-4 contains the dollar sales per square foot of selling space for each company from 1993 through 2001. Watch this statistic because it often provides good trend information by measuring the selling effectiveness of the company. Occupancy costs are the second largest expense to a merchandiser, especially those that buy or lease expensive space in malls. Many retailers include numerous operating statistics in their annual reports to stockholders including the sales per square foot of selling space, number of stores, the number of stores leased and owned, plus other information. Look in the Management Discussion and Analysis section for many types of additional information.

What Do You Think?

12-11 Did a change in company profits occur before, during, or after the year in which sales per square foot changed for each company?

12-12 How well does the change in sales per square foot correlate with the change net income?

12-13 If the change in sales per square foot does not correlate with the change in net income, what might be the other factors that would have an effect on net income?

As you can see, no simple way exists to predict the future of an enterprise's earnings. Uncertainty is the risk that investors take when they invest in a particular company. The best defense against risk is to stay informed and watch for any signs that the company will lose value.

Exhibit 12-4
Dollar Sales per Square Foot of Selling Space per Year

	1993	1994	1995	1996	1997	1998	1999	2000	2001	2002
Sears	N/A	N/A	N/A	321	318	317	327	333	319	303
JCPenney	123	133	131	134	136	130	130	127	133	140
The Gap	463	444	425	441	463	532	548	482	394	349
Kmart	182	181	195	201	211	222	233	236	235	N/A

Importance of External Information to Creditors

Creditors lend money to a company on either a short-term basis of five years or less or a long-term basis of more than five years. Short-term creditors and long-term creditors have different objectives and look for different attributes in the borrowers. Short-term creditors include trade creditors and commercial lending institutions.

Trade creditors provide goods and services to a business and expect payment within normal trade terms for the industry, usually between 30 and 60 days. Trade creditors seldom charge interest. Because the credit they extend to a company is essentially an interest-free loan, they check the firm's credit history and payment history to determine whether that company consistently pays its bills on time. Short-term creditors analyze a company's financial statements looking for evidence of profitability and liquidity to ensure the firm should be able to pay timely in the future. At times, trade creditors offer to accept a trade note for a longer repayment time than normal trade terms. Some trade notes include a provision for interest charges, especially when the terms are for a year or longer.

Lending institutions offer commercial loans to support the operating activities of a business. Unlike trade creditors, banks charge interest on every loan and require interest payments periodically. Some may also require that the principal be paid periodically in installments. The lending institutions have the same information needs to make their decisions as trade creditors. The only difference is the length of the loan may be as long as 5 years instead of 60 days. Lending institutions will also pay close attention to the solvency ratios, especially the coverage ratio.

Long-term creditors also seek assurance of receiving prompt payments, but from a different perspective. Generally banks and corporate bondholders lend money to companies for relatively long periods of time. Therefore, long-term creditors' principal objectives are to determine whether the company will be able to make its periodic interest payments and to repay the loan when required. Long-term creditors will focus on profitability and solvency ratios and pay close attention to the level of operating cash flows.

All creditors pay attention to the profitability, liquidity, and solvency of their borrowers. Short-term and long-term creditors review borrowers' financial statements annually or quarterly. Trade creditors monitor their customers' financial position frequently by analyzing their payment record. As long as the bills are paid on a timely basis, they seldom require much information from the buyer. When a customer fails to make timely payments, the creditor begins to monitor it more closely. Frequently, it is too late by that time. This is not to say creditors are lax. Most trade creditors have a thorough screening process for new accounts and grant credit only to those with good credit ratings. Unfortunately, some businesses experience financial problems within a very short time frame. If the creditors are not aware, they can get caught with a loss from a previously good customer.

● **trade creditors**
Providers of goods and services to a business who expect payment within normal trade terms for the industry, usually between 30 and 60 days.

Importance of External Information to Regulators

Regulators include the IRS, the SEC, state taxation agencies, utility rate-setting agencies, and other government agencies. Regulators depend on periodic reports from the organizations they oversee as evidence of compliance with the rules and regulations they are charged with monitoring. Frequently, the information includes financial statements and other accounting reports. In most instances, the chief officers of the company submitting the reports must swear under penalty of perjury that the information contained in the reports is true and correct to the best of their knowledge.

The United States operates on a philosophy of self-reporting to regulatory agencies, instead of announced or unannounced government inspections. Regulators do not have the staff to thoroughly inspect each report they receive. Reports are examined randomly, unless a company has submitted an erroneous report in the past or has been flagged for attention due to the unusual nature of its report. Companies with a history of prior troubled submissions will be checked more thoroughly and more frequently. Regulatory agencies rely on the integrity of the reports submitted to keep our system of self-reporting in place. When the agency determines that the number of fraudulent reports rises dramatically, the freedom and luxury of self-reporting might be jeopardized. Unannounced audits create an atmosphere of distrust and fear in which most businesspeople do not wish to operate.

Regulatory agencies also develop guidelines for measuring how well the information submitted conforms to norms the agency has developed from past submissions. Say, for example, the IRS knows that most taxpayers with incomes between $50,000 and $100,000 contribute between 3 percent and 5 percent (not real amounts) of their gross income to charities. If a taxpayer submits a return with 20 percent of his or her gross income claimed as charitable deductions, the return is flagged for possible audit. If the examiner looks at the taxpayer's prior returns and sees that each year this taxpayer has contributed 20 percent of income to charity, the examiner may remove the audit flag if the taxpayer was audited twice and provided proof of the contributions.

The SEC also looks for financial reports that appear to be unusual when compared to the historical submissions from that particular company or reports that differ greatly from the rest of the companies in the industry. Every publicly held company submits five major reports each year: four quarterly 10-Q reports and an annual 10-K report. The SEC has too few accountants and auditors to review each submission made. Knowing that the SEC cannot audit all submissions, can unscrupulous company managers submit false financial statements to its auditors and the SEC and go undetected? Of course they can, and they can possibly get away with it for some time. Well-hidden management fraud can go undetected by teams of external auditors and government regulators for a while, but the truth usually comes out because the fraud eventually undermines the viability of the organization. Sometimes the failure is the first hint that something is wrong.

Ethical Considerations of External Financial Reporting

In a free-market nation, ethics should be the cornerstone of conducting business and reporting its results. Good ethics is good business. Over a long period of time, ethical companies last the longest. James Cash Penney named his company "The Golden Rule Company" when he started in 1902. That name makes a powerful statement about the ethics he embraced. He did so in a time when the phrase *business ethics* was considered an oxymoron. If you believe that today's business climate lacks ethics, study business history in the 19th century and the early 20th century. The rise of social responsibility began in the second half of the 20th century. Not everyone joined the cause.

Unfortunately, as management operates a company and reports its financial statements, some managers choose unethical behavior in hopes of winning at any cost. Few, if any, succeed. Their road to disgrace is littered with the shattered economic lives of innocent investors, employees, consumers, and competitors. Some try to skirt the ethical line by paying more attention to managing the financial statements than managing the company. Sadly, some managers fail to learn that a well-managed company can be much more profitable than a company with well-managed financial statements.

What Do You Think?

12-14   Explain what you think this statement "a well-managed company can be much more profitable than a company with well-managed financial statements" means.

12-15   What, if any, are the ethical boundaries in managing the financial statements?

Should managers care about what goes into external financial statements? Of course they should. They should analyze the financial statements as we indicated in Chapters 7 and 8. But more important than "what" the financial statements reveal is "why" the financial statements indicate those results. "Management by financial statements" is a poor way to run a company. A well-run company will show evidence of such in its financial statements.

Even the best-managed company may perform poorly at times. Remember those political and economic influences on business? What happened to Adolph Coors Company during the 1920s? How did it survive Prohibition? It survived not by secretly manufacturing illegal goods, but by making glassware and producing malt for candy and malted milkshakes. A firm in trouble because of outside influences can demonstrate that it has staying power by adapting to its environment, appropriately changing course, and refocusing its strategic plans. Falsifying the financial statements is not part of a successful strategy. Again, good ethics is good business.

Now that you understand the importance of financial information to external users, let's turn our attention to what you need to understand about some of the information contained on those statements.

External Reporting Valuations

As you read a balance sheet, all the assets, liabilities, and equity accounts are expressed in terms of dollars, or other currency values. The asset or liability is not dollars, of course, but bricks and mortar, or an obligation to deliver services or goods or to repay dollars in the future. How are the equivalent values of noncash assets, liabilities, and equity assigned? As you learned in Chapters 5 and 6, fair values are assigned at the time of the transaction and recorded into the accounting system. These values become the historical cost of the transaction. Historical cost is but one of the valuations that find their way to the balance sheet. Other valuation methods include net realizable value, lower of cost or market, fair value or market value, and present value. Each of these other valuation methods represent a departure from the historical cost principle. We will discuss the appropriate use of each of these other valuation methods.

Historical Cost

In Chapter 2 you learned that one of the basic accounting principles is historical cost. Accountants use historical cost because it is reliable, comparable, and consistent. Economists argue that it is not relevant because it is historical. It is, however, reliable, and it is based on the fair value at the time of the transaction. This does not present too much trouble for the income statement and the statement of cash flows because fair values normally do not change much within one year. The trouble arises with the balance sheet and statement of stockholders' equity, both of which use historical cost as the main reporting basis.

To illustrate the use of historical cost, let's look at Sears. Sears opened the Sears Tower in Chicago in 1973 after three years of construction at a cost of $150 million. Regardless of its market value, the building remains on Sears' books at a cost of $150 million. The company records depreciation on it each year to allocate the cost of using the building to produce revenues. Assume that Sears decided to depreciate the building on a straight-line basis over 50 years. On the balance sheet for 2003, the building might indicate the following value:

To learn more about the Sears Tower, visit its Web site at **www.Sears-Tower.com.**

| Building | $150,000,000 | |
| Less: accumulated depreciation | $ 90,000,000 | $60,000,000 |

Does an informed reader believe that the building is currently worth $60 million? Probably not. What is the value of the building on December 31, 2003? For the sake of argument, assume that the fair market value of the building in 1993 was $250 million. On December 31, 2001, the value of the building might have been $50 million because few people wanted to work in the tallest building in the world. On December 31, 2003, the fair value might be $150 million after fear subsided about the height of the building.

What Do You Think?

12-16 Who can determine the fair market value of the Sears Tower on each of the dates mentioned above? Would this person be willing to certify the value? Does this person require payment for issuing an opinion on the value of the Sears Tower? If so, what would you estimate the fee to be?

12-17 If Sears issues a balance sheet three months after the appraisal discussed in question 12-16, should the appraisal be updated?

12-18 What would happen if the appraiser gives an erroneous value?

If Sears has no intention of ever selling the building, does its market value have any meaning? It seems that a market value might be irrelevant if it is never marketed. As accountants have considered the pros and cons of using a value other than historical cost, they have raised all these questions. Historical cost has become a default value on the balance sheet and in the general ledger because many types of market value are elusive. How many people or organizations are capable of buying the Sears Tower? Is a market value verifiable, reliable, relevant, consistent, or comparable?

The one thing you know when you read a balance sheet is that the assets listed should be the minimum values of the assets in a going concern. Any time the value of an asset permanently falls below its **book value**, historical cost minus accumulated depreciation, the accountant should record an asset impairment. An **impairment** is a permanent decline in the fair value of an asset below its book value.

When the accounting profession or the SEC decides that historical cost is an inappropriate reporting valuation for an account, accountants use a different valuation technique.

Net Realizable Value

Accounts and Notes Receivables are reported at **net realizable value**, the amount the firm expects ultimately to collect. As you learned in Chapter 6, some receivables may not be collectible, and we record an Allowance for Doubtful Accounts to reduce the receivables to the net realizable value. Reporting at net realizable value complies with the conservatism assumption and reports the true value of the asset. The Allowance for Doubtful Accounts represents the impairment of the historical value of the receivables. Exhibit 12-5 contains a note to a financial statement for Perry Ellis International, Inc. concerning its accounts receivable.

The Company carries accounts receivable at the amount it deems to be collectible. Accordingly, the Company provides allowances for accounts receivable it deems to be uncollectible based on management's best estimates. Recoveries are recognized in the period they are received. The ultimate amount of accounts receivable that become uncollectible could differ from those estimates.

The Perry Ellis note describes in great detail how its management reduces its receivables to a net realizable value. As you read this note to the financial statements, notice that management analyzes the receivables each year to see whether it can identify the type of accounts that will not be received. An accounts receivable manager can accomplish this by creating an aged accounts receivable as we discussed in Chapter 6. The Perry Ellis receivables' manager must have spotted a problem in 2000 because the beginning 2001 allowance balance was more than $1 million. In 2001, management declared that almost $1 million in specific accounts receivable were worthless and would not be collected. The ending allowance balance in 2001 fell below the beginning

● **book value (of an asset)**
Historical cost minus accumulated depreciation.

● **impairment**
A permanent decline in the fair value of an asset below its book value.

● **net realizable value**
The amount the firm expects ultimately to collect.

You can learn more about the Perry Ellis company by visiting its Web site at **www.perryellis.com**.

Exhibit 12-5
Perry Ellis International, Inc. Accounts Receivable Note

Perry Ellis International, Inc. and Subsidiaries
Notes to Consolidated Financial Statements
For Each of the Three Years in the Period Ended January 31, 2003

4.   Accounts Receivable
Accounts receivable consist of the following as of January 31:

	2002	2003
Trade accounts	$ 47,778,539	$ 75,676,880
Royalties and other receivables	4,506,696	5,888,000
Total	52,285,235	81,564,880
Less: Allowance for doubtful accounts	(1,914,990)	(2,075,141)
Total	$ 50,370,245	$ 79,489,739

The activity for the allowance for doubtful accounts is as follows:

Allowance for doubtful accounts	2001	2002	2003
Beginning balance	$ 1,014,576	$ 427,965	$ 1,914,990
Provision	330,435	1,575,000	280,620
Write-offs net of recoveries	(917,046)	(87,975)	(120,469)
Ending balance	$ 427,965	$1,914,990	$ 2,075,141

The Company maintains an allowance for doubtful accounts for estimated losses resulting from the inability of our trade customers to make required payments. We provide an allowance for specific customer accounts where collection is doubtful and also provide a general allowance for other accounts based on historical collection and write-off experience. Judgment is critical because some retail customers are currently operating in bankruptcy or have experienced financial difficulties. If their financial condition were to worsen, additional allowances might be required.

---

amounts signaling that the manager(s) did not anticipate a large number of bad accounts in the following year. Once again the manager anticipated a major loss in 2002, although the specific write-offs in 2002 and 2003 were comparatively small.

Lower of Cost or Market Value

Inventories are normally recorded at historical cost in the general ledger. Not all items in an inventory are fresh, new products that customers want to buy. Firms often have clearance sales to rid themselves of merchandise that is less attractive to buyers. Some firms clear any remaining inventory by selling it to a special type of wholesaler, often called a "rag buyer" in the clothing industry. Rag buyers pay stores much less than their historical cost and can then sell to stores that offer deep discounts to the public, such as T.J. Maxx or Ross Stores, Inc.

Whereas most merchandisers plan on the cost of inventory to increase over time due to inflationary trends, a few industries find their product costs actually decrease over time. Such has been the trend in the computer products industry for the past decade. Each new generation of computer is more powerful and costs less than the previous generation. Companies in the computer business, such as International Business Machines Corporation (IBM) may find that unsold inventory has a market value less than its cost. Conservatism dictates that the value shown on the balance sheet be historical cost unless the market value is a lesser amount. This is the concept of **lower of cost or market (LCM)**. IBM's 2002 notes to consolidated financial statements have two notes that refer to inventories as shown in Exhibit 12-6.

Manufacturing companies such as IBM normally disclose the amount of each type of inventory and whether the value shown is cost or the lower of cost or market. IBM has defined its market value as the net realizable value. It means the same for inventory as it does for receivables—an amount that will ultimately be collected. The

To learn more about IBM, visit its Web site at **www.IBM.com**.

● **lower of cost or market (LCM)**
The value shown on the balance sheet should be historical cost unless the market value is a lesser amount.

Exhibit 12-6
Notes to Financial
Statement for Inventories

Notes to Consolidated Financial Statements
INTERNATIONAL BUSINESS MACHINES CORPORATION
AND SUBSIDIARY COMPANIES (AUDITED)

For the Years Ended December 31, 2002 and 2001

Note A   Significant Accounting Policies

Inventories
Raw materials, work-in-process, and finished goods are stated at the lower of average cost or net realizable value.

Note E   Inventories

(DOLLARS IN MILLIONS)

AT DECEMBER 31:	2002	2001
Finished goods	$ 960	$ 1,259
Work in process and raw materials	2,188	3,045
Total	$ 4,304	$ 4,304

accountants have determined for each item or type of inventory whether the cost exceeds its market value. The lower of the two amounts is totaled to obtain the final inventory amount.

Current Market Value or Fair Value

We record temporary investments in the marketable securities of other companies in the books and records of the company at historical value. Prior to the 1990s, accountants valued marketable securities portfolio on the balance sheet at the lower of cost or market to be conservative. In the early 1990s, the SEC asked the FASB why marketable securities could not be valued at market value regardless of whether the market value was higher or lower than historical cost. After all, the market value of traded securities was easy to obtain from the business pages of a newspaper, the *Wall Street Journal*, or the Internet. In addition, little or no cost was involved in obtaining the value and the listed price each workday was verifiable and unbiased. The SEC believed the only accounting principle it violated was the historical cost principle, which can be overridden with justification as you have seen in prior paragraphs. Since 1994, management reports on the balance sheet the fair market value of its portfolio of temporary investments in marketable securities of other firms. Management also includes additional information in the notes to financial statements such as the Johnson & Johnson disclosure in Exhibit 12-7.

Investments in marketable securities of subsidiary companies are recorded and reported, not at market value, but on an equity basis that reflects the corresponding value reported on the subsidiary's books. Investments in bonds that a company intends to hold to maturity are recorded and reported on the balance sheet at cost as adjusted for amortization of a premium or discount. (See the appendix to Chapter 3 for details on amortization of premium and discounts.) We also reduce an investment in subsidiaries or bonds held to maturity for permanent declines, or impairments, in value.

Johnson & Johnson, for example, reports on its balance sheet that it has $4,581 million in current marketable securities and $121 million in noncurrent marketable securities at December 30, 2002, and $4,214 million in current and $969 million in noncurrent marketable securities at December 30, 2001. The balance sheet refers the reader to notes 1 and 14. Exhibit 12-7 reproduces a portion of note 1 and all of note 14, which explain the nature of the investments. As you see, the totals in note 14 do not

Exhibit 12-7

Johnson & Johnson Notes to Financial Statements on Marketable Securities

Notes to Consolidated Financial Statements   *Johnson&Johnson*

1 Summary of Significant Accounting Principles

Investments

Short-term marketable securities are carried at cost, which approximates fair value. Long-term debt securities that the Company has the ability and intent to hold until maturity are carried at amortized cost, which also approximates fair value. Investments classified as available-for-sale are carried at estimated fair value with unrealized gains and losses recorded as a component of accumulated other comprehensive income.

Management determines the appropriate classification of its investment in debt and equity securities at the time of purchase and re-evaluates such determination at each balance sheet date. The Company periodically reviews its investments in non-marketable equity securities for impairment and adjusts these investments to their fair value when a decline in market value is deemed to be other than temporary.

14 Marketable Securities

(Dollars in Millions)	December 28, 2003				December 29, 2002			
	Net Cost	Unrealized Gains	Unrealized Losses	Estimated Fair Value	Net Cost	Unrealized Gains	Unrealized Losses	Estimated Fair Value
Money market funds	$1,559	—	—	1,559	701	—	—	701
Commercial paper	330	—	—	330	35	—	—	35
Time deposits	663	—	—	663	754	—	—	754
Government securities and obligations	2,844	1	—	2,845	1,976	3	—	1,979
Bank notes	22	—	—	22	18	—	—	18
Corporate debt securities	2,235	—	—	2,235	2,791	6	—	2,797
Total current marketable securities	$7,653	1	—	7,654	6,275	9	—	6,284
Government securities	25	—	—	25	14	—	—	14
Bank notes	6	—	—	6	27	—	—	27
Corporate debt securities	6	—	—	6	—	—	—	—
Investments held in trust	47	—	—	47	80	—	—	80
Total non-current marketable securities	$ 84	—	—	84	121	—	—	121

Current marketable securities include $3.5 billion and $1.7 billion that are classified as cash equivalents on the balance sheet at December 28, 2003, and December 29, 2002, respectively.

equal the amounts reported on the balance sheet for current marketable securities. Look carefully at the sentence at the bottom of note 14. It tells the reader that part of the investments is included in cash on the balance sheet. We can make the following calculations:

(dollars in millions)	2002 Estimated Fair Value	2001 Estimated Fair Value
Total current securities	$6,284	$6,902
Less: amount on balance sheet	4,581	4,214
Difference	$1,703	$2,688
Rounded to nearest tenth billion	$1.7 billion	$2.7 billion

Indeed the note provides correct information for the reader. What is the difference between a marketable security and a cash equivalent? A **cash equivalent** is a marketable security maturing in 90 days or less at purchase, with little or no risk of

● **cash equivalent**
A marketable security maturing in 90 days or less at purchase, with little or no risk of change in the value at maturity due to interest rate change.

change in the value at maturity due to interest rate change. Cash equivalents include investments such as certificates of deposit, savings accounts, money market accounts, and U.S. Treasury bills.

So now you know that several valuation methods are used to provide financial statement users quality information. In addition to different valuations, management may also choose among alternative accounting principles. External users must know which principle management selected when comparing the results to other companies' results. When two firms use different methods, we cannot compare them effectively unless we consider the difference the principle selection makes.

Alternative Accounting Principles

We meet one of the challenges of understanding financial statement reporting when we compare two companies that use different acceptable accounting principles. Why not make all companies throughout the world use exactly the same principle for each account or account type? Because not all businesses are alike. Many have different reporting requirements due to the nature of their industry. As you recall, we discussed the constraint of industry practices in Chapter 2. A general retail merchandiser is a very different type of operation than an electric utility, a hospital, a bank, or an oil and gas producer. Alternative accounting principles developed from such differences along with different levels of risk aversion and conservatism among business leaders and accountants.

Americans also hold dear the freedom of choice. As a profession, accountants believe that some elements of choice should exist among accounting principles when no long-run difference exists in reporting income or financial position. Using one accounting method instead of another should not make a material difference in economic decision-making. Three required accounting concepts keep the choice of method from creating such material differences. First is the concept of consistency. Once a firm selects an accounting principle, it may not change to another principle without complete disclosures to the financial statement users. If a company's management could switch accounting principles each year, they might be able to manipulate net income. Intentional manipulation not only violates representational faithfulness, but also is highly unethical and can be illegal. We will examine the required reporting for changes in accounting principles in more detail in Chapter 13.

Second, the concept of full disclosure requires management to provide any information relevant to the reader's decision-making, such as the choice of accounting principles. The first note in the notes to financial statements must clearly identify the accounting principles the company selected for all its reporting so that readers can assess both the selected principles and whether each has been consistently used during each of the prior reported years. Some firms report every accounting policy selected in note 1 and others disclose them in separate notes. To illustrate the differences in reporting these alternate accounting policies, examine Exhibit 12-8, which contains a list of selected accounting policies and how four companies disclosed them in their 2001 annual reports.

To view the notes to financial statements of these companies, go to their Web sites and look for their annual report. The notes to financial statements follow the financial statements: **www.target.com,** **www.walmartstores.com**, **www.daimlerchrysler.com,** and **www.pg.com**

As you can see, Wal-Mart Stores, Inc., DaimlerChrysler AG, and the Procter & Gamble Company include many of the same items in the first footnote about significant accounting policies. Target Corporation, on the other hand, discloses many of the same items in separate notes. These are large companies with many complex transactions. The accounting policies of a small, nonpublic company might only have 5 to 10 such items listed.

Exhibit 12-9 gives examples of similar wording found in different companies' notes about cash equivalents and the use of estimates. Each company may have different disclosures, but many similarities in wording appear. As you can see, little difference exists in the meaning of the notes among the four companies. The AICPA and the FASB have sample disclosures provided in various publications, which many accountants copy

Exhibit 12-8
Notes to Financial Statements on Significant Accounting Policies

ISSUE	TARGET CORPORATION	WAL-MART	DAIMLER CHRYSLER	PROCTER & GAMBLE
Organization	X			
Consolidation	X	X	X	&
Use of estimates and assumptions	X	X	X	X
Fiscal year	X			
Reclassifications	X	X		X
Cash and cash equivalents	&	X		X
Financial instruments		X	X	X
Interest during construction		X		
Property, plant, and equipment	&	X	X	X
Goodwill and intangibles	&	X	X	X
Foreign currency translation		X	X	X
Revenue recognition	&	X	X	X
Operating expenses		X		
Advertising costs	&	X		
Pre-opening costs		X		
Insurance/self-insurance		X		
Depreciation and amortization		X		
Earnings per share	&	X	X	
Accounting principle change		X	&	
New accounting pronouncements		X	X	X
Basis of presentation			X	X
Receivable sales	&		X	
Estimated credit losses			X	
Product-related expenses (warranties)			X	
Research and development			X	
Sales of newly issued subsidiary stock			X	
Leasing/leased assets	&		X	
Marketable securities			X	
Inventories	&		X	X
Accrued liabilities			X	

X = Included in significant accounting policies note.
& = Included in separate note.

almost verbatim. Management frequently tries to standardize its wording, both to avoid misinterpretation by the reader and to reduce the risk of improper disclosure.

Third, financial statements must be representationally faithful. The message the financial statements project should not mislead the reader into perceiving a financial picture different from the true one. Clearly, from the scandals of the early years of the 21st century, a few companies have prepared misleading financial statements. Regardless of rules, regulations, and laws, some members of society will always cheat. The Association of Certified Fraud Examiners (ACFE) asserts in its publications that some people will never cheat or steal, some people will always cheat and steal, and the rest of the people will cheat or steal in certain situations.

When a new form of income or revolutionary new business type arises, such as e-commerce, no manual exists about how to represent the financial reality of the transactions. Managers of revolutionary new businesses may not find GAAP that apply to their operations. One example occurred when airlines first offered frequent flier miles in the last quarter of the 20th century. Even the U.S. Congress and the IRS did not know what to do with that phenomenon. During the period of time it takes to develop a generally accepted accounting principle managers may report differently. Then they will

For more information about fraud, visit the Association of Certified Fraud Examiners' Web site at **www.cfe.com**.

Exhibit 12-9
Similarities in Wording of Notes Among Companies

USE OF ESTIMATES

Target:
The preparation of our financial statements, in conformity with accounting principles generally accepted in the United States, requires management to make estimates and assumptions that affect the reported amounts in the financial statements and accompanying notes. Actual results may differ from those estimates.

Wal-Mart:
The preparation of consolidated financial statements in conformity with generally accepted accounting principles requires management to make estimates and assumptions. These estimates and assumptions affect the reported amounts of assets and liabilities. They also affect the disclosure of contingent assets and liabilities at the date of the consolidated financial statements and reported amounts of revenues and expenses during the reporting period. Actual results may differ from these estimates.

Daimler Chrysler:
Preparation of the financial statements requires management to make estimates and assumptions that affect the reported amounts of assets and liabilities and disclosure of contingent assets and liabilities at the date of the financial statements and reported amounts of revenues and expenses during the reporting period. Actual results could differ from those estimates. Due to current economic conditions and events in 2001, it is possible that these conditions and events could have a significant effect on such estimates made by management.

Procter & Gamble:
Preparation of financial statements in conformity with accounting principles generally accepted in the United States of America requires management to make estimates and assumptions that affect the amount reported in the consolidated financial statements and accompanying disclosures. These estimates are based on management's best knowledge of current events and actions the Company may undertake in the future. Actual results may ultimately differ from estimates.

CASH AND CASH EQUIVALENTS

Target:
Cash equivalents represent short-term investments with a maturity of three months or less from the time of purchase.

Wal-Mart:
The Company considers investments with a maturity of three months or less when purchased to be cash equivalents.

Daimler Chrysler:
Cash and cash equivalents are mainly comprised of cash at banks, cash on hand and checks in transit.

Procter & Gamble:
Highly liquid investments with a maturity of three months or less when purchased are considered cash equivalents.

have to correct prior statements, which may cause readers to believe they have done something wrong. In some cases, a change in principle may even have significant effects on reported income.

Managers can be tempted to prepare fraudulent financial statements to hide previous mistakes, to manipulate income amounts, or to achieve predicted results. Frequently the fraud is small in the beginning and managers find the idea of committing a small fraud less objectionable than admitting they failed to achieve an earnings projection or they made a mistake. Most believe it will correct itself in the near future and no one will ever know. Regardless of the level of fraud perpetrated, however, it will eventually become known. Would the elimination of choice among acceptable accounting principles reduce the amount of deception in reporting? Absolutely not.

The two most common differences managers use in reporting arise in inventory valuation methods and depreciation rates. Let's discuss each one separately.

Differences in Depreciation Methods

As you recall, depreciation is an allocation of the cost of using a long-lived asset over the time the firm uses the asset. Over time, the depreciation process transfers the historical cost of the asset from the balance sheet to depreciation expense on the income statement to match more closely the expenses with the revenues they help produce. The actual total cost of using the asset is the difference between its historical cost and the amount received when the company disposes of the asset. For example, if the officers of Elevation Sports, Inc. purchase equipment for $75,000 and sell it for $25,000, it cost the company $50,000 to use the equipment. The $50,000 cost would be a fact. The main problem with this fact is that it is unknown until the asset disposal occurs. Managers cannot know this fact when they purchase the asset. They can only estimate how long the asset will be useful and how much they might be able to sell it for when they no longer find it useful.

The Effect of Estimates

Estimates of the length of the asset's useful life and the amount of its residual value directly affect the amount of depreciation expense recognized each year. Megan assumed that Elevation's equipment would last for five years and would be worth $15,000 when it was sold. This provided a straight-line depreciation expense of $12,000 per year. She could also have made the following assumptions:

	Residual Value	Useful Life	Annual Depreciation
a.	$10,000	5 years	$13,000
b.	20,000	4 years	13,750
c.	—0—	3 years	25,000

As you can see, the depreciation would have been different in each situation with a maximum variation of $13,000 from the $12,000 that Megan estimated. If the company actually sold the equipment for $25,000 at the end of year 3, none of the depreciation amounts would have been correct. Does this mean that the depreciation was wrong and the SEC will require the company to restate its prior years' income? No, because no one can predict the future. In reality, the company would compute a gain or loss on the sale of the asset as follows:

Original cost	$75,000
Less: Depreciation to date	36,000 (3 years @ $12,000)
Book value	$39,000
Sales price	25,000
Loss on the asset sale	$14,000

The recognition of the gain or loss on the equipment corrects the net income of the company to reflect the total cost of using the equipment over time:

Depreciation to date	$36,000
Loss on the asset sale	14,000
Total cost of using the equipment	$50,000

The company recognizes the cost over its three-year use of the asset as follows:

Year	Depreciation	Loss	Total
1	$12,000		$12,000
2	12,000		12,000
3	12,000	$14,000	26,000
Total	$36,000	$14,000	$50,000

Obviously, the better the company estimates the residual value and useful life of the asset, the less gain or loss it will report on the income statement. If Megan had used option C for depreciation, she would have reported the following:

Original cost	$75,000
Less: Depreciation to date (3 years @ $25,000)	75,000
Book value	—0—
Sales price	25,000
Gain on the asset sale	$25,000
Depreciation to date	$75,000
Gain on the asset sale	(25,000)
Total cost of using the equipment	$50,000

Year	Depreciation	Loss	Total
1	$25,000		$25,000
2	25,000		25,000
3	25,000	$25,000	—0—
Total	$75,000	$25,000	$50,000

Although the amount of each year's reduction of income is very different from one estimate to the other, the $50,000 is the same for both assumptions. In fact, all three assumptions would provide the same total result as follows:

Method	a	b	c
Depreciation year 1	$13,000	$13,750	$25,000
Depreciation year 2	13,000	13,750	25,000
Depreciation year 3	13,000	13,750	25,000
(Gain) or loss	11,000	8,750	(25,000)
Total cost	$50,000	$50,000	$50,000

Would the same hold true if the company elected to use a different method of computing depreciation? Let's explore some different methods of computing depreciation.

Most companies have more than one type of depreciable asset and many firms use more than one depreciation method. You now understand the effect that estimates of residual value and useful life have on the amount of depreciation expensed each year for straight-line depreciation. You should also understand the effect the choice of depreciation method has on financial statements. We will compare and contrast the two most commonly used depreciation methods—straight-line depreciation and double-declining-balance depreciation.

Straight-Line Depreciation

● **straight-line depreciation**
A method of depreciation that assumes an asset is used equally in each time period of its useful life.

According to *Accounting Trends and Techniques 2001*, 96 percent of the 600 SEC-registered companies surveyed in 2000 use straight-line depreciation for all or part of long-lived assets. **Straight-line depreciation** assumes an asset is used equally in each time period of its useful life. Other methods, collectively called **accelerated depreciation methods**, record a large amount of depreciation expense in the early years of an asset's life and reduce that amount each year. At least 13.7 percent of the companies the compilers of *Accounting Trends and Techniques 2001* surveyed used some type of accelerated depreciation.[1] Some companies use more than one type of method. In addition, the IRS requires that businesses use either the straight-line method or a prescribed accelerated depreciation method called the **modified accelerated cost recovery system** (MACRS) for tax purposes. MACRS does not conform to GAAP, which, therefore, requires companies to use two methods—one for tax purposes and another for financial statement purposes. As the name implies, MACRS is an accelerated depreciation method. Knape & Vogt Manufacturing Company uses straight-line depreciation for financial accounting and MACRS for Income taxes. Contrast this with the Stanley Works, which uses more than one depreciation method. Exhibit 12-10 contains the footnotes for both companies. If you were to try to compare these companies, their income might not be comparable due to the depreciation.

In Chapter 4, when Megan figured the depreciation for Elevation Sports' production equipment, costing $75,000 with a residual value of $15,000, the annual depreciation amount was $12,000. Look at the following five-year pro forma income statements and balance sheets for Elevation Sports computed using the straight-line method in Exhibit 12-11. The income statements and balance sheets are condensed and show only changes related to income, cash, net equipment, and retained earnings holding all other numbers constant. Notice that the depreciation amount is the same each year in the income statement; likewise, the accumulated depreciation increases by the same amount each year on the balance sheet.

Now let's consider the same situation using an accelerated depreciation.

Double-declining-balance depreciation is an accelerated depreciation method that calculates depreciation expense at twice the straight-line rate applied to the beginning book value of the asset. The following are the simple steps to calculating double-declining-balance method each year:

1 Figure the straight-line rate in percentages. ($100\% \div N$, where N = number of years in the asset's useful life.)
2 Double the straight-line percentage.
3 Multiply the doubled percentage by the asset's book value.
4 Deduct the depreciation from the beginning book value to find the ending book value.
5 Do not depreciate below the residual value.

● **accelerated depreciation methods**
Methods of depreciation that record a large amount of depreciation expense in the early years of an asset's life and reduce that amount each year.

● **modified accelerated cost recovery system (MACRS)**
The accelerated depreciation method prescribed by IRS for business use for tax purposes.

● **double-declining-balance depreciation**
An accelerated depreciation method that calculates depreciation expense at twice the straight-line rate applied to the beginning book value of the asset.

Knape & Vogt Manufacturing Company

Property, Equipment and Depreciation:
Property and equipment are stated at cost and depreciated, for financial purposes, using the straight-line method over the estimated useful lives of the assets. For income tax purposes, accelerated depreciation methods and shorter useful lives are used.

The Stanley Works

Long-Lived Assets:
Property, plant and equipment are stated on the basis of historical cost less accumulated depreciation. Depreciation is provided using a combination of accelerated and straight-line methods over the estimated useful lives of the assets.

Exhibit 12-10
Depreciation Disclosures

---

1. Andy Mrakovcic, ed., *Accounting Trends & Techniques 2001*, 55th ed. (New York: American Institute of Certified Public Accountants, 2001), p. 359.

Exhibit 12-11
Elevation Sports, Inc. Straight-Line Depreciation

Elevation Sports, Inc. Pro Forma Income Statement For the Years Ended May 31					
	2002	**2003**	**2004**	**2005**	**2006**
Income before depreciation	$117,300	$117,300	$117,300	$117,300	$117,300
Depreciation	12,000	12,000	12,000	12,000	12,000
Income before taxes	$105,300	$105,300	$105,300	$105,300	$105,300
Income tax expense	42,120	42,120	42,120	42,120	42,120
Net Income	$ 63,180	$ 63,180	$ 63,180	$ 63,180	$ 63,180

Elevation Sports, Inc. Pro Forma Balance Sheet May 31					
	2002	**2003**	**2004**	**2005**	**2006**
Cash	$132,880	$208,060	$283,240	$358,420	$433,600
Other current assets	61,800	61,800	61,800	61,800	61,800
Equipment	75,000	75,000	75,000	75,000	75,000
Less: Accumulated depreciation	(12,000)	(24,000)	(36,000)	(48,000)	(60,000)
Other assets	34,300	34,300	34,300	34,300	34,300
Total Assets	$291,980	$355,160	$418,340	$481,520	$544,700
Total liabilities	$128,800	$128,800	$128,800	$128,800	$128,800
Common stock	100,000	100,000	100,000	100,000	100,000
Retained earnings	63,180	126,360	189,540	252,720	315,900
Total Liabilities and Stockholders' Equity	$291,980	$355,160	$418,340	$481,520	$544,700

What Do You Think?

12-19 Based on Exhibit 12-11, how much is the change in retained earnings each year? Why is it that amount?

12-20 What is the book value of the equipment at the end of each fiscal year? What will the book value of the equipment be at the end of fiscal year 2007?

As an example, apply the double-declining-balance method to Elevation Sports' equipment for the first year. Each step follows the previous directions:

1 Figure the straight-line percentage.
$$\frac{100\%}{5} = 20\%$$

2 Double the straight-line percentage.
$$20\% \times 2 = 40\%$$

3 Multiply the doubled percentage by the asset's book value.
$$40\% \times \$75,000 = \$30,000$$

4 Deduct the depreciation from the beginning book value to find the ending book value.

$$\$75,000 - \$30,000 = \$45,000$$

5 Do not depreciate below $15,000 of book value.

The following chart indicates the depreciation amount each of the five years of the equipment's life.

Year	Beginning Book Value	Depreciation Expense	Ending Book Value
2002	$75,000	$30,000	$45,000
2003	45,000	18,000	27,000
2004	27,000	10,800	16,200
2005	16,200	1,200	15,000
2006	15,000	—0—	15,000

Notice that the asset is not depreciated in the last year and the fourth year does not equal 40 percent of the beginning book value because we reached the residual value part way through the fourth year.

Exhibit 12-12 uses the information in the table to illustrate the same scenario in Exhibit 12-11 except it substitutes the double-declining-balance depreciation. Compare the results in Exhibit 12-12 to those in Exhibit 12-11.

Exhibit 12-12
Elevation Sports, Inc. Double-Declining-Balance Depreciation

Elevation Sports, Inc. Pro Forma Income Statement For the Years Ended May 31					
	2002	**2003**	**2004**	**2005**	**2006**
Income before depreciation	$117,300	$117,300	$117,300	$117,300	$117,300
Depreciation	30,000	18,000	10,800	1,200	0
Income before taxes	$ 87,300	$ 99,300	$106,500	$116,100	$117,300
Income tax expense	34,920	39,720	42,600	46,440	46,920
Net Income	$ 52,380	$ 59,580	$ 63,900	$ 69,660	$ 70,380

Elevation Sports, Inc. Pro Forma Balance Sheet May 31					
	2002	**2003**	**2004**	**2005**	**2006**
Cash	$140,080	$217,660	$292,360	$363,220	$433,600
Other current assets	61,800	61,800	61,800	61,800	61,800
Equipment	75,000	75,000	75,000	75,000	75,000
Less: Accumulated depreciation	(30,000)	(48,000)	(58,800)	(60,000)	(60,000)
Other assets	34,300	34,300	34,300	34,300	34,300
Total Assets	$281,180	$340,760	$404,660	$474,320	$544,700
Total liabilities	$128,800	$128,800	$128,800	$128,800	$128,800
Common stock	100,000	100,000	100,000	100,000	100,000
Retained earnings	52,380	111,960	175,860	245,520	315,900
Total Liabilities and Stockholders' Equity	$281,180	$340,760	$404,660	$474,320	$544,700

What Do You Think?

12-21 Compare the balance of Retained Earnings on each balance sheet in Exhibits 12-11 and 12-12. Why are the balances unequal until the final year?

12-22 Is the sum of the net income for the five years using accelerated depreciation less than, more than, or equal to the sum of the net income using straight-line depreciation?

12-23 If you had to select a method of depreciation for your business or as a part of your job responsibilities, which would you select? Why?

As you see when you review these two exhibits, over time, the method of depreciation management selects has no permanent effect on the company's cumulative income. The only effect is a timing effect on the income between years. Because in the final result different depreciation methods are irrelevant, depreciation methods are choices available among GAAP. Management must, however, select a method for a particular type of asset and continue to use that method so that the company cannot manipulate income from year to year.

Let's look at one final indicator we can glean from management's disclosures about long-lived assets.

Age of a Firm's Long-Lived Assets

By examining the notes to the financial statements for long-lived assets you may be able to determine the approximate age of the company's assets. Exhibit 12-13 contains Oneida Ltd.'s note disclosure for its property, plant, and equipment. Just by looking at the numbers, you might assume that its equipment is more than half depreciated. Making this determination, however, requires you to know the method of depreciation used. In the accounting policies note, Oneida's management discloses it uses "generally the straight-line method." Knowing that Oneida uses straight-line depreciation, we might conclude that the assets have less than one-half of their useful lives remaining.

Our conclusion does not, however, give us clues to how long the remaining life might be. By finding information on the cash flow statement and the balance sheet, we might be able to estimate the remaining useful life. The note indicates that depreciation for the year was $11,417,000. If we divide the net assets of $73,675,000 by $11,417,000, we can estimate the remaining life at approximately 6.5 years.

We can conclude that Oneida might have to replace its assets within the next decade.

Exhibit 12-13
Oneida Ltd. Long-Lived Asset Disclosure

7. PROPERTY, PLANT AND EQUIPMENT		
Property, plant and equipment by major classification are as follows:		
(Thousands)	2004	2003
Land	$ 6,242	$ 6,248
Buildings	61,620	64,017
Machinery and equipment	139,787	158,419
Tooling	26,602	28,821
Total	234,251	257,505
Less accumulated depreciation	160,576	155,139
Property, plant and equipment—net	$ 73,675	$102,366
Depreciation expense totaled $11,417, $13,899 and $12,373 for 2004, 2003 and 2002, respectively.		

What Do You Think?

12-24   Describe other ways to determine the amount of depreciation from the financial statements.

Let's now turn our attention to differences in accounting for inventories.

Differences in Inventory Methods

Only a very small percentage of the products manufactured are unique because we live in an era of mass production. If a business sells unique items, of which no two are alike, it is easy to identify which product is being sold and which remains in inventory. A store such as Wal-Mart may have as many as 10,000 products, few of which are unique or have unique serial numbers. How does a Wal-Mart manager determine which specific units were sold?

Physical Flow of Goods

Inventory is normally kept in a warehouse or distribution center. The warehouse may not always be a building with four walls and a roof. The natural differences among products causes the warehousing function to differ. Consider the following examples:

1   wheat delivered to a silo
2   gravel stored in a pit
3   oil placed in an underground storage tank
4   cars, trucks, and vans parked on a lot

When a farmer delivers wheat to a silo, he deposits the wheat in the top of the silo and receives payment from the grain dealer. When the grain dealer sells the wheat to a customer, the customer extracts the wheat from the bottom of the silo. Silos function because of the law of gravity, so the oldest wheat is on the bottom of the silo and the newest wheat is in the top of the silo (see Exhibit 12-14). Therefore,

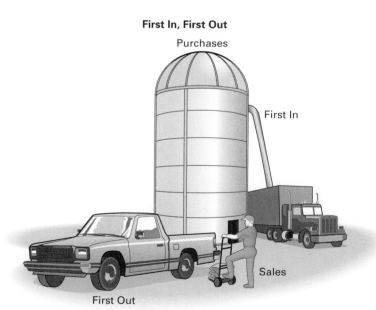

First In, First Out

Purchases

First In

Sales

First Out

Exhibit 12-14
First-In, First-Out Inventory

Exhibit 12-15
Last-In, First-Out Inventory

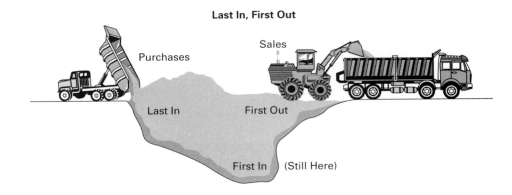

Last In, First Out

first-in, first-out (FIFO) method
An inventory flow concept based on the assumption that the first units of inventory acquired are the first sold.

the physical movement of the wheat is on a **first-in, first-out (FIFO) method**, an inventory flow concept based on the assumption that the first units of inventory acquired are the first sold.

In contrast to wheat dealers, gravel dealers frequently keep the gravel inventory in a pit. When new gravel arrives at the dealer's location, the truck driver dumps the gravel into the pit. When the gravel dealer makes a sale, he removes the gravel from the top of the pit because he cannot access the bottom of the pit (see Exhibit 12-15). The physical movement of the gravel is on a **last-in, first-out (LIFO) method**, an inventory flow concept based on the assumption that the last goods acquired are the first ones sold.

last-in, first-out (LIFO) method
An inventory flow concept based on the assumption that the last goods acquired are the first ones sold.

Still another type of goods storage commingles old inventory with new inventory. When an oil producer delivers oil to a customer, it frequently delivers the oil to an aboveground storage tank. Because of the physical properties of oil, it blends with other oil when added into a container. So when oil enters a storage tank, it mixes with other oil and loses its unit identity. Therefore, any oil extracted from the tank is a mixture of all oil added to the tank. We might say that extracted oil represents an average of the oil inventory (see Exhibit 12-16). The **average cost method** is an inventory flow assumption that assigns an average cost to the units of inventory on hand at the time of each sale.

average cost method
An inventory flow assumption that assigns an average cost to the units of inventory on hand at the time of each sale.

Finally, look at a dealer's lot of cars, trucks, and vans. Each vehicle has unique characteristics and a serial number. The dealer places the vehicles wherever there is room and moves the vehicles around. Customers purchase their choice of vehicle, based not on its location, but on its ability to suit the customer's needs. The customer specifically identifies the vehicle he or she wants. The physical movement of the vehicles is based on the specific identification of the desired unit (see Exhibit 12-17). With the **specific identification method**, the inventory cost is based on the actual cost of the item sold.

specific identification method
An inventory method that assigns the actual cost of the item sold.

Exhibit 12-16
Average Cost Method of Inventory

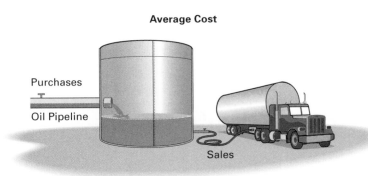

Average Cost

Exhibit 12-17
Specific Identification Inventory

What Do You Think?

12-25 For what types of products would it be important that the first units purchased be the first ones sold? Explain.

12-26 Describe five categories of products for sale in a grocery store. How do store personnel typically restock the shelves for each of these products? Why?

12-27 If you owned a retail computer store, what reasons would you have for insisting that your employees sell the first computer received before ones that arrived at the store later?

Flow of Inventory Cost

We have discussed the physical flow of units in and out of inventory. But what about the cost of these units? As a company purchases inventory, we add its cost to inventory in the accounting records. Likewise, as the firm sells the merchandise, we remove its cost from inventory on the balance sheet and transfer it to cost of goods sold on the income statement. You might suppose that accounting rules require the flow of costs through a company's accounting records to reflect the reality of the way the physical units flow through the company's inventory. Accounting rules, however, do not require that the cost flow for inventory mirror the flow of physical units. Regardless of how physical units actually flow through inventory, a company may select any of the four cost flow assumptions it chooses.

To illustrate the difference each method makes on the income statement and the balance sheet, let's consider the example of the Harwood Equipment Company. The following is the inventory activity for Harwood during September.

Date	Transaction	Units	Unit Cost	Unit Selling Price
9–1	Beginning inventory	1	$ 800	
9–3	Purchase	2	1,025	
9–17	Sale	1		$1,500
9–22	Purchase	1	1,100	
9–26	Purchase	1	1,200	
9–29	Purchase	1	1,450	
9–30	Sale	2		1,500

You can analyze the information based on your knowledge of inventory cost, cost of goods sold, and gross profit.

1 Harwood sold three units at $1,500 for a total of $4,500.
2 Harwood had a beginning inventory of one unit that cost $800.

3 Harwood purchased the following items:

9–3	2 @ $1,025	$2,050
9–22	1 @ $1,100	1,100
9–26	1 @ $1,200	1,200
9–29	1 @ $1,450	1,450
Total purchases		$5,800

4 The cost of goods available for sale is $6,600 (beginning inventory of $800 plus purchases of $5,800).

The goods available for sale will be $6,600 regardless of which method we use to determine the cost of goods sold and the ending inventory.

First-In, First-Out Method

Using the FIFO cost method, we assume that the first units owned were sold, and the last units purchased comprise the ending inventory. Harwood had six units to sell during September, sold three, and had three remaining at the end of the month.

Under the FIFO method, we assume that the first three units owned were sold:

Beginning inventory	1 @ $800	$ 800
9–3 purchase	2 @ $1,025	2,050
Cost of units sold		$2,850

Likewise, the ending inventory comes from the last purchases:

9–29 purchase	1 @ $1,450	$1,450
9–26 purchase	1 @ $1,200	1,200
9–22 purchase	1 @ $1,100	1,100
Cost of ending inventory		$3,750

By using the cost of sales calculation, we can determine from an accounting viewpoint the cost of units that were sold and the cost of those that remain in inventory:

FIFO	Units	Cost
Beginning inventory	1	$ 800
Purchases	5	5,800
Goods available for sale	6	$6,600
Ending inventory	3	3,750
Cost of goods sold	3	$2,850

Last-In, First-Out Method

Using the LIFO cost method, we assume that the last units owned were sold, and the first units purchased comprise the ending inventory—exactly the opposite of the FIFO method. Harwood had six units to sell during September, sold three, and had three remaining at the end of the month. Under LIFO, we assume that the last three units purchased were sold:

9–29 purchase	1 @ $1,450	$1,450
9–26 purchase	1 @ $1,200	1,200
9–22 purchase	1 @ $1,100	1,100
Cost of units sold		$3,750

Likewise, the ending inventory comes from the first units owned:

Beginning inventory	1 @ $800	$ 800
9–3 purchase	2 @ $1,025	2,050
Cost of ending inventory		$2,850

By using the cost of sales calculation we can determine from an accounting viewpoint the cost of units sold and the cost of units that remain in inventory:

LIFO	Units	Cost
Beginning inventory	1	$ 800
Purchases	5	5,800
Goods available for sale	6	$6,600
Ending inventory	3	2,850
Cost of goods sold	3	$3,750

Average Cost Method

Instead of separating the inventory cost into two groups, the average cost method assigns the same cost to each inventory unit. It is simple to apply. Divide the cost of goods available for sale by the number of units available to determine the average unit cost. Harwood owned six units of inventory that cost $6,600.

$$\frac{\text{Average}}{\text{cost}} = \frac{\text{Total goods available for sale}}{\text{number of units available}} = \frac{\$6,600}{6} = \$1,100/\text{unit}$$

Use the cost of sales calculation to measure the cost of the units sold and the cost of the units remaining from an accounting viewpoint:

	Units	Cost
Beginning inventory	1	$ 800
Purchases	5	5,800
Goods available for sale	6	$6,600
Ending inventory	3	3,300
Cost of goods sold	3	$3,300

Comparison of Methods

We stated earlier that the three assumptions produced different results. Exhibit 12-18 indicates these differences in cost of goods sold, ending inventory, and gross profit. As you may have concluded, the differences among methods occur because of the changing prices. As prices rise, LIFO produces the highest cost of sales and the lowest ending inventory and net income. As prices fall, the opposite occurs and FIFO produces the highest cost of sales and the lowest ending inventory and net income. Normally, the average cost method will produce costs in between LIFO and FIFO.

Notice in Exhibit 12-18 that the inventory on the balance sheet matches the amount calculated in the previous discussion. Also note that the net income follows the predictions during a time of rising prices. LIFO produces the lowest net income at $500, FIFO the highest net income at $1,450, and average cost is in between at $1,000. If we try to compare two companies that use different methods, the initial comparison may be misleading.

Reporting Inventories in the Notes to Financial Statements

According to *Accounting Trends & Techniques 2001*, 64 percent of firms use FIFO, 49 percent use LIFO, and 30 percent use average cost. Only 4 percent of companies use LIFO for all inventories, but 25 percent use LIFO for 50 percent or more of inventories.[2] The percentage of firms using LIFO has decreased 9 percent in the past decade, whereas the percentage of firms using FIFO has decreased 1 percent and the percentage using average cost has remained the same.[3] As you see from the statistics, unlike the case for depreciation, firms use a variety of inventory methods.

---

2. Andy Mrakovcic, ed., *Accounting Trends & Techniques 2001*, 55th ed. (New York: American Institute of Certified Public Accountants, 2001), p. 359.

3. Gerard L. Yarnall, CPA, ed., *Accounting Trends & Techniques 1997*, 51st ed. (New York: American Institute of Certified Public Accountants, 1997), p. 154.

Exhibit 12-18
Comparative Financial Statements for FIFO, LIFO, and Average Cost Methods

---

HARWOOD EQUIPMENT COMPANY
Income Statement
For the Month Ended September 30, 2004

	FIFO	LIFO	AVERAGE COST
Sales	$4,500	$4,500	$4,500
Cost of Goods Sold	2,850	3,750	3,300
Gross Margin	$1,650	$ 750	$1,200
Operating Expenses			
Warehouse rent	200	200	200
Net Income	$1,450	$ 500	$1,000

HARWOOD EQUIPMENT COMPANY
Balance Sheet
August 31, 2004 and September 30, 2004

		FIFO	LIFO	AVERAGE COST
Assets	August 31		September 30	
Cash	$21,000	$22,300	$22,300	$22,300
Accounts receivable	1,500	4,500	4,500	4,500
Merchandise inventory	800	3,750	2,850	3,300
Total Assets	$23,300	$30,550	$29,650	$30,100
Liabilities and Stockholders' Equity				
Accounts payable	$ —0—	$ 5,800	$ 5,800	$ 5,800
Common stock	15,000	15,000	15,000	15,000
Additional paid-in capital	8,000	8,000	8,000	8,000
Retained earnings	300	1,750	800	1,300
Total Liabilities and Stockholders' Equity	$23,300	$30,550	$29,650	$30,100

Before IRS instituted the LIFO Conformity Rule, many firms used FIFO inventory for financial statements and LIFO inventory for tax purposes. FIFO provides the highest net income in times of rising prices and LIFO the lowest net income. So the financial statements going to stockholders indicated a higher net income and the tax return indicated a lower net income and, therefore, a lower tax. Because most inventories physically move on a FIFO basis, managers looked at the FIFO financial statements as the true income and the LIFO tax returns as a way to minimize taxes. Seems like a smart move. The LIFO Conformity Rule changed this practice by requiring firms to use the same inventory method for tax purposes that they used for financial statement purposes. Not wishing to pay a fortune in recalculated income taxes, most companies switched the financial statement method to conform to the LIFO tax method. Now new companies select the single method they wish to use for both.

Exhibit 12-19

Family Dollar Stores, Inc. and Target Corporation Comparison of Inventory Disclosures

---

Family Dollar Stores, Inc. and Subsidiaries
Notes to Consolidated Financial Statements
Years Ended August 30, 2003, August 31, 2002 and September 1, 2001

1. Description of Business and Summary of Significant Accounting Policies:

Merchandise inventories:
Inventories are valued using retail prices less markon percentages, and approximate the lower of first-in, first-out (FIFO) cost or market.

Target Corporation and subsidiaries

NOTES TO CONSOLIDATED FINANCIAL STATEMENTS

Inventory

We account for inventory and the related cost of sales under the retail inventory accounting method using the last-in, first-out (LIFO) basis. Inventory is stated at the lower of LIFO cost or market. The cumulative LIFO provision was $52 million and $64 million at yearend 2002 and 2001, respectively.

Inventory

(millions)	February 1, 2003	February 2, 2002
Target	$3,748	$3,348
Mervyn's	486	523
Marshall Field's	324	348
Other	202	230
Total inventory	$4,760	$4,449

How do we compare two firms that use different inventory methods? The largest difference would be between a company using LIFO and another firm using FIFO inventory. LIFO companies take care of this in the notes to the financial statements. Exhibit 12-19 contains the notes from Family Dollar Stores, Inc. and Target Corporation.

As you can see, Family Dollar uses FIFO inventory and Target uses LIFO. The information helps us to compare the two companies. The last sentence of Target's information tells us the amount of the beginning and ending LIFO reserve. Combined with the beginning and ending LIFO inventory from the balance sheet, $4,248 million and $4,449 million, respectively, this information lets us compute what the beginning and ending inventory would have been using the FIFO method as follows:

(in $ millions)	LIFO	+	LIFO Reserve	=	FIFO
Beginning inventory	$4,449		$64		$4,513
Ending inventory	4,760		52		4,812

Likewise, we can compute the FIFO cost of goods sold in two steps, using the cost of goods sold calculation and the cost of goods sold from the income statement of $29,260 million. First, use the cost of goods sold calculation to compute the amount of purchases made during the year. By working backward, you can find the goods available for sale and then purchases.

(dollars in millions)		Solution
	Beginning inventory (LIFO)	$ 4,449	$ 4,449
+	Purchases	?	29,571
=	Goods available for sale	$?	34,020
−	Ending inventory (LIFO)	4,760	4,760
=	Cost of goods sold	$29,260	$29,260

Using the amount of the purchases, you can determine the amount of cost of goods sold under FIFO as follows:

(dollars in millions)		Solution
	Beginning inventory (FIFO)	$ 4,513
+	Purchases	29,571
=	Goods available for sale	$34,084
−	Ending inventory (FIFO)	4,812
=	Cost of goods sold	$29,272

The cost of goods sold of $29,272 million is more than the LIFO method, which would lower the gross profit by $12 million. Target's use of LIFO decreased its cost of goods sold because enough goods fell in price to reduce the LIFO reserve. When the conversion from LIFO to FIFO changes the inventory and cost of goods sold amounts, it will also change the ratio calculations for at least three ratios: gross profit percentage, inventory turnover, and profit margin before income taxes.

Implications of LIFO on Ratio Comparisons

We computed the ratios for Family Dollar in Chapter 8, from which we can extract the profit margin before taxes and the inventory turnover ratios. We can compute the gross profit margin and recalculate the FIFO ratios for Target from the following data:

(dollars in millions)	Family Dollar	Target (LIFO)	Target (FIFO)
Sales	$4,750	$43,917	$43,917
Cost of sales	3,146	29,260	29,272
Gross margin	$1,604	$14,657	$14,645
Profit before taxes	$ 390	$ 2,676	$ 2,664
Ending inventory	$ 854	$ 4,760	$ 4,812

Gross Profit Percentage

The gross profit percentage is the gross margin divided by net sales. The following are the gross profit percentage calculations for Family Dollar and Target LIFO and FIFO:

(dollars in millions)	Family Dollar	Target (LIFO)	Target (FIFO)
Gross margin	$1,604	$14,657	$14,645
Sales	$4,750	$43,917	$43,917
= Gross profit %	33.77%	33.37%	33.35%

We see little difference in the gross profit percentage because of the small change in gross margin due to using LIFO. Will we also see little difference in the profit margin before taxes?

Profit Margin Before Income Taxes

The profit margin before income taxes is the profit before income taxes divided by sales. The following are the calculations:

(dollars in millions)	Family Dollar	Target (LIFO)	Target (FIFO)
Profit before taxes	$ 390	$ 2,676	$ 2,664
Sales	$4,750	$43,917	$43,917
= Profit margin before taxes	8.21%	6.09%	6.07%

Again we see that the magnitude of change on sales is minimal and makes little difference in the profit margin before taxes. Prices did not change a lot in 2002. If prices change dramatically during a year, we could see an important difference. Shall we conclude that no significant difference will occur in the inventory turnover?

Inventory Turnover

Inventory turnover is cost of goods sold divided by inventory. Let's see if we find a measurable difference in the LIFO and FIFO inputs for this ratio:

(dollars in millions)	Family Dollar	Target (LIFO)	Target (FIFO)
Cost of sales	$3,146	$29,260	$29,272
Inventory	$ 854	$ 4,760	$ 4,812
= Inventory turnover	3.68	6.15	6.08
Days inventory (365 + Inventory turnover)	99.18	59.35	60.03

The difference is small but accounts for an additional day of inventory on hand. Target does not have a very large LIFO reserve, partly because we have not seen a lot of inflation in the past 20 years. Say, for example, Target had a $1,052 million and $1,064 million LIFO reserve. The difference between the LIFO ratios and the FIFO ratios would be as follows:

(dollars in millions)	Target (LIFO)	Target (FIFO)
Gross margin	33.37%	33.35%
Profit margin before taxes	6.09%	6.07%
Inventory turnover	6.15	5.04
Days inventory	59.35	72.42

As you can see, the difference would be dramatic, resulting in an inventory turnover of 5.04 with 13 days' difference in the number of days of inventory on hand. You can see why the LIFO disclosures are important when comparing two firms. Without the conversion to FIFO, the comparison might be very misleading.

After studying this chapter, you probably realize that freedom of choice allows firms to select appropriate alternative accounting principles. The user of accounting information must take time to read and understand the complete financial statements, including the notes to financial statements. As we stated in Chapter 8, no one specific datum, statistic, or ratio can determine whether a company is a good investment. An understanding of the industry, the economy, and the political environment, however, provides good perspective when analyzing a company. In Chapter 13 you will discover more about the annual reports sent to stockholders and investors containing information the SEC requires.

CHAPTER SUMMARY

The objective of accounting is to provide information that is useful in decision making. External users of financial information make economic decisions after performing some type of analysis on the information. External information is useful to shareholders, creditors, and regulators. Ethics should be the cornerstone in both the conducting of business and the reporting of its results.

The valuations used on the balance sheet may vary and include historical cost, net realizable value, lower of cost or market value, and current (fair) market value. The use of alternative accounting principles often makes the comparison of two companies complex. Information about the significant accounting policies are found in the notes to the financial statements.

The two most common differences found in reporting are depreciation and inventory valuation methods. Depreciation is an allocation of the cost of long-lived assets to the periods used. The depreciation process transfers over time the historical cost of an asset from the balance sheet to the income statement to better match expenses with revenues. The use of estimates is important in determining depreciation. The use of accelerated methods of depreciation increases expense in the early years of life, which decreases the net income in the early years of the life of the asset. Over the life of the asset, the total transferred to the income statement is exactly the same regardless of the depreciation method used.

When we are valuing the ending inventory, the cost flow assumption selected determines the amount of the inventory on the balance sheet and the cost of goods sold and net income for the income statement. Similar to the choice of depreciation methods, the choice of inventory method makes no difference in the net income over the life of a firm. It does make a difference from one year to the next, however. Companies may select from among the following methods: first-in, first-out (FIFO), last-in, first-out (LIFO), average cost, and specific identification. Companies that use LIFO for tax purposes must use LIFO for financial statement purposes. Analysts can convert LIFO to FIFO with the LIFO reserve note.

Visit the Web site *www.prenhall.com/terrell* for additional study help with the Online Study Guide.

REVIEW OF CONCEPTS

A Explain the importance of external financial information to financial statement users.

B Describe the valuation methods used to prepare financial statements.

C Provide three examples of long-lived depreciable assets.

D Describe the depreciation process.

E Explain the depreciable base of a fixed asset. Describe two estimates management makes that will affect the amount of depreciation recorded each period.

F Explain how an accelerated depreciation method differs from straight-line depreciation.

G Explain how the amount of depreciation expense is calculated using straight-line depreciation and describe the process of determining depreciation expense using the double-declining-balance method.

H Explain what an asset's book value means. Explain how the amount of accumulated depreciation factors in to the book value.

I Compared to straight-line depreciation, describe the effect of an accelerated depreciation method on the balance sheet and on the income statement.

J Regardless of which depreciation method is used, explain at what point an asset is considered fully depreciated.

K Describe how a gain or loss on the sale of an asset is calculated, and indicate on which financial statement gains and losses appear.

L Explain why an investor would want to determine the average life of a firm's long-lived assets. Explain how this would help make a better investment decision.

M Distinguish among the methods of accounting for and valuing inventories.

N Describe the effects the methods of valuing inventory have on the balance sheet and income statements.

O Discuss why the LIFO method of valuing inventory is preferred for tax purposes in periods of rising prices.

P Explain why the FIFO method of valuing inventory is preferred for financial statement purposes.

Q Describe what the LIFO reserve means and what impact it has on the computation of gross profit.

APPLICATION EXERCISES

12-28 As a prospective investor in a manufacturing company, would you be concerned if the financial statements reported that the fixed assets were reported at their fair market value rather than their historical cost? Why or why not?

● **LO 1**
Information

12-29 As a prospective lender to a manufacturing company, would you be concerned if the financial statements reported that the fixed assets were reported at their fair market value rather than their historical cost? Why or why not?

● **LO 1**
Information

12-30 As a prospective lender to Sears, what would you expect to find out about how the accounts receivable are valued on the balance sheet?

● **LO 1**
Information

12-31 Describe the method of valuation used for each of the following accounts:
a. cash
b. accounts receivable
c. merchandise inventory
d. equipment
e. land
f. investments in equity securities

● **LO 2**
Valuation

12-32 Describe the method of valuation used for each of the following accounts:
a. accounts payable
b. common stock
c. additional paid-in capital
d. bonds payable
e. retained earnings
f. treasury stock

● **LO 2**
Valuation

12-33 Evaluate the following statement: "The depreciation process is a process designed to value fixed assets on the balance sheet."

● **LO 3**
Depreciation Process

12-34 Jim Garcia and Company purchased a lathe for use in its manufacturing operation. The machine cost $150,000, has a five-year estimated useful life, and will be depreciated using the straight-line method. The only thing remaining to be determined before yearly depreciation expense can be calculated is the estimated residual value. The alternatives are:
1. $10,000 estimated residual value
2. $20,000 estimated residual value
3. $30,000 estimated residual value

● **LO 3**
Computation
of Depreciation

Required:

a. Calculate the yearly depreciation expense for the new lathe under each of the alternatives given.
b. Which of the three alternatives will result in the highest net income?
c. How long will the new lathe be useful to Garcia and Company?

LO 3
**Computation
of Depreciation**

12-35 John Henry, Inc. has just purchased a minicomputer for use in its manufacturing operation. The machine cost $75,000, has a four-year estimated useful life, and will be depreciated using the straight-line method. The only thing remaining to be determined before yearly depreciation expense can be calculated is the estimated residual value. The alternatives are:
1. $7,500 estimated residual value
2. $12,500 estimated residual value
3. $17,500 estimated residual value

Required:

a. Calculate the yearly depreciation expense for the new minicomputer under each of the alternatives given.
b. Which of the three alternatives will result in the lowest net income?
c. How long will the new minicomputer be useful to John Henry?

LO 3
**Computation
of Depreciation**

12-36 Burt Machine Company purchased a new milling machine for a total installed cost of $700,000. The milling machine will be depreciated straight line in accordance with corporate policy. Lori Burt, the corporate controller, is trying to decide on an estimated useful life and an estimated residual value for the asset. The alternatives are:
1. a six-year estimated useful life with a $40,000 estimated residual value
2. a five-year estimated useful life with a $100,000 estimated residual value
3. a four-year estimated useful life with a $140,000 estimated residual value

Required:

a. Calculate the yearly depreciation expense for the new printing press under each of the alternatives given.
b. Which of the three alternatives will result in the lowest yearly net income? Which of the three alternatives will result in the highest yearly net income?
c. What should the deciding factor be in selecting among the three alternatives?

LO 4
**Computation
of Double-Declining-
Balance Depreciation**

12-37 Wedtech Company purchased a high-tech assembler on January 2, 2006, for a total cost of $600,000. The assembler has an estimated useful life to the company of five years. Wedtech thinks it can sell the used assembler for $40,000 after five years. The company chose to depreciate the new assembler using the double-declining-balance method.

Required:

a. Prepare a schedule showing the amount of depreciation expense for each of the five years of the estimated useful life.
b. What will the book value of the assembler be at the end of the five-year estimated useful life?
c. What does book value represent?

LO 4
**Computation
of Double-Declining-
Balance Depreciation**

12-38 Gopher Company purchased an earthmoving machine on January 2, 2006, for a total cost of $900,000. The earthmover has an estimated useful life to the company of four years. The company believes it can sell the used earthmover for $80,000 after four years. The company uses double-declining-balance depreciation.

Required:

Prepare a schedule showing the amount of depreciation expense for each of the four years and the book value of the end of each year.

12-39 Swinton Company purchased a very sophisticated stamping machine on January 2, 2005, for $480,000. The estimated useful life of the stamping machine is six years. Eric Swinton, the CFO, estimates the machine's residual value is $40,000.

LO 4
Computation
of Depreciation

Required:

a. Calculate the yearly depreciation expense for the stamping machine assuming the company uses the straight-line depreciation method.
b. Prepare a schedule showing the amount of depreciation expense for each of the six years of the estimated useful life assuming the company uses the double-declining-balance depreciation method.
c. How should Eric decide which to use?

12-40 WebbCo, Inc. purchased a pasteurizing machine on January 2, 2005, for $375,000. The estimated useful life of the machine is four years with a residual value of $45,000.

LO 4
Computation
of Depreciation

Required:

a. Calculate the yearly depreciation expense for the machine assuming the company uses the straight-line depreciation.
b. Prepare a schedule showing the amount of depreciation expense for each of the four years assuming the company uses double-declining-balance depreciation.

12-41 Pepco Inc. purchased a fleet of delivery trucks on January 2, 2005, for $700,000. The estimated useful life of the fleet is four years, after which Pepco's president estimates she can sell the entire fleet for $50,000.

LO 3 and 4
Computation
of Depreciation

Required:

a. Calculate the yearly depreciation expense for the fleet assuming the company uses straight-line depreciation.
b. Prepare a schedule showing the amount of depreciation expense for each of the four years assuming the company uses double-declining-balance depreciation.
c. Double-declining-balance calculates depreciation at twice the straight-line rate. Why is the amount of depreciation expense in 2005 under double-declining-balance not exactly twice the amount under straight-line for 2005?
d. Over the four-year useful life of the vehicles, how much depreciation expense will be charged against income using the straight-line method? How much will be charged against income using the double-declining-balance method? Discuss the impact on the net income of each method of depreciation in the first two years of life of the asset.
e. Compute the gain or loss on the sale of the asset assuming straight-line depreciation and double-declining-balance depreciation if the fleet sells for $50,000 on January 3, 2009.
f. What is Pepco's total cost of using the fleet during its ownership period?

12-42 Cruse Company purchased a machine for $200,000 on January 2, 2005. The machine had an estimated useful life of five years and an estimated residual value of $25,000. The company uses straight-line depreciation. It is now June 30, 2008, and management decides to dispose of the machine.

LO 4 and 5
Computation of Gain
or Loss

Required:

a. Calculate the book value of the machine as of June 30, 2008.
b. Calculate the gain or loss on the sale of the machine assuming Cruse sells it for $102,000.
c. Calculate the gain or loss on the sale of the machine assuming Cruse sells it for $25,000.
d. What is the impact of the gain or loss in parts b and c on the 2008 balance sheet and income statement?

12-43 Farr Company purchased a machine for $150,000 on January 2, 2006. Management determined the machine had an estimated useful life of four years and an

LO 4 and 5
Computation of Gain
or Loss

estimated residual value of $10,000. The company uses straight-line depreciation. It is now September 30, 2008, and management has decided to dispose of the machine.

Required:

a. Calculate the machine's book value on September 30, 2008.
b. Calculate the gain or loss on the sale of the machine assuming Farr sells it for $172,000.
c. Calculate the gain or loss on the sale of the machine assuming Farr sells it for $25,000.
d. What is the impact of the gain or loss in parts b and c on the balance sheet and income statement for 2008?

LO 4, 5, and 6
Impact of Depreciation Methods on Gains and Losses

12-44 Millie and Maude are twins, and each has her own company. Three years ago, on the same day, they each purchased high-speed copiers for their companies to use. The machines were identical and cost $28,000 each. Both machines had estimated useful lives of five years and residual values of $3,000. The only difference was the depreciation method selected. Millie chose to depreciate her copier using the straight-line method, whereas Maude selected an accelerated depreciation method.

Due to rapid technological developments in the machines, Millie decided at the end of two years to sell her machine and buy a new one. Maude decided to do the same thing. In fact, they each received $16,500 when they sold their machines. Later, while they were having lunch together, Maude mentioned that when she sold her copier, she had a gain of more than $6,000 on the sale. Millie didn't say anything, but she thought something was wrong because she knew she had sold her copier for exactly the same amount Maude had, yet the sale of her copier had resulted in a loss of $1,500.

Required:

a. Did Millie do better than Maude?
b. Explain how Millie could have had a loss of $1,500 on the sale of her copier whereas Maude had a sizable gain. Support your conclusions with computations.

LO 4, 5, and 6
Impact of Depreciation Methods on Gains and Losses

12-45 Redd and Fred each ran an automotive repair shop. Each bought a new piece of equipment costing $10,000 on January 2. The equipment is expected to have a five-year life and no salvage value. Redd used straight-line depreciation and Fred used double-declining-balance depreciation. At the end of three years, each sold his machine for $5,500.

Required:

a. Compute the depreciation for both Redd and Fred through the third year.
b. Compute the gain or loss that each would recognize on the sale of the machine.
c. If the gain or loss is different, explain why.
d. Did one do better than the other? Explain.

LO 4, 5, and 6
Impact of Depreciation Methods on Gains and Losses

12-46 Ethel and Lucy each ran a cooking school. Each bought a new piece of equipment costing $20,000 on January 2. The equipment is expected to have a five-year life and no salvage value. Ethel used straight-line depreciation and Lucy used double-declining-balance depreciation. At the end of three years, each sold her machine for $11,000.

Required:

a. Compute the gain or loss that each would recognize on the sale of the machine.
b. If the gain or loss is different, explain why.
c. What is the total cost of using each machine?

LO 5 and 6
Comparison of Cost Flow Assumptions

12-47 Cox Company buys and then resells a single product as its primary business activity. This product is called the Whatzit and is subject to rather severe cost fluctuations. Following is information concerning the company's inventory activity for the Whatzit product during July 2005:

July 1   431 units on hand, $3,017.
July 2   Sold 220 units.

July 9   Purchased 500 units @ $11 per unit.
July 12   Purchased 200 units @ $9 per unit.
July 16   Sold 300 units.
July 21   Purchased 150 units @ $6 per unit.
July 24   Purchased 50 units @ $8 per unit.
July 29   Sold 500 units.

Required:

Calculate the cost of goods sold (units and cost) for July 2005 and ending inventory (units and cost) at July 31, 2005, using the following:
  a. FIFO method
  b. LIFO method
  c. average cost method (round all unit cost calculations to the nearest penny)
  d. Which of the three methods resulted in the highest cost of goods sold for July? Which one will provide the highest ending inventory value for Cox's balance sheet?
  e. How would the differences among the three methods affect Cox's income statement and balance sheet for the month?

12-48   The Frank Naifeh Company buys and then resells a single product as its primary business activity. Following is information concerning the company's inventory activity for the product during October 2004:

LO 5 and 6
Comparison of Cost
Flow Assumptions

October 1   216 units on hand @ $4 per unit.
October 5   Sold 80 units.
October 7   Purchased 150 units @ $7 per unit.
October 11   Purchased 100 units @ $11 per unit.
October 15   Sold 200 units.
October 21   Purchased 300 units @ $13 per unit.
October 25   Purchased 50 units @ $18 per unit.
October 29   Sold 350 units.

Required:

  a. Calculate cost of goods sold (units and cost) for October using the following:
    1. FIFO method
    2. LIFO method
    3. average cost method (round all unit cost calculations to the nearest penny)
  b. Which of the three methods resulted in the highest cost of goods sold for October? Which one will provide the highest ending inventory value for Naifeh's balance sheet?
  c. How would the differences among the three methods affect Naifeh's income statement and balance sheet for the month?

12-49   The David Harris Company buys and then resells a single product as its primary business activity. Following is information concerning the company's inventory activity for the product during August 2006:

LO 5 and 6
Comparison of Cost
Flow Assumptions

August 1   216 units on hand @ $18 per unit.
August 5   Sold 80 units.
August 7   Purchased 150 units @ $13 per unit.
August 11   Purchased 100 units @ $11 per unit.
August 15   Sold 200 units.
August 21   Purchased 300 units @ $7 per unit.
August 25   Purchased 50 units @ $4 per unit.
August 29   Sold 350 units.

Required:

  a. Calculate cost of goods sold (units and cost) for August using the following:
    1. FIFO method
    2. LIFO method
    3. average cost method (round all unit cost calculations to the nearest penny)

b. Which of the three methods resulted in the highest inventory amount for Harris' August 31 balance sheet?

c. How would the differences among the three methods affect Harris' income statement and balance sheet for the month?

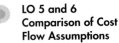

LO 5 and 6
Comparison of Cost Flow Assumptions

12-50 The Dennis Lee Company buys and then resells a single product as its primary business activity. Following is information concerning the company's inventory activity for the product during July 2004:

July 1 216 units on hand @ $4 per unit.
July 5 Sold 80 units.
July 7 Purchased 150 units @ $4 per unit.
July 11 Purchased 100 units @ $4 per unit.
July 15 Sold 200 units.
July 21 Purchased 300 units @ $4 per unit.
July 25 Purchased 50 units @ $4 per unit.
July 29 Sold 350 units.

Required:

a. Calculate cost of goods sold (units and cost) for July using the following:
   1. FIFO method
   2. LIFO method
   3. average cost method (round all unit cost calculations to the nearest penny)
b. Which of the three methods resulted in the highest cost of goods sold for July?
c. Describe the differences among income statements and balance sheets prepared under the three cost-flow assumptions.

LO 6
LIFO Reserve

12-51 Nash Company reports inventories based on the FIFO cost flow assumption. Rambler Company reports inventories based on the LIFO cost flow assumption. Both Nash and Rambler operate within the same industry. The following information is from the companies' individual annual reports.

	Nash	Rambler
Sales	$2,500,000	$5,000,000
Cost of goods sold	1,800,000	3,000,000
Gross profit	700,000	2,000,000
Beginning inventory	400,000	600,000
Ending inventory	450,000	750,000
Beginning LIFO reserve		300,000
Ending LIFO reserve		350,000

Required:

a. Compute the inventory turnover ratio and the gross profit percentage for each company. How do the ratios compare?
b. Using the LIFO reserve, recalculate the gross profit, ending inventory, the inventory turnover, and the gross profit percentage for Rambler to see how the companies compare.
c. Compare the two companies based on the information presented after adjusting the inventories for the LIFO reserve.

LO 6
LIFO Reserve

12-52 Shryock Company reports inventories based on the LIFO cost flow assumption. Shreck Company reports inventories on the FIFO cost flow assumption. Both companies are in the same industry and are approximately the same size. The following information relates to each company and was taken from their annual reports.

	Shryock	Shreck
Sales	$1,000,000	$1,100,000
Cost of goods sold	710,000	770,000
Gross profit	320,000	330,000
Beginning inventory	180,000	185,000
Ending inventory	200,000	225,000
Beginning LIFO reserve	95,000	
Ending LIFO reserve	110,000	

Required:

a. Compute the inventory turnover ratio and the gross profit percentage for each company. How do the ratios for the two companies compare? Does one of the companies look more attractive as an investment? Why?

b. Using the LIFO reserve recalculate the gross profit, ending LIFO inventory, the inventory turnover, and gross profit percentage for Shryock.

c. How do the two companies compare based on the information presented after adjusting the inventories for the LIFO reserve?

12-53 The Benny Blades Company and the Emeril Behar Company both began operation on January 2, 2005. Both companies experienced exactly the same reality during 2005: They purchased exactly the same number of units of merchandise inventory during the year at exactly the same cost, and they sold exactly the same number of inventory units at exactly the same selling price during the year. They also purchased exactly the same type and amount of property, plant, and equipment and paid exactly the same amount for those purchases.

At the end of 2001, the two companies prepared income statements for the year. Blades reported net income of $92,000 and Behar reported net income of $55,000.

Required:

List and discuss all items you can think of that might have caused the reported net income for the two companies to differ.

LO 1–6
Comprehensive

12-54 Pete Rush and Company is a merchandiser. The company's accounting records yielded the following schedule for October 2005:

		Units	Cost
	Beginning inventory, October 1	200	$ 600
+	Purchases during October	1,700	5,100
=	Goods available for sale	1,900	$5,700
	Cost of goods sold	1,500	4,500
=	Ending inventory, October 31	400	$1,200

LO 1–6
Comprehensive

On October 31, 2005, the company conducted a physical count of its inventory and discovered only 375 units of inventory actually on hand.

Required:

a. Show Rush's schedule of cost of goods sold and ending inventory as it should be, to reflect the results of the physical inventory count on October 31.

b. Explain how the company's income statement and balance sheet will be affected by changes you made in part a.

c. What are some possible causes of the difference between the inventory amounts in the company accounting records and the inventory amounts from the physical count?

LO 7
Comprehensive

12-55   Go to the The Kroger Co. Web site at *www.kroger.com* and locate the annual report. Read the accounting policies note for inventories and depreciation of property, plant, and equipment.

Required:

a. What inventory method does Kroger use?
b. What depreciation method(s) does Kroger use for plant and equipment?
c. Estimate the remaining life of its depreciable assets.
d. Explain how the information contained in the accounting policies note might help the average investor or lender.

LO 7
Comprehensive

12-56   Go to the Adolph Coors Company Web site at *www.coors.com* and locate the annual report.

Required:

a. Look up the notes to financial statements. Read the summary of significant accounting policies section to find the methods used for inventory evaluation and depreciation of property and equipment.
b. Calculate the change in the inventory turnover ratio and days inventory when you convert LIFO to FIFO. Is the difference material in amount?
c. Estimate the average remaining life of the depreciable assets. Looking at the cash flow statement, do you think Coors will be able to replace its assets from operations or will it be required to borrow?

LO 7
Comprehensive

12-57   Go to the following Web sites to find the annual reports for JCPenney at *www.jcpenney.com* and Sears at *www.sears.com*

Required:

Both companies use LIFO inventory and straight-line depreciation. From information contained in the financial statements, answer the following questions for each company:

a. For property, plant, and equipment:
  1. Estimate the remaining life of depreciable assets.
  2. Do you think they will have to borrow for any future replacements of long-lived assets? Explain.
b. For inventory:
  1. Compute the gross profit percentage, inventory turnover, and days inventory as the statements are presented.
  2. Compute the gross profit percentage, inventory turnover, and days inventory after converting each company into FIFO inventory.
  3. Describe the difference in the ratios between LIFO and FIFO. What do the differences, or lack thereof, tell you about each company?
c. If you could select only one of the companies for your portfolio, which would you choose? Explain your rationale.

To investigate more about Pepsi, go to its Web site at *www.pbg.com*.

12-58   Comprehensive Ethics

The following appears in the 2001 annual report for the Pepsi Bottling Group, Inc.:

Note 3: Comparability of Results

Asset Lives

At the beginning of fiscal year 2000, we changed the estimated useful lives of certain categories of assets primarily to reflect the success of our preventive maintenance programs in extending the useful lives of these assets. The changes, which are detailed in the table below, lowered total depreciation cost by approximately $69 million, or $0.13 per diluted share in 2000. In 2001, we are utilizing the same asset lives as in 2000.

Estimated Useful Lives *in years*	2000	1999
Manufacturing equipment	15	10
Heavy fleet	10	8
Fountain dispensing equipment	7	5
Small specialty coolers and specialty marketing equipment	3	5 to 7

Reported net income and earnings per share for three years were:

Year	Net Income	Basic ESP
2001	$305,000,000	$1.07
2000	$229,000,000	$0.78
1999	$118,000,000	$0.46

Required:

a. Assume that you are a lender processing a loan for the Pepsi Bottling Group. How would you use this information?
b. What accounting concept(s) did the company violate when it made the changes? In this case, are the violation(s) acceptable? Why or why not?
c. Was the company's action unethical? Why or why not?
d. Was the company required to make this disclosure? Explain.

12-59 The CEO of Barnes, Inc. is concerned about repaying a bank loan due this year. The CFO instructs the chief accountant to reduce depreciation expense by 50%. He instructs the accountant to change the estimated lives of the assets and salvage values to accomplish this reduction. The CFO believes the increased net income will make the bank loan committee willing to renegotiate the existing loan.

 Ethics

Required:

a. Were the actions of the CFO unethical? Explain.
b. What would the chief accountant have to do to the salvage values and estimated lives to accomplish the CFO's request?
c. If you were the chief accountant, how would you respond to the CFO?

CHAPTER 13

LEARNING OBJECTIVES

After completing this chapter you should be able to:

1 Determine the role of ethics in business reporting and the implications of the Sarbanes-Oxley Act of 2002.

2 Understand the information found in a typical annual report and required in the Form 10-K.

3 Gather information about a company and obtain an annual report.

4 Decipher items found on balance sheets and in the notes to financial statements of large or complex companies.

5 Explain why recurring and nonrecurring items are presented separately on the income statement.

6 Interpret the net of tax disclosure of extraordinary items, discontinued operations, and accounting changes on the income statement.

7 Discuss the importance of skepticism in using financial information.

External Reporting for Public Companies

After unprecedented growth in the 1990s, the U.S. stock market has had a difficult time in the new millennium. Although many people blame personal greed, corporate greed, fraud, and/or audit failures, the truth is that these and many other social, economic, and political factors contributed to the problem as well. The U.S. Congress created the SEC in 1934 to prevent abusive practices and give investors and stockholders comprehensive information about companies. The SEC, however, cannot require investors to study public information about a company before making the decision to invest. Day trading became one of those factors in the unparalleled increase in stock market prices during the 1990s. It seems doubtful that most day traders conducted detailed studies of the companies' management integrity and the fairness of the financial information provided by the companies in which they traded. Many of the day traders subjected themselves to the very risks Congress tried to protect them from when it created the SEC.

Although we cannot be sure of every factor that contributed to the stock market's problems, ignorance about the companies did not have to be one. Remember that the financial statements for firms that have declared bankruptcy reflected economic difficulties, unless management prepared fraudulent financial statements that their auditors either failed to uncover or uncovered but ignored. For example, Kmart Corporation's financial decline was evident from three to five years before the company filed for Chapter 11 bankruptcy.

Visit **www.prenhall.com/terrell** to view the "McDonald's International" video.

Visit **www.kmart.com** to view Kmart's annual reports.

Visit **www.amazon.com** to read the financial history of the company in their financial statements.

Most of the dot-com firms that collapsed had never shown a profit. A company that has never shown a profit is probably not a good investment. Amazon.com is one of the companies that may have survived the dot-com disaster. It may, however, depend on your perspective. If you had bought Amazon.com stock when it was issued in 1997 at $1 per share and you sold on March 5, 2004, for $44, you would have experienced a 44-fold profit in seven years. If, however, you had purchased stock in 1999 when the price was $112, you would have experienced an 61 percent decline. Many investors believed Amazon.com would be the International Business Machines Corporation (IBM) or Microsoft Corporation success story of the new century. By the end of 2001, when the price was less than $5 per share, investors simply hoped it would survive.

To fight ignorance about the financial health of a company, one step is to locate and read its entire annual report. It contains a wealth of information, both written and implied.

Let's see how to go about it.

Format of 10-K Forms

Visit the SEC Web site to obtain information on many companies.

The SEC requires public companies to file an annual Form 10-K along with quarterly 10-Q forms. It also requires the company to send an annual report to its stockholders. All three of these reports are public information that can be obtained in a variety of ways. Today, most firms have their annual report and SEC filings available for download from their Web sites. The SEC has a public Web site at *www.freeedgar.com*. Through that site, you can view the public filings for each of the more than 15,000 companies registered with the SEC.

According to the Office of Management and Budget, the Form 10-K requires an average of 430 hours to complete. It consists of the four parts detailed in Exhibit 13-1. The SEC requires management to include the annual report sent to stockholders. Because both have common elements, the Form 10-K can refer to the annual report,

Exhibit 13-1
Summary of Form 10-K

> **SUMMARY OF FORM 10-K**
>
> **PART I:** Discussion of the business, its properties, any legal proceedings, and submission of matters to a vote of security holders.
>
> **PART II:** Market of common equity and stockholder matters, selected financial data, management's discussion and analysis of financial condition and operating results, disclosure about market risk, financial statements and supplementary data, and changes in and disagreements with accountants on financial disclosure.
>
> **PART III:** Directors and executive officers, executive compensation, security ownership by certain owners and management, and related-party transactions.
>
> **PART IV:** Exhibits, financial statement schedules, and reports in Form 8-K.

thus eliminating duplicate work. Likewise, smaller companies frequently send the Form 10-K with a glossy cover and additional information to stockholders in lieu of a traditional annual report.

Reporting Scandals

Since trade began, some businesspeople have used unethical business practices. In England in 1700, when the first stock companies were formed, the South Seas Company scandal so shook the faith of many in this new form of business ownership that England banned the sale of stock for a century. Three hundred years later, unethical business behavior still exists.

Why do some managers cheat, lie, and steal? Most do so to achieve a personal goal of success or to accumulate wealth. Two of the most visible cases of the past few years illustrate distinctly different roads to disaster and demonstrate how critically important it is for management and auditors to maintain the highest level of ethical standards.

The Enron Corp. Case

During the 1990s, Enron, an energy trading company, was soaring to new heights of success. Its managers could see no end in sight. But when success inevitably became harder to sustain, management began to engage in creative financing that skirted legal boundaries. Apparently ignoring any unethical aspects of its actions, Enron's financial reporting also broke the substance-over-form rule of accounting, which requires that a firm's financial statements be representationally faithful in reporting the true effect of transactions. Enron's gas futures contracts created future liabilities that might cause significant future losses. At first, management structured the contracts to follow the letter of the law, using narrowly applied accounting rules that allowed the company to report the liabilities off the balance sheet in the notes to the financial statements. Eventually, managers failed to comply with the specific accounting rules, but they continued to report as if they had complied. The result of all these fraudulent activities was tremendous inflation of Enron's profits and underreporting of its liabilities. When the gas markets dropped dramatically, Enron incurred all the possible losses and the institution collapsed.

Big Five accounting firm Arthur Andersen LLP was Enron's auditor, but unfortunately also served as Enron's consulting firm for technology and other business concerns. Because its consulting relationship with Enron was so lucrative for the accounting firm, Andersen lost its objectivity and independence at some point in its accounting dealings with Enron, and it either contributed to the unethical financial reporting or conveniently ignored its client's ethical lapses.

When members of Andersen's Houston office eventually discovered the reporting problems at Enron in 2002, the accounting firm went to the SEC, blew the whistle, and began to restate its client's financial statements for the past few years in an effort to correct the fraudulent reporting. Enron soon collapsed into bankruptcy. When it looked as if Andersen might be implicated in the commission of the frauds, the Houston office began to shred evidence to protect itself. This action cast serious doubts on the credibility and integrity of the Houston office.

The WorldCom, Inc. Case

Instead of hiding liabilities off the balance sheet and inflating revenues as Enron did, WorldCom, the nation's second largest domestic long-distance telephone carrier, now known as MCI, decided to increase assets and reduce expenses to inflate its net income while it was slowly sliding toward bankruptcy. Over a period of three years, WorldCom apparently recorded more than $9 billion of false assets to reduce expenses and show small profits. Because the "assets" consisted of buried communications cables and lines, it was not easy to physically observe them.

As the auditor for WorldCom, Andersen appeared to put too much faith in its client's integrity and did not probe deeply enough to discover the fraud. It remains to be seen whether Andersen's failure represented professional negligence or consummate incompetence, but in either case Andersen obviously breached its standards of due professional care.

The Enron and WorldCom cases illustrate the need for accountants and auditors to adhere to their strict code of conduct. The SEC sanctioned a handful of unscrupulous or negligent auditors, and it finally suspended Andersen's license to work for SEC clients. A once proud and respected century-old firm disintegrated within a few months, leaving thousands of its innocent employees without jobs and helping to destroy the public trust accountants are required to protect.

The Sarbanes-Oxley Act of 2002

The Sarbanes-Oxley Act of 2002 created the Public Companies Accounting Oversight Board (PCAOB). The PCAOB sets standards of conduct and approves all accounting firms who can audit SEC-regulated companies. To gain approval, large firms must have their audit practices inspected annually, small firms triennially. The PCAOB is proving itself to be very strict. The efforts of members of the profession, the AICPA, the SEC, and the PCAOB have succeeded in restoring public confidence in CPAs. Speaking in February 2004, AICPA Chairman Scott Voynich stated that CPAs enjoyed their highest-ever ratings for public trust, even higher than before the Enron and WorldCom scandals.

The Sarbanes-Oxley Act of 2002 increased management's responsibility for the representational faithfulness of the financial statements of public companies. According to the act, the CEO and CFO of the company must certify each 10-K and 10-Q form, declaring that:

1. they have reviewed the statements and there is no material untrue or omitted information that would mislead readers;
2. the financial statements present fairly the financial condition and operating results of the company; and
3. they have carefully reviewed the internal controls for effectiveness to ensure that material information is known.

The act makes it illegal for any officer or director to mislead, coerce, influence, or manipulate an auditor of the financial statements. The CEO or CFO must also forfeit any stock option or incentive-based income or profits made on stock for one year following the issuance of incorrect financial statements. Time will tell if the new rules make corporate officers and directors think seriously before issuing financial statements that might be tainted with fraud or incorrect information. Knowledge of accounting rules and principles will be more valuable than ever.

Increased Ethics

The Sarbanes-Oxley Act assigns direct responsibility to the officers and directors of public companies for honesty in financial reporting. Will it lead to increased levels of corporate ethical behavior? Cynics say no. Optimists believe it will. If you recall, the ACFE believes that some people are honest all the time, some are never honest, and the majority of people are honest most of the time. People who are never honest will not suddenly become ethical in their corporate dealings. If those people who are mostly honest think much harder before doing anything that might remotely be considered illegal or unethical, the Sarbanes-Oxley Act may prevent fraud and reduce the amount of fudging in the gray areas.

Some managers have played the game of doing as much as they can to manipulate the financial statements, believing that if the auditors could not find it, they were out of danger of being caught. The Sarbanes-Oxley Act requires each company to adopt a code of ethics for the CFO, controller, and chief accountant. In addition, the **audit committee**, a subcommittee of the board of directors that hires and works with the independent auditor, must have at least one member who is a financial expert. The SEC, likewise, must review each company's filings at least once every three years. Currently, the SEC reviews mostly smaller companies and companies with questionable reporting in the past. The added mandatory reviews may discourage intentional misrepresentations because the odds of detection will rise dramatically.

● **audit committee**
A subcommittee of the board of directors that hires and works with the independent auditor.

One additional factor may help the reliability of public financial statements. For the last three decades, auditors have looked for laborsaving techniques to reduce the amount of time required to determine the fairness of management's financial statements. Clients pressured accountants to reduce audit fees because many felt that the audit was a necessary but expensive nuisance that added no value to the company. Some audit firms tried to perform value-added audits to give management feedback about the effectiveness of their strategic planning. But many firms simply used more audit detection software programs to reduce the labor costs of performing the audit. Enron and WorldCom, among others, lie in the wake of such thinking. Many auditors will revisit more old-fashioned, labor-intensive audit techniques to substantiate the integrity of the general audit software in determining errors and manipulations.

What happens when the auditor believes that management should report differently than the statements read? The auditor's objective is to express an opinion on the overall fairness of the financial statements. The auditor is bound by the Code of Professional Conduct and must follow the standards established by the Auditing Standards Board of the AICPA.

The AICPA Code of Professional Conduct consists of principles and rules. The principles include responsibilities, public interest, integrity, objectivity and independence, and due care in the performance of professional services. The rules set forth the conduct that conforms with and breaches those principles. Remember from Chapter 1 that auditors are expected to be independent of the client for whom they perform their services. Auditors must also maintain a confidential relationship with respect to their clients, observe a high degree of integrity and objectivity, and follow strict guidelines when advertising their professional services. CPAs working as independent auditors must also refrain from accepting contingent fees or commissions for referral services.

So, back to the question, what happens when the auditor, bound by all these rules, disagrees with the client? He or she has a major dilemma—whether to uphold professional ethics or to please the client. The only course of action open to an ethical auditor is to persuade the client to change the report or to issue a qualified or adverse opinion. In hindsight, auditors for WorldCom and Enron should clearly see the errors of their actions.

The major reporting instrument for the shareholders is the annual report. The Sarbanes-Oxley Act also affects the annual report.

What Do You Think?

13-1   What effect do you believe the Sarbanes-Oxley Act will have on corporate reporting during the next five years? After five years? Why?

13-2   What effect do you believe the Sarbanes-Oxley Act will have on the behavior of corporate officers and directors during the next five years? After five years? Why?

Format of Annual Reports

No two annual reports are exactly alike. Some imitate comic books, coloring books, magazines, file folders, owner's manuals, or small books. Some include discs, coupons, mouse pads, or phone cards. Lengths vary from 30 to 100 pages. Exhibit 13-2 lists the common elements found in an annual report. Those items marked with a bullet are required by the SEC; many of these are also included in the Form 10-K.

The Sarbanes-Oxley Act added a requirement for a management report on internal control that assesses the effectiveness of the internal control structure and the company's procedures for financial reporting. The independent auditor must also attest to the validity of management's assessment of its internal control.

Many of the items contained in an annual report you will recognize and understand easily. Let's discuss some of the less familiar ones.

Five-Year Selected Financial Data

Visit IBM's Web site at **www.ibm.com** to learn more about the company.

Some companies' annual reports, such as Family Dollar Stores, Inc., and Wal-Mart Stores, Inc., give more than five years of selected financial data. Family Dollar provides 10 years and Wal-Mart 11 years. The SEC only requires five. Most of the information provided concerns elements of the income statement and major items on the balance sheet. These are the elements that most financial analysts use for ratio or trend analysis. Exhibit 13-3 contains the five-year financial data for IBM.

Exhibit 13-2
Annual Report Common Elements

ANNUAL REPORT COMMON ELEMENTS

   Letter to shareholders from the chairman, CEO, or president
- Brief description of the business
   Financial Highlights
   Promotional information about the company, customers, products, supply chain, and locations
- Five-Year Selected Financial Data
- Management's Discussion and Analysis of financial condition, operating results, and internal control
- Independent Auditors' Report
- Consolidated Statement of Earnings for three years
- Consolidated Balance Sheet for two years
- Consolidated Statement of Cash Flows for three years
- Consolidated Statement of Shareholders' Equity for three years
- Notes to Consolidated Financial Statements
- Three-year financial information about industry segments and geographical segments
- Quantitative and qualitative disclosures about market risk
- Directors' and officers' identity, occupation, and principal employer
- Markets in which the company's securities are traded
- High and low market prices for each quarter of the most recent two years
- Dividends paid on common stock for the two most recent years
- An offer to provide a free copy of the 10-K to shareholders unless the report contains all disclosures of the 10-K

* = Elements required by the SEC.

Exhibit 13-3
IBM Five-Year Selected Financial Data

Five-Year Comparison of Selected Financial Data

International Business Machines Corporation and Subsidiary Companies

(dollars in millions except per share amounts)

FOR THE YEAR:	2003	2002	2001	2000	1999
Revenue	$ 89,131	$ 81,186	$ 83,067	$ 85,089	$ 83,334
Income from continuing operations	7,613	5,334	8,146	7,874	7,359
(Loss)/income from discontinued operations	(30)	(1,755)	(423)	219	353
Net income	7,583	3,579	7,723	8,093	7,712
Earnings/(loss) per share of common stock:					
Assuming dilution:					
Continuing operations	4.34	3.07	4.59	4.32	3.93
Discontinued operations	(0.02)	(1.01)	(0.24)	0.12	0.19
Total	4.32	2.06	4.35	4.44	4.12
Basic:					
Continuing operations	4.42	3.13	4.69	4.45	4.06
Discontinued operations	(0.02)	(1.03)	(0.24)	0.12	0.20
Total	4.40	2.10	4.45	4.58 *	4.25 *
Cash dividends paid on common stock	1,085	1,005	956	909	859
Per share of common stock	0.63	0.59	0.55	0.51	0.47
Investment in plant, rental machines and other property	4,398	5,022	5,660	5,616	5,959
Return on stockholders' equity	29.9 %	15.5 %	35.3 %	40.0 %	39.1 %
AT END OF YEAR:					
Total assets	$ 104,457	$ 96,484	$ 90,303	$ 90,412	$ 89,571
Net investment in plant, rental machines and other property	14,689	14,440	16,504	16,714	17,590
Working capital**	7,098	7,502	7,484	7,474	3,577
Total debt	23,632	26,017	27,151	28,576	28,354
Stockholders' equity	27,864	22,782	23,448	20,550	20,426

* Does not total due to rounding.
** Prior years reclassified to conform with 2003 presentation.

What Do You Think?

13-3 Do you notice anything unusual about the balance sheet amounts in Exhibit 13-3? If so, do you assume there is an error?

13-4 When you find information in an annual report that does not seem to be correct, where do you look to confirm your suspicion or allay your fears?

Management Discussion and Analysis

The SEC requires that management discuss the company's financial results presented in the annual report. The management discussion and analysis (MD&A) frequently represents management's best effort to tell its story positively in three to five pages of the report. The disclosures frequently include additional statistics and information not found in the financial statements or in the notes to the financial statements. Financial statement users should always read the MD&A for a more complete, although possibly biased, picture of the company. If the user's perceptions of the financial statements vary measurably from management's, it might indicate that management is less than honest about the company's financial picture. Independent auditors do not express an opinion on the MD&A.

Industry and Geographical Segments

To learn more about Altria Group, Inc. visit its Web site at *www.altria.com*.

Many large public companies operate in more than one industry. Consider, for example, the Altria Group, Inc., formerly known as Phillip Morris Companies, Inc. It operates in six industry or geographical segments including food, tobacco, beer, and financial services. Exhibit 13-4 contains information from a section of *Note 14. Segment Reporting* in the notes to financial statements for 2003. Most would agree, these are diverse groups. You recall from our discussions of financial statement analysis, ratio comparisons are made to industry standards. For a company such as Altria Group, to what industry do you compare? The segment information allows an analyst to compare the profitability ratios for each segment to the correct industry.

Disclosures about Risk

A public company must make disclosures about four types of risk that might significantly affect the amounts reported on the current financial statements. Such disclosures describe the risks associated with the:

1. nature of its operations;
2. use of estimates to prepare accrual financial statements;
3. use of certain estimates that on occurrence of future events have a reasonable possibility of making a material change to the current statements within a short period of time; and
4. vulnerability due to concentrations of customers, revenues, suppliers, or geographical area.

Let's examine each of these types of risks.

Nature of Operations

To learn more about Coors, visit its Web site at *www.coors.com*.

Some industries are more vulnerable to legal problems, societal changes, political disfavor, or consumer boycott. Alcohol-related businesses were declared illegal during Prohibition between World War I and World War II. Adolph Coors Company survived

Exhibit 13-4
Altria Group, Inc. Segment Information

Note 14			
Segment Reporting:			
Segment data were as follows:			
(in millions)	**2003**	2002	2001
Net revenues:			
Domestic tobacco	**$17,001**	$18,877	$19,902
International tobacco	**33,389**	28,672	26,517
North American food	**21,907**	21,485	20,970
International food	**9,103**	8,238	8,264
Beer		2,641	4,791
Financial services	**432**	495	435
Net revenues	**$81,832**	$80,408	$80,879
Earnings before income taxes, minority interest and cumulative effect of accounting change:			
Operating companies income:			
Domestic tobacco	**$ 3,889**	$5,011	$ 5,264
International tobacco	**6,286**	5,666	5,406
North American food	**4,920**	4,953	4,796
International food	**1,282**	1,330	1,239
Beer		276	481
Financial services	**313**	55	296
Amortization of intangibles	**(9)**	(7)	(1,014)
General corporate expenses	**(771)**	(683)	(766)
Operating income	**15,910**	16,601	15,702
Gain on Miller transaction		2,631	
Interest and other debt expense, net	**(1,150)**	(1,134)	(1,418)
Earnings before income taxes, minority interest and cumulative effect of accountingchange	**$14,760**	$18,098	$14,284

this period by continuing to produce and market malt, an ingredient used in brewing beer. Coors marketed malt for malted milk shakes, candy, and other baking uses. It also produced glass bottles for milk and even glassware for home use. In the last quarter of the 20th century, tobacco companies faced drastic reductions in demand in the United States and looked to foreign markets for sales. Tobacco companies merged with companies in other industry segments to protect themselves. Environmentalists frequently target businesses that endanger the environment, such as the tuna companies that were targeted because they inadvertently trapped dolphins in their nets. Some tuna cans now have a picture of a dophin and the words "Dolphin Safe." Countries have been boycotted because of their political views or for the inhumane treatment of its citizens. Some mutual funds restrict their investments to companies that do not deal with abusive governments, harm the environment, or sell tobacco products or other controversial products and services.

Use of Estimates in Financial Statements

Visit *www.buckle.com* to learn more about The Buckle's operations.

As you learned in Chapter 6, making adjustments for accrual accounting frequently requires using estimated amounts. Estimates are carefully made so that any differences are minor and do not affect the integrity of the statements. Most companies include a statement similar to that in Exhibit 13-5 from The Buckle, Inc.'s note to financial statements, January 31, 2004. The risk of misstating the financial statements in a significant way using such estimates should be remote.

Use of Significant Estimates

To learn more about this issue, go to *www.ford.com* and *www.bridgestone.com*. News accounts are also available on the Web.

Companies sometimes encounter major events that require the estimation of losses and liabilities. The exact amount of the final loss may not be known for several years. GAAP require that losses be reported as soon as they can be estimated. Consider the recent problem with Bridgestone/Firestone tires and Ford Explorers. At stake were the replacement of tires, auto design questions, wrongful death and injury claims, and vehicle replacements and repairs. Because many lawsuits had been and would be filed, final determination of liability could not be known at December 31, 2000. Ford Motor Company management contended that the problem was tires alone, and therefore belonged to Bridgestone Corporation. Ford made no loss accrual. Bridgestone accrued a loss of $754 million and included a two-page note disclosure in its annual report on the state of the lawsuits and recall of the tires. It stated:

> *However, there can be no assurance that BFA [Bridgestone/Firestone Affiliates] will be able to resolve product liability suits and claims as currently envisioned and, accordingly, the ultimate liability could be higher. . . . in the opinion of management, the ultimate disposition of these product liability suits and claims could possibly be material to the results of the operations in any one accounting period but will not have a material adverse effect on either BFA's or the Company's consolidated financial position or liquidity.*

In 2001, Bridgestone accrued another $661 million loss after settling litigation with the U.S. Attorney General representing all 53 jurisdictions. A 2002 loss left Bridgestone with $132 million net income and more than $6 billion in net worth. Ford and Bridgestone have severed relations and Bridgestone will no longer supply tires for Ford in the Americas after existing contracts expire. Although the 2001 estimate of loss was only about half of the eventual loss, management's risk analysis was basically correct that additional losses were not anticipated to have a material adverse effect on liquidity or financial position.

Exhibit 13-5
The Buckle, Inc. Note Disclosure for the Use of Estimates

> **Use of Estimates** >> The preparation of financial statements in conformity with accounting principles generally accepted in the United States of America requires management to make estimates and assumptions that affect the reported amounts of assets and liabilities and disclosure of contingent assets and liabilities at the date of the financial statements and the reported amounts of revenues and expenses during the reporting period. Actual results could differ from these estimates.

What Do You Think?

13-5 Ford and Bridgestone/Firestone have blamed each other for the failure of the tires on the Ford Explorer. If another brand of tires subsequently failed on the Explorer and Ford were found to be responsible for part of the tire failure, should Ford estimate the liability in that year? Why or why not?

13-6 If Ford were found liable for defective vehicle design, how could the amount of the loss logically be estimated?

Concentrations of Risk

Concentrations of risk represent a lack of diversification in customers, revenues, markets, suppliers, or customers' ability to pay, which increases the risk of failure because a particular group of companies fails to perform their part of contracts. Most large companies manage such risks by diversifying customer bases and products, granting credit only to customers with high credit ratings and using multiple suppliers. Smaller companies may not have that luxury and are therefore more vulnerable to failure.

A good example of a smaller company is Claire's Stores, Inc., a retailer of fashion accessories with stores in many mall locations throughout the United States, Canada, the Caribbean, Europe, and Japan. In its February 1, 2003, annual report, Claire's management reports a long list of risk factors for its business, as follows.

Certain Risk Factors Relating to Our Business

- Fluctuations in consumer preference and economic conditions affect the demand of our products.
- Purchases in advance of merchandise inventory, excessive markdowns, interruptions in distribution and material inventory shrinkage may negatively impact our profitability.
- A disruption of imports from our foreign suppliers may increase our costs and reduce our supply of merchandise.
- Fluctuations in same-store net sales may affect the price of our stock.
- Store operations and expansion may affect our ability to increase net sales and operate profitability.
- The failure to execute our international expansion or successfully integrate our international operations may impede our strategy of increasing net sales and adversely affect our operating results.
- The useful life and value of our goodwill and intangible assets will continue to be reevaluated and could result in a write-down of our goodwill and intangible assets in a future period.
- Changes in the anticipated seasonal business pattern could adversely affect our sales and profits, and our quarterly results may fluctuate due to a variety of factors.
- Our industry is highly competitive.
- A decline in number of people who go to malls could reduce the number of our customers and reduce our net sales.
- The recent terrorist attacks have heightened security concerns and could result in lower customer traffic in our stores.
- We depend on key personnel.

● concentrations of risk
A lack of diversification in customers, revenues, markets, suppliers, or customers' ability to pay, which increases the risk of failure because a particular group of companies fails to perform their part of contracts.

Visit Claire's Web site at *www.clairestores.com* to learn more about its operations and read the full text of its risk factors.

- Litigation matters incidental to our business could be adversely determined against us and our insurance coverage may not be adequate to protect our assets and operations.
- The price of our stock may fluctuate in the future.
- Control by our chairman.
- Our wage expenses may increase as a result of increases in federal minimum wage laws.

As you can see, they have listed almost every conceivable risk factor. Most companies do not provide such an exhaustive list of risk factors. Claire's disclosure seems to provide for almost any risk of failure. It may be that the management is risk averse and has gone overboard in identifying risk factors to protect itself.

You will find that annual reports contain a great deal of information about a company. As you examine the financial statements, you will probably find items that we have not discussed in previous chapters. These items appear on the financial statements of large public companies, and we will discuss these individually.

Accounting Elements Found on Complex Corporations' Financial Statements

Public companies frequently engage in complex transactions that create accounts not usually found in smaller firms. As we explore these accounting elements, we will look at each financial statement, beginning with the balance sheet.

Balance Sheet Accounts

Marketable Securities and Investments

When a company has cash that exceeds its current operating needs, its management often invests the cash in **marketable securities**, which are government or corporate bonds and stocks of other corporations. Management invests in securities for three purposes:

1 short-term use of excess cash,
2 long-term use of excess cash, and
3 to own significant investments in other firms

Management classifies the investments as either current or noncurrent assets. Current investments in marketable securities can be classified as either trading securities or available-for-sale securities. **Trading securities** are debt and equity securities traded on organized exchanges that management has intentions of selling within a very short time. **Available-for-sale securities** are debt and equity securities traded on organized exchanges that management may keep for an indefinite time. Exhibit 13-6 reproduces the current asset section of the balance sheet for Nathan's Famous, Inc., a restaurant group found in airports, universities, stadiums, and theaters. It also includes the note disclosure that explains the types of investment, bonds, and partnership interests, as well as the cost, fair market value, and any unrealized holding gains and losses.

Noncurrent investments include two types of securities. The first is **held-to-maturity securities**, investments in corporate or government bonds that management intends to hold until the bonds mature. Management can also make long-term investments in the equity of another company. The investment may be an influential or

● marketable securities
Government or corporate bonds and stocks of other corporations.

● trading securities
Debt and equity securities traded on organized exchanges that management has intentions of selling within a very short time.

● available-for-sale securities
Debt and equity securities traded on organized exchanges that management may keep for an indefinite time.

To see the entire annual report, visit **www.nathansfamous.com**.

● held-to-maturity securities
Investments in corporate or government bonds that management intends to hold until the bonds mature.

Exhibit 13-6

Nathan's Famous, Inc. & Subsidiaries Marketable Securities Disclosure

CONSOLIDATED BALANCE SHEETS
(in thousands, except share amounts)

	March 30, 2003	March 31, 2002
ASSETS		
Current Assets		
Cash and cash equivalents	$ 1,415	$ 1,834
Marketable securities and investment in limited partnership	4,623	8,819
Notes and accounts receivable, net	2,607	2,808
Inventories	389	592
Assets available for sale	799	1,512
Prepaid expenses and other current assets	642	1,269
Deferred income taxes	2,079	1,747
Total current assets	12,554	18,581

Nathan's Famous, Inc. & Subsidiaries 2003 Annual Report   12 / 13

Note E—Marketable Securities and Investment in Limited Partnership

The cost, gross unrealized gains, gross unrealized losses and fair market value for marketable securities by major security type at March 30, 2003 and March 31, 2002 are as follows:

	Cost	Gross Unrealized Gains	Gross Unrealized Losses	Fair Market Value
2003:				
Available for sale securities:				
Bonds	**$ 4,513**	**$181**	**$ (71)**	**$ 4,623**
2002:				
Trading securities:				
Bonds	$7,821	$ —	$(20)	$7,801
Investment in limited partnership	1,020	—	(2)	1,018
	$8,841	$ —	$(22)	$8,819

Proceeds from the sale of available for sale and trading securities and the resulting gross realized gains and losses included in the determination of net income are as follows:

	2003	2002	2001
Available for sale securities:			
Proceeds	$6,088	$ —	$ —
Gross realized gains	12	—	—
Gross realized losses	(2)	—	—
Trading securities:			
Proceeds	$ 767	$2,933	$2,564
Gross realized gains	—	8	—
Gross realized losses	(252)	(1)	(2)

Effective April 1, 2002, the Company transferred the Company's bond portfolio formerly classified as trading securities to available for sale securities due to a change in the Company's investment strategies. As required by FASB Statement No. 115, "Accounting for Certain Investments in Debt and Equity Securities," the transfer of these securities between categories of investments has been accounted for at fair value and the unrealized holding loss previously recorded before April 1, 2002 of $20 from the trading category has not been reversed. The unrealized gain for the fiscal year ended March 30, 2003 totaling $64 net of income taxes has been included as a component of comprehensive income. Investments classified as trading securities are recorded at fair value and the unrealized gains or losses are recognized as a component of investment and other income in the consolidated statement of operations. During the fiscal year ended March 30, 2003, the Company liquidated its investment in limited partnership and received proceeds of $767 and recorded a loss of $252 which is included as a component of investment and other income in the accompanying consolidated statement of operations for the fiscal year ended March 30, 2003.

● influential investment
Represents an ownership interest sufficient to influence, but not control, the decision-making process of the investee firm.

● controlling investment
Investor has an ownership interest greater than 50 percent of the outstanding stock and controls the decision-making process in the investee firm.

● consolidated financial statements
The combined statements of two or more entities that comprise one economic entity as defined by the economic entity assumption.

● minority interest in consolidated subsidiaries
The equity of other owners, outside of the consolidated entity, in the subsidiaries the parent company controls.

Visit *www.world.sony.com* to see the whole balance sheet and its note disclosure about minority interests.

● operating lease
A lease that gives the lessee control of an asset for only a portion of its useful life and is treated as rent expense.

● capital lease
A lease that gives the lessee the primary incidents of ownership such that the substance of the transaction is an asset purchase financed by the long-term lease instrument.

Visit *www.famousdaves.com* to look at the entire annual report.

controlling interest of that firm. An **influential investment** represents an ownership interest sufficient to influence, but not control, the decision-making process of investee firm. Influential investments appear in the noncurrent section of the balance sheet. A **controlling investment** indicates that the investor has an ownership interest greater than 50 percent of the outstanding stock and controls the decision-making process in the investee firm.

When a company owns a controlling interest in another firm, the financial statements are consolidated. When you see the terms *consolidated balance sheet, consolidated statement of income*, or **consolidated financial statements**, you recognize that these are the combined statements of two or more entities that comprise one economic entity as defined by the economic entity assumption. You will not, however, see the investment of a controlled firm on the consolidated statements because the assets and liabilities of the controlled, or subsidiary, firm are added to the balance sheet of the controlling, or parent firm. One item you might see on a consolidated balance sheet is the **minority interest in consolidated subsidiaries**, an amount that represents the equity of other owners, outside of the consolidated entity, in the subsidiaries the parent company controls. Such amounts represent the claims of the outside owners against the consolidated assets. You find the amounts listed between the liabilities and stockholders' equity sections on the balance sheet. Exhibit 13-7 shows Sony Corporation's liabilities and equity section in its March 31, 2004 balance sheet. Notice the minority interest indicated just before the stockholders' equity section. Owners outside Sony Corporation have a $220 million claim on the consolidated assets of $87,410 million.

Leased Assets

Leases are of two types. A lease may be classified as an operating lease or it may be a capital lease. An **operating lease** gives the lessee control of an asset for only a portion of its useful life and is treated as rent expense. An operating lease is not reported on the balance sheet because it only represents a monthly expense the business entity must pay, such as when management rents an office for three years.

Contrast this with a firm that leases a new building for its remaining useful life under a capital lease. The **capital lease** gives the lessee the primary incidents of ownership such that the substance of the transaction is an asset purchase financed by the long-term lease instrument. Therefore, not only is the capital lease reported as an asset, but also the lease liability is reported on the balance sheet. The expense of using the asset appears as depreciation on the income statement.

Some firms prefer to report a lease as an operating lease to keep the liability off the balance sheet. You must be careful in reading all notes regarding leases to understand the operation of the entity, and when comparing two companies in the same industry, it is critical to understand the total obligations for leases assumed by each company. Consider, for example, Famous Dave's of America, Inc. Exhibit 13-8 on page 514 contains the balance sheet and accompanying notes for a sale-leaseback and the lease liability. The balance sheet indicates that Famous Dave's owns $47,147,000 of plant, property, and equipment net of accumulated depreciation; a $4,500,000 financing lease obligation, and a $105,000 lease obligation. Note 7 explains the $4.5 million financing lease obligation arises from the sale of three restaurant buildings, which were immediately leased back by the company. Because the substance of the lease was a loan, using the buildings as collateral, the company elected to treat the transaction as a loan, regardless of the lease form of the transaction. The note also contains the minimum payments required by the "lease" and indicates that the company treats the payments as interest on the loan and continues to depreciate the building.

According to Note 8, Famous Dave's also uses lease financing for leasehold improvement and equipment that cost $4.3 million with accumulated depreciation of $3.7 million. The total payments due in the next five years are $530,000 including $37,000 of interest. The principal of the future payments total $493,000, of which

Exhibit 13-7
Sony Corporation Partial Consolidated Balance Sheet

Consolidated Balance Sheets

Sony Corporation and Consolidated Subsidiaries - March 31

	Yen in millions		Dollars in millions (Note 3)
	2003	2004	2004
LIABILITIES AND STOCKHOLDERS' EQUITY			
Current liabilities:			
Short-term borrowings (Note 11)	¥124,360	¥91,260	$878
Current portion of long-term debt (Notes 8, 11 and 13)	34,385	383,757	3,690
Notes and accounts payable, trade (Note 6)	697,385	778,773	7,488
Accounts payable, other and accrued expenses (Notes 5 and 14).	864,188	812,175	7,809
Accrued income and other taxes	109,199	57,913	557
Deposits from customers in the banking business (Note 12)	248,721	378,851	3,643
Other (Notes 20 and 23)	356,810	479,486	4,610
Total current liabilities	2,435,048	2,982,215	28,675
Long-term liabilities:			
Long-term debt (Notes 8, 11 and 13)	807,439	777,649	7,477
Accrued pension and severance costs (Note 14)	496,174	368,382	3,542
Deferred income taxes (Note 20)	159,079	96,193	925
Future insurance policy benefits and other (Note 10)	1,914,410	2,178,626	20,948
Other	255,478	286,737	2,758
	3,632,580	3,707,587	35,650
Minority interest in consolidated subsidiaries	22,022	22,858	220
Stockholders' equity (Note 15):			
Subsidiary tracking stock, no par value–			
Authorized 100,000,000 shares, outstanding 3,072,000 shares	3,917	3,917	38
Common stock, no par value–			
2003–Authorized 3,500,000,000 shares, outstanding 922,385,176 shares	472,361		
2004–Authorized 3,500,000,000 shares, outstanding 926,418,280 shares		476,350	4,580
Additional paid-in capital	984,196	992,817	9,546
Retained earnings	1,301,740	1,367,060	13,145
Accumulated other comprehensive income –			
Unrealized gains on securities (Note 7)	17,658	69,950	672
Unrealized losses on derivative instruments (Note 13)	(4,793)	(600)	(6)
Minimum pension liability adjustment (Note 14)	(182,676)	(89,261)	(858)
Foreign currency translation adjustments	(302,167)	(430,048)	(4,135)
	(471,978)	(449,959)	(4,327)
Treasury stock, at cost			
(2003 – 1,573,396 shares, 2004 – 2,468,258 shares)	(9,341)	(12,183)	(117)
	2,280,895	2,378,002	22,865
Commitments and contingent liabilities (Notes 8 and 23)			
	¥8,370,545	¥9,090,662	$87,410

The accompanying notes are an integral part of these statements

Exhibit 13-8
Famous Dave's of America, Inc. and Subsidiaries Abbreviated Balance Sheet and Note Disclosure for Leases

FAMOUS DAVE'S OF AMERICA, INC. AND SUBSIDIARIES
CONSOLIDATED BALANCE SHEETS
DECEMBER 28, 2003 AND DECEMBER 29, 2002
(in thousands, except per share date)

ASSETS	2003	2002
Current Assets	$16,350	$13,550
Property, equipment and leasehold improvements, net	47,147	51,861
Other Assets	10,270	9,406
	$73,767	$74,817

LIABILITIES AND SHAREHOLDERS' EQUITY		
Current Liabilities	$ 7,309	$ 7,781
Long-term debt, less current obligation	12,349	12,422
Capital leases, less current portion	105	432
Financing leases	4,500	4,500
Other liabilities, net	2,632	2,390
Total liabilities	$26,895	$27,525
Commitments and contingencies (note 16)		
Shareholders' equity	46,872	47,292
	$73,767	$74,817

FAMOUS DAVE'S OF AMERICA, INC. AND SUBSIDIARIES
NOTES TO CONSOLIDATED FINANCIAL STATEMENTS
DECEMBER 28, 2003, DECEMBER 29, 2002 AND DECEMBER 30, 2001

(7) FINANCING LEASE OBLIGATION
We have a $4.5 million financing obligation involving three existing restaurants as a result of a sale/leaseback transaction. Under this financing, we are obligated to make monthly interest payments of $42,917 (which increases 4.04% every two years) for a minimum of 20 years. We have the option to purchase the leased restaurants for the greater of $4.5 million or fair market value of the properties at the date of purchase at any time or renew the lease for two additional five-year terms. Based upon our continued involvement in the leased property and its purchase option, the transaction has been accounted for as a financing arrangement. Accordingly, the three existing restaurants are included in property, equipment and leasehold improvements and are being depreciated, and a portion of the monthly payments are accounted for as interest expense in the consolidated statements of operations. The principal financing lease obligation payment of $4.5 million is due in March 2019.

(8) CAPITAL AND OPERATING LEASE OBLIGATIONS
Our assets under capital leases consist of agreements for furniture, equipment and leasehold improvements. Capital leases outstanding under this agreement bear interest at an average rate of 8.1% and expire through February 2006. The obligations are secured by the property under lease. Total cost and accumulated amortization of the capital leased assets were approximately $4.3 million and $3.7 million at December 28, 2003, and approximately $4.3 million and $2.8 million at December 29, 2002, respectively.

We have various operating leases for existing and future restaurants and corporate office space with lease terms ranging from 3 to 35 years, including lease options. Eight of the leases require percentage rent of between 3% and 7% of annual gross sales, typically above a natural breakeven point, in addition to the base rent. All of these leases contain provisions for payments of real estate taxes, insurance and common area maintenance costs. Total occupancy lease cost for fiscal years 2003, 2002 and 2001, including rent, common area maintenance costs, real estate taxes and percentage rent, was approximately $5.6 million, $4.6 million, and $4.3 million, respectively. Percentage rent was approximately $128,000, $145,000 and $188,000 for fiscal years 2003, 2002 and 2001, respectively.

Future minimum lease payments existing at December 28, 2003 were:

Fiscal Year	Operating Leases	Capital Leases
2004	$ 2,530,000	$ 418,000
2005	2,587,000	104,000
2006	2,674,000	8,000
2007	2,666,000	—
2008	2,639,000	—
Thereafter	31,72 ,000	—
Total future minimum lease commitments	$44,823,000	$ 530,000
Less: Interest at 4.9% - 15.4%		37,000
Total capital lease obligations		$ 493,000

$389,000 is due in the next fiscal year. These carefully explained notes to the financial statements let the reader understand the nature of the obligations and the accounting treatment Famous Dave's used.

What Do You Think?

13-7   After reading Famous Dave's Note 7, why do you think the balance sheet shows a $4.5 million liability for the financing lease obligation? Be specific in your reasoning.

13-8   How much of the financing liability from question 13-7 is a current obligation? Why?

13-9   Famous Dave's Note 8 indicates that $418,000 of the capital lease obligation is currently due. Where is that shown on the balance sheet?

Goodwill

Goodwill represents the excess paid for the assets of another entity over and above the fair market value of those assets. Goodwill is an intangible asset that exists in many businesses, but, according to GAAP may be recorded only when it is purchased. If you think about the name recognition of McDonald's Corporation, you immediately realize the market value associated with the name. This represents an element of goodwill to the company, but would never be recorded unless McDonald's sold the restaurants and its name to The Walt Disney Company. Disney would record the goodwill it paid in excess of the market value of the net assets. Management tests the value of goodwill at least once each year to determine if its value is impaired, and if so, its loss in value must be treated as an impairment loss and reduce the value of goodwill on the balance sheet.

● **goodwill**
The excess paid for the assets of another entity over and above the fair market value of those assets.

Exhibit 13-9 contains Sony's 2003 note about goodwill. Sony determined that its indefinite life assets, including purchased goodwill, had suffered no impairment in value and did not write them down. Impairment losses appear on the income statement as part of operating expenses.

Deferred Income Taxes

Deferred income taxes represent either an asset or a liability to the organization. **Deferred income taxes** arise because the tax laws in effect for any year often differ from GAAP, which dictate how the financial statement information is to be reported. A common difference between income tax laws and GAAP occurs in the computation of depreciation. Companies often report accelerated depreciation on the income tax return compared to straight-line depreciation on the financial statements. This will provide for a temporary lowering of the income taxes in the early years and will subsequently be reversed in the later years of life of the asset. By using accelerated depreciation for the income tax return, the entity is only delaying for a period of time the taxes it otherwise would have paid if it had used the straight-line method of depreciation for tax purposes. As a result the company will report an amount of deferred taxes as a liability on the balance sheet that will ultimately be paid in later years.

● **deferred income taxes**
Liabilities that arise because the tax laws in effect for any year often differ from GAAP, which dictate how the financial statement information is to be reported.

A company can also pay income taxes in advance and have a deferred tax asset. This occurs, for example, when a company receives rent in advance and must pay income taxes on the receipt before recognition in the income statement. Exhibit 13-10 contains the note disclosure for Darden Restaurants, Inc. for fiscal year 2003. Darden has both deferred tax assets and liabilities. The note describes how the current and deferred taxes are computed on the income statement and details the amounts of timing differences for both deferred tax assets and deferred tax liabilities for the balance sheet. Exhibit 13-11 includes sections of the 2003 income statement and balance sheet. As you can see, the note disclosure details the $115,488 shown on the income statement and $101,331 (net) on the balance sheet.

Go to **www.darden.com** to view the entire annual report for Darden Restaurants, Inc.

Exhibit 13-9
Sony Corporation Partial Balance Sheet and Note Disclosure for Goodwill

---

Sony Corporation Annual Report 2003

Consolidated Balance Sheets
March 31

	Yen in millions		Dollars in millions
	2002	2003	2003
Other assets:			
Intangibles, net	233,088	**258,624**	**2,155**
Goodwill, net	317,240	**290,127**	**2,418**

9. Goodwill and intangible assets   to

Intangible assets acquired during the year ended March 31, 2004 totaled ¥35,840 million ($345 million), which are subject to amortization and primarily consist of music catalogs of ¥2,526 million ($24 million), acquired patent rights of ¥7,903 million ($76 million) and software to be sold, leased or otherwise marketed of ¥13,632 million ($131 million). The weighted average amortization period for music catalogs, acquired patent rights and software to be sold, leased or otherwise marketed is 21 years, 8 years and 3 years, respectively.

Intangible assets subject to amortization comprise the following:

	Yen in millions				Dollars in millions	
	March 31				March 31,	
	2003		2004		2004	
	Gross carrying amount	Accumulated amortization	Gross carrying amount	Accumulated amortization	Gross carrying amount	Accumulated amortization
Artist contracts	¥89,078	¥(69,281)	¥80,675	¥(68,300)	$776	$(657)
Music catalog	120,242	(48,447)	109,795	(47,610)	1,056	(458)
Acquired patent rights	46,758	(18,024)	52,996	(23,172)	510	(223)
Software to be sold, leased or otherwise marketed	17,848	(7,267)	31,983	(13,577)	308	(131)
PlayStation format	11,873	(7,719)	11,873	(10,094)	114	(97)
Other	45,257	(20,499)	43,175	(17,328)	414	(166)
Total	¥331,056	¥(171,237)	¥330,497	¥(180,081)	$3,178	$(1,732)

The aggregate amortization expenses for intangible assets for the years ended March 31, 2002, 2003 and 2004 were ¥25,554 million, ¥27,871 million and ¥28,866 million ($278 million), respectively. The estimated aggregate amortization expense for intangible assets for the next five years is as follows:

	Yen in Millions	Dollars in Millions
Year ending March 31,		
2005	¥26,863	$258
2006	2 1,401	206
2007	13,958	134
2008	12,269	118
2009	11,705	113

Total carrying amount of intangible assets having an indefinite life comprise the following:

	Yen in Millions		Dollars in Millions
	March 31		March 31
	2003	2004	2004
Trademarks	¥57,410	¥57,384	$552
Distribution agreement	18,834	18,834	181
	¥76,244	¥76,218	$733

In addition to the amortizable and indefinite-lived intangible assets shown in the above tables, intangible assets at March 31, 2003 and 2004 also include unrecognized prior service costs totaling ¥22,561 million and ¥21,376 million ($206 million), respectively, which were recorded under FAS No. 87, "Employer's Accounting."

Exhibit 13-10
Darden Restaurants, Inc. Deferred Tax Liability Note Disclosure

NOTE 12
Income Taxes

The components of earnings before income taxes and the provision for income taxes thereon are as follows:

| | Fiscal Year | | |
	2003	2002	2001
Earnings before income taxes:			
U.S.	$345,496	$359,947	$296,160
Canada	2,252	3,362	5,058
Earnings before income taxes	$347,748	$363,309	$301,218
Income taxes:			
Current:			
Federal	$ 68,178	$ 88,063	$ 79,285
State and local	11,396	14,582	13,049
Canada	24	133	134
Total current	$ 79,598	$102,778	$ 92,468
Deferred (principally U.S.)	35,890	22,743	11,750
Total income taxes	$115,488	$125,521	$104,218

During fiscal 2003, 2002, and 2001, we paid income taxes of $65,398, $56,839, and $63,893, respectively. The following table is a reconciliation of the U.S. statutory income tax rate to the effective income tax rate included in the accompanying consolidated statements of earnings:

| | Fiscal Year | | |
	2003	2002	2001
U.S. statutory rate	35.0%	35.0%	35.0%
State and local income taxes, net of federal tax benefits	3.0	3.1	3.1
Benefit of federal income tax credits	(4.5)	(3.9)	(4.1)
Other, net	(0.3)	0.4	0.6
Effective income tax rate	33.2%	34.6%	34.6%

The tax effects of temporary differences that give rise to deferred tax assets and liabilities are as follows:

	May 25, 2003	May 26, 2002
Accrued liabilities	$ 12,616	$ 19,052
Compensation and employee benefits	55,935	52,804
Asset disposition and restructuring liabilities	2,004	2,584
Other	2,638	2,392
Gross deferred tax assets	$ 73,193	$ 76,832
Buildings and equipment	(116,148)	(93,752)
Prepaid pension costs	(25,987)	(18,096)
Prepaid interest	(1,454)	(3,478)
Deferred rent and interest income	(13,117)	(12,496)
Capitalized software and other assets	(16,115)	(12,127)
Other	(1,703)	(2,465)
Gross deferred tax liabilities	$ (174,524)	$(142,414)
Net deferred tax liabilities	$(101,331)	$(65,582)

Exhibit 13-11

Darden Restaurants, Inc. Balance Sheet and Income Statement Excerpts

Consolidated Statements of Earnings

	Fiscal Year Ended		
(In thousands, except per share data)	May 25, 2003	May 26, 2002	May 27, 2001
Earnings before income taxes	347,748	363,309	301,218
Income taxes	115,488	125,521	104,218
Net earnings	$ 232,260	$ 237,788	$ 197,000

Consolidated Balance Sheets

(In thousands)	May 25, 2003	May 26, 2002
ASSETS		
Current assets:		
Cash and cash equivalents	$ 48,630	$ 152,875
Short-term investments	–	9,904
Receivables	29,023	29,089
Inventories	173,644	172,413
Assets held for disposal	–	3,868
Prepaid expenses and other current assets	25,126	23,076
Deferred income taxes	49,206	52,127
Total current assets	$ 325,629	$ 443,352
LIABILITIES AND STOCKHOLDERS' EQUITY		
Total current liabilities	$ 639,909	$ 601,014
Long-term debt	658,086	662,506
Deferred income taxes	150,537	117,709
Other liabilities	19,910	19,630
Total liabilities	$ 1,468,442	$ 1,400,859

What Do You Think?

13-10 Refer to Exhibit 13-10. One of the highlighted sentences discloses the amount of taxes paid in each of the three years presented in the annual report. Where else would you expect to find this information? Go to the company's Web site to see if the disclosure is where you expect to find it.

13-11 The amounts of deferred tax assets and deferred tax liabilities in Exhibit 13-10 do not seem to agree with the amounts listed on the balance sheet in Exhibit 13-11 for either year. Does some relationship exist between the numbers?

The final disclosure we will examine is for pension liabilities.

Pension and Postretirement Benefits

When a firm offers employees compensation and benefits after retirement, it increases the current cost of employing those workers. When we apply the matching principle to current revenue, the expenses include foreseeable future costs earned by the current laborers for their current service. This includes employee benefits. Many firms offer a 401(k)-type of retirement plan. A 401(k) is a **defined contribution pension plan**, a plan that sets aside current dollars in an individual retirement account for an employee to accumulate over time to give the employee a pension fund at retirement. The amount of the retirement benefits depends on the amount accumulated through investments. The cost of such a benefit is easy to determine. The plan usually calls for a set percentage of each employee's total earnings for the year. So if a firm pays $2,000,000 in salaries and wages during a year and must contribute 10 percent to the pension plan for each employee, it must pay a total of $200,000 to the employees' pension accounts. If current costs are paid in a timely manner, no pension liability accrues.

Many firms adopt a **postretirement benefits plan** for employees that continues to pay medical and life insurance benefits for retirees, their survivors, or both. Those costs will be paid in the future, at amounts and for time periods that are currently unknown. Firms can also adopt a **defined benefit pension plan**, which gives an employee a pension at retirement of a certain monthly or annual benefit. For example, when you retire, you will receive 50 percent of the average of your highest three years' annual salary. If you are currently age 25 and you can retire at age 55, do you know now how much you will make during your highest three years of service? Management makes certain assumptions about the annual increase in wages and the amounts the pension fund can earn. They provide a pension consultant this information along with an employee census, containing the date of birth and length of service. The pension consultant uses actuarial science to combine these bits of data with mortality rates to determine the present value of a fund necessary to provide such benefits in the future.

The employees, the IRS, and the pension plan trustees must make sure that the defined benefit pension plan and postretirement benefit plan remain properly funded and actuarially sound so that the retirees will receive their promised benefits. GAAP requires that the notes to financial statements contain certain disclosures to allow readers to determine the soundness of each plan. The IRS requires similar disclosures be given, at least annually, to each participant. Exhibit 13-12 details the pension and postretirement benefits disclosure for Yum! Brands Inc. for 2003. Yum! is the parent company of Taco Bell, Kentucky Fried Chicken, and Pizza Hut.

Yum! has a defined benefit pension plan and a postretirement medical plan benefit plan. Notice, however, that the company has discontinued its plans for employees hired after September 30, 2001. The current expense for the pension plan and postretirement benefit plan amounts to $40 million and $8 million, respectively. The current value of the future benefits owed to pension plan participants total $629 million and the estimated liability for future medical benefits total $81 million. The fair value of the trust's plan assets is $251 million, and the postretirement medical costs are not funded. Does this mean that retirees must worry that the plan will fail for them? Not really. First, if all the currently covered employees quit on the balance sheet date, their accumulated benefits would amount to only $563, the accumulated benefit obligation. The benefit obligation of $629 is based on their projected future benefits. Second, the stock market suffered unusual losses in 2002 that may reverse in future years, improving the fair value of the plan assets. Third, companies are not required to fund postretirement benefits, so Yum! has done nothing wrong by not funding the medical plan. Finally, the plan requires the company to provide enough for future benefits. Security will rest in the integrity of the company. As you can see, the benefit obligation increased a great deal between 2002 and 2003, a normal phenomenon in defined benefit plans. New employees will not enjoy these same benefits, which may make the current plan participants more secure because new entrants would only make the funding needs increase.

- **defined contribution pension plan**
A pension plan that sets aside current dollars in an individual retirement account for an employee to accumulate over time to give the employee a pension fund at retirement. The amount of the retirement benefits depends on the amount accumulated through investments.

- **postretirement benefits plan**
A benefit plan for employees that continues to pay medical and life insurance benefits for retirees, their survivors, or both.

- **defined benefit pension plan**
A pension plan that gives an employee a pension at retirement of a certain monthly or annual benefit.

Visit the Web site at *www.yum.com* to learn more about the company.

Exhibit 13-12
Yum! Brands Inc. 2003 Pension and Postretirement Benefits Disclosure

NOTE 17   Pension and Postretirement Medical Benefits

Pension Benefits

We sponsor noncontributory defined benefit pension plans covering substantially all full-time U.S. salaried employees, certain hourly employees and certain international employees. The most significant of these plans, the YUM Retirement Plan (the "Plan"), is funded while benefits from the other plan are paid by the Company as incurred. During 2001, the Plan was amended such that any salaried employee hired or rehired by YUM after September 30, 2001 is not eligible to participate in the Plan. Benefits are based on years of service and earnings or stated amounts for each year of service.

Postretirement Medical Benefits

Our postretirement plan provides health care benefits, principally to U.S. salaried retirees and their dependents. This plan includes retiree cost sharing provisions. During 2001, the plan was amended such that any salaried employee hired or rehired by YUM after September 30, 2001 is not eligible to participate in this plan. Employees hired prior to September 30, 2001 are eligible for benefits if they meet age and service requirements and qualify for retirement benefits.

On December 8, 2003, the Medicare Prescription Drug, Improvement and Modernization Act of 2003 (the "Act"), which introduces a Medicare prescription drug benefit as well as a federal subsidy to sponsors of retiree health care benefit plans that provide a benefit that is at least actuarially equivalent to the Medicare benefit, was enacted. On January 12, 2004 the FASB issued Financial Staff Position No. 106a, "Accounting and Disclosure Requirements Related to The Medicare Prescription Drug, Improvement and Modernization Act of 2003" ("FSP 106a") to discuss certain accounting and disclosure issues raised by the Act. We have elected to defer the measurement and disclosure requirements under the provisions of FSP 106a until specific authoritative guidance is issued by the FASB later in 2004. The reported accumulated benefit obligation and net periodic benefit costs of our postretirement plan do not reflect the effects of the Act. The authoritative guidance, when issued, could require revisions to previously reported information. While we may be eligible for benefits under the Act based on the prescription drug benefits provided in our postretirement plan, we do not believe such benefits will have a material impact on our Consolidated Financial Statements.

We use a measurement date of September 30 for our pension and post-retirement medical plans described above.

Obligation and Funded status at September 30:

	Pension 2003	Benefits 2002	Postretirement Medical Benefits 2003	Postretirement Medical Benefits 2002
Change in benefit obligation				
Benefit obligation at beginning of year	$ 501	$ 420	$ 68	$ 58
Service cost	26	22	2	2
Interest cost	34	31	5	4
Plan amendments	—	14	—	—
Curtailment gain	(1)	(3)	—	—
Benefits and expenses paid	(21)	(16)	(4)	(3)
Actuarial loss	90	33	10	7
Benefit obligation at end of year	$ 629	$ 501	$ 81	$ 68
Change in plan assets				
Fair value of plan assets at beginning of year	$ 251	$ 291		
Actual return on plan assets	52	(24)		
Employer contributions	157	1		
Benefits paid	(21)	(16)		
Administrative expenses	(1)	(1)		
Fair value of plan assets at end of year	$ 438	$ 251		

Funded status	$(191)	$(250)	$(81)	$(68)
Employer contributions	—	25[a]	—	—
Unrecognized actuarial loss	230	169	28	18
Unrecognized prior service cost	12	16	—	—
Net amount recognized at year-end	$ 51	$ (40)	$(53)	$(50)

(a) Reflects a contribution made between the September 30, 2002 measurement date and December 28, 2002.

Amounts recognized in the statement of financial position consist of:

Accrued benefit liability	$(125)	$(172)	$(53)	$(50)
Intangible asset	14	18	—	—
Accumulated other comprehensive loss	162	114	—	—
	$ 51	$ (40)	$(53)	$(50)

Additional information

Other comprehensive loss attributable to change in additional minimum liability recognition	$ 48	$ 76

Additional year-end Information for pension plans with accumulated benefit obligations in excess of plan assets

Projected benefit obligation	$ 629	$ 501
Accumulated benefit obligation	563	448
Fair value of plan assets	438	251

While we are not required to make contributions to the Plan in 2004, we may make discretionary contributions during the year based on our estimate of the Plan's expected September 30, 2004 funded status.

Components of Net Periodic Benefit Cost

	Pension Benefits		
	2003	2002	2001
Service cost	$ 26	$ 22	$ 20
Interest cost	34	31	28
Amortization of prior service cost	4	1	1
Expected return on plan assets	(30)	(28)	(29)
Recognized actuarial loss	6	1	1
Net periodic benefit cost	$ 40	$ 27	$ 21
Additional loss recognized due to:			
Curtailment	$ —	$ 1	$ —
Special termination benefits	—	—	2

	Postretirement Medical Benefits		
	2003	2002	2001
Service cost	$ 2	$ 2	$ 2
Interest cost	5	4	4
Amortization of prior service cost	—	—	(1)
Recognized actuarial loss	1	1	—
Net periodic benefit cost	$ 8	$ 7	$ 5

Weighted-average assumptions used to determine the net periodic benefit cost for fiscal years:

	Pension Benefits			Postretirement Medical Benefits		
	2003	2002	2001	**2003**	2002	2001
Discount rate	**6.85%**	7.60%	8.03%	**6.85%**	7.58%	8.27%
Long-term rate of return on plan assets	**8.50%**	10.00%	10.00%	—	—	—
Rate of compensation increase	**3.85%**	4.60%	5.03%	**3.85%**	4.60%	5.03%

Prior service costs are amortized on a straight-line basis over the average remaining service period of employees expected to receive benefits. Curtailment gains and losses have generally been recognized in facility actions as they have resulted primarily from refranchising and closure activities.

Weighted-average assumptions used to determine benefit obligations at September 30:

	Pension Benefits		Postretirement Medical Benefits	
	2003	2002	**2003**	2002
Discount rate	**6.25%**	6.85%	**6.25%**	6.85%
Rate of compensation increase	**3.75%**	3.85%	**3.75%**	3.85%

Our estimated long-term rate of return on plan assets represents a weighted-average of expected future returns on the asset categories included in our target investment allocation based primarily on the historical returns for each asset category, adjusted for an assessment of current market conditions.

Assumed health care cost trend rates at September 30:

	Postretirement Medical Benefits	
	2003	2002
Health care cost trend rate assumed for next year	**12%**	12%
Rate to which the cost trend rate is assumed to decline (the ultimate trend rate)	**5.5%**	5.5%
Year that the rate reaches the ultimate trend rate	**2012**	2011

There is a cap on our medical liability for certain retirees. The cap for Medicare eligible retirees was reached in 2000 and the cap for non-Medicare eligible retirees is expected to be reached between the years 2007–2008; once the cap is reached, our annual cost per retiree will not increase.

Assumed health care cost trend rates have a significant effect on the amounts reported for our postretirement health care plans. A one-percentage-point change in assumed health care cost trend rates would have the following effects:

	1-Percentage-Point Increase	1-Percentage-Point Decrease
Effect on total of service and interest cost	$ —	$ —
Effect on postretirement benefit obligation	$ 4	$ (3)

Plan Assets

Our pension plan weighted-average asset allocations at September 30, by asset category are set forth below:

Asset Category	2003	2002
Equity securities	**65%**	62%
Debt securities	**30%**	37%
Cash	**5%**	1%
Total	**100%**	100%

Our primary objectives regarding the pension assets are to optimize return on assets subject to acceptable risk and to maintain liquidity, meet minimum funding requirements and minimize plan expenses. To achieve these objectives we have adopted a passive investment strategy in which the asset performance is driven primarily by the investment allocation. Our target investment allocation is 70% equity securities and 30% debt securities, consisting primarily of low cost index mutual funds that track several sub-categories of equity and debt security performance. The investment strategy is primarily driven by lower participant ages and reflects a long-term investment horizon favoring a higher equity component in the investment allocation.

A mutual fund held as an investment by the pension plan includes YUM stock in the amounts of $0.2 million and $0.1 million at September 30, 2003 and 2002 (less than 1% of total plan assets in each instance).

Let's take one last look at where pension and postretirement benefits appear on the financial statements. Exhibit 13-13 on page 522 shows Yum! Brands's Income Statement for 2003. The expenses of $40 million and $8 million are included in employee benefits costs in the "Costs and Expenses, net" section on the income statement. In the middle of the reconciliation of the funded status appears a section titled, "Amounts recognized in the statement of financial position consist of." It outlines three locations of amounts included on the balance sheet. The accrued benefit liabilities of $125 million and $53 million appear as part of other current and long-term liabilities. The intangible asset of $14 million is included in other intangible assets. The accumulated other comprehensive loss can be found, net of applicable taxes, on the statement of stockholders' equity. Unfortunately for the reader, no single amount is included on the balance sheet for pension and postretirement liabilities.

Now let's turn our attention to special items found on the income statements of many more complex firms.

Income Statement

Investors, lenders, and other income statement users expect some predictive value in the amount of net income, assuming that current net income reflects an achievable future income. This can only be true when the income statement contains nothing unusual. Unusual events occur, however, and accounting reporting rules clearly state what is considered recurring income and what is nonrecurring. GAAP identifies special items and three kinds of nonrecurring events that receive different treatment on an income statement.

Special Items

● **special items**
Events that are either unusual or not likely to recur and are disclosed separately in the operating expenses on the income statement.

Special items report events that are either unusual or not likely to recur and are disclosed separately in the operating expenses on the income statement. Exhibit 13-13 contains the income statement for Yum! for 2003. The highlighted line is labeled "AmeriServe and other charges (credits)." According to information provided in the notes to financial statements, these items include recoveries of previously recognized losses caused by the bankruptcy of a supplier, settlement costs of litigation, acquisition costs, and severance costs of closing certain support functions. Each of these items represent one-time events, but they are not unusual in nature. The separate reporting of these special items allows the reader to make decisions and judgments using the information.

Exhibit 13-13
Yum! Brands Inc. Income Statement for 2003

Consolidated Statements of Income

Fiscal years ended December 27, 2003, December 28, 2002 and December 29, 2001

(in millions, except per share data)	2003	2002	2001
Revenues			
Company sales	**$ 7,441**	$ 6,891	$ 6,138
Franchise and license fees	**939**	866	815
	8,380	7,757	6,953
Costs and Expenses, net			
Company restaurants			
Food and paper	**2,300**	2,109	1,908
Payroll and employee benefits	**2,024**	1,875	1,666
Occupancy and other operating expenses	**2,013**	1,806	1,658
	6,337	5,790	5,232
General and administrative expenses	**945**	913	796
Franchise and license expenses	**28**	49	59
Facility actions	**36**	32	1
Other (income) expense	**(41)**	(30)	(23)
Wrench litigation	**42**	—	—
AmeriServe and other charges (credits)	**(26)**	(27)	(3)
Total costs and expenses, net	**7,321**	6,727	6,062
Operating Profit	**1,059**	1,030	891
Interest expense, net	**173**	172	158
Income Before Income Taxes and Cumulative Effect of Accounting Change	**886**	858	733
Income tax provision	**268**	275	241
Income before Cumulative Effect of Accounting Change	**618**	583	492
Cumulative effect of accounting change, net of tax	**(1)**	—	—
Net Income	**$ 617**	$ 583	$ 492
Basic Earnings Per Common Share	**$ 2.10**	$ 1.97	$ 1.68
Diluted Earnings Per Common Share	**$ 2.02**	$ 1.88	$ 1.62

See accompanying Notes to Consolidated Financial Statements.

Nonrecurring Events

A **nonrecurring event** is an event that is both unusual in nature **and** not expected to recur. Nonrecurring events are separated from continuing income. Following are the three general types of nonrecurring items, listed in their order of presentation on the income statement:

● **nonrecurring event**
An event that is both unusual in nature **and** not expected to recur.

1 discontinued operations
2 extraordinary items
3 cumulative effect of changes in accounting principles

Proper classification of items as recurring or nonrecurring is critical to the usefulness of the accounting information. A company might be tempted to treat an item as nonrecurring because it reduces net income or to include an item with recurring revenues when it increases net income. To prevent companies from confusing the users of financial statements this way, the accounting profession restricts the items that may be considered nonrecurring. We will consider the criteria for each of these items after we discuss the income tax effects of these nonrecurring items.

Income Tax Disclosure. The income tax amount shown in the income from continuing operations section of the income statement is the amount of tax expense associated with the ongoing, recurring operation of the business. But how should a company disclose the income tax effect of the nonrecurring items shown on the income statement? The nonrecurring events cannot escape income tax consequences, and those consequences must be disclosed. Because we present nonrecurring items separately from continuing operations, lumping their tax effect with the tax expense shown for continuing operations would distort the information.

To illustrate this distortion, consider the 2003 income statement of Yum! Brands. Suppose in that same year, Yum! had a $950 million gain on a nonrecurring event and the income before taxes did not change. The following depicts how it would change the income statement if the tax were included with the income tax for continuing operations:

Single Income Tax Amount

(in millions)	
Income from continuing operations before tax	$ 886
Provision for income taxes*	588
Income from continuing operations	$ 298
Nonrecurring gain	950
Net income	$1,248

*Computed at 32.05%.

Contrast this approach with one that reports the nonrecurring event **net of tax**, which is the amount shown for a nonrecurring event that has been adjusted for any income tax effect.

● **net of tax**
The amount shown for a transaction that has been adjusted for any income tax effect.

Net of Tax Approach

(in millions)	
Income from continuing operations before tax	$ 886
Provision for income taxes*	284
Income from continuing operations	$ 602
Nonrecurring gain, net of $304 tax effect	646
Net income	$1,248

*Computed at 32.05%.

Reporting nonrecurring items leaves the income from continuing operations amount undisturbed, and reports the true amount of recurring income.

What Do You Think?

13-12 Using the preceding net of tax illustration, how much income tax expense would Yum! have theoretically incurred if it experienced a $950 million nonrecurring gain?

13-13 Is the amount you calculated in 13-12 the same as, greater than, or less than the amount in the single income tax amount illustration? Explain.

To eliminate any distortion or confusion, GAAP requires that the only tax expense shown on the income statement as a separate line item will be the amount associated with continuing operations. Therefore, the three major types of nonrecurring items included on the income statement are shown "less income tax effect," or "net of tax effect." The tax effect applies to both nonrecurring gains and losses.

● **discontinued operations**
The results of operations for a component of the company sold and any gain or loss from the actual disposal of the business component that are reported as a nonrecurring event on the income statement.

● **business component**
A portion of an entity whose assets, results of operations, and activities can be clearly distinguished, physically and operationally, and for financial reporting purposes, from the other assets, results of operations, and activities of the entity.

To learn more about Big Lots, Inc.'s disposal of KB Toys, visit *www.biglots.com*.

● **extraordinary event**
An event that is *both* unusual in nature and infrequent in occurrence for a specific entity.

Discontinued Operations. If a company disposes of a component of its business, the results of operations for the component of the company sold and any gain or loss from the actual disposal of the business component are reported as a nonrecurring event called **discontinued operations** on the income statement. The portion of the business being eliminated is considered a **business component,** provided that its assets, results of operations, and activities can be clearly distinguished, physically and operationally, and for financial reporting purposes, from the other assets, results of operations, and activities of the entity. For an example, consider the income statement of Big Lots, Inc. in Exhibit 13-14. The note disclosure describes the sale of KB Toys in fiscal year 2000. Part of the sale included an insurance claims liability Big Lots retained. In the fourth quarter of fiscal year 2001, the company discovered that the amount estimated in the 2000 loss on the disposal of the KB Toys division exceeded the actual claims by $8,480,000 and recorded a gain on the disposal for fiscal 2001. The income before discontinued operations for all years presented reflects the results of operations for Big Lots excluding any operations of the KB Toys division or its disposal loss.

Notice also that the disclosure includes the EPS for 2001 income before discontinued operations $(0.25), the discontinued operations $0.07, and net income $(0.18) for fiscal 2001. Stockholders find the EPS disclosures to be very helpful in their analyses.

Extraordinary Events. GAAP defines an **extraordinary event** as one that is *both* unusual in nature and infrequent in occurrence for a specific entity. The statement preparer must exercise judgment when deciding whether or not to classify the result of an event as an extraordinary event or a special event in continuing operations. When applying the criterion of "unusual in nature," the accountant must consider the operating environment of the business entity. The environment of an entity includes factors such as the characteristics of the industry or industries in which it operates, the geographical location of its operations, and the nature and extent of government regulation. Thus, an event or transaction may be unusual in nature for one entity but not for another because of differences in their respective environments (*APB Opinion No. 30,* paragraph 21). Therefore, a gain or loss that would be considered unusual for one company might be considered an ordinary event for another company. Accountants must also consider the operating environment of the entity when applying the criterion of "infrequent in occurrence." To be considered infrequent, an event must not be expected to recur in the foreseeable future. The following events or transactions meet the criteria of both unusual and infrequent and should therefore be presented as extraordinary items on the income statement:

● A hailstorm destroys a large portion of an orange grove in an area where hailstorms are rare.

Exhibit 13-14

Big Lots, Inc. Income Statement Disclosure for Discontinued Operations

Consolidated Statements of Operations

	Fiscal Year		
	2002	**2001**	**2000**
(In thousands, except per share amounts)			
Net sales	$ 3,868,550	$ 3,433,321	$ 3,277,088
Costs and expenses:			
Cost of sales	2,236,633	2,092,183	1,891,345
Selling and administrative expenses	1,485,265	1,368,397	1,200,277
Interest expense	20,111	20,202	22,947
	3,742,009	3,480,782	3,114,569
Income (loss) from continuing operations before income taxes	126,541	(47,461)	162,519
Income tax expense (benefit)	49,984	(18,747)	64,195
Income (loss) from continuing operations	76,557	(28,714)	98,324
Discontinued operations		8,480	(478,976)
Net income (loss)	$ 76,557	$ (20,234)	(380,652)
Income (loss) per common share — basic:			
Continuing operations	$ .66	$ (.25)	$ 88
Discontinued operations		.07	(4.30)
	$ .66	$ (.18)	$ (3.42)
Income (loss) per common share — diluted:			
Continuing operations	$ .66	$ (.25)	$ .87
Discontinued operations		.07	(4.26)
	$ .66	$ (.18)	$ (3.39)

The accompanying notes are an integral part of these financial statements.

- A tornado destroys a manufacturing company in northern California, where tornados have never occurred.
- A company operating a manufacturing plant in Ghana learns that the country will expropriate all foreign businesses in three months.
- An earthquake, rare in Louisiana, destroys one of the oil refineries owned by a large multinational oil company.

Because extraordinary events enter the income statement after income from continuing operations and discontinued operations, we present them net of tax. Examine Exhibit 13-15 to see how ExxonMobil disclosed an extraordinary gain in fiscal year 2001. ExxonMobil had gains in both 2001 and 2000. Notice that ExxonMobil treated

Visit ExxonMobil's Web site at
www.exxon.com.

Exhibit 13-15
ExxonMobil Disclosure of an Extraordinary Gain

Summary Statement of Income

	2003	2002	2001
		(millions of dollars)	
Revenues and other income			
Sales and other operating revenue (1)	237,054	200,949	208,715
Income from equity affiliates	4,373	2,066	2,174
Other income	5,311	1,491	1,896
Total revenues and other income	246,738	204,506	212,785
Costs and other deductions			
Crude oil and product purchases	107,658	90,950	92,257
Production and manufacturing expenses	21,260	17,831	17,743
Selling, general and administrative expenses	13,396	12,356	12,898
Depreciation and depletion	9,047	8,310	7,848
Exploration expenses, including dry holes	1,010	920	1,175
Merger related expenses	–	410	748
Interest expense	207	398	293
Excise taxes (1)	23,855	22,040	21,907
Other taxes and duties	37,645	33,572	33,377
Income applicable to minority and preferred interests	694	209	569
Total costs and other deductions	214,772	186,996	188,815
Income before income taxes	31,966	17,510	23,970
Income taxes	11,006	6,499	8,967
Income from continuing operations	20,960	11,011	15,003
Discontinued operations, net of income tax	–	449	102
Extraordinary gain, net of income tax	–	–	215
Cumulative effect of accounting change, net of income tax	550	–	–
Net income	21,510	11,460	15,320
Net income per common share (dollars)			
Income from continuing operations	3.16	1.62	2.19
Discontinued operations, net of income tax	–	0.07	0.01
Extraordinary gain, net of income tax	–	–	0.03
Cumulative effect of accounting change, net of income tax	0.08	–	–
Net income	3.24	1.69	2.23
Net income per common share – assuming dilution (dollars)			
Income from continuing operations	3.15	1.61	2.17
Discontinued operations, net of income tax	–	0.07	0.01
Extraordinary gain, net of income tax	–	–	0.03
Cumulative effect of accounting change, net of income tax	0.08	–	–
Net income	3.23	1.68	2.21

(1) Sales and other operating revenue includes excise taxes of $23,855 million for 2003, $22,040 million for 2002 and $21,907 million for 2001.

The information in the Summary Statement of Income shown above is a replication of the information in the Consolidated Statement of Income in ExxonMobil's 2004 Proxy Statement. For complete consolidated financial statements, including notes, please refer to pages A21 through A46 of ExxonMobil's 2004 Proxy Statement. See also management's discussion and analysis of financial condition and results of operations and other information on pages A6 through A19 of the 2004 Proxy Statement.

What Do You Think?

13-14   Determine whether each of the following would be an extraordinary or special event. Explain your reasoning.

(a) earthquake damage in Los Angeles
(b) flood damage in Iowa from the Mississippi River
(c) freeze damage to the strawberry crop in southern California
(d) hurricane damage to Corpus Christi, Texas
(e) hurricane damage to San Francisco, California
(f) fire damage in a paint manufacturing plant

13-15   Could the destruction of a manufacturing plant by fire or tornado ever create an extraordinary gain? Explain.

the extraordinary gains much like Big Lots treated the disclosures of the discontinued items, including separation from regular income and separate EPS. Were a firm to have both discontinued operations and an extraordinary gain or loss, the discontinued item would be listed first and the extraordinary event second. Each would have a separate EPS amount.

The final nonrecurring event is the cumulative effect of an accounting principle change.

Changes in Accounting Principles.   One important factor in the usefulness of accounting information is consistency. In Chapter 2 we discussed how the need for this quality discourages companies from randomly changing their accounting methods. However, business entities occasionally find it necessary to make changes. In fact, the FASB views changes in accounting principles or standards as part of accounting's natural progression.

Disclosure of the effects of these changes results in the third major type of nonrecurring item that is shown on the income statement net of tax: cumulative effect of a change in accounting principle. This nonrecurring item can result from either of two scenarios. Bear in mind, however, that in both cases the company must be changing from one acceptable accounting treatment to another acceptable treatment. The first scenario involves the adoption of a newly required accounting standard. When a company applies a new accounting method required by the implementation of a new FASB standard, net income is often adversely affected. This effect on net income must be reported in the year of implementation of the new rule. However, often the impact of a new standard is actually a cumulative effect, so the presentation represents how the new standard would have affected income if it had been in place throughout the life of the company. Whenever a new standard is implemented, the effect is considered to be a nonrecurring item and is presented net of tax on the income statement just before net income.

The second scenario occurs because a company has many acceptable choices to measure its transactions and events. A company may also choose to change from one acceptable method of accounting for an item to another acceptable method. For instance, in Chapter 12 we discussed two methods for calculating periodic depreciation expense—the straight-line method and the double-declining-balance method—and we presented three methods of accounting for the flow of inventory costs—FIFO, LIFO, and average cost. The choice among these methods can have a significant effect on reported net income for a period. Therefore, changes among these methods require proper presentation of the effect of the change on the income statement. The choice to change accounting methods should be made after careful consideration of all ramifications of such an action. Investors, creditors, the SEC, and the IRS are skeptical of companies that voluntarily change specific methods more than once.

The required presentation for a cumulative effect of a change in accounting principle is the same whether the change was caused by a new accounting rule or was a

To learn more about Snap-On
Incorporated, visit
www.snapon.com.

discretionary choice. Exhibit 13-16 contains an illustration of changes in accounting principles for Snap-On Incorporated that had not one but three changes in accounting principles. In fiscal year 2002 the company elected to adopt a new FASB standard for accounting for goodwill, which increased net income. The before- and after-tax amount of the cumulative effect was $2.8 million because the goodwill was not a tax-deductible item.

Exhibit 13-16
Snap-On Incorporated Change in Accounting Principle Disclosure

SNAP-ON INCORPORATED

Consolidated Statements of Earnings

(Amounts in millions except per share data)	2002	2001	2000
Net sales	$ 2,109.1	$ 2,095.7	$ 2,175.7
Cost of goods sold	(1,144.2)	(1,146.7)	(1,178.9)
Gross profit	964.9	949.0	996.8
Operating expenses	(799.2)	(848.7)	(792.6)
Net finance income	37.7	35.7	38.1
Restructuring and other non-recurring charges	(5.1)	(49.4)	(12.3)
Operating earnings	198.3	86.6	230.0
Interest expense	(28.7)	(35.5)	(40.7)
Other income (expense) — net	(8.4)	(3.5)	3.3
Earnings before income taxes	161.2	47.6	192.6
Income taxes	58.0	26.1	69.5
Earnings before cumulative effect of a change in accounting principle	103.2	21.5	123.1
Cumulative effect of a change in accounting principle, net of tax	2.8	(2.5)	25.4
Net earnings	$106.0	$19.0	$148.5
Net earnings per share — basic			
Earnings before cumulative effect of a change in accounting principle	$1.77	$.37	$2.11
Cumulative effect of a change in accounting principle, net of tax	.05	(.04)	.43
Net earnings per share — basic	$1.82	$.33	$2.54
Net earnings per share — diluted			
Earnings before cumulative effect of a change in accounting principle	$1.76	$.37	$2.10
Cumulative effect of a change in accounting principle, net of tax	.05	(.04)	.43
Net earnings per share — diluted	$1.81	$.33	$2.53
Weighted-average shares outstanding			
Basic	58.2	57.9	58.4
Effect of dilutive options	.3	.2	.2
Diluted	58.5	58.1	58.6
Pro forma amounts of a change in accounting for pensions in 2000			
Net earnings	$106.0	$19.0	$123.1
Net earnings per share — basic	1.82	.33	2.11
Net earnings per share — diluted	1.81	.33	2.10

See Notes to Consolidated Financial Statements.

In fiscal year 2001, the company elected to adopt a new FASB rule that changed its method of accounting for derivative instruments. A **derivative** is a security that has value based on another security or transaction, such as an option. An **option** is a contract to purchase something in the future at a guaranteed price. Frequently, companies offer employees stock options to purchase the company's stock at a reduced price. The option derives its value from the discount it will provide the option holder in purchasing the share of stock. The change to the new standards created a $4,100,000 loss recognition less its $1,600,000 tax savings.

In fiscal 2000, Snap-On changed a defined benefit pension plan to a defined contribution pension plan. The change reduced the accrued pension expense by $41,300,000 and increased income tax expense by $15,900,000. This change significantly affected net income and EPS in fiscal 2000, whereas the fiscal 2001 change made a minor change in the 2001 net income and EPS.

Let's also discuss another disclosure made on the Snap-On statement of earnings—diluted EPS.

● **derivative**
A security that has value based on another security or transaction, such as an option.

● **option**
A contract to purchase something in the future at a guaranteed price.

Diluted Earnings per Share

When a company such as Snap-On grants stock options to employees, those potential future shares of stock represent a dilutive threat to the shares current stockholders own. There are two fundamental types of **dilutive securities**, securities that will reduce the percentage of ownership of current stockholders—convertible securities and options. **Convertible securities** are bonds payable or preferred stock that owners may, at their option, convert to common stock. When option holders exercise their rights to buy shares or convertible securities, owners covert their securities into common shares, the earnings must then be shared among more stockholders, and the EPS will decrease. To clearly notify shareholders or investors of such a threat, the company reports **diluted earnings per share**, which indicates the potential impact of any issued dilutive securities on per share earnings. When we calculate the diluted EPS, we modify the formula as if the exercise or conversion took place in the beginning of the year.

Recall the EPS formula we introduced in Chapter 6:

$$EPS = \frac{\text{net income}}{\text{common stock outstanding shares}}$$

We will expand this equation to the **basic earning per share**, calculated based on conditions as they exist on the balance sheet date:

$$\text{Basic EPS} = \frac{\text{net income} - \text{preferred dividend requirements}}{\text{weighted average common stock outstanding}}$$

If we apply that to the earnings Snap-On reported, we see how management derived the basic EPS amount:

$$\text{Basic EPS} = \frac{\text{net income} - \text{preferred dividend requirements}}{\text{weighted average common stock outstanding}}$$

$$\text{Basic EPS} = \frac{\$106,000,000 - \$0}{58,200,000} = \$1.821 = \$1.82 \text{ per share}$$

Management provided the earnings and weighted average shares outstanding amounts on the earnings statement. The diluted EPS takes into account convertibles and options that will increase the number of shares outstanding, as follows:

$$\text{Diluted EPS} = \frac{\text{net income} - \text{preferred dividend requirements}}{\text{common stock outstanding assuming dilution}}$$

● **dilutive securities**
Securities that will reduce the percentage of ownership of current stockholders.

● **convertible securities**
Bonds payable or preferred stock that owners may, at their option, convert to common stock.

● **diluted earnings per share**
A calculation that indicates the potential impact of any issued dilutive securities on per share earnings.

● **basic earning per share**
An EPS calculation based on conditions as they exist on the balance sheet date.

Applied to Snap-On, we arrive at the following amount:

$$\frac{\text{Diluted}}{\text{EPS}} = \frac{106,000,000 - \$0}{58,200,000 + 300,000} = \$1.812 = \$1.81 \text{ per share}$$

You can compute both basic and diluted EPS for income before the cumulative effect of an accounting principle change with the same formula by substituting income before the extraordinary event for net income. Do the same for the effect of the discontinued operations, extraordinary events, and cumulative effect of accounting principles changes by omitting the preferred dividend requirements. To test this, apply the formulas to Snap-On's information as follows:

Income before extraordinary event:

$$\text{Basic EPS} = \frac{\$103,200,000 - \$0}{58,200,000} = \$1.773 = \$1.77 \text{ per share}$$

$$\text{Diluted EPS} = \frac{\$103,200,000 - \$0}{58,200,000 + 300,000} = \$1.764 = \$1.76 \text{ per share}$$

Cumulative effect of an accounting principle change:

$$\text{Basic EPS} = \frac{\$2,800,000 - \$0}{58,200,000} = \$.048 = \$.05 \text{ per share}$$

$$\text{Diluted EPS} = \frac{\$2,800,000 - \$0}{58,200,000 + 300,000} = \$.048 = \$.05 \text{ per share}$$

We can reconstruct Snap-On's final presentation on the earnings statement:

Net earnings per share — basic			
Earnings before cumulative effect of a change in accounting principle	$1.77	$.37	$2.11
Cumulative effect of a change in accounting principle, net of tax	.05	(.04)	.43
Net earnings per share — basic	$1.82	$.33	$2.54
Net earnings per share — diluted			
Earnings before cumulative effect of a change in accounting principle	$1.76	$.37	$2.10
Cumulative effect of a change in accounting principle, net of tax	.05	(.04)	.43
Net earnings per share — diluted	$1.81	$.33	$2.53

When you look at the Snap-On EPS amounts, it seems pointless to provide both computations. The amounts, when rounded, differed by only $0.01 or less, so could the company have presented only the basic EPS amounts? When, however, you examine the prior two years' results, you discover that the amounts are very different in 2000. Also, when you look at the amounts we calculated, you see that the options do have a dilutive effect on earnings, although the amounts are only one cent in 2002.

Snap-On provided the weighted average number of common shares outstanding. You can compute the weighted average shares by determining the number of shares outstanding at the beginning of the year, adjusting the number each time it changes, and weighting each number of shares by the length of time they are outstanding. Consider for example the Carter-Abshire Company. On January 1 it has 100,000 common shares outstanding. On April 1 and August 1 the company issues 20,000 new shares. Compute the weighted average as follows:

Date	(A) Number of Shares Outstanding	(B) Period of Time	(A) X (B)
January 1	100,000	3/12	25,000
April 1	120,000	4/12	40,000
August 1	140,000	5/12	58,333
	Weighted average shares		123,333

Investors and stockholders should use the diluted EPS from continuing operations for decision making. It represents the worst-case scenario about the earnings of the company.

We have examined many of the unusual items found on balance sheets. Before we conclude this chapter and the book, let's discuss one final topic—the need to be skeptical.

Be a Skeptical User of Financial Information

We hope that by this time you would not blindly invest your savings or retirement funds in stocks or bonds of any companies without using your newly acquired financial investigative tools. Please add a healthy dose of skepticism to your toolbox. Annual reports are usually written by company insiders who present the material in the most favorable way possible, so always read with a note pad in hand ready to take notes. Look for the following red flags:

- **Read the auditor's report for any explanatory paragraphs, adverse opinion, or refusal to express an opinion.** An adverse opinion indicates that the auditor has strong evidence that the statements do not present a fair financial picture. Refusal to express an opinion usually signifies that the company did not cooperate with the auditors. The only reason not to cooperate is to cover questionable accounting. If the auditor attached an explanatory paragraph to qualify the opinion, be sure to understand why it is included. For example, the Snap-On opinion had several explanatory paragraphs explaining the changes in accounting principles, two required by new FASB rules, another because the company adopted a new type of pension plan, and two to explain the change of auditors from Arthur Andersen LLP to Deloitte & Touche LLP. Andersen ceased operations after the fiscal year 2001 opinion was issued. None of these explanations would be alarming to readers if they carefully read the explanations.
- **Carefully read and analyze the financial statements, referring to the notes to the financial statements for clarification.** Make notes about your conclusions. Then, read the CEO's letter to the stockholders and compare it to the MD&A. Both of these company reports should give you the same impression of the company's operations for the year, so look for disparities between the two reports. Finally, compare the CEO's and management's analysis to yours. If you discover major differences, thoroughly investigate those differences. When you cannot understand the discrepancies, be wary.
- **Look at the five-year (or longer) sales trends of the company and the industry in which it operates.** Be suspicious of a company whose sales trend does not approximate the industry trend. How does the company explain the difference in the trend? Surprisingly enough, some companies have reported fraudulent sales and even paid income tax on them to falsely inflate stock prices. We are always amazed that a company can make people believe it is highly profitable even when no one they know uses its products. For example, say that a company reports sales sufficient to indicate that every U.S. household used at

least a dozen of its products each year. Yet when you go to your local store, its product is on clearance and neither you nor anyone you know has used even one during the past year. Something is probably wrong with the sales amounts reported.

● **See if a company has very little debt compared to other companies in its industry.** Look at the operating cash flows for the past 5 to 10 years. Have the operating cash flows been sufficiently positive to provide the funds necessary for expansion, to pay dividends to stockholders, and pay the principle on any long-term debt? If so, the low debt is probably justified. Be careful, however, to read carefully because the company might have hidden liabilities by not reporting them on the balance sheet. Remember Enron? Read the notes to financial statements carefully for terms such as *operating leases*, *special purpose entities, limited partnership interests*, and *joint ventures*. Those might be signs of off-balance-sheet financing.

● **Compute the ratios for the company and compare them to the industry averages.** Beware of a pattern of ratios that make no sense because none of them match the industry averages and the pattern is erratic. Most ratio analyses follow a rational pattern in which the company's strengths and weaknesses become evident. If the analysis makes no sense, something may be amiss.

Finally, remember the adage, "When it looks too good to be true, it probably is." Your common sense, armed with knowledge and understanding of the financial statements, will go a long way toward protecting you from poor investments.

CHAPTER SUMMARY

Two major consumers of corporate financial reports are stockholders and government regulators, most notably the SEC. The most comprehensive presentation of financial reporting to stockholders is the annual report. The SEC has specific disclosure requirements for information provided in the annual report and the Form 10-K, required annually for publicly traded companies. The SEC prescribes the rules for the form and content of the financial statements and other information included in the 10-K. The Sarbanes-Oxley Act of 2002 increased the management's responsibility for the financial statements and tightened the regulation of external auditors.

You can gather information about publicly traded companies on the Internet, in the library, or from news sources. Some of the special elements found in the annual report include five-year selected financial data, the management discussion and analysis (MD&A), industry and geographical segments, and disclosures of risk.

Balance sheets of large companies include several accounting elements not found in small companies. Marketable securities are temporary or long-term investments in debt and equity securities of other companies. Companies frequently use temporary investments to earn revenue on idle cash. Long-term equity investments often represent permanent investments in subsidiary companies.

Leased assets are often treated as if they were a purchase because the substance of the transaction is a financing arrangement. Assets leased for short periods are treated as operating leases and the cost is expensed as rent expense.

Goodwill represents the excess of the purchase price of a company over the market value of its net assets. A company must test the value of the goodwill each year for impairments to its value. If value is impaired, the company recognizes a loss from the impairment.

Deferred income taxes arise from differences in the tax rules and accounting rules and create timing differences in the recognition of revenues and expenses between tax reports and financial statements. Pension and postretirement benefits costs require lengthy note disclosure to assure participants that the company has recognized the current expense amounts and future liabilities for the benefits due the participants in defined benefit plans.

Income statements often include items that are not part of the company's normal operations and are not expected to recur. Inflows or outflows of this type must be separated from results of activities that are expected to recur as part of the company's normal, ongoing operations. A nonrecurring item that is unusual in nature or unlikely to recur, but not both, appears as a special item in the continuing operations section of the income statement. Three major types of nonrecurring items (discontinued operations, extraordinary items, and changes in accounting principles) are both unusual in nature and unlikely to recur and are presented after income from continuing operations and shown net of tax.

The income statement should contain EPS amounts for income from continuing operations, all nonrecurring items, and net income. If the company has convertible stocks, bonds, or options that are dilutive securities, it must report both basic and diluted EPS for all three types of income.

Users of financial statements should be skeptical of financial information. Any information that appears to be contradictory or unbelievable should be investigated carefully using financial analysis tools.

Visit the Web site *www.prenhall.com/terrell* for additional study help with the Online Study Guide.

REVIEW OF CONCEPTS

A Describe the importance of ethics in business reporting.

B Describe the information required in Form 10-K and how each item helps the user of the financial statements.

C Explain the impact of the Enron and WorldCom scandals on the accounting profession and investors' trust.

D Describe the implications of the Sarbanes-Oxley Act of 2002 for corporate officers and external auditors.

E Describe the typical format of the annual report and contrast it to the Form 10-K.

F Identify the basic information provided in the five-year selected financial data. Why do you think each item was included?

G Explain what is required in the management discussion and analysis section of the annual report. What level of skepticism should be attached to management's report?

H Discuss why the disclosures about the four types of risk are required of corporations.

I Explain the process a reader should use to understand items such as marketable securities, investments, and leased assets on the balance sheets and in the footnotes of complex companies.

J Explain the meaning of goodwill.

K Describe the meaning of deferred income taxes.

L Describe pension and postretirement benefits and explain what information their presentation in the notes to financial statements gives the readers.

M Define a special item and describe how to report it on the income statement.

N Compare the presentation of recurring and nonrecurring items on the income statement.

O Describe why extraordinary items, discontinued operations, and accounting changes are reported net of taxes on the income statement.

P Explain the type of transactions that cause discontinued operations, extraordinary items, and the cumulative effect of accounting changes to be reported on the income statement.

Q Discuss the importance of skepticism in the use of financial statements.

APPLICATION EXERCISES

LO 1
Financial Reporting

13-16 Your uncle, who owns a small business, knows that you are taking a course in accounting. He tells you that his banker is requiring that he provide audited financial statements for the last fiscal year. He does not understand why the bank is requiring this, and he asks you why they would want an audit of his financial statements. What do you tell him?

LO 2
Annual Reports

13-17 Following are the items the SEC requires to be included in the annual report, along with some items not required but normally included.

Required:

Identify each of the items as either required (R) or optional (O).

R = Required   O = Optional

a. _____ audited financial statements
b. _____ the principal market in which the securities of the firm are traded
c. _____ industry segment disclosures for the last three fiscal years
d. _____ the management report
e. _____ offer to provide a free copy of Form 10-K to shareholders on written request, unless the annual report complies with Form 10-K disclosure requirements
f. _____ report on corporate citizenship
g. _____ MD&A of financial condition and results of operations
h. _____ five-year selected financial data
i. _____ brief description of the business
j. _____ letter to the stockholders
k. _____ identification of directors and executive officers with the principal occupation and employer of each
l. _____ high and low market prices of the company's common stock for each quarter of the two most recent fiscal years and dividends paid on common stock during those years

LO 2
Annual Reports

13-18 Identify and describe the basic information one would expect to find in an annual report of a publicly traded company.

LO 2 and 3
Annual Reports

13-19 Use the information in the most recent annual report of GAP Inc. at *www.gap.com* to answer the following:

Required:

a. Which CPA firm audited the financial statements?
b. What type of opinion did the firm render?
c. Which paragraph of the audit report identifies the party responsible for the financial statements?
d. Which paragraph of the audit report identifies who is responsible for the audit of the financial statements?
e. Which paragraph of the audit report actually reports the expression of an opinion?

LO 2 and 3
Annual Reports

13-20 Use the information in the most recent annual report of the May Department Stores Company at *www.maycompany.com* to answer the following:

Required:

a. List the title of each financial statement included in the annual report.
b. Which financial statement lists the assets, liabilities, and stockholders' equity?
c. Which financial statement reports the sales, cost of goods sold, and the operating expenses?

13-21 Use the information contained in the most recent annual report of IHOP Corporation at *www.ihop.com* to answer the following:

LO 2 and 3
Annual Reports

Required:

  a. Who wrote the letter to the stockholders? In your opinion, what were the three most important messages in the letter?

  b. What are the segments of IHOP Corporation for reporting purposes? For each segment, calculate the percentage of income each provides to the corporation.

13-22 The Buckle sells clothing to young people in upscale malls around the nation. Known for its fashion sense, The Buckle has little debt, high profits, and a successful marketing strategy. Read the latest annual report of The Buckle at *www.thebuckle.com* to see if they make any mention of community service work or social responsibility.

LO 2 and 3
Financial Reporting
Cases

Required:

  a. What conclusions might you draw about The Buckle's social responsibility if you read The Buckle's annual report?

  b. List three questions you would ask The Buckle's president about the company's social responsibility if he came to the store where you were shopping.

  c. What advice would you give the president?

13-23 Use the information in the most recent annual report of Eastman Kodak Company at *www.kodak.com* to answer the following:

LO 2 and 3
Annual Reports

Required:

  a. Which CPA firm audited the financial statements?

  b. What type of opinion did the auditor firm render?

  c. Who does the audit report identify as the party responsible for the financial statements?

  d. Does the audit opinion contain an explanatory paragraph? If so, describe its meaning.

  e. What did the auditor report about the internal control of Kodak?

  f. Comment on Kodak's stability of earnings and operating cash flows over the past five years.

13-24 Locate the latest annual report of the Southwest Airlines Corporation at *www.southwest.com* and read the letter to the stockholders.

LO 2 and 3
Financial Reporting

Required:

  Summarize the main points of the CEO's message. Read the MD&A for any information that supports or fails to support the information the CEO provides. Discuss any variances between the two. In your opinion, did the CEO present the information in a way that unfairly created a favorable impression? If so, describe.

13-25 Locate the latest annual report of Disney at *www.disney.go.com* and read the letter to the stockholders.

LO 2 and 3
Financial Reporting
Cases

Required:

  Summarize the main points of the CEO's message. Read the MD&A for any information that supports or fails to support the information the CEO provides. Discuss any variances between the two. In your opinion, did the CEO unduly manipulate his information? If so, describe.

LO 2 and 3
Financial Reporting Cases

13-26 Locate the latest annual report of the Clorox Company at *www.clorox.com* and read the letter to the stockholders.

Required:

In what types of community projects does Clorox participate? What does this tell you about the culture of this company? Is this the type of company in which you would seek a career? Why or why not?

LO 2 and 3
Financial Reporting

13-27 Locate the latest annual report for the General Electric Company at *www.ge.com*. Read the disclosure about the risks the company faces.

Required:

After reading this disclosure prepare a brief summary of the risks GE is facing. How would those risks affect your decision of whether or not to invest in GE?

LO 2 and 3
Financial Reporting

13-28 Locate the latest annual report for the Boeing Company at *www.boeing.com*. Read the disclosure about the risks the company faces.

Required:

After reading this disclosure, prepare a brief summary of the risks facing Boeing. How would those risks affect your decision of whether or not to invest in Boeing?

LO 2 and 3
Financial Reporting

13-29 Locate the latest annual report for the JCPenney Company at *www. jcpenney.com* and for the Jim Walters Corporation at *www.jimwalterhomes.com*. Read the disclosure about the risks each company faces.

Required:

After reading these disclosures, prepare a brief summary comparing and contrasting the risks each company faces.

LO 3 and 4
Balance Sheet Items

13-30 Pick a company that you are interested in learning more about and obtain a copy of its latest annual report.

Required:

a. Read the footnote disclosures concerning marketable securities, goodwill, and leases as applicable.
b. Summarize the footnotes.
c. Describe how this information does or does not help you to understand this company better.

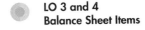

LO 3 and 4
Balance Sheet Items

13-31 Locate the latest annual report for the Motorola Company at *www.motorola.com*. Find the footnote disclosure for the pension plan and postretirement benefits.

Required:

a. What type of retirement plan does Motorola have for its employees?
b. Summarize the footnote.
c. Explain how the footnote helps you understand the pension plan that the company has for its employees and its pension liability.

13-32   Use the Internet to find the information necessary to complete this application exercise.

LO 3 and 4
Balance Sheet Items

Required:

   a. Pick two companies within the same industry and compare and contrast the information you find about each company with respect to each of the following:
      1. marketable securities and investments
      2. leased assets
      3. goodwill
      4. deferred tax assets and liabilities
   b. How has the information you discovered affected your opinions about each of these companies?

13-33   Locate the annual reports for 2002 and 2003 for Target Corporation at *www.target.com*.

LO 3, 5, and 6
Financial Reporting
Cases

Required:

   a. If Target is reporting any nonrecurring items on the income statement, identify them and explain the treatment on the income statement.
   b. If you were able to identify any nonrecurring items on the income statement, explain the net of tax disclosure treatment and the impact on the reported net income.

13-34   Locate the annual reports for 2002 and 2003 for the Hewlett-Packard Company at *www.hp.com*.

LO 3, 5, and 6
Financial Reporting
Cases

Required:

   a. If Hewlett-Packard is reporting any nonrecurring items on the income statement, identify them and explain the placement of these items on the income statement.
   b. If you were able to identify any nonrecurring items on the income statement, explain the net of tax disclosure treatment and the impact on the reported net income.

13-35   A client contacts you and asks you to advise him on a potential investment in the Lauer Company. On reviewing the ratios for Lauer, you noticed that many of the financial ratios were significantly higher than the industry averages and that the company's ratios had increased significantly over the previous year. You also investigated the industry and found that many companies within the industry were having a difficult year while Lauer was reporting record profits.

LO 7
Skepticism

Required:

   Explain to your client why you are skeptical of the information that you found regarding Lauer.

13-36   Using the library and the Internet, find articles detailing the downfall of WorldCom.

LO 7
Skepticism and Ethics

Required:

   a. Using the information you find, write a summary report explaining how the poor ethics of management brought about the collapse of the company.
   b. Examine the information to see what part the auditors' lack of skepticism, lack of ethics, or both might have played in the debacle.

LO 7
Skepticism and Ethics

13-37 Using the library and the Internet, find articles on the downfall of Global Crossings Corporation.

Required:

a. Using the information you find, write a summary report explaining how the poor ethics of management brought about the collapse of the company.
b. Examine the information to see what part the auditors' lack of skepticism, lack of ethics, or both might have played in the debacle.

LO 7
Skepticism and Ethics

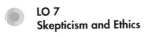

13-38 Using the library and the Internet, find articles chronicling the downfall of Enron.

Required:

a. Using the information you find, write a summary report explaining how the poor ethics of management brought about the collapse of the company.
b. Examine the information to see what part the auditors' lack of skepticism, lack of ethics, or both might have played in the debacle.

LO 7
Skepticism and Ethics

13-39 Using the library and the Internet, find articles comparing the downfalls of Enron and WorldCom.

Required:

a. Using the information you find, write a summary report comparing and contrasting how each company collapsed.
b. Examine the information to see what part the auditors' lack of skepticism, lack of ethics, or both might have played in each debacle.

Ethics

13-40 Ed Able, controller of Fatboys Motorcycles, suspects the CEO and the CFO are perpetrating a major financial statement fraud. The suspected fraud involves a significant overstatement of sales. Able has asked for your help in verifying that this fraud does exist.

Required:

a. Based on all you have learned, what steps or procedures might you recommend to uncover this fraud?
b. If you determine that this fraud does exist, what should Able do?

Comprehensive Annual Report Project

13-41 Comprehensive Annual Report Project

Required:

Complete the following information about a company from its annual report.

I. General Information
  A. Name of company.
  B. Identify the company's industry.
  C. List the major products or services.
  D. Exchange on which the company's stock is listed.
  E. Name of the auditing firm. Did the auditors give a good report about the statements?
  F. List the three major points of the CEO's or president's message.
  G. List the three most important other pieces of promotional information in the report.
  H. Identify the company's year-end date.

II. Capital Structure

    A. List the **total** liabilities and the **total** stockholders' equity for each year presented on your balance sheet (no need for detailed information).

    B. Determine which is greater, liabilities or equity.

    C. Capital stock

        1. List the following information for each year shown in the report:

	Year 1	Year 2
Common stock		
# shares outstanding		
Par value		
Preferred stock		
# shares outstanding		
Par value		

        2. Determine whether the company has any treasury stock. If so, identify:

            a. The number of shares:

                Year 1

                Year 2

            b. Describe why you think the company acquired it.

        3. List the stock market prices (common and preferred) shown in the annual report.

III. Assets

    A. *Inventories*. List the kind of inventories the company has.

    B. *Property, plant, and equipment*. List the company's long-term assets.

    C. Describe depreciation method(s) the company uses.

    D. List the following for each year shown on the balance sheet:

	Year 1	Year 2
Total current assets		
Total long-term assets		
Total assets		

IV. Cash Flows

    A. List the **total** for the following:

	Year 1	Year 2	Year 3
Operating cash flows			
Investing cash flows			
Financing cash flows			
Net change in cash			

    B. Operating cash flows

        1. Have the operating cash flows been positive?

        2. Have they increased or decreased in the years shown in the statement?

        3. Are the operating cash flows sufficient to pay principal and interest on debt and meet investing requirements?

        4. Must the company obtain cash from financing to meet its cash requirements?

    C. Investing cash flows

        1. What type of investments has the company made?

        2. Does the company appear to be growing or contracting? How can you tell?

D. Financing cash flows
    1. What are the major sources of financing cash?
    2. Has the company paid dividends each year?
    3. Does the amount listed on the cash flow statement for dividends equal the amount shown as dividends on the statement of equity? Why or why not?
E. Does the company enjoy positive cash flows?

V. Analysis
  A. Compute the 13 ratios from Chapter 8 for the last year of the annual report. Compare these to the industry averages and describe if the company's average is better or worse than the industry average. Use the following headings for your analysis:

      Ratio Name
      Company Ratio
      Industry Average
      Better/Worse

  B. Prepare a common-size balance sheet using the major sections of the balance sheet for the past two years.
  C. Prepare a common-size income statement and trend analysis of the major sections of the income statement for the past three years.
  D. Describe three internal strengths of this company.
  E. Describe three internal weaknesses of this company.
  F. Describe three external opportunities for this company.
  G. Describe three external threats to this company.

VI. Oral Report

In five minutes or less, report your conclusions about this company. Give specific information to support your analysis.

Comprehensive Annual Report Project

13-42 Comprehensive Annual Report Project

With this project, you will learn everything you can about one company using its annual report, the Internet, media reports, stock market results, and contact with company officials. You will prepare a well-organized, bound report for final submission. Your instructor may require an oral presentation at the end of the semester. By the end of the project, you will decide whether this company is a good stock or bond investment, vendor, customer, or employment prospect.

Select a publicly traded company that interests you as an investment or employment prospect. Obtain two copies of the annual report. Give one copy to your instructor. Prepare a detailed listing of the annual report to become familiar with its contents. List each page including the outside front cover, inside front cover, inside back cover, and outside back cover. For each page listed, write a brief list of the information contained on that page. For example:

    Page 2   CEO's letter to the stockholders
    Page 24   Consolidated balance sheet

Your project will consist of the following sections:
   I. General Information
  II. SWOT Analysis
 III. Capital Structure
 IV. Assets
  V. Cash Flows
 VI. Financial Ratio Analysis
VII. Summary and Conclusions

Required:

1. General Information
   A. Identify the Internet address.
   B. Identify the company's industry.
   C. Identify the industrial classification code.
   D. Identify the stock exchange or exchanges where the stock is traded.
   E. Identify the ticker symbol.
   F. Identify the name of the audit firm.
   G. Briefly summarize the CEO's message.
   H. Read any other promotional or informational material about the company. Often this information relates the firm's views on social responsibility. Briefly summarize this information as provided in the annual report.

II. Complete a SWOT (strengths, weaknesses, opportunities, threats) analysis on the company. Analyze the following for both strengths and weaknesses. After completing the analysis of each item, write at least a two-paragraph summary of your analysis of the internal environment of the company. A major source of the information for the analysis may be found in the annual report's MD&A.

   A. Corporate Structure
      1. Does the structure improve decision making?
      2. Does the structure fit the current business environment?
   B. Corporate Culture
      1. What are the beliefs, values, and expectations of management and employees?
      2. Is the corporate mission clear to all concerned?
      3. Is the corporate mission consistent with the corporate beliefs and values?
      4. Is the mission carried out well?
   C. Corporate Resources. How strong or weak are the following resources:
      1. Human resources
      2. Financial resources
      3. Management information system
      4. Manufacturing
      5. Research and development
      6. Marketing
      7. Distinctive competencies

List the specific opportunities and threats in the external environment in the following areas:

   D. Industry Environment
      1. Customers
      2. Suppliers
      3. Competitors
      4. Substitute products or services
   E. Macroenvironment. What specific problems or opportunities exist for the company in the following areas:
      1. Economic
      2. Changes in societal trends and attitudes
      3. Political and legal
      4. Technology
      5. Globalization
      6. Demographics
   F. After listing the attributes of the company, write at least a two-paragraph summary of your analysis of the external environment of the company. Write a summary of your overall conclusions concerning the SWOT analysis.

III. Capital Structure
  A. What are the company's total liabilities?
  B. Comment on how the mix of liabilities and equities relates to or affects the company.
  C. How many outstanding shares of common and preferred stock are listed for each year shown in the report?
  D. How many shares of treasury stock are presented for each year? Explain why you think the company bought back the stock.
  E. List the stock market prices quoted in the annual report.

IV. Assets
  A. Inventories
    1. If applicable, list the company's different inventories.
    2. Identify the method or methods the company used to value the inventories.
    3. List the total dollar value of inventory for each balance sheet presented in the company's annual report.
    4. Compute the percentage of inventories to total assets for each year of the annual report's balance sheets.
    5. Are the company's inventories growing as a percentage of assets?
    6. List the cost of goods sold and the gross profit for each income statement appearing in the annual report.
    7. Calculate the percentage of cost of goods sold to net sales and the percentage of gross profit to net sales for each period presented.
    8. Have the cost of goods sold and gross profit percentages remained relatively stable for the income statements appearing in the report? If not, describe the changes.
  B. Property, Plant, and Equipment
    1. List the total of property, plant, and equipment for the years listed in the annual report.
    2. List the total of accumulated depreciation associated with property, plant, and equipment for the years listed in the annual report.
    3. Identify the method or methods of depreciation the company used.
  C. List the total of all assets for the years listed in the report.
  D. List the total of the current assets for the years listed in the report.
  E. Is the company capital intensive; that is, does it have many more long-term assets than other assets?
  F. Does the company appear to be growing in terms of long-term assets?
  G. In the periods presented on the balance sheet, has the company had significant changes in asset structure, such as major purchases of other companies, investments, or discontinued operations?
  H. If the company acquired long-term assets, how were they financed?
  I. Describe any significant assets the company has that it does not list on the balance sheet, such as brand names or significant human resources.

V. Cash Flows
  A. List the total for operating, investing, and financing cash flows for each of the years shown in the report's statement of cash flows.
  B. Examine the operating cash flows. Have the operating cash flows been positive? Have the operating cash flows increased or decreased in the years presented? Are the operating cash flows sufficient to pay principal and interest on debt and meet other cash requirements?
  C. Examine investing cash flows. For each line presented in the investing section, discuss how the line relates to another part of the annual report. Include the page number where you found the information. The MD&A may be a good place to find this information.

D. Examine the financing cash flows. For each line presented in this section, trace the amount or find a discussion of the amount elsewhere in the report. The statement of stockholders' equity may be a good place to look. Document by page reference where you found the information.

E. What method is used to prepare the cash flow statement, direct or indirect?

VI. Ratio Analysis

A. Compute the 13 basic ratios presented in Chapter 8 for the last two years and present them in tabular form.

B. Locate the industry averages according to the NAIC code and include them in the table prepared in part A. Be sure to find the time period that most closely matches the company's year end.

C. Evaluate your company's profitability, liquidity, and solvency, comparing them to industry averages.

VII. Summary and Conclusions

A. Summarize your conclusions about the company using all the information gathered for this report. Include a recommendation of whether or not to invest in this company.

B. Assemble your report, bind it, and submit it in to your instructor.

GLOSSARY

A

accelerated depreciation methods Methods of depreciation that record a large amount of depreciation expense in the early years of an asset's life and reduce that amount each year.

account The history of all increases and decreases in an accounting element.

account receivable A customer's legal promise to pay cash in the future.

accountant An information specialist who provides a variety of accounting and consultation services to businesses and individuals.

accounting A system for analyzing and recording business transactions, transforming the resulting data into information useful for decision making, and reporting to the proper stakeholders.

accounting cycle The sequence of steps repeated in each accounting period to enable a company to analyze, record, classify, and summarize its transactions into financial statements.

accounting data The raw results of economic transactions and events.

accounting equation Assets equal liabilities plus equity.

accounting information The product of accountants' organization, classification, and summarization of economic transactions and events so that it is useful to economic decision makers.

accounting system A system that gathers data from source transactions to create the books and records that transform the data into a manageable format and eventually produces useful information in the form of financial statements.

accruals Adjustments made to recognize items that should be included in the income statement period but have not yet been recorded.

accrued expense Expense incurred during the financial statement period that has not yet been recognized.

accrued revenue Revenue earned and realizable during the financial statement period that has not yet been recognized or recorded.

activity-based costing (ABC) system A cost system that identifies specific activities that cause costs to occur and uses those activities as the bases for common cost allocation.

additional paid-in capital The amount paid to a corporation for stock in excess of its par value.

administrative costs All costs of operating a business that are not product and selling costs. Includes support functions such as accounting, finance, executive, and human resources.

aged accounts receivable schedule A listing of accounts receivable by customer to confirm the total of receivables and determine the extent to which any accounts are past due.

amortization Allocation of costs of intangible assets to the time periods benefited.

analytical review techniques Tools financial analysts use to identify relationships among financial data.

annuity A stream of cash flows where the dollar amount of each payment and the time intervals between each payment are uniform.

articles of incorporation An application for incorporation that generally includes: (1) basic information about the corporation and its purpose; (2) the names of the incorporators; and (3) details concerning the types and amounts of corporate stock authorized for sale.

articulation The linkage between the financial statements.

assets Things an entity owns or controls that have future value.

assurance services Independent professional services that improve the quality of information, or its context, for decision makers.

attestation Involves the evaluation of one party's assertion to a third party.

audit committee A subcommittee of a board of directors that hires and works with an independent auditor.

auditing A process of gathering objective evidence, evaluating the evidence against specific criteria, and reporting the results to the users of the information.

authorized shares The maximum number of shares the charter allows the corporation to issue.

available-for-sale securities Debt and equity securities traded on organized exchanges that management may keep for an indefinite time.

average cost method An inventory flow assumption that assigns an average cost to the units of inventory on hand at the time of each sale.

B

balance sheet The financial statement that provides information about the present condition of a business at a specific point in time. A balance sheet consists of three accounting elements: assets, liabilities, and equity.

bank statement A summary of the cash inflows and outflows processed by the bank.

basic earning per share An EPS calculation based on conditions as they exist on the balance sheet date.

bill of material A listing of the quantity and description of each direct material item used to produce one unit.

blended cost of capital The combined cost of debt and equity financing.

board of directors A group of people who have ultimate responsibility for managing the corporation.

bond A type of long-term note payable, usually a $1,000 interest-bearing debt instrument.

bond indenture A legal document that details the agreement between the company issuing the bonds and the buyers of the bonds, including the timing and amount of the interest payments and repayment of the bond principal.

book value (of an asset) Historical cost minus accumulated depreciation.

bottom-up budgeting An approach to budgeting for which lower-level managers and employees prepare the initial budget.

breakeven Occurs when a company's operating income is zero.

break-even point The sales volume required to achieve breakeven.

budget performance report A report that compares the actual amounts spent against the budgeted amounts for a budget category.

budget variance The difference between the actual and budgeted amounts for a budget category.

budgeted balance sheet A presentation of estimated assets, liabilities, and owners' equity at the end of the budget period.

budgeted cash flow statement A statement of a company's expected sources and uses of cash during the budget period.

budgeted income statement A pro forma income statement that shows the expected net income for the budget period.

business The process of producing and distributing goods and services to those who desire them.

business component A portion of an entity whose assets, results of operations, and activities can be clearly distinguished, physically and operationally, and for financial reporting purposes, from the other assets, results of operations, and activities of the entity.

business plan Details of a firm's business goals and its action plan to achieve those goals.

C

capital assets Long-lived assets such as land, buildings, machinery, and equipment.

capital budget The budget that outlines how a firm intends to allocate its scarce resources over a 5-year, 10-year, or even longer time period.

capital budgeting The planning and decision process for making investments in capital projects.

capital investments Business expenditures made to acquire expensive assets that will be used for more than one year. Also called **capital projects**.

capital lease A lease that gives the lessee the primary incidents of ownership such that the substance of the transaction is an asset purchase financed by the long-term lease instrument.

cash budget A budget that shows whether the expected amount of cash operating activities generated will be sufficient to pay anticipated expenses during the budget period.

cash equivalent A marketable security maturing in 90 days or less at purchase, with little or no risk of change in the value at maturity due to interest rate change.

cash payments schedule A schedule that details the amount of cash a company expects to pay out during the budget period.

cash receipts schedule A schedule that details the amount of cash a company expects to collect during the budget period from the sales of its product.

cash to total assets ratio A ratio that measures the percentage of total assets made up of cash.

certified public accountant (CPA) An individual who meets the educational and professional criteria required to be licensed by a state board of accountancy.

chart of accounts A list of all the accounts used by a business entity.

chief financial officer (CFO) A person who directs the firm's financial affairs.

chief operating officer (COO) The corporate officer who directs the daily operations of the corporation.

collateral Something of value that must be forfeited to the lender if the borrower fails to make payments as agreed.

commercial paper A corporate promissory note that investors buy from the corporation.

common costs Costs shared by a number of cost objects.

common stock The voting stock of a corporation.

common-size statement An analysis that converts each element of the balance sheet from dollar amounts to percentages of total assets and each element of an income statement from dollar amounts to percentages of sales.

comparability The quality of information that allows users to identify similarities and differences between two sets of accounting information.

compound interest Interest calculated on the investment principal plus all previously earned interest at the end of each compounding period.

compound journal entries Journal entries with more than two accounts listed.

compounding Determining the future value of an amount invested today.

compounding period The frequency with which interest is calculated and added to the principal, such as annually, semiannually, quarterly, monthly, or daily.

comprehensive income The change in equity arising from any non-owner source.

concentrations of risk A lack of diversification in customers, revenues, markets, suppliers, or customers' ability to pay, which increases the risk of failure because a particular group of companies fails to perform their part of contracts.

conservatism Choosing alternatives that are least likely to overstate assets and income or understate liabilities when uncertainty or doubt exists.

consistency Conformity from period to period of accounting policies and procedures.

consolidated financial statements The combined statements of two or more entities that comprise one economic entity as defined by the separate entity assumption.

consulting services Activities in which an accountant provides data, decision information, and other advice that helps the client manage the business.

contribution income statement An income statement that classifies expenses by cost behavior.

contribution margin The difference between operating revenues and variable costs, which measures the amount of revenues remaining after variable costs to contribute toward fixed costs and profits.

contribution margin ratio (CMR) The contribution margin divided by sales.

controlling investment Investor has an ownership interest greater than 50 percent of the outstanding stock and controls the decision-making process in the investee firm.

convertible securities Bonds payable or preferred stock that owners may, at their option, convert to common stock.

core competency An activity at the center of the organization's purpose that it performs very well.

corporate bylaws Basic rules for management to follow in conducting the corporation's business.

corporate charter A certificate that creates a legal corporate entity and entitles the corporation to begin operations.

corporate culture An organization's values and beliefs.

corporate mission A statement that describes the organization's purpose.

corporate secretary The corporate officer who maintains the minutes of the board of directors' and stockholders' meetings and may also represent the company in legal proceedings.

corporate stock Evidence of a share of ownership in a corporation.

corporate vision A statement that articulates the organization's values and intentions.

corporation A separate legal entity with the rights and obligations of a person.

cost accounting A narrow application of management accounting dealing specifically with procedures designed to determine how much a particular item (usually a unit of manufactured product) costs.

cost driver The activity that causes an expense to occur.

cost object An activity, product, service, project, geographic region, or business segment for which management wants separate cost measurement.

cost of capital The cost of obtaining financing from all available financing sources. Also called the **required rate of return** or the **hurdle rate**.

cost of debt capital The interest a company pays to its creditors.

cost of equity capital The return equity investors expect to earn from a combination of dividends received and the appreciation in the market value of the stock.

cost of goods sold The cost of merchandise transferred to a customer in the entity's primary business activity.

cost of goods sold budget A budget that calculates the total cost of all the products a company estimates it will sell during the budget period. Also called a **cost of services budget** for a service business.

cost-benefit relationship The benefit from knowing information should exceed the cost of providing that information.

cost-volume-profit (CVP) analysis The analysis of the relationships between cost and volume, and the effect of those relationships on profit.

coverage ratio A ratio that indicates a company's ability to make its periodic interest payments. Also called the **times interest earned ratio**.

current ratio A ratio that measures a company's ability to meet its current liabilities with cash generated from current assets.

D

debt financing Borrowing funds for business operations.

debt ratio A ratio that measures what proportion of a company's assets is financed by debt.

default Failure to repay a loan as agreed or to abide by other requirements of a lending agreement.

deferrals Postponements of the recognition of a revenue or expense even though the cash has been received or paid.

deferred expense An asset created when cash is paid before an expense has been incurred.

deferred income taxes Liabilities that arise because the tax laws in effect for any year often differ from GAAP, which dictate how the financial statement information is to be reported.

deferred revenue Unearned revenue created when cash is received before the revenue is earned.

defined benefit pension plan A pension plan that gives an employee a pension at retirement of a certain monthly or annual benefit.

defined contribution pension plan A pension plan that sets aside current dollars in an individual retirement account for an employee to accumulate over time to give the employee a pension fund at retirement. The amount of the retirement benefits depends on the amount accumulated through investments.

deposits in transit Deposits recorded in the books that have not been included in the bank statement.

depreciation The allocation of the cost of long-lived assets to the periods benefited by its use.

derivative A security that has value based on another security or transaction, such as an option.

diluted earnings per share A calculation that indicates the potential impact of any issued dilutive securities on per share earnings.

dilutive securities Securities that will reduce the percentage of ownership of current stockholders.

direct costs Costs easily traced to one cost object.

direct labor The wages of persons who transform direct materials into finished goods.

direct labor efficiency standard The estimated number of direct labor hours required to produce one unit.

direct labor efficiency variance A variance that measures whether production consumed more or fewer hours than the standard direct labor hours to manufacture the actual quantity produced during the month.

direct labor rate standard The expected hourly wage paid to production workers.

direct labor rate variance A variance that measures the effect of unanticipated wage rate changes by calculating the difference between the actual wage rate paid to employees and the direct labor rate standard.

direct material price standard The anticipated price to be paid for each direct material item.

direct material price variance The difference between the amount the company expected to pay for direct material and the amount it actually paid.

direct material quantity standard The amount of direct material required to make one unit of product.

direct material quantity variance The difference between the standard and actual consumption of direct material for the number of units actually manufactured.

direct materials Raw materials and purchased components that are measurable in quantity and cost.

direct method A method of preparing the operating section of the cash flow statement that presents the amount of cash inflows from customers, interest earned on loans, and dividends received and the cash outflows for merchandise, wages, operating expenses, and interest.

discontinued operations The results of operations for a component of the company sold and any gain or loss from the actual disposal of the business component that are reported as a nonrecurring event on the income statement.

discount Occurs when a bond sells for less than par value.

discounted note A loan arrangement in which a bank deducts the full interest in advance from the loan proceeds.

discounting Determining the present value of an amount of cash to be received in the future.

discounting cash flows Determining the present value of cash to be received in future periods.

distributions to owners Transfers of cash or other company assets to owners that result in a reduction of equity.

dividend A distribution of part of a firm's after-tax profit to its shareholders.

double-declining-balance depreciation An accelerated depreciation method that calculates depreciation expense at twice the straight-line rate applied to the beginning book value of the asset.

E

earned equity The total amount a company has earned since its beginning, less any amounts distributed to its owner(s).

earnings per share (EPS) A ratio that reveals how much of a company's net earnings is attributable to each share of common stock.

e-commerce Business transactions that are conducted through the Internet and other electronic media.

effective interest rate The actual interest rate the lender earns and the borrower pays.

effective interest rate of a bond The actual interest rate that the bondholder will earn over the life of the bond, also called the **yield rate** or **market interest rate**.

empower To give employees the authority to make decisions concerning their job responsibilities, including decisions about items in the operating budget.

entrepreneurship Creativity, willingness to accept risk, and management skills necessary to combine natural resources, human resources, and physical capital into business activity.

equity The difference between an entity's assets and its liabilities.

equity financing Acquiring funds for business operations by selling ownership interests in the company.

error corrections Corrections made by adjusting entries when an accountant reviews a trial balance and notices errors in the recording or posting process.

ethics A system of standards of conduct and moral judgment.

expenses Sacrifices of the future value of assets used to generate revenues from customers.

external decision makers People outside the company who make decisions *about* the company from limited information furnished by the entity's management.

external environment The industry environment and the macroenvironment in which a company operates.

extraordinary event An event that is *both* unusual in nature and infrequent in occurrence for a specific entity.

F

factors of production The four major items needed to support economic activity: natural resources, human resources, physical capital, and entrepreneurship.

factory overhead All other manufacturing costs that are not direct materials or direct labor.

feedback value The quality of information that allows users to substantiate or amend prior expectations.

final consumer The final user of a product.

financial accounting Provides historical financial information to internal and external decision makers.

Financial Accounting Standards Board (FASB) The organization principally responsible for establishing accounting guidelines and rules in the United States.

financial statement analysis The process of looking beyond the face of financial statements to gain additional insight into a company's financial health.

financial statement audit An examination by an independent CPA of enough of a company's records to determine whether the financial statements were prepared in accordance with GAAP and demonstrate a fair representation of the company's financial condition.

financing activities Activities that involve the borrowing and repayment of cash and changes in equity from owners' transactions.

first-in, first-out (FIFO) method An inventory flow concept based on the assumption that the first units of inventory acquired are the first sold.

fiscal year A year that differs from the calendar year but normally coincides with the end of the normal business cycle for an industry.

fixed cost A cost that remains the same regardless of the volume of sales or production.

fixed manufacturing overhead budget variance A variance that measures the difference between actual total fixed manufacturing overhead and budgeted fixed manufacturing overhead.

fixed manufacturing overhead volume variance A variance that measures utilization of plant capacity.

FOB point The old shipping term *free on board* defines the point where title passes and a purchase/sales transaction legally occurs.

forecasted financial statements Financial statements that estimate what may happen in the future instead of what actually happened from past transactions. Also called **pro forma financial statements**.

free cash flows The operating cash flows remaining after capital expenditures and dividends.

full disclosure principle Requirement that information necessary for an informed user of the financial statements of a business enterprise to make an economic decision must be made available to the statement users.

future value The value of a payment, or series of payments, at a future point in time, calculated with an interest rate.

G

gains Increases in net assets (equity) that result from incidental or other peripheral events that affect the entity, except for normal revenues and investments by owners.

general journal A journal for recording all transactions that cannot be recorded in a special journal.

general ledger The entire group of accounts in an accounting system.

generally accepted accounting principles (GAAP) Guidelines for presentation of financial accounting information designed to serve external decision makers' need for consistent and comparable information.

going-concern assumption In the absence of any information to the contrary, a business entity will continue to remain in existence for an indefinite period of time.

goodwill The excess paid for the assets of another entity over and above the fair market value of those assets.

gross profit Sales minus cost of goods sold.

H

held-to-maturity securities Investments in corporate or government bonds that management intends to hold until the bonds mature.

high-low method A model that separates the fixed and variable components of a cost element by using the mathematical differences between the highest and lowest levels of activity within a relevant range of production volume.

historical cost principle Requires that balance sheet items be reported at the total cost at acquisition instead of a current value.

human resources Mental and physical efforts of all workers who produce the goods and services for a society.

hybrid company A company that participates significantly in more than one type of business activity.

I

impairment A permanent decline in the fair value of an asset below its book value.

imposed budget A budget for which upper management sets budget amounts for all operating activities with little possibility of negotiation.

income statement A financial report that provides information about an entity's financial performance during a specific time period.

incorporators Persons who submit a formal application to create a corporation and file it with the appropriate state agency.

incremental budgeting The process of using the prior year's budget or the company's actual results to build the new operating budget.

independence A requirement that an accountant have no personal or financial interest (direct or indirect) in the client being examined.

indirect labor The cost of supervisory, janitorial, maintenance, security, and other personnel who do not work directly on production but assist direct laborers.

indirect materials Supply items used in manufacturing in small quantities that are impractical to measure.

indirect method A method of preparing the operating section of the cash flow statement that begins with net income and adjusts it for all items that did not generate or use cash.

industry A group of companies that form a sector of the economy.

industry environment A company's relationships and relative power position with its customers, suppliers, competitors, special interest groups, and the extent of substitute products and services.

industry practices Certain industries may require departure from GAAP because of the peculiar nature of the industry or a particular transaction, to ensure fair presentation of the financial information within that industry.

influential investment An ownership interest sufficient to influence, but not control, the decision-making process of an investee firm.

information Data that are put into some useful form for decision making.

intangible assets Assets consisting of contractual rights.

interest The cost of borrowing money that represents rent paid to use another's money. It is revenue to the lender and expense to the borrower.

internal control structure A process designed to provide assurance that an entity can report reliable financial information, comply with laws and regulations, operate efficiently and effectively, and safeguard its assets.

internal decision makers People within the organization who make decisions *for* the company and have almost unlimited access to accounting information.

internal environment An organization's culture and resources.

internal rate of return (IRR) The calculated expected percentage return promised by the project.

International Accounting Standards Board (IASB) An independent organization responsible for establishing international accounting standards and rules of statement presentation.

inventory turnover ratio A ratio that indicates the number of times total merchandise inventory is purchased (or finished goods inventory is produced) and sold during a period.

investing activities Activities that provide the resources that support operations.

investments by owners The amount invested by the company's owner(s) to get it started or to finance its expansion.

issued shares Shares of stock sold to stockholders.

J

journal A book of original entry in which a chronology of the business entity's transactions is recorded.

journalizing The act of recording accounting transactions into a journal.

L

last-in, first-out (LIFO) method An inventory flow concept based on the assumption that the last goods acquired are the first ones sold.

liabilities The obligations of an entity to transfer assets to, or perform services for, a third party.

limited liability company (LLC) A corporation in which stockholders enjoy the limited liability status of a corporation but are taxed as partners in a partnership.

limited liability partnership (LLP) A partnership that limits the liability of a general partner to his or her own negligence or misconduct, or the behavior of persons he or she controls.

limited partnership A partnership that consists of at least one general partner and one or more limited partners.

liquidation The process of going out of business during which all assets are sold and all liabilities are settled.

liquidity The ease with which an asset can be converted to cash.

liquidity ratios Ratios that evaluate a company's ability to generate sufficient cash to meet its short-term obligations.

long-term financing Borrowing with a repayment period that extends past five years.

losses Decreases in net assets (equity) that result from incidental or other peripheral events that affect the entity, except for normal expenses and distributions to owners.

lower of cost or market (LCM) The value shown on the balance sheet should be historical cost unless the market value is a lesser amount.

M

macroenvironment The current and future state of, and likely changes in, the economic climate, the political climate, demographics, technology, and societal trends and attitudes.

management accounting Provides detailed financial information and nonfinancial information to internal decision makers.

manufacturing The business activity that converts raw materials into a tangible, physical product.

marketable securities Government or corporate bonds and stocks of other corporations.

matching principle Requirement that a company match revenue with the expense of producing that revenue.

materiality Something that will influence the judgment of a reasonable person.

merchandising The business activity of selling finished goods produced by other companies.

minority interest in consolidated subsidiaries The equity of other owners, outside of the consolidated entity, in the subsidiaries the parent company controls.

mixed cost A cost that has both a fixed component and a variable component.

modified accelerated cost recovery system (MACRS) The accelerated depreciation method prescribed by IRS for business use for tax purposes.

monetary unit assumption Economic activities are measured and expressed in terms of the appropriate legal currency for a business.

monopolistic practices Taking advantage of consumers by raising prices unfairly because a business is the main supplier of a particular good or service.

mortgage A document that states the agreement between a lender and a borrower who has secured the loan with collateral.

N

natural resources Include air currents, water, land, and things that come from the earth such as timber, minerals, oil, and natural gas.

net cash flow The project's expected cash inflows minus its cash outflows for a specific period.

net income The difference between the rewards (revenues and gains) and the sacrifices (expenses and losses) for a given period of activity.

net loss Occurs when the expenses and losses for the period are greater than the revenues and gains for the period.

net of tax The amount shown for a transaction that has been adjusted for any income tax effect.

net present value (NPV) The present value of cash inflows minus the present value of cash outflows associated with a capital budgeting project.

net realizable value The amount the firm expects ultimately to collect.

net sales to working capital ratio A ratio that indicates the level of sales generated for a given level of working capital.

neutrality Absence of bias to influence reported information.

nominal interest rate The interest rate that the issuing corporation agreed to pay in the bond indenture, stated as a percentage of the par value of the bond.

nonrecurring event An event that is both unusual in nature **and** not expected to recur.

no-par stock Stock authorized without a par value.

normal balance Defines the type of entry that increases the account; debits increase debit balance accounts and credits decrease debit balance accounts.

note payable A written agreement or debt instrument between a lender and a borrower that creates a liability for the borrower to repay both principal and interest.

not-for-profit firms Generally benevolent organizations formed to serve the needs of society instead of earning profits to distribute to owners.

NSF checks Customers' checks that their banks dishonor for insufficient funds and return to the depositors' banks.

O

operating activities Activities centered around the company's primary business activities.

operating budget The plan for a firm's operating activities for a specified period of time. Also called a **master budget**.

operating cash flows to average current liabilities ratio A ratio that measures the ability to pay current debt from operating cash flows.

operating cash flows to average total liabilities ratio A ratio that measures the ability to pay total debt from operating cash flows.

operating lease A lease that gives the lessee control of an asset for only a portion of its useful life and is treated as rent expense.

opportunity cost The value of what is relinquished because of choosing one alternative over another.

option A contract to purchase something in the future at a guaranteed price.

outsourcing Buying services, products, or components of products from outside vendors instead of producing them.

outstanding checks Checks that were written through the end of the month but did not appear on the bank statement.

outstanding shares The number of shares of stock currently held by stockholders.

P

par value An arbitrary dollar amount placed on the stock by the incorporators at the time of incorporation.

par value for a bond The principal of the loan, which is the amount that must be repaid at maturity.

par value stock Stock that carries a par value.

participative budget A budget approach in which managers and employees at many levels of the company are engaged in setting performance standards and preparing the budget.

partnership A business with two or more owners who all share in the risks and profits of the entity.

payback period method A capital budgeting technique that measures the length of time a capital project must generate positive net cash flows that equal, or "pay back," the original investment in the project.

period costs The costs of operating a business that are not product costs.

periodicity assumption Measurement of economic activity over an arbitrary time period, such as a year or month, for the purpose of providing useful information.

permanent accounts All asset, liability, and equity accounts, except for the dividend account.

perpetual budgeting A budgeting approach in which as one month ends, another month's budget is added to the end of the budget so that, at any time, the budget projects 12 months into the future. Also called **rolling budgeting**.

physical capital Buildings, equipment, tools, and infrastructure required to produce goods and services.

post-closing trial balance A trial balance prepared after the closing entries are posted to prove that the closing entries zeroed the temporary accounts and the remaining accounts are in balance.

posting Recording each journal transaction into the general ledger account it changes.

posting reference column A column in the general journal that contains a reference to the general ledger account number affected by each transaction.

postretirement benefits plan A benefit plan for employees that continues to pay medical and life insurance benefits for retirees, their survivors, or both.

predatory pricing Marking prices so low that competitors are forced to drop out of the market because they cannot remain profitable.

predictive value The quality of information that assists users to increase the probability of correctly forecasting the results of past or present events.

preferred stock Stock that offers certain preferential treatment to its owners over common stockholders for dividends and in the event of liquidation.

premium Occurs when a bond sells for more than par value.

present value (PV) of a project The amount the future cash inflows is worth today when discounted at the appropriate discount rate.

present value (PV) of an investment The amount an investment is worth today evaluated at the appropriate interest rate.

price discrimination Charging different prices to different customers to lessen competition.

price fixing When a group of competitors agree to set a uniform market price to increase their profits.

primary securities market Sales of newly issued stocks and bonds between the issuing corporation and investors in which the corporation receives the proceeds of sales.

principal In the case of notes and mortgages, the amount of funds actually borrowed.

product costs All costs of acquiring or manufacturing goods to make them available for sale to customers.

production budget A budget which plans for the cost and number of units that must be manufactured to meet the sales forecast and the desired quantity of ending finished goods inventory.

profit The excess of revenues over expenses.

profit margin after income tax ratio A ratio that measures the after-tax net income each sales dollar generates.

profit margin before income tax ratio A ratio that measures the profitability of sales before income taxes.

profitability The ease with which a company generates income.

profitability index An index of the values of alternative but acceptable capital budgeting projects, whose index values we calculate by dividing the present value of the project's cash inflows by the present value of its cash outflows.

profitability ratios Ratios that measure a firm's past performance and help predict its future profitability level.

promissory note A legal promise to repay a loan.

purchases budget A budget which plans for the cost and number of units that must be purchased to meet the sales forecast and the desired quantity of ending finished goods inventory.

Q

qualitative factors Nonnumerical attributes that affect decision alternatives.

quantitative factors Considerations that affect business decisions and are represented by numbers.

quick ratio A stringent test of liquidity that compares highly liquid current assets to current liabilities. Also called the **acid-test ratio**.

R

ratio analysis A technique for analyzing the relationship between two items from a company's financial statements for a given period.

receivables turnover ratio A ratio that measures the liquidity of accounts receivable.

regression analysis A mathematical model that uses all the items in the data set to compute a least squares regression line that equals the total cost formula.

relevance A characteristic of useful accounting information that requires the information to pertain to and make a difference in a particular decision situation.

relevant cost A future cost that is pertinent to a particular decision and differs between two decision alternatives.

relevant costing The process of determining which dollar inflows and outflows pertain to a particular management decision.

relevant net cash flows Future cash flows that differ among decision alternatives.

relevant range A range of business activity in which cost-behavior patterns remain unchanged.

relevant revenue A future revenue that differs between two decision alternatives.

reliability A characteristic of useful accounting information that requires the information to be reasonably unbiased and accurate.

representational faithfulness Validity or agreement between a measure or description and the event that it represents.

return on assets ratio A ratio that measures how efficiently a company uses its assets to produce profits. Also called **return on total assets**.

return on equity after taxes ratio A ratio that indicates how much after-tax income was generated for a given level of equity.

return on equity before taxes ratio A ratio that calculates how much before-tax income was generated for a given level of equity.

revenue recognition principle Revenue recognition occurs when the revenue is earned and an enforceable claim exists to receive the asset traded for the revenue.

revenues Increases in net assets (equity) that occur as a result of an entity's selling or producing products and performing services for its customers.

S

sales budget A budget that details the expected sales revenue from a company's primary operating activities during the budget period.

sales forecast The prediction of sales for the budget period.

scarce resources The limited amount of funding available to spend on capital projects.

secondary securities market Trading that occurs on organized stock exchanges among buying and selling investors and from which the corporation receives nothing.

Securities and Exchange Commission (SEC) The government agency empowered by Congress to regulate securities sales and establish accounting rules, standards, procedures, and the form of published financial reporting.

selling and administrative expense budget A budget that calculates all costs other than the cost of products or services required to support a company's forecasted sales.

selling costs Period costs related to advertising, selling, and delivering goods to customers.

selling price of a bond The amount for which a bond actually sells. Also called the **market price**.

sensitivity analysis A technique used to determine the effect of changes on the CVP relationship.

separate entity assumption The assumption that economic activity can be identified with a particular economic entity and that the results of the activities will be separately recorded.

service A business activity that provides specific work or a job function as its major operation.

short-term financing Borrowing that must be repaid within five years.

simple interest Interest calculated only on the original principal.

social responsibility Attitudes and actions that exhibit sensitivity to social and environmental concerns.

sole proprietorship A business that is owned by a single individual and is not legally separate from the owner.

solvency A company's ability to meet the obligations created by its long-term debt.

special items Events that are either unusual or not likely to recur and are disclosed separately in the operating expenses on the income statement.

special journals Journals that record a specific type of transaction such as sales.

special order An order that is outside the normal scope of business activity.

specific identification method An inventory method that assigns the actual cost of the item sold.

stakeholder Any person or entity affected by the way a company conducts its business.

standard A preestablished benchmark for desirable performance.

standard cost system A system in which management sets cost standards and uses them to evaluate actual performance.

standard direct labor cost The total expected cost of labor used to produce one unit, calculated by multiplying the direct labor efficiency standard by the direct labor rate standard.

standard direct material cost The total expected cost of each material used to produce one unit, calculated by multiplying the standard quantity of direct material by the standard price.

standard fixed manufacturing overhead rate An overhead rate calculated by dividing the budgeted fixed manufacturing overhead cost by the appropriate cost driver.

standard fixed overhead cost The expected fixed overhead cost to produce one unit, calculated by multiplying the standard fixed manufacturing overhead rate by the direct labor efficiency standard.

standard variable manufacturing overhead rate An overhead rate calculated by dividing the budgeted variable manufacturing overhead cost by the budgeted direct labor hours.

standard variable overhead cost The expected variable overhead cost to produce one unit, calculated by multiplying the standard variable manufacturing overhead rate by the direct labor efficiency standard.

statement of cash flow A financial statement that details cash provided and used by the three major functions of a firm—to operate, to invest resources, and to finance the operations and investments.

statement of stockholders' equity The financial statement that reports the change in the entity's equity during a period of time.

stock Certificates of ownership in a corporation.

stock certificate A legal document providing evidence of ownership and containing the provisions of the stock ownership agreement.

stockholder A person or entity who owns shares of stock in a corporation and usually has the right to vote on how to operate the business and to receive profit distributions. Also called a **shareholder.**

straight-line depreciation A method of depreciation that assumes an asset is used equally in each time period of its useful life.

strategic plan The plan that describes the organizational approach the senior management of a company will employ to fulfill the corporate mission and vision and achieve the stated goals by allocating financial resources and directing human resources.

sunk costs Past expenditures that current or future actions cannot change.

supply-chain management The business process of ordering, handling, and managing inventory.

T

T-account An abbreviated general ledger account that has only two columns and no explanations.

temporary accounts All revenue, expense, gain, and loss accounts that are part of net income plus the dividend account.

term The length of time between borrowing and repaying a loan.

time value of money The increase in the value of cash over time due to the accumulation of investment income.

timeliness Having information before it is too late to influence decisions.

top-down budgeting An approach to budgeting in which senior executives prepare the budget, and lower level managers and employees work to meet that budget.

total asset turnover ratio A ratio that calculates the amount of sales produced for a given level of assets used.

trade creditors Providers of goods and services to a business who expect payment within normal trade terms for the industry, usually between 30 and 60 days.

trade organizations Organizations that collect information about an industry, act as a spokesperson for the industry, interface with government agencies, and promote the products and services marketed by the industry.

trading securities Debt and equity securities traded on organized exchanges that management has intentions of selling within a very short time.

transposition errors Number reversals that cause errors that are always evenly divisible by nine.

treasurer The corporate officer who is responsible for managing the company's cash.

treasury stock Shares of stock reacquired by the corporation and held in its treasury.

trend analysis A technique that indicates the amount of changes in key financial data over time.

trial balance A listing of each general ledger account balance to verify that the general ledger, and therefore the accounting equation, is in balance.

V

variable cost A cost that changes proportionately with the volume of sales or production.

variable manufacturing overhead efficiency variance A variance that measures the difference between the variable manufacturing overhead cost attributable to planned and actual direct labor hours worked.

variable manufacturing overhead spending variance A variance that measures the difference between what was actually spent on variable manufacturing overhead and what should have been spent, based on the actual direct labor hours worked.

verifiability The ability of information to be substantiated by unbiased measures.

W

working capital The difference between current assets and current liabilities.

worksheet A tool accountants use to accumulate the data required to prepare financial statements.

Z

zero-based budgeting An approach to budgeting where managers start from zero when preparing a new budget, and they must justify each item on the budget every year as though it were a new budget item.

INDEX